Publications
Of
The Colonial Society of Massachusetts

VOLUME LXXXVI

The Papers of Francis Bernard

Governor of Colonial Massachusetts, 1760-69

VOLUME 4: 1768

Sir Francis Bernard, 1772. By John Singleton Copley.
By permission of the Governing Body, Christ Church, Oxford.

EDITED BY COLIN NICOLSON

The Papers of Francis Bernard
Governor of Colonial Massachusetts, 1760-69

VOLUME 4: 1768

Research Assistants:
Stuart Salmon
Christopher Minty
Robyn Leith Stewart

BOSTON   THE COLONIAL SOCIETY OF MASSACHUSETTS   2015
Distributed by the University of Virginia Press

DEDICATION

To Owen Dudley Edwards

CONTENTS

APPENDICES

ILLUSTRATIONS

ACKNOWLEDGEMENTS

I am delighted once again to thank everyone who has assisted in the publication of this volume of *The Bernard Papers*. Firstly, my sincere thanks to the Colonial Society of Massachusetts for financing the project, and to John W. Tyler, editor of publications, for his guidance and encouragement. Owen Dudley Edwards and Neil Longley York diligently read the manuscript. The book is all the better for their generosity. My thanks also to Stuart Salmon, Christopher Minty, and Robyn Leith Stewart for their excellent research assistance: they helped transcribe documents, check facts, and proof-read drafts with little fuss and much care. John Catanzariti, former editor of the Jefferson Papers, shaped editorial policy, while colleagues contributed in various ways, notably Emma Macleod and Ben Marsh. Key support was provided by the UK Arts and Humanities Research Council; a generous Research Fellowship provided relief from teaching commitments during 2011, enabling me to conduct research for this volume. My sincere thanks also to Jeanne Abboud for her splendid work in designing this volume, and to Kyriaki Tsaganis at Scribe for the digital edition. I am especially pleased to acknowledge the many librarians and archivists who answered my enquiries at the Houghton Library, Harvard University, the Massachusetts Historical Society, the UK National Archives, the National Library of Scotland, the University of Stirling, and the William L. Clements Library of the University of Michigan.

Permission to publish material from the following collections is herewith acknowledged: the private collections of Robert Spencer Bernard; the Massachusetts Archives Collection, courtesy of the Massachusetts Archives; the Thomas Gage Papers, by permission of the William L. Clements Library.

This volume is dedicated to Owen Dudley Edwards, whose erudition and enthusiasm have been inspirational throughout my academic career. I am deeply grateful to Owen for his many insights regarding this and other projects. My last debts are the greatest: to my dear wife Catherine and my wonderful daughters, Catriona and Kristen.

LIST OF ABBREVIATIONS

Acts and Resolves	*The Acts and Resolves, Public and Private of the Province of Massachusetts Bay, 1692-1776.* 21 Vols. Boston, 1896-1922.
Adams, *American Independence*	Thomas R. Adams, *American Independence, The Growth of an Idea: A Bibliographical Study of the American Political Pamphlets Printed Between 1764 and 1776 Dealing with the Dispute Between Great Britain and Her Colonies.* Providence, R.I., 1965.
APC	*W. L. Grant and James Munro, eds., Acts of the Privy Council of England: Colonial Series, 1613-1783.* 6 Vols. Vols. 4-6. London, 1909-1912.
Appeal to the World	*Samuel Adams, An Appeal to the World; or A Vindication of the Town of Boston, From Many False and Malicious Aspersions Contain'd in Certain Letters and Memorials, Written by Governor Bernard, General Gage, Commodore Hood, the Commissioners of the American Board of Customs, and Others, and by Them Respectively Transmitted to the British Ministry. Published by Order of the Town.* Boston: Edes and Gill, 1769.

Barrington-Bernard	Edward Channing and Archibald Cary Coolidge, eds., *The Barrington-Bernard Correspondence and Illustrative Matter, 1760-1770.* Harvard Historical Studies Series. Vol. 17. Cambridge, Mass., 1912.
Bernard Papers	Colin Nicolson, ed., *The Papers of Francis Bernard, Governor of Colonial Massachusetts, 1760-69.* 6 Vols. The Colonial Society of Massachusetts; distributed by the Univ. of Virginia Press. Boston, 2007-.
BL	The British Library.
BL: Add	The British Library: Additional Manuscripts.
Boston Gazette	*Boston Gazette and Country Journal.*
BP	Bernard Papers, 13 Vols. Sparks Papers, MS 4. Houghton Library, Harvard University.
Bowdoin and Temple Papers, Loose MSS.	Bowdoin and Temple (Winthrop Papers). Loose Manuscripts, 1580-1900. MHS.
Bowdoin and Temple Papers	*The Bowdoin and Temple Papers. Collections of the Massachusetts Historical Society*, 6th ser. Vol. 9. Boston, 1897.
CO 5	Colonial Office Records, Colonial Office Series. TNA.
CO 5/757	Massachusetts, Original Correspondence of Secretary of State, 1767-1768. CO 5/757. TNA.
CO 5/766	Letters to Secretary of State, 1766-1768. CO 5/766. TNA.

CO 5/823

Massachusetts, Council Executive Records, 1760-1766. CO 5/823. TNA.[1]

CO 5/827

Massachusetts, Council Executive Records, 1766-1769. CO 5/827. TNA.

CO 5/828

Council in Assembly, Massachusetts, 1767-1768. CO 5/828. TNA.[2]

CO 5/893

New England, Original Correspondence of Board of Trade, 1767-1770. CO 5/893. TNA.

Coll. Mass. Papers

Collection of Papers relating to Massachusetts History, 1749-1777. Ms. N-2193. Massachusetts Historical Society.

Copies of Letters from Governor Bernard to Hillsborough

Copies of Letters from Governor Bernard, &c. to the Earl of Hillsborough. [Boston: Edes and Gill], 1769.[3]

Correspondence of Gage

Clarence E. Carter, ed., *The Correspondence of General Thomas Gage and the Secretaries of State, 1763-1775.* New Haven, 1931.

Customs GB II

Great Britain Commissioners of Customs letters [typescripts], 1764-1774. Formerly cataloged as "G.B. Customs II." Includes typescripts of the Bowdoin and Temple Papers. Massachusetts Historical Society.

DCB

Dictionary of Canadian Biography Online. Toronto, 2003, http://www.biographi.ca.

Dorr Collection	The Annotated Newspapers of Harbottle Dorr Jr. 4 Vols. Online edition. Massachusetts Historical Society, http://www.masshist.org/dorr/.
Early American Imprints, Series 1	*Early American Imprints, Series 1: Evans, 1639-1800.* Online edition. Readex, Archive of Americana. Newsbank Inc., http://infoweb.newsbank.com.
ECCO	Eighteenth Century Collections Online. Available at Historical Texts published by JISC Collections https://historicaltexts. jisc.ac.uk/#!/home.
FB	Francis Bernard (1712-79).
Gage	Thomas Gage Papers. American Series. 139 Vols. Vols. 73-88 (1768-1769). William L. Clements Library.[4]
GC3-327	Massachusetts Council Executive Records, 1692-1774. 13 Vols. GC3-327. Vols. 15 and 16. Massachusetts Archives. Transcripts of originals in TNA (CO 5/823 and CO 5/827).
HCJ	*Journals of the House of Commons, 1688-1834.* 89 Vols. Vols. 30-34. London, 1803-1835. House of Commons Parliamentary Papers. ProQuest and University of Southampton, http://parlipapers.chadwyck.co.uk.

HLJ	*Journals of the House of Lords, 1688-1834*. 66 Vols. Vols. 30-32. London [1771-1808].[5] House of Commons Parliamentary Papers. ProQuest and University of Southampton, http://parlipapers.chadwyck.co.uk.
HLL	House of Lords Library
HLL: American Colonies Box 1	The House of Lords Library: American Colonies Box 1, 28-30 Nov. 1768. HL/PO/JO/10/7/286.
HLL: American Colonies Box 2	The House of Lords Library: American Colonies Box 2, 28-30 Nov. 1768. HL/PO/JO/10/7/287.
HLL: American Colonies Box 3	The House of Lords Library: American Colonies Box 3, 28-30 Nov. 1768. HL/PO/JO/10/7/288.
Hutchinson Transcripts	Malcolm Freiberg, ed. and comp., Transcripts of the Letterbooks of Massachusetts Governor Thomas Hutchinson. Edited transcripts of originals in the Massachusetts Archives Collection. Vols. 25-27. Microfilm P-144. 3 Reels. Massachusetts Historical Society.
JBT	*Journal of the Commissioners for Trade and Plantations*. 14 Vols. London, 1920-1938.
JHRM	*The Journals of the House of Representatives of Massachusetts, 1715-1779*. 55 Vols. Boston, 1919-1990.
KJV	Authorized or King James Version of The Bible.

Legal Papers of John Adams	L. Kinvin Wroth and Hiller B. Zobel, eds., *Legal Papers of John Adams*. 3 Vols. Cambridge, Mass., 1965.
Letters to Hillsborough (1st ed.)	*Letters to the Right Honourable the Earl of Hillsborough, from Governor Bernard, General Gage, and the honourable His Majesty's Council for the Province of Massachusetts-Bay. With an appendix, containing divers proceedings referred to in the said letters.* Boston: Edes and Gill, 1769.[6]
Letters to Hillsborough (repr.)	*Letters to the Right Honourable the Earl of Hillsborough, from Governor Bernard, General Gage, and the honourable His Majesty's Council for the Province of Massachusetts-Bay. With an appendix, containing divers proceedings referred to in the said letters.* Boston: Edes and Gill, 1769; repr. London: J. Almon, [1769?].[7]
Letters to the Ministry (1st ed.)	*Letters to the Ministry from Governor Bernard, General Gage, and Commodore Hood. And also Memorials to the Lords of the Treasury, from the Commissioners of the Customs. With sundry letters and papers annexed to the said memorials.* Boston: Edes and Gill, 1769.[8]
Letters to the Ministry (repr.)	*Letters to the Ministry from Governor Bernard, General Gage, and Commodore Hood. And also Memorials to the Lords of the Treasury, from the Commissioners of the Customs. With sundry letters and papers annexed to the said memorials.* Boston: Edes and Gill, 1769; repr. London, J. Wilkie, 1769.[9]
M-Ar	Massachusetts Archives. Boston.

Mass. Archs.	Massachusetts Archives Collection, Records, 1629-1799. 328 Vols. SC1-45x. Massachusetts Archives.
MH-H	Houghton Library, Harvard University.
MHS	Massachusetts Historical Society.
MiU-C	William L. Clements Library. University of Michigan.
MP	Member of Parliament.
ODNB-e	*Oxford Dictionary of National Biography Online.* London, 2004-2006, http://www.oxforddnb.com.s
OED	*Oxford English Dictionary Online.* London 2004-2006, http://dictionary.oed.com.
NEP	Papers Relating to New England, 1643-1768. 4 Vols. Sparks Papers, MS 10. Houghton Library, Harvard University.
Papers of John Adams	Robert J. Taylor, Mary-Jo Kline, Gregg L. Lint, et al., eds., *Papers of John Adams.* 17 Vols. to date. Cambridge, Mass., 1977-.
PDBP	Peter D. G. Thomas and R. C. Simmons, eds., *Proceedings and Debates of the British Parliament respecting North America, 1754-1783.* 6 Vols. Millwood, N.Y., 1982.
Procs. MHS	*Proceedings of the Massachusetts Historical Society*, 3d ser.
Prov. Sec. Letterbooks	Province Secretary's Letterbooks, 1755-74, Secretary's Letterbooks, 1701-1872. 4 Vols. SC1-117x. [Vols. 1, 2, 2A, & 3]. Massachusetts Archives.

Reports of the Record Commissioners of Boston	*Reports of the Record Commissioners of the City of Boston.* 38 Vols. Boston, 1876-1909.
Select Letters	[Francis Bernard], *Select Letters on the Trade and Government of America; and the Principles of Law and Polity, Applied to the American Colonies. Written by Governor Bernard in the Years 1763, 4, 5, 6, 7, and 8.* London, 1774. First edition. W. Bowyer and J. Nichols. London, 1774.[10]
T 1	Treasury Board Papers and In-Letters, 1557-1922. T 1. TNA.
T 28/1	Treasury "America Book," 29 Oct. 1765-5 Sept. 1778. T 28/1. TNA.
Temple Papers, 1762-1768: JT Letterbook	Bowdoin and Temple (Winthrop Papers). Bound MSS. Temple Papers, 1762-1768: Letter book of John Temple and other manuscripts. MHS.
TH	Thomas Hutchinson (1741-80).
TNA	The National Archives of the UK, London.
WMQ	*The William and Mary Quarterly: A Magazine of Early American History and Culture,* 3d ser.
Works of John Adams	Charles Francis Adams, ed., *The Works of John Adams, Second President of the United* States. 10 Vols. Boston, 1850-1856.

1. The Council's record books are Council Executive Records, 1760-1769, CO 5/823 and CO 5/827. There is also a set of nineteenth-century transcripts in Council Executive Records, 1692-1774, 13 vols. [vols. 2-14]. GC3-327, M-Ar. The corresponding volumes for 1760-69 are vols. 15 and 16.

2. There are two contemporaneous sets of the Council's legislative records. One was kept in Boston and is in Council Legislative Records, 1692-1774, 24 vols., GC3-1701x, vols. 23-28, M-Ar. The other was sent to London: Council in Assembly, Massachusetts, 1760-1769, CO 5/820-CO 5/828. This project utilizes the London copies, for it was this set that was prepared for and consulted by ministers and officials.

3. This was the first publication in the Bernard Letters pamphlet series, printing six of Bernard's letters to the earl of Hillsborough **Nos. 706**, **708**, **709**, **711**, **717**, and **718**, *Bernard Papers*, 5: 96-101, 103-109, 111-114, 128-135; and Thomas Gage to Hillsborough, Boston, 31 Oct. 1768. The compositors' copy texts were transcripts of copies of original correspondence presented to Parliament on 20 Jan. 1769;* the transcripts were prepared and authenticated by the clerk of the papers of the House of Commons on 27 Jan. William Bollan, acting as London agent to the Massachusetts Council, sent them to Samuel Danforth, the "president" of the Council, on 30 Jan.; the parcel arrived on 8 Apr. and Danforth subsequently passed them to fellow councilor James Bowdoin, in whose keeping they remained. Thus, the printed versions of the first batch of Bernard Letters were three steps removed from the original letters received by the secretary of state: the differences between them generally are not substantive (viz. missing or additional words, grammatical alterations) and consistent with accidental copying errors (misspellings) or incidental practice (orthography, punctuation). There are three imprints, listed as items 68a-68c in Adams, *American Independence*, 51-52. Copies of all the imprints are available in *Early American Imprints, Series 1*, nos. 41911, 11178, and 11179. The first was an unnumbered four-page folio pamphlet, the second a sixteen-page quarto, and the third a twenty-eight-page quarto. The first imprint was published between 10 and 17 Apr.; all three would have been distributed to newspapers for reprinting.

    * These are no longer extant. The Parliamentary archives in the House of Lords Library holds the American correspondence laid before Parliament on 28 Nov. but not the letters presented on 20 Jan. 1769. HLL: American Colonies Boxes 1-3.

4. The Gage Papers were being reorganized when this volume was in preparation. I have retained the abbreviation "Gage" for consistency across the *Bernard Papers* series but have added additional information to this section summarizing the collection.

5. The editors of this online resource advise that "the Journals of the House of Lords follow the same model as for those of the House of Commons. . . The volumes are from the Hartley Library [*Univ. of Southampton*], but give no information as to date, order or printer." http://parlipapers.chadwyck. co.uk/infoCentre/about_long18.jsp. The first thirty-one volumes (covering the period up to 1767) were published between 1771 and 1777; vol. 36, published in 1808, took the series up to 1779. See H. H. Bellot, "Parliamentary Printing, 1660-1837," *Bulletin of the Institute of Historical Research* 9 (1933-34).

6. The Boston first edition included all the correspondence printed in *Copies of Letters from Governor Bernard to Hillsborough*, and added several documents framing and constituting the Massachusettsís Council's response to their governor's reports: James Bowdoin's letter to Hillsborough dated 15 Apr. 1769; the Council's letters to Hillsborough of 15 Apr. and 12 Jun. 1769;*; and an appendix of the Council's proceedings, Jun-Dec. 1768. For copy text the printers again used the transcripts made by the House of Commons' clerk plus author copies of the Council's documents, both sets probably supplied by James Bowdoin. Publication was advertised in the *Boston Weekly News-Letter*, 27 Jul. 1769. The first edition is listed as 68d in Adams, *American Independence*, 53. Several US libraries have copies of this rare pamphlet, including the Library of Congress and the Boston Public Library. The project utilized the digitized version available in *Early American Imprints, Series 1*, no. 49926 (digital supplement).

    ***Appendices 3** to **5**, *Bernard Papers*, 5: 325-358.

7. The London reprint is listed as 68e in Adams, *American Independence*, 53. The British Library microfilm copy (166p in reel no. 1870) is available in ECCO. The page sequence is different from the first edition, but the content is the same. It was first advertised for sale at 3s. in the *Public Advertiser*, 31 Oct. 1769.

8. Pamphlet 69a in Adams, *American Independence*, 53. The project used the digitized version of the pamphlet held by the Bodleian Library (Oxford) available in ECCO. This was a new edition of correspondence based on a second batch of transcripts supplied by the Commons' clerk of papers and again transmitted to Boston by William Bollan, on 21 Jun. It included thirty of Bernard's letters to the secretaries of state for the American Colonies (the earls of Shelburne and Hillsborough)* and two in-letters from Hillsborough (**Nos. 722** and **727**, *Bernard Papers*, 5: 142-143, 153-157); Gage to Hillsborough, Boston, 3 and 5 Nov. 1768; letters received by Philip Stephens, the secretary of the Admiralty, from Royal Navy officers stationed in Boston (including Commodore Samuel Hood, 22 Nov. to 7 Dec. 1768); memorials of the American Board of Customs to the Treasury (including **Appendix 6**) and their enclosures, and correspondence with Gov. Bernard (**Nos. 624** and **626**). It was first advertised for sale in the *Massachusetts Gazette and Boston Weekly News-Letter*, 7 Sept. 1769 and the *Boston Evening-Post*, 11 Sept. 1769.

   * In this volume: to Shelburne: **Nos. 585, 589, 593, 596, 600, 601**, plus FB's letter of 2 Feb. 1768, CO 5/757, f 24 (omitted from this volume because it merely acknowledged receipt of correspondence); to Hillsborough: **Nos. 623, 630, 632, 633, 638, 646, 648, 654, 656, 660, 663, 664, 668, 672, 681, 686, 690**, and **691**. To Hillsborough: **Nos. 694, 698, 700**, and **703**, *Bernard Papers*, 5: 63-68, 75-77, 79-82, 86-90.

9. Pamphlet 69c in Adams, *American Independence*, 53. The project used the digitized version of the copy in the Houghton Library (Harvard), (146p in microfilm reel no. 1471), in ECCO. The London reprint included three additional letters from Commodore Hood to Philip Stephens. Advertised for sale at 2s. 6d. in the *Public Advertiser*, 15 Nov. 1769.

10. A second edition was published in 1774 with a variant title and additional papers. *Select Letters on the Trade and Government of America; and the Principles of Law and Polity, Applied to the American Colonies. Written by Governor Bernard, at Boston, In the Years 1763, 4, 5, 6, 7, and 8. Now first published: To which are added The Petition of the Assembly of Massachuset's Bay against the Governor, his Answer thereto, and the Order of the King in Council thereon* (London: T. Payne, 1774). It was reprinted in Boston by Cox and Berry and advertised for sale on 27 Oct. 1774.

INTRODUCTION

That it should be left to any one . . . to ask for Troops to come here . . .
will be the Wonder of the future readers of the History of these Times
(Francis Bernard to John Pownall, Boston, 11 Jul. 1768).

History has not been kind to Francis Bernard (1712-79), governor of colonial Massachusetts, and with good reason. The governor's historical reputation rests largely on the part he played in pushing the American colonists toward revolution. His enemies considered him a myopic imperialist pursuing a centralizing agenda, his friends thought him a stumbling functionary bereft of political know-how. Historians have been more understanding of Bernard's predicament and how he managed to alienate foes and disappoint friends. Bernard was the kind of government official without whom revolutions might not occur: a thwarted modernizer, despairing of metropolitan inertia and resentful of local power shifts that undermined his own authority, he sought and found retribution in a hostile portrayal of his opponents and critics. The odds were always against Bernard winning the political struggle with the American colonists or obtaining the full co-operation of provincial institutions for British colonial reforms, but not against him triumphing in a war of information.[1]

The colonists and their governor vied to control information flowing to London. That struggle illuminates both what they made of each other and the wider contest over British imperial authority unfolding around them—what historians call the Imperial Crisis. The propaganda war began in 1765, when Bernard was caught in the cross-fire of controversy generated by Parliament's attempt to impose direct taxation on the American Colonies by means of the Stamp Act. Bernard's detailed reports of riots and demonstrations in Boston proved so alarming to British ministers that they believed a revolt was near certain in the Massachusetts capital. While these reports were discussed by the cabinet, the king, and Parliament, Americans never had the opportunity to read them; but they deduced how antagonistic they must have been from private correspondence and occasional reports of Parliament's debates. In 1768, the British government again fretted about insurrection in Boston, though the circumstances were rather different from what they had been three years earlier. The colonists too feared that Bernard once more was misrepresenting their cause to the British. They were right. But it was over a year before the colonists found evidence to support their accusations, and even then managed to read and acquire but a fraction of what the governor and his British correspondents were saying about them. The evidence is presented in full for the first time, in this fourth volume of the *Bernard Papers* series, and continues in the fifth, as is the story of how the colonists used the evidence to further their own agenda.

By 1768, Bernard's administration drew little local political support largely because of widespread discontent with Parliament's American Revenue Act, passed the previous summer. The Revenue Act (better known as the Townshend duties act) taxed several articles of trade (glass, paper, painter's colors, lead, and tea). But whereas the 1765 act imposing a range of stamp duties was never properly implemented in America because of widespread opposition, the Townshend duties were collected and the trade laws (commonly known as the Navigation Acts) enforced with greater rigor than hitherto. These successes owed much to the diligence of the American Board of Customs based in Boston and the host of customs officers under its command. Unable to prevent enforcement of the 1767 Revenue Act, the colonists concentrated on persuading the British to repeal it and other American revenue acts, as well as other obnoxious legislation known collectively as the Townshend Acts.[2] During this phase of the Imperial Crisis, colonial opposition was sustained by broad-based popular movements.[3] The campaign in Massachusetts was managed by the Whig party and channeled through the provincial legislature and town meetings. Opposition to taxation was far less violent than it had been in 1765, and was again contained by local leaders known as Sons of Liberty: merchants like John Hancock, keen to free commercial activity from the restrictions of mercantilism; intellectuals like James Otis Jr., a popular leader since 1761 when he challenged the legality of customs officers' writs of assistance; Samuel Adams, a down-at-heel tax collector and clerk of the House of Representatives, who, by 1768, was with Otis the best known of the governor's many radical critics; elected representatives from the country towns who filed into Boston's Town House (known today as the Old State House), where the assembly met, to condemn their governor's misdeeds; wealthy councilors like James Bowdoin, who led and coordinated with Adams opposition in the Governor's Council; and, by contrast, working men and women who supported and enforced the boycotts of British imports and consumer goods. None of these people trusted Francis Bernard.[4]

Bernard mustered no more than token assistance from friends of government in defending parliamentary authority, and lurched from one issue to another before finally retreating. More than anything, Bernard wanted out; another posting in the colonies or a job in England was eminently preferable to enduring another few years in Boston. Bernard did not concede ground gracefully, however, and mounted a vituperative counter-offensive against the colonists—not in any public forum, but privately and secretly in his official correspondence. The documents published in the *Bernard Papers* chart not only the rise of colonial opposition and Bernard's gubernatorial tribulations but his studied attempts to precipitate British intervention. This fourth volume reveals how Bernard manufactured a crisis for his superiors' consumption, one apparently so deep as to warrant immediate punitive measures to allay an incipient rebellion and structural reforms to reinvigorate imperial power. Bernard got none of the reforms he wanted, yet managed to persuade the British government to send regular soldiers to Boston, ostensibly to protect Crown officials and in reality to cow the spread of radicalism. We can only speculate as to how history might have turned out had the British not sent soldiers to Boston; but we do know that when Regulars stepped ashore on 1 Oct. 1768 Bostonians' and New Englanders' respect for the instruments and agencies of imperial power started to decline markedly. And yet, while Bernard was conscious of his own failings in coping with American resentment and British neglect, he was never mindful of the possible consequences of his own actions in turning British ministers against the colonists and helping turn the colonists against the British.

History was not on Bernard's side, yet Bernard has bequeathed history and historians a cornucopia of documentation. From brief commentaries on the famous and the obscure—many of whom, he was convinced, secretly favored independence—to studied evaluations of why the colonies were on the cusp of revolt, Bernard's correspondence was a valuable source of information for colonial policymakers in London. Governor Bernard may have been the official communicant of news concerning provincial affairs but ministers also received and relayed information coming in from numerous other sources, some of which were controlled by the governor's enemies. The contest to control the flow of information back and forth across the Atlantic was thus a central aspect of the Imperial Crisis.

It is a truism to attribute some of the misunderstandings and errors of judgment on both sides to the slowness of transatlantic communication, which at best was four weeks on journeys eastward and six weeks westward. Official mail sent by the packet from Falmouth (the southern English port farthest from London) to New York generally took two weeks longer than if sent with merchantmen sailing from London to Boston or Rhode Island (on account of less favorable ocean currents), on top of which officials in Boston had to wait another six days for their papers to arrive overland by couriers.[5] The mail packets from England were frequently delayed: in 1768, those leaving in January, February, and June were all several weeks later than anticipated. Major policy documents and secret orders could therefore take months to reach the recipient, notably instructions to Governor Bernard announcing that troops were being dispatched to Boston (**No. 622**: dated 11 Jun. received 14 Sept.; **No. 661**: dated 30 Jul. received 18 Sept.)

These vagaries inevitably complicated governors' tasks of replying to official letters and bringing London up-to-date with developments in America. Commenting on eastward conveyances, the secretary of state for the Colonies Wills Hill, the first earl of Hillsborough, writing at his desk in Whitehall, remarked that

> it frequently happens, that Intelligence of public Transactions in the Colonies is received by private Persons in this City, long before any official Communication of it comes to me for His Majesty's Information. (**No. 651**.)

Thus Hillsborough instructed colonial governors to send dispatches by the "first Opportunity that offers" and thence duplicates and copies by the next mail packet (which even then occasionally arrived before the original dispatch). Governors did not have the luxury of being able to delay outgoing shipping until they could write replies to incoming mail. In the case of vessels departing Boston a day or two after arriving, Bernard was usually able to dash off a single page letter before sailing (for example, **No. 609**). Usually he had to search for vessels sailing direct to England or transmit his dispatches to the postmaster at New York for carriage by the mail packet, for which they might lie in wait for several days or even weeks. On the whole, Bernard tended to compose his replies shortly after receiving a letter; sometimes delays occasioned by the absence of suitable conveyance gave him time to add a postscript or compose a rejoinder, and brood upon insults and threats real and imagined.[6]

The practicalities of managing communications indubitably influenced the substance of transatlantic exchanges. All royal governors were obliged to follow the instructions received with their commission and others sent out intermittently by the secretary of state. But until otherwise directed by the secretary, governors were obliged to act independently of London. While governors could not anticipate or preempt the secretary of state's directives, they could aspire to use replies to influence ministerial deliberations. Bernard, however, often worried that his out-going correspondence was subject to espionage. He generally considered merchantmen and Royal Navy ships securer than the mail packet, but he had become wary of committing letters to ships owned by merchants whom he counted among his political opponents; ships' masters were "easily" corrupted (**No. 672**). Bernard prided himself on his candid style of reporting, yet even he was reticent to put names to the people whom he criticized or denigrated in his letters (though not James Otis, whom he continued to disparage openly and with relish). The governor's prose was sometimes coded by allusive metaphor, drawing upon scripture or classical history, which substituted for direct explanation; alternatively, his writing resorted to dramatic description. Both devices served to convey the seriousness of the point being discussed. Sometimes shrouded meaning meant recipients misunderstood, and requested additional clarification, as Hillsborough was obliged to do when he struggled to separate fact from fiction in Bernard's reports of the *Liberty* riot and other disturbances in June 1768 (**No. 661**). At the same time, Bernard was careful to enclose files of supporting documentation: copies of correspondence, newspaper clippings, extracts of the proceedings of the assembly, minutes of Council meetings, depositions, and so on. Generally, he assumed the evidence spoke for itself, but he often provided commentaries on the material. All of this—the vivid reporting style and the weight of material evidence—was calculated to shape the perceptions of ministers and officials in London. But Bernard was not without rivals contesting his version of events—men and women just as angry and often more eloquent.

Boston, January 1768

In January, when the Massachusetts House of Representatives petitioned King George III to repeal the Townshend Revenue Act, it set out what amounted to the mainstream Whig position on British colonial policy. Taxation was a gift of the people, long recognized as such in English constitutional history and law; and the right of taxing the American Colonies lay not with the Parliament in London, but with the colonial legislatures. Several supplications on this theme were delivered by Massachusetts and other colonies to the King and Parliament between 1767 and 1770. It was not the case that each new petition was progressively more assertive than its predecessor, but cumulatively the petitions mounted a significant challenge to the doctrine of parliamentary supremacy. Bernard fully understood that the question in dispute was not just about parliamentary taxation but colonial rights of self-government and the sovereignty of the King-in-Parliament. (For a discussion see **No. 580**.) Contrived distinctions between "internal" or direct taxes and "external" taxes or trade duties to some Britons promised a *modus vivendi* to draw a line under the prolonged controversy over the hated Stamp Act. Now, under the penetrating gaze of the "Pennsylvania Farmer" (the Philadelphia lawyer John Dickinson), distinctions between types of taxes were quickly dispensed with. Whigs now denied Parliament's authority to legislate any taxes for America. The Farmer's "Masterly Writings," widely printed in colonial newspapers (**No. 578**), Bernard thought amounted to a "Bill of Rights" for the American Colonies (**No. 590**). Indeed, after attacking the Townshend duties colonists proceeded to call for the repeal of all American revenue acts and the dismantling of the entire mercantilist system on the basis of their constitutional rights and liberties.

The governor's adversaries in Massachusetts easily by-passed official channels of communication with London. After petitioning the king in January, the House of Representatives directly dispatched a series of letters to leading British statesmen setting forth the case for repeal of the Townshend duties (**Nos. 579, 580, 581, 589,** and **591**).[7] The House also appointed its own agent, Dennys DeBerdt,[8] in the expectation that he would lobby ministers and parliamentarians as well as transmit the House's remonstrances. Bernard might not have been concerned at this circumvention had not his enemies also advanced an alternative narrative in which they accused him of misrepresenting the province's interests. These accusations became shriller as the year passed. Conducted by Adams, Otis, and other Whig writers, the campaign to expose the governor began in earnest in the first few months of 1768 and did not end until his departure in Aug. 1769.

London, January to February

British politics was not a closed book to Bernard in 1768, but after ten years in the colonies he little understood the political landscape. Bernard's understanding of British politics had been shaped by the Whig hegemony of the 1750s, ended by the accession of George III in 1760. When the earl of Halifax relinquished responsibility for the colonies in 1765, Bernard lost more than a reliable patron.[9] Halifax epitomized the centralizing tendency that Bernard believed was missing from British-American relations and whose absence had weakened British imperial power and authority. Halifax was also a tangible connection to the certainties of mid-eighteenth-century politics that Bernard knew. Bernard had been loyal to the Whig magnate the duke of Newcastle, whose partnership with William Pitt had brought Britain to victory in the Seven Years' War.[10] As governor, Bernard had tried to emulate Newcastle's penchant for a "broad bottom" administration before the Stamp Act Crisis brought a shuddering realignment in Massachusetts politics that undermined support for the provincial government.[11] Struggling to adapt to this situation, Bernard failed to comprehend developments in Britain, notably Pitt's championing the American cause in 1766, Rockingham's strategy in repealing the Stamp Act, and why the ministries of Grenville and Rockingham were so brief.[12] Shelburne's term as secretary for the Colonies in Chatham's administration Bernard found unsettling, and it took him the best part of a year to appreciate that London could not be depended upon to uphold the reputation and authority of royal governors.[13] (Newsworthy events from the London papers, such as the controversial trial and parliamentary electioneering of John Wilkes, he followed intermittently.) In short, by 1768 Bernard concluded that the British political establishment was unprepared to aid him in thwarting the growth of radicalism.

Bernard's sense of being cast adrift also reflected the uncertainty in colonial policymaking during Chatham's administration, 30 Jul. 1766-14 Oct. 1768. Policy, such as it was, was haphazard and reactive, owing to the priorities accorded domestic and European business to the exclusion of American affairs. Chatham himself was largely absent because of illness. Also, cabinet, government, and Parliament all assumed that the American Declaratory Act (passed on 18 Mar. 1766 in conjunction with the act repealing the Stamp Act) ought to have put an end to American gripes, considering the colonists had no option but to accept the principles that Parliament could pass legislation for America in any and "in all cases whatsoever" and that the sovereignty of the King-in-Parliament was unassailable. Until the appointment of Wills Hill (1718-93), first earl of Hillsborough, as secretary of state for the Colonies (a new post) in January 1768, Bernard must sometimes have supposed British colonial policy moribund. His initial concern was not that the British government and Parliament would concede on principles but that they would heed the clamor for a repeal of the Townshend Revenue Act. While Bernard did not have any particular interest in sustaining parliamentary taxation per se, he had a vested interest in shoring up this particular piece of legislation: for the act promised Crown salaries for the colonial governors, to be paid out of the tea duty as and when the government in London decided.

For sure, Bernard had friends near the center of British high politics. John Pownall, the senior administrator in the Plantation Office, remained loyal to Bernard throughout the Imperial Crisis (**No. 647**). He was not a political appointee but a civil servant, although the re-organization of the colonial office under Hillsborough for a while left him uncertain of his future; nonetheless he prospered under Hillsborough and his successors.[14] His erudite brother Thomas Pownall, a former Massachusetts governor (although Bernard's junior by a decade) and probably the Briton best-informed on American affairs, was more of an enigma to Bernard; in the course of the next eighteen months they came to distrust each other.[15] Bernard's correspondence with Richard Jackson, a member of Parliament, lost some of the intimacy that characterized their exchanges when Jackson was province agent in 1765 (**No. 590**).[16] Bernard knew that whatever he said to these men would likely be verbally conveyed to ministers, and, latterly in Thomas Pownall's case, also to the opposition and friends of America. But it was to his only true British confidant, Lord Barrington, his wife's cousin and secretary-at-war,[17] that Bernard frankly expressed his deep misgivings as to his own capacity for fulfilling London's expectations that he should keep the colonists quiet (**No. 583**).

Behind the scenes, Lord Barrington continued to represent Bernard's interests whenever possible. His office did not bestow a position in the cabinet and Barrington was often a peripheral figure in policymaking. But in 1768 and 1769, he was a prominent contributor to parliamentary debates on the exclusion of John Wilkes, first elected MP for Middlesex in March 1768. Barrington's close political friendship with Hillsborough was an additional avenue for the transmission of Bernard's views. Barrington thought Bernard's advocacy of American representation in Parliament irrelevant to the Imperial Crisis, yet nonetheless warmed to some of the governor's other suggestions for strengthening imperial power at the cost of colonial autonomy (**Nos. 583, 584**, and **597**). Barrington regarded himself a hard-liner on American affairs, fearing "with Grief, but not with surprise, the open attempts towards independency making in New England" since the repeal of the Stamp Act (**No. 605**).

Bernard could never afford to take the support of British ministers for granted. He simply could not predict how the British government might react to the colonial petitions and remonstrances. Several current government ministers, when in opposition, had genuinely sympathized with the colonists in their distaste for the Grenville administration attempting to tax them without direct representation; they had listened attentively to the colonists throughout the Stamp Act Crisis and championed the act's repeal. They included such political heavyweights as the lord chancellor, the earl of Camden, and the prime minister, the earl of Chatham,[18] both of whom Bernard presumed were misinformed of the colonists' true intentions, though the governor was never in direct contact with either man in 1765 nor 1768. The colonists, Bernard believed, had misconstrued their eminences' public condemnation of the Stamp Tax as unequivocal support for American self-government (**Nos. 577, 579**, and **580**). On both counts Bernard was partially correct: Chatham and his followers, when in opposition and government, never conceded the minimum of what the Americans were wanting by 1768—exemption from all parliamentary taxation and strict limits on the scope of parliamentary authority. Bernard was more troubled by the earl of Shelburne, secretary of state for the Southern Department and a confirmed critic of the governor's confrontational style. When official news of the transfer of colonial responsibilities from Shelburne's office to Hillsborough's was delayed, Bernard continued to send dispatches direct to Shelburne.[19]

For the past year, Shelburne had been advising Bernard that he should avoid antagonizing the House of Representatives and do his utmost to reconcile the colonists to parliamentary supremacy. Theirs was a difficult relationship, with Bernard resenting the interference of a minister whom he believed knew little about imperial administration and Shelburne only reluctantly abandoning plans to recall Bernard.[20] Bernard was necessarily more circumspect in his correspondence with Shelburne than he was with his British friends. Shelburne could have removed Bernard peremptorily, after the governor consented to a provincial indemnity act and in doing so exceeded his powers (the act having promised the Stamp Act rioters immunity from prosecution).[21] Nonetheless, Bernard was didactic when the opportunity presented, and retained his composure to pen a justification for his professedly candid style of reporting. His letter of 21 Jan. reminded Shelburne that it was the governor—as the king's representative—and not the assembly who deserved respect as the prime source of information.

> The King in all matters relating to America has great
> reliance on the Reports of his Governors, who being
> appointed by him & accountable to him are under the
> greatest obligations not to deceive him. But if the As-
> semblies are allowed to represent matters to the King,
> without the privity of the Governors, the King must
> either lose the Advantage of having the opinion of his
> Governors upon the Subject matter, or must delay his
> judgement untill he can order his Governor to report
> his Opinion. . . . It is my Duty to report proceedings
> which appear to me to require Animadversion, at the
> time that they happen: it is your Lordships province
> to fix the time when they shall be taken into consid-
> eration; for which I shall allways wait with due defer-
> ence. (**No. 581.**)

Bernard was spared having to explain his pertinent disregard of "due deference"
when writing this particular letter. For American affairs were removed from Shelburne's ministerial portfolio on the very day Bernard was writing and given over to a
new colonial department headed by Wills Hill, first earl of Hillsborough. Hillsborough's appointment as the first secretary of state for the Colonies (21 Jan. 1768-15
Aug. 1772), which Bernard learned of in late February, he thought an indication
the administration were taking greater interest in American affairs.[22]

To the British, Massachusetts and Virginia seemed always to be one step ahead
of the other colonies in pushing the case for legislative autonomy.[23] While other
lower houses of assembly were occasionally more forthright in challenging parliamentary authority, the Massachusetts House of Representatives undeniably
upset the British government with a circular letter of 11 Feb. to the speakers of
other assemblies urging intercolonial opposition to the Townshend Revenue Act
(**Appendix 1**). The Circular Letter's articulation of colonial rights was an adept
compromise: it leaned toward a moderate position in explicitly accepting Parliament's legislative supremacy, and toward the radicals in protesting that rights of
taxation lay with the colonial assemblies. But Hillsborough's impulsive reaction
bestowed iconoclastic status on this document (**Appendix 1**). Prompted by Hillsborough, Chatham's cabinet insisted that the House vote approving the circular
be rescinded, even though the letter had been distributed. Thus did the British
government unwisely commit Bernard to a contest of wills with the Massachusetts
legislature that, despite initial optimism, the governor knew he could never win
(**Nos. 585, 589**, and **No. 591**).

Hillsborough exerted a profound influence on the Imperial Crisis, pushing
the colonists and the British further apart. His reputation as a hard-liner rested

largely on his responsiveness to information being supplied him by colonial governors, Bernard preeminently, and the Treasury, who forwarded him the reports of the American Board of Customs in Boston. Bernard was not aware of Hillsborough's appointment until 20 Feb. at the earliest, but thereafter wrote all his official letters—including and especially those to Shelburne—with Hillsborough in mind. (Official confirmation arrived on 11 May). Their correspondence printed in this volume and the next is a comprehensive dialogue exploring the several issues bedeviling British-colonial relations in 1768: opposition to the Townshend duties, nonimportation, the rescinding of the Circular Letter, the *Liberty* riot in Boston, the Convention of Towns, and the arrival and quartering of the British Regulars.[24] On these and other matters, Bernard's reports contained information of strategic importance to ministers. British policy, in short, was not to give way on matters of principle, despite American objections, and to bolster colonial governors' dwindling authority whenever possible. At stake, according to Hillsborough—echoing the central message of Bernard's missives—was the credibility of British imperial power. As an Anglo-Irish absentee landlord, Hillsborough's personal fortune derived from his extensive Irish estates, whose origin in seventeenth-century land confiscation from the Catholics was felt to necessitate ruthless implementation of the law in theory if not always in practice.

Boston, February

Bernard's bullishness, however, was evident before he knew of Hillsborough's appointment. The duplicate of a delayed letter from Shelburne, dated 17 Sept. 1767 and approving his conduct, arrived on 2 Feb. (**No. 566**).[25] The following day, it was read to the House of Representatives by the province secretary. On 16 Feb., Bernard agreed to surrender extracts to Thomas Cushing, Speaker of the House. A few days earlier the Speaker had given Bernard a copy of the Circular Letter, which Bernard then dispatched to Shelburne enclosed in **No. 589**. Bernard's subsequent explanation (in **No. 591**) did not suggest that he had traded correspondence with Cushing in order to obtain the Circular Letter, but stressed that he had followed the secretary of state's advice that he could use the letter of 17 Sept. as he saw fit: thus, Bernard continued, by disclosing to the House he had the minister's backing he hoped to discourage faint-hearted Whigs and encourage stout-hearted friends of government. (He had done much the same thing with a letter from Shelburne's predecessor, Henry Seymour Conway, warning that repeal of the Stamp Act had raised British expectations that the colonists should cease complaining about taxation.)[26] But there was a trade-off of sorts. In gifting Shelburne's letter to his enemies Bernard ought to have expected the Whigs to press him to release more information (as they did), unless he was hopelessly naïve. In presenting the Circular Letter to the British (as he was obliged to do, though not immediately), he also would have appreciated that it would open up old wounds. Neither action was the outcome of astute political calculation, but of carelessness, and together kept Bernard in the cross-fire of imperial politics—as indeed he might also have anticipated.

Bernard was certainly not inured to the criticism swirling around him, but from February onwards he detached himself from the political game and indulged in hollow imperialist imperatives. He could not conceive "any Danger of the Parliament's giving Way," he declared to Lord Barrington (**No. 587**). "The Impeachment of the Power of Parliament has been Continually extending since the Time of the Stampt-Act," he informed Barrington in March, "& will not stop 'till the Parliament interposes with Effect" (**No. 592**). Bernard and Barrington were increasingly pessimistic about the Chatham administration being able to restore equilibrium to British-American relations without Parliament adopting some signal measures to curb the protest movement. While they did not always specify the kind of measures they had in mind, reforming the colonial governments was certainly top of their private agenda; repealing the Townshend Revenue Act was not, and neither was it yet on the government's list. There was much in Bernard's correspondence that would have appealed to Britons like Barrington who believed that British errors of judgment had only encouraged Americans' pretensions of self-government.

Having emotionally abandoned provincial politics Bernard concentrated on playing imperial politics, by trying to influence from afar the deliberations of the British government and Parliament. His demands for British intervention took form during the early spring and summer and were, on this occasion, calculated to attract ministers' attention—which he did, some of it warranted but all of it unwanted by the Americans. As he might also have expected, his past and present conduct as governor was thenceforth subjected to scrutiny: in Massachusetts by the Whig "Faction" in the House of Representatives and the Boston town meeting, and Whig polemicists writing in the province newspapers; and in Britain by the secretary of state, the cabinet, and the Parliament.

London, March to April

On reading Bernard's last letters to Shelburne, which started arriving in the first week of March, Hillsborough would have been struck by two features of Massachusetts politics: the boldness of the Whig party and the impermanence of any opposition to the Whigs. On the first count, Hillsborough may not have appreciated that the Whig party in the House of Representatives was so extensive. Bernard's reports would have reinforced the notion that opposition could be put down to a faction and the influence exerted by two of Boston's representatives, James Otis Jr.

and Samuel Adams. Otis and Adams were impressive leaders, the former largely as an orator, the latter as a political manager, and both as political writers. Bernard's communications with the Whig leaders were largely conducted through the Speaker, Thomas Cushing (**No. 581**), a more moderate Whig than Otis or Adams. The several remonstrances issued by the House during January and February were produced by committees, although Adams and Otis took lead roles in crafting and writing the papers, bringing a persuasive, forthright logic that on perusal by the British would have seemed to brook no compromise.[27] The assumptions underpinning the Circular Letter, Bernard reported, stood "equally conclusive against all Acts of Parliament," while the Letter itself accused him of misrepresenting the province to ministers (**No. 589**).

The second point, regarding the lack of support for the provincial government, was more obvious to Hillsborough. The radical Whigs were only momentarily encumbered by initial objections from conservative Whigs and friends of government. After delaying the adoption of the Circular Letter, these critics simply melted away (**Nos. 585** and **589**). It is uncertain if Hillsborough knew much if anything about the divisions within the Whig ranks that Bernard revealed to Richard Jackson in **No. 586**. (Notably between James Otis Jr. and Joseph Hawley, who did not yet share his colleague's radical enthusiasm and was probably experiencing the self-doubts that had once troubled Otis.) Bernard's most recent report, while intimating widespread distaste for scurrilous newspaper articles voicing "blasphemous abuse of Kingly Government itself," was not heartening. It emphasized the high degree of coordination among the governor's enemies in the House, town, and newspapers. So, while a "Virulent Libell" in the *Boston Gazette* (by Dr. Joseph Warren) could elicit sympathy for a victim as unpopular as the governor and stir resentment against the radicals for abusing press freedoms, legal redress could not be expected (**No. 593**). But how to help the king's governor sustain his administration and maintain parliamentary authority? Unbeknown to Bernard, Chatham's cabinet had no intention of making concessions to the colonists or—for now at any rate—heeding their complaints about the king's governor. On 4 Apr., Hillsborough assured Bernard that he "entirely agree[d]" with the necessity of preserving the primacy of official channels of communication (**No. 603**). (Hillsborough kept his word in so far as he refused to recognize the agents appointed separately by the Massachusetts House and Council.) After praising Bernard for aiding the rejection of the Circular Letter (**No. 603**), news of its adoption, arriving on 15 Apr. (**No. 589**), jolted Hillsborough into action. First, he presented the Circular Letter to the cabinet. Thereupon, with his colleagues' approval, Hillsborough issued his own circular to the colonial governors insisting they ignore the Massachusetts Circular Letter and denouncing its "dangerous and Factious Tendency" to "promote" an illegal combination "in open Opposition to, and denial of, the authority of Parliament."[28] In a separate letter of 22 Apr., Hillsborough instructed Bernard to have the House of Representatives rescind the original vote of approval (**No. 608**).

Hillsborough's instruction to Bernard was an impulsive gesture, a warning to colonial radicals. He would have known from Bernard's letters that it would commit the governor to a political struggle he could only win by scaring the House into submission. The requirement to rescind the vote was a high-handed demand that the Whig members repudiate intercolonial politics and work through and with the governor's office in making obedient supplications for a redress of grievances. It is likely that the British government's proposal to create a baronetcy for Bernard (first broached through Barrington in **No. 610**), was more than an incentive or reward for Bernard. It too was a public signal to Bernard's critics in both America and Britain that the governor still had the confidence of the Chatham administration and the king; yet it also enabled Hillsborough to recall Bernard with grace should the rescinding instruction prove a failure. The secretary was already thinking of moving him to another province. Hillsborough, however, was demanding too much of others and too little of himself. The instruction to rescind was an error of judgment (**Appendix 1**). Bernard did not receive the rescinding instruction until 15 Jun., along with a caveat from Barrington that "Things are coming apace to crisis: My friend Lord Hillsborough will have his hands full." Bernard, he advised, really ought to get out of the province as soon as he could (**No. 605**).[29] When Bernard presented Hillsborough's instruction to the House of Representatives later that month, the ensuing confrontation demonstrated not the fractiousness but the unity of the Whigs in trying to get the Townshend duties repealed.

Boston, March to April

Bernard's first reports of popular protests against the Townshend duties instinctively and explicitly drew comparison with the Stamp Act riots and demonstrations of 1765. While the previous disturbances were generally nonviolent, the destruction of Thomas Hutchinson's house and the intimidation of other government officials, had led Bernard to conclude that mobbism was a weapon of choice for the Sons of Liberty.[30] He was not blind to Whig endeavors to control crowds, in which they were largely successful, but overly-sensitive to menacing behavior. Rioters and politicians had defeated the Stamp Act, he concluded, mainly by threatening retribution against officials duty-bound to enforce the law; in the winter of 1765-66 he believed he had no choice other than to close the law courts and Customhouse—unless he were to instruct officials to break the law by ignoring an act of Parliament. First with the Stamp Act, and then the Townshend Acts, Bernard was convinced that mobs would be called upon to aid the Whigs' campaign for repeal, in which, once again, "they propose to suspend the Execution of the Laws." (**No. 592**.)

Writing in haste—whether contrived or not—reinforced the comparison and conveyed immediacy for the reader. This example to John Pownall:

> I have not Time now to write to you as fully as I could wish: I can only say that it looks as if the Same Disorders which attended the Stampt-Act are coming on apace. People seem determined not to Submit to the Laws of Trade; They now declare against all Laws which impose Duties; The Molasses Act of which was formerly a Favour is as great an Object of Opposition as any. The Officers of the Trade are threatned, Mobbings Continu^a^lly expected, The Commissioners in the most precarious Situation not knowing how to order the Execution of the Laws or how to let it alone. I am just as defenceless as ever. &c &c. God grant that the Opinion which has prevailed at home that the Colonies would come to Rights of themselves may not prove a fatal Deception. (**No. 595**.)

Bernard's talent for dramatic anticipation was more pronounced in his letters to his British friends than it was to the secretaries of state. This to Richard Jackson:

> Every Things here is running into Confusion; People here are ready to refuse to submit to any Laws of Trade imposing Duties; the Officers are threatened; Mobbs are expected; the Commissioners are frightned; the Government is defenceless; &c &c. These are the Effects of America (or rather Boston) being left to Right itself. You shall here more soon. (**No. 594**.)

Perhaps though, Bernard was deceiving himself, for unlike the Stamp Tax the Townshend duties were being collected. Collection proceeded apace under the American Board of Customs, established at Boston in November 1767. The tea duty and other trade duties brought into the king's Treasury around £40,000 per annum (minus officials' salaries). The nonimportation agreements adopted by the colonies, beginning in Boston in March, over the next eighteen months reduced by half the value British imports and with it revenue from duties payable in the colonies: gross receipts from duties were £39,512 in 1768, £42,787 in 1769, and £36,668 in 1770. Full trade resumed in 1770 (with the notable exception of duted tea); within two years the value of imports was more than double what it had been five years earlier and revenue collection peaked at £49,113.[31] Smuggling, however, particularly of Dutch tea, was widespread (judging by anecdotal evidence) but it is difficult to establish any specific impact on Crown revenues. Consumers habituated to contraband and merchants accustomed to evading trade duties were naturally hostile toward customs officers, and their assiduous efforts to enforce the boycotts of British goods enabled popular participation in the protest movement.[32] But direct action to prevent customs officers enforcing the trade laws was uncoordinated and not sustained beyond the locale of occurrence. Nothing in the Whigs' campaign against the Townshend Acts overtly proposed coercing government officials into suspending imperial laws. What Bernard and the Customs Board initially reported were shady "rescues" of goods impounded by customs officers and the outrageous defiance of smuggler Daniel Malcom in preventing an authorized search of his property (**Appendix 2**).[33]

However, it was the Customs commissioners, not the governor, who, in a memorial of 12 Feb., first divined a sinister purpose to the insults trafficked in the town meetings and routinely hurled at them from outside the Customhouse building in King Street. "At these meetings the lowest mechanics discuss upon the most important points of government with the utmost freedom; which, being guided by a few hot and designing men, become the constant source of sedition." (**Appendix 2**.) Bernard was not privy to the commissioners' private deliberations nor to the proceedings of the Board; indeed, he soon found reason to resent the commissioners' arrogance toward provincial officers. Even so, there is evidence to suggest some collusion between the governor and the commissioners—at least in so far as making sure their stories tallied. Confiding in Barrington, Bernard wrote on 3 Mar. "The present Suspence is a very disagreeable one: the Commissioners see that they must wait till a violent Opposition is made to their Officers; & yet they dread the Experiment. I must be involved with them more or less," having promised them "Asylum" at Castle William. (**No. 592**.)

On 18 Mar., when Boston Whigs noisily celebrated the second anniversary of the Stamp Act's repeal, the Customs commissioners alerted the governor to the possibility that the effigies of Commissioner Paxton and Inspector General Williams, found hanging on Liberty Tree, were "a presage of some open Acts of Violence" (**No. 599**). That same day, Bernard wrote Shelburne and Hillsborough, expressing disappointment that the Council seemed dismissive of the entire incident and would not join him in condemning the disturbances as a precursor of "Insurrection." But as both the Council and Thomas Hutchinson appreciated, when local Whigs removed the effigies they defused the situation and ensured that the celebrations would pass off peacefully (**No. 600**). The governor and the commissioners may have colluded in their epistolary counter-attack, but it was Bernard who seemed to relish the task of dramatizing the Board's present predicament (of which his recent letters to Pownall and Jackson had given notice). There is no doubt that his letters of 18 Mar. were intended to elicit a strong reaction, perhaps the strongest possible in the circumstances: the direct deployment of British Regulars.

Nothing was to be gained from asking the Council to join him in making such a request of the British commander in chief, General Thomas Gage, based at New York.[34]

> I have once before [*in 1765*] tried the Experiment when the Danger was more urgent and immediate than it is now and the Success then fully convinced me that it is to no Purpose ever again to repeat the Question. His Majesty's Ministers have within these three Years been fully acquainted with the defenceless State of this Government; and therefore I trust that I shall be excused leaving it to the Administration to determine upon a Measure which they are much more able to judge of and be answerable for than I can be. (**No. 600**.)

By likening spontaneous acts of resentment to the intimidation offered government officials prior to the Stamp Act riots, Bernard hoped to persuade Hillsborough to order General Gage to dispatch troops to Boston. This rationale also underpinned Bernard's subsequent reports on the *Liberty* riot of 10 Jun. wherein he connected evasion of the trade laws to the Whigs' wider political agenda. Bernard and the Customs commissioners, in short, were able to convince Hillsborough and the Treasury that the resurgence in crowd action threatened a violent turn, evinced a propensity for lawlessness, and, more worryingly still, threatened insurrection; thus they let the British deduce that the provincial government and Customhouse now required the protection of British soldiers and that inaction would jeopardize imperial power.

Meanwhile, the death of the Bernards' fourth son, fifteen year-old Shute, on 5 Apr. after "a short Illness of four days," shook the governor to the core.[35] "I find that a Number of Children does not so much reconcile one to the Loss of one, as might be imagin'd. However I ought not to repine, when I have 9 hopeful Children left," he confided to Barrington, striving to maintain composure (**No. 606**). The Bernards would lose two other boys: Frank (the eldest) who died in Boston in 1770, and William, the seventh child, lost at sea in 1776. Shute's death doubtless made the governor and his wife Amelia all the more determined to get out of Boston. But it is otherwise difficult to ascertain how it might have affected Bernard's handling of public affairs during the spring; perhaps it rendered him altogether more impatient with critics whose antics he believed jeopardized the beguiling ordinariness of daily life.

To former governor Thomas Pownall, Bernard complained that colonists expected their governor should "Side with them in their Pretensions against the Parliament" (**No. 607**). For Pownall also, securing American representation in Parliament was one way to end the interminable disputes over taxation. But what Bernard did not tell Pownall was that he believed the Americans were intent on a more "desperate Defiance of Great Britain;" and he had no intention of exposing his "Family" to "a much greater risk . . . to another insurrection." It was vital, Bernard pleaded with Barrington, that he be accorded leave to report in person and get his family out. To underline the point, a "secret" postscript to a letter delivered by a secure conveyance asserted unequivocally that it was the "intention of the Faction here to cause an Insurrection against the Crown Officers" as soon as "their extravagant Demands" on self-taxation were refused (**No. 609**). These concerns Barrington obligingly forwarded to Hillsborough.[36] Not until mid-September (when fresh instructions arrived from Hillsborough) did Bernard give up the expectation of being allowed to return to England that year.

These, then, were the sentiments of a beleaguered imperial official. What support Bernard could muster in the spring of 1768 came from a dwindling band. With the friends of government in the House out-muscled by the Whigs and the Council becoming more unpredictable, Bernard relied heavily on his cabinet of advisers: principally Thomas Hutchinson (the lieutenant governor and chief justice), Andrew Oliver (the province secretary), Robert Auchmuty (judge of the Vice Admiralty Court), and—for a while at least—Jonathan Sewall (the advocate general of Vice Admiralty and the province attorney general).[37]

Of his deputy Hutchinson Bernard was pleased to claim later that there was always a "Union of Sentiments & Coalition of Interests between us" (**No. 788**).[38] While his advisers generally supported the governor in his run-ins with the assembly, these Massachusetts-born men nevertheless evinced their own provincial perspectives, Hutchinson most prominently. Of Hutchinson, Bernard remarked that "It gives me great pleasure to say that I can depend upon his resolution & steadiness as much as I can Upon My own" (**No. 596**). That Hutchinson did not share Bernard's deep-seated anxieties about popular violence (as his comments in **No. 600** imply) points to a tension—but not a fracture—in their relationship. The hostility Bernard felt toward the province radicals was rooted in fear that what Hutchinson endured in 1765 might also happen to him in 1768. Even so, senior provincial officers escaped maltreatment in 1768, and no Customs officer was manhandled until the seizure of Hancock's *Lydia* in April or physically attacked until the *Liberty* riot of 10 Jun.

For all that Hutchinson was the governor's confidant and privy to some of the governor's correspondence, he was not fully aware of what exactly Bernard was telling the British about the colonial opposition during 1768. Hutchinson noted later that

> The Governor has but in very few Instances acquaint-
> ed me with the Letters he has wrote. I dont know
> that I ever saw any thing he wrote to Lord Hillsboro.
> He must undoubtedly have wrote some things which
> ought not to be published.[39]

Hutchinson and Bernard, in fact, disagreed about many things, not least the governor's preference for a royally-appointed Council and his colonialist attitude toward
provincial law and law enforcement. Hutchinson must have experienced pressure
from friends as well as enemies to cease defending the governor, if not to abandon
him. After Hutchinson justified Bernard's handling of the Stamp Act riots to former
province agent William Bollan,[40] Bollan's riposte was scathing about Hutchinson's
loyalty to "your little great man . . .

> whatever you may think of your favourite, I am per-
> suaded that his law, justice and policy will be found
> wanting when weigh'd in a just balance, at the same
> time believing that if some parts of his conduct were
> known to you they wou'd fall under your censure as
> well as mine.[41]

Bernard never took Hutchinson's loyalty for granted, knowing truthfully that it was
Hutchinson, not he, who brought a deep understanding of colonial history and
society to government. Bernard's jealously was manifest in the delusion that it was
he and not Hutchinson who managed the government side. "I certainly have many
friends more strongly attached to me than they are to him," Hutchinson intimated
to a family member, "tho my friends in general are his also." [42] Hutchinson, Bernard
could rely on, but others gave him increasing cause for concern.

The lengthy dispute between the Customs commissioners and his chief law
officer, Jonathan Sewall, the province's attorney general and the advocate general
of Vice Admiralty, was the most serious of any internal rift that Bernard had to deal
with in his nine-year administration. Sewall owed his rapid rise to Bernard's patronage, but appeared to stall when asked to pursue the Whig printers of the *Boston
Gazette*, Benjamin Edes and John Gill (**No. 596**). When it came to enforcing the
trade laws, Sewall evinced a strict constructionist interpretation of the laws of
admiralty that upset the Customs commissioners. Matters came to a head in the
spring when he delivered his opinion on the *Lydia* case with a panache that exposed
the commissioners' ignorance of the law yet also saved them (and himself) from
embarking on an ill-founded prosecution of the vessel's owner, the Whig merchant
John Hancock. By the summer Sewall was threatening to resign, believing (rightly)
that the commissioners had questioned his competency. The dispute between the

commissioners and Sewall seemed always to intrude at the very moment when the governor was pre-occupied with grave matters of state and where Sewall's assistance was most needed: in the pursuit of Hancock after the seizure of his sloop *Liberty* and on the eve of the Regulars' arrival (**No. 678**).

Sewall resented the fact that the Customs commissioners seemed to regard him as a political servant. No matter that their cause was to humble a high-profile Whig, Sewall genuinely doubted that, after seizing the *Liberty*, there was sufficient evidence to convict Hancock for evading the trade laws (**No. 672**). Sewall stood to benefit financially from any successful prosecution in the Vice Admiralty Court, as did Bernard as governor, and with exorbitant fines being levied and punitive penalties sought, the trial, from Nov. 1768 to Mar. 1769, became a *cause célèbre*. Sewall abandoned the case for lack of evidence.[43] As the dispute between Sewall and commissioners dragged on, Bernard had good cause to resent Sewall's stubbornness and the commissioners' vindictiveness. But Sewall's independence of mind also led Bernard, by the end of 1768, to question his loyalty and exclude him from his cabinet council.[44] Bernard never knew the full story of Sewall's spat with the Customs commissioners until the following January, by which time it was clear to him that his attorney general had compromised his own integrity as much as he had been compromised by the commissioners.[45]

Boston, May to June

Mid-May brought Bernard official confirmation of Hillsborough's appointment and with it news that the secretary fully approved his conduct in office. Hillsborough's first business letter praised everything the governor had tried in order to limit the Whigs' influence, notably his refusal to recognize the House's agent and his tactical veto on radicals elected to the Council (**No. 588**). The secretary's subsequent communications were equally supportive (**No. 603** etc.). These endorsements boosted Bernard's self-confidence. While accepting that the "political Barometer" stood unchanged, there was "less appearance of violence" and he dared hope that "Vigorous measures" could yet "give a great turn to the politicks of this place" (**No. 617**).

Bernard's replies to Hillsborough exhibited a freedom, if not a talent, for insulting the colonists. He invited sympathy for the victims of "Terror," identified his own tribulations with British neglect, and exhorted Hillsborough to action.

> I therefore do not expect that this Government will recover itself, untill these Men have received some signal Check from Great Britain, such as will open the Eyes of their deluded followers. Their being suffered for near 3 years with Impunity to govern this Town by a trained Mob, and to set Great Britain at Defiance

> & treat the supreme imperial Power with a Contempt
> not only indecent but allmost treasonable has caused
> a great Despondency among the Officers and Friends
> of Government, and has brought the Kings Authority
> very low. (**No. 614**.)

Hitherto, Bernard's venom had been directed primarily at Boston representative James Otis Jr. The Whig party's electoral successes, its domination of the House of Representatives, and the inroads it was making in the Council still owed much to the disgruntled Otis family, with whom Bernard ruled out any possible compromise (**Nos. 616**, **617**, and **619**). But the commitment and organizational skills of other Whig leaders were equally worthy of comment. Bernard did not always name them, preferring to cast them as revolutionary phantasms for Hillsborough's amusement: "3 or 4 Persons bankrupt in Reputation as well as in Fortune, and equally void of Credit in Character & in Property." (**No. 614**). This slur was an unmistakable acknowledgement of Samuel Adams's emergence as a formidable driver of the opposition in both the House and the Boston town meeting. Other local Whigs took a lead role in the enforcement of Boston's nonimportation agreements of March and August, and one of Bernard's early reports hints at the growing commitment of Boston's workers to the scheme (**No. 615**). The weight of evidence Bernard presented Hillsborough thus far pointed to an ably-led opposition movement feeding on broad-based popular support. This was not, in the parlance of the time, the faction of thwarted ambitious men that British parliamentarians habitually fooled themselves were fomenting the troubles in America. If Hillsborough had genuinely believed the fallacy, Bernard's letters ought to have dispelled it.

The governor eyed the prospect of remaining in post only as long as was necessary. He still expected to be granted leave of absence, though when that might be he could only guess; and he still supposed that Barrington could find him another, less troublesome posting in America. Having dutifully informed the British of the political, constitutional, and even social aspects of the colonial protest movement and suggested appropriate remedies Bernard was prepared to bide his time until he could get out of Boston. For all that he hoped the British government would offer "some signal Check"—ideally the cantonment of a regiment of troops in Boston and the appointment of a royal Council (**No. 658**)—he probably did not expect London to move so quickly.

With the arrival on 17 May of HMS *Romney*, a fifty-gun, fourth-rate ship captained by John Corner, Bernard probably felt more secure than he had in years (**No. 634**). Bostonians, on the other hand, viewed with trepidation the movements of Royal Navy vessels in and out of the harbor during the next two months.[46] Corner's press gangs provoked immediate resistance (**No. 618**) that spilled over into a riot on Friday, 10 Jun., following the seizure of John Hancock's sloop *Liberty*.

These disturbances fit the wider patterns of colonial crowd action and did not in themselves threaten civil disorder or exhibit revolutionary tendencies.[47] But Bernard returned to his insurrectionist theme when he declared the events of 10 Jun. a "great Riot" in which lives were threatened (but not lost), property damaged (though not much), and customs officers beaten (yet not endangered) (**No. 623**). It is difficult to judge the veracity of Bernard's accounts of the *Liberty* riot. When it comes to ascertaining crowd motivation and intention historians have rightly questioned the probity of the governor's reports.[48] Bernard's motivation, however, can reasonably be deduced from correspondence printed in this volume (**Nos. 620-636**) and a selection of the papers of the Customs Board (**Appendices 6 and 7**). These transcripts confirm in detail for the first time historians' suspicions[49] that Bernard and the Customs commissioners used the *Liberty* riot to manufacture a sense of crisis in the hope of bringing British soldiers to Boston. All of this should aid historians' understanding of how one of the major flashpoints of the Imperial Crisis had an impact upon British policymaking.[50]

Bernard's first report to London (**No. 623**) omitted details as to what had triggered the riot: the seizure of John Hancock's sloop *Liberty*. Hancock may have been under surveillance since early May, the Customhouse suspecting him of routinely smuggling Madeira wine, molasses, and other goods. But senior customs officers only seized the *Liberty* at Hancock's Wharf after one of their junior officers admitted that—several weeks previously—he had been physically restrained by Hancock's men while attempting an inspection of the vessel. Fearing a violent attempt to rescue the *Liberty* or its cargo, customs officers Benjamin Hallowell and Joseph Harrison arranged for boats from the HMS *Romney* to tow the *Liberty* from the wharf to the warship. On their return to the waterfront, Hallowell, Harrison, and Harrison's son were met with a hail of insults and stones from a crowd initially numbering upwards of three hundred. Doubtless it was a terrifying enough ordeal for the officers coming ashore, but on making their way back to the Customhouse and to their homes had to pass through a much larger crowd swollen by observers and angry townsfolk. Governor Bernard's narrative captures the officers' progress through a gauntlet of blows. The crowd proceeded to Boston Common to burn a "pleasure Boat" belonging to Harrison. There the people were "harangued by a Leader" to defend their "liberties" and keep faith in "the Strength of our ^own^ Arms and God." Further violence, Bernard concluded, was averted only when the rum ran out, though the day's events seemed a "Prelude to greater Mischiefs." That, in sum, constituted the "great Riot" Bernard described to Hillsborough.

While the drama of the *Liberty* riot matched the first Stamp Act riot, of 14 Aug. 1765, the sequel Bernard anticipated was conspicuously absent. Three years previously, the mobs had progressed from intimidating officials to destroying Thomas Hutchinson's mansion house. But there was no escalation this time, with local

Whigs carefully restraining hotheads and even seeking Bernard's assistance to end impressment (**Nos. 629**, **631**, and **632**). Bernard's subsequent letters proffered only signifiers of intent to commit violence, not actual evidence of intent. On 12 Jun., he "heard some loose Reports that there was to be another rising." Advertisements by the Sons of Liberty summoned the people to an open air meeting on Tuesday 14 Jun. and handbills threatened retribution. Rumors abounded that the seizure of the *Liberty* was premeditated and provocative: that the commissioners, the governor, and the naval commander together had hatched a plot to incite the populace to violence in order to justify the misrepresentations they had already made to Britain (**No. 630**). A year hence, Samuel Adams read copies of official correspondence documenting the *Liberty* riot, including Bernard's report in **No. 623**, and, writing in the pamphlet *Appeal to the World*, concluded that he had been right all along about the governor: that he was involved in a conspiracy to disseminate disinformation.

By retreating to the *Romney* and thence to Castle William for nigh on five months, the Customs commissioners projected another narrative for Bernard to consider. When would it be safe for them to return to the Customhouse? What was Bernard doing to ensure their safety? Bernard and the commissioners compiled their own files documenting the exchanges between them lest they have to justify their respective decisions at a future date (**Nos. 624** to **627**). John Temple, however, did not accompany the other commissioners to Castle William and remained in town. Consequently his signature is absent from many of the Board's documents, but Temple's already strained relationship with his colleagues deteriorated further as they came to suspect him of leaking information to his Whig friends via his father-in-law James Bowdoin, the Whig leader in the Council. To his enemies, including Bernard, it seemed as if Temple was motivated by animus and incapable of forming professional relationships.[51]

Discussions between the governor and the Council, meanwhile, focused less on the dwindling prospect of violence and more on the perceived state of the province (**No. 628**). So too did debates in the House of Representatives and Boston town meeting. Whigs feared that the commissioners and Bernard were providing the British with a plausible rationale for sending in soldiers; as might be expected, the "state" of Massachusetts figured prominently in the governor's correspondence with Britain (**No. 630**). In short, the Customs commissioners were pressing Bernard to resolve the issue by asking the Council to join him in requesting military assistance from General Gage.

Bernard first raised the idea with the Council on 13 Jun. but did not put a formal question to them until 27 Jul. Gage, however, was concerned, on learning from the Customs commissioners, that the commissioners "had received no Assurances of Protection" (**No. 637**). He provided Bernard with sealed orders that he could use to expedite the deployment of soldiers from Halifax, Nova Scotia (**No. 639**). Bernard knew little of Gage personally, but after the Stamp Act riots was impressed by the general's readiness to offer military assistance. For his part, Gage probably supposed the civilian governor indecisive.[52] Bernard may have been hoping that Gage would make that difficult decision for him and briefly confused himself, wrongly supposing that Gage had indeed ordered troops direct to Boston (**No. 641**). (Gage's letters concerning the deployment of troops to Boston were not previously printed in the *Correspondence of Gage*).

In the meantime, on 18 Jun. Bernard dispatched a letter to Hillsborough with a plaintive cry for intervention:

> the retreat of the Commissioners has been very time-ly and well circumstanced & their security is now ef-fectually provided for. Your Lordship may wonder at my dwelling upon this; but if there is not a Revolt the Leaders of the Sons of Liberty must falsify their Words & change their purposes. For my part when I consider the Defenceless State of this Town I cannot think they will be so mad as to attempt to defend it against the King's Forces: but the Lengths they have gone already are scarce short of Madness. (**No. 632.**)

Replying to Barrington, Bernard noted that "Your Lordship observes that Things are coming apace to a Crisis: I am sure they are with us; and I fear the Bostonians will get the Start of you" (**No. 634**).

The governor and the Customs commissioners on the one hand and the Council, the Whigs, and the town meeting on the other viewed the retreat of the American Board of Customs to HMS *Romney* after the *Liberty* riot from different perspectives. Both sides thought it sent a dangerous signal to the British govern-ment that law and order in Boston was being challenged and that royal officials were in jeopardy. While Bernard and the Customs commisioners exaggerated the threat of crowd action in so far as the insurrection they espied did not exist (as historian Dirk Hoerder has shown), the entire episode—the riot caused by the seizure of the *Liberty* and the impressment of sailors—illustrated the inability of the provincial government and imperial establishment to enforce authority in the face of resistance to imperial agencies. The "conditions of law," according to his-torian John P. Reid, were now largely determined by Whig politicians in the van of the colonial protest movement. (Some of these Whigs were "new men" as Ber-nard recognised, although the leadership pool did not substantively expand at this time.)[53] In the months ahead, and against a backdrop of increasingly hostile public opinion, Bernard expended considerable effort trying convince Hillsborough of the rectitude of his observations on crowd action and his worth as a commentator on the protest movement.

On 15 Jun., in the midst of the brouhaha over the *Liberty* riot, Bernard received Hillsborough's instruction to have the House of Representatives rescind the vote approving the Circular Letter. The news was unwelcome in itself, for it committed Bernard to a contest he knew he could not win.

> I cannot foresee what will be done upon the occasion; whether Prudence will get the better of Faction, or not. I know not how to hope that they will comply; if they do not, your Lordship may depend upon it I will obey my orders (**No. 633**).

If the House refused to rescind the vote, Bernard had no option but to dissolve the assembly and send a report of its proceedings to Hillsborough; such documents the secretary had threatened to lay before Parliament so that "such Provisions as shall be found necessary may be made to prevent for the future a Conduct of so extraordinary & unconstitutional a Nature" (**No. 608**).

The instruction's arrival was also decidedly untimely, for it significantly complicated Bernard's response to the *Liberty* riot. Both controversies aided his enemies in constructing a convenient fiction: that since the beginning of the year, at least, Bernard had deliberately misled ministers as to the state of the province in order to persuade them to intervene. The rescinding instruction was in essence an over-reaction to the reports Hillsborough had been receiving from Bernard and the Customs commissioners. But the Whigs' conspiracy theory was based entirely on suspicion, supposition, and a welter of ideological premises. Their deductions reflected the course of events, but their judgments were formed in the heat of political battles. The governor's correspondence with Shelburne and Hillsborough, they well knew, might contain the requisite evidence, yet for the moment was out of reach, save a single abridged letter Bernard agreed to hand over to the House of Representatives (**No. 566**).[54]

That Bernard *had* engaged in hostile reporting can be established from the documentation printed in this volume. That he *had* urged the British to take special measures is also evident. But did he do so with malign intent? Historiography allows some leeway for misunderstandings on both sides, and the documentary evidence from the first six months of 1768 is not enough to convict the governor of disinformation in the court of historical opinion.[55] The governor dramatized local crises he could not manage, but he did not create or invent them. He did impugn the characters of Whig leaders James Otis Jr. and Samuel Adams, but did not personally accuse them of sedition or treason. This ought to count as misrepresentation and misinformation, as the House alleged (**Appendix 9**); but it was not the conspiracy of disinformation that Samuel Adams later claimed. However, the rescinding controversy and *Liberty* riot together constituted a watershed in the governor's reporting of events and developments. For, thereafter, Bernard thought and wrote strategically, moving with deliberation, purpose, and perspicacity to endanger his enemies: this was more counter-offensive than conspiracy, and traded in whatever intelligence and information he could accumulate.

Bernard began his account of the rescinding controversy (**No. 638**) on 25 Jun. four days after presenting the House with an extract of Hillsborough's letter demanding a vote to rescind the Circular Letter. He finished the letter a week later, on the day after the House divided. Bernard did not tell the House he was empowered to dissolve the assembly in the event of noncompliance and that Hillsborough might initiate an inquiry by Parliament; he did not wish to resort to "Threats in the first Instance, before their Minds were known." His brief account of the debate seemed to bear this explanation out. When Otis delivered a "Rhapsody" of abuse against the king's ministers and parliamentarians, the governor hoped he might alienate moderate and conservative Whigs. But "All were involved in one common Obloquy," Bernard wrote despairingly. Thereupon, when the House demanded an unexpurgated copy of Hillsborough's instruction (**No. 608**) and copies of other letters to the governor, Bernard released those paragraphs of the instruction letter that contained the "Threats." The House thus knew what the consequences would be of defying the rescinding instruction. The prospect of escalation prompted the members to seek a recess to ascertain the views of their constituents, and only when refused by Bernard did they proceed to vote. The question to "rescind or not rescind" was decided in the negative by ninety-two votes to seventeen, on 30 Jun. It was the clearest indication to date of the assembly's determination to withstand imperial power.

Defiance of British colonial policy now defined mainstream Whig opinion. Bernard attributed the prime leadership role to James Otis, though the governor was cognizant of the differences that existed between Otis and Samuel Adams. Otis's demagoguery, he believed, reflected the mood of the other members, though Bernard misunderstood some of the historical allusions in Otis's speeches. The House's formal reply to Bernard's message nonetheless was calculated to appeal to a broad base of opinion: it defended their and the colonies' rights of redress and petition and accused the governor of "Misinformation and Misrepresentation," [56] prompting the appointment of a committee to petition for the governor's removal. Dissolution prevented any formal progress on the matter, and the House had to be content with the milder censure delivered in a letter to Hillsborough (**Appendix 9**).

When Bernard dissolved the assembly he knew that the locus of opposition would shift from the House of Representatives to the Council, which continued to meet with him in its advisory capacity. He knew too that his conduct would become the focus of attention in the Boston town meeting. The rescinding instruction was the last time the Crown would require Bernard to make specific demands of the assembly. It was also the beginning of the end for Bernard. "I apprehend that I shall be drove to execute my orders in a manner that may make me personally offensive," he wrote Barrington, "I therefore a good deal depend upon my obtaining leave of absence." (**No. 640**.) Bernard wanted out, as quickly as possible. Barrington had already got him what he desired: an instruction permitting leave of absence (**No. 636**), which Bernard received in mid-September, together with the offer of the governorship of Virginia.[57]

London, May to July

Wills Hill (1718-93), first earl of Hillsborough and first secretary of state for the Colonies (1768-72), was one of the most controversial British figures of the Imperial Crisis, largely because of his decision to send British troops to Boston in 1768. Hillsborough had been the colonial secretary for just four months when letters arrived in May and June illustrating the apparently precarious position of the king's servants in Boston (**Appendix 2**, **Nos. 596** and **600**). From such accounts, Hillsborough finally realized the strength and reach of the colonial opposition (of which the rescinding instruction seemed unaware). News of fresh outrages reinforced his determination to thwart colonial radicalism. His initial reaction was calm though not pedestrian: governors were exhorted to provide full assistance to the Customs Board (**No. 612**). Hillsborough also assumed full managerial control of American affairs, gathering information with a view to clarifying governors' responsibilities (**No. 635**), channeling all communications through his office (**No. 651**), and reserving the right to present governor's correspondence to Parliament as required (**No. 653**) and regardless of Bernard's previous objections. Bernard was granted a discretionary leave of absence so that he could update Hillsborough in person (**No. 636**). Customs officer Benjamin Hallowell,[58] however, was already crossing the Atlantic, bearing accounts of the *Liberty* riot by the Customs commissioners (**Appendix 6**) and Bernard (**Nos. 623, 630, 632**, and **633**).[59]

There is no comprehensive biography of Hillsborough, despite him leaving a substantial array of primary documentation[60] covering a long political career.[61] He had more than twenty-five years' experience of British politics before his appointment as colonial secretary. Hillsborough's three years as president of the Board of Trade[62] did not kindle a particular interest in American affairs or equip him with the deep knowledge acquired by his predecessor Charles Townshend.[63] Hillsborough's elevation to secretary of state, according to one historian, had more to do with his availability for office, having "sustained a political presence through persistence, not talent."[64] While Hillsborough lacked the brilliance and charisma of the earl of Shelburne, he was able to keep allies on side rather than alienate them, as Shelburne tended to do when secretary of state.

The political ambitions of neither Shelburne nor Hillsborough lay in management of American affairs. Much the same could be said of any cabinet minister whose portfolio ever included the colonies. Both Shelburne and Hillsborough rose quickly to high political office, and, more obviously in Hillsborough's case, attended to the consolidation of their own and British power in Ireland. Shelburne and Hillsborough were scions of the Anglo-Irish aristocracy. After resigning office in October 1768, Shelburne spent years in opposition until joining Rockingham's second administration of 1782 and succeeding Rockingham as prime minister to lead his own five-month administration. Hillsborough never led a British administration, and his (unfulfilled) ambition was to become lord lieutenant of the kingdom of Ireland, the king's representative and the head of government.[65] Shelburne's lands were in the Gaelic Catholic south-west, Hillsborough's in County Down in the heavily Protestant North-East. In Shelburne's case this probably induced some sympathy for the American colonists (if only because of the imperative to remain alert to their grumbling). Hillsborough's estate and wealth lay in a region whose frontier situation had been so explosive and which now (from landowners' standpoints) needed ruthless attention, taking no chances on disaffection.

The extent to which these socio-psychological drivers shaped their handling of American affairs remains to be established. In sum, Shelburne stood for conciliation with the Americans, having supported Rockingham's repeal of the Stamp Act; but that also entailed firmly defending the principle of parliamentary supremacy, as demonstrated by his reaction to the New York Assembly's defiance of the Quartering Act.[66] Hillsborough was for bullying recalcitrant Americans; as a Grenvillite, he had opposed making concessions to the Americans and remained committed to the ideal of strengthening the imperial bonds whenever possible. Hillsborough reputedly behaved like a "pompous" courtier (Horace Walpole), his insincerity and "duplicity" even upsetting the phlegmatic colonial agent Benjamin Franklin.[67] Hillsborough patently lacked leadership qualities. He "panicked," historian John Brooke has written, for he was "a weak man, totally unfitted by convictions or character to be in charge of American affairs."[68] In sending troops to Boston, Robert Middlekauf concluded, "Hillsborough prepared the way for colonial action; some colonists said that he left them no choice."[69]

On the face of it, much of the invective historians have directed at Hillsborough seems facile and irrelevant to the government's decision to send Regulars to Boston. Moreover, Governor Bernard had already "crafted a case for direct British intervention in colonial affairs" before Hillsborough took office. He argued consistently in letters to Hillsborough's predecessor, the earl of Shelburne, that crowd action and radical opposition to the Townshend duties were undermining the enforcement of imperial law.[70] But Bernard's impatience with Shelburne and Shelburne's distrust of Bernard were never absent from their correspondence during 1767. Thus, Bernard welcomed Hillsborough's appointment, because he assumed, like many British commentators, that Hillsborough would take a hard-line toward the American Colonies, and that he would be more supportive of the governors than Shelburne. Such an opinion was not misplaced and was fed by Barrington's early reports that Hillsborough was a man of "prudence firmness & temper." (**No. 605**.) Barrington, moreover, advised that he himself was a conduit to the secretary of state, informing Bernard that he had "communicated your most ingenious thoughts about American Affairs to my friend Lord Hillsborough" (**No. 597**). He later transmitted Hillsborough's offer of a baronetcy and the lieutenant-governorship of Virginia (which was not a demotion) (**No. 610**), though the latter was quickly withdrawn for political reasons (**No. 665**). Hillsborough already knew a little of Bernard's reform plans[71] and sought the opinions of Barrington and Pownall as to Bernard's reliability as a political commentator. Hillsborough evidently trusted the veracity of Bernard's reporting more than Shelburne did.

Peter D. G. Thomas's detailed account of British policymaking has revealed how far the cabinet's response to the situation in Boston, and the colonies more generally, was guided by Hillsborough. The colonial secretary relied on a wealth of information provided by imperial officials, notably Bernard and the American Board of Customs. Despite the time lag in receiving and responding to information Hillsborough correctly concluded that Bernard's letters revealed an escalation in opposition to the Townshend Acts during 1768. Hillsborough was obliged to sift through the reports and to decide what merited action and what did not, then consider *modus operandi* that the cabinet (and later the Parliament) would likely approve.[72] Hillsborough was inclined merely to express support for Bernard in his tussles with the Massachusetts House of Representatives (**No. 603**). He decided to intervene, however, upon learning of the House's efforts to organize intercolonial opposition to the Townshend duties act. He instructed Bernard to require the House to rescind the vote approving its circular letter to the speakers of the colonial assemblies (**No. 608**), thus setting his governor on a collision course with the House (**No. 638**). But it was news of the demonstrations in Boston in March and Bernard's and the Customs commissioners' apprehensions of violence that finally prompted Hillsborough and the cabinet to consider a military response.

On 8 Jun., the earl of Hillsborough issued orders to the British commander in chief in North America that would change the course of history (**Appendix 4**). Gage was instructed to send to Boston two of the sixteen regiments presently stationed in North America:[73] one to be quartered in the town, and the other at Castle William. For this task Gage selected the 14th and 29th Regiments of Foot based at Halifax, Nova Scotia. Furthermore, five Royal Navy vessels were ordered to Boston harbor to assist the American Board of Customs in carrying out its duties.[74] Hillsborough communicated the cabinet's decision to Bernard in a letter of 11 Jun. (**No. 622**). Reports on the *Liberty* riot (notably **No. 632** and **Appendix 6**) brought to London on 19 Jul. by Benjamin Hallowell initiated a further round of cabinet discussions. On 30 Jul., Hillsborough ordered two additional regiments to Boston, the 64th and 65th Regiments stationed in Ireland and already scheduled for a tour of duty in Nova Scotia the following spring (**No. 661**).

Ministers were not seeking a military solution to the Imperial Crisis, but presumed that the presence of the Regulars would restore respect for imperial authority which, like Bernard, they seemed to think was in decline. Recent events in London demonstrated the British government's readiness to use the military as a police force. On 10 May dragoons deployed upon Barrington's orders dispersed a rally at St. George's Fields, London, held in support of the incarcerated John Wilkes, returned to Parliament in March at the general election. Six people were killed by the soldiers, whose actions Barrington publicly lauded. The situations in London and Boston were by no means comparable. Both political prudence and the law dictated that with Boston, Hillsborough and Barrington leave it to the civil government—in this case the Governor and Council—to decide if and when they required soldiers to break up riots. Ministers calculated that billeting the troops in the town itself would be a sufficient deterrent to rioters. In that sense, the British viewed the relocation of the soldiers not as a military expedition but a temporary cantonment (as Bernard himself had long urged).[75]

How far cabinet deliberations on the troop deployment were driven by the colonial secretary is open to debate, but Bernard's reports were considered carefully by Hillsborough and his colleagues. Hillsborough's letter to Bernard of 11 Jun. (**No. 622**) stressed that the decision to send two regiments to Boston was based "upon the most mature Consideration of what has been represented by yourself, and by the Comm[rs] of the Customs established at Boston." He specifically cited Bernard's letter on the disturbances in Boston of 18 Mar. (**No. 600**) and the Customs commissioners' memorials (**Appendices 2** and **3**). According to John P. Reid, Hillsborough was "misled" by exaggerated accounts of crowd action framed by officials whose anxieties clouded the probity of the evidence.[76]

Alternatively, it could be suggested that Hillsborough was obliged to make a judgment call as to whether or not the situation in Boston warranted troop deployment. He was probably confused (rather than "misled") by Bernard's unsubstantiated reports that insurrection was intended in Boston. Hillsborough wished that Bernard "had been more explicit" in discerning and providing unambiguous evidence:

> a very full and confidential Communication of what
> you have heard, concerning the Designs and Inten-
> tions of those, whose Opposition to Measures of Con-
> ciliation render them justly suspected as Enemies to
> all Government, would have been more satisfactory
> than the alarming and dark hint you give. (**No. 622**.)

Hillsborough was bemused by Bernard's insistence on obtaining the agreement of
the Council in requesting military assistance, reminding Bernard (correctly) that
if civil government was actually endangered he could make such a request on his
own authority.[77] However, Hillsborough continued, the government's decision to
dispatch troops rested on the credibility of Bernard's interpretation.

> It is but too evident, not only from the Accounts con-
> tained in your last Letters, but also from a Revision of
> the State of your Government for some Times past,
> that the Authority of Civil Power is too weak to en-
> force Obedience to the Laws, and preserve that Peace
> and good Order, which is essential to the Happiness
> of every State.

Hillsborough thus accepted Bernard's proposition that civil government was weak,
irrespective of the fact that imperial laws, including the Townshend duties act, were
being enforced (though the trade laws were being circumvented by smugglers).
Furthermore, the colonial secretary erroneously assumed that political opposition
routinely encompassed criminal behavior. So, by reducing the Imperial Crisis to
questions of law and order, Hillsborough accepted the rationale that Bernard and
the American Board of Customs had constructed to justify the deployment of the
Regulars in the first place.

Boston, July

Bernard to Gage, 2 Jul. 1768:

> The State of Affairs in Boston is full as bad as the re-
> ports you have received can make it.[78] All real power
> is in the hands of the people of the lowest class; Civil
> Authority can do nothing but what they will allow. I
> have been obliged, after having in Vain applied to the
> Council for advice & assistance to tell the Commis-
> sioners of the Customs that I can give them no pro-
> tection. (**No. 641**.)

Bernard's plaintive evocation of his government's weakness was at best disingenu-ous, at worst deliberately misleading. Boston was not controlled by the mob; nor had Bernard formally asked the Council to join him in a request for military assistance. Gage interpreted the letter as a tacit request for military back up, and, judging by his subsequent correspondence with Bernard, that would appear to have been Ber-nard's intention (**Nos. 643**, **652**, and **655**). Moreover, having received the sealed orders from Gage, Bernard transmitted them to the commander at Halifax, Lt. Col. William Dalrymple, still assuming that Dalrymple was being instructed to deploy his men to Boston. Anxious to preserve a veneer of deniability in the face of public hostility, he observed that

> my Situation requires that I should appear to know as little of and act as little in the Proceedings of this Kind as can well be. I should therefore be obliged to you if in conducting a Business of this Kind you would let me appear a Stranger to it untill it becomes necessary to communicate it to me officially. (**No. 642**.)

Rumors were getting wilder (Castle William could be invested, **No. 644**); law enforcement was in the hands of local Whigs (smugglers who rescued impounded cargoes returned them to the Customhouse at the behest of town officials, **No. 648**); customs officers were regularly threatened (one defended himself with fire-arms, **No. 656**). A climax was nigh (a "Time of Trial, whether this Town &c will or will not submit to Great Britain," **No. 649**). Emotions ran high. Everyone expected the Regulars were imminent. While Bernard did not anticipate an "insurrection" the troops' arrival would nevertheless be a moment of reckoning with the Sons of Liberty ("whoever procures Troops . . . will be destroyed.")

> That it should be left to any one ~~here~~ to ask for Troops to come here at this Time of Day, will be the Wonder of the future readers of the History of these Times. (**No. 649**)

When, on 16 Jul., Bernard was disabused of the notion that troops were on the way (**No. 652**) he turned his attention to the Council. Having transmitted the Council's petition to the king protesting American taxes, he hoped the moderates would be more amenable to his situation (**No. 654**). Lest there be any further confusion, he made sure that Gage would not move any troops without the authori-zation of the Governor and Council (**No. 655**). But he did not expect the Council to join him in writing Gage, and with no further news from Hillsborough wrote despondently to Barrington:

> now all the Burthen is to be laid upon me and, as if I
> was not at present sufficiently loaded with Dangers &
> Difficulties, I alone am to be made answerable to the
> Fury of the People for introducing Troops here illegally
> & unconstitutionally; for so they will call the requiring
> them without the Advice of Council. (**No. 658**.)

Bernard's brief account of the Council's rejection, on 29 Jul., of his proposal to request troops conclusively established that "all expectation of troops coming to Boston, untill orders arrive from England is over." But he continued to press Hillsborough, aiming to convince him that Chatham's desire of avoiding the "Appearance of forcible & compulsive Measures" since 1766 had not pacified the Americans: that the only realistic alternative was for London to send the troops into Boston (**No. 660**).

Boston, August to September

With the assembly in abeyance, Bernard prepared himself for an uncomfortable but endurable few months until he could take his leave. Seeking direction from Hillsborough, he lamented that the "state of this Government . . . is brought so low, that It can never recover itself by any internal means without a sacrifice of the rights of the imperial Power" (**No. 663**). He warned too that on 8 Aug., the Boston merchants voted to pursue a unilateral boycott of British imports, the town once more setting the pace of colonial opposition (**No. 664**) and pandering to the mob with popular celebrations of the Stamp Act's repeal (**No. 668**). He was still uncertain as to how Hillsborough would receive his reports on provincial politics and crowd action, for the June mail from London was unseasonably late (**No. 668**), and did not arrive until mid-September. Until then he worried that he might be recalled without the promise of relocation, and hesitated in responding to Barrington's inquiry (**No. 610**) about accepting a baronetcy lest he be saddled with the costs of the patent or embarrassed by the offer's withdrawal (**No. 666**). Thus, hopeful of obtaining a leave of absence, a signal reward for his services, and a posting elsewhere, Bernard made ready to return to England in the fall (**No. 667**), with, presumably, his family following later.

The arrival of the July mail packet on 3 Sept. complicated his situation. First, Hillsborough reminded Bernard that he would present to Parliament whatever items of correspondence he saw fit regardless of the governor's concerns that his enemies would use the information against him (**No. 653**). The governor's "Enemies," Hutchinson observed later, expected that the British government would eventually have to justify their American policy to Parliament and were confident "that by some means or other they shall come to the knowledge of" the governor's letters[79]—as they did, and with great effect.[80] A second letter (**No. 622**) confirmed that Bernard was granted leave of absence and announced that Hillsborough had issued troop orders to Gage (**Appendix 4**). Bernard received the duplicate of **No. 622** from Capt. William Sherriff, who arrived in Boston on 3 Sept. bearing a missive from Gage explaining the terms of his orders and requesting the governor's advice on the "number" of troops that "will be necessary" (**No. 669**). Gage had already ordered the 14th and 29th Regiments of Foot to Boston, plus one company from the 59th Regiment and one artillery company with five field pieces.

Bernard had some discretion in their deployment, that is to say, how the troops were to be divided between the town of Boston and Castle William. **No. 622** stated that "at least" one regiment was to be placed in the town itself (for which purposes he assumed that Castle Island was outside the town boundary). The problem of finding sufficient barracks in the town seemed much less important than placating the local populace. Initially, he favored putting one entire regiment into the Castle, alongside the provincial garrison, weakly hoping this might assuage some of the hostility toward the British soldiers. To deflect some of the anger sure to come his way, Bernard planned to maintain the fiction that he was a functionary implementing Hillsborough's instructions. He asked Gage for a "public" copy of his orders and which he intended showing the Council when he requested quarters for the soldiers (**No. 671**). A more difficult problem was how to break the news of the regiments' imminent arrival. Rather than risk inciting the populace with a sudden public announcement, he counted on his confidants spreading the news quietly before the Council met. "I have therefore purposely let it transpire that I expect to receive orders for providing quarters for 2 regiments." Even so, he predicted, "There will be a disturbance more or less upon this occasion." (**No. 672**). So, when the town meeting asked him if he knew for certain that troops were on the way, Bernard intimated that he only had "private Intelligence," not official confirmation (**No. 677**).

Bernard's disingenuity compensated for an intelligence failure. While the governor and his advisers anticipated some form of opposition to the troops' arrival, of what kind they were unable to assay. While they did not expect organized armed resistance, they could not discount hot-heads assailing the governor or raising the rural populace to impede the landings. Bernard had been using informers within the Whig movement, and was well-informed about the opinions and the transgressions of local politicians, Otis included, but not about plans to confront the soldiers—if ever there were any. The first probative issue for British ministers, therefore, concerned the governor's interpretation of evidence gathered from informers; the second concerned the veracity of the evidence itself, which was largely unverifiable. In replying to Hillsborough on 9 Sept., Bernard intimated that he dare not risk endangering his men concealed among the Whig ranks (**No. 672**)—no matter what Hillsborough had said about the necessity of acquiring evidence to expose the

Whig leaders. Bernard continued to rely upon informers in the year ahead (see the source note to **No. 672**).

Bernard's government also faced a systemic problem when it came to investigating criminal acts associated with or arising from popular opposition to unpopular imperial laws. Many times since the Stamp Act riots Bernard had alleged radical polemics were overtly seditious and that crowd action had insurrectionist tendencies: evidence for the former invariably comprised annotated newspaper clippings; for the latter, reports of rumors of activity in Boston and beyond and accounts of protests—all of it covered by Bernard's own interpretations.[81] Hillsborough would have preferred hard evidence and less interpretation:

> a very full and confidential Communication of what you have heard, concerning the Designs and Intentions of . . . suspected . . . Enemies to all Government, would have been more satisfactory than the alarming and dark hint you give, when you say, *that you dare not to repeat what you have heard, till their Purposes become more apparent.* (**No. 622**.)

By the time he read this, Bernard's allegations of sedition and insurrectionism had become bolder, and he now addressed some of Hillsborough's concerns, if only to highlight the difficulties he faced in gathering evidence. In part, the tendency to overstate crowd action in letters to London (**Nos. 623**, **640**, etc.) compensated for the political bias of colonial juries. There was never much chance of the province attorney general being able to obtain indictments against Whigs facing criminal charges or peddling libels about the governor (**Nos. 593** and **719**).[82] Bernard's patience with Jonathan Sewall was severely tested by Sewall's dispute with the Customs commissioners' (albeit about matters arising from Sewall's role as advocate general of Vice Admiralty), and he harbored doubts as to Sewall's capacity for the attorney general's job (albeit that Bernard thought his chief law officer ought to function as an instrument of government, as in England, more than its adviser). Sewall's independently-minded legal advice had not been heartening thus far. When no one could be found willing to testify against any of the *Liberty* rioters, Bernard was led to "suppose the Attorney-general was not Very earnest in endeavouring to procure Evidence." Bernard placed greater value on his "acquaintance with some of the Sons of Liberty; by which means I sometimes get at useful intelligence," though he was not prepared to reveal his sources or commit their evidence to paper lest it be "intercepted here (which is easily done by corrupting a Master of a Ship)" (**No. 672**). Having abandoned the pursuit of the rioters, Bernard subsequently assisted the American Board of Customs to prosecute John Hancock and five of his men in the Vice Admiralty Court, again with the seemingly reluctant assistance of the attorney general.

Meanwhile, Bostonians seethed in anger. Bernard's reports to London captured the bitterness on display at the tempestuous town meeting of 12 Sept. held at Faneuil Hall. They not only supplement the town records but enliven this moment in history with accounts of speeches so rousing "it appeared as if they were acting a play, evry thing, both as to matter & order, seeming to have been preconcerted before hand." The proceedings were choreographed, to the extent that the musket chests were opened up and the weapons laid out on the floor as a prop for the "Orators". The word *"Enemy"* was thrice spoken, ostensibly referring to the French but consciously reiterated to bring the British into mind.

> But this flimsy Veil was not allways kept on: it was often said that they had a right to oppose with arms a military force which was sent to oblige them to submit to unconstitutional Laws; and when it was required to be more explicit, the Chairman [*James Otis Jr.*] said that they understood one another Very well, & pointing with his hand added "there are the Arms; when an attempt is made agst your liberties they will be delivered; our Declaration wants no explication:" and indeed it does not. (**No. 681**.)

Some of the spontaneous speeches were so threatening that the hot-heads had to be "silence[d]" by their own party. Otis's own measured theatricality, according to one informer's précis, also bordered on sedition. "That in case Great Britain was not dispos'd to redress their Grievances after proper applications, that the Inhabitants had then nothing more to do, but gird the Sword to the thigh and shoulder the Musquet" (**No. 681**). The histrionics continued when the town declared Boston was facing subjugation by a standing army, which it declaimed an infringement of the Bill of Rights of 1689. Nonetheless, the grandstanding masked genuine apprehension among townspeople as to what the immediate future held, and fear of what proximity to the Regulars might entail.

Bernard claimed to have reliable evidence of sedition. First, there was the document by which the Boston selectmen summoned a convention of towns. It was a "daring . . . Assumption of the royal Authority" to summon an assembly that, he asserted inaccurately, imitated the House of Representatives. Second, the governor claimed he would be able to compile a list of the leaders among the five hundred citizens who had pledged to invest Castle William to prevent its occupation against the Regulars (**No. 681**). However, Bernard may never have drawn up a list of insurgents, for no such document has survived and there is no record of its composition. Third, there were the town meeting speeches (previously mentioned) that Bernard summarized as hearsay. The second and third items of evidence were not readily admissible in a court of law without additional witness testimony, as a trained lawyer like Bernard well knew. The only tangible evidence of wrongdoing the governor forwarded to London was the circular of the Boston selectmen acting *ultra vires* in summoning the Convention of Towns (**Appendix 13**). (Bernard found the Convention's resolves characterized by "moderation so Very different from the temper of those who called this meeting.").[83]

Knowing what he knew, Bernard confessed to Gage that he would not stick around to welcome the soldiers. Now that he had his discretionary leave of absence he planned to be on his way home within three weeks (**No. 680**), and later revealed that he "had fixed upon the Ship & the Day of embarking, Oct 1ˢᵗ." (**No. 716**.)[84] As fate would have it that was the day the first of the Regulars came ashore, and Bernard was obliged to oversee their settlement after receiving fresh instructions from Hillsborough on 18 Sept. (**No. 661**). In one sense, Bernard was running scared, fearful of retribution, but also evading responsibility for the consequences of his actions.

> Ever since I have perceived that the Wickedness of some and the folly of others will in the End bring Troops here, I have conducted myself so as to be able to say, and swear to, if the Sons of Liberty shall require it, that I have never applied for Troops. (**No. 592**.)

Bernard's crudely fashioned disavowal rested on a conviction that he been proven right. Once, he had told Gage that

> For my own part, I cant look back upon the 3 years last past, without wondering that there have not been Troops at Boston for the last 2 of them. I am sure they have taken pains enough ^at Boston^ to show the Necessity of such an Arrangement. (**No. 655**.)

Bravado in the streets and town halls and beacons atop the hills did not frighten Gage. He and the regimental commanders made preparations for dealing with whatever resistance they met, with or without the governor's assistance.

Boston, September

Bernard and the Customs commissioners overstated the case for bringing Regulars to Boston. Their overblown accounts of the *Liberty* riot reinforced their earlier alarmist messages concerning radicalism and popular protest, and were sent in ignorance of the fact that the British government had already decided to send troops. This was an unavoidable but not unforeseeable contingency, although neither Bernard nor the commissioners anticipated getting four regiments—nearly 2,200 troops on paper—to garrison and patrol a town of 16,000 souls. On 18 Sept., Bernard received Hillsborough's latest instructions, dated 30 Jul., intimating that the ministry expected the governor to remain in place to await the arrival of the British soldiers, including the regiments on their way from Ireland. "No Remissness of Duty will be excusable, upon Pretence of Terror and Danger in the Execution of Office." Moreover, Bernard was directed to reform the province magistracy and conduct an investigation into the causes of the *Liberty* riot. He was to apprehend rioters and arrest those who had encouraged "a Resistance to the Laws" with a view to transporting criminals to England for trial in the Court of the King's Bench under a treason statute of Henry VIII (**No. 661**). Talk of reconciliation being achieved through firmness would have struck the Americans as absurd if the mention of treason trials was not so downright dangerous; but the Americans never got to read this letter themselves before the Revolution and in most instances were obliged to second guess the full content of Hillsborough's instructions to Bernard or accept whatever précis Bernard proffered.

The responsibility for bringing the soldiers lay heavy upon his shoulders when Bernard announced Hillsborough's latest orders (**No. 661**) to the Council, on 19 Sept. He knew that he had failed to extricate himself from a crisis that, while not entirely of his own making, was all the more serious for what he had done to exacerbate tensions. If Bernard experienced remorse, he buried it in self-validating arguments citing Hillsborough's justification of the "Necessity" for "strengthening the Hands of Government." (**No. 661**). None of the other remedial measures Hillsborough proposed were appealing, for each promised only to implicate the governor in further public contests sure to sully an already tarnished reputation. His enemies were gunning for him, metaphorically for sure and perhaps (he feared) literally too.

> I am indeed a good Deal worn with my former Service, which has been severe & dispiriting for 3 Years past; & I had Expectations that I was even now going to receive my Reward in being placed in a Station where I should have Health Peace & Competence. I carried my Expectations so far as to engage a Cabbin & fix upon a Day for embarking. But since the Kings Service requires that I should continue here in further station, I submit cheerfully to my Destination; & hope I have Strength enough to serve another Campaign. If the Dispute lasts much longer, it will be too much for me. (**No. 684**.)

Bernard still had a few weeks before the troops arrived. With the Convention of Towns meeting at meeting at Faneuil Hall between 22 and 29 Sept., he anticipated this illegal congress would stir anger in the province at large and focus resentment upon him (**No. 691**).

He was less prepared for the Council's skilful evasion of Parliament's Quartering Act, which required the province to provide barracks or billets for the Regulars (**No. 686**). Gage must have pondered the governor's insouciance in ever supposing that the general's subordinate officers could have negotiated the provision of barracks without a governor's assistance (regardless of Hutchinson's abilities), especially when Bernard apprised him of the Council's opposition to fitting out public buildings (**No. 687**). Bernard was unprepared for the Council's forthright opposition, coordinated by James Bowdoin, and applied his own brand of reverse logic to assert they "are desirous to lend an hand to the Convention to bring about a forfeiture of the Charter." (**No. 690**.) Out of necessity, Bernard appropriated the town's Manufactory House without any guarantee that the province would reimburse costs (**No. 692**). In fact no troops were ever quartered in that building, and the governor and the regimental commanders were obliged to put the soldiers into tents and other public buildings until they could hire private premises sufficient to accommodate two of the four regiments.

The kind of government Bernard expected to run when the troops arrived might be gleaned from his disappointment in describing the Council as the last "Citadell" of the provincial government to fall to the Whigs. He began recording how each councilor voted (**Nos. 690** and **693**). While meetings of the Governor and Council would continue, and the Council would continue to exercise executive and judicial functions, the province legislature had been dissolved and would not meet again until he summoned it. Under the Province Charter the governor was obliged to call at least one meeting annually to seat representatives, elect councilors, and vote the annual supply acts and salary acts (including his own). The assembly did not meet again until May 1769. To Bernard's enemies, this was government by royal fiat.

The Regulars came ashore on 1 Oct. and within a few weeks were followed by the 64th and 65th Regiments from Ireland. Inevitably, many Bostonians came to perceive the soldiers as an army of occupation.

Nor did the situation in London that winter seem to promise reconciliation. The king's speech of 8 Nov. proclaimed Boston to be "in a state of disobedience to all law and government."[85] In February, Parliament adopted a series of resolutions condemning the proceedings of the General Court, the Boston town meeting, and the Convention of Towns for evincing a "design . . . to usurp a new constitutional authority." [86] How much of this was Hillsborough's doing is not clear, for criticism by the king and colleagues (notably Camden, Conway, Grafton, and Shelburne) obliged the cabinet to shelve any program for the reform of colonial government Hillsborough may have had in mind. In the end it came down to Bernard to act upon Hillsborough's directive to mount an investigation into the colonists' treasonable activities.[87] From the beginning of his secretaryship in 1768 to his resignation four years later,[88] and thence to the close of the War of Independence, Hillsborough steadfastly refused to make concessions to the Americans on matters respecting parliamentary authority.[89] Never had he known a "man of less judgment," opined King George, after the loss of the American Colonies.[90]

Neither did Governor Francis Bernard fully understand his American opponents. Reading the history of pre-revolutionary Massachusetts in the *Bernard Papers* reveals the emergence of an amorphous popular movement that came to dominate the provincial assembly and local politics in Boston; astute leaders and committed citizens campaigned against both the governor and Great Britain, and were able not only to contain popular violence but fitfully exploit the fear of violence to undermine the confidence of government officials. Crown servants were prone to exaggerate such threats because, like other targets of crowd action through the ages, they genuinely believed that escalation was always likely. All of that is just part of the story of the origins of the American Revolution, however.

Reading the history of the Imperial Crisis requires scholars to delve beyond state papers, to explore the private papers of individuals and the newspapers of the day, and to construct representations of that past from the materials available. Documenting that story necessarily requires an editor to collate various sources, compare different accounts of the same event, and evaluate conflicting interpretations. The editorial commentaries in the *Bernard Papers* cross-reference the transcripts to accounts by the governor's critics, notably Samuel Adams, the House of Representatives, the Boston town meeting, and the province Council. That process is complex and intricate, and unavoidably raises as many questions as it purports to answer.

Reading Governor Bernard's accounts on their own would provide a rather skewed picture of the Imperial Crisis, and raises a historiographical problem. Why did the British government choose to believe Bernard's version of events over that of the Americans? It is not just the case that the governor was trusted because he was the king's representative; multiple channels of communication were available, through private individuals, unofficial agents, and the provincial assembly. The question ought to be re-stated: why did Bernard's version prevail?

The answer lies partly in the fact that the *Bernard Papers* is not just the story of a beleaguered English colonialist, but also touches upon the lives of the men and women caught up in the events of the pre-revolutionary years, from the Stamp Act riots, through the *Liberty* riot and nonimportation movement, to the Boston

Massacre. We see their participation in the colonial protest movement through the governor's eyes. Governor Bernard's reactions to popular protest were typically hostile (as too were the responses of the officials of the American Board of Customs). Thus, the British government responded to a representation of popular politics that was probably not unfamiliar to them—of rambunctious, noisy, and self-confident crowds intoxicated by radical notions of rights and liberties, engulfing government officers in Boston in scenes not so different from the crowds swarming the London streets during the height of the Wilkite movement, 1767-71. When pressed, regardless of his own persistent liberalism, Bernard reached for atavistic descriptors to denigrate the politics of the street, as he had being doing since the Stamp Act riots of 1765. Bernard's antagonistic depiction of the colonial leadership was also well-established by 1768. His descriptions of James Otis, Samuel Adams, James Bowdoin, and others add color to what historians already know and provide some insight into the tensions among the leadership. Most important, however, is what the *Bernard Papers* divulges about Bernard's reaction and how it influenced the British government.

By 1768, Bernard was caught up in a maelstrom of protest, and projected his own predicament into the arena of British policymaking. He manufactured a crisis. Not the crisis over taxation—which was of Britain's making, not his—but a crisis of government. He argued that the colonists had undermined not only his administration but government itself. For sure, the Whigs were the dominant political group in the assembly and town meetings, and their arguments had been radicalized: their claims of exemption from parliamentary authority in matters of taxation had progressed to claims of right, questioning the legitimacy of parliamentary legislation and challenging the doctrine of parliamentary supremacy. This, in Bernard's estimation, was a popular movement with revolutionary credentials. His Whig enemies, on the other hand, professed only to confront innovations, and thwart innovators, and preserve what liberties they had always claimed to enjoy.

Bernard's version of events sometimes lacked credibility, and his integrity was openly questioned by critics. But it prevailed in British government circles because it had a champion. Bernard's interpretation was not accepted uncritically, but under Hillsborough's stewardship, American policy was susceptible to the external stimuli provided by the governor. The problem for the Americans was that Hillsborough listened more to his officials on the ground than to them or their representatives in America or London. When this became known, the colonists were obliged to defend themselves. In 1768, they were not aware exactly of what Bernard and Hillsborough had written about them or the province, but suspected they had been portrayed as rebels. The Whigs fought back, accusing Bernard of having misrepresented both them and the province. In correcting Bernard's version of events the

Whigs aimed to provide the British with a convenient scapegoat, whose removal might help to restore good feelings.

The story of this fourth volume of the *Bernard Papers* is how, in 1768, Bernard controlled the flow of information to London. For the remainder of his administration, the governor and his enemies fought to control how information was interpreted in London and re-interpreted in Boston. In the winter of 1768-69, the British government was obliged to defend American policy in Parliament for the first time in more than two years. Official American correspondence, above all Bernard's letters, was used to justify policy and provide a *raison d'être* for the troop presence in Boston. That story the fifth volume of the *Bernard Papers* considers in detail.

EDITORIAL APPARATUS

Editorial policy has aimed to preserve the integrity of manuscripts by printing them in full (except where noted) and depicting their content as accurately as possible with limited editorial intervention.

Whenever possible, autograph out-letters and in-letters have been used as authoritative texts—the actual manuscripts upon which the transcripts are based. When the receiver's copy (**RC**) or its duplicate were not extant, contemporary copies were substituted from the preserved record in the receiver's or author's letterbook (**RLbC** and **LbC**). In the absence of a letterbook, the transcript was based on a copy of an original made by a third party; printed versions (**PC**) were used in the last resort—contemporary imprints taking precedence over modern imprints and transcriptions

Bernard's letters to the secretaries of state were his primary means of communication with the British government. He wrote regularly to the secretary of state for the Southern Department, whose portfolio included the American Colonies, and then, from 1768, to the newly-created secretary of state for the Colonies, whose first occupant was the earl of Hillsborough. Bernard usually wrote out his own letters to the secretaries of state in a fine, easy to read script. Numbered sequentially, his first official letter to Hillsborough is dated 12 May 1768; he restarted the sequence at the beginning of 1769. In-letters from the secretary of state were numbered in sequence regardless of the year or the minister, reaching No. 11 before Shelburne left office and No. 27 by the time Bernard returned to England. This volume has printed most but not all of the extant correspondence between Bernard and the secretaries of state dated 8 Jan. to 30 Sept. 1768, omitting letters of acknowledgment (of appointments or receipt of correspondence) and several circulars (which are mentioned in the editorial commentaries and listed in **Appendix 14**).

The secretaries of state probably read every one of Bernard's holographs before passing the letters to their clerks so copies could be made and the originals filed. Letters to the earl of Halifax, to Henry Seymour Conway, and to the earl of Shelburne are in CO 5/755-CO 5/757; letters to the earl of Hillsborough are in CO 5/758. The secretaries' clerks were not required to keep a minute-book (as was the case with clerks attached to the Board of Trade and the Board of Admiralty); nor did they maintain correspondence entrybooks (either a ledger or letterbook). However, correspondence that the secretary of state referred to other departments (that is, the Treasury, the Privy Council, the Admiralty, the War Office, and the Board of Trade) can usually be traced in the administrative record of these departments.

The filing system for original incoming letters was thorough, by the standards of the day. The secretary of state's clerks routinely endorsed in-letters on the back leaf of the letter when folded (usually its last verso page) thus providing a convenient docket for filing. A date of receipt was written at the top, sometimes with one or two lines summarizing the letter's subject matter; a filing reference was added at the bottom. For example, Bernard's letter to the earl of Hillsborough of 26 Dec. 1768 (**ALS**, **RC**) is endorsed "Governor Bernard (N$^\circ$. 37) R 24th: Feby 1769. B.9." The first figure, "N$^\circ$. 37", indicates that this letter was the thirty-seventh that Bernard had sent to Hillsborough in 1768. "R" prefaces the date of receipt and "B.9." is the bundle of correspondence in which the letter was filed. The numbering of letters was established by the earl of Shelburne in 1766, but the docketing procedure was operational before then. Bernard's letters were later re-bound but the original ordering of materials in the collections was preserved, more or less. The letter to Hillsborough is now contained in a bound volume of papers, CO 5/758, with a modern folio reference, ff 38-39.

In the aftermath of the Stamp Act Crisis, colonial governors were required to communicate directly with the secretary of state in all matters. Bernard continued to send copies to the Board of Trade, but with one important difference: the addressee was the secretary of state, not the Board. For example, the Board's file copy of Bernard's letter to Hillsborough of 26 Dec. 1768 is in CO 5/893, ff 92-94; it is a letter handwritten by a clerk and signed by the governor (**dupLS**, **RC**). I have catalogued it not as a distinct item of correspondence but as a variant of the original letter in CO 5/758. This particular manuscript was laid before a meeting of the Board of Trade on 6 Dec. 1769 (*JBT*, 13: 35) and subsequently endorsed by a clerk in the Plantation Office: "Boston Decr. 26. 1768 Govr Bernard (N$^\circ$ 37) Dup Reced Read Dec^r: 6. 1769. N.n. 28."

Several people were involved in the composition of the original letters and papers authored by Bernard. Bernard himself wrote out the majority of his out-letters; not only the originals going to the secretary of state and to the Board of Trade, but also the duplicates and the triplicates of these letters that were conveyed separately. He also made letterbook copies of much of this material. Before 1768, Bernard was also heavily reliant on clerks to make letterbook copies of routine correspondence and prepare copies of out-letters for dispatch. But concerns over security meant that he became increasingly dependent upon his third son Thomas Bernard (27 Apr. 1750-1 Jul. 1818). From 1 Jan. 1768 to 2 Aug. 1769, when his father left the province, Thomas was responsible for over 65 per cent of letterbook entries and over 12 percent of out-letters, including duplicates (with Bernard penning over 40 percent of out-letters).

In transcribing manuscripts for *The Bernard Papers*, the authoritative texts were systematically compared with the extant variants composed by the clerks. Substantive differences in content were rare. Contemporary emendations to letterbook copies (**LbC**) were usually incorporated in the fair versions dispatched to and received by correspondents (**RC**). Major differences among the variant texts are discussed in the endnotes and source notes, and an editorial comment clarifies scribal involvement. Near-contemporaneous transcripts[91] and modern versions, including *Barrington-Bernard*, are listed only when cited or discussed.

Transcripts are presented in chronological order, according to the first given date. Non-epistolary enclosures follow the covering letter, while letters that were themselves enclosures have been placed in sequence by date. With letters bearing the same date, out-letters take precedence over in-letters (unless the out-letter is a reply to the in-letter); thereafter, out-letters are sorted by the likely order of composition (for which Bernard's letterbooks provide a rough guide); date of receipt has been used to sort in-letters; the remainder have been sorted alphabetically by correspondent. Transcripts have been allocated numbers in a sequence than runs across the series of published volumes, in this volume beginning with **No. 577**.

Editorial practice is to show the whole text plus any substantive emendations made by the author—the person(s) on whose authority a document was prepared or under whose signature it was sent—and by any clerk who drafted or copied the document. (Noncontemporaneous annotations on manuscripts have been excluded.) Obvious slips of the pen have been ignored. When the source note reports "minor emendations not shown," the editor is referring to corrections of oversights and grammatical errors made by the scribe or author of the manuscript that have no bearing on the meaning of the text or the author's perceived intention. Generally, original emendations, including scribal corrections, are reconstituted when this might help to illuminate authorial intention or when the additions suggest ambiguity or invite alternative interpretations: the representations follow the editorial apparatus set out in Table 1.

Grammar and spelling were transcribed with limited modernization. Orthographical idiosyncrasies have been retained, save for the kind of transparent mistakes mentioned above. Abbreviations, contractions, and terminal punctuation (and its absence) follow the manuscript, as does capitalization (when the writer's intention can be determined) and the underlining of dates. Emphasis is rendered in italics. Superscripts have been preserved but with all accompanying punctuation lowered to the line. Accidentally conjoined words have been separated. Eighteenth-century spelling, such as "highth" for "height," is readily understood; however, instances confusing to the reader are clarified by an interpolation or an endnote. Original forms have been reproduced, such as the ampersand (&) and the thorn ("y" for "th"), but not the long "s." Confusing punctuation in numbers has been silently corrected, with period separators being replaced by commas (thus "20.000" becomes "20,000"). Where symbols are used in the original to indicate pounds sterling, they are lowered to the line, and silently corrected to "£ s. d." Clarification on currency and monetary values is provided in endnotes.

The layout of the transcripts has preserved some common features of manuscripts and standardized others. The location and punctuation of salutations and datelines have been preserved, but placed in one line; the addressee's name is at the end of the closure (where it usually is) and above the postscript regardless of its location in the manuscript. Original lineation has not been retained but paragraphing sequencing has. Epigraphs, foreign language phrases, and postscripts have been formatted. Closures have been centered, except those running on from the last sentence of a letter. Tabulated information is presented in a form as close to the original as possible. Quotation marks placed at the beginning of every line of quoted material have been silently relocated to the beginning and end; block quotations have been indented. Flourishes have been omitted, as have brackets in dockets and closures. All transcripts have been given a caption; original titles have been transcribed and placed with the main body of text except entrybook titles, which are given in the notes.

The source note at the end of each transcript provides information about the provenance and location of the authoritative text. Table 2 is a list of descriptive acronyms used to indicate the typology of authoritative texts. The acronyms representing manuscript collections and archives are explained in the List of Abbreviations, above. (Pagination and folio descriptors have been omitted except when required by a repository's citation style.) Where possible, the source note provides some clarification as to the processes of composition and preservation, noting among other things differences in handwriting styles, the extent of authorial emendation, and the location of variant texts. Endorsements added by the recipient confirming receipt and dockets added by the sender have been transcribed in accordance with editorial method. These are not enclosed in quotation marks but are easily recognizable since they are prefixed with "endorsed" or "docket" and offset from the editor's comments. When Bernard marked a letter with "r" he meant "received" and with "a" "answered." Extant enclosures are briefly described, and should be assumed to be manuscript copies (usually third-party copies) unless otherwise indicated. Relevant historical and administrative information is provided at the end of the source note. Guidance is given as to where to find any replies and rejoinders. The order of discussion varies, according to the requirements of each transcript.

Endnotes to source notes follow in sequence those for the transcript. Endnotes aim to clarify obscurities in the transcript and direct the reader to additional material. Cross-references to transcripts published in this volume are indicated by bold numerals, thus, **No. 577**. Citations of manuscripts not printed in this volume direct the reader to the authoritative version; in many cases there is only one extant manuscript; source text typology is included where it may help the reader. "Not found" is used to signal the absence of a manuscript.

Appendix 14 is a list of Bernard's extant correspondence for the period covered by this volume. This list is an interim calendar. The information has been checked as fully and thoroughly as all the other material printed in this volume; it is possible, however, that some typological classifications may change, if further handwriting analysis can identify the clerks who scribed the copies. Any such revisions will be reported in the Calendar volume.

Acts of the English, Irish, Scottish, and British parliaments are cited according to regnal year, with dates where appropriate, and with modernized titles; the index provides both the dates and a short-title. Provincial legislation is not normally calendared by regnal year but by date, although Bernard's contemporaries used regnal codes when referring to historic acts.

Biographical information is provided at the first mention of a person in the correspondence; rare sources are cited but standard reference works are not.[92] Online directories and newspaper collections proved to be particularly useful.[93] Francis Bernard is referred to throughout as "FB" and Thomas Hutchinson as "TH".

I have tried to record information and transcribe manuscripts as accurately as possible, but it is inevitable that there will be errors in a project of this scale. I am grateful to everyone who has helped me to correct them, and I take full responsibility for those that remain.

TABLE 1
EDITORIAL SYMBOLS

Additions (insertions, interlineations, and substitutions) are marked with carets "^"at the intended location. When it is necessary to distinguish different hands or differentiate between insertions and substitutions the following will be used: ↑roman↓.

Bold type or heavily-inked letters are set in **bold**.

Canceled text is shown in ~~strikethrough~~ font.

Confusing passages are described "thus in manuscript" in an endnote.

Conjectured readings for illegible material that can be inferred from the source text are in [roman text within square brackets]; there is a question mark before the closing bracket if there is considerable doubt as to the accuracy of the reading, [roman?].

Editorial interpolations have been italicized and placed in square brackets, [*editor's comment*].

Ellipses signify material that is either illegible or missing. The number of suspension points corresponds to the number of missing letters or numbers, e.g. [. . .] for three letters missing. Missing words are rendered thus, [_ _ _].

Emphasis is conveyed by *italics* and double underlining by SMALL CAPITALS.

Lacunae are represented by [*blank*].

Passages marked for deletion are indicated by <angled brackets>.

Underlining in authorial tables, numbers, dates, and punctuation has been retained.

TABLE 2
SOURCE TEXT TYPOLOGY

The first set of acronyms in table 2 describes the nature of the authoritative text on which the transcript is based. The second set categorizes documents by their administrative history and preservation.

ADft	Author's Draft Manuscript.
AL	Autograph Letter (text in the hand of the author, but unsigned).
ALS	Autograph Letter Signed (text and signature in the hand of the author).
AMs	Autograph Manuscript (text in the hand of the author but unsigned).
AMsS	Autograph Manuscript Signed (text and signature in the hand of author).
Dft	Draft
dup/trip	duplicate/triplicate
extract	An extract of a source text.
L	Letter (text not in the hand of the author and unsigned).
LS	Letter Signed (text not in the hand of the author but signed by the author).
Ms	Manuscript.
MsS	Manuscript Signed.
précis	A summary.
noted	A documentary record of the existence of a nonextant source text.
Prt	Contemporary Printed version of manuscript.
AC	Author's Copy (loose file or bound copies usually found in a personal collection).
Copy	Third Party Copy.
LbC	Author's Letterbook or Entrybook
PC	Published Copy.
RbC	Recordbook Copy.
RC	Receiver's Copy.
RLbC	Receiver's Letterbook Copy.

ENDNOTES

❧❧❧ ❦❦❦

1. See Colin Nicolson, *The 'Infamas Govener': Francis Bernard and the Origins of the American Revolution* (Boston, 2001).

2. The 1767 Townshend Acts were the American Revenue Act, 7 Geo. 3, c. 46; the Commissioners of Customs Act, 7 Geo. 3, c. 41; the Mutiny in America Act, 7 Geo. 3, c. 55; the New York Suspending Act, 7 Geo. 3, c. 59. They are briefly discussed in *Bernard Papers*, 3: 24-28. The best account is Peter D. G. Thomas, *The Townshend Duties Crisis: The Second Phase of the American Revolution, 1767-1773* (Oxford, 1987).

3. See Merrill Jensen, *The Founding of a Nation: A History of the American Revolution, 1763-1776* (New York, 1968); Pauline Maier, *From Resistance to Revolution: Colonial Radicals and the Development of American Opposition to Britain, 1765-1776* (London, 1973; ed. 1988); Dirk Hoerder, *Crowd Action in Revolutionary Massachusetts, 1765-1780* (London, 1977); John W. Tyler, *Smugglers & Patriots: Boston Merchants and the Advent of the Revolution* (Boston, 1986); Marc Egnal, *A Mighty Empire: The Origins of the American Revolution* (Ithaca, NY, 1988).

4. James Otis Jr. (1725-83), representative for Boston, 1761-69 and 1771; Samuel Adams (1722-1803), representative for Boston between 1765 and 1774; James Bowdoin (1726-90), elected to the Council 1757-68, 1770-73.

5. Memorial of the American Board of Customs to the lords commissioners of the Treasury, Boston, 12 May 1768, T 1/465, ff 60-61.

6. Some of FB's letters were composed over several days. In this volume: **Nos. 590, 591, 609, 623, 632, 633, 638, 640, 656,** and **686.** In the next volume notably **Nos. 779** and **792,** *Bernard Papers*, 5: 274-275, 295-296.

7. These are printed in *JHRM*, 44: 217-250.

8. Dennys DeBerdt (d.1770), a Dissenter and London merchant, was appointed agent of the House of Representatives on 12 Mar. 1767, ostensibly to represent the province in the border dispute with New Hampshire, but without the concurrence of the Governor and Council, as was normal when appointing the province agent. Neither FB nor the British government recognized DeBerdt's position.

9. George Montague-Dunk (1716-71), second earl of Halifax, was a reform-minded first lord commissioner (that is, president) of the Board of Trade, 1748-61; secretary of state for the Northern Department, 1762-63 and 1771, and for the Southern Department, Aug. 1763-10 Jul. 1765. On Halifax and Bernard see *Bernard Papers*, 3: 5, 11.

10. Thomas Pelham-Holles (1693-1768), first duke of Newcastle, was first lord of the Treasury from 1754 to 1762. He was leader of his own administration between 1754 and 1756, and thereafter formed a coalition with William Pitt (1708-78) until 1761. As the prime minister, Pitt chose to hold the secretaryship of state for the Southern Department until his resignation on 5 Oct. 1761. Pitt formed his second administration on 30 Jul. 1766, succeeding the marquess of Rockingham, and having been raised to the peerage as first earl of Chatham. He resigned office in Oct. 1768, after suffering chronic illness.

11. Nicolson, *The 'Infamas Govener'*, 38, 70-72.

12. George Grenville (1712-70) was first lord of the Treasury and chancellor of the Exchequer in the administration he led from Aug. 1763 to 10 Jul. 1765. Charles Watson-Wentworth (1730-82), second marquess of Rockingham, entered office as first lord of the Treasury on 13 Jul. 1765 and left office on 30 Jul. 1766.

13. On Shelburne's term as secretary of state for the Southern Department, 30 Jul. 1766 to 21 Jan. 1768, and his handling of American affairs see *Bernard Papers*, 3: 20-22, 26, 29-32.

14. John Pownall (1724/5-95) was secretary to the Board of Trade, 1745-68, and undersecretary of state at the American Department, Jun. 1768-Aug. 1772. On Pownall's career see Franklin B. Wickwire, "John Pownall and British Colonial Policy," *WMQ* 20 (1963): 543-554.

15. Thomas Pownall (1722-1805) had been governor of Massachusetts, 1757-60, and was author of the widely respected *The Administration of the Colonies* (London, 1764), of which several editions were published during the Imperial Crisis (and are available in ECCO). His career is best followed in John A. Schutz, *Thomas Pownall: British Defender of American Liberty* (Glendale, Calif., 1951); G. H. Guttridge, "Thomas Pownall's *The Administration of the Colonies*: The Six Editions," *WMQ* 26 (1969): 31-46. Bernard's concerns that Pownall was corresponding with the Boston Whigs are mentioned in **No. 742**, *Bernard Papers*, 5: 198-202.

16. Richard Jackson (1721/2-87) was a barrister and MP for Weymouth and Melcombe Regis until 1768; he was currently province agent for Connecticut (1760–70) and Pennsylvania (1763–69), having also served Massachusetts between 1765 and 1766. Jackson's letters to Bernard have not survived intact to enable a fuller evaluation of the nature of their correspondence. W. P. Courtney, "Jackson, Richard (1721/2–1787)," rev. J.-M. Alter, in *ODNB-e* (http://www.oxforddnb.com.ezproxy.stir.ac.uk/view/article/14546, accessed 29 Mar. 2014).

17. William Wildman Barrington (1717-93), second Viscount Barrington, MP for Plymouth, and secretary at war, 1755-61 and 1765-78. His career can be followed in Tony Hayter, *An Eighteenth Century Secretary at War: The Papers of William, Viscount Barrington* ([London], 1988).

18. Charles Pratt (1714-94), baron (later earl) of Camden was lord chancellor from 1766 to 1770. On Pitt and America see Jeremy Black, *Pitt the Elder* (1993); Neil Longley York, "When Words Fail: William Pitt, Benjamin Franklin and the Imperial Crisis of 1766," *Parliamentary History* 28 (2009): 341-374.

19. William Petty (1737-1805), second earl of Shelburne, had been secretary of state for the Southern Department since 30 Jul. 1766, serving in both Chatham's and Grafton's administrations. He relinquished responsibility for colonial affairs on 21 Jan. 1768, when they were taken over by the new Colonial Department. Shelburne remained at the Southern Department until resigning from the government on 21 Oct. 1768. John Cannon, "Petty, William, second earl of Shelburne and first marquess of Lansdowne (1737–1805)," *ODNB-e* (http://www.oxforddnb.com/view/article/22070, accessed 2 Mar. 2012). Lord Edmond Fitzmaurice, *Life of William, Earl of Shelburne, afterwards First Marquis of Lansdowne, with extracts from his Papers and Correspondence* (London, 1912).

20. See *Bernard Papers*, 3: 20-23, 28-31.

21 The Massachusetts Indemnity Act of 1766 was disallowed by the Privy Council. Bernard was instructed to procure another act, which he safely avoided when the Townshend duties controversy engulfed his administration. *Bernard Papers*, 3: 258.

22. Historians often refer to Hillsborough's position as secretary of state for the *American* Colonies and his office as the *American* Department. The correct terms are "secretary of state for the Colonies" and the "Colonial Department." The terms "colonial secretary" and "American secretary" are commonly interchangeable when referring to the secretary of state. The secretary of state for the Colonies was regarded as a junior appointment to the secretaries of state for the Southern and Northern Departments. Administrative efficiency only partly drove the creation of the new office, for Shelburne's critics within the government saw in it an opportunity to undermine his influence (on which point I am grateful for the advice of Neil Longley York). The Colonial Department was abolished in 1782. See Margaret Spector, *The American Department of the British Government* ([New York], [1940]); Sainty, et al., *Officeholders in Modern Britain*, 2: 22-58; Thomas, *The Townshend Duties Crisis*, 45-47.

23. See Charles R. Ritcheson, *British Politics and the American Revolution* (Norman, Okla., 1954); John Derry, *English Politics and the American Revolution* (London, 1976); Thomas, *Townshend Duties Crisis*.

24. I have included forty-one and omitted four of Bernard's letters to Hillsborough. One of the omissions is an original version of a letter to Shelburne (**No. 600**); two others are letters of introduction for colonists visiting England (dated 21 Jul. and 8 Aug., BP, 7: 12 and CO 5/757, ff 371-372); and one has not been found (of 23 Sept., noted in *HCJ*, 32: 76). Of the twenty-two extant letters from Hillsborough five been omitted because they duplicated information provided elsewhere (which was the case of state papers Nos. 4, 8 and 17 dated 20 Feb., 30 Apr., and 13 Aug. in BP, 11: 141-144, 175-176, 285) or transmitted other documentation ("No. 5", dated 5 Mar., BP, 11: 149-152); "No. 2" was a circular notifying the governors of Hillsborough's appointment. BP, 11: 123-126.

25. *Bernard Papers*, 3: 407-409.

26. **No. 462**, *Bernard Papers*, 3: 134-138.

27. John K. Alexander, *Samuel Adams: The Life of an American Revolutionary* (Lanham, Md., 2011), 64-68; Harry Alonzo Cushing, *The Writings of Samuel Adams*, 4 vols. (New York, 1904), 1: 134-198. On Otis's contribution see **No. 581**n5.

28. The earl of Hillsborough, circular to the colonial governors, Whitehall, 21 Apr. 1768. CO 5/241, f 28.

29. For an account of cabinet deliberations on the Circular Letter see Thomas, *Townshend Duties Crisis*, 78-83.

30. Thomas Hutchinson (1711-80) held several senior positions in Massachusetts: lieutenant governor, 1760-69; chief justice of the Superior Court of Judicature, 1760-71; acting governor 1769-71, and governor, 1771-74. Referred to as "TH" in the editorial commentaries below.

31. *Bernard Papers*, 3: 25, 421-422; James F. Shepherd and Gary M. Walton, *Shipping, Maritime Trade, and the Economic Development of Colonial North America* (Cambridge, 1979), 104, 113, 143; an account of the gross receipt, payments, and net produce of the Customs in North America, 1767-1774, T 1/461, f 1.

32. The best account of the nonimportation controversy in Boston is Tyler, *Smugglers & Patriot*, 109-170.

33. For Bernard's early reports on rescues and Malcom see **Nos. 454, 493, 504, 537**, *Bernard Papers*, 3: 120-121, 204, 232-234, 338.

34. Thomas Gage (1721-87), British military commander in chief in North America, 1764-75.

35. *Boston Post-Boy and Advertiser*, 11 Apr. 1768.

36. According to **No. 665**.

37. Andrew Oliver (1706-74) was province secretary, 1756-70. Robert Auchmuty (1724-88), was appointed judge of the Vice Admiralty Court in New England in 1768. Jonathan Sewall (1729-96) was the province attorney general, 1767-75, and the advocate general of Vice Admiralty, 1767-68. He was also appointed solicitor general on 24 Jun. 1767 and may have nominally continued in office following his appointment as attorney general until his replacement by Samuel Quincy (1735-89) on 21 Mar. 1771. William H. Whitmore, *The Massachusetts Civil List for the Colonial and Provincial Periods* (Albany, 1870), 125.

38. *Bernard Papers*, 5: 290-291.

39. TH to unknown, Boston, 14 Nov. 1768, Mass. Archs., 26: 327, in Hutchinson Transcripts, 2: 679.

40. TH to William Bollan, 15 Oct. 1767, quoted in *Bernard Papers*, 3: 189-190.

41. William Bollan to TH, London, 18 Dec. 1768, Mass. Archs, 25: 254-255a, in Hutchinson Transcripts, 1: 250-251.

42. TH to Nathaniel Rogers, Milton, 31 May 1768, Mass. Archs., 25: 258-259, in Hutchinson Transcripts, 1: 258.

43. See the source note to **No. 623** in this volume; **Nos. 710** and **715** in *Bernard Papers*, 5: 109-111, 121-124.

44. **No. 719**, *Bernard Papers*, 5: 134-138.

45. See **No. 728**, *Bernard Papers*, 5: 154-158.

46. Commodore Hood, the commander of the North Atlantic Station, ordered several Royal Navy ships (listed in **No. 634**n4) to Boston harbor after requests for assistance from the American Customs.

47. Hoerder, *Crowd Action in Revolutionary Massachusetts*, 166-169.

48. On crowd action generally see Pauline Maier, "Popular Uprisings and Civil Authority in Eighteenth-Century America," *WMQ* 27 (1970): 3-35; Maier, *From Resistance to Revolution*; Hoerder, *Crowd Action in Revolutionary Massachusetts*; William Pencak, Matthew Dennis, and Simon P. Newman, *Riot and Revelry in Early America*, (University Park, 2002); Paul A. Gilje, *Liberty on the Waterfront: American Maritime Culture in the Age of Revolution* (Philadelphia, PA, 2004). On the *Liberty* riot see John Philip Reid, *In a Rebellious Spirit: The Argument of Facts, The Liberty Riot and the Coming of the Revolution* (Univ. Park, Penn., 1979).

49. Especially Reid, *In a Rebellious Spirit*.

50. Researchers should also consult the entire file of Customs Board's papers on the *Liberty* riot which contains numerous depositions and correspondence with the Treasury, Capt. John Corner, and FB. T 1/465, ff 124-193.

51. John Temple (1731-98). The Boston-born Temple had been surveyor general of Customs for the Northern District before his appointment to the American Board of Customs. Temple's professional relationship with FB broke down in 1764 after he accused the governor of fraud (for which see *Bernard Papers*, 2: 216, 488, 502-504). He came to dislike his fellow commissioners partly because of their association with the governor. Married to Elizabeth Bowdoin (1750-1809), daughter of Whig councilor James Bowdoin, Temple was distrusted by his colleagues who suspected him of being a Whig sympathizer. Temple's working relationship with the other commissioners broke down when the Board returned to Boston in Nov. 1768, and by February was beyond repair. Temple was replaced in 1771.

52. **No. 387**, *Bernard Papers*, 2: 349-350.

53. Hoerder, *Crowd Action in Revolutionary Massachusetts*, 164-176, quotation at 145. Nicolson, *The 'Infamas Govener'*, 169-171; John Philip Reid, *In a Defiant Stance: The Conditions of Law in Massachusetts Bay, the Irish Comparison, and the Coming of the American Revolution* (University Park, Penn., 1977). See also Reid's *In a Rebellious Spirit*.

54. *Bernard Papers*, 3: 407-409.

55. See Nicolson, *'The Infamas Govener'*, 167-173.

56. Message of the House of Representatives, 30 Jun. 1768, *JHRM*, 45: 91-94.

57. These FB acknowledged with **No. 682**.

58. Benjamin Hallowell (1724-99), comptroller of Customs at Boston, 1764-70, and a commissioner of Customs from 1771. His house was attacked during the Stamp Act riot of 26 Aug. 1765.

59. The papers brought by Hallowell were reviewed by the Treasury on 21 Jul. and Hillsborough on 23 Jul. They were considered by the cabinet on 27 Jul. Thomas, *Townshend Duties Crisis*, 85-86.

60. Hillsborough's personal papers in the Public Record Office of Northern Ireland contain little material of relevance to the imperial crisis. His correspondence is also scattered throughout numerous collections in the British Library. Hillsborough's state papers from the imperial crisis, however, are well preserved in the Colonial Office Documents (CO 5) at TNA, and in the Bernard Papers (BP), vols. 11 and 12, in Sparks MS 4, at the Houghton Library. There are transcripts of some of his letters in the Frederick Lewis Gay Transcripts, 1632-1786, 69 vols. MHS.

61. The most important of Hillsborough's numerous offices were president of the Board of Trade, 1763-65 and 1766; joint postmaster-general, 1766-68; secretary of state for the Colonies, 21 Jan. 1768-13 Aug. 1772; secretary of state for the Southern Department from 25 Nov. 1779 until his resignation on 27 Mar. 1782 after the fall of the North administration. The best biography is Peter Marshall, "Hill, Wills, first marquess of Downshire (1718–1793)," *ODNB-e* (http://www.oxforddnb.com.ezproxy.stir.

ac.uk/view/article/13317, accessed 20 Aug. 2013). On Hillsborough and America see Sian E. Rees, "The Political Career of Wills Hill, Earl of Hillsborough (1718-1793) with particular reference to his American policy," unpublished PhD diss., Aberystwyth University, 1976.

62. Hillsborough was the first lord commissioner of the Board of Trade, 17 Sept. 1763-c.12 Aug. 1765 and 18 Aug. to 4 Dec. 1766. The president's role was discontinued by the Chatham administration, and from 12 Jul. 1768 the secretary of state for the Colonies was *ex officio* chairman. Sainty, et al., *Office-holders in Modern Britain,* 3: 28-37.

63. See *Bernard Papers*, 3: 25-27.

64. Marshall, "Hill, Wills," *ODNB-e.*

65. Wills Hill succeeded his father as second (Irish) Viscount Hillsborough in 1742. The earldom of Hillsborough was a creation in the Irish peerage for Hill in 1751 (he was also created Viscount Kilwarlin). He sat in the House of Commons as MP for Warwick, from 1741 to 1756, when he was created Lord Harwich in the British peerage; thereafter he sat in the House of Lords. His title of earl of Hillsborough was admitted to the British peerage in 1772 when he was also created Viscount Fairford; in 1789, he was created marquis of Downshire in the Irish peerage. The lord lieutenant of Ireland between 1767 and 1772 was George Townshend (1724–1807), first Marquess Townshend and older brother of Charles Townshend (1725-67), Chatham's chancellor of the Exchequer.

66. *Bernard Papers*, 3: 29-31.

67. Don Cook, *The Long Fuse: How England Lost the American Colonies, 1760-1785* (New York, 1995), 162.

68. John Brooke, *The Chatham Administration, 1766-1768* (London, 1956), 332, 336.

69. Robert Middlekauff, *The Glorious Cause: The American Revolution, 1763-1789* (New York, 1982), 175.

70. *Bernard Papers*, 3: 2, 19-23.

71. *Bernard Papers*, 2: 87-88, 98, 100, 144, 480.

72. Thomas, *Townshend Duties Crisis*, 80-120.

73. "Disposition and State of the Forces in North America . . . 1766," MiU-C: Charles Townshend Papers, box 8/23.

74. For the ships' movements in and out Boston harbor see **No. 694**, *Bernard Papers*, 5: 63-68.

75. Nicolson, *The 'Infamas Govener'*, 172-173; Thomas, *Townshend Duties Crisis*, 82.

76. Reid, *In a Rebellious Spirit*, 127.

77. The Governor-in-Council was the appropriate civil authority to make such a request of either Hillsborough or Gage. FB was unwilling to take such action on his own without the Council's express support, though he did not require it cases of emergency, such as rebellion or insurrection. Instructions clarifying the procedure were circulated to colonial governors on 24 Oct. 1765, following the Stamp Act riots.

> You will not . . . fail to use your utmost Power for repelling all Acts of Outrage, and Violence, and to provide for the Maintenance of Peace and good Order in the Province, by such a timely Exertion of Force, as the Occasion may require; for which Purpose You will make the proper Applications to General Gage, or Lord Colville, Commanders of His Majesty's Land & Naval Forces in America.

No. 405, *Bernard Papers*, 2: 385-387.

78. FB is referring not only to the newspaper reports but also to the American Board of Customs's letter to Gage, 15 Jun. **Appendix 5**.

79. TH to unknown, Boston, 14 Nov. 1768, Mass. Archs., 26: 327, in Hutchinson Transcripts, 2: 679.

80. See **Introduction** to *Bernard Papers*, 5: 1-39.

81. On sedition see *Bernard Papers*, 3: 384-386, 397-398, 400-405, 409; on insurrectionism see ibid., 68-70, 79, 219, 384-385, 393-396, 404, 424.

82. *Bernard Papers*, 5: 75-77. See also Reid, *In a Defiant Stance*, 20-54.

83. **No. 698**, *Bernard Papers*, 5: 75-77.

84. *Bernard Papers*, 5: 125-127.

85. *HJL*, 32: 165-166 and *HCJ*, 32: 21-22.

86. *HLJ*, 32: 209-210; *HCJ*, 32: 151. Parliament's proceedings on America are discussed in *Bernard Papers*, 5: 11-22.

87. Ian R. Christie and Benjamin Woods Labaree, *Empire or Independence, 1760-1776: A British-American Dialogue on the Coming of the American Revolution* (Oxford, 1976), 124-129; Reid, *In a Rebellious Spirit*, 77-80; Lawrence Henry Gipson, *The British Empire before the American Revolution*, 15 vols. (Caldwell, Id, 1936), 11: 235-241.

88. Hillsborough resigned following a disagreement with his cabinet colleagues over western expansion in America. He strenuously opposed a proposal to establish a new colony along the Ohio River but undermined his own credibility when it was revealed that he had encouraged applicants to submit a land grant for an unfeasibly large territory in the expectation that it would be refused, thus jeopardizing the scheme. Marshall, "Hill, Wills," op. cit.

89. See Theodore Draper, *A Struggle for Power: The American Revolution* (New York, 1997), 318-319, 347-349, 359.

90. Quoted in Cook, *The Long Fuse*, 128.

91. George Chalmers, "Papers relating to New England, 1643-1786," Sparks MS 10, MH-H; John Almon, *A Collection of Interesting, Authentic Papers, relative to the Dispute between Great Britain and America; shewing the causes and progress of that misunderstanding, from 1764 to 1775* (London, 1777).

92. Standard biographical directories include: Mark Mayo Boatner, ed., *Encyclopedia of the American Revolution* (New York, 1966); Joseph Foster, ed., *Alumni Oxonienses: the Members of the University of Oxford, 1715-1886*, 4 vols. (Oxford and London, 1888); Edward A. Jones, *The Loyalists of Massachusetts: Their Memorials, Petitions and Claims* (London, 1930); David E. Maas, ed. and comp., *Divided Hearts: Massachusetts Loyalists, 1765-1790: A Biographical Directory* (Boston, 1980); Sir Lewis Namier and John Brooke, eds., *The House of Commons, 1754-1790*, 3 vols. (London, 1964); John A. Schutz, ed., *Legislators of the Massachusetts General Court* (Boston, 1997); Search & ReSearch Publishing Corp, *Early Vital Records of the Commonwealth of Massachusetts to About 1850* (Wheat Ridge, Conn., 2002); John L. Sibley, Clifford K. Shipton, Conrad Edick Wright, Edward W. Hanson, eds. *Biographical Sketches of Graduates of Harvard University* [title varies], 18 vols. to date (Cambridge, Mass., 1873-); James H. Stark, *The Loyalists of Massachusetts and the Other Side of the American Revolution* (Boston, 1910); Nancy S. Voye, *Massachusetts Officers in the French and Indian Wars, 1748-1763* (microfiche, Boston, 1975).

93. *American National Biography Online* (New York, 2005-, at http://www.anb.org); *Dictionary of Canadian Biography Online* (Toronto, 2003-, http://www.biographi.ca); Newsbank Inc., *America's Historical Newspapers. Archive of Americana. Early American Newspapers Series 1, 1690-1876* (2008-, available via subscription at GenealogyBank.com, http://www.genealogybank.com/gbnk/newspapers/); *Oxford Dictionary of National Biography Online* (London, 2004-2006, http://www.oxforddnb.com) (hereafter *ODNB-e*). The British Army Lists, published annually since 1740, are not online, but Worthington C. Ford, *British Officers Serving in America, 1754-1774* (Boston, 1894) is available at the Internet Archive. com. Also useful for establishing dates of British government appointments is the authoritative J. C. Sainty, et al., eds., *Officeholders in Modern Britain, 1660-1870*, 11 vols. (London, 1972-2006), available at British History Online (via http://www.british-history.ac.uk/catalogue). Contemporary almanacs and court-registers are accessible through ECCO. For example, *The Court and City Kalendar: or, Gentleman's Register, for the year 1766* . . . (London, 1765).

The Papers of
Governor Francis Bernard

8 JANUARY-30 SEPTEMBER 1768

577 | To John Pownall

Boston Jan. 8 1768

Dear S^r.

I avail myself of an Opportunity to inform you that on Dec. 30 I opened the Winter Session of the Genl. Court.[1] As Nothing is as yet ripe enough to occasion my troubling the ~~Secretary~~ Minister of State, I have only to send Copies of my Speech for the Secretarys Office and for that of your Board. Its cheif Excellency is that it is perfectly inoffensive, for so it has been allowed to be by all Parties. For my Oratory is now so reduced as to found its Merit in saying little & meaning less.[2] But this Kind of Eloquence has its Use: for the Assembly has now sat 10 Days & shown no ill humour. But they say it is to come; and will appear in two Instances: 1 in censuring the Cheif Justice for an unanimous Act of the superior Court which has been approved of by every reasoning Man in the Province and was indeed necessary to the very Existence of the Court; 2. In remonstrating against the late Act of Parliament for raising a Revenue in America for paying Judges & Govr &c: great Pains are taken and no little by me to prevent any Imprudent Assertions of Rights which the Parliament cannot admit or avoid resisting.[3] I am in hopes that they will have some Weight, and that Prudence and Moderation will prevail in the House more than they have of late Used. I shall not be surprised when the House comes to be really divided, to find that the Friends of Government will be more numerous, than they have of late appeared to be. But this is all Conjecture and depends upon Events not now known.

I was favoured with your Letter by Captn. Spry.[4] By very unlucky Accidents he came in here in such Distress as gave me an Opportunity of being very serviceable to him, for which I am sufficiently paid by his own Acknowledgements.[5] I will own to you that among the Difficulties I have had to struggle with, my general Want of Instructions Directions & Advice has been a considerable Part. But I cannot expect from my Friends what they have not to give me nor from my Superiors what they don't think proper to impart. I wish you every Thing that is desirable: but however have so much Selfishness in me that I can't tell how to regret my still corresponding with you in your old Character.

I am Dear Sir &c

John Pownall Esq.

L, LbC   BP, 6: 55-56.

In handwriting of Thomas Bernard. Enclosures: FB's speech to the Council and the House of Representatives, 30 Dec. 1767 (not found) for which see *JHRM*, 44: 88.

Shortly before FB wrote this letter to John Pownall (1724/5-95), the Grafton ministry announced that the earl of Hillsborough was to lead a new Colonial Department with responsibility for the American Colonies, commencing on 21 Jan.[6] FB learned of Hillsborough's appointment a month afterward, on 20 or 21 Feb. (**No. 590**).

The last paragraph of FB's letter to Pownall alludes to their mutual concerns about the management of colonial affairs under the stewardship of the earl of Shelburne, secretary of state for the Southern Department in Grafton's administration.[7] Pownall had been secretary of the Board of Trade since 1745: under his daily management, the Board had been closely involved in colonial policymaking as an advisory body to the secretary of state, the Treasury, and the Privy Council; it was kept up-to-date about developments in Massachusetts via regular correspondences with FB and the other royal governors. Lately, however, the Rockingham and Chatham administrations[8] had sidelined the Board by concentrating power in the hands of the secretary of state; regular communications from the Board of Trade to the governors had ceased in Aug. 1766, though FB continued a personal correspondence with Pownall. In complaining of "Want of Instructions Directions & Advice," FB was accusing Shelburne of neglect. While he exempted Pownall from blame he hinted that the Board's secretary knew more than he was able or cared "to impart" (Pownall having earlier expressed concerns about his future career at the Board).[9] Hillsborough eventually supplanted the Board altogether, relieved governors of their obligation to keep the Board informed of their activities (**No. 645**), and secured the appointment of Pownall as an under-secretary of state in the Colonial Department.[10]

---

1. The second session of the legislature ran from 30 Dec. 1767 to 4 Mar. 1768.

2. FB's opening speech invited the assembly to consider the report of the boundary commissioners examining the province border with New York, and the relevant correspondence with governors Sir Henry Moore and John Wentworth. The sense of ennui pervading FB's observation about his "Oratory" indicates the shallowness of his promise to the assembly to "be always ready to assist in all Measures which shall appear to me to be conducive to the true Honor and real Interest of this Province." *JHRM*, 44: 88.

3. Both issues were probably raised in the course of a day's debate on the Townshend duties, on 30 Dec. The "censure" of TH was offered in criticism of his role in the Superior Court's decision of Oct. 1767 to disbar Joseph Hawley (a leading Whig) from legal practice. See **No. 586n4**.

4. **No. 564,** *Bernard Papers*, 3: 401-402.

5. British army officer William Spry, captain lieutenant in the military branch of Ordinance, had arrived in Boston on 7 Nov. 1767 en route to his new posting as commander of the artillery at Halifax. But the ship in which he traveled carried smallpox, necessitating the quarantining of passengers and crew by the town authorities. FB intervened to procure Spry's release, doubtless upon learning that the captain was immune. *Bernard Papers*, 3: 402.

6. *Lloyd's Evening Post*, 1 Jan. 1768; *Public Advertiser*, 5 Jan 1768.

7. William Petty (1737-1805), second earl of Shelburne, was secretary of state for the Southern Department, 30 Jul. 1766-21 Oct. 1768. He relinquished responsibility for colonial affairs on 21 Jan. 1768, when they were taken over by the new Colonial Department under the earl of Hillsborough.

8. Charles Watson-Wentworth (1730-82), second marquess of Rockingham, accepted the king's invitation to form an administration in succession to George Grenville's on 10 Jul. 1765, entering office as first lord of the Treasury on 13 Jul. and continuing until 30 Jul. 1766. The succeeding administration of William Pitt (1708-78), first earl of Chatham and Lord Privy Seal, ended with his resignation on 14 Oct. 1768. Augustus Henry Fitzroy (1735-1811), third duke of Grafton, led the administration as first lord of the Treasury during Chatham's long illness; after Chatham's resignation, he formed his own administration as prime minister until 30 Jan. 1770.

9. **No. 572**, *Bernard Papers*, 3: 342, 419.

10. Pownall held the position from 24 Jun. 1768 until 5 Apr. 1776.

William Pitt, first Earl of Chatham and prime minister, 1766-68. After Richard Brompton.
© National Portrait Gallery, London.

578 | To John Pownall

Boston Jan 9 1768

Dear S^r.

I send you the enclosed Papers containing the four first Letters of a Pensylvanian Farmer as a Specimen of an American System of Politicks. These Letters are reckoned to be and undoubtedly are the most Masterly Writings ~~of~~ on that Side of the Question. As it is not probable that they are really the Produce of Pensylvania, various Conjectures are made from whence these ~~Conjectures~~ Papers come. Some have derived them from this Town and have pointed out the Author. But it seems certain that the Faction here had not a Writer of Abilities equal to this Work. Others impute them to Mr Dulany of Maryland; but without any other Authority than the internal Evidence of the Writing being suitable to his Abilities, and agreeable to his Manner, both as to Stile, & the unnecessary Quotation of Authorities.[1] Whoever is the Author, People's Curiosity is not a little Attentive to the Reception these Papers will meet with in England. For it seems pretty plain that if what is laid down in them is the Law of America, the Parliament of Great Britain need not give themselves much more trouble to make Laws for this Country. They are printed in the Pensylvanian Chronicle in the first Instance, & from thence copied in the New York & Boston Papers and I suppose in all others upon this Continent. What I now send you are one in the Original and three others in different Papers.[2] As the first Letter dwells so much upon the N York Act[3] I am enclined to think they originate from Thence: tho' this Reason is not conclusive. If you have not met with these before you receive this, they will afford Amusement if they are of no other Use.

I am &c

J Pownall Esq:

L, LbC   BP, 6: 59-60.

Probably in handwriting of Thomas Bernard. Enclosures (not found) were the first four "Letters from a Farmer in Pennsylvania" published in the *Pennsylvania Chronicle* and other newspapers. The first of twelve letters by the "Pennsylvania Farmer" appeared in the *Pennsylvania Chronicle and Universal Advertiser* of 30 Nov.- 3 Dec. 1767 and the last on 15 Feb. 1768; they were reprinted in the *Boston Gazette*, the *Boston Chronicle*, and the *Boston Evening-Post* between 21 Dec. 1767 and 29 Feb. 1768. FB probably enclosed reprints of the second, third, and fourth letters in the series (spanning a four week period from 2 to 26 Dec. in the *Pennsylvania Chronicle*) which were reprinted as follows: no. 2, *Boston Gazette*, 28 Dec.; no. 3, *Boston Evening-Post*, 28 Dec. and 11 Jan., and *Boston Gazette*, 4 Jan.; no. 4, *Boston Gazette*, 11 Jan., and *Boston Chronicle*, 28 Dec.-4 Jan.[4] FB continued to send Pownall copies of the "Letters" as they appeared in print.[5]

FB heralded the appearance of one of the best known works of the pre-revolutionary period, praising the "Letters from a Farmer in Pennsylvania" as the "most Masterly Writings" on the "American side." Serialized in colonial newspapers and reprinted in several pamphlet editions, the essays were read throughout America and Europe, prompting historian Forrest McDonald to declaim that their "impact and their circulation were unapproached by any publication of the revolutionary period except Thomas Paine's *Common Sense.*"[6] FB was more curious than intrigued by the mystery surrounding the identity of the "Pennsylvania Farmer," but was convinced the author was a New Yorker (**No. 579**). By mid-July (at the latest), authorship was attributed to the Pennsylvania legislator John Dickinson (1732-1808), whose popular "Liberty Song" was being performed at gatherings of the Boston Whigs.[7] Dickinson's major contribution to the political debate was to deliver an accusatory argument that in seeking to tax the colonists directly the British were dangerous constitutional innovators; that the assertion of Parliament's legislative supremacy in the Declaratory Act of 1766 presaged an empire where taxes could be imposed with impunity. While Dickinson urged conciliation, his arguments, together with British entrenchment, "forced everyone on both sides to face and give a firm answer to a forbidden question: what is the nature and distribution of power in the imperial system?"[8] FB's reluctance to consider local Whig writers capable of producing such a "Masterly" work might be redolent of the snobbish disdain with which he had previously dismissed colonial literature. But FB was not blind to the rhetorical merits of Whig political writing, professing to admire the Farmer's "Abilities"—his exposition and learning—if not his principles, in mounting the most serious ideological challenge yet to imperial authority.

---

1. Daniel Dulany (1722-97), a Maryland lawyer was the author of a well-known attack on the Stamp Act, *Considerations on the Propriety of Imposing Taxes in the British Colonies, for the purpose of raising a revenue, by act of Parliament* (Annapolis, 1765). The pamphlet was a forceful attack on parliamentary taxation, and was subsequently published in Boston, London, and New York. See John Eliot Alden, "The Boston Edition of Daniel Dulany's Considerations on the Propriety of Imposing Taxes," *The New England Quarterly* 13 (No. 4, 1940): 705-711. I am grateful to Christopher F. Minty for drawing my attention to Alden's article. Dulany eventually became a Loyalist, a transition that was not uncommon among conservative Whigs in Massachusetts (and exemplified by councilors John Erving Sr., Harrison Gray, and Isaac Royall).

2. The underlining of this sentence is probably noncontemporaneous.

3. The New York Suspending Act, 1767 (7 Geo. 3, c. 59).

4. I am grateful to Christopher Minty for researching the publication dates.

5. BP, 6: 82.

6. Forrest McDonald, ed., *Empire and Nation: Letters from a Farmer in Pennsylvania (John Dickinson). Letters from the Federal Farmer (Richard Henry Lee)* (Indianapolis, 1999), chapter: "Introduction," accessed from http://oll.libertyfund.org/title/690/102298 on 27 Feb. 2013.

7. Arthur Schrader, "Songs to Cultivate the Sensations of Freedom," in *Music in Colonial Massachusetts, 1630-1820*, ed. Sheldon B. Cohen (Boston, 1980), 105-156, at 113-116.

8. McDonald, *Empire and Nation*.

579 | To John Pownall

Private

Boston Jan. 16 1768

Dear S[r]

Together with the Duplicates of my former Letters[1] & inclosures I send you a 5th Farmer's Letter, which seems not to be wrote by the same Hand as the others, but certainly comes from the same Junto.[2] The Printers of the Faction here own that they have had them in Manuscript; which they have made plain by printing some of them before they arrived here from other Presses, they also own they know the Author; and it is allmost admitted by them that they originate at N York. I in my own Mind have fixed upon the Man, being one of Rank & Ability: but the Circumstance from whence I derive this Notion is so minute accidental & confidential that it will not Justify the using ~~the~~ a Name: however it serves to confirm the Opinion that they originated at N York.

On the back of the 5th Letter you will see a Speech of L_ C_m.[3] This was reprinted at N York under the Name of L_ C_n:[4] and it was read in our House last Thursday[5] as a Speech made very lately. It is said to have given a final Turn to the Resolution of sending a Remonstrance against the Acts,[6] which has past the House and will probably be sent by the same Ship which carrys this. I have not been able to get a sight of it; but I have heard of some very bold Passages in it. All the Arguments used upon this Occasion are derived from the Reasoning against the Right of taxing the Colonies in Parliament and the Distinctions used between external and internal Taxes. This is carried to such a Length by the Popular Writers here, that they have declared that every Appropriation of Port Duties to the Purposes of a revenue make it an internal Tax and as such, an Infringment of ^their^ Rights. So here is an End of Port Duties, at least such thereof as raise Money.

I told the Speaker[7] a few Days ~~ago~~ before the Session that if they were determined to remonstrate, they should do it in such a Manner, as the high Terms with which they treat the Matter might not be made publick, for that the Parliament was at present by no means disposed to bear patiently any further Arraignments of their Authority.[8] I am told this Business is conducted so that M[r] Deberdt will be at Liberty to strike out the Offensive Parts,[9] if he intends to make use of the Substance in Parliament. ~~These~~ People declare against an American Representation, and yet conduct their Business as if their sole Purpose was to inforce it. I told the Speaker that they would drive the Ministry into this Measure, whether they liked it or not: and the Leaders must design so to do; otherwise they would not be continually enlarging their Pretensions, and giving for reason their not being represented; they would not exult in L_ C_n's Speech, the whole Argument of which concludes for the Necessity of such a Representation. For my own Part I have long been convinced of the Expediency of such a Measure: but it now appears to be the only Thing left to reconcile the two Countries upon Principles admissible by both

I am &c

J Pownall Esq:

L, LbC   BP, 6: 62-65.

In handwriting of Thomas Bernard. Enclosures (not found): "Duplicates" of **Nos. 577** and **578** and copies of their enclosures; FB's speech to the Council and the House of Representatives, 30 Dec. 1767 (for which see *JHRM*, 44: 88). FB stated that he enclosed a copy of the fifth essay in "Letters from a Farmer in Pennsylvania." His comments on New York in the first paragraph of this letter to Pownall might indicate that he was referring to a reprint in one of the New York newspapers (for which see note 2 below). However, for reasons given in note 3 it is possible he enclosed the first imprint in the *Pennsylvania Chronicle*, 21-28 Dec. 1767. FB later dispatched pamphlet copies of the Farmer's "Letters" which he described as a "Bill of Rights" for the American Colonies on account of its central argument attacking the Townshend duties: that any parliamentary tax imposed on the colonists, regardless of kind, was unconstitutional.[10] No direct reply from Pownall has been found.

"L_C_m" referred to William Pitt (1708-78), created earl of Chatham on 30 Jul. and prime minister from that day until 14 Oct. 1768. Pitt's speeches of 14 Jan. 1766 advocating repeal of the Stamp Act marked him out as the Americans' leading advocate in Parliament. The main thrust of Pitt's argument was that taxation was a gift of the people and therefore Parliament had no right to tax Americans who were not directly represented in that body. Pitt also advanced the distinction between "external" and "internal" taxes, mentioned in FB's letter, in part to justify trade duties under the first heading and repudiate direct taxes under the second. As FB rightly observed, Americans' "Reasoning" against the Townshend duties was predicated on accepting Pitt's original proposition that parliamentary taxation of unrepresented Americans was inherently unjust.[11] On 20 Jun. 1766, the Massachusetts House of Representatives passed a vote of gratitude for his part in procuring the Stamp Act's repeal.[12] On 2 Feb. 1768, the House wrote Chatham in the hope, if not expectation, that he could be persuaded to repeal the Townshend duties that his administration had introduced the previous summer.[13]

"L_C_n" in this letter was Charles Pratt (1714-94), created baron (later earl) of Camden on 10 Jul 1765. He was appointed lord chancellor in Chatham's administration and raised to the peerage. Camden's arguments for repealing the Stamp Act were generally similar to Chatham's, but he was more outspoken in expressing his opposition to parliamentary taxation per se, declaring it unconstitutional, and did not make distinctions between "external" and "internal" taxes as Chatham did. He also spoke against the introduction of the American Declaratory Act, on 11 Mar. 1766.

The speeches of both political heavyweights were reprinted in the American Colonies. Extracts of Pitt's speeches against the Stamp Act appeared in several newspapers over the summer of 1766.[14] But unlike Pitt, Camden showered praise on FB for his reporting of the Stamp Act riots.[15] The exact date of Camden's pro-Bernard speech cannot be established, but it was sometime between his pro-American maiden speech of 3 Feb. and his attack on the Declaratory Bill of 11 Mar.[16] That latter speech, his most famous, was first published in the London *Political Register*, 3 Oct. 1767, and reprinted in colonial newspapers under the erroneously titled "L—C—m's *Speech on the declaratory Bill of the Sovereignty of* Great-Britain *over the Colonies.*"[17] The Massachusetts House probably expected more from Camden than from Chatham, judging by the letter dispatched on 29 Jan. 1768. The lord chancellor was reminded of what he had said previously about the unconstitutionality of American taxation, and asked to consider that Townshend's Revenue Act (1767) and all American "Port Duties" were taxes "in effect" (as Dickinson's "Farmer" argued). Equally obnoxious was Townshend's provision for paying Crown salaries from the taxes collected.

> It is humbly submitted to your Lordship, whether subjects can be said to enjoy any degree of freedom, if the Crown in addition to its undoubted authority of constituting Governors, should be authorized to appoint such stipends for them, as it shall judge proper, at their expence and without their consent. This is the unhappy state to which his Majesty's subjects in the Colonies are reduced.[18]

---

1. **No. 577**.

2. "Letters from a Farmer in Pennsylvania," V was first published in the *Pennsylvania Chronicle and Universal Advertiser*, 21-28 Dec. 1767, and reprinted in New York and Boston, including the *New-York Mercury*, 11 Jan., the *New-York Gazette, or Weekly Post-Boy*, 11 Jan., the *Boston Gazette*, 18 Jan., and the *Boston Chronicle*, 11-18 Jan. 1768.

3. Lord Chatham. Appended to the fifth letter printed the *Pennsylvania Chronicle*, 21-28 Dec. 1767, was a note that ought to have been included as a footnote to the fourth letter printed in the newspaper's issue for 14-21 Dec. It contained author John Dickinson's commentary on William Pitt's House of Commons speech of 14 Jan. 1766 in which Pitt urged the repeal of the Stamp Act. Dickinson reviewed the distinction that Pitt had reputedly made between "external taxes" for the regulation of trade and "internal taxes" for raising revenue, which many contemporaries had come to accept. Dickinson, however, concluded that the distinction was not so much erroneous as irrelevant, since any tax was, by definition, a revenue raising measure; therefore, the Townshend duties, though designated "Port Duties," were as unconstitutional as the Stamp Tax since Americans had not consented to their imposition. The footnote was relocated to its correct place in the first pamphlet edition printed by David Hall and William Sellers. John Dickinson, *Letters from a Farmer in Pennsylvania, to the Inhabitants of the British Colonies* (Philadelphia, 1768).

    In the seventh letter, published in the *Pennsylvania Chronicle* on 11 Jan. and reprinted in the *New-York Journal*, 16 Jan., Dickinson, quoted further extracts from parliamentary speeches, including Pitt's famous declamation of 14 Jan. 1766 that "this kingdom has no right to lay a tax upon the colonies" and Camden's attack on the proposed Declaratory Act from 11 Mar. 1766. For Camden, Dickinson's source was "L—C—m's *Speech on the declaratory Bill of the Sovereignty of* Great-Britain *over the Colonies,*" *Pennsylvania Chronicle*, 21-28 Dec. 1767; this version was reprinted in the New York and Massachusetts newspapers.

4. Lord Camden. "L—C—m's *Speech on the declaratory Bill of the Sovereignty of* Great-Britain *over the Colonies,*" in the *New-York Gazette, or Weekly Post-Boy*, 4 Jan. 1768. FB seems to confuse the earl of Chatham with Lord Camden, because the newspapers wrongly attributed Camden's speech of 11 Mar. to "L—C—m" (Chatham). FB's comment that members of the House of Representatives supposed the "Speech [*was*] made very lately" indicates some uncertainty as to the speech's provenance. But in a letter to Jackson written on the same date (**No. 580**), he unequivocally (and accurately) attributed the printed speech to Camden.

5. On 14 Jan. James Otis Jr. spoke on Camden's speech (**No. 580**).

6. FB is referring specifically to the House of Representatives' petition to the king, 20 Jan. 1768. *JHRM*, 44: 217-219. But the House also prepared a series of "Representations" to leading British politicians, for which see *JHRM*, 44: 219-250 and the list in **No. 593**n3. The House's instructions to Dennys DeBerdt (d.1770)—who had been appointed House agent on 17 Mar. 1767—were delivered in a long letter of 12 Jan., *JHRM*, 44: 241-250.

7. Thomas Cushing (1725-88), representative for Boston between 1761 and 1774, and Speaker of the House of Representatives, 1766-70 and 1772-74.

8. The publication of "Letters from a Farmer in Pennsylvania" had heightened FB's anxiety that differences between Britain and the colonies over imperial power and parliamentary authority were becoming irreconcilable. See **No. 578**.

9. See **Nos. 580** and **581**.

10. FB to John Pownall, 28 Mar. 1768, BP. 6: 104-105.

11. Historians have debated whether or not Pitt actually meant what he said and indeed what he actually said. The most recent investigation by Neil Longley York points to Pitt deliberating the constitutionality of the Stamp Tax as an "internal" tax, and famously deciding that taxation of the unrepresented Americans was unconstitutional. Pitt had not questioned Parliament's legislative supremacy in the American Colonies. But FB's reference to "Reasoning against the Right of taxing the Colonies in Parliament" in the second paragraph of the letter printed here is indicative of the direction of colonial arguments used against the Townshend duties. Neil Longley York, "When Words Fail: William Pitt, Benjamin Franklin and the Imperial Crisis of 1766," *Parliamentary History* 28 (2009): 341-374, at 343-345.

12. *JHRM*, 43 pt.1: 108-109.

13. *JHRM*, 44: 144.

14. Reports of Pitt's speeches against the Stamp Act appeared in many colonial newspapers over the summer of 1766. Some were contained in published letters from England, such as that printed in the *Pennsylvania Gazette*, 1 May 1766. One particular letter, dated 30 Jan. 1766, was reprinted in the *Newport Mercury*, 5 May; the *Boston News-Letter*, 8 May; the *Boston Evening-Post*, 12 May; and other papers. A fuller version was printed in *The Celebrated Speech of a Celebrated Commoner* ([London], 1766), though it was not advertised in colonial newspapers. Pitt was widely honored as a national hero for masterminding Britain's victory over France in the Seven Years' War, and was further lauded by the American colonists for saving them from the Stamp Act. As prime minister and Lord Privy Seal, Chatham's American policy was avoiding making any concessions to the Americans in matters respecting parliamentary authority, despite what the Massachusetts Whigs hoped; policy was largely shaped by other members of his cabinet during long periods of illness and absence, notably Chancellor of the Exchequer Charles Townshend and First Lord of the Treasury Grafton. Nonetheless, Americans would look to Chatham again when war threatened in 1774 and 1775 to effect a reconciliation with Britain. See *Bernard Papers*, 3: 24-27; John Brooke, *The Chatham Administration, 1766-1768* (London, 1956).

15. Camden's speech extracted in the *New-York Mercury*, 26 May 1766; *Boston Evening-Post*, 26 May 1766. See *Bernard Papers*, 3: 151, 153, 155n.

16. These speeches are summarized in William Cobbett, *The Parliamentary History of England from the earliest period to the year 1803, from which last-mentioned epoch it is continued downwards in the work entitled "The parliamentary debates,"* 36 vols. (London, 1806-1820), 16: 168-169, 177-181.

17. *Pennsylvania Chronicle*, 28 Dec. 1767; the *New-York Gazette, or Weekly Post-Boy*, 4 Jan. 1768; and the *Boston Evening-Post*, 18 Jan. 1768.

18. *JHRM*, 44: 229-231.

580 | To Richard Jackson

N° 2[1]

Boston, Jan 16 1768

Dear S^r:

I have not as yet had Time to open your Letters for the Purpose of giving them a general Answer:[2] but I am desirous of improving every little Opportunity to fling in a few Lines to you.

I still continue quiet, no Attempts having as yet been made by the House to make me a Party to their Disputes. They have been employed ever since the ~~Begin~~ ^ope^ning the Session in preparing a Remonstrance against the late Acts for imposing Duties &c; & have but just now, in 18 Days finished it. A few Days before the Session, the Speaker asking my Opinion upon that Subject, I advised him by all Means to conduct the Business, so that the high Terms and Pretensions, which I supposed they would make Use of might not necessarily be made public; for that the Parliament at present was by no Means disposed to bear with Patience further Impeachments of their Authority. And I understand that the Business is so managed that the Remonstrance is addressed to M^r De Berdt, with Directions to lay the whole before the Ministry, or prepare a Memorial from it, as he shall see Occasion. And no Copies of it are allowed to be taken here: So that he will have it in his Power to oppress the Offensive Passages, Some of which, as they have been reported to me, are indeed very violent.[3]

I have sent Mr Pownall some Political News Papers[4] in which the present Pretensions of America are enforced in a better Manner than common. The whole Arguments are derived from the reasoning in Parliament against the Taxation of America & the Distinction between external & internal Taxes; which latter is carried to such a length here as to exclude all Port Duties which produce Money. Altho the Americans in general don't seem to desire a Representation yet the popular leaders seemed determined to drive the Parliament into granting one. How is this to be reconciled? The cheif Demagogues propose to themselves to be their Representatives, and yet don't dare avow their Intention. This was very evident in the House two Days ago: Otis produced a Speech of Lord Campdens on the declaratory Bill in April 1766, which has been reprinted from the political Magazine in the Name of L_d C_m;[5] This he told them was made a little while ago; & he triumphed upon it most immediately. Now the whole Conclusions of this Speech make for the Necessity of an American Representation. For my own Part; I have ~~so strong~~ long seen the Expediency of such a Measure; but now the Necessity of it is so apparent, that it seems plain to me, that an American Representation for Matters relative to the whole Empire, & inferior Legislatures subordinate to Parliament for domestic Business is the only Thing left to reconcile the two Countries upon principles admissible to both. I have no Time to argue upon this now; but shall probably touch upon it again in some future Letter.

I am &c

R Jackson Esqr

L, LbC   BP, 6: 65-67.

In handwriting of Thomas Bernard.

---

1. Hitherto, FB had not numbered his letters to Jackson. The first in the series was dated 8 Jan. 1768. BP, 6: 57-59. FB ceased the practice by mid-March.

2. These letters from Jackson have not survived. Jackson remained a key contact for FB in spite of his removal from the province agency in 1767 (for which see *Bernard Papers*, 3: 266) notwithstanding his own opposition to DeBerdt's appointment as House agent and disappointment at Jackson's dismissal.

3. FB was hoping Jackson would be able to persuade DeBerdt to censor any documents he received from the House of Representatives, before presenting them to the king or secretary of state. FB could not be sure that the British would ignore DeBerdt's credentials as House agent, even though he had opposed the appointment on constitutional grounds. DeBerdt was not hidebound by protocol, but he would not have assumed he had authority to alter any documents unless so directed by the Speaker of the House, Thomas Cushing, his principal contact. However, DeBerdt had already criticized the House for delaying voting compensation to the victims of the Stamp Act riots. FB thought the House's recent letter to DeBerdt might also have alarmed him with its provocative references to exploitative taxes and standing armies. *Bernard Papers*, 3: 230; House of Representatives to Dennys DeBerdt, 12 Jan., 1768, *JHRM*, 44: 241-250. See **No. 581**n4.

4. See source notes to **Nos. 578** and **579**.

5. Lord Camden's speech of 11 Mar. 1766 was printed in the English *Political Register*, 3 Oct. 1767, and reprinted in colonial newspapers under the title "L—C—m's *Speech on the declaratory Bill of the Sovereignty of* Great-Britain *over the Colonies.*" *Pennsylvania Chronicle*, 28 Dec. 1767; the *New-York Gazette, or Weekly Post-Boy*, 4 Jan. 1768; and the *Boston Evening-Post*, 18 Jan. 1768. See the source note to **No. 579**.

581 | To the Earl of Shelburne

Nº 1

Boston Jan 21. 1768

My Lord

I found it necessary to call the Assembly sooner than I intended & they accordingly met on Dec 30. I deferred giving your Lordship any account of their proceedings till they should become intresting enough to deserve your Lordship's notice. The first 18 days were Spent in preparing remonstrances against the Act for imposing new Duties & directing the application of them for the support of the Administration of justice & the Government. A few days before the meeting of the Assembly The Speaker of the House was with me & in the course of Conversation informed ^me^ that it was intended to remonstrate against the late Acts & asked my Opinion upon it. I told him that if they were determined upon that step, I would advise them to do it in such a manner that the Terms of their Remonstrance might not necessarily come before Parliament. For I knew that however cautiously it might be worded, it could not be free from a claim of a right to an Exemption from Acts of this kind. And I was well assured that however favorable the Parliament had been to them heretofore, It was at present by no means disposed to bear with a farther Dispute of their Authority so soon after it had been so solemnly declared to be inherent in them;[1] & especially in the present cause, which was of port duties, which had heretofore been admitted to belong to parliament, & now were to be taken away by a refinement, which, however it might read in American news papers,[2] would never be heard in the two Houses;[3] which allowed of no distinctions in what they should think fit to enact for America. I added, that if they should think proper to address his Majesty's Secretary of State upon this occasion, it was my Official Business to take the charge of it & I should faithfully remitt it whatever the contents were. And if they put it into other hands, I should remonstrate against it as being irregular & unconstitutional for any addresses to pass from an Assembly (where the King has a representative presiding) to his Majesty either directly or indirectly, except thro' the mediation of his Representative.[4]

As soon as the Assembly met the House ordered the Commission of the Commissioners of the Customs, which was registred in the Secretary's office, to be brought in & read & then appointed a Committee to consider the state of the Province & report.[5] This Committee reported a Letter to Mr Deberdt their Agent[6] & another to your Lordship. These being Very lengthy took many days' consideration, in which many Offencive passages were struck out; tho' I am told there still remain, at least, in the letter to M[r] Deberdt, sevral bold & imprudent expressions.[7] These two Letters took up 18 days; after which the Committee reported an Address to the King, which was concluded & agreed upon in 4 or 5 days more.[8] When the two first Letters were finished I directed the Secretary to ask the Speaker to let me have a sight of them, as I had been allways used to do in like cases, without ever being refused. The Speaker said that he must advise about it, & afterwards told the Secretary that there was an order of the House that no Copies should be taken;[9] & therefore He could not let me have them. The Secretary replied that that was no objection to my seeing them; for that I did not want any Copy & would give him any assurance that no Copy should be taken, whilst in my hands; & advised him to see me. The Speaker came to me & repeating his difficulties offered to take the Opinion of the House. I told him He should not move the House in my name, for I would not put in their Power to refuse me this: that I had allready Waited five days for a sight of these papers; and if he would not let me have it now, I should take it as a refusal, & should acquaint the Secretary of State with it. He still said that He would endeavour to get leave to show them to me; but nothing has been done. I must add that I by no means apprehend this to be an Affront to my person but my Office: for at this time the Speaker himself seemed uncommonly desirous by some other means to persuade me of his respect; And the House from the time of the opening the Session to this day has shown their disposition to avoid all disputes with me, ev'ry thing having passed with as much good humour as I could desire; except only their continuing to act in addressing the King remonstrating to the Secretary of State & employing a separate Agent; as if they were the States general of the Province, without a Governor or a Kings Council.[10]

It is the Importance of this Innovation, without any Wilfulness of my own, which induces me to make this remonstrance to your Lordship, at a time when I have a fair prospect of having in all other business nothing but good to say of the proceedings of this House; I mean so far as their disposition has hitherto appeared. It is of great Consequence that the Assemblies of America should be prevented making an Usage of addressing the King or his Ministers of State upon general affairs of the Government without the intervention of the Governor, which is ^the^ official Medium of all Representations from the general Assemblies to the Crown. I know not that it has ever been attempted in Any other province but this; and in this It has been ^allways^ a Symptom of a disorder in the State & has ever been discountenanced by the Government at home. In my Letter to your Lordship N[o] 11 dated March 28 1767 [11] I quote a Letter from the Lords of Trade to the Gov[r] of Mass[ts] Bay dated May 26 1704 wherein mentioning an Address to have been sent over without the concurrence of the Governor they add "We can by no means approve their proceding in this manner; it is very unfit that Assemblies should make representations to his Majesty by particular Agents of their own, without the consent & knowledge of his Majesty's Governor &c". When I wrote that Letter I had not been refused the inspection of any papers which I desired to see. In the present case I am not allowed to see papers addressed to the King or his Minister, which have been publickly read for 18 days together in an Assembly of 100 members with a Gallery in it Constantly filled with people more or less, have been communicated without doors to whomever the Clerk of the House has pleased, in public as well as in private Companies & ^are^ made a Secret to no one but to the Governor & Council.

I would not presume to dictate to your Lordship what is the proper time to correct this irregularity; nor have I any doubt but that the impropriety of it appears to your Lordship in the same light that it does to me. I would avoid repeating what I have urged in my foremention'd letter; but would rather trouble your Lordship to review that when you take this into Consideration. I will only mention two reasons against admitting this practice; one of which has been urged before, but in the present case has received fresh force.

1. The King in all matters relating to America has great reliance on the Reports of his Governors, who being appointed by him & accountable to him are under the greatest obligations not to deceive him. But if the Assemblies are allowed to represent matters to the King, without the privity of the Governors, the King must either lose the Advantage of having the opinion of his Governors upon the Subject matter, or must delay his judgement untill he can order his Governor to report his Opinion. In the latter Case the Worst is Delay & Trouble, but in the former the King will be liable to be & frequently will be deceived. And where the Assembly shall take particular Care to keep their Representations Secret from the Governor, they must (if they do not intend to deceive the King) intend to prevent his having the Opinion of his Governor; that is to deprive him of full information. 2. When an Assembly is sitting, The Governor, as the King's Representative has the Officiality of reporting to his Majesty all the proceedings of such Assembly. But if either of the Houses address the Secretary of State upon provincial business separately & privately from the Governor, the Secretary of State in that instance becomes the Governor, & there are at the same time two royal Presidents to one Assembly. I would not be understood to mean to limit the extent of the Power of your Lordship's Office: but I am perswaded that it must be disagreeable as well as inconvenient for your Lordship to be obliged to take upon you the business of a subordinate Office, the passing by of which mediation must often occasion Deception & Confusion.

But after all I am sensible that great Allowance should be made for the late unsettled state of the Country, which it has not yet recovered itself from. And I do not mean to precipitate your Lordship's determination of these or any other Matters which have been represented by me. It is my Duty to report proceedings which appear to me to require Animadversion, at the time that they happen: it is your

Lordships province to fix the time when they shall be taken into consideration; for which I shall allways wait with due deference.

I am with great respect, My Lord Your Lordships most obedient
& most humble Servant

Fra Bernard

The right honble The Earl of Shelburne

ALS, RC   CO 5/ 757, ff 18-21.

Endorsed: Boston Jan^{ry} 21st: 1768. Govr Bernard's (N°. 1) R. 7. March A.4. Variants: CO 5/893, ff 33-36 (dupLS, RC); CO 5/766, ff 98-14 (L, RLbC); BP, 6: 256-262 (L, LbC); three extracts in Coll. Mass. Papers, 1768; *Letters to the Ministry* (1st ed.), 3-5; *Letters to the Ministry* (repr.), 2-6. The duplicate was considered by the Board of Trade on 6 May 1768. *JBT*, 13: 26. Extracts were laid before both houses of Parliament on 28 Nov. 1768. HLL: American Colonies Box 1. Hillsborough formally replied to FB's letter with **No. 603**.

On the same day FB wrote this letter, Shelburne demitted responsibility for the American Colonies to the earl of Hillsborough, recently appointed secretary of state for a new Colonial Department. Shelburne's last official letter to FB was dated 14 Nov. 1767 (**No. 574**, *Bernard Papers*, 3: 419).[12] Hillsborough, in due course, responded to the letters FB had sent Shelburne over that winter.[13]

FB had had a difficult relationship with the earl of Shelburne. When FB purposefully set out to convince the secretary of state of the Americans' proclivities for radicalism and rebellion, Shelburne advised moderation and caution, and for a while considered removing FB. Shelburne eventually endorsed FB's conduct as governor, but it was patently obvious to FB that the secretary did not fully trust him.[14] When FB wrote Shelburne on 21 Jan., he had yet to receive Shelburne's approval for vetoing the election of radical councilors and refusing a separate House agent. Shelburne's letter arrived on 2 Feb. (**No. 566**).[15] Until then, as **No. 581** reveals, FB pressed the secretary of state to consider his position as the king's representative untenable since "the passing by of which mediation [*in communication with London*] must often occasion Deception & Confusion." Subsequent letters, the last dated 21 Mar. 1768 (**No. 601**), were bleaker assessments of imperial decline. But in January, FB had not given up hope of being able to reverse that slide, as he shortly advised Barrington: "I have shown the Assembly the natural and constitutional Power of a Governor here, whilst he keeps himself Blameless and is supported from home." (**No. 583**).

Hillsborough's reply (**No. 603**) intimated that the king "entirely" approved his conduct, while also censuring the House of Representatives' for withholding information from the governor. Hillsborough, moreover, delayed presenting the House's petition to the king.[16]

---

1. By the American Declaratory Act, 6 Geo. 3 c. 12 (1766).

2. FB also considered the "refinement" in the colonial case against parliamentary taxation in his letters to Pownall, **Nos. 578** and **579**. Here he is referring to newspaper articles by the "Pennsylvania Farmer" and commentators upon them that shaped the ensuing debate.

3. That is, the Houses of Parliament.

4. Notably, when FB transmitted to the then secretary of state, the earl of Halifax, the assembly's petition to the House of Commons protesting the introduction of the Sugar Act and stamp duty, his covering letter provided detailed commentary on each of the petition's main points. **No. 315**, *Bernard Papers*, 3: 161-167. Preventing FB from reading a petition was one way that the Massachusetts House of Representatives could limit his interference, but there was no guarantee that the secretary of state would recognize the legitimacy of DeBerdt's appointment as House agent—in fact Hillsborough did not—or accept any paper not transmitted by the governor.

5. The committee appointed on 30 Dec. 1767 included the four Boston representatives: Speaker Thomas Cushing, Samuel Adams (1722-1803), James Otis Jr. (1725-83), John Hancock (1737-93). They were joined by FB's old enemies Jerathmeel Bowers (1717-99), Samuel Dexter (1726-1810), Joseph Hawley (1723-88), and Edward Sheaffe. All were prominent radicals. The committee proceeded to prepare instructions for House agent Dennys DeBerdt (on 12 Jan.), a letter to Shelburne (15 Jan.), a petition to the king (20 Jan.), and several letters to leading British statesmen (22 Jan. to 22 Feb.). A full list is provided in **No. 593**n3. These documents were the work of the committee, but Samuel Adams, as clerk of the House, took the lead role in their composition, as he did with most other official papers issued by House from early 1768 onwards. *JHRM*, 44: 89; Alexander, *Samuel Adams*, 64-68; Cushing, *Writings of Samuel Adams*, 1: 134-198. The recollections of John Adams provide a corrective to the tendency of Samuel Adams biographers to minimize or ignore the contributions of co-authors, notably Otis. John Adams, who was very familiar with the writing styles of both James Otis and Samuel Adams, suggested that Otis's input to the documentary series was substantive. Having analyzed several passages in the documents, John Adams concluded that Otis's "hand" was "visible . . . demonstrative . . . indelible." In a letter to his former clerk William Tudor Sr., John Adams first suggested that "these letters," which he read in pamphlet form, "from beginning to end, demonstrate the rough case of James Otis and the polish and burnish of Samuel Adams." But in the same letter, Adams concluded that

    > upon an attentive and careful review of all these letters, I can find nothing to ascribe to Mr. [*Samuel*] Adams. Every sentence and every word of them appears to me to be Mr. Otis's. They are but an abridgment, a concise compendium of Mr. Otis's argument against the execution of the acts of trade in 1761, seven years before these letters were written. If Mr. Otis himself had not informed me that he had given them all to Mr. Sam Adams to be revised, I should not have suspected that Mr. Adams had any thing to do in the composition of them; for Mr. Otis was as severe a critic, and as capable of writing well, as any man of that time. He only did not love to revise, correct, and polish. If Mr. Adams had really any share in these compositions, it must have been only in the collocation of words.

    John Adams to William Tudor Sr., Quincy, 7 Mar. 1819, *Works of John Adams*, 10: 367-375. FB's various comments in this and other volumes of the *Bernard Papers*, respecting the House's public papers, suggest that he considered Otis and Adams as lead authors. The problem of ascertaining their respective contributions can be left to their future biographers to resolve.

6. The committee reported the draft letter to DeBerdt on 6 Jan. and the letter to Shelburne on 15 Jan. *JHRM*, 44: 99, 114. The House ordered that they should be sent immediately and that they should be copied into the journals. House of Representatives to Dennys DeBerdt, 12 Jan., 1768, ibid., 241-250; to the earl of Shelburne, 15 Jan. 1768, ibid., 44: 219-224.

7. The letter to DeBerdt framed the case against parliamentary taxation in terms of natural rights philosophy, asserting what colonists would call their "unalienable" or "inalienable" rights. House of Representatives to Dennys DeBerdt, 12 Jan., 1768, *JHRM*, 44: 241-250. While Samuel Adams's biographers have assumed that the letter was crafted by the clerk of the House, John Adams supposed that "every line" was a "diamond" to prove his case that James Otis was the sole author of this particular document. *Works of John Adams*, 10: 374.

8. The House of Representatives, petition to the king, 20 Jan. 1768. *JHRM*, 44: 217-219. The petition

was not as explicit as the letters to DeBerdt and Camden in disputing the legitimacy of parliamentary taxation. The eighth paragraph acknowledged Parliament's legislative supremacy and "superintending authority" in "all cases." John Adams later suggested that this passage reflected the handicraft of James Otis, whereas Samuel Adams had already moved toward a more radical position in challenging Parliament's legislative supremacy. While the "superintending authority" clause may also have been a concession to Otis's constitutional principles, it was also a convenient means of implying (thus avoiding explicitly stating) that Parliament's authority was contested not only in the matter of the Townshend trade duties but colonial taxes generally. For (again in a passage characteristic of Otis), the petition protested vociferously at colonists being taxed without representation.

> If these Acts of Parliament [*including the 1767 Revenue Act*] shall remain in force: and your Majesty's Commons in Great Britain shall continue to exercise the power of granting the Property of their fellow subjects in this Province, your people must then regret their unhappy fate in having only the name left of free subjects.

JHRM, 44: 218; *Works of John Adams*, 10: 367.

9. No such order is recorded in the journals, and FB was given a copy of the letter on 23 Feb. *JHRM*, 44: 190.

10. FB had previously alluded to the States General of the Netherlands in a letter to John Pownall, **No. 430**, *Bernard Papers*, 3: 58n11. The States General were formally referred to as "Their High Mightinesses," and FB probably expected Shelburne to pick up the allusion.

11. **No. 542**, *Bernard Papers*, 3: 345-351.

12. Shelburne continued as secretary of state for the Southern Department in Grafton's administration until resigning on 21 Oct. 1768. FB received the first news of Hillsborough's appointment between 20 and 22 Feb. but continued writing Shelburne until 21 Mar. See source note to **No. 582**.

13. For a list of correspondence and Hillsborough's reaction see **No. 588**.

14. For a summary see *Bernard Papers*, 3: 37-30.

15. *Bernard Papers*, 3: 407-409.

16. See **No. 712**, *Bernard Papers*, 5: 115-118.

582 | *Circular From the Earl of Hillsborough*

Nº. 1.

Whitehall, January 23, 1768.

Sir,

His Majesty having been graciously pleased to appoint me to be One of His Principal Secretaries of State, and to commit to my Care the Dispatch of all such Business relative to His Majesty's Colonies in America, as has been usually dispatched by the Secretary of State for the Southern Department, I have His Majesty's Commands to signify this Arrangement to You, and His Majesty's Pleasure that your Dispatches be for the future addressed to me, conformable to the Rule of Correspondence prescribed in His Majesty's Order in Council of the 8ᵗʰ of August 1766,[1] a Copy of which is herewith transmitted to you.

It is His Majesty's Intention, in making the present Arrangement, that all possible Facility and Dispatch should be given to the Business of His Colonies, and as nothing can more effectually contribute to this salutary purpose than a frequent and full Communication of all Occurences that may happen, and a regular and punctual Transmission of all Acts and Proceedings of Government and Legislature, and of such Papers as have any Relation thereto; I have it in Command from His Majesty to recommend this to your particular Attention.[2] His Majesty having observed with Concern that this essential Part of the Duty of His Officers in America has scarcely any where been duly attended to.

I have nothing further to add but to express my earnest Wishes, that, by the utmost Attention and Application I can give, I may be able to fulfil His Majesty's most gracious Intentions, and I take the Liberty to assure You, that I will not omit to lay your Dispatches as soon as I receive them before The King, and to forward and assist, as far as I am able, your Measures for the Public Service.

I am, with great Truth and Regard, Sir, Your most obedient humble Servant

Hillsborough.

Governor of Massachuset's Bay.

PS.

You will be pleased to continue to number each Letter you address to me, in the same manner as in your Correspondence with the Earl of Shelburne, beginning your first Letter to me with Nᵒ. 1.

H.

NB. I send you inclosed for your information pieces of several Acts relating to America, which passed in the last Session of Parliament.[3]

LS, RC   BP, 11: 115-118.

Endorsed by FB: Earl of Hillsborough d Jan 23 1768 r. May 11. Docket by Thomas Bernard: His Appᵗ _ with Orders to Correspond only with the Secrʸ of State __   Enclosed an order of His Majesty in Council, Court of St. James's, 8 Aug. 1766, BP, 11: 119-121; the list of acts of Parliament has not been found. This circular is the first official letter from Wills Hills, the earl of Hillsborough, appointed secretary of state for the Colonies on 21 Jan., heading up a new Colonial Department whose business largely concerned America.[4] While FB did not receive Hillsborough's circular letter until 11 May,[5] he was aware of Hillsborough's appointment from news brought by incoming vessels, between 20 and 21 Feb. (**No. 590**) and again on 6 or 7 Mar.[6] Until he received formal confirmation, however, FB continued writing Shelburne (his last dated 21 Mar.)[7] His first formal reply to Hillsborough was dated 12 May (**No. 611**).

Hillsborough's cabinet colleagues considered his office as being junior to the secretaries of state for the Northern and Southern Departments.[8] Hillsborough, however, as British observers like Lord Barrington expected, emerged as the driving force in colonial policymaking in Chatham's cabinet; he remained in position in the duke of Grafton's administration and in Lord North's administration until resigning in 1772.[9] FB welcomed Hillsborough's appointment, supposing (rightly) that he would be more communicative than Shelburne and inclined to consider the reform of colonial government. Royal instructions issued in 1766 obliged FB to communicate directly with the secretary of state in the first instance, rather than with the Board of Trade, and thereafter send to the Board duplicate copies of his letters to the secretary of state.[10] Hillsborough's circular continued this practice, although in July he relieved the governors of the obligation to supply the Board of Trade with duplicates (**No. 645**), thus concentrating the administration of colonial affairs in the Colonial Department.

---

1. Left marginalia: virgule indicating the enclosure.

2. Left marginalia: the paragraph is marked by a line (probably added by FB) from the beginning until "Attention," with a closing vertical line marking the section end.

3. The current session was the seventh session to the twelfth Parliament of Great Britain; it commenced on 24 Nov. 1767 and finished on 10 Mar. 1768. By "last Session" Hillsborough may have meant the sixth session, from 11 Nov. 1766 to 2 Jul. 1767. Legislation relevant to America passed during the regnal year 7 Geo. 3 included the Free Importation of Wheat and Flour from the American Colonies Act (c. 4); the Free Importation of Rice from the American Colonies Act (c.30); the Colonial Trade Act (c.35); the Revenue and Customs Duties Act (c.46), also known to posterity as the Townshend Duties Act, which imposed duties on tea, glass, paper, lead, and painter's colors; an act allowing a drawback of duties on the exportation of tea to Ireland and America (c.56). Owen Ruffhead, *The Statutes at Large, from Magna Charta to the twenty-fifth year of the reign of King George the Third*, 10 vols. (London, 1786), preface to vol. 8.

4. Wills Hill (1718-93), first earl of Hillsborough and first secretary of state for the Colonies, 21 Jan. 1768-15 Aug. 1772.

5. The duplicate of Hillsborough's short second letter, also dated 23 Jan., arrived on 15 May. BP, 11: 123-126.

6. **No. 595**n2.

7. **Nos. 591**, **593**, **596**, **600**, and **601**, to which Hillsborough replied with **No. 622**.

8. The earl of Shelburne remained as secretary of state for the Southern Department until 21 Oct. 1768.

9. Arthur Herbert Basye, "The Secretary of State for the Colonies, 1768-82," *American Historical Review* 28 (1922): 13-23.

10. *Bernard Papers*, 2: 15-16; Leonard Woods Labaree, ed., *Royal Instructions to British Colonial Governors, 1670-1776*, 2 vols. (London, 1935), 2: 748-751.

Wills Hill, first Earl of Hillsborough and Secretary of State for the Colonies, 1768-72.
Line engraving after unknown artist, published 1781. © National Portrait Gallery, London.

583 | To Lord Barrington

Boston Jan. 26 176[8][1]

My Lord

I have just now received the Duplicate of your Lordships Letter dated Oct: 6,[2] the Original not being come to hand, as the Oct[r]: Mail is not yet arrived. I am also indebted for your Lordships Letter dated July, 8, which did not arrive till Oct[r]:10.[3] I had deferred acknowledging the last mentioned, in Expectation that I ~~did not~~ should recieve some advises which might direct my Answer to Your Lordship; ~~that~~ but they are not arrived ^yet^ tho' daily expected. However I have so many matters to write upon to your Lordship, that I shall begin now; And as my Subjects are various I shall digest them into separate letters; in which the preference will be due to that which is of the most public & interesting concern.

Your Lordship[4] observes that there is a strong Desire that America should become quiet, & that no disputes should arise between the Mother Country & its Colonies or between Governors & their Assemblies. I have had many hints & have given the utmost attention to them & pursued their purpose as far as I could do consistently with that Rule wisely laid down by Your Lordship that nothing should be given up on this Side the ~~water~~ Atlantick which is materially valuable on yours. To prevent disputes between the Mother Country & its Colonies must be the Work of Great Britain; No Man in the Colonies, not all the Governors in America, tho' they could act with one Mind and with the best Understanding can of themselves bring about so desirable an Event. Upon this Subject I shall write to your Lordship by a seperate Letter.[5]

The preventing Disputes between the Governors and their Assemblies is easily effected, at least will probably be soon brought about in this Province. I have shown the Assembly the natural and constitutional Power of a Governor here, whilst he keeps himself Blameless and is supported from home;[6] And have falsified that prevailing Notion that a Governor of this Province cannot withstand a popular Clamour. Otis himself has given up the Question and says it is to no purpose any longer to oppose me: And some of his Colleagues have allready made peace with me. The Assembly has now sate[7] a full Month & have not shown the least Intimation to Dispute; on the Contrary they have shown a good Disposition to avoid and to remove the Causes which have occasioned it before. So that it is probable that America may become apparently quiet notwithstanding their present pretensions. But, my Lord wounds may be skinned over without healing; and a Calm may be more dangerous than a Storm. It is my Opinion that Great Britain will never be safe till the Wounds are probed to the Bottom and a Remedy applied that will prevent the Return of the Disorder. This must be the work of Parliament, and tho more difficult than it was some Time ago, is still very practicable; in what Manner, I will explain in my Next

I am &c

Viscount Barrington

L, LbC   BP, 6: 67-70.

In handwriting of clerk no. 3.

The warning that he had "so many matters to write upon" was FB's way of re-energizing his epistolary friendship with Lord Barrington, having being obliged to accept that Barrington's patronage was not unconditional. (See **Nos. 472** and **541**).[8] The correspondence that flowed during the next two years explored the problems of imperial administration and colonial government, starting with FB's next letter to Barrington (**No. 584**).

1. First written as "6" then corrected to "7".
2. **No. 568**, *Bernard Papers*, 3: 409-411.
3. **No. 553**, ibid.: 375-376.
4. First written as "Lordship's" before the apostrophe and last letter were (partially) erased.
5. **No. 584**.
6. Silently corrected following scribal interlineation. May have been first written as "hope".
7. Thus in manuscript.
8. *Bernard Papers* 3: 162-163, 344-345.

584 | *To Lord Barrington*

Boston Jan 28 1768.

My Lord

I understand that it is a prevailing Opinion on your side of the Ocean that America, if let alone will come to herself & return to the same Sense of Duty & obedience to Great Britain which she professed before. But It seems to me that observing & considerate Men on this side the water expect no such thing. If indeed the Ill temper of the Americans had arose from accidental Causes, & exercised itself without meddling with fundamental principles, the Cause ceasing the Effects might also cease; & the subject of complaint being removed, a perfect & durable constitution might be restored.

But when the Dispute has been carried so far as to ~~take~~ involve in it ~~questions~~ matters of the highest importance to the ^imperial^ Sovereignty, when it ^has^ produced questions which the Sovereign state cannot give up, & the dependent states insist ^upon^ as the terms of a reconciliation; when the imperial state has so far given way as to flatter the dependent states that their pretensions are admissible; Whatever terms of reconciliation Time Accident or Design ~~shall~~ ^may^ produce, if they ~~have~~ ^are^ deficient in settling the true relation ~~between~~ ^of^ Great Britain ~~&~~ ^to^ her Colonies, & ascertaining the bounds of the Sovreignty of the one & the dependency of the other, Conciliation will be no more ^than a^ suspension of Animosity; the seeds of which will be left in the ground ready to start up again whenever there shall be a new occasion for the Americans to assert their ~~pretensions against~~ ^independence of^ the Authority of parliament, that is whenever the parliament shall make ordinances which the Americans shall think not for their intrest to obey.

It was easy to be foreseen that the distinctions used in parliament in favour of the Americans would be adopted by them & received as fundamental laws. It would signify nothing by what numbers these distinctions were rejected: the respectableness of the Names of the promoters of them, & the apparent intrest of ye Americans in maintaining ^them^ would outweigh all authority of Numbers for the contrary Opinion. It was also to be foreseen that the Americans would carry these Distinctions much farther than the promoters could possibly intend they should be. But yet these ~~distinctions~~ never gave me any concern, because they carried their remedy with them: if they were hurtful to the constitution, they ~~carried their remedy with them;~~ ^had an antidote at hand and^ like the antient Spear, if they wounded the Sovereign state they produced a rust to cure it.[1] If the Parliament cant ^tax^ the Americans because they are not represented, it may allow them representatives, & the Authority is compleat.

I have been used & ~~am still~~ always disposed to set an high~~er~~ value upon the Wisdom of statesmen ^perhaps so much higher^ than ~~they~~ ^~~perhaps~~ it may^ deserve; and I am still desirous rather to err on that side than the opposite. When the great Man^~~for~~^ ~~for~~ ^~~of~~ of^ whose political Ability I then had & still have the highest reverence, ~~pronounced for the~~ ^founded his^ impeachment of the power of parliament to tax the Americans upon the want of American representatives,[2] It appeared to me to be a stroke of refined policy. I considered this difficulty to be started, in order to enforce the necessity of allowing the Americans to send representatives to parliament. I considered not only the Advantages which would arise from such an ordinance for the present by removing all objections to the power of parliament; but also the benefit which must arise for the future by ~~an Union of the two~~ ^incorporating ~~the~~ American^ with Great Britain in an Union which must more effectually prevent a Separation than can be provided ~~against~~ by any other means. If this Objection had been pursued to this conclusion, The Author of it would have been deservedly esteemed the benefactor of both Countries. Without this conclusion It is not easy to see how ^this Contravention of the Authority of parliament can be of service^ ~~it can produce any good~~ to either.

Let us state the positions urged in parliament on the behalf ~~in the behalf~~ of the Americans & the use which has been made of them in America, & see how far the chain of reasoning can be extended. It was said in parliament, that 1. The parliament has no right to tax the Americans, because the Americans have no representatives in parliament. 2. But they have a right to impose port duties or external[3] taxes, because such duties are for the regulation of trade. 3. The difference between an external and an internal tax is that the former is imposed for the regulation of trade & the latter for raising a Revenue. From these premises the Americans have drawn the following conclusions. 1. Port duties imposed for raising a Revenue are internal Taxes. 2. Port duties of which the produce is to be paid into the Exchequer for the use of Government. 4. All the Port Duties ^imposed upon America^ are internal Taxes. The only Difference between the Port duties declared to be for raising a Revenue, & those of which ~~of~~ no such declaration is made is that in one the Intention is explicit; in the other it is implied: they both come within the definition of internal taxes, & there are no taxes left for the distinction to operate upon.

This is not a fictitious Argument but a real one now urged & insisted upon as the terms of a good agreement between great Britain & her Colonies. For proof of which I refer your Lordship to the Farmer's Letters, in which you~~r Lordship~~ will find the whole of this argument laid down either positively or consequentially. What then shall be done? shall the parliament make a new declarative Act? See! here are counter declarations to the former act. shall they take no notice of these American Pretensions? they will then be confirmed in the minds of the Americans & become really, what they are now proclamed[4] to be, a Bill of American rights. The right Way to get rid of these difficulties, which have arose out of the political dissentions at Westminster, is to allow the Americans to send representatives. This will be a full Answer to all their pretensions: it has been for some time past expedient; it is now become necessary.

In one of the ^news-^papers inclosed with this is a Speech said to have been spoke in the House of Lords, which has been reprinted from a London pamphlet. The whole Argument of this does not tend to show that the Americans ought not to be taxed; but that previously to their being taxed, they ought to be allowed to send representatives. This has been extremely well received here, altho' the conclusion is for an American representation. If this was really a Speech of a Lord of that House, it might have been properly answered by admitting the conclusion and thereby avoiding a dispute about the premises. If the Americans should be allowed Representatives, it would become a Question merely speculative, whether Representation is necessary to Taxation or not.

And yet the Americans in general do not desire a representation, tho' the publications on their behalf all tend to that conclusion; and some of them seem calculated to force the parliament into that measure as the only one which will satisfy them[5] ~~pretensions~~. The truth is that ^tho'^ the Leaders of the People set out with a view of obtaining a representation & have never lost sight of it; it has but lately occurred to the people ^in general^ that this may be a probable consequence of their denying the Authority of parliament. The former have ^had^ no objection to being representatives; but the people have not as yet seen their intrest in sending them. It is from this disposition in the demagogues, as well as ^from^ the support they received in parliament turning upon the same question, that the Americans have founded all their Arguments against the Authority of parliament in their want of representatives in it; and a System for separating them from parliament is formed upon a proposition which it is in the power of the parliament at [*blank*] pleasure to convert into the means of more closely uniting them with it. But the mutual intrest of the two Countries seems to be equally misunderstood on both sides of the Water.

I will illustrate this Account of the Ideas of the Americans by fresh facts. At the opening of the present Session of the Assembly of this province, a Member who had distinguished himself by carrying the objections to the Authority of parliament to their present length, now in a set speech retracted all his former Opinions, & said that he had fully informed himself of the relation between Great Britain & her Colonies, & was convinced that the power of parliament over her colonies was absolute, with this qualification, that they ought not to tax them untill they allowed them to send representatives; & that if the Colonies had representatives the power of parliament would be as perfect in America as it was in England. He then argued for an ^American^ Representation, & said it was now become a Measure necessary both to Great Britain & the Colonies, for the healing the breaches between them.

This surprised the House: but their Eyes began to open. A Member on the side of Government charged the Opposition with an intention to make an American Representation necessary by their denying the authority of Acts of parliament over them because they were not represented. The proofs he adduced & the equivocal Answers of the other party left little doubt of this. Upon this an old Member[6] (whose name & Character is well known in England) said that as they were determined to have representatives, He begged leave to recommend ^to them^ a Merchant who would undertake to carry their representatives to England for half what they would sell for when they arrived there.

It ~~This~~ has been a serious Objection that American representatives would be subject to undue influence: ^but are not English representatives so? & is that an argument ag^st^ having parliaments?^ Another is that the Colonies would not be able to maintain them. Both these, which contradict each other, would be easily answered: but the most intresting Objection, which is not avowed & therefore cannot receive a formal Answer, is that an American Representation will take away all ~~take all~~ pretences for disputing the Ordinances of Parliament. The Admission of American representatives into parliament will allow of the continuing the provincial Assemblies for the purposes of domestic Œconomy; & therefore no Objections have been drawn from the cessation of the inferior legislatures; the supposition of which would create infinite difficulties.

Upon the whole, My Lord, if there was no Necessity for the appointment of American representatives (which I think there is & that very pressing) the Idea of it greatly enlarges my View of the Grandeur of the British Empire. And if there is an Danger of its falling to pieces, which surely cannot be too much guarded against, it seems to me that nothing could so effectually provide against so fatal an Event, as binding the Colonies to the Mother Country by an incorporating Union, & giving them a share in the Sovereign legislature. If this was done there could [be] no dispute ^about^ the rights & priviledges of Americans in contradistinction to those of Britons; and an Opposition ^by force^ to the Government of Great Britain would have but one name. And then We might expect a longer Duration to the entire British Empire than desponding politicians are willing to promise at the present time, & in its present state.

AL, AC   BP, 11: 127-136.

Minor emendations not shown. Docket: Letter to Lord Barrington [_]:[7] not sent In favour of American Representation.[8]   The version printed here is a final version of a scribal draft, heavily corrected by FB, in BP, 6: 70-77 (Dft, LbC). The differences between them are numerous and substantive. The corrected scribal draft in the letterbooks was probably a first draft and the unsigned author's copy printed here (AC) was likely a fair copy of a second, improved draft (but which is not extant). For that reason the differences between the scribal draft and author's copy have not been fully explained in the notes to this transcript. The AC version was printed in *Select Letters*, 53-60, and *Barrington-Bernard*, 245-252. While FB marked this version "not sent" one fair copy was sent; Barrington acknowledged receipt of a dupRC in **No. 605** and its enclosure, a copy of the *Boston Evening-Post*, 18 Jan. 1768, which reprinted Lord Camden's parliamentary speech of 11 Mar. 1766.

In the version printed above, FB returned to the theme of securing American representation in Parliament, which he had first discussed in his essay "Principles of Law and Polity" (1764).[9] FB hoped that American representation would dampen criticism of parliamentary authority, though as this letter concedes Camden's and Pitt's defense of the colonists' case against the Stamp Act had encouraged the colonial Whigs' in their entrenchment. Few Whigs saw any practical constitutional benefits in securing direct representation in Parliament, and the colonial assemblies, together with the Massachusetts Convention of Towns and Boston Sons of Liberty, argued for colonial legislative autonomy by challenging Parliament's legislative supremacy in the colonies. FB delivered a cogent summary of these arguments in this letter, for Barrington's edification. But it was the hostile reaction of ministers to events in Massachusetts that finally prompted Barrington to dismiss FB's scheme for American MPs as irrelevant. On 16 Apr., he advised FB to "put that Plan entirely out of the

Question." "Things are coming apace to crisis," he noted, as Hillsborough devised Britain's response to the Massachusetts Circular Letter (**No. 605**).[10] In the rejoinder (**No. 634**), FB avoided engaging Barrington in debate and briefly reported his preoccupation with his own crisis occasioned by the *Liberty* riot.

---

1. The spear of Achilles, from Greek mythology: the rust from which Achilles used to cure his wounded enemy King Telephus, thus fulfilling a prophecy that Telephus would guide the Greeks on their way to Troy. The story was probably post-Homeric, and formed the subject of *Telephus*, a play by Euripides (c.480–406 BC) now lost. Shakespeare refers to the tale in *Henry VI, Part 2*, where York claiming the Crown says "a king's smile and frown, like to Achilles' spear,/Is able with the change to kill and cure." (5:1.100-101). I am grateful to Owen Dudley Edwards for the reference in Shakespeare.

2. William Pitt (later the earl of Chatham), in his speeches to Parliament of Jan. 1766. See York, "When Words Fail: William Pitt, Benjamin Franklin and the Imperial Crisis of 1766," 341-374.

3. First written as "internal".

4. Thus in manuscript.

5. First written as "their".

6. Timothy Ruggles (1711-95), a former brigadier-general of provincial regiments, was the long-serving representative for Hardwick, Worcester Co., and a provincial delegate at the Stamp Act Congress. His condemnation of the Congress's petitions prompted the House to censure him, which matter FB reported to the Board of Trade and friends in England. *Bernard Papers*, 3: 113, 115, 119, 126.

7. Obscured by tight binding.

8. The docket is followed by a noncontemporaneous annotation: "It was *sent*, and is printed in his 'Letters', p. 53."

9. *Bernard Papers*, 2: 461-481.

10. On Hillsborough see the source note to **No. 608**.

585 | To the Earl of Shelburne

[Nº 2][1]

Boston Jan 30 1768

My Lord

I received your Lordship's Letter No 11[2] by the Novʳ Mail which arrived here this day sevnight: the October mail, which has other Letters of your Lordship for me is not arrived here, tho' by the accounts We have, it is daily expected.[3] I have therefore at present only to say that I shall regard the letter now received rather for my own instruction than a Direction to others. The time is not yet come, when the House is to be moved against popular printers however profligate & flagitious: it comes too home to some[4] (2 or 3 at the most) of its own Members. But, if there was a View of success, I should by no means think it proper to make such an attempt now, when the House shows so good a disposition to reconciliation to Government; of which they have given good proof since the date of my former Letter.[5] They have acted in all things, even in their remonstrance (as far as I, who have not been allowed a Sight of it can learn) with temper & Moderation; they have avoided some subjects of dispute & have laid a foundation for removing some Causes of former altercations. I speak this only from private report; nothing of this kind Very material having as yet come up to me.

But in one thing The House has shown itself contraagent to the Faction who want again to embroil America. There is no Doubt but that the principal Design in forming this Remonstrance was to set an Example to the rest of America, & produce a general Clamour from evry other Assembly against the late Acts. This was partly defeated by my refusing to call the Assembly before the usual time;[6] & again by the House resolving to form their remonstrance in such a manner that it should not of necessity be made publick. But tho' this last intention was quite inconsistent with the purpose of communicating the Substance of their remonstrance to the other Assemblies yet it did not discourage the party from attempting it. The House was accordingly moved that a day be assigned to take into consideration the propriety of informing the other Governments with their proceedings against the late Acts, that, if they thought fit; they might join therein. Upon the day this was strongly opposed & fully debated: it was said by the opposers of the Motion, that they would be considered at home as appointing another congress; and perhaps the former was not yet forgot. Upon the close of the debate it was carried in the negative by at least 2 to 1.[7] No one transaction in the House has given me ^so great hopes^ that they are returning to a right Sense of their Duty & their true intrest as this has done; and I hope it will make some attonement for their remonstrance.

I am with great respect My Lord, Your Lordships most obedient
& most humble Servant

Fra Bernard

The Right honble The Earl of Shelburne.

ALS, RC   CO 5/757, ff 22-23.

Endorsed: Boston Jan^ry 30th: 1768. Governor Bernard. (N°. 2) R 7th. March. A.5.   Variants: CO 5/893, ff 37-38 (LS, RC); CO 5/766, ff 104-106 (L, RLbC); BP, 6: 263-264 (L, LbC); Coll. Mass. Papers, 1768 (L extract, Copy); *Letters to the Ministry* (1st ed.), 5-6; *Letters to the Ministry* (repr.), 6-7. Hillsborough replied with **No. 603**. Considered by the Board of Trade on 6 May 1768. *JBT*, 13: 26. Extracts were laid before both houses of Parliament on 28 Nov. 1768. HLL: American Colonies Box 1.

FB's sanguine expectations for the House of Representatives contrast markedly with earlier reports on "the unsettled state of the Country." (**No. 581**). But they were short-lived, for the House approved a circular letter on 4 Feb., calling on the colonies to unite in opposition to the Townshend duties.

---

1. Faint.

2. Dated 14 Nov., this was Shelburne's last official letter to FB. **No. 574**, *Bernard Papers*, 3: 419. Shelburne had cautioned FB not to proceed with any prosecution of libels unless he could command "a great Degree of Unanimity" in the assembly, including cases where "any Member of that Assembly could be discovered to be concerned in Publications." FB, it can be deduced, had no intention of pursuing James Otis Jr. or Samuel Adams without the full backing of both the British government and the assembly, neither of which seemed likely in the near future.

3. **No. 581**.

4. Thus in manuscript.

5. **No. 581**, 21 Jan. 1768.

6. The first session of the General Court ran from 27 May to 25 Jun. 1767; the second session ran from 30 Dec. 1767 to 4 Mar. 1768.

7. Thomas Cushing's letter to Hillsborough of 30 Jun. (**Appendix 9**) confirms that the motion proposing a circular letter was defeated on 21 Jan., the day after the House approved its petition to the king. It was proposed again on 4 Feb., and this time passed in the affirmative. *JHRM*, 44: 122-135. The rejection of the first motion was also expunged from the journals, on 4 Feb. **No. 589**. For a copy of the Circular Letter, dated 11 Feb., see **Appendix 1**.

586 | To Richard Jackson

N° 3

Boston Feb 1 1768

Dear S^r:

I find myself obliged still to apologise to you for not writing in full to you: I attempt it with every Packet, but find myself prevented in Spite of my Teeth.[1] I have very little Time for this, unless the Wind tomorrow Morning shall give me more: I will improve it as well as I can.

Among other Symptoms of the good Disposition of the House to retrieve their past Conduct is a Sense of Shame for their Treatment of you. before the opening of the Session the Speaker expresst his Desire to me that a suitable Grant should be made to you; and after the Session was opened, He told me that it was proposed to make a Grant to you & Mr Debert upon the same paper & asked if I would pass it so. I answered that it would not come up to me; for I knew the Council would not pass it in that form, being resolved not to pass any more double Votes; & I should not persuade them to depart from a Rule which I myself had recommended. But to resolve the Difficulty, I assured him that if I knew that it was the Intention of the House that these two Grants should stand or fall together, I would take no Advantage of their being upon seperate papers, but would consent to both or negative both. However in Regard to the Grant to Mr Debert, I desired it might be understood that if I consented to Mr Deberts grant, it would be only as a Measure of Reconciliation, & they must not expect that I will consent to any more Grants of a Salary to an Agent of the House which they know to be an ~~irregular~~ ^uncon-stitutional^ Appointment.

In the Course of Conversation I had read to the Speaker some Passages in your Letters relating to this Business. He desired that I would let him have extracts of them. I advised with Mr Oliver, and with his Approbation, let the Speaker have Copies of such as would be of use, as Mr Oliver did a Passage in a Letter to him, signifying that you opposed the Salary Bill: they were all carefully castrated.[2] These had a surprising Effect in the House & Every one was loud in your Commendation, & some of the Opposition in as much as any. They passed one Vote for a Grant to you & Mr Deberdt of £300 sterling p^r an each for 2 Years Salary as Agents, you to be accountable for the £200 you had received by Bills & Charges.[3] Old Otis moved that this should be in full of all Accounts in Order to exclude your 3 Years Councellorship from Compensation. But this was generally rejected, young Otis giving it up; And it was declared that your pay as Councellor was not to be included in this. They also passed a Vote of general Approbation of your whole Conduct, & appointed a Committee to write to you. They have not sent these Votes up as yet it being intended to seperate them, to satisfy the Board, to which I hear Otis jun^r: has consented. I have told the Speaker that they must put the Compensation for your three Years Councelling ~~life~~ into some Way of liquidation, before I can pass ~~the liquidation before I can pass~~ these Votes: And I expect it will be done.

Soon after the Opening the Session Maj^r Hawley[4] (A man of ability but of violent & Changeable Passions, who about 15 months ago left the Government party & joined Otis & came the most violent opposer of the Right of Parliament to legislate for America as he called it) in a set Speech told the House that he had taken Pains to enquire into the Right of the British Parliaments & found they were the sovereign Legislators of America & had a Right to bind the Colonies by their Acts with this Exception that if they taxed them they ought to allow them Representatives, and when the Parliament had allowed the Colonies representatives, their Legislative power over them would be as complete & absolute as it was over any part of England. He added that an American Representation was now become necessary to both Countries, as there was no other Measure that would so effectually conciliate & unite Great Britain & her Colonies to each other. Otis treated this as the revery of a Madman.[5] (H. having a little wildness in his Constitution) being directly contradictory to his repeated assertions during all the ^last^ winter Sessions. Upon this Ruggles pulled out of his pocket one of Otis's books published near 3 Years ago, & red there out paragraphs which confirmed every thing that Hawley had said. This was truly *Argumentum ad hominem*.[6]

This Doctrine was new to the House & Surprized them; but they soon had a further explanation of it. The Government party could not prevent the Remonstrances against the late acts passing; but by frequently canvassing them, they got a great part of the most offensive matter struck out.[7] The House also voted that no Copies of their letters should be allowed to be taken; under which order the Speaker refused me a sight of the Letters, without first moving the House, which I would not permit. Nevertheless the Faction would not give up their original design of making these remonstrances an alarm to the Other Governments. It was moved in the House that a day be assigned to consider of informing the Assemblies of the other Governments of their proceedings against the late Acts. Upon the Day[8] the debate was very long & extremely well managed on the side of Government, it being carried in the negative by above [9] 2 to 1. The Faction has never had so great a Defeat as this has been; nor so great a disappointment, as it cuts off their hopes of once more inflaming the whole continent.

In the course of this Debate a member charged the cheifs of the Faction with a fixed design to enforce an American representation, by making the Want of representatives a reason for disobedience to all Acts of Parliament that are now enacted, & supported his charge with such proofs, as being confirmed by the loose & equivocal answer given on the other Side, convinced the generality of the House that it was so. And Brig[r] Ruggles said that as it was time[10] to begin canvassing for representatives, He had a proposal to make from a Merchant of this Town, who desired to have the honor of fitting out a Ship to carry home their representatives; which he offer'd to do for half what they would sell for when they got there. I am obliged to stop hastily & am D[r] S[r] &c.

R Jackson Esq.[11]

L, LbC   BP, 6: 77-81.

In handwriting of Thomas Bernard.

---

1. That is to say, despite what FB intended: "in despite of the teeth of all rhyme and reason." Falstaff in *The Merry Wives of Windsor*, 5:5.125-126.

2. The actual letters to FB cannot be identified, but probably included those concerning the Stamp Act controversy (dated 8 to 21 Nov. 1765), from which extracts were laid before the House of Representatives on 6 Dec. 1766. *JHRM*, 43, pt.1: 213. Copies ordered by Andrew Oliver are in Prov. Sec. Letterbooks, 3: 38-47. Jackson's letter to Andrew Oliver was dated 9 Jan. 1767. Mass. Archs., 5: 273.

3. Orders allowing £600 to DeBerdt and Jackson were passed on 5 Feb. 1768. *Acts and Resolves*, 17: 289. Before Jackson's dismissal in Feb. 1767, FB had argued that he be properly compensated for his services to the province. He evidently enjoyed informing Jackson of the assembly's resolve, as well as the vote of general approbation (that Jackson had acted with "Diligence and Fidellity") passed on 1 Feb 1768. As FB intimates, these favorable outcomes were calculated to win him over in the matter of releasing province monies to support DeBerdt, whose status as House agent he continued to dispute. *JHRM*, 44: 143; *Bernard Papers*, 3: 265-266, 359.

4. Joseph Hawley (1723-88) represented Northampton in the House of Representatives in 1751, 1754-55, and 1766 to 1780. A graduate of Yale (1742), his legal career brought him to political prominence when he represented ten rioters from Lanesborough, Berkshire Co., the only Stamp Act rioters in the province to be prosecuted. They had tried to rescue debtors detained in prison because court officials were unable to process the documents required to release them on bail. The case therefore illustrated the problematic consequences of the Crown's refusal to instruct court officials to proceed to business without stamped papers. The rioters were convicted by the Berkshire County inferior court on 26 Nov. 1765, but their case was appealed to the province's Superior Court, where Hawley represented one of the rioters, Seth Warren. Hawley did not win the case; but the rioters were subsequently fined just £3, and in early December Hawley was able to persuade the assembly and governor to pass an indemnity law granting the rioters immunity from prosecution. John Philip Reid, "In a Defensive Rage: The Uses of the Mob, the Justification in Law, and the Coming of the American Revolution," *New York University Law Review*, 49 (1974): 1043-1091 at 1055-1062.

    Hawley's part in the case was the subject of close inspection by Jonathan Sewall, writing as "Philanthrop," FB's defender in the newspapers. *Boston Evening-Post*, 5 Jan. 1767; *Bernard Papers*, 3: 311. Hawley responded with two detailed accounts of the trials in the *Boston Evening-Post* on 3 and 27 Jul. 1767. However, the articles were deemed libelous for criticizing the Superior Court justices, and in October, the court disbarred Hawley from practicing for two years. The suspension was lifted upon petition, in 1769. *Bernard Papers*, 3: 80; *JHRM*, 44: 89; *Legal Papers of John Adams*, 1: ci.

5. FB obviously enjoyed the irony of Otis, who suffered from mental illness, accusing Hawley of being a "Madman." Hawley's support for American representation in Parliament flew in the face of the Whigs' tactical attack on parliamentary taxation. Otis may also have been concerned that FB would entice other Whigs to support the scheme, though he would not have known how assiduously FB was promoting American representation as a practical solution to the dispute over taxation. See **No. 584**.

6. Trans.: "an argument against the man," meaning that, in this case, Ruggles was exposing the folly and inconsistency of James Otis Jr. On Otis see *Bernard Papers*, 2: 263n; 3: 280-281, 416, 425.

7. On 20 Jan. 1768. *JHRM*, 44: 121-122, 124; the petition is printed at 217-219.

8. The actual date is unknown.

9. Editorially altered. The scribe used colons to signify hyphenated line breaks, thus rendering "above" as "a:bove". All such breaks have been removed in accordance with editorial method.

10. This word was corrected by the scribe.

11. Run-on closure and recipient's name in FB's hand.

587 | To Lord Barrington

Boston Feb. 7. 1768

My Lord

I come now to answer, the first Part of your Lordship's last Letter intimating the favourable Disposition towards me:[1] and in order to give this Subject a full Latitude, it will be proper to go back to the first movements of it.

It was in Sept[r]. 1766 that I wrote to your Lordship to sollicit a Removal from hence.[2] I was then in a State very distressful, not only uneasy in my Administration but exposed & threatned with personal Danger. And yet under all those Difficulties, I expressed a Desire that I might be made easy here, by supporting my Government & augmenting my Salary. The Truth is I did not know where to go or what to ask for. The best Governments in the King's Gift are in my Opinion the least Desirable, as the Emoluments are, in general, much overballanced by the unhealthiness of the Climates. There were several of the very best Governments vacant at that Time; Jamaica, Leeward Islands, & Barbadoes. I then absolutely declined the two first, altho' the very best Governments in the Kings Gift. Barbadoes I expressed a great Desire for: and indeed it is the only one among the Islands that I have desired. Now that as well as the other two is but just filled:[3] so that the only Object of my Desire in the West Indies is now out of the Question.

In Regard to the Continent, in the Same Letter I intimated that South Carolina, altho' upon Account of the Climate far from being desirable, would in my present Situation (if I had no Prospect of being quieted with an adequate Salary) be more agreeable than to be left here. Soon after I sent away that Letter, I wrote to M[r] Jackson to disclaim S Carolina,[4] upon Account of the disagreeable Inform[ns]:[5] of the Climate which I had then received; of which we have frequently visible Evidence from the sallow Complexions of those Carolineans who come hither to recover their Health. I will here apologise for my exceptiousness[6] in Regard to Climates, by assuring your Lordship that it is not so much on my own account (tho' my Life is made valuable by the tender Age of most of my Children) as it is for the Sake of M[rs] Bernard, whose frame, naturally delicate, has been much weak'ned since she came here. To follow the Governments along the Continent N Carolina is much in the same Predicament as its Name Sake, & is now full with a new Governor.[7] Virginia being a L[t]: Government would be no advancement, New Jersey (my favourite in Regard to Situation) would be a degradation. We now come to N York ~~my favourite with Regard to Situation~~ now full of a new Governor also:[8] I should ^gratefully^ accept of this if it was to become vacant and be offered to me: but should like better ^& I think it would be better^ for me to be properly supported in this Government. They are both of them liable to be harrast by the Spirit of Jealousy of and Opposition to Government which prevails in both & has for some Time past been whetting itself upon each other. But there is this Material Difference between the two Provinces: in N York that Spirit actuates Men of Rank and Ability, in Massachusets it works only with Men of Middling or low Rank; in the Latter the Govr has the generality of respectable Men on his Side; in the former they are more generally against Government. Without entring into more particulars, It appears to me than the Administration of N York is more difficult than that of Mass^tts: especially as I can plainly perceive that this Government has received Strength from the Spirited & steady use which I have made of my negativing power & the public Approbation it has received. This, with the great additional Strength which it will gain from that wise Parliamentary Measure for providing for the Support of the Governors & Crown Officers, will make it full as necessary for the Leaders of the People to court the Governor as it will be for the Governor to court them.

This leads us to the ballancing the Question. Since the Time when I applied to be removed from hence one Event then despairred of has happened; The Parliament has made a Provision for the Payment of the Governor,[9] & tho' it has not been declared what the Salary will be, yet we must suppose that it will be adequate to the Importance of the Government. Another good event is coming on apace[10] Reconciliation between me & the Malecontents. The Assembly has now sat near 6 Weeks, & not the least Disrespect has been shown to me, even ^by those^ who were used to be most forward at other Times. On the contrary All such Businesses, as I might be Supposed to have an Intrest or a Will in, have been done in such a Manner as I could desire. And yet they still pursue an Opposition to the late Acts of Parliament by Remonstrances: and at the same Time appears an evident Disposition to restore the Peace of this Government. This will not be disappointed by the Defeat of their Purposes in Parliament; it will be much more probably improved by it. As for the Salary, a Gentleman of very good Authority assures me it will be £2500; tho' others report that it will be but £2000. If it is the least of these Sums, it will (together with a Restoration of the good Humour of the Government) make a Removal from hence not desirable; especially when the Cheif Governments have been so lately filled as to afford little Prospect of a valuable Vacancy. It is true this ~~Prospect~~ ^Expectation^ may be ~~interrupted~~^vented^:[11] for tho' The Act is passed, yet Nothing has been done in Pursuance of it; and it may be repealed before any Thing is done; As the Assembly of the Massachusets are now endeavouring to engage all the other Assemblies on the Continent to join in remonstrating against it.[12] But I cannot think that there is any Danger of the Parliament's giving Way to such a Combination[.] They have seen too much allready of the Abuse of the former Repeal, for which a strong Necessity was to be pleaded, to give Way to another Dictation of the Colonies which is itself one of the Abuses of the former Indulgence. If they ^should^ give

Way, they may as well at once Repeal all the former Acts of Trade which impose Duties for they are all included in the same Chain of reasoning.

You see, my Lord, that it is very probable that this Government may be made more desirable to me than another; or at least that I must wait till the Salary of it is settled before I can properly compare it with another. So that all I can resolve upon now is to desire your Lordship, after accepting my most gratefull Thanks for your Kind Care of me, to endeavour to keep alive the favourable Disposition of advancing me, till I can determine what Occasion I shall have for it. In the mean Time I would avail myself of it, with your Lordships Approbation, to obtain leave of Absence for a Year, to be left to my own Discretion whether I shall use it presently or not. For two Things must happen before I should chuse to go to England: I must wait till the Salary of this Government is fixed & put in a Way of Payment: And I should chuse to see the Peace of the Government perfectly restored before I leave this Place. Both these may probably happen before next Midsummer: the first of them will be known to your Lordship much sooner than it will to me; and when it does happen, I think with Submission, that it will be a proper Time to Make the Request, leaving to me to make Use of the Licence as the other Event shall turn out, more or less, One Thing your Lordship may be assured of, that I will not leave the Province at a Time when my Presence here appears in any Way necessary. But when we get into a little good humour with one another a Short Seperation may make us meet again better Friends than before. Besides I shall by this Means have an Opportunity to Consider effectually how I can best avail myself of the favourable Disposition towards me, which my present Distance makes Difficult. I have not as yet wrote to the Minister upon this Subject; and shall not 'till I dismiss the Assembly: When I do your Lordship shall be informed of all Particulars. If Leave should be obtained, it will be very expedient that it should be kept secret till I shall Think it Time to make Use of it. I am wth: great Grat: & Resp^{ct}:

My Ld your Ldships most obed^t: humble Servant

Visc^t: Barrington

L, LbC   BP, 6: 82-87.

In handwriting of Thomas Bernard. Minor emendations not shown. Interlineations in FB's hand.

When writing Barrington, FB was still optimistic that colonial governors would receive a hefty Crown salary, paid for by the Townshend duties. This might explain FB's refusal of another posting and his renewed determination to confront colonial radicals in the House of Representatives. Doubts concerning British intentions soon set in, however. No provision was made for FB or other governors when, in June, TH was offered an annual grant as lieutenant governor. FB's expectations were never realized, and he remained financially dependent on the assembly for the duration of his administration.

FB never did raise the question of his leave of absence with Shelburne, and the remainder of his letters to the minister dealt with the political troubles that engulfed his government. As this letter indicates, FB instead relied upon Barrington to make the case for him. This he did, and Hillsborough approved FB's leave of absence on 22 Jun. (**No. 636**), which FB received in September. But the arrival of the Regulars and subsequent events prevented FB from returning to England until Aug. 1769.

---

1. **No. 568**, *Bernard Papers*, 3: 409.

2. On 1 Sept., **No. 497**, ibid., 213-216.

3. Samuel Rous was acting governor of Barbados, 1766-68, following the departure of Charles Pinfold and until the arrival of William Spry.

4. **No. 532**, *Bernard Papers*, 3: 319-321. The current governor of South Carolina was Lord Charles Greville Montagu (1741-84), second son of the third duke of Manchester; he was governor 1765-73.

5. A contraction of "Informations".

6. Scribal correction: first written form is indecipherable.

7. William Tryon (1729-88), governor of North Carolina, 1765-71, and of New York, 1771-80.

8. Sir Henry Moore (1713-69) had taken over as governor of New York in Jul. 1765.

9. An act for granting certain duties in the British Colonies and Plantations in America . . . , 7 Geo. 3, c. 46 (1767), known variously as the American Revenue Act, the Revenue and Customs Duties Act, or the Townshend duties act.

> V. And be it further enacted by the Authority aforesaid, That his Majesty and his Successors shall be, and are hereby, impowered, from Time to Time, by any Warrant or Warrants under his or their Royal Sign Manual or Sign Manuals, countersigned by the High Treasurer, or any Three or more of the Commissioners of the Treasury for the Time being, to cause such Monies to be applied, out of the Produce of the Duties granted by this Act as his Majesty, or his Successors, shall think proper or necessary, for defraying the Charges of the Administration of Justice, and the Support of the Civil Government, within all or any of the said Colonies or Plantations.

10. This word is smudged.

11. "Intervented": obscure, meaning "to come between, obstruct, thwart." *OED*.

12. On 4 Feb., the House approved a motion to write a circular letter to the speakers of the other assemblies. *JHRM*, 44: 122-135. For a copy of the letter, dated 11 Feb., see **Appendix 1**.

588 | *From the Earl of Hillsborough*

(N°. 3)

Whitehall. February the 16th 1768.

Sir,

Since the Earl of Shelburne's Letter to you of the 14th: last November:[1] your Letters to His Lordship N° 25. 26. 27. 28. & 29. have been received, & laid before the King.[2]

His Majesty collects from them with great Satisfaction, that the idle and groundless Jealousies and Discontents, which have so long disturbed the Tranquillity of the Province, having been industriously fomented by weak and ill-designing Men, are at length subsided; and that the Minds of His good Subjects of the Massachuset's Bay are restored to that Confidence in his Government, which the Justice and Lenity of It so amply entitles it to. That even those whose erroneous and intemperate Zeal had carried them Lengths most unjustifiable in themselves, and dangerous to the Well-being of the Province, are returned to a dispassionate and calm Temper of Mind, and begin at last to discover what has ever been clear to all Mankind, that His Majesty is the tender & affectionate Father of all His Subjects, and that the real Interest of Great Britain and her Colonies, ever was, is, and always must be, One and the same.

His Majesty gives all the Merit and Approbation due to your Prudence and Conduct in these critical Circumstances, and I am to recommend to you to cultivate and improve the becoming Dispositions which have of late appeared. An inflexible Adherence to your Duty, attended by every conciliating & persuasive Method you can devise, to convince Those who are within your Province, that their Happiness, in common with That of all His Subjects, is the great Object of His Majesty's Government, will most effectually conduce to the Completion of this very desireable End. You have my most hearty Wishes for your Success, at the same Time that I congratulate You upon the Progress you have already made towards it.[3]

Since my Appointment to my Office, the Lords of Trade have transmitted to me their Representation to His Majesty upon those Parts of your Letters to Lord Shelburne N° 11. & 17.[4] which relate to the Claim of the House of Representatives to appoint an Agent for the Affairs of the Province independent of the Governor and Council.

I have had the Honor to lay this Representation before the King, who has commanded me to transmit to You the inclosed[5] Copy of it, not doubting but that the House of Representatives will be induced, from a Consideration of the Propriety of what is set forth in It, to recede from a Claim that appears to His Majesty to be neither supported by Reason ^nor^ justified by Precedent, and to adopt that Mode of Appointment of an Agent, which has been adjudged, upon the fullest Examination, to be the most regular and constitutional in all Cases, and seems, in a more particular Manner, to correspond with the Principles of the Charter, on which the Government of the Colony of Massachuset's Bay is founded.

I am &c[a]

Hillsborough.

Governor of Massachusetts Bay

LS, RC   BP, 11: 137-140.

Endorsed by FB: Earl of Hillsborough 16 feb. 1768 Sundries.   Variants: CO 5/766, ff 107-109 (précis, RLbC); CO 5/757, ff 15-17 (LS, AC). Enclosure not found. FB received this letter on 11 May[6] and replied with **No. 614**.

  As this letter indicates, FB had won the confidence of His Majesty's ministers, Hillsborough above all. FB would have been pleased to note that the British government accepted his (fallacious) view that opposition to British colonial policies was principally the work of "ill-designing Men," who had inflamed popular opinion, and that he had acted with the leniency and moderation recommended by previous secretaries of state. Hillsborough's refusal to recognize DeBerdt's status as House agent reinforced FB's expectations that under Hillsborough's charge British policymaking would be more interventionist. Knowing that Hillsborough fully supported him, FB was prepared to take a harder line in tackling his "indefatigable" enemies in the House during May and June, as he revealed in his reply (**No. 614**).

---

1. **No. 474**, *Bernard Papers*, 3: 165-166.

2. **Nos. 569, 570, 571, 573**, and **575**, respectively, were laid before the Board of Trade on 4 Feb. 1768. *JBT*, 13: 9-10.

3. Left marginalia: direction indicator (☞) pointing to the phrase "Progress . . . It." The next two paragraphs are marked by a virgule.

4. FB's letters **Nos. 542** and **551** were discussed on 2 and 4 Feb. 1768. *JBT*, 13: 9-10.

5. The Board of Trade, representation to the king, Whitehall, 4 Feb. 1768, CO 5/757, ff 7-8.

6. According to **No. 611**.

589 | To the Earl of Shelburne

Duplicate

N°. 4

Boston, Febr^y 18th, 1768.

My Lord,

By my Letter N°. 2, I informed your Lordship,[1] that a Motion in the House for circulating a Copy of their proceedings against the late Acts of Parliament to all the Assemblies on the Continent, had been rejected by above 2 to 1; & that I formed promising Conclusions from this Defeat of the factious Party. But I was too hasty in my Approbation of the Conduct of the House: this was too great a point to be given up; The Party therefore resolved to make another effort, & having prepared the way by privately tampering with, & influencing particulars, they moved that all the former proceedings upon this business should be obliterated out of the Journal, which being agreed[2] to, the way became clear for another Motion, that a Committee should be appointed to prepare a Circular letter to the sevral[3] Speakers of the Assemblies upon the Continent containing an Abstract of their remonstrances against the late Acts, & a desire that the other Assemblies would join with them. A Letter was presently reported & agreed to by the House.[4]

As soon as I knew that this was past (the House) I got the Speaker to come to me, & in the presence of the Secretary, required a Copy of the Circular letter, that I might transmit it to your Lordship, to whom I said I should be obliged to send an account of this extraordinary proceeding, which I feared would be thought similar to the Congress in 1765. He said that He did not doubt but that it would easily be obtained with the leave of the House. He accordingly asked the leave of the House the next day, which he not only obtain'd for the Copy in question, but also for the other proceedings of which he had refused me the sight some time before.[5] But this was designed for serving a particular purpose, as I shall hereafter inform your Lordship in another letter upon another Subject.[6]

I now send your Lordship a Copy of this Circular letter, which I would animadvert upon if the time would permit. at present I will only make two observations: 1. That this present undertaking is calculated to inflame the whole Continent, & engage them to join together in another Dispute with the Parliament, about the Authority of the latter; altho' the present Subject Matter was professedly allowed by the Americans themselves to be within the bounds of the power of Parliament at the time of the former dispute. 2. That the Distinctions, by means of which they now transfer the Matters contained in the late Act of Parliament from the range of what they before conceded to Parliament to that of what they before denied, is equally conclusive against all Acts of Parliament imposing duties in the American

Ports, & consequently if the last Act should be given up to those pretensions All other acts of American revenue must follow. I shall write fully to your Lordship upon this Subject, when I have leisure to review the proceedings of this Session.

I am, with great respect, My Lord, Your Lordships. Most Obed[t]
& most humble Servant,

Fra Bernard

The Right Honble, The Earl of Shelburne.

dupALS, RC   CO 5/757, ff 28-29.

Variants: CO 5/766, ff 107-109 (précis, RLbC); BP, 6: 265-268 (L, LbC);[7] Coll. Mass. Papers, 1768 (L extract, Copy); *Letters to the Ministry* (1st ed.), 7-8; *Letters to the Ministry* (repr.), 8-9. The duplicate, printed here, may have been sent under cover of **No. 595**. The RC (not found) enclosed a copy of the House of Representatives' circular letter to the speakers of the colonial assemblies, 11 Feb. 1768, CO 5, 757, ff 30-33 (**Appendix 1**). The Circular Letter and extracts of FB's cover letter to Shelburne (**No. 589**) were laid before both houses of Parliament on 28 Nov. 1768. HLL: American Colonies Box 1. A copy may have been sent to Gen. Gage under cover of **Appendix 4**.

Historians have rightly viewed the passage of the Massachusetts Circular Letter of 11 Feb. 1768 as a milestone in British-colonial relations, partly because it re-energized inter-colonial opposition and partly because of the ensuing controversy over the House's refusal to rescind it.[8] FB's objections are considered in the source note to **Appendix 1**. For FB personally, the Circular Letter marked another turning point in his relations with the Whigs. FB had had some limited success in persuading moderates to join friends of government in repudiating radical initiatives, notably when the motion for a circular letter was first rejected; when put to the House a second time the motion was carried in a House that was probably just as full.[9] The Circular Letter commented upon the governor asserting (accurately, though without evidence) that "Enemies of the Colonies have represented them to his Majesty's ministers and to the Parliament, as factious, disloyal, and having a disposition to make themselves independent of the mother Country." (**Appendix 1**.)

1. **No. 585**.
2. First written form indecipherable.
3. On 4 Feb 1768. *JHRM*, 44:148.
4. On 11 Feb 1768. *JHRM*, 44: 157. See **Appendix 1**.
5. These were the several remonstrances the House had prepared in January, for which see **No. 593**n3.
6. **No. 591**.
7. This copy is wrongly dated Feb. 16.
8. For example, Middlekauff, *The Glorious Cause*, 161; Maier, *From Resistance to Revolution*, 174-175.
9. For more information about the vote of reconsideration see the source note to **No. 638**.

590 | To Richard Jackson

No. 5

Boston Feb. 20. 1768

Dear Sr:

I was in hopes by this Opportunity to have wrote to you fully; especially as Mr Bromfield, a Gentleman not unknown to you and much esteemed by me has engaged to take my present Packet.[1] Since my last[2] Things have not gone so well in the Assembly as when I wrote to you last. Otis's Party has recovered itself since the Defeat of the Motion to write circular Letters to the rest of the American Assemblies to desire them ^to join them^ in their Opposition to the late Act of Parliament. Factious Men have great Advantages over fair dealers; the former can practise many Tricks which the latter despise; these are much sooner tired than the other are; and such is the Depravity of Mankind, that there is generally less perseverance in good Pursuits than in bad. So it has happened here: The Friends of Government are allways tired out with the extended Length of the Winter Session, which the Factious Lengthen for that among other Purposes. Hence it is that the Faction generally recovers Ground at the End of ~~the~~ a Session; & in this they have got the House to expunge from their Journal all that passed before concerning a Circular Letter and afterwards they obtained a Vote for a Circular Letter, a Copy of which I hereby send you: I have no Time to make Remarks upon it, but shall leave it to you[r] own Judgement for the present.

As for your Business it stands pretty much as it did: the Obstacles which have prevented its Conclusion, have arose entirely from the two Otises, who have been as perverse and malicious as possible; The Speaker tho of that Party, has done evry thing in his Power to bring it to an End as honourable to you & themselves as possible. About a Week ago the House appointed a Committee to be joined by a Committee of the Board to write a Letter to you in the Name of the general Court.[3] This was reported in as handsome Terms as possible; in it was a Clause informing you that your Pay as Councellor was not included in this Grant but left to a further Consideration untill they could learn what was due upon that Account. This was approved by the Council & sent down to the House; the Clause aforementioned was objected to by the Otises, who urged, that the first Motion of that Business ought to come from you by making a Charge of what was due to you. After a long Debate they rejected the reported Letter & appointed a Member (a cheif Speaker on our Side)[4] to draw a Letter to you from the House; which he did immediately in Terms respectable to you, but omitting mention of the Contested Clause: and the House has, as I understand, passed this Letter, and keep the Letter reported to themselves.[5] The Board is much exasperated at this Treatment & will probably resent it: but they ^deserve^ this and more for their timid Submission to the many Insults which they have received from the House since Otis has prevailed in it; & for their acquiescing in the House doing the Provincial Business by a seperate Agent of their own for 2 Years past & thereby excluding the Council from having any Share in the Management of the Concerns of the general Court in England. After having given this Detail which I can carry no further, I have only to add that the Grants still lie before me & that I shall not part with them till I have past upon them; which most probably will be in the affirmative at all Events.[6]

I hereby send you a compleat Set of the Pensylvania Farmer's Letters: I sent two Sets to Sec[ry]. Pownall, thereby avoiding the Appearance of Officiousness in troubling the Secr[y]: of State with political Newspapers & of Negligence in taking no Notice of Writings which perhaps may be thought to deserve a public Animadversion. Certain It is that if this System of American Policy, which is artfully wrote, and apparently derived from great Authority in England, and universally circulated, should receive no Refutation (as it is impossible it should in America), it will become a Bill of Rights in the Opinion of the Americans. In such Case the Parliament may enact declaratory Acts as many as they please; but they must not expect any real Obedience. When you have perused all these Letters, you will I beleive see with me the Necessity of immediately granting the Americans a Representation: If this had been done two Years ago, America would have been quiet by this Time; if it is delayed two Years longer it will become more difficult: It is at present the only Remedy left; in a few Years more there will be neither this nor any other. For you may assure yourself that whoever depends upon America coming to rights of its own accord will find themselves deceived in the End: and very fatal, probably, will be the Disappointment.

I was in Hopes that this Session would have passed without any Dispute: but the Otises would not let it go off So. I received a Letter from Ld Shelburne which had been long and impatiently expected by the Friends of Government which approved my Conduct in negativing the elected Councellors & disapproved the Occasion they gave for it by rejecting the[7] principal Officers of Government & assured me of his Majesty's Support. The Nature of the Letter required that it should be communicated & yet I was in Doubt in what Manner to do it. I therefore ^advised with the Council from whom it was^[8] proposed that I should direct the Secretary to read it in the House, & afterwards that I should give the Speaker a Copy with a Restriction that he should allow no Copy to be taken. I did so, & it seemed to pass on very quietly for some Days. But after they had gained the Vote for sending the Circular Letter, they grew so elate that they immediately attacked the Sec[ry]: of States Letter, & after a preparatory Message and a gentle Answer from me, they have this Day delivered a Message to me so wild unreasonable & outrageous, that it exceeds all Bounds of Discretion & common Prudence & outdoes even Otis's outdoings. I shall find myself obliged to let them have the free Use of the Letter, & also to give a Answer to the Message; but it will be very short and as gentle as the Case will permit. I send my Lord Shellburne Copies by this Ship; & will send the same to you either by this or the next.[9]

I am &c

PS. You will observe that I have numbered this Letter 5. I reckon from the New Year and the Number will stand thus N° 1 Jan 8, N° 2 Jan 16, N° 3 Feb. 1, N° 4 Feb. 8;[10] If you'll observe this Method, you'll find it of use.

R Jackson Esq:

PS to the Letter to Mr Jackson dated Feb. 20 No 5

Vide Page 2[11]

Feb. 22.

Yesterday arrived here Capt Jenkinson in 19 days from the Lands end; who brings the first advice of the charges of the Ministry. I hope this Event considering Lord B^s intimacy with Lord H^illsborough^ will be favorable to me, & by its stability to great Britain & America also.[12] The Otises having got the advantage of a thin House, are grown quite mad. They have this afternoon been passing a Letter to Lord Shelburne upon the subject of his Letter to me which as I am told is beyond all things for folly & madness. The Majority upon this occasion was but one third part of the whole House you shall have a full account of this,

L, LbC   BP, 6: 90-94, 96.

In handwriting of Thomas Bernard. Minor emendations not shown. May have enclosed copies of the documents dispatched under cover of **No. 591**. "Letters from a Farmer in Pennsylvania" were originally published in the *Pennsylvania Chronicle and Universal Advertiser* in a series of twelve letters between 30 Nov. 1767 and 15 Feb. 1768. Hitherto FB had been sending copies to John Pownall (**Nos. 578** and **579**). The "compleat Set" that he now sent Jackson may have been compiled from the *Pennsylvania Chronicle* and/or from reprints in the New York and Massachusetts newspapers: Letters I-IX and XI and XII were reprinted in the *Boston Gazette,* 21 Dec. 1767-29 Feb. 1768; nos. I, III, and VIII in the *Boston Evening-Post*, 28 Dec.-8 Feb.; and nos. IV-IX, and XI in the *Boston Chronicle*, 28 Dec.-7 Mar. A reprint of the tenth letter in the series has not been located. The Farmer's "Letters" were also printed in pamphlet form in Philadelphia, New York, and London during 1768, and were issued by Edes and Gill in late March, following a public declaration of gratitude by the Boston town meeting.[13] This FB later dispatched to Barrington (along with a similar complete set of letters, dispatched in batches).[14]

1. Probably one of the Bromfield brothers, Henry (1727-1820) or Thomas (b.1733), Boston merchants.

2. Dated 8 Feb. 1768. BP, 6: 88-89.

3. On 13 Feb. *JHRM*, 44: 164.

4. Identity unknown.

5. On 17 Feb., ibid. 172; CO 5/828, f 142; Andrew Oliver to Richard Jackson, 23 Feb. 1768, Mass. Archs., 56: 541-542.

6. FB had written Jackson on 8 Feb. stating he was anxious of "bringing this Business to a tolerable Conclusion." BP, 6: 88-89. He signed the grants on 26 Feb. 1768, awarding DeBerdt £600 and Jackson £500. *Acts and Resolves*, 17: 289.

7. **No. 566**, *Bernard Papers*, 3: 407-409.

8. Interlineation in FB's hand.

9. **No. 594**.

10. The letter of 8 Jan. 1768 in BP, 6: 57-59; **Nos. 580** and **586; 8 Feb.** in BP, 6: 88-89.

11. This cross-reference takes the reader to the last page of the main text in the letterbook, at p. 94. The postscript is on p. 96.

12. Writing Lord Barrington, FB concluded "that knowing your Lordship's Connexion with that noble Lord, I have Reason to congratulate myself upon the Event." Boston, 20 Feb., BP, 6: 95.

13. *Letters From A Farmer in Pennsylvania, to the Inhabitants of the British Colonies* (Printed and sold by Edes and Gill, in Queen-Street [Boston], 1768); *Reports of the Record Commissioners of Boston*, 16: 241.

14. On 28 Mar. 1768. BP, 6: 105-106.

591 | *To the Earl of Shelburne*

Duplicate

N⁰ 5.

Boston Feb. 20. 1768.

My Lord

I informed your Lordship that I had received your Lordships Letter No 8[1] & added that I should make such a prudent & proper use of it as I hoped would perfectly restore the peace & tranquillity of this Province. I thought it best to advise the Council concerning the Manner of communicating it to those whom it concerned. I therefore read it to the Council & observed that I could not send a Copy of it to the House,[2] upon Account of the Abuse which all such communications were subject to, that of being publish'd in the News Papers, which if the House dont expressly order they notoriously permit.[3] Upon which it was proposed by a Councellor that I should let the Secretary carry the Letter into the House & read it there; & it was afterwards thought proper that I should give the Speaker a copy, to be communicated to such Members as desired it without suffering a Copy to be taken. When this was done I took some pains to make it understood, that the Caution I used that this Letter should not be made public arose from a Desire that there should be no Triumph on my Part; but that it should be used for the purpose for which it was designed, Conciliation; as It was rather intended as a Directory for future Proceedings than a Censure of the Past.

But all this Caution signified nothing: the Heads of the factious Party for many Days seemed to acquiesce: and I expected no other than good effects from this Communication. But after the Party had carried their Point in ordering a Circular Letter[4] to the several Assemblies on the Continent; they became elate, & resolved to make a Dispute concerning your Lordships' Letter. The Occasion they took to move this matter was my applying to the Speaker for a copy of the circular Letter to trans-mitt to your Lordship, which the Speaker proposed to the House, not by my Direc-tion but of his own Motion. Upon this Occasion Otis said it was as reasonable[5] that they should have Copies of my Letters which were referred to by your Lordship: & accordingly the Message No. 1 of the enclosed was dressed up & sent to me.[6]

There certainly never was such a request made by an Assembly to a royal Gover-nor since America was colonised, as is contained in the last words of this Message.[7] It was attempted by Otis once before; but then it failed.[8] However I determin'd to give it as soft an answer as possible; & therefore when I had formed it,[9] I showed it to the Lieut. Governor, the Secretary &c, & struck out every word that the most cautious Man could apprehend liable to be taken hold of to give Offence.[10] But it signified nothing: they had prepared the House (which had been before evacu-ated of some of the most able Men on the Side of the Government, tired out with the Length of the Session) by private Cabals & determined to go to the greatest Lengths. They accordingly prepared a Message,[11] in the words as inclosed, & after a long Debate carried a vote for it & it was delivered to me this Morning.[12]

I shall not make any Observations on it at present; but only inform your Lord-ship that I cannot wholly pass it by unnoticed. For as it is professedly designed to be publish'd I must give some answer to it, but it shall be as short cautious & soft as the Case will admit. For your Lordship may depend upon it that it is not in the Power of these People to move my Temper or to make me depart from that Steady Conduct which his Majesty's Service & the present state of this Province so abso-lutely require. All I am concerned at is that, I shall, I fear, be obliged to consent to your Lordship's letter being enter'd in the Journals of the House; from whence it will probably find its way to the Press. This is in plain Terms required by the last Message; & if I should find myself obliged to concede to it, my best apology for it must be that I cannot see that the Publication can do any Harm, & it probably will have very good Effects. Upon the whole, tho this Fracas has seemingly interrupted the good humor of the Session, yet I am persuaded it will do the Cause of the Faction no real Service; & they will still find it necessary to lower their sails. Nor do I think this Dispute merely accidental: It has been the constant way of the Faction since it first raised its head, to create a Dispute at the end of the last Session, in order to find matter for influencing the ensuing Elections in favor of the popular Cause. If this had not come in their way they would have found some other Subject of a Dispute. Perhaps this may be as ineffectual as some other would have been. I am

> With great Respect My Lord, Your Lordship's Most obedient
> & most humble Servant

Fra. Bernard

The right honble The Earl of Shelburne

PS. Feb. 22.

This morning I found the message deliverd to me last Saturday published in the Boston Gazette,[13] as indeed I expected it would. I thereupon orderd the Secretary to deliver a verbal Message from me in the Terms as enclosed.[14] I am informed that this Afternoon the Faction has been passing a Letter to your Lordship complaining of misrepresentations from which your Lordship's Letter was formed.[15] I will not say any thing of it, as it will come to your Lordship as soon as my Report of it could. I have only to desire that your Lordship would suspend your Judgement of it, till you hear further from me which will be as soon as I have prorogued them, which I hope will be in a few days.

dupLS, RC   CO 5/757 ff 34-35.

In handwriting of clerk no. 3. Endorsed: Boston Feb^ry 20th: 1768. Govr Bernard (N°. 5). R 15 April Dup^l original not recd.   The endorsement indicates that the autograph original was not received. However, on 4 Apr., Hillsborough acknowledged having received and read a letter from FB, which was likely a copy of the original.[16] The duplicate printed here may have been sent under cover of **No. 595**. Variants: CO 5/766, ff 115-121 (L, RLbC); BP, 6: 269-273 (L, LbC); a copy may have been sent to Gen. Gage under cover of **Appendix 4**. Enclosures: FB's messages to the House of Representatives, 16 and 22 Feb. 1768; messages of the House to FB, 13 and 18 Feb.; a copy of the House of Representatives to the earl of Shelburne, 22 Feb. 1768 (not found, for which see *JHRM*, 44: 239-240.) The only extant enclosure from this particular set is FB's message of 22 Feb. in CO 5/757, f 36. FB added the postscript after receiving news of Hillsborough's appointment,[17] but that information does not appear to have had any substantive bearing on the postscript's brief report of the House's proceedings.
     This letter is a reply to **No. 566**, dated 17 Sept. 1767, in which Shelburne communicated to FB official approval of the governor's conduct during 1766 and 1767, notably his vetoing radicals elected to the Council and his refusal to recognize the appointment of a separate House agent. *Bernard Papers*, 3: 407-409. FB had received Shelburne's letter

c.2 Feb. Only in retrospect does FB's decision to release Shelburne's letter to the House (in return for a copy of the Circular Letter) appear a mistake. Shelburne's letter, although supportive of FB, also indicated that their governor had had some influence upon the secretary of state.[18] The House's message of 18 Feb. proposed that "Surely" Shelburne would not have censured the House

> but upon what he thought to be the best authority . . . . Your Excellency then must allow the House to believe, until they shall be convinced to the contrary, that your several letters, to which his Lordship refers, are so fully expressed as to have left his Lordship no room to suspect that he could be mistaken.[19]

The House reiterated the point in a letter to Shelburne, approved on 22 Feb. But they also controversially requested Shelburne to order FB to lay before the House copies of his correspondence with the secretary of state, specifically those out-letters that had informed Shelburne's judgments in **No. 566**.

> As the House think they have just grounds of suspicion, that his Excellency's letters to your Lordship contain, at least, an implication of charge and accusation against them, which they are kept in ignorance of; they rely upon your known candor and justice, that upon this their humble request, you will be pleased to give Orders that copies be laid before the House of Representatives; that they may have the opportunity of vindicating themselves and their constituents, and of happily removing from your mind an opinion of them, grounded, as your Lordship might then reasonably judge, upon good information, as having behaved in a manner unbecoming the character of loyal subjects. They hope you will be so favorable as to suspend your further judgment of them, till they can be made acquainted with the matters that may have alledged against them, and can make their defence.[20]

Releasing Shelburne's letter (**No. 566**), then, failed to quash suspicions that FB had misrepresented the province to the secretary of state. The galleries were not cleared when the letter was read aloud in the House. According to the printers of the *Boston Gazette*, Shelburne's letter "was said to have been handed about in private companies." Edes and Gill were ostensibly justifying the House's decision to publish its own letter to Shelburne.[21] But the *Gazette*'s carefully worded rationale would equally have been useful in defending any subsequent decision to print Shelburne's letter to FB (**No. 566**), as it did, on 7 Mar.[22]

FB fully expected that Shelburne's letter would be published, and acquiesced in the expectation that he might use the dispute to his advantage. Hitherto he had relied upon a general acceptance of the idea that the governor was the king's symbolic representative as well as his proxy, whereas the House had come to think of him as an officer bereft of gravitas and increasingly unworthy of respect. It was a moment of revolutionary potential, and one to which FB was attuned. The libels in the *Gazette* became more daring while his enemies in the House openly plotted his downfall, investigating with greater thoroughness the nature of FB's reports to British ministers. Hillsborough acknowledged receipt of **No. 591** with **No. 608**, and issued fresh instructions requiring the House to rescind the vote approving the Circular Letter.

1. **No. 566**, *Bernard Papers*, 3: 407-409.

2. FB received Shelburne's letter (**No. 566**) c.2 Feb. The discussion in Council is not mentioned in the formal record, and probably occurred on 3 Feb. Later that day the province secretary read Shelburne's letter to the House. *JHRM*, 44: 147.

3. Notably, Secretary Conway's letter of 31 Mar. 1766, announcing the repeal of the Stamp Act (**No. 462**): it was printed in the *Boston Evening-Post*, 9 Jun. 1766, without FB's express consent, though he did not prevent it, thinking it "could but be of good Service." *Bernard Papers*, 3: 172.

4. On 4 Feb., with the letter being approved on 11 Feb.

5. Thus in manuscript.

6. On 13 Feb. *JHRM*, 44: 164.

7. The committee were instructed to request copies of Shelburne's letter and of all correspondence with FB referred to in the letter. Ibid.

8. See note 3 above.

9. Left marginalia: authorial annotation, "2". The sequence of annotations is from 1 to 4 but the leaf edge is torn and the first number is missing.

10. Shelburne's letter of 17 Sept. (**No. 566**) was read to the House on 3 Feb. by the province secretary, after which FB gave the Speaker an edited copy of the letter on condition that no further copies were made. *JHRM*, 44: 147. (This version was subsequently entered in the journals, ibid., 250-251.) The House demanded a copy of the whole letter in a message of 13 Feb. FB's carefully crafted reply of 16 Feb. allowed that the Speaker could communicate Shelburne's letter "in any manner which is consistent" with the "restriction" he had imposed upon the Speaker; in other words, the Speaker could read the letter again but not distribute authentic copies (though members could write down what they heard). Ibid., 171. FB excised one passage from his draft message justifying his refusal to surrender copies of his other correspondence with Shelburne:

    > It is by no means the Intention of the Secretary of State that the Subject of those former proceedings, of which he has for my guidance signified his disapprobation, should be revived; and I shall not contribute to it.

    Mass. Archs., 110; 321 (ADft, AC).

11. Annotation: "3".

12. The message to FB was approved on 18 Feb. 1768, *JHRM*, 44: 176-178.

13. *Boston Gazette*, 22 Feb. 1768.

14. Annotation: "4 no duplicate".

15. The House of Representatives to the earl of Shelburne, 22 Feb. 1768, *JHRM*, 44: 239-240.

16. **No. 603**.

17. See source note to **No. 582**.

18. Nicolson, *The 'Infamas Govener'*, 162.

19. *JHRM*, 44: 178.

20. Ibid., 239-240.

21. *Boston Gazette*, 22 Feb. 1768, p. 2.

22. On 7 Mar. 1768, in the *Boston Evening-Post*, the *Boston Gazette*, and the *Boston Post-Boy and Advertiser*.

592 | *To Lord Barrington*

Boston Mar. 4 1768

My Lord

In my Letter of Jan 28[1] I informed your Lordship to what Lengths the Americans had carried their Improvements of the Arguments which had been used in England in favour of their being exempt from a parliamentary Taxation. I there mention that the Pretensions were not expressly carried to the Length that they were Consequentially. But, my Lord, the little Interval of Time between the Dates of that Letter and this has afforded Instances of these Pretensions being actually carried to the full Length they are capable of. The Traders here are now associating in the same Manner that they did at the Time of the Stamp Act; with what Success remains to be determined: however there is now a Subscription opened to import no British Goods (except for the Fishery) for 18 Months.[2] If this was all, we Crown Officers should be ~~very~~ well Content: but it is given out among them that they will not submit to the Laws in the Mean Time; & violent methods of Opposition are every Day expected. One Man has unloaded a Cargo without entring it at the Custom House: it was done in the Night with a strong hand; but it is as publickly known as if it had been at Noon Day. The Officers either do not or dare not know where the Goods are carried. Many Merchants say they will not suffer Custom House Officers to go on board their Ships; one of them declared ^so^ in the House of Representatives. When they are asked what will satisfy them, the Answer is a total Repeal of the Laws of Trade imposing Duties and nothing less. And untill such Repeal shall be made they propose to suspend the Execution of the Laws, as they did in the Stampt-Act, which is now made a Precedent. However there has not as yet been a violent Opposition to the Officers; but it is hourly expected.

Your Lordship may imagine that such a State of this Town must be very disagreeable to the Commissioners of the Customs who are strangers in this Country. There have been Nights fixed by Common Report for a Tumult twice within these 10 Days. Upon one of them Mr Burch[3] one of ^these^ Gentlemen had a large Number of Men with Clubs assembled before his Door great Part of the Evening, and he was obliged to send away his Wife & Children by a back Door.[4] This was afterwards turned to a Joke & said to be nothing but to intimidate them; but if it was only a Joke it was a very cruel one. The Commissioners have asked me what Support I can give them, if there should be an Insurrection; I answer none at all.[5] They then desire me to apply to the general[6] for Troops; I tell them I cannot do it; for I am directed to Consult the Council about requiring Troops; & they will never advise it let the Case be ever so desperate. Indeed I no more dare apply for Troops than the Council dare advise me to it. Ever since I have perceived that the Wickedness of some and the folly of others will in the End bring Troops here, I have conducted myself so as to be able to say, and swear to, if the Sons of Liberty shall require it, that I have never applied for Troops. And therefore, my Lord, I beg that Nothing I now write may be considered as such an Application. The present Suspence is a very disagreeable one: the Commissioners see that they must wait till a violent Opposition is made to their Officers; & yet they dread the Experiment. I must be involved with them more or less: I have promised them an Asylum at the Castle & possibly may want it myself. Tho' the more moderate of the Opponents to the Laws of Trade say that they will hurt No body; but when they find that they are not like to be redressed, they will put the Commissioners & all their Officers on board a Ship & send them back to England. This is the Talk used to prevent Riots: a Short Time will determine it. I shall drop the Subject here having said enough to shew how probable it is that the Officers of the Crown will soon be in the same situation which they were above 2 Years ago; and how deceitful that Opinion is like to prove, that America will come to Rights of its own Accord. The Impeachment of the Power of Parliament has been Continually extending since the Time of the Stampt-Act; & will not stop 'till the Parliament interposes with Effect.

Having said so much for the public there is little remaining for myself. Your Lordship may imagine that whilst the Faction are attacking the Authority of Parliament they won't let the Governor alone. They accordingly picked a Quarrel with me about the Middle of the Session: But they have chose an unfortunate Subject and managed it ^very^ ill. I found myself obliged to make it the Subject of a Speech at the End of the Session; as the Faction have shown their Intention, to hurt me with the People by the Publication of the Papers of their House followed with an Infamous Libell. But they are both fully answered by my Speech and an Address of the Council; both of which joined together on this Occasion will I hope open the Eyes of the People to the Wickedness of these Fellows.[7]

I am &c

The Right honble The Ld Visc^t: Barrington

P S

If your Lordship should think proper to communicate any Part of this Letter, you will spare my Name as much as possible.

L, LbC   BP, 6: 96-99.

In handwriting of Thomas Bernard. Minor emendations not shown. The RC may have been sent under cover of a letter to John Pownall, dated 14 Mar.[8] Barrington acknowledged receipt with **No. 605**.

This letter exhibits the essence of FB's case for persuading the British government to send regular soldiers to Boston. The first point in his argument was that the colonists were determined to "suspend the Execution of the Laws" in order to force the repeal of the

Townsend Revenue Act and all trade duties. By "Laws," FB meant more than unpopular acts of Parliament and drew a parallel with the Stamp Act Crisis wherein public officials were prevented from carrying out a range of legal obligations and functions because of widespread defiance of a single parliamentary act. In short, he imagined the rule of law to be in jeopardy. Second, to that end the Bostonians had instituted an illegal combination, another nonimportation agreement, and threatened violence against senior Crown servants. Third, while he did not think any of this would persuade the Council to join him in requesting military assistance, FB hoped that any actual violence would lead the British authorities to order the Regulars direct to Boston. "The Commissioners see that they must wait till a violent Opposition is made to their Officers; & yet they dread the Experiment. I must be involved with them more or less." FB and the Customs commissioners accepted that only a personal attack upon their officers or persons might induce the British to intervene. This raises the possibility, extreme though it is, that the seizure of John Hancock's vessels *Lydia* in April and *Liberty* in June were intended not only to make an example of a leading Whig, but to provoke violence from Hancock's men, as Whigs later alleged, even though such would and did expose customs officers. Finally, the resurgence in colonial opposition now underlined the failure of Rockingham's policy of conciliation. FB maintained that having repealed the Stamp Act the British ought to have strengthened royal government in the colonies. For in FB's formulation, opposition to the Townshend Acts had become a test of the principle of parliamentary supremacy espoused by the Declaratory Act. The British government and many parliamentarians quickly came to share that view. Once again, FB asked Barrington to transmit his views to British ministers but without any qualms about his letter being published in the British press if it might elicit the desired response.

---

1. **No. 584**.

2. The subscription proposed that nonimportation take effect on 1 Jun. 1768 and was circulated to traders in the first week of March. FB provided more details about the merchants' "first movement" against the Townshend duties in **No. 601**.

3. Little is known of William Burch (d.1796), who had come from England to join the American Board of Customs.

4. The Customs commissioners were apprehensive of mob violence when they arrived during the Pope's Day celebrations of 5 Nov. 1767, but such fears were quickly allayed. Nonetheless, FB here proffered the first report of actual intimidation, albeit of a kind far milder than the tarring and feathering soon experienced by inferior customs officers and informers. *Bernard Papers*, 3: 421. On 18 Mar. (the anniversary of the Stamp Act's repeal), the commissioners reported that on hearing of effigies being hoisted on the Liberty Tree they feared "some open Acts of Violence." **Appendix 2**. The effigies were removed by the Sons of Liberty, leading TH to conclude that there was no plan to assault the commissioners; nevertheless, he noted, "the Least hint from their Leaders would encourage them to any degree of violence and how soon that hint may be given we know not." TH to Richard Jackson, Mass. Archs., 26: 295-296 and Hutchinson Transcripts, 2: 610. FB provided more details of the events in a letter of 4 Mar. (**No. 600**).

5. These proceedings are discussed in **Appendix 3**.

6. Gen. Thomas Gage.

7. For these proceedings see **No. 593**.

8. BP, 6: 101-102.

Samuel Adams, c.1772. Oil on canvas by John Singleton Copley. Photograph © 2015 Museum of Fine Arts, Boston.

593 | *To the Earl of Shelburne*

N° 6

Boston Mar 5. 1768

My Lord

Yesterday I prorogued the general Assembly after a Session of above 9 weeks, greatest part of which was spent in animadverting upon & counterworking the late Acts of parliament concerning the Revenue: so that there was ^not^ time enough to do the provincial business, nor even all of that which I recommended to them at the opening [*of*][1] the Session.[2] Some of the productions of these Animadversions will come to your Lordship directly from the Speaker of the House;[3] their Letter to their Agent I could have procured a Copy of,[4] but have declined it, as there is no occasion, nor is it my desire, to make their case worse than it need be by the Communication of a confidential Correspondence. The Circular Letter to the rest of the Colonies I have allready sent to your Lordship.[5] There is a Letter, I am told, from the House to the Lords of the Treasury; but there is no occasion for my communicating that.[6] I now send a Copy of the Resolves of the House upon importations & Manufactures;[7] It is so decently & ^cautiously^ worded that at another time It would scarce have given offence: But the Faction boast of it, as it was meant to be, as a confirmation of the Boston Resolves.[8]

In my letter N° 5 & the postscript therein, I informed your Lordship of the proceedings upon your Lordships letter of Sept[r] 17th, as far as Feb 22.[9] On Feb 28 appeared in the Boston Gazette a Virulent Libell[10] against me founded upon the insinuations flung out by the faction that your Lordship's Censure of the proceedings of the general Court in turning the Lieut Governor Secretary &c out of the Council was founded on misrepresentations made by me. There is no occasion for such supposition as the Causes of such censure were sufficiently assigned in the letter itself.[11] They durst not attack the letter directly & therefore were obliged to do it thro' me: And having founded the Message of the House upon groundless suppositions; these suppositions are used as undoubted truths to ground their libell upon. For your Lordship must know that two of the cheif leaders of the Faction in the House (Otis & Adams) are the principal Managers of the Boston Gazette. Hence it is that the drawers of the Messages & Remonstrances of the House & ^the writers of^ the Libellous & Seditious Letters in the Newspaper are generally ~~written by~~ the same. Thus in the present Case the Libell is nothing but a Corollary drawn from the Message.[12]

I had never before taken any notice of the libells published in the Boston Gazette: But this was attended with so many circumstances of flagitiousness; founded upon a letter of the Secretary of state wrote by order of his Majesty &

communicated by his Governor to the general Court; &, besides the general falsity & Malice of it, concluded with a blasphemous abuse of Kingly Government itself;[13] that I did not think I could with safety to the Government, pass it by unnoticed. I therefore next morning laid it before the Council at a very full board there being 20 present which is the whole number but 3.[14] It was received with general detestation; most of the gentlemen spoke to testify their Abhorrence of it; and it was remarkable that some of those who heretofore had been inclined to the popular side were most loud in their resentments of this Outrage. In the end they ^unanimously^ advised me to lay before the two Houses of the general Court,[15] that is, themselves in their legislative capacity & the House of Representatives. This I did by a Message to each,[16] in the terms inclosed,[17] which are the same except in the proper distinctions.

The Board appointed a Committee to prepare an answer to my Message,[18] which was reported & agreed upon unanimously by the same number as before mentioned. In the House, which was grown thin & evacuated by the friends of Government in greater proportion than the opponents, It had not the same Success: the faction laboured with all their might to prevent the paper being censured. It was debated a whole afternoon & adjourned to the next morning, during which interval all the usual practices of tampering with the members were employed, & ^the next Day^ upon a Vote the Consideration of the libell was dismissed.[19] The cheif Argument used for this purpose was that as there was no Name used, it was not a libell in law & would not be considered So in a court of justice. It was finally agreed that the Message, as inclosed,[20] should be sent to me. The Faction carried their points by small Majorities: upon the last question The Numbers were 39 to 30; the greater of which is about one third part of the whole House.[21] Otis upon this Occasion behaved in the House like a Madman; he abused evry one in Authority & especially the Council in the grossest terms. The next morning[22] He came into the Council chamber before the board met, & having read the Councils Address, he with Oaths & imprecations Vowed Vengeance upon the whole Council at the next Election, & told one Councellor, who happened to be there, that He should never sit at that board after his year was out. This is the Man, who makes such a disturbance about my using My Negative in the appointment of Councellors; the annual Election ^of whom^ is the Cankerworm[23] of the Constitution of this Government.

It may be expected that after such strong declarations against this libell the Council would have joined with me in the prosecution of the printers. But that could not be brought about: it was known that I intended to move that business; & therefore One of the board in the Name of some of my friends was sent to me to advise the contrary.[24] It was suggested that It would be better to leave the Matter where it stood with a continued unanimity of the (allmost) whole Council, than by proceeding farther to divide them, especially as it was thought probable that a

Vote for a prosecution might not be obtained.[25] I was satisfied with these reasons, & declined making any further Motion. This is one of the Consequences of that fatal ingredient in this Constitution[,] the election of ye Council; which will allways weaken this Government, so that the best Management will never make its weight capable of being put in the Scales against that of the people, tho' the late Act of parliament will ^do^ much towards it. However I ordered the Attorney general[26] to procure informations so that if a prosecution may be hereafter thought advisable, it may be practicable. But after all, these printers are answerable to the Government of Great Britain an hundred times more than they are to this; & whilst that Debt remains unsatisfied we ought not to complain, that it is not paid here.

I had intended, when I prorogued the general Court to have made a short Speech to ye House in answer to their last Message on your Lordship's Letter. But their publishing that Message in one of their papers, & that Virulent libell in the next, showed such a determined Design to misrepresent me to the people, that I was obliged to enter more fully into my justification than I intended to have done at first; & accordingly I delivered the Speech inclosed.[27] I flatter myself it will have Very good Effects, from the general approbation it has received from all parties in this Town. It is intended to open the Eyes of the people to the Wickedness of this factious junto; tho' perhaps they will not see it clearly till they feel some of the Effects of its Machinations; which cannot fail of coming upon them in some shape or other as they are now going on.

I shall not trouble your Lordship with a Vindication of myself against the complaint which the House has sent against me; but shall trust to my Speech for that. I hope however that their request of Copies of my Letters will receive such a reprehension as it deserves; and that it will be done otherwise than by the honor of a Letter from your Lordship to the House: in which, besides the general objection to such a correspondence, there is this further impropriety, that before such letter can arrive there will be a new House, which possibly may differ considerably from this both in Men & Manners. I shall proceed to inform your Lordship of other things which it may be proper for me to report, as fast as I can get time & Materials.

I am with great respect, My Lord, Your Lordships most obedient
& most humble Servant

Fra Bernard

The right honble The Earl of Shelburne.

ALS, RC   CO 5/757, ff 38-41.

Endorsed: Boston March 5th: 1768 Govr. Bernard. (N^o6) R 18 April A.9   Enclosures: a copy of the House of Representatives' message to FB, 13 Feb. 1768, CO 5/757, ff 42-46;

[Francis Bernard], [Proceedings of the Massachusetts Council, 1-4 Mar. 1768], [4 Mar. 1768] ibid., ff 47-51; *Boston Gazette*, 29 Feb. 1768, ibid., 52-54; resolve of the House of Representatives, 28 Feb. 1768 (for which see *JHRM*, 44: 198-199). Variants of letter in: CO 5/766, ff 121-127 (L, RLbC); BP, 6: 272-277 (L, LbC); *Letters to the Ministry* (1st ed.), 8-10; *Letters to the Ministry* (repr.), 10-13. The RC may have been sent to John Pownall under cover of **No. 595** and the duplicate (not found) with another letter to Pownall of 14 Mar.[28] FB finished writing this RC before receiving confirmation on 6 or 7 Mar. (**No. 595**) that the earl of Hillsborough had superseded Shelburne. He does not appear to have made any changes to the letter subsequent to receiving this news. An extract and the enclosures were laid before both houses of Parliament on 28 Nov. 1768. HLL: American Colonies Box 1.

Dr. Joseph Warren's anonymous and venomous attack on FB's reputation in the *Boston Gazette* on 29 Feb. presented an opportunity of sorts to rally support in the Council and the House. At the Council's urging, FB presented the article to both houses of the assembly for consideration. He did not expect the assembly to recommend that the author be prosecuted by the province attorney general for traducing the governor's reputation or his disrespectful treatment of "Kingly Government." But he hoped the assembly would support him in taking action against the printers of the *Boston Gazette* (Benjamin Edes and John Gill), who FB believed were being managed by James Otis Jr. and Samuel Adams. There is no detailed record of the discussion in the House of Representatives, but the House evidently considered a series of questions as to whether or not the article was libelous and seditious. By a majority of nine the House voted to take "no further action," and in replying to FB defended the liberty of the press. The House could not protect the printers or author from prosecution but they did screen them whilst also insulting the governor. In the event of a prosecution, the only line of defense was for the printer and author to prove the truth of any alleged libel. But at this juncture in the Imperial Crisis, the Whigs did not have substantive evidence that the governor was conspiring against the colonists, yet by refusing to take or endorse legal action the House effectively implied that there was some truth in the article's allegation. Had the vote gone the other way, the friends of government might have proposed a further motion to censure the printers. Thus, FB noted, the "faction laboured with all their might to prevent the paper being censured," Otis even entering the Council Chamber to lambast and insult those councilors who had sided with the governor. FB could have instructed the attorney general to prosecute Edes and Gill without the support of the assembly—and was ready to do so—but he was mindful of Shelburne's advice to have the backing of the assembly in such cases.[29] He did not let the matter lie. Chief Justice Hutchinson presented the article to a grand jury of the Superior Court; the jury instructed the attorney general to prepare a bill of prosecution, but the following day refused to pass it. FB attributed their change of mind to the printers of the *Boston Gazette* and their Whig allies intimidating the jury. (**No. 596.**)

FB's closing speech to the assembly of 4 Mar. was a signal turn in his engagement with his critics. Privately, he had pressed the case for British intervention; publicly he now sought to exculpate himself from any wrongdoing. FB did not engage the arguments the House had made against the Townshend Revenue Act, concentrating instead on his critics' efforts to undermine his reputation. He began by praising the "Moderation and good Temper" he had witnessed during the first weeks of the late session, blaming the "Lovers of Contention" for fomenting opposition by making "extraordinary and indecent Observations" on his correspondence with Shelburne.

> If you think that this Censure [*by Shelburne*] is singular, you deceive yourselves; and you are not so well informed of what passes at *Westminster* as you ought to be, if you do not know that it is as general and extensive as the Knowledge of the Proceedings to which it is applied: And therefore all your Insinuations against me, upon false Suppositions of my having misrepresented You, are vain and groundless, when every Effect is to be accounted for from plain Narrative of Facts which must have appeared to the Secretary of State from your own Journals.

This bitter and sarcastic vindication might have alarmed everyone, not just FB's Whig opponents. Doubtless all were left wondering as to what their governor had actually said about the province in his letters to Shelburne and apprehensive as to what he might now say about those he deemed "false Patriots . . . sacrificing their Country to the Gratification of their own Passions."[30] Thereafter, FB's conduct as governor remained center stage in provincial politics for the duration of his administration. At the same time, the more FB was regarded as a flawed person and vulnerable official than as the monarch's representative, King George III once more became a venerable object in American minds.

---

1. Supplied from LbC.

2. The second session of the legislative year ran from 30 Dec. 1767 to 4 Mar. 1768.

3. In early 1768, Speaker Thomas Cushing signed a series of letters on behalf of the House of Representatives protesting the Townshend Acts: to Dennis DeBerdt, 12 Jan.; to the earl of Shelburne, 15 Jan.; to the marquess of Rockingham, 22 Jan.; to the earl of Camden, 29 Jan.; to the earl of Chatham, 2 Feb.; a circular letter to the speakers of the colonial assemblies, 11 Feb.; to Henry Seymour Conway, 13 Feb.; to the lords commissioners of the Treasury, 17 Feb.; to the earl of Shelburne, 22 Feb. See *JHRM*, 44: 217-250. For discussion see **Nos. 579** to **581, 589**, and **591**.

4. House of Representatives to DeBerdt, 12 Jan. 1768, *JHRM*, 44: 241-260. The contents are discussed in **No. 580**n4 and **No. 581**n6-8.

5. **Appendix 1** enclosed in **No. 589**.

6. House of Representatives to the lords commissioners of the Treasury, 17 Feb., *JHRM*, 44: 233-236.

7. Annotation in left margin: "5". On Friday 26 Feb., eighty-two members voted to approve a resolve to "discountenance the use of foreign superfluities" and to encourage native manufactures, with only Timothy Ruggles dissenting (for which act of Toryism his name was emblazoned in capitals in the copy printed in the *Boston Gazette*, 28 Feb. 1768). *JHRM*, 44: 198-199. Boston's nonimportation subscription was being circulated when FB wrote this letter, but support for nonimportation was not so prevalent among the representatives, as FB's comments about the careful wording of the House resolves indicate.

8. On 13 Jan., the Boston town meeting had pledged to revive a plan to produce sail cloth at the Manufactory House, using unemployed or poor laborers. *Reports of the Record Commissioners of Boston*, 16: 230-232.

9. **No. 591** written in reply to Shelburne's letter of 17 Sept. 1767, **No. 566**, *Bernard Papers*, 3: 407-409.

10. Annotation: "6". The correct date of publication was Monday 29 Feb.

11. In **No. 566**, Shelburne had censured the House for "improper Excesses" and "private Resentments" in excluding Crown officers from the Council, writing that "It cannot, under such Circumstances be surprizing" that FB had vetoed councilors chosen in their stead. *Bernard Papers*, 3: 407.

12. Printed in the *Boston Gazette* (on 29 Feb.), the House's message to FB of 18 Feb. claimed that in censuring the House, Shelburne could only have been acting in response to advice tendered by FB. The implication was that FB had misrepresented the motives of his opponents. The article by "A True Patriot"* went further in criticizing FB by personalizing the accusation that he had misled Shelburne. *Boston Gazette, Supplement,* 29 Feb. 1768. Warren demonized FB, accusing him of harboring an "Enmity" toward the province, delighting in his "Cruelty" and "Malice," and exhibiting a "diabolical Thirst for Mischief." His "Jesuitical Insinuations" were designed to corrupt the secretary of state. The other issue that concerned FB was to establish a clear linkage between the House and the *Boston Gazette* before pursuing the Whig leaders for libel. He was following both Shelburne's advice in **No. 574** to obtain evidence and his own desire to exact revenge. (*Bernard Papers*, 3: 422-424.) It was natural for FB to suppose that the piece had been authored or influenced by either James Otis Jr. or Samuel Adams, both prolific political writers. But the "True Patriot" in the *Boston Gazette* of 29 Feb. was in fact Dr. Joseph Warren, whose authorship (unknown to FB) can be established from an annotation in the Dorr Collection, 2: 38.

   * The "True Patriot" pseudonym had been employed earlier by a writer from "Swanzey" in the *Massachusetts Gazette and Boston News-Letter*, 24 Sept. and the *Boston Evening-Post*, 28 Sept. 1767. Both of these pieces were putative productions of a pro-government writer. It is possible, however, that the "True Patriot" from "Swanzey" was in fact a Whig writer, who ironically affected to mock Otis's "Blustering" style as a means of eliciting sympathy for the harassed Whig leader. Alternatively, FB or a government supporter may have written these pieces, although there is no evidence to confirm this. Nicolson, '*The Infamas Govener*', 273n129.

13. The last lines were.

    > We never can treat good and patriotic Rulers with too great Reverence—
    > But it is certain that Men total abandoned to Wickedness, can never merit
    > our Regard, be their Stations ever so high.
    >
    > 'If such Men are by God appointed,
    > The Devil may be the Lord's anointed.'

    The pro-American British Dissenter Thomas Hollis rightly identified the source of the quotation as "*Rochester's Satires.*" *The True Sentiments of America Contained in a Collection of Letters Sent from the House of Representatives*, (London, 1768), 84. The quotation is from one of the earl of Rochester's posthumously published satires on King Charles II, *The Restauration: Or the History of Insipids: a Lampoon* (1707), 26.5-6. One historian described the invective in the *Boston Gazette* "as vicious as any colonial governor was ever subjected to." Jensen, *Founding of a Nation*, 254.

14. Present in given order were: Samuel Danforth, Isaac Royall, Benjamin Lincoln, John Erving Sr., William Brattle, James Bowdoin, Gamaliel Bradford, Thomas Hubbard, Nathaniel Sparhawk, Harrison Gray, James Russell, Thomas Flucker, Nathaniel Ropes, John Bradbury, Timothy Paine, Royal Tyler, John Chandler, Samuel White, Jeremiah Powell, and James Pitts. Absent were Samuel Dexter, John Hill, and John Worthington. We can only speculate if among the Whigs who condemned the article by the "True Patriot" were FB's vocal critics Brattle, Bowdoin, Gray, Tyler, and Pitts.

15. Annotation: "7".

16. On 1 Mar.: annotation: "8".

17. On 1 Mar.: annotation: "10".

18. Annotation: "9". These proceedings are not fully reported in the Council's legislative records for 1 Mar. (CO 5/827, f 40). But FB kept his own minute which he enclosed with this letter, CO 5, 757, ff 47-49; this document, prepared by an unknown clerk, was used to date the proceedings discussed above.

19. On 4 Mar.

20. The Council message of 4 Mar. is in CO 5/ 757, ff 48-49; annotation: "11".

21. The assembly's proceedings of 3 and 4 Mar. are in *JHRM*, 44: 213-215.

22. 4 Mar.

23. *OED.* "A highly malignant and corrupting influence that spreads and consumes, in the manner of a cankerworm.*" * A moth caterpillar that feeds on fruit trees.

24. The identity of this councilor is unknown, but may have been one of FB's cabinet of advisers. See *Bernard Papers*, 3: 73n9.

25. Afterward, the "True Patriot" delivered an unrepentant explanation that claimed the moral high ground in a Ciceronian fashion by purporting to expose a conspiracy against colonial liberties.

> There are circumstances, in which not justice alone, but humanity itself, obliges us to hold up *the villain to view*, and to expose his guilt, to prevent his destroying the innocent.

Thus did Warren artfully craft a case that led readers inexorably to compare FB to Catiline, the notorious leader of the conspiracy against the Roman Republic thwarted by the consul Cicero and exposed in the Senate in 63 BC. Claiming that his criticism had not been overtly personal, denying any disloyalty to the king, and protesting that the "profaneness" of his article's last two lines had been misunderstood, Warren nonetheless left readers and FB in no doubt that personal integrity was at the heart of the matter:

> Whoever he is, whose conscience tells him he is not the monster I have portraited, may rest assured, I did not aim at him; but the person who knows the black picture exhibited, to be his own, is welcome to take it to himself. . . . My design was to compare wicked men, and especially wicked magistrates, to those enemies to mankind, the devils, and to intimate that the devils themselves might boast of divine authority to seduce and ruin mankind.

The Biblical allusion here to "devils" tempting wicked magistrates was obviously to Job 2, by implication equating FB's supposed American victims with Job whose sufferings were unmerited and whose patience was proverbial. The author finished with a pledge to continue writing "sentiments with freedom" and "publish whatever I think conducive to the general emolument." *Boston Gazette*, 7 Mar. 1768.

26. Jonathan Sewall (1729-96) had succeeded Jeremiah Gridley as province attorney general on 18 Nov. 1767.

27. On 4 Mar.; annotation: "12".

28. BP, 6: 101.

29. "I should be led to hope that the Assembly would vindicate their own Honor, and make the Guilty feel the Displeasure of an injured Province." Shelburne to FB, 14 Nov. 1767, **No. 574**, *Bernard Papers*, 3: 423.

30. *JHRM*, 44: 214-215.

594 | To Richard Jackson

N°. 6

Boston Mar 6. 1768

Dear S^r.

My time since the Adjournment of the Court has been so fully employed in public Dispatches that I have nothing left for a Letter to you by this Packet. I have only to say that I have passed your Grant of £600 and will write to you more fully upon the Subject.[1] I send you inclosed printed Papers which will explain a Squabble Otis has raised in the House.[2] I will only say that as he was determined to raise a Quarrel, he has hit upon a Subject as favourable to me as could be. Every Things[3] here is running into Confusion; People here are ready to refuse to submit to any Laws of Trade imposing Duties; the Officers are threatened; Mobbs are expected; the Commissioners are frightned; the Government is defenceless; &c &c. These are the Effects of America (or rather Boston) being left to Right itself. You shall here more soon.

Yours &c.

R Jackson Esq_r

L, LbC   BP, 6: 101.

In handwriting of Thomas Bernard. Enclosures (not found) but likely included a copy of the *Boston Gazette*, 28 Feb. 1768.

The frenetic last five lines of this letter echoed the unease of FB's recent letter to Barrington, **No. 592**.

1. On 26 Feb., the General Court awarded £600 to Jackson for services as province agent. *Acts and Resolves*, 17: 289. FB probably did not keep his promise to provide a more detailed account (at least, no such letter is extant); perhaps notification of payment precluded reason for further discussion.

2. FB assumed wrongly that Otis was the author of a libel printed under the pseudonym of "A True Patriot". See **No. 593**n12.

3. Thus in manuscript.

595 | To John Pownall

Boston Mar 7 1768

Dear Sir,

I am now making up a Packet for your Board which will contain duplicates of two Letters to the Earl of Shellburne with its Enclosures.[1] I have also an Original to the same noble Lord,[2] whom I find myself obliged to continue to Address, tho I know of the Appointment of the Earl of Hillsbourough;[3] as the Notices of such an Appointment has not Come to me in any Authentick Way, not even by a Paragraph in the Gazette.[4] You will also receive some Newspaper Publications, which will Sufficiently explain the Occasion of a Quarrel which Otis has raised in the House and the Manner.[5] I have not been able to avoid, as much as I have desired Speaking & publishing upon this Occasion: I think it will have a good Effect.

I have not Time now to write to you as fully as I could wish: I can only say that it looks as if the Same Disorders which attended the Stampt-Act are coming on apace. People seem determined not to Submit to the Laws of Trade; They now declare against all Laws which impose Duties; The Molasses Act of which was formerly a Favour is as great an Object of Opposition as any.[6] The Officers of the Trade are threatned, Mobbings Continu^a^lly expected, The Commissioners in the most precarious Situation not knowing how to order the Execution of the Laws or how to let it alone. I am just as defenceless as ever. &c &c. God grant that the Opinion which has prevailed at home that the Colonies would come to Rights of themselves may not prove a fatal Deception.

I shall do my Duty in the best Manner I can, but expect a great Deal of Trouble untill Releif from Home can come

I am &c

J: Pownall Esqr:

L, LbC   BP, 6: 99-100.

In handwriting of Thomas Bernard. The original of this letter and a large packet of enclosures were sent by the New York packet.[7] Enclosures (not found): copies of **Appendix 1** and FB's message to the House of Representatives, 22 Feb. 1768 (for which see *JHRM*, 44: 188); House of Representatives to the earl of Shelburne, 22 Feb. 1768 for which see ibid., 239-24. May also have enclosed the RC of **No. 593**, and the duplicates of **Nos. 589** and **591** along with copies of their enclosures.

While FB welcomed Hillsborough's appointment on the firm assumption that the new secretary of state would take a harder line with colonial opposition, he was still determined to leave Massachusetts as soon as he could obtain permission (see source note to **No. 609**).

1. Probably **Nos. 589** and **591**.

2. The RC of **No. 593**.

3. Thus in manuscript.

4. FB here confirms that he had just received unofficial news (probably in the previous twenty-four hours) that the earl of Shelburne had been replaced. He had known since 20 or 21 Feb. that Hillsborough was being appointed to head up a new department (**No. 590**). The *Boston Evening-Post* announced a change of secretary on 7 Mar. but did not name Hillsborough as secretary of state for the Colonies until 14 Mar. The *London Gazette* did not carry the announcement.

5. FB made the same unfounded assertion in **No. 594**.

6. FB is recalling the 1733 Molasses Act, which imposed a 6d. duty on a gallon of molasses imported to America. By "Favour" he meant that the Molasses Act was not rigorously enforced, at least until the introduction of the Sugar Act (1764), which also lowered the duty to 3d. The American Revenue Act of 1766 further reduced the duty to 1d. But other aspects of the mercantilist system, notably restrictions on colonial trade with Southern Europe and duties on wines imported from the Azores, Madeira, and Portugal continued to rankle American merchants. See Tyler, *Smugglers & Patriots*, 96-99.

7. BP, 6: 101.

596 | *To the Earl of Shelburne*

N° 7

Boston Mar 12 1768

My Lord

Since I wrote my last the Superior Court has been opened at Boston: upon which occasion the Cheif Justice (Lᵗ Govʳ) made a long & forcible charge to the Grand Jury upon the Subject of the Libells published in the Boston Gazette[1] & particularly that ^which^ has been lately animadverted upon by the Council.[2] This so sensibly affected the Grand Jury & all the hearers of it, that it left no doubt in the mind of any one present that the grand Jury would find a bill against the printers. And they themselves had so little doubt of it, that as soon as they came out of Court they sent for the Attorney general[3] & directed him to prepare a Bill against the next Morning. But in the interval The Faction who conducts that paper was indefatigable in tampering with the Jury; so that when the Business was resumed the next day, the Bill was opposed so effectually that it passed in the Negative by a small Majority, some say of one only. Upon this occasion the Managers of the paper were seen publickly to haunt the grand Jury men wherever they went; & the Arguments which were used in the grand Jury chamber were allmost Word for Word the Same which Otis had before used in publick.[4]

Sensible People who have a regard for their Country are much concerned at this defeat of justice. They say that it is a Symptom of such extream Weakness in the Government, that it affords little hopes of it's recovery. And indeed I do not expect that the Government will ever recover its Authority without Aid from Superior powers. If the Opposition was directed only against persons & Measures a Reconciliation might & soon would take place & all might be well again. But Men & Measures are only nominal defendants: The Authority of the King, the Supremacy of Parliament, the Superiority of Government are the real Objects of the attack; and a general levelling of all the powers of Government, & reducing it into the hands of the whole people is what is aimed at, & will, at least in some degree, succeed, without some external assistance. The Council, which formerly used to be revered by the people has lost its weight, & notwithstanding their late spirited exertion, is in general timid & irresolute, especially when the Annual Election draws near. That fatal ingredient in the Composition of this Constitution is the bane of ^the^ whole: and never will the royal Scale be ballanced with that of the people 'till the Weight of the Council is wholly put into the former. The making the Council independent of the people (even tho' they should still receive their original Appointment from them) would go far to cure all the disorders which this Government is Subject to.

But, my Lord, whilst I am treating of the constitutional imbecillity of the Council I must not forget my promise that I would represent to his Majesty the public spirited Conduct of the Council during this last Session. I must therefore beg leave to assure your Lordship that in many transactions in this last Session the Council have in general shown great attention to the Support of the Government & the Wellfare of the people, & have upon many occasions shown a resolution & steadiness in promoting his Majesty's Service, which would have done honour to his Majesty's appointment if they had wholly held their places under it. Which makes it more to be lamented that such Men should be subjected to be continually threatened to be turned out of their places, whenever they exercise the dictates of their own judgements in contravention to the Fury of a Seditious Demagogue.

I must not omitt to do justice to the spirited Conduct of the Lieut Governor in his function of Cheif Justice: It gives me great pleasure to say that I can depend upon his resolution & steadiness as much as I can Upon My own; & am assured that there will be no Want of a due enforcement of the Laws to the correction of the present abuses. Where there is a failure of this Exertion It will arise either from the defaults of juries or from the Comptroll which in this defenceless Government the common people sometimes exercise over the Laws; especially the Laws of Great Britain. The cheif Justice has been much prest to print his charge, but has hitherto declined it. However He has reduced it to writing, that if it should be misrepresented in the Boston Gazette (as from the great Licentiousness which reigns here is very probable) he may be able to justify himself. In the Mean time as He has begun with these printers, He will, I dare say, pursue his purpose; and as the publication of this paper is a Crime committed in evry County in the Province, It is probable that another Grand Jury may not be so regardless of their Oath & their duty to their Country as this has been.

I am, with great respect, My Lord, Your Lordship's most obedient
and most humble Servant

Fra Bernard

The right honble The Earl of Shelburne

ALS, RC   CO 5/757, ff 64-65.

Endorsed: Boston March 12th: 1768. Governor Bernard (N[o]. 7) R. 3[d]. June. A.11.   Variants: CO 5/893, ff 39-41 (dupLS, RC); CO 5/766, ff 146-150 (L, RLbC); BP, 6: 278-280 (L, LbC); *Letters to the Ministry* (1st ed.), 10-12; *Letters to the Ministry* (repr.), 13-16. Enclosed a copy of the *Boston Gazette*, 29 Feb. 1768 (not found). The original and duplicate were forwarded under cover of a letter to John Pownall, dated 14 Mar.[5] One of these variants was considered by the Board of Trade on 6 Jul. 1768. *JBT*, 13: 34. Extracts were laid before both houses of Parliament on 28 Nov. 1768. HLL: American Colonies Box 1. A copy may have been sent to Gen. Gage under cover of **Appendix 4**.

   The politicization of colonial juries seriously troubled FB and the province attorney general during 1768. Juries were selected by local constables and generally would not indict Whigs on any matter concerning the enforcement of imperial law. FB and the American Board of Customs began to consider other (more controversial) means of instituting criminal proceedings in common law courts, for example, by filing an "information" against persons (see **No. 719**).[6]

---

1. "A True Patriot," (Dr. Joseph Warren), *Boston Gazette, Supplement*, 29 Feb. 1768. See **No. 593**n12.

2. For the proceedings of the Council and the House on the offending article see **No. 593**.

3. Attorney General Jonathan Sewall was not actually present on that "first day" in court, and TH's subsequent comments on Sewall's absence were implicitly critical. Sewall was not obliged to attend all court proceedings and may not have been a party to TH's and FB's plans to pursue Edes and Gill. But the fact was he only prepared a bill of indictment against the printers for presentation to the jury on the second day. TH confirmed that, "in the interval" (as the governor noted), "Otis and his creatures . . . prevaild upon so many of the Jury to change their voices." At FB's request, TH "committed" the charge from "memory" to paper for future use, ruing that "ever since" the people "were more enragd against me than ever." The pursuit of Edes and Gill was abandoned for the moment, and TH sent his copy of the charge to a correspondent in England. TH to Thomas Whately, Boston, 5 Oct. 1768, Mass. Archs., 25: 281, in Hutchinson Transcripts, 1: 278.

4. Otis had defended the freedom of the press and denounced as the governor's lackeys those councilors who favored censuring the printers. See **No. 593**.

5. BP, 6: 101-102.

6. "There are three simple and related points about the conditions of law in prerevolutionary Massachusetts that have sometimes been misunderstood: a political majority [*in the town meetings*] could control [*the selection of*] Massachusetts juries; juries were the judges of law as well as of fact [*in considering indictments*]; and courts had little power to control and no power to overrule jury verdicts." Reid, *In a Defiant Stance*, 28. For a detailed discussion of the "civil traverse jury" see ibid., 20-40, and for the "management" of juries, ibid., 41-54.

597 | *From Lord Barrington*

Cavendish Square March 12. 1768

Dear Sir

Last Packett which arrived two or three days ago brought me two Letters from you, dated the 26th. & 28th. of January:[1] I am very much obliged to your Excellency for both, but I am unable to answer them as I ought. The Packett to North America goes off tonight, and the Election orders which go all over Great Britain at the same time, make such full Employment for the War Office, that I have been thoroughly busyed for some days past: I also set out for my own Election at Plymouth tomorrow.[2]

I have communicated your most ingenious thoughts about American Affairs to my friend Lord Hillsborough. I am sorry to find that a man so knowing in what relates to that Country as your self, is of opinion that nothing can put a real end to our difference with our fellow Subjects there, but a representation from thence.[3] Without entering into that subject, I may venture to say that the proposed expedient is impracticable, as no Influence could make ten Members of either House of Parliament agree to such a Remedy.

I hope this Letter will find you and all my Cousins perfectly well. I rejoyce that your prudence & spirit have conquer'd faction in New England:[4] I most cordially wish it were subdued on this side of the Ocean. I am with the greatest truth & regard Dear Sir

Your Excellencys most faithful & most obedient Servant

Barrington

ALS, RC   BP, 11: 157-160.

Endorsed by FB: Lord Barrington d Mar 12 1768 r May 15.

Barrington did not have his troubles to seek in the months ahead. His brutal suppression of political demonstrators in the St. George's Field Massacre of 10 May was scrutinized in Parliament and without. He was execrated by the pseudonymous satirist "Junius," whose first letter appeared in January 1769.

1. **Nos. 583** and **584**.

2. Parliament closed on 10 Mar. 1768 and the general election commenced on 15 Mar. The new Parliament opened on 10 May. Barrington had represented Plymouth since 1754, and continued as the town's MP until 1778.

3. That is, the direct representation of Americans in Parliament.

4. Barrington's unguarded praise for FB was probably intended to compensate for his rejection of the governor's proposal regarding American representation. It is possible, however, that Barrington's optimism also reflected the mood of government ministers more generally with regard to the situation in the American Colonies, before FB's pessimistic reports recounting his squabbles with the House of Representatives began arriving in London from April through June. **Nos. 589, 591** to **593, 595,** and **596**.

598 | To Richard Jackson

Boston March 14 1768

Dear S^r

I sent you a Short Letter in a Packet to Mr Pownal which I dispatched to New York a Week ago for the Packet Boat.[1] I am now Sending some duplicates to Newport to go by a Ship from thence: as this Port is more than ever I knew it at this time void of Ships ready for England, I can add only a few lines as a Supplement to my former.

Since I wrote last the Superiour Court has opened here: upon which Occasion the Cheif Justice gave a most forcible & energetick Charge to the grand jury upon the Subject of the Libells published in the Boston Gazette. It so affected all that hear'd it, that it was Universally Concluded that the Grand Jury could not avoid finding a Bill against the Printers. They themselves thought so: for as soon as they came out of Court they sent for the Attorney General & as it seemed unanimously, directed him to prepare a Bill for that Purpose against their next meeting. But this Interval was so fully employ'd by the Faction in tampering seperately with the Persons of the Grand Jury, that when they came together again, they rejected the Bill by a Small majority, some say of only one; to the great Disappointment of all who are concerned for the Wellfare of The Province & the Authority of the Government.[2]

The Cheif Justice has been much pressed to Print his charge but has hitherto declined it. However he has had the caution to reduce it immediately to Writing that he may have it in his power to Vindicate himself from the Misrepresentations which must be expected from the Writers of that infamous Paper. So it is probable that the malice of his Enemies will bring that into the Public which the Solicitations of his Friends could not Obtain. Now he has entered into this Business he will most Probably pursue it: & there is no doubt but the Writers of the Paper will give him Opportunity to revive the Subject; for it is much more Probable they will be elated with the Success than be cautioned by their Escape. And as their Crime is indictable in any County it is probable that their paper will come before another Grand Jury who will treat [it][3] as it deserves.[4]

I send you a protest of Brig[r] Ruggles which is another Confirmation of the Integrity & Steadiness of this good Man in persevering in his Maxim that submission to great Britain is the true Interest of the Colonies.[5] He ought to have some publick notice taken of him by the Great Men at home. I have just hear'd of your Fathers death:[6] I can neither condole nor congratulate; for I do not think that the easy passage out of this Life which a fullness of Years procures, a Subject of the one, nor accession of riches to a Man Who already has enough, a Cause for the Offense. However if it shall enable you to change the Scene of your Life more to your mind, I shall rejoice at the Consequence. I am &c

R. Jackson Esq[r]__

L, LbC   BP, 6: 103-104.

Possibly in handwriting of John Bernard. Minor emendations not shown. The RC was forwarded under cover of a letter to John Pownall, dated 14 Mar.[7] Enclosure (not found): the protest of Timothy Ruggles, 29 Feb. 1768, printed in *Boston Post-Boy and Advertiser*, 14 Mar. 1768.

1. **No. 595**.

2. See also **Nos. 593** and **596**.

3. Obscured by tight binding.

4. See **No. 596**.

5. Timothy Ruggles (1711-95) had been a firm friend of government during the Stamp Act Crisis. See *Bernard Papers*, 2: 373-372; 3: 15, 113, 253. Ruggles was the only dissenter when the House of Representatives resolved on 26 Feb. to support domestic manufacturing, protesting that the British government would view the resolve as a "threat" and likely to cause a "breach" between Britain and the American Colonies. Ruggles's request that his protest be entered in the House journals was voted down by the chamber; that is probably why he published it in a newspaper friendly to the government (there being no evidence that FB had any part in this). *Boston Post-Boy and Advertiser*, 14 Mar. 1768. See also **No. 593**n7.

6. Richard Jackson Sr. (d.1768).

7. BP, 6: 101-102.

599 | From the American Board of Customs

Copy

Sir,

We have avoided representing to your Excellency the Apprehensions we have for sometime been under of Indignity being offered to his Majesty's Commission, in which we have the Honour to act, but as an open Insult was this Morning offered to a Member of this Board and a principal Officer Acting under it, namely M[r] Paxton[1] and M[r] Williams,[2] by affixing Effigies said to represent them upon a Tree in this Town, and as the Alarm was given this Morning at Day break, by discharging of Guns, beating of Drums and hoisting Colours, We cannot help considering the Same as a presage of some open Acts of Violence whereby his Majesty's Commission may be dishonoured, more especially as it has been currently reported for some time past that a Riot would happen on this Night.

We therefore pray that your Excellency will be pleased to take such Measures as you may judge necessary to maintain the Peace of the Town and prevent any Outrage upon Ourselves or our Officers.

Your Excellency will receive this Letter by M[r] Wootton[3] one of our Inspectors, who will inform you of an Insult he met with last night.[4]

We remain &[ca]

WB. HH. JT. CP. JR.[5]

18th M[ch] 1768

His Excellency Gov[r] Bernard in Council

L, Copy   T 1/465, f 28.

Endorsed: Copy of a Letter to His Excellency Gov[r] Bernard in Council Dated 18th. March 1768 From the Comm[rs] of the Customs. Another copy at T 1/465, f 34.

This letter was delivered to FB on the morning of Thursday 18 Mar. while the Governor's Council was deliberating the local celebrations commemorating the second anniversary of the Stamp Act's repeal (see **No. 600**). Whereas the commissioners evidently suspected that the effigies of Charles Paxton and John Williams left hanging from a flagstaff fixed to the Liberty Tree "presage[d]" violent riots, the Council did not, blaming the incident on "some insignificant people" and voting unanimously that they believed the commissioners were not in any danger. After customs officer William Wootton communicated the commissioners' letter, the Council adjourned to 4 PM to await further information from the commissioners; none received, the Council reaffirmed the vote taken that morning. Votes were not usually recorded in Council minutes, but on this occasion and subsequently both the governor and the Council were more careful in preserving a formal record, and FB himself began to keep a note of divisions. CO 5/827, ff 41-42.

Both the Council and the *Boston Gazette* wrongly supposed that local Sons of Liberty were firmly in control of popular demonstrations, as historian Dirk Hoerder has shown. The effigies were the work of Loammi Baldwin (1744-1807), a twenty-three year-old carpenter from Woburn, who had been active in the Stamp Act riots and was to become a prominent civil engineer and revolutionary officer. Baldwin protested to the Boston selectmen that he and his friends intended no harm, and refused to remove the flagstaff. The effigies were re-moved by "Neighbours without any opposition" (**No. 600**), though whether this was before or after the selectmen's interview with Baldwin is uncertain (**Appendix 3**). In any case, their peaceful removal persuaded TH that their display "was no part of a concerted plan" to mobilize protest.[6] In the evening, a crowd of around eight hundred people (according to Hoerder) paraded through Boston's streets, with banners, drums, and fireworks, briefly gathering outside the homes of FB, the Customs commissioners, and Inspector General John Williams. These incidents FB discussed in **No. 600**. No one was attacked, but the fact that the demonstrations occurred indicated that the Sons of Liberty were "successful" only in their "controlled . . . reporting" of the events of 18 Mar. not in their direction.[7]

---

1. Charles Paxton (1704-88) was a confidant of FB and an effective (and for that a deeply unpopular) customs officer in Boston before his appointment as a commissioner of the American Board of Customs.

2. John Williams, the senior inspector general to the Customs Board, was an American by birth and former receiver general of Customs at Martinique. See Joseph R. Frese, "The Royal Customs Service in the Chesapeake, 1770: The Reports of John Williams, Inspector General," *The Virginia Magazine of History and Biography* 81 (1973): 280-318.

3. William Wootton was the second inspector general.

4. Described in Wootton's deposition filed in CO 5/893, f 48.

5. William Burch (d.1794), Henry Hulton (1732-91), John Temple (1732-98), Charles Paxton (1704-88), and John Robinson (d.1783).

6. TH to Richard Jackson, Boston, 23 Mar. 1768, Mass. Archs., 26: 295-296.

7. Hoerder, *Crowd Action in Revolutionary Massachusetts*, 158-159.

600 | *To the Earl of Shelburne*

duplicate

Boston March 19 1768

My Lord

I expected that the Appointment of the Commissioners of the Customs in America would have made it unnecessary for me to have troubled your Lordship with any Representations upon the Subject of the Customs. But I see such an Opposition to the Commissioners and their Officers and such a Defiance of the Authority by which they are appointed continually growing, that I can no longer excuse my informing your Lordships of the Detail of Facts from whence the most dangerous Consequences are to be expected.[1]

It is sometime since there have been frequent Reports of Insurrections[2] intended, in which it has been said the Houses of one or more of the Commissioners and their Officers would be pulled down: two were more particularly fixed on. Upon one of these Nights a Number of Lads, about 100, paraded the Town with a Drum and Horns, passed by the Council Chamber whilst I was sitting in Council, assembled before M[r] Paxton's (a Commissioners) House and huzzaed; and to the Number of at least 60 lusty Fellows (as I am assured) invested M[r] Burch's (another Commissioner's) House for some Time; so that his Lady and Children were obliged to go out of a back Door to avoid the Danger which threatened.[3] This Kind of Disturbance was kept up all the Evening; and after all was treated as the Diversion of a few Boys, a Matter of no Consequence. This was I think on March 4.

After this it was reported that the Insurrection was postponed till March 18 which was the Anniversary of the repeal of the Stamp Act; upon which Day Effigies were to be exhibited; and two Persons, M[r] Paxton a Commissioner and M[r] Williams one of the Inspectors general were mentioned as devoted to the Resentment of the Mob. I took all the Pains I could to discover the Truth of this Report; but could get no other Answer but Assurances that no such ^thing^ would be done or suffered. On the very Day before I spoke with the most knowing Men I could procure; who were very positive that no Effigies would be hung up. And yet late that Evening I had certain Advice that Effigies were prepared: but it was too late to do any Thing, and my Information was of that Nature that I could not make Use of it in Public.[4]

Early the next morning, the Sheriff[5] came to inform me that the Effigies of M[r] Paxton and M[r] Williams were hanging upon Liberty Tree. I had the Day before appointed a Council to meet, and I now sent round to get them together as soon as possible it might be. Before I went to Council I learnt that the Effigies had been taken down by some of the Neighbours without any opposition. At Council I set forth in strong Terms the Notoriousness[6] of this Insult,[7] the danger of it's being followed by actual Violence and the Necessity there was of providing for the Defence of the Town.[8] But all I could say made no Impression upon the Council: they persevered in treating the Affair as of no Consequence, and assuring me that there was no Danger of any Commotion. After they had given their Opinion as in the inclosed Copy of the Minutes, I received a Letter from the Commissioners[9] setting forth the Insult they had received, the Danger they apprehended, and desiring the Protection of the Government. I communicated this to the Council[10] and proposed that they should reconsider this Business; but finding them not inclined to depart from their opinion, as before given, I adjourned the Reconsideration till the Afternoon. In the Afternoon the Question being again put to them, They adhered to their former Opinion.

I should have mentioned before that under all their Assurances I had that there would be no Disturbances, it was never understood that the Day, the Anniversary of the Repeal of the Stamp Act should not be celebrated.[11] Accordingly at Break of Day there were beating of Drums and firing of Guns heard; and the whole Town was adorned with Ships Colours: and to add to the Celebration, the Feast of S[t]: Patrick being the day before was postponed to this Day. However great Pains were taken by the Select Men of the Town and some other Gentlemen that the Festivity should not produce a Riot in the Evening: and so far it succeeded that it produced Terror only and not actual Mischeif. There was a Number of Gentlemen dined at two Taverns near the Townhouse, upon the Occasion of the Day: these broke up in good Time. After which many of the same and other Gentlemen kept together at the Coffee House (one of the Taverns)[12] all the Evening. These prevented a Bonfire in that Street, which was several Times attempted, and would probably have been a Prelude to Action. But the assembling a great Number of People of all Kinds Sexes and Ages, many of which shewed a great Disposition to the utmost Disorder, could not be prevented. There were many hundred of them paraded the Streets with Yells and Outcries which were quite terrible. I had in my House M[r] Burch (one of the Commissioners) and his Lady & Children, who had the Day before moved to our House for Safety. I had also with me the Lieut: Governor and the Sheriff of the County. But I had taken no Steps to fortify my House, not being willing to shew an Apprehension of Danger to myself. But at one Time there was so terrible a Yell from the Mob going by, that it was apprehended that they were breaking in; but it was not so. However it assumed the same Terror as if it had been so; and the Lady, a stranger to this Country, who chose our House for an Asylum, has not recovered it as yet — They went on and invested M[r] Williams' House but he shewed himself at a Window and told them that he was provided for their Reception,[13] and they went off; and either did not intend or dared not to attack his House. They also at two different Times about Midnight made outcrys about M[r] Paxtons House out of mere Wantonness to terrify his Family.[14] The whole made it a very terrible Night to those who thought themselves Objects of Popular Fury: and yet if I should complain of it, I should be told that it was nothing but the common Effects of Festivity and rejoicing; and there was no Harm intended.

Your Lordship will perhaps ask what I have been doing all this while, that this Spirit of Disorder is got to such a Pitch: I answer, every Thing in my Power to prevent it. Since first these Tumults were apprehended, the Commissioners, with whom (I mean 4 of the 5)[15] I am upon the most intimate Terms, have often asked me what Support to their Office or Protection for themselves I can afford: I answer none in the World. For tho I am allowed to proceed in the ordinary Business of the Government without Interruption; in the Business of a popular Opposition to the Laws of Great Britain founded upon Pretensions of Rights and Priviledges, I have not the Shadow of Authority or Power. I am just now in the Situation I was in above two years ago, sure to be made obnoxious to the Madness of the People by the Testimony I am obliged to bear against it and yet left exposed to their Resentment without any possible Resort for Protection. I am then asked why I don't apply for Troops as well to support the Kings Government as to protect the Persons of his Officers. I answer because I dont think it proper or prudent to make such Application upon my own Opinion only. All the Kings Governors are directed to take the Advice of the Council in Military Movements. And in this Government, where the Governor is in a more peculiar Manner obliged to have the Advice of the Council for allmost every Thing he does, it would be dangerous to act in such an important Business without such Advice. And it is in vain to put such a Question to the Council: for considering the Influence they are under from their being Creatures of the People and the personal Danger they would be subject to in assisting in the restraining them, it is not probable that the utmost Extremity of Mischief & Danger would induce them to advise such a Measure. I have once before tried the Experiment when the Danger was more urgent and immediate than it is now[16] and the Success then fully convinced me that it is to no Purpose ever again to repeat the Question. His Majesty's Ministers have within these three Years been fully acquainted with the defenceless State of this Government; and therefore I trust that I shall be excused leaving it to the Administration to determine upon a Measure which they are much more able to judge of and be answerable for than I can be. I shall have trouble and Danger enough when such Orders arrive, tho' I keep ever so clear of advising or promoting them. These my Lord are the Answers I have given to the Commissioners in the Course of Conversation; which I have thought proper to recapitulate in this Place for my own Vindication if it Shall be needful.

I should have mentioned before but for not interrupting the Narrative, that in the Debate at the Council one Gentleman said there were Associations formed for preserving the Peace of the Town. I said that I had not been made acquainted with them: that if there were any such they ought to have been formed with my

Privity and confirmed by my Authority. That if a general Association for supporting the Authority of the Government and preserving the Peace of the Town could be brought about, it would be of great Service, and I should be glad to see it set about immediately. Upon this a Councellor got up with Vehemence and said that such a Subscription was illegal and unconstitutional, and he should protest against it as tending to bring an Opprobrium on the Town. I said that at a Time when a Subscription was handed about the Town in direct Opposition to the Parliament and People of Great Britain and was every Day enforced by Menaces and other unfair Methods, it was very extraordinary at that Board to hear a Subscription for the Support of Government and Preservation of the Peace called illegal. That I should not endeavour to press a Measure which would derive its cheif Efficacy from being so Voluntary but I feared they would see the Expediency of such a Measure when it was too late. From this and the Generality of the Assurances that no Mischief would be done, I am to understand that the Preservation of the Peace of this Town is to depend upon those who have the Command of the Mob and can restrain them (and of Course let them loose) when they please; and civil Authority is not to interpose in this Business. And indeed I have with Attention observed, that all the Assurances that no Mischief was intended at present are founded upon the Impropriety of using Violence at a Time when they were applying to the Government and Parliament of Great Britain for redress. But it is inferred and sometimes expressly declared that when they have Advice that the Redress which they expect is denied, they will immediately proceed to do themselves Justice: and it is now become common Talk that they will not submit to Duties imposed by Parliament, not only those by the late Acts but all others which raise a Revenue. This is publick Talk: as for the Sanguine Expectations which the Faction from whose Cabinet all these Troubles have arose, has formed for controlling and triumphing over Great Britain, I dare not repeat what I have heard till their Purposes become more apparent.

In this Narrative I have taken no Notice of the Town Meetings of Merchants, Subscriptions for not importing English Goods, Proposals for Manufactures &c which have been carrying on before and during the whole forementioned Time. I intend to make a Seperate Letter upon these Subjects; which possibly may accompany this, as I am not as present apprised of a Conveyance safe enough to trust this by.

I am, with great Respect, My Lord, your Lordships most obed^t:
and most humble Servant

Fra Bernard

The Right honble The Earl of Shelburne

dupLS, RC   CO 5/893, ff 41-45.

Possibly in handwriting of John Bernard. Endorsed: *Massachusets*. Duplicate of a Letter N°. 8. From Francis Bernard Esqr. Govr. of Massachusets Bay, to the Earl of Shelburne, dated March 19. 1768, relative to the opposition made to the Commissioners of the Customs, and their Officers. Nn 13. Recd. June 24. Read July 6th. 1768. 2 papers.   Enclosures: minute and resolution of the Massachusetts Council of 18 Mar. 1768, CO 5/893, ff 46-47; deposition of William Wootton, 18 Mar. 1768, ibid., f 48. Variants of letter: CO 5/766, ff 150-160 (L, RLbC); BP, 6: 280-288 (L, LbC); *Letters to the Ministry* (1st ed.), 12-17; *Letters to the Ministry* (repr.), 16-22. A copy was made for Hillsborough, probably by a Plantation Office clerk, and is filed at CO 5/757, ff 66-71; substantive differences are itemized in the notes below. The duplicate received by Shelburne was considered by the Board of Trade on 6 Jul. 1768. *JBT*, 13: 34. Copies of the letter together with the enclosures were laid before both houses of Parliament on 28 Nov. 1768. HLL: American Colonies Box 1. Read by Privy Council, with enclosures, 26 Jun. 1770. *APC*, 5: 247.

While FB was writing specifically for Shelburne, he would also have had Hillsborough in mind, knowing that he had charge of American affairs.[17] FB presumed that Hillsborough would take a firmer line with the colonists' petitions and protests than Shelburne. This letter (and its continuation in **No. 601**) dramatized recent events in Boston; alarmist terms such as "Insurrection" and "Terror" were carefully chosen to elicit a reaction from Hillsborough. Yet, while FB was exaggerating the threatening aspects of crowd action to manufacture a sense of crisis, the episode itself—not just how he reported it—illustrated how far the "conditions" of law with regard to crowd control were subject to Whig influence.[18] "I am to understand that the Preservation of the Peace of this Town is to depend upon those who have the Command of the Mob and can restrain them (and of Course let them loose) when they please."

1. The town of Boston later declaimed this passage "false and malicious," for rather than defying the king's authority the people had all submitted to the revenue laws (which, smugglers excepted, was true) while awaiting the outcome of the colonists' petitions for repeal. *Appeal to the World*, 3-4.

2. "Few if any among us ever heard of such reports . . . it is very much to be questioned whether he received his intelligence from any other persons, but the Commissioners themselves." *Appeal to the World*, 4.

3. Ann Burch (d.1806), wife to William Burch. Writing about this incident, Samuel Adams later offered a rare gender perspective on the British imperial elite:

    > It has been usual for the Commisioners to affect an Apprehension of Danger to themselves and their Families, to serve the purposes they had in View. There is indeed no accounting for the real Fears of Women and children. The ladies however can sometimes vie with their husbands in Intrigue, and are thoroughly vers'd in the Art even of *political* Appearance. And it is said that *all* are Politicians in this Country: Whether this lady, whom Gov. Bernard has *politely* ushered into the View of the Public, *really* thought herself in Danger or not, it is incumbent on him to show that there were just Grounds for her Apprehensions.

    Appeal to the World, 5.

4. It is possible that the Boston selectmen mentioned in the source note to **No. 599** alerted FB, but more likely that the governor had an informer of consequence among the Whigs.

5. Stephen Greenleaf (1704-95), sheriff of Suffolk County from 1757 to 1776.

6. Hillsborough's copy (CO 5/757, f 67): "Atrociousness".

7. The minute of the Council meeting of 18 Mar. does not adequately reflect the strength of feeling generated by this issue and vented in this letter. Nor does the minute aid identification of the speakers to whom FB refers. The day's proceedings commenced with FB presenting the Council with information about the effigies "exhibited" at Liberty Tree. A debate followed, at the end of which FB put the following question: "whether they apprehended there was any danger of a disturbance in the town in y^e. evening?" The Council answered in the negative, to which FB responded with a second question: "whether they would in time advise him to take any measures for securing ye peace of the town and what?" The Council delivered the unanimous reply that since "there is no danger of any disturbance, they do not think any measures necessary to be taken for that purpose." CO 5/827, f 41. Samuel Adams later asked "where could be the Danger of . . . actual Violence, when some of the Inhabitants themselves had taken down the Effigies, with at least the tacit Consent of the whole Community[?]" *Appeal to the World*, 7.

8. Hillsborough: "preservation of the Peace of the Town."

9. **No. 599**.

10. On 18 March 1768. CO 5/827, f 41.

11. On this point Harbottle Dorr added the following annotation to his copy of *Letters to the Ministry* (1st ed.): "Truth is sometimes extorted even from the Devil!" MHS catalogue reference E187, f 844.

12. The British Coffee House. The other inn mentioned here was probably the Bunch of Grapes Tavern, frequented by leading Whigs and province lawyers. Both were situated in King Street.

13. Presumably Williams declared that he was armed.

14. "This is Painting indeed, much beyond the Life: but Mr. Bernard has the Art in Perfection." Gen. Thomas Gage, Adams noted correctly, later described the incident as "trifling," but without acknowledging the context: Gage was explaining to Hillsborough that the term was used by "Those who would justify or rather palliate the proceedings of the people here." *Appeal to the World*, 9; *Copies of Letters from Governor Bernard to Hillsborough*.

15. Temple was the exception.

16. *Bernard Papers*, 2: 324, 332, 339-340.

17. See source note to **No. 582**.

18. On this wider issue see Reid, *In a Defiant Stance*.

601 | To the Earl of Shelburne

N° 9

Boston Mar 21. 1768

My Lord

In my last letter[1] I omitted giving your Lordship an account of the meetings of the Merchants &c within the time I was describing, as I reserved it for a separate letter: as the two subjects are not necessarily connected & I cant say how far they are really so. These proceedings however so immediately followed a particular transaction that it is necessary to begin the Narrative with that.

About the middle of febry[2] one Malcolm (a little trader, who about 18 months before made himself famous by a Violent & riotous resistance to the Custom house officers endeavouring to search his house for uncustomed goods, of which there is a Very full Account in your Lordship's office)[3] expecting a Schooner laden with Fyal[4] Wines to come in, asked an Officer of the Customs, what indulgence he might expect in regard to the duties. The Officer answered him, none at all; he must pay the whole duties; Malcolm replied, he was glad he knew what he had to trust to. Some days after the Schooner came in & was ordered to anchor among the Islands 5 miles below the Town. From thence the Cargo consisting, as is said, of above 60 pipes of Wine was landed in the night & carried in drays to different cellars, each load being guarded by a party of Men with clubs. This business employed a Number of Men the greatest part of the night & was as notorious, by the Noise it occasioned for many hours together, as if it had been done at noon day. The lading of the Schooner was also publickly known & talked of long before She arrived, She appeared plainly when She came up to Town by well known marks to have been lightened a yard or more, & was evidently too light to bear the Sea. Nevertheless the Master went to the Custom house & swore that She came from Surinam in ballast & had landed nothing since She left that Port.

Two or three days after, this Malcolm procured a meeting of some Merchants & traders at which he presided. Their Deliberations were Sanguine & full of high pretensions: but nothing was determined upon, but to call a general Meeting of the Merchants on fryday Mar 4. This may be said to be the first movement of the Merchants against the Acts of parliament: all the proceedings before were carried on at town meetings,[5] & were rather ^upon^ refinements of policy than concern for Trade. There never was less reason for the Merchants to complain of the regulations of trade than at present; there never was a greater plenty of Money or a more apparent Ballance of trade in their favor; of which the State of Exchange with London, which now is & for a long time has been at par is an irrefragable Evidence.

However The Merchants are at length dragged into the Cause; their intercourse & Connection with the politicians & the Fear of opposing the Stream of the people have at length brought it about against the Sense of an undoubted Majority both of members property & weight. Accordingly the Result of this meeting was that a Subscription for not importing any English goods, except for the fishery ^for 18 months^, should be prepared & carried round the Town; & a Committee was appointed for that purpose. This was the same night that the little mob with the Drum passed by the Town house.

Upon the Subscription Paper first going round the Town It met with no great Success: a great many declined it; as indeed it cannot fail being ruinous to the generality of traders. Upon this all Engines were set to work to increase the Subscription: Some were told they would be obnoxious to the lower sort of people, others were threatned with the resentment of the higher. Some were made affraid for their persons & houses; others for their trade & credit. By such means the Subscription has been filled by numbers who if at liberty would protest against the force put upon them & neither intend nor can comply with the terms. And there are still remaining Enough of the most respectable Merchants in the Town non subscribers, to defeat this Scheme, even if the subscribers were to keep to their promise: and it never can be carried into execution, without the interposition of the Mob. But it is scarce a Secret with any of them that the cheif intent of this Subscription is to raise an alarm among the Merchants & Traders of Great ^Britain^ & by means of popular discontent there to oblige the parliament to submit to their Terms in America. As this Game has been once before plaid with success, it is no Wonder that they have great dependence upon it Now.[6]

There is such Confidence in the Success of this Combination, that the Business of Manufactures seems to be dropped; at least it is not now talked of.[7] I cannot be answerable for all America; it is possible that in Pensylvania, which advances much faster in Acts than other Colonies there may be some rivalry with Great Britain.[8] But for New England to threaten the Mother Country with Manufactures, is the idlest Bully that ever was attempted to be imposed upon sensible people. Notwithstanding all the puffs flung in the Newspapers, there is not as yet the least apparent advance of any one Work. They have neither materials nor hands nor inclination for such works. All the Wool in the province would not make 2 pair of stockings a year for each person. It allways has been worked up, cheifly in the families where it grows, & there used, not being fit for any Market: All the advantage being its being done in the dead time of the Year, when there is no Work to be done out of doors. There is no probability of any increase or improvement in this than what has been time out of mind. There has been an attempt to make nails; it is found they cannot be brought within a saleable price: paper, there is but one Mill, that can scarce keep itself going. There is now an attempt to set up a

Manufactory of Duck or Sail cloath at Boston, in order to employ the poor who are so ill managed as to be a great burthen: If that should succeed, it can only be by the Town making good the loss in the price of labour & thereby gaining something in aid of the poor rate. And this, as it is a foreign Manufacture, cannot hurt Great Britain. Whatever therefore may be the Motives to induce Great Britain to Submit to the present advanced claims of the Americans, let not the Fear of American Manufactories be one of them.[9]

And indeed a temporary Stoppage of the importation of British goods to America, if it could be done without alarming the Manufactors, would be advantageous to the British Trade as things stand now in this part of America. For the English Merchants have brought themselves under difficulties in regard to their American Debtors, which the peaceable & Submissive conduct of the Americans, if it had happened to be so, would not have removed. Formerly The Merchants of Boston were of the same nature with those of London, importers & dealers by whole-sale & by no means retailers. Then the Merchants of London dealt for small profit that the Merchants of Boston might have a reasonable profit in retailing. But for some years past the London Merchants for the sake of advancing their profits, have got into dealing immediately with the retailers, & have thereby abolished the distinction of Merchants at Boston: so that at present ev'ry Merchant is a Shop keeper & ev'ry Shop keeper is a Merchant. Hence instead of dealing with respectable & creditable houses, the London Merchants are engaged in a great number of little Shops; and for the sake of the advantage derived from treating with people who cannot dispute the terms prescribed to them, they have extended their credit beyond all bounds of prudence, & have sacrificed Security to profit; and they have also glutted this Country with goods much more than its real Wants ^required^.[10] It must therefore be expected that whenever a Ballance is struck between the traders of Great Britain & New England, there will be a considerable deficiency in the latter; not from the Country itself, for that is in as good Ability as ever it was, but from particular persons who have been credited beyond their powers & resources. It is therefore the Intrest of Great Britain that this ballance should be struck as soon as may be; and a Suspension or other regulation of the importation is one necessary Step towards striking such a ballance. What is said here of Boston & New England is generally applicable to the other Colonies, tho' I can't exactly say how far to each. The Conclusion of this Detail is that if the British Merchants should incur Any great losses by their trade to America they ought not to be imputed to the parliament or the administration of Great Britain, but to their own indiscretion, in giving too great credit to America & overstocking its markets.

To illustrate the foregoing Narrative, I send your Lordship their own Account of the meeting on the 18th with a list of the toasts, as usual. There is also in the same paper a piece containing a Sneer upon the late proceedings of parliament;[11]

the whole Wit of which arises from the common assertion that the parliament has no right to impose Duties in the American Colonies – no more than they have in portugal. In the same is also the Letter to your Lordship, as the Address to the King is in another of the same papers & in others.[12] This shews that the cheif Use of these Letters is to inflame the other Colonies: for unless they preferred this Service to the obtaining redress from home, they could not be so deficient in duty respect & even common civility, as to publish in America an Address to the King & a Letter to his Minister of State, before they could have come to hand in England. Heretofore ^even^ a complimentary Address to the King never used to be published in America, till it appeared there in the Gazette. In short, your Lordship may depend upon it that Nothing less than the abolition of all Acts imposing Duties, is proposed. When that is done the transition to all other Acts of Parliament will be Very short & easy.

I am, with great respect, My Lord, Your Lordships most obedient
and most humble Servant

Fra Bernard

The right honble The Earl of Shelburne

ALS, RC   CO 5/757, ff 74-77.

Endorsed: Boston March 21. 1768 Gov[r] Bernard (N[o]. 9) R 3[d]. June. A.13.   Enclosed copies of the *Boston Gazette* and the *Boston Post-Boy and Advertiser*, 21 Mar. 1768, CO 5/757, ff 78-80. Variants of the letter: CO 5/893, ff 50-53 (dupALS, RC); CO 5/766, ff 160-168 (L, RLbC); BP, 6: 288-295 (L, LbC); *Letters to the Ministry* (1st ed.), 17-19; *Letters to the Ministry* (repr.), 22-25. Hillsborough replied to the RC with **No. 622**. The duplicate, received on 24 Jun., was considered by the Board of Trade on 6 Jul. 1768. *JBT*, 13: 34. Extracts of the letter together with the enclosures were laid before both houses of Parliament on 28 Nov. 1768. HLL: American Colonies Box 1. A copy may have been sent to Gen. Gage under cover of **Appendix 4**.

---

1. Dated 19 Mar. 1768. CO 5/757, ff 66-71.

2. The exact date is uncertain. The passage of time that elapsed between Daniel Malcom's approach to Inspector General John Williams (the unnamed "Officer of the Customs" mentioned) and the merchants' meeting of 4 Mar. is signified by two connected phrases: "Some days after" and "Two or three days after" that. In total, perhaps a week separated the two events. In referring to their memorial of 12 Feb., the commissioners of Customs noted that ". . . On the next day" Malcom's vessel arrived in the harbor; and that night the sixty pipes of wine were unloaded. **Appendix 3**.

3. See **No. 504**, *Bernard Papers*, 3: 232-236.

4. From the Portuguese island of Faial in the Azores archipelago.

5. Nonimportation was first proposed at a town meeting on 28 Oct. 1767, and implemented after a town meeting held on 1 Mar. 1768. See notes 6 and 7 below.

6. [Samuel P. Savage], "A List of the Subscription of Those Gentlemen who are immediately concerned in importing Goods from great Britain, That they will not import any for a year from the date excepting such as are coming this Spring, taken from the Committee,⁵ List as reported March 9ᵗʰ. 1768," Samuel P. Savage II Collection, MHS. Initial responses to the subscription were considered at a merchants' meeting at the British Coffee House on 9 Mar. The agreement was to take effect on 1 Jun. 1768 and remain in force for eighteen months or until the Townshend duties were repealed. One hundred and sixty-six Boston firms were asked to subscribe (over half the total number in the town) but nearly one-third either did not subscribe or stipulated conditions. Nevertheless, by the end of April, only eight firms still refused to sign and thirteen others continued to insist on conditions. Tyler, *Smugglers & Patriots*, 112-113.

7. On 28 Oct., the town had voted to encourage American manufactures and discourage "foreign" imports (including British manufactures). The resolves condemned the "excessive use of Foreign Superfluities" and compiled a list of goods and products for nonimportation: loaf sugar; cordage; anchors; coaches, chaises and carriages; horse furniture; hats, gloves, shoes; ready-made cloathing; sole leather; sheathing and deck nails; gold and silver thread; lace; gold and silver buttons; wrought plate; diamond stone and paste ware; snuff; mustard; broad cloths above 10s. per annum; cambric; cheese; gauze; glue; lawns; linseed oil; malt liquor; "millenary ware"; muffs, furs, and tippets; pewterer's hollow ware; silk "of all kinds for Garments"; silk and cotton velvets; starch; stays; silversmith's and jeweller's wares. The resolves further urged domestic production of those goods subject to the Townsend duties which could be produced in the colonies: glass and paper. *Reports of the Record Commissioners of Boston*, 16: 220-224. The subscription attracted 665 signatories, men and women from across the social spectrum, for which see the printed copy with signatures in the Houghton Library, AB7.B6578.767w, at http://pds. lib.harvard.edu/pds/view/46431739 (accessed 19 Aug. 2013).

8. The New York merchants adopted nonimportation on 27 Aug. 1768, the agreement taking effect on 1 Nov.; the Philadelphia merchants approved nonimportation on 6 Feb. 1769.

9. The scheme to convert the town workhouse into a "Manufactory House" was approved at the annual town meeting of 14 Mar. In October, local Whigs and townspeople occupied the building to prevent it being converted into a barracks for British troops. *Reports of the Record Commissioners of Boston*, 16: 239.

10. FB's perceptive observations reflect a significant change in the composition of Boston's mercantile community since the Seven Years' War. The emergence of retailers as importing merchants, sustained by British credit, opened up a major fault line between shopkeepers (many of whom were recently arrived from Britain) and wholesale merchants (including prominent Whigs); the former accused the latter of using nonimportation to drive them from the market in British dry goods. This conflict of interest was at the heart of local disputes over the continuation and enforcement of the nonimportation agreements until the fall of 1770. The best account is Tyler, *Smugglers & Patriots*, 109-138.

11. *Boston Gazette*, 21 Mar 1768, p. 2. "Democritus" offered a satirical piece on the popular British argument that the defense of the colonies alone justified the imposition of taxes, supposing that since the Royal Navy had long protected Portugal, as it had the American Colonies, then Portugal too should be subject to parliamentary taxation.

12. The House of Representatives to Shelburne, 15 Jan. 1768, *Boston Gazette*, 21 Mar. 1768, p. 1. The House's petition to the king of 20 Jan. 1768 was printed in the *Boston Post-Boy and Advertiser*, 21 Mar. 1768.

602 | To Michael Francklin

Boston March 24 1768

S^r.

Upon the Receipt of your Letter of feb^{ry}: 29.[1] I communicated it with its Inclosure to the cheif Justice of this Province & desired him to enable me to answer it effectually. This he engaged to do: but as the Superior Court was then setting, I could not expect it 'till the Business was over. I have now received it & enclose it together with the Papers it refers to & suppose that it will remove the Difficulties your cheif Justice lies under.

I must observe that Writs of Assistance were first granted in this Province by Cheif Justice Sewell many Years ago.[2] Upon cheif Justice Hutchinson coming to the Bench, there was a formal Opposition to the Renewing them after the Demise of the late King, which was prosecuted with such Earnestness, that the hearing lasted 3 Days successively. The Court was unanimous ~~for~~ ^in^ the Opinion for granting them as the Laws then stood.[3]

It is not improbable but that, [as?][4] there is now a Commission of Customs in America, the Form of the Writ may be alterd so as to be made more conformable to that used in England. But no Steps have been taken towards this as yet.

I am &c

The hon Lt Govr Franklin[5]

L, LbC   BP, 5: 260-261.

In handwriting of Thomas Bernard. Enclosure from TH not found.

Lt. Gov. Michael Francklin had evidently sought FB's advice about the correct form a writ of assistance should take. But this letter is also an early indicator of the Customs commissioners' concern about the effectiveness of the writs of assistance, a type of warrant issued to customs officers by the colonial courts enabling them to acquire the assistance of local magistrates when searching for contraband. American merchants were perturbed by the fact that the writ needed to be issued only once to a named customs officer. The officer did not have to reapply to the court (which in Massachusetts was the Superior Court) as he was obliged to do for other writs and for a stated period; writs of assistance remained in effect until the monarch's death.[6] Moreover, the writ of assistance enabled the officer to search any premises without requiring him to state the reasons for the search or the objects being sought (though it did not, as some critics alleged, grant the holder "unlimited power"). The legality of the writs was hotly contested in Massachusetts in two hearings before the Superior Court, in Feb. and Nov. 1761, with James Otis Jr. and Oxenbridge Thacher famously contesting the legality of the instrument in the American Colonies.[7] When that failed, Otis led the House of Representatives in a vain attempt to substitute a provincial warrant that FB, who vetoed the bill, regarded as "wholly inefficacious."[8] The writs of assistance remained in force, a much-hated instrument of royal authority, deriving from three English statutes and issued with the full force of English law.[9] Nevertheless, writs were resisted every time smugglers staged a rescue of goods seized by customs officers or a crowd hampered a search. Daniel Malcom's success in preventing law officers searching his premises in Sept. 1766 illustrated how a single trader supported by a defiant crowd might defy the letter of the law.[10] As FB reveals, the commissioners of Customs were complaining about their officers being refused the writs by colonial courts. In June, the commissioners delivered a report condemning the obstructionism of courts in Pennsylvania and Connecticut.[11] They were anxious to protect their officers from damage suits (often brought against them by the merchants they had been pursuing under the writ, as had been the case in Massachusetts during the early 1760s). Subsequent generations of Americans came to venerate colonial resistance to the writs as being symbolic of the colonists' struggle for Liberty, whereas for government officials at the time resistance was both a cause and symptom of the weakness of imperial power.

---

1. Not found.

2. Stephen Sewall (1702-60), chief justice of the Massachusetts Superior Court, 1752-60.

3. The "3 Days" to which FB referred was probably the first of two hearings by the Massachusetts Superior Court in 1761 concerning the legality of the writs of the assistance. The first was prompted by petitions from Thomas Lechmere, surveyor general of Customs, and officers including Charles Paxton, whose applications for writs were being challenged by the Boston merchants. The hearing commenced on Tuesday 24 Feb., with Jeremiah Gridley speaking for the Crown and James Otis Jr. and Oxenbridge Thacher for the merchants. Judgment was delayed while Chief Justice Hutchinson sought guidance and advice from Britain. The second hearing took place on Wednesday 18 Nov. with the Court ruling in favor of the writ.

4. Obscured by tight binding.

5. Michael Francklin (1733-83) had been appointed lieutenant governor of Nova Scotia in 1766 and had assisted FB and his partners obtain land grants in the St. Croix Bay area.

6. King George II died on 25 Oct. 1760.

7. For detailed accounts and analysis of the legal arguments see *Legal Papers of John Adams*, 2: 106-146; Daniel R. Coquillette and Neil Longley York, eds., *Portrait of a Patriot: The Major Political and Legal Papers of Josiah Quincy Junior. Vol. 4. The Law Reports, Part One (1761-1765)*, 194-205. On the political and legal contexts see Maurice Henry Smith, *The Writs of Assistance Case* (Berkeley, 1978), 17-40, 95-148, and passim.

8. **No. 99**, *Bernard Papers*, 1: 194.

9. 12 Car. 2, c, 19 (1660), 13 & 14 Car. 2, c. 11 (1662); 7 & 8 Will. 3, c. 22 (1696).

10. **No. 504**, ibid, 3: 232-235.

11. American Board of Customs to the Treasury, 3 Jun. 1768, T 1/465, ff 81-102. The Board supplied the Treasury with further reports, filed in T 1/485, ff 306-309.

603 | *From the Earl of Hillsborough*

(N°. 6.)

Duplicate

Whitehall April 4th, 1768.

Sir,

I have received, and laid before The King, your Letters to the Earl of Shelburne, dated the 21st and 30th January, and 3[d] of February 1768, which you have marked (I presume on Account of the Commencement of a new year) 1, 2, and 3.[1]

His Majesty entirely approves your Conduct, in Relation to the Proceedings of the House of Representatives for preparing a Representation (which they presume to stile a Remonstrance)[2] against some late Acts of Parliament; at the same Time His Majesty does very much disapprove those Proceedings, and consider the Assembly's Refusal of all Communication with You upon this Occasion to be as irregular, as it was disrespectful to the Person and Office of His Governor.[3]

I entirely agree with you in Opinion as to the Impropriety of allowing the Assemblies in the Colonies to pass by their Governors in presenting Representations to His Majesty or any of His Ministers; nor do I believe that The King will allow any to be received which shall be presented in that manner. That which is the Subject of your Letter has not yet been offered to me; if it should be offered, I shall think it my Duty not to receive it; in the first Place, because it has not been first communicated to You, and, in the next, because M[r]. DeBerdt is not the regular Agent of the Colony.

At the same Time that The King cannot but disapprove the Proceedings in this Case, it is with great Pleasure and Satisfaction His Majesty observes the Account You give in your two subsequent Letters of the Temper and Disposition of the Assembly,[4] in the Case of the Proposition for offering a Correspondence with the other Governments on the Subject of their Deliberations.

The Manner, in which that Proposition was received and rejected, does Honor to the very great Majority which appeared against it; and The King considers it as one very good Effect of your commendable Endeavours to convince the People, that their true Interest lies in a due Subordination to the Laws of this Kingdom.

I am, with great Truth and Regard, Sir, your most obedient humble Servant

Hillsborough.

Governor Bernard

dupLS, RC   BP, 11: 163-166.

Endorsed by FB: Earl of Hillsborough d Ap 4 1768 r Aug 20 Upon a proposed Remonstrance of this Assembly _   Variants: CO 5/765, ff 4-5 (L, LbC); CO 5/757, ff 26-27 (L, Copy). Extracts were laid before both houses of Parliament on 28 Nov. 1768. HLL: American Colonies Box 1.

While Hillsborough was concerned by the procedural irregularities surrounding the adoption of the House of Representatives' petition, he was alarmed by the colonists' increasingly strident arguments against the Townshend Acts, notably in John Dickinson's *Letters from a Farmer in Pennsylvania*.[5] The Townshend Acts were implemented, however, unlike the Stamp Act, though this letter acknowledged that FB was facing sustained opposition with dwindling political support. Yet Hillsborough's next letter to FB (**No. 608**), prompted by news of the Massachusetts Circular Letter, was a major policy document obliging FB to challenge the House.

1. The first two are **Nos. 581** and **585**. The third of FB's out-letters to Shelburne was dated 2 Feb. not 3 Feb., CO 5/757, f 24.

2. FB was evidently unsettled by the term, given its historical associations with the English Parliament's Grand Remonstrance of 1641 which listed their many grievances with King Charles I and advocated a program of reform for both Church and State, and which the king opposed.

3. Hillsborough refused to present the petition to the king. See **No. 712**n6, *Bernard Papers*, 5: 117.

4. **Nos. 589** and **591**, dated 18 Feb. and 20 and 22 Feb.1768, respectively.

5. Thomas, *Townshend Duties Crisis*, 78-81.

604 | To Nathaniel Ropes

Boston Ap 9 1768

S[r]:

Your Letter came to me at a Time when I was very unfit for Business.[1] However I communicated it and Col. Pickman's[2] Letter to one of the Comissioners; who has since been with me and told me that the superseding M[r] Nutting[3] is entirely a mistake which will be set right very soon. In the mean Time M[r] Nutting need be under no Concern: for he has been so well recommended to the Board that there is much more probability of an Addition being made to his Former appointments than their being diminished. And I am authorised to ~~tell~~ ^assure^ you that it will be proposed, when this Matter is redressed to make his Appointment more beneficial to him than it has hitherto been.

I am S[r] &c.

The Honble N. Ropes Esq[4]

This you will please to communicate to Col Pickman

L, LbC   BP, 5: 258.

In handwriting of Thomas Bernard. Minor emendations not shown.

---

1. Ropes's letter has not been found. FB's incapacity was owing to the death of his son Shute, on 5 Apr. See the source note to **No. 605.**

2. Benjamin Pickman (1708-73) was a wealthy Salem merchant and colonel of the militia.

3. John Nutting (1739-1800), originally of Cambridge, was a carpenter by trade and a master builder of some renown by the time of the Revolution, employing some fifty men. He was evidently seeking some redress from the American Board of Customs. A future Loyalist, Nutting nevertheless tried to live out the war peacefully in Salem, but was obliged to leave after protests by angry neighbors in 1775, and he played a leading role in the failed British attempt to establish the Loyalist colony of New Ireland in Maine, between 1778 and 1780. Samuel Francis Batchelder, "Adventures of John Nutting, Cambridge Loyalist," *Proceedings of the Cambridge Historical Society* 5 (1910): 55-98.

4. Nathaniel Ropes (1724-74) had been a member of the Council since 1761 and chief justice of the Essex County superior court since 1766.

605 | *From Lord Barrington*

Cavendish Square April 16. 1768.

Dear Sir,

I was yesterday favour'd by several Letters from you, and as the Packett sets out this Evening I have not time to answer any of them as I wish: I have indeed scarce been able to read them; for the same conveyance brought me some material pub-lick Dispatches which require answers, and I have only a few hours to write them. I cannot however suffer this days Post to go, without carrying my acknowlegments of your kind Attention to me, and of the material information you send me.

Three of your Letters dated the 28th. 26th of January and the 20th of Feb: are duplicates.[1] One of them contains a very ingenious but in my poor opinion imprac-ticable plan for representing the Colonies in Parliament.[2] I acquainted you with my opinion on that Subject by last Packett.[3] I then knew how such a proposal however right would be received on this side the Water, and the Act of Assembly dated feb 11th. shews how much it would be abhor'd on your side, at least in your Govern-ment, so we must put that Plan entirely out of the Question.[4]

I see with Grief, but not with surprize, the open attempts towards independency making in New England & I conclude the other northern Colonies. A man must have been blind who did not foresee that consequence, from the repeal of the Stamp Act. Things are coming apace to crisis: My friend Lord Hillsborough will have his hands full, but for the sake of the publick I am glad America is in his hands. He has prudence firmness & temper: The times want them all.[5]

I am persuaded you are in the right in your dispute with the Assembly; but that dispute makes it eligible for *you*, (tho' not for this Country) that you should be removed to a better Government; especially as no steps are taking towards granting a fixt salary to the Governors of the Northern Colonies. I will watch every Circumstance that can make for your benefit, and your Letter dated 9th. february[6] ~~will~~ ^has^ informed me of your wishes. I am with great truth & esteem & with my best Comps. to my Cousins

Dear Sir Your Excellency's Most faithful & obedient humble Servant

Barrington

PS.

In my hurry I had forgot to acknowlege your Letter of the 4th. March[7] which is of the most serious importance. The contents will not be neglected by me & I will make the proper use of them without *committing* the writer so as to hurt him.

ALS, RC   BP, 11: 167-170.

Endorsed: Lord Barrington d Ap 16 1768 r June 15.

Barrington was not a member of the cabinet, but in rejecting FB's "Plan" for American representation in Parliament (**No. 584**),[8] presumed or knew that such a proposal had no appeal to ministers. Hillsborough was already in discussion with the cabinet about fashioning a response to the Massachusetts Circular Letter (news of which had just been received).[9] Moreover, Barrington's disappointing news that the Chatham administration was not inclined to pay governors a salary out of the Townshend duties was confirmed by **No. 610**, which FB received on 20 Aug.

1. **Nos. 584** and **583**, and BP, 6: 94-96, respectively.

2. **No. 584**.

3. **No. 597**.

4. The passage of the House of Representatives' circular letter to the speakers of the colonial assemblies, 11 Feb 1768, *JHRM*, 44: 157-158.

5. This is probably an allusion to Cicero's famous declamation in the first oration against Catiline. "O *tempora, o mores!*" *Orationes In Catilinam*, 1.1.

6. This is an error for FB's letter of 7 Feb. **No. 587**.

7. **No. 592**.

8. The idea of American representation in Parliament was more popular in Britain than Barrington implies. Thomas Pownall was probably its most prominent advocate following discussion in *The Administration of the American Colonies* (4th ed. 1768).

9. See the source note to **No. 608**.

606 | To Lord Barrington

Boston Apr: 20 1768

My Lord

I take this Opportunity to inform your Lordship that we've lost our fo^u^rth Son Shute who died at Cambridge, where he was placed for his Studies, on the 5th inst.: after 4 Days Illness in the 16 Year of his Age. I find that a Number of Children does not so much reconcile one to the Loss of one, as might be imagin'd. However I ought not to repine, when I have 9 hopeful Children left.

Yesterday I received your Lordship's Letter recommending M.ʳ Chaumier:[1] Immediately after which I had an Opportunity of shewing my Desire of serving him by removing some difficulties in the Way of his obtaining an Indulgence from the Board of Customs, which I hope has been effectually done.

Both the Mails of Janry & Febry are still due, tho the latter should have been in by this Time. I have no Advice in an Official Way of the Appointment of Lord Hillsborough: so I am now in an Interval between the closing my Correspondence with Ld Shellburne, & opening one with L.ᵈ Hillsborough.[2] The Officers of the Crown & Friends of the British Government are now in a distressed State, hoping that, but not knowing how or when, they shall be relieved.

In a former Letter I proposed that I should have a discretionary Leave to come home.[3] Altho Things are very much alter'd since I wrote that Letter, yet it still becomes very advisable to the Government, & desirable to me, that I should have leave to come to England. I must run a Risk in it: But the Times are growing so bad, that I am not like to have any Choice in it. The good Inclinations of the Ministry towards me, I am satisfied will have no good Effect untill I can have an Interview with them. As soon as the Mail comes in, I will write more fully to your Lordship upon these Subjects; in the mean Time I could wish that the Purpose of obtaining a discretionary Leave for my coming home might be pursued.

I am &c

The Right honble L.ᵈ Visc.ᵗ: Barrington

L, LbC BP, 6: 106-107.

In handwriting of Thomas Bernard.

In this letter, FB acknowledges his distress at the death of his son Shute (b.26 Jul. 1752), on Tuesday 5 Apr. 1768, after "a short Illness of four days." He was "intern'd" at Cambridge on the Friday following, probably at the Old Burying Ground. *Boston Post-Boy and Advertiser*, 11 Apr. 1768. Little is known of Shute Bernard, including the cause of his death. He was residing at Cambridge when he died, "where he was placed for his Studies," FB noted; this was probably a reference to his attendance at Harvard College.[4] Shute's passing coincided with a watershed in FB's dialogue with the secretary of state; henceforth FB communicated directly with the earl of Hillsborough.

1. This may be a reference to Barrington's letter of 8 Jan. which could have been carried by Robert Chamier, who was appointed surveyor and searcher at the Boston Customhouse. BP, 11: 111-114. Robert Chamier was probably a kinsman of Anthony Chamier (1725-80), a financial adviser to the British government. Connected by marriage to Thomas Bradshaw (1733-74), secretary to the Treasury from 1767, Anthony Chamier acquired a succession of government positions with the assistance of Barrington, whom he served as deputy secretary-at-war 1772-75.

2. FB's last letter to Shelburne was dated 21 Mar. 1768 (**No. 601**), and his first to Hillsborough 15 May (**No. 611**).

3. **No. 587**

4. Shute Bernard's name has not been found in the Overseer's Records at Harvard Archives, though at fifteen years-old he would have been of age to enter the college. His older brother Thomas had graduated in 1767. For age profiles of graduates see Conrad Edick Wright, *Revolutionary Generation: Harvard Men and the Consequences of Independence* (Amherst, 2005), 14.

607 | To Thomas Pownall

Boston Ap. 20 1768

Dear S^r:

I have made myself severely censured by myself for so long neglecting to acknowledge my Sense of your Kindness in your Letter of Sep 3.[1] I was desirous to write at Leisure & many Things have happened upon that Account as well as others which have occasioned my postponing it from Day to Day; untill it has become a Burden upon my Conscience.

Before I received your kind Advice I had begun to act upon your Plan. I have kept wholly upon the defensive for a year & a half. But I have to do with such a wicked Set of People, that they won't allow a Governor to be neutral in their Disputes with Great Britain, but expect that he shall Side with them in their Pretensions against the Parliament. It is in Vain therefore, untill all the Disputes with the Parliament are over for a Governor (in these Parts at least) to endeavour to be popular. Besides, the independent Salary which would greatly increase the Powers of Government, seems to be postponed to latter Lammas.[2] I know not which is the greatest, the Encouragement which that Act gave to the Friends of Government, or the discouragement they have received from the non Execution of it. Certain it is that the Kings Cause has suffered greatly by the Delay of carrying that Act into

Execution: From hence the Opposers of Government have received great Assurances that they shall be able to overturn that Act.

You judge perfectly right of the Expediency of giving Representations^ves^ to the Americans. Above two years ago I recommended that (not Officially) as a very advisable Measure, at which Time others might have been pursued with good Effect.[3] At present if the Question was to be put, I would pronounce it to Be the only Measure left to prevent a Seperation of America from Great Britain. It will indeed be attended with Difficulties; but at this Time what can be proposed that will not. For the Proof of this read the Farmers Letters, which will now form the American Political Creed; read the Letters from our House; & see how they can be effectually answered but by giving them Representations which pulls up all their Pretensions by the Root. I could carry this Subject to a great Length, if I had time, but must stop for the present.

I will take Care to have every Thing done at S[t] Croix in the best Manner consistent with Œcononony.[4] You mentioned D[r]: Franklin as a Partner.[5] I know not how this is; I have never received a Warrant for him; nor do I know of any Grant made to him: and I have allways understood the Partnership to be confined to the Bay of S[t] Croix. If there is any Thing left unlocated there besides the 120,000 Acres, the Lieut: Gov[r]: of Nova Scotia is my very good Friend[6] and will do any Thing in his Power to assist our Partnership.

All our Disappointments in wild Hemp[7] have arose from the Indians: Nothing has being left undone by me or Col Goldthwait.[8] All I was able to get last Summer was a little Seed, which I shall sow & send you some of the produce: you will perceive I write in a Hurry: my public Business is so increasing by the Disorders of the Country that I am scarce ever out of one.

I am &c

Tho Pownall Esq[r]:

L, LbC BP, 6: 107-110.

In handwriting of Thomas Bernard.

Thomas Pownall, the former Massachusetts governor and one of the most intelligent commentators on American affairs, had evidently advised FB to be less outspoken in his dealings with the assembly and to remain "upon the defensive." Such a plan might have worked had the factions been equal in terms of power and numbers, as they were during Pownall's administration, 1758-60. But, as FB pointed out, there had been a major realignment since then, and the Whigs, now in the ascendancy, were pressing to dominate the executive at every opportunity. The two governors were not close friends, though Pownall's experience had been instructive during the early days of FB's administration. FB evidently admired his predecessor's *The Administration of the Colonies* (London, 1764), which he read critically. Pownall's proposal for a reformed imperial parliament containing American representatives, advanced in the fourth edition of the *Administration* (1768), harmonized with FB's proposal for American representation mooted in the "Principles of Law and Polity" (1764). But Pownall, an MP for Tregony, Cornwall (1767-74), probably lost FB's respect with his occasional speeches in the House of Commons defending American liberty.[9]

1. Not found.

2. Lammas was the annual harvest festival of 1 Aug., but "latter Lammas" is here meant ironically as a humorous phrase for "a day that will never come". *OED*.

3. **No. 413**, *Bernard Papers*, 2: 413-419.

4. Thus in manuscript; a scribal error for "Œconomy."

5. Pownall probably discussed the role of Benjamin Franklin (1706-90) in his letter of 3 Sep. 1767 and in a letter that FB received previously, between Jan. and Mar. 1766. See **No. 456**, *Bernard Papers*, 3: 123-124.

6. Michael Francklin (1733-83).

7. See **No. 454**, *Bernard Papers*, 3: 127-130.

8. Thomas Goldthwait (1718-79), the commander of Fort Pownall, had aided FB's enquiries in trying to source hemp seeds from the Penobscot tribe.

9. Nicolson, *The 'Infamas Govener'*, 93-99; *Bernard Papers*, 2: 481n1 and n3; Schutz, *Thomas Pownall,* 195-214.

608 | *From the Earl of Hillsborough*

(Nº. 7)

Whitehall. April the 22d: 1768.

Sir

I have received, and laid before the King, Your Letters to the Earl of Shelburne Nˢ. 4. 5. & 6.[1] with the Inclosures.

It gives great Concern to His Majesty to find that the same Moderation, which appeared by Your Letter (Nº: 3)[2] to have been adopted at the Beginning of the Session in a full Assembly, had not continued, and that, instead of that Spirit of Prudence and Respect to the Constitution, which seemed at that Time to influence the Conduct of a large Majority of the Members, a thin House at the End of the Session should have presumed to revert to, and resolve upon, a Measure of so inflammatory a Nature, as that of writing to the Other Colonies on the Subject of their intended Representations against some late Acts of Parliament.

His Majesty considers this Step as evidently tending to create unwarrantable Combinations to excite an unjustifiable Opposition to the constitutional Authority of Parliament, and to revive those unhappy Divisions and Distractions which have operated so prejudicially to the true Interests of Great Britain and the Colonies.

After what passed in the former Part of the Session, and after the declared Sense of so large a Majority, when the House was full, His Majesty cannot but consider this as a very unfair Proceeding, and the Resolutions ^taken^ thereupon to be contrary to the real Sense of the Assembly, and procured by Surprize, and therefore it is the King's Pleasure, that so soon as the general Court is again assembled at the Time prescribed by the Charter, You should require of the House of Representatives, in his Ma^js^ty's Name, to rescind the Resolution which gave Birth to the Circular Letter from the Speaker, and to declare their Disapprobation of, & Dissent to that rash and hasty Proceeding.[3]

His Majesty has the fullest Reliance upon the Affection of His good Subjects in the Massachusett's Bay, and has observed with Satisfaction that Spirit of Decency and Love of Order which has discovered itself in the Conduct of the most considerable of It's Inhabitants, and therefore His Majesty has the better Ground to hope that the Attempts made by a desperate Faction to disturb the public Tranquillity will be discountenanced, and that the Execution of the Measure recommended to You will not meet with any Difficulty.

If it should, and if notwithstanding the apprehensions which may justly be entertained of the ill Consequence of a Continuance of this factious Spirit, which seems to have influenced the Resolutions of the Assembly at the Conclusion of the last Session, the new Assembly should refuse to comply with His Majesty's reasonable Expectation; It is the King's Pleasure that you should immediately dissolve them, & transmit to me, to be laid before His Ma^js^ty, an Account of their Proceedings thereupon, to the End that His Majesty may, if he thinks fit, lay the whole Matter before His Parliament, that such Provisions as shall be found necessary may be made to prevent for the future a Conduct of so extraordinary & unconstitutional a Nature.

As it is not His Majesty's Intention that a faithful Discharge of Your Duty should operate to Your own Prejudice, or to the Discontinuance of any necessary Establishments, proper Care will be taken for the Support of the Dignity of Government.

I am, with great Truth & Regard, Sir, Your most obedient humble Servant

Hillsborough

LS, RC   BP 11: 171-174.

Endorsed by FB: [_ _ _][4] Earl of Hillsborough r June 15 1768 d Ap 22 directing to dissolve the Assembly if they refuse to rescind &c[5]   Variants: BP, 11: 171-174 (LS, RC); CO 5/765, ff 6-8 (L, LbC). The copy presented to the House omitted the salutation, the first sentence, the last two paragraphs of the main text, and the closure. *JHRM*, 45: 68-69. Extracts of the RC were laid before both houses of Parliament on 28 Nov. 1768. HLL: American Colonies Box 1.

Hillsborough learned of the Massachusetts Circular Letter on 15 Apr. and immediately presented it to the cabinet, who, "despite Shelburne's opposition" Peter D. G. Thomas notes, agreed the course of action proposed by Hillsborough.[6] On 21 Apr., Hillsborough sent a circular to the colonial governors (though FB's RC has not survived). He denounced the Massachusetts Circular Letter for its "dangerous and Factious Tendency" to "promote an unwarrantable Combination, & to excite and encourage an open Opposition to, and denial of, the authority of Parliament." He urged governors simply to ignore the Massachusetts letter (though he could not prevent the speakers replying).[7] On 22 Apr., Hillsborough wrote the letter printed here: it was to embroil the governor in a dispute with the House of Representatives over withdrawing retrospectively the vote approving the Massachusetts Circular Letter.

The secretary of state's circular to the colonial governors of 21 Apr. and his letter to FB of 22 Apr. constitute the first major policy initiative since Hillsborough took office. It echoed Shelburne's reaction to the New York Assembly when ministers pushed through the New York Suspending Act of 1767 after the colony had defied the American Quartering Act. While that contest was resolved without recourse to enforcing the act (prohibiting the assembly meeting), it doubtless reinforced Hillsborough's conviction that if confronted the House of Representatives would back down. Historians of British policymaking have contextualized Hillsborough's harder line toward the Americans with reference to anxieties induced by the New York incident, the Wilkes controversy in Britain, and advances in the colonists' constitutional arguments. Hillsborough, moreover, "claimed full personal responsibility" for the policy shift that saw Britain insisting that the vote of the Massachusetts House of 11 Feb. approving the Circular Letter be rescinded immediately.

But it is important also to consider why Hillsborough made it abundantly clear to FB that it was the governor's reports which had convinced the king and his ministers that colonial radicalism was resurgent. Of particular note, is the deflated optimism with which Hillsborough received FB's letters of 20 and 22 Feb. (**No. 591**) and 5 Mar. (**No. 593**). Such an acknowledgement of FB's influence, however, was double-edged, for it underlined that Hillsborough could, at any time, blame the governor's reporting of events for the policy shift. The instruction to have the House rescind the vote, when it arrived, united the House in opposition to the governor and in defiance of Hillsborough. It would be reading too much into this course of events to suggest that Hillsborough anticipated this outcome, though not to suggest that he supposed FB could be made a scapegoat for such an eventuality. In that respect, the administration's subsequent decision to award FB a baronetcy provided additional cover for removing FB from Massachusetts, should opposition escalate, as well as due and proper public recognition of his endeavors to maintain British imperial authority. Barrington was asked to ascertain FB's preferences for a new position (**No. 610**).

FB's account of the House of Representatives' refusal to rescind the Circular Letter is in **No. 638**.

---

1. **Nos. 589**, **591**, and **593**, respectively.

2. Dated Boston, 2 Feb. 1768. CO 5/757, f 24.

3. Annotation: "it is the King's Pleasure . . . Proceeding." This passage is marked by a pencil line in the left margin and lines at the beginning and end of the passage. They may have been added by FB.

4. Obscured by tight binding.

5. The docket description is in the hand of Thomas Bernard and was probably added at a later date.

6. The best account of these deliberations is Thomas, *Townshend Duties Crisis,* 78-83, quotation at 81.

7. The earl of Hillsborough, circular to the colonial governors, Whitehall, 21 Apr. 1768. CO 5/241, f 28.

609 | To Lord Barrington

Boston May 9 1768

My Lord

The Febry Mail is not yet come in: so that at this Time, 4 Months after his Appointment, I have received no Letter from Lord Hillsborough.[1] As upon this Account I must still defer writing to him, I am now aware that I shall not have Time to apply to him for Leave to go to England; so as to expect an Answer in Time to set out soon enough to keep clear of the Winter: and a Winter Voyage in these Seas is to be avoided by all Means possible.

I must therefore beg of your Lordship that I may be favoured with your Lordships Application (with as little Loss of Time as may be) that I may have an Order or Leave to come to England before Winter. An order it will be if the Minister sees the Expediency of calling me to make a Report in Person of the present State of New England; in which Way I am convinced I can be more serviceable to his Majesty than I can by continuing here without real Authority. It seems to me that the Omission of the most proper Means to quiet America, if there has been any such, must be imputed to the Administration having wanted proper Informations of the State of the Country; which for many Reasons cannot be communicated by Letters.

Considering this as a License granted to me, It will still partake of the Nature of a publick Business. For if my Service has received the Approbation with which I have been flattered, I hope it will create a Merit, which will exempt me from being again exposed to the same Dangers, which I so firmly withstood & so happily escaped. In the Winter 65-6, I was sevral Times drove to the very Brink of Deserting my post; & in the Spring following the Lieut: Gov: told me that nothing surprised him more than to see me in this Town at that Time. And if we are to beleive the Heads of the Faction here, if Concessions from Great Britain are not soon made, the next Winter will be as dangerous to Crown Officers as any which have passed.

I have not at present any Dispute of my own or of any Kind but what arises from the Opposition to Great Britain. At present the Faction is cheifly employed in insulting affronting & threatning the Commissioners of the Customs & their Officers. The Instances are gross & notorious: I shall not at present mention Particulars, as I suppose the Commissioners themselves will fully report them to their Superiors.[2] It is sufficient that these Proceedings necessarily involve me in continued Disputes,[3] as I cannot dispense with paying due Respect to Gentlemen bearing Commission under the great Seal & station'd in my Government. And yet this is in a Manner required of me, as the Terms of being ~~loved~~ ^spared^ myself. It therefore seems unavoidable that when they rise against the Commissioners (which they publickly declare they will do, as soon as they learn that their applications to the Government at home are successless) the Governor must be involved in the Dispute & partake ^of^ the Difficulty & Danger.

For these Reasons its well as others, I much desire that I may have leave to come to England next winter. I am sensible that I run a risk of hurting my Family Stock, & much so, if I cannot obtain an appointment under the late Act with an early Commencement. But my Family Will run a much greater risk from my being left exposed to another insurrection, which will undoubtedly be attended with much more mischeif than the former , as it will be accompanied with a desperate Defiance of Great Britain. This Event seems unavoidable if measures are not already taken to prevent it. _ If an Order should be obtained, I beg it may be forwarded with all Expedition, & a duplicate & triplicate by other Ships.

I am &c.

The Right Hon The Ld Vis^t^. Barrington.

PS. May. 12.

Yesterday I recieved my Lord Hillsboroughs first Packet,[4] & as the Ship which is to carry this is to sail to morrow I shall have no time to write Lord Hillsborough except to acknowledge the Reciept of his Letters.[5] I shall probably be able to write upon my subject in about a weeks time: but as the Time of that will be uncertain I shall stand in need of Your Lordships interposition in the same manner as if this Packet had not arrived. And it is the more to be desired as it will be proper to prepare his Lordship for an Address directly from myself; which latter I shall most probably inclose to your Lordship, that you may judge of the propriety of it before it be presented. I should have mentiond before that I have recieved your Lordships Letter of Jan. 8[6] & am obliged to you for your kind information.

secret

As I have a Confidence in the Conveyance of the inclosed, I will venture to add a few Lines, which I should not chuse to trust to the common Post: I am well assured that it is the intention of the Faction here to cause an Insurrection against the Crown Officers, at least of the Custom house, as soon as any Kind of Refusal of their extravagant Demands against Great Britain shall furnish a Pretense for so extraordinary a Step; & that they depend upon being join'd & supported in this by some of the other Colonies. I am advised of this by one of their Party whose name I can never use, as he is not suspected of communing with me.[7] I asked him if they were likely to confine themselves to the Custom House officers, or would extend their operations to the other Crown officers & especially the Governor. His answer was, "if I was Governor Bernard I would get out of the way whenever any Commotion began, especially if it arose from the Expectation or the arrival of regular Troops." The same Person told me they were waiting for the success of their application to other Colonies to join them in an actual opposition. Since this I have learnt that they greatly exult in Advices they have lately recieved from other Colonies. All this is continually confirmed by frequent Declarations that they will do themselves Justice; that they will remove the Commissioners & their officers; that no Pensioner of Great Britain, no, not one that recieves a Stipend from ~~Great Britain~~ thence shall live in this Province; & it has been publickly declared upon Charge that if the Commissioners were not recalled before the beginning; of the Winter, they will be shipped of for England. The Situation of these Gentlemen (& indeed of all the Crown Officers) is become very gloomy; especially as they cant learn from England or New York that any Relief is intended to be sent to protect them from this desperate Gang. I should have observed before, that it cannot be concieved that they would treat the Parliament of Great Britain with the Insolence & Contempt which their News Paper is frequently fill'd with, if they did not mean to set her at Defiance, & dare her to express a resentment. This is the present State of this unhappy distracted Town.

L, LbC   BP, 6: 110-115.

The first two pages of the manuscript are in Thomas Bernard's handwriting and the remainder in FB's. Minor emendations are not shown.

This letter reveals FB's growing exasperation with the American Board of Customs, whose commissioners he was obliged to assist in enforcing the trade laws. "Disputes" arising from the operations of the Customs Board had begun to trouble his administration, notably the commissioners' antagonism toward FB's chief law officer, Jonathan Sewall, the province's attorney general and the advocate general of Vice Admiralty.[8] Nevertheless, FB agreed with the commissioners' aim of trying to persuade Hillsborough to dispatch British Regulars to Boston. "The reducing this Country into good order," he opined, "is now become the most arduous task, that perhaps [*the present*] Administration was ever engaged in." (**No. 611**.) In case their entreaties were successful, FB wanted out of Boston as quickly as possible.

On learning of Hillsborough's appointment as secretary of state for the Colonies, FB began to suppose that he would be allowed leave to return home. Ostensibly he wished to report on the state of the province but in reality hoped to be relocated to another colony or appointed to a position in Britain. Lord Barrington and John Pownall had earlier dissuaded

FB from requesting leave of absence from Hillsborough's predecessors.[9] On this occasion, Barrington relayed FB's concerns to Hillsborough (**No. 665**). FB's hopes of securing leave were raised upon receiving Hillsborough's approbation of his conduct on 11 May (**No. 588**), and, a letter from Barrington on 20 Aug. communicating Hillsborough's promise of a baronetcy; but there was also disappointing news that the administration was not introducing Crown salaries for governors (**No. 610**). FB's expectation of obtaining leave of absence was not dashed until he received, on 18 Sept., Hillsborough's notification of the imminent arrival of British Regulars (**No. 661**).

---

1. The vessel carrying the dispatches arrived on Wednesday 11 May. **No. 611**.

2. See **Appendices 2** and **3**.

3. From here the writing is in FB's hand.

4. **No. 582**.

5. **No. 611**. FB's first substantive letter was **No. 614**.

6. BP, 11: 111-114.

7. Richard Silvester and Nathaniel Coffin are obvious candidates for FB's informer. See **Nos. 732** and **733**, *Bernard Papers*, 5: 171-173. However, the phraseology of the report might equally suggest a prominent Whig willing to discuss the governor's predicament with a third party trusted by both the informer and the governor.

8. See the source note to **No. 678**.

9. **Nos. 499** and **529**, *Bernard Papers*, 3: 218-220, 306-308.

610 | *From Lord Barrington*

Cav: Square May the 9th. 1768.

Dear Sir,

Lord Hillsborough told me the other day that he thought it very right you should receive an immediate mark of the King's favour, and approbation of your Services, and ask'd me whether you would have any objection to being created a Baronet. I said that I never had observed any thing in you which made me conceive you were fond of Titles, and that it cost three or four hundred pounds to be a Baronet; but that I would enquire of you, & let him know your Inclinations. I beleive there is no Government in America which if vacant you might not have, with the greatest care; but at present there is nothing to be disposed of but the Lieutenant Government of Virginia. This I am authorised to offer you, with or without the Title of Baronet.[1] Lord Hillsborough conceives it to be the same as a Government in point of Rank as the Governor never resides, and that in point of value it is better than what you have: In ease & comfort it is infinitely preferable. I do not find there is any prospect of paying the Governors of America out of the funds created last year, and which were then created only to give the late Chancellor of the Exchequer a little momentary eclat.[2] I ask'd Lord H. who he would propose to be Your Successor: He said it would be a great distress to this Country, whenever you left the Massachusets, but that his Views went[3] of Mr. Hutchinson the present Lieut. Governor; and this in the strictest confidence I was allow'd to tell you. In short my dear Sir, You have now the whole before you for consideration, and no man can determine better. My Lord H. has promised me to write you such a private Letter as will authorise you to come hither on leave, if you should chuse it. I am with my best Compliments to all my Cousins

Your Excellency's must faithful & most obedient Servant

Barrington.

ALS, RC   BP, 11: 183-186.

Endorsed: Lord Barrington May 9 1768 r Aug 20.   Variant in BP, 11: 177-180 (dupALS, RC). FB replied on 27 Aug. with **No. 666**.

Once again, Barrington revealed himself as FB's unofficial contact with the British government. On this evidence, Hillsborough was keen to remove FB from Massachusetts, with Virginia the most likely of destinations. It was not that Virginia was any less problematic than Massachusetts, or that the British supposed that FB might somehow quieten the opposition there; rather that the recent death of the lieutenant governor and acting governor, Francis Fauquier, had created an opening and opportunity for Hillsborough to rotate the governors.

The proposal to elevate FB to the English baronetcy probably originated with Hillsborough, and had the full backing of King George III. The official letter of notification supposed honoring FB would "teach the Americans" that loyalty and duty were the "means of obtaining rewards," although Hillsborough's motivation also reflected policy imperatives. (See the source note to **No. 608**.) It was, nevertheless, a signal honor: a baronetcy was hereditary and conferred the honorific title of "Sir." It was inferior to a peerage and usually awarded English notables with estates far outstripping FB's, but ranked above a knighthood which was the highest honor a serving governor might usually expect. Barrington's comment that FB was not overtly "fond of Titles" invites a modern reader to speculate that FB may have harbored some resentment toward the English nobility; however, the viscount was actually alluding to FB's lack of ambition in that direction and his aversion to having to pay substantial transaction fees on the patent for a baronetcy of over £300. FB had had to renew his governor's commission twice at a cost of £800.[4] His request for compensation had been refused, and there was little prospect of the Grafton administration paying his baronet's fees. He waited three months before formally accepting with **No. 682**, without knowing that the administration would pay for all associated costs. The baronetcy was created on 5 Apr. 1769.

1. The Virginia governorship was a sinecure and the governor often an absentee, with the actual duties carried out by the lieutenant governor. The present governor was Sir Jeffrey Amherst (1717-97), but Amherst had left the American Colonies in 1763 without ever attending to his duties as governor, leaving Lt. Gov. Francis Fauquier (1703-68) to continue as acting governor, a role which he had filled since 1758. Fauquier's death on 3 Mar. led to the temporary elevation of John Blair (c.1687-1771). The governorship was eventually filled by the appointment of Norborne Berkeley (c.1717-70), fourth Baron Botetourt; appointed as a full governor on 12 Aug. 1768, Botetourt held the position until his death on 15 Oct. 1770.

2. *OED*: "to make an éclat: to 'make a noise in the world', create a sensation." Townshend's 1767 Revenue Act (7 Geo. 3, c. 46), proposed using the monies raised by trade duties to pay the salaries of Crown officials in the American Colonies. The salaries of the American Board of Customs were paid in this way, but not governors and lieutenant governors (who continued to rely upon annual provincial grants). Important revisions were made to this practice from 1768 onwards, for which see the source note to **No. 766**, *Bernard Papers*, 5: 250-252. The implication that Charles Townshend's policies were primarily dramatic gestures merits further attention from historians in so far as he raised governors' expectations and inadvertently incited colonial anger.

3. Here "went" means "favored," the adjective deriving from a now obscure noun meaning "course of action or plan." *OED*.

4. *Bernard Papers*, 3: 71; Nicolson, *The 'Infamas Govener'*, 171-172; Sir Thomas Bernard, *Life of Sir Francis Bernard* (London, 1790), 170.

611 | To the Earl of Hillsborough

Boston May 12 1768

N° 1

My Lord

Yesterday in the afternoon I received the first dispatches I have been honoured with from your Lordship containing your Letters N° 1 2 & 3[1] with the inclosures. I beg leave to congratulate your Lordship upon your appointment to the American Department;[2] which will afford a large field for the exercise of those abilities by which your Lordship is distinguished: as the reducing this Country into good order is now become the most arduous task, that perhaps Administration was ever engaged in.

I shall be Very punctual in the regular transmission of the Acts & proceedings of this Government.[3] I hope that I have been allways so, & may flatter myself that I may afford some exception to the general Observation of the Neglect of that Duty. I myself have been more apprehensive of my being too voluminous in my letters & transmissions than deficient.

Upon a view of this subject, It cannot escape your Lordship's penetration that the publick Use which has been made of the Letters of Governors &c must tend to destroy that confidentiality in informing the Minister which is so necessary to the Service. The Communicating them to Parliament was unavoidable, tho' that might have been done with more regard to the safety of the writers than was then shown.[4] But the suffering Copies to be taken & published in News papers & pamphlets,[5] has done much hurt to the King's Service, as well by furnishing factious Men with Matter to abuse Government, as by discouraging Governors writing freely for the future. However I have not, as yet, restrained myself upon that account, in confidence that this proceeding has been better considered since than it was at the time.

As there is a Ship now ready to sail, I have only time to send this acknowledgement of the receipt of your Lordship's Letters. I shall take the earliest Opportunity to answer them in full.

I am, with great respect, My Lord, Your Lordship's most obedient
& most humble Servant.

Fra Bernard

The right honble The Earl of Hillsborough

ALS, RC   CO 5/757, ff 88-89.

Endorsed: Boston. May 12th: 1768 Governor Bernard. (N°. 1) R. 24 June. A.14.   Variants: CO 5/766, ff 170-171 (L, RLbC); BP, 6: 295-297 (L, LbC) Hillsborough replied with **No. 653**.

---

1. **No. 582**; circular from the earl of Hillsborough, Whitehall, 23 Jan. 1768. BP, 11: 123-126; **No. 588**.

2. Hillsborough assumed the office of secretary of the state for the Colonies on 21 Jan. 1768. FB knew of the appointment by 21 Feb. See source note to **No. 582**.

3. Hillsborough's second letter had complained of the "Want of complete collections of the Laws of the . . . Colonies" and requested each governor to forward an entire set of provincial laws pertaining to their province. BP, 11: 123. Province Secretary Andrew Oliver had been punctual in observing this requirement. The acts and resolves of the General Court during FB's administration that Oliver sent to Britain are filed in CO 5/778-CO 5/784.

4. FB's correspondence on the Stamp Act riots was presented to Parliament in Jan. 1766 and cited in the House of Lords' debates on the repeal of the Stamp Act. See *Bernard Papers*, 3: 13, 90, 127–130, 151, 153-155.

5. FB is referring to Shelburne's letter, **No. 566**, published in the Boston newspapers, which is discussed in **No. 591**.

612 | *Circular From the Earl of Hillsborough*

Circular (N°: 9.)

Duplicate.

Whitehall. May the 14th. 1768.

Sir,

The Commissioners of His Majesty's Customs in America having represented that their Officers meet with great Obstructions, and are deterred from exerting themselves in the Execution of their Duty;[1] I have it in Command from His Majesty to signify to you His Pleasure, that you do give them all the Assistance and Support in your Power in the Discharge of their respective Offices, & in carrying the Laws of Trade and Revenue into due Execution.

I am, with great Truth & Regard, Sir, Your most obedient humble Servant.

Hillsborough.

Governor of Massachuset's Bay.

dupLS, RC   BP, 11: 181-182.

Endorsed: Earl of Hillsborough Circular No 9 Duplicate d May 14 1768 To assist the Commr^s.   Received c.29 Aug. 1768.[2] Variant in CO 5/241, f 31 (L, LbC).

Hillsborough's directive was not an admonition but an exhortation. Following receipt of the Customs commissioners' memorials to the Treasury highlighting evasions of the trade laws (including **Appendix 2**), the secretary of state for the Colonies had no option but to reiterate governors' responsibilities to provide customs officers with every assistance.

---

1. **Appendix 2** and **No. 599**.
2. According to **No. 668**.

613 | To John Pownall

Boston May 17. 1768

Dear S[r]

I hereby transmit the duplicates of the Acts passed last Session.[1] I dont See any occasion for me to make observations upon any of them. The Liberty I take of rejecting Acts which are in any ways exceptionable makes this service less frequent than It has heretofore been.

I also send you some copies of the proceedings of the Commissaries for Settling the Line between Our province & that of New York.[2] I am to write upon this subject & intend to do it fully: but as We have no Agent,[3] & the Meeting of the new Assembly is so near,[4] I have thought fit to postpone it till We see what will [be][5] done in the appointment of an Agent. In the mean ^time^ I must beg that this Matter may not be brought upon the carpet untill We are ready for the support of our pretension;[6] which is Nothing more than to have that Line established which was reported by the Lords of trade some years ago[7] & has been acquiesced in by our province ever since. This I apprehend cannot well be done without a proper Agent, which may be appointed next Session & may not: for if an improper person should be chosen against the general opinion of the Council, I shall not consent to him. In such case We must make out our defence in the best manner We can.

I am S[r] Your most faithful & obedient Servant

Fra. Bernard

John Pownall Esq[r] Secretary &c.

ALS, RC   CO 5/893, ff 54-55.

Endorsed: *Massachusets*. Letter from Francis Bernard Esq[r] Gov[r]. of Massachusets Bay, to The Secry, dated May 17. 1768, relative to Acts & to Commissaries for settling the boundary Line between that Province & New York Nn 17. Reced Read July 6th. 1768. 1 paper.   Variant in BP, 6: 297-298 (L, LbC). Enclosures: *A Conference between the Commissaries of Massachusetts-Bay and the Commissaries of New-York at New-Haven in the Colony of Connecticut, 1767* (printed by Richard Draper: Boston, 1768), CO 5/893, ff 56-75.

The long-running boundary dispute between Massachusetts and New York had been complicated by land riots and cross-border depredations against squatters conducted by New York landowners. FB had tried to maintain diplomatic momentum and supported the joint commission that the earl of Shelburne insisted be held to resolve the matter. However, as FB notes in this letter, Massachusetts still held to the Board of Trade's view (set down in1757) that it was the Crown's responsibility to settle the boundary line, not the provinces'. The boundary dispute was not resolved until 1773.[8]

THE PAPERS OF GOVERNOR FRANCIS BERNARD

1. See *Acts and Resolves*, 4: 977-994; *JHRM*, 44: 87-214.

2. Read in the House of Representatives, 4 Mar. 1768. *JHRM*, 44: 212.

3. That is, FB refused to recognize the authority of the House-appointed agent, Dennys DeBerdt, who had previously been given responsibility for representing the province in settling the boundary with New Hampshire. *Bernard Papers*, 3: 348.

4. 25 May.

5. Editorially supplied.

6. For an explanation see *Bernard Papers*, 3: 377-378.

7. In 1757. See *Bernard Papers*, 3: 261.

8. See *Bernard Papers*, 3: 31, 192-193, 199–200, 209, 211, 259–260, 378, 336, 343.

614 | To the Earl of Hillsborough

Duplicate

Nº: 2

Boston May 19 1768

My Lord

In your Letter Nº 3[1] your Lordship is pleased to give me Credit for my Service in the Restoration of the Minds of the People here to that Confidence in his Majesty's Government, which it is entitled to. But alas, my Lord, my Merit is confined to earnest Endeavours to bring about that much wish'd for Event favoured by a little Self-flattery at one Time that I had succeeded. At the Time I wrote the Letters mentioned,[2] The Faction had not recovered their Power & I was in hopes they never would. For the first Month of the Winter Session. They behaved decently towards Government, and had not Power enough in the House to carry a Question for this Province taking the lead in an Opposition to the late Acts of Parliament. But indefatigable in Mischief they kept continually tampering with Particulars in Private, untill they had poisoned the Minds of many of the well meaning but ignorant Countrymen, of whom the House is in some Measure composed. Having filled their Imaginations with Fears and Jealousies which they were incapable of judging truly of, they produced the circular Letters Addresses Remonstrances &c which your Lordship ~~has~~ by ^this^ Time has been fully acquainted with. The Friends of Government could do nothing more than to prune these Writings, and cut off the most Offensive Parts, which they did to a Great Degree; tho' perhaps it had been better let alone. Upon this Occasion, as upon others for the same Purposes, their Success and Triumph upon the Repeal of the Stamp-Act was held out as a Precedent for the present Business, and an Incentive to pursue the same Measures, as before; which they say must oblige the Parliament to repeal these Acts also.

It has been a Subject of Wonder how the Faction which harrasses the Town and through it the whole Continent, which is know[n][3] to consist of very few of the lowest kind of Gentry and is directed by 3 or 4 Persons bankrupt in Reputation as well as in Fortune, and equally void of Credit in Character and in Property, should be able to keep in Subjection the Inhabitants of such a Town as this, who posses an hundred Times the Property & Credit (I might say much more) of those who rule them with a Rod of Iron. This Paradox is at once solved by showing that this Town is governed by the lowest of the People and from the Time of the Stamp Act to this Hour has been and is in the Hands of the Mob: and tho' these Troops have not been employed in Actual Service of late, yet they have been frequently paraded in a Manner most suitable to strike Terror, to let People know that this Corps is still kept up for the Punishment of delinquents. I make no Doubt but above half of those who signed against the Importation of British Goods were brought to it by Intimidation. It has been common for a Person, who had signed, to excuse himself by saying "What, would you have my House pulled down". And some Gentlemen of a more firm make, when they refused signing said "you may pull my House down, if you please; but I won't subscribe." so closely connected were the alternative ^Ideas^ of submitting to the Faction or being exposed to its Resentment.

It would carry me too far to show how the Despotism which is exercised over this Town is made subservient to the Cause of the Faction in the House of Representatives. But it is certain that sevral Representatives who have acted with them have been brought to it by Intimidation: I have had it from some of their own Mouths. The Faction cannot indeed threaten distant Places with their Troops of Execution; tho' their Terror has been made Use of a great Way from Boston: but they can ruin a Mans Reputation and make him Obnoxious to his own Townspeople by public Libells and private Insinuations. And in these Practices they have been so successful that a great many of the best Men in the Province remain excluded from the House by these means. And thus Intimidation has, among other Causes, contributed to subject the House to the dictature of a few desperate Men who having little or nothing to lose dare to do any thing without fearing Consequences.

I therefore do not expect that this Government will recover itself, untill these Men have received some signal Check from Great Britain, such as will open the Eyes of their deluded followers. Their being suffered for near 3 years with Impunity to govern this Town by a trained Mob, and to set Great Britain at Defiance & treat the supreme imperial Power with a Contempt not only indecent but allmost treasonable has caused a great Despondency among the Officers and Friends of Government, and has brought the Kings Authority very low. I have indeed preserved the Citadel, I mean the Council Chamber: otherwise they would have been in Possession of the whole Government before now. I shall continue to exert myself as I have hitherto done: but shall be very watchful to lay hold of any Occasion which may produce a Reconciliation of these Men to the Kings Government. Hitherto it has been ^im^practicable without wounding the Honour of the King & the Dignity of Government. And I suppose they will continue intractable till they hear of the Success of their Remonstrances against the late Acts of Parliament. If they should be disappointed, they will become either outrageous or submissive: they themselves say it will be the former; I beleive the latter; especially If the rejection of their Claim is accompanied with measures to oblige them to be obedient: which they may well expect, as they have given notice that they will not acquiesce in the Decision of Parliament, if it is against them. But this Threat will prove like that of the Manufactures when it comes to be put to Trial.[4] I am with great Respect,

My Lord, your Lordships most obedient & most humble Servant.

Fra Bernard

The Right honble The Earl of Hillsborough

dupLS, RC   CO 5/757, ff 104- 106.

In handwriting of Thomas Bernard. Endorsed: Boston 19th: May 1768. Governor Bernard. (N[o]. 2). R 13th: July. (Duplicate Orig[l]. not received).   Variants: CO 5/766, ff 172-177 (L, RLbC); BP, 6: 300-34 (L, LbC).

The Stamp Act Crisis of 1764-66 had brought about a political re-alignment in the province resulting in the ascendancy of the Whig or popular party in the House of Representatives. While colonial parties did not resemble modern organizations, the Whigs' ideological cohesiveness in protesting infringements of the colonists' rights and liberties made them a formidable opposition party during 1768, notably when preparing remonstrances against the Townshend Acts (**Nos. 579** to **581**) and pushing through the Circular Letter (**No. 589**). The friends of government, in contrast, had dwindled to insignificance. FB also faced determined opposition in the Council (**No. 600**), behind which he observed James Bowdoin's skillful direction (**No. 654**). As this letter indicates, FB attributed the success of the Whigs to the co-ordinating role of the Boston Faction. Hitherto, FB tended to highlight James Otis Jr.'s dynamic leadership but in this letter observed that the drivers were "3 or 4 Persons bankrupt in Reputation as well as in Fortune, and equally void of Credit in Character & in Property." This depiction does not fit Otis's profile or that of the merchant Bowdoin, but it does correspond to Samuel Adams, Boston's representative and clerk of the House, who had experienced financial difficulties. Adams's personal finances were in jeopardy and his reputation was being undermined by alleged irregularities in his role as a Boston tax collector.[5] Adams's great success as a political manager, according to his several biographers, was to co-ordinate opposition to the administration being undertaken by several institutions: the Boston caucuses, the Boston town meeting, the House of Representatives, and the merchant committees. He also constituted an important link to those who organized out-of-doors protests, as FB's class-laden depiction of political tensions implied.[6] In FB's purview, behind Adams stood the mob, an interpretation endorsed by friends of government like Nathaniel Coffin and later propagated by Loyalists.[7]

1. **No. 588**.

2. **Nos. 569, 570, 571, 573**, and **575**, *Bernard Papers*, 3: 411-416, 420-422.

3. Faint.

4. FB is referring to the initial reluctance of many Boston merchants to embrace nonimportation and sustain domestic manufacturing, which agreement would take effect on 1 Jun. (and about which he informed Shelburne in **No. 601**).

5. In 1767, the town had brought a successful action against Adams for the non-collection of £1,463 in taxes requiring him to repay the outstanding total by Mar. 1768. He was then given additional time to repay, and cleared some of the debt with donations received; in 1772 the town waived his obligation to return the outstanding amount of £1,100. Ibid., 69. For judicious accounts see Catherine S. Menand, "The Things That Were Caesar's: Tax Collecting in Eighteenth-Century Boston," *Massachusetts Historical Review* (1999): 49-77; Alexander, *Samuel Adams*, 68-69.

6. See John C. Miller, *Sam Adams: Pioneer in Propaganda* (Stanford, Calif., 1936); Pauline Maier, "A New Englander as Revolutionary: Samuel Adams," *The Old Revolutionaries Political Lives in the Age of Samuel Adams* (New York, 1980), 3-50; Ira Stoll, *Samuel Adams: a Life* (New York, 2008); Alexander, *Samuel Adams* (2011).

7. See Colin Nicolson, "'McIntosh, Otis & Adams are our demagogues': Nathaniel Coffin and the Loyalist Interpretation of the Origins of the American Revolution," *Procs. MHS* 108 (1996): 73-114.

615 | *To the Earl of Hillsborough*

Duplicate[1]

N° 3

Boston May 21 1768

My Lord

In Answer to your Lordship's Letter N° 4,[2] I have the Honor to inform you, that in Obedience to Orders signified by the Lords of Trade by my Letter dated Nov[r] 15th 1766 I transmitted the most particular & exact Account of the Manufacturers set up & carried on in this Government since they year 1734, and of the public Encouragements given thereto, that I could procure; all the Transactions relating thereto happening before I came to the Government. It is not necessary to trouble your Lordship with a Copy of this Letter as every account of the setting up of a Manufacture concludes with the Failure of it; and they were all deceased before I arrived here.

I did not think it necessary to send an annual Account where I had nothing to inform of. But as of late Manufacturers have been mentioned as a threat against Great Britain by my Letter dated March 21 last past;[3] I showed that this Threat of Manufacturers was an idle Bully without the least Foundation. I therein mentioned that a Manufactory of Duck[4] was proposed to be set up, and a Committee was appointed to sollicit a Subscription for that Purpose. But after having tried the Town round, they could not raise half the money wanted: so this child is dead born.

I will use one Argument to shew the Impossibility of setting up Manufactures in this Town arising from the Price of Labor in it. The Staple Manufacture of this Town (if it may be so called) used to be Shipbuilding. This was so encouraged that the Ship builders when they had nothing bespoke, would set Vessels upon the Stocks on their own Account. But for some years past this Business has been leaving the Town and transporting itself to other Parts of the Province where they build cheaper. The under working of Boston may in some Degree arise from the easier acquisition of Timber; but it is much more occasioned by the extravagant Rise of Wages of the Workmen at Boston. A Ship builder at Boston some Months ago was applied to by a Number of Ship Carpenters who were out of Business & desired that he would put up a Keel upon his own Account in order to employ them. He said he would, if they would work for 2s. 3d. sterl^g a day. They said they could not work under 3s. sterl^g a day: he replied that he could not build Ships at that Rate: so they remained Idle. What are the Manufactures which will bear Wages at the Rate of 3s. a day for handicraft Labor?[5]

> I am with great Respect My Lord, your Lordships most obedient
> and most humble Servant

Fra. Bernard

The Right honourable The Earl of Hillsborough

dupLS, RC   CO 5/757, ff 107-108.

Endorsed: Boston May 21st 1768. Governor Bernard (N.º 3) R 13th: July. (Duplicate Orig^l not reced.) A.17 Encl^d.   Variants: CO 5/766, ff 177-180 (L, RLbC) and BP, 6: 298-300 (L, LbC).

The skilled workmen FB mentions may or may not have been firm supporters of the nonimportation agreement. What is certain is that shipbuilders for whom they worked later supposed that high(er) wages might tempt craftsmen and laborers to give up their support for the scheme; both the shipbuilders and FB underestimated workers' commitment to the boycott, which remained largely solid, despite rising levels of unemployment and underemployment on the Boston waterfront occasioned by nonimportation.[6]

1. This line in FB's hand.

2. Dated Whitehall, 20 Feb. 1768. BP, 11: 141-144. This one-sentence circular letter to the colonial governors enclosed a copy of the House of Commons' address to the king of 27 Mar. 1766, which had required governors to provide "exact Accounts" of manufactures established in their province since 1734. The request for information was driven by the government's interest in removing some of the restrictions on colonial manufacturing. The Board of Trade had already requested the information (**No. 509**, *Bernard Papers*, 3: 248-250), and which FB supplied, when Hillsborough distributed his circular.

3. **No. 601**.

4. "Duck" was the common name for untwilled linen or cotton used for small sails and sailor's trousers. *OED*.

5. Three shillings per day was equivalent to the average weekly wage of an unskilled laborer. Gary B. Nash, *The Urban Crucible: Social Change, Political Consciousness, and the Origins of the American Revolution* (Cambridge, Mass., 1979), 12.

6. Colin Nicolson, "A Plan 'to banish all the Scotchmen': Victimization and Political Mobilization in Pre-Revolutionary Boston," *Massachusetts Historical Review* 9 (2007): 55-102, at 72-74. While the nonimportation subscription was offered to merchants and shopkeepers in March, other Bostonians had already demonstrated their commitment to the protest movement by signing the nonconsumption agreement of 28 Oct. 1767. See **No. 601** n6 & n7.

616 | *To the Earl of Hillsborough*

Duplicate

N° 4.

Boston May 30 1768

My Lord

If your Lordship has informed yourself of my proceedings in negativing several Councellors elect at every Election since the Repeal of the Stamp Act, you must know that it took its Rise from the Party which got uppermost by Means of the Troubles arising from the Stamp Act, excluding from the Council at the Election in 1766 the Lieut. Governor the Secretary the Judges and the Attorney general merely & professedly for their being Officers of the Crown. This was done immediately after they had received Advice of the Repeal of the Stamp Act, and therefore it appeared to me such a notorious Instance of undutifullness and Insolence, that I thought myself obliged to resent it on Behalf of the Crown. I therefore negatived 6 of the new elected Council, whom I thought most instrumental in turning out the Lieut Govr &c; 2 of whom were councellors the former Year[1] & the other 4 Members of the House distinguished by nothing more than an Attachment to the Party which set them up.[2]

At the Election in 1767, I caused it to be understood, that if the Party would join in electing the Lieut Governor & Secretary I would accept at least as many of the negatived, & probably should be induced to fill up the Board.[3] This was treated with Contempt, & it was given out by the Faction that I had been reprimanded for what I had done before and durst not use my Negative again. As soon as the Election was over, some of the principal Members of the House, supporters of Government waited on me & desired that I would keep to my Purpose of negativing these Men, while they persisted in their repeating this Affront to the King.[4] This Request perfectly agreeing with my own Opinion, I negatived 5 of the Persons before negatived, the other being one of the two former Councellors having conciliated himself by a very decent Behaviour.[5]— I have thought proper to prefix this Detail to what I have now to write, to save your Lordship the Trouble of going back to my Letters wrote upon these Occasions.

I did not expect myself that this new Assembly would be much better disposed to Government than the former. Such infinite Pains had been taken by the Faction to keep up the Jealousy against the Government of Great Britain and such continual Improvement was made of every accidental & incidental Matter for the Purpose of Contention, that I had little Hopes that the Occasional Change of Men which a new Election produces would make a Change of the Measures, especially whilst the Spirit of Opposition to the Acts of Parliament was kept up & remained unchecked. It was generally beleived that the Lieut Governor would be chosen; on the other Hand 4 or 5 Councellors for promoting the Address to me last Session testifying the Councils Abhorrence of the Libell against me,[6] and assured themselves of turning them out. Both these Purposes were very near accomplished.

Your Lordship must understand that in New England a different Mode of Election prevails from what is used in Britain. Here it is not sufficient for a Man to have a greater Number of Votes than the Rest of the Candidates; but he must also have a Majority of the whole Number of Electors. By this Rule the Lieut Governor has twice out of 3 Times lost his Election. In the present Case in the Choice of the first 18 he was the 18th in the Order of Election; but wanting 3 of a Majority of the whole Electors, he was to be put up again.[7] In this Interval the two Cheif Heads of the Faction (Otis and Adams) told the House that the Lieut Governor was a pensioner of Great Britain & averred that he had a Warrant from the Lords of the Treasury for £200 a year out of the new Duties which they were then opposing.[8] This being urged in a Manner which left no Opportunity or Time for Refutation or Explanation, gave a Turn against him so that upon the second polling he had 10 Votes less than before: This obliged his Freinds to give up his Cause. I must observe to your Lordship that this £200 a year has been ordered as an Addition to his Salary as cheif Justice: which Addition will make the whole Income clear of Expences, scarce more than £300 a year; a scanty Appointment for a cheif Justice of a Province so populous & extensive as this & scarce an equivalent for the Abuse his Fidelity to the Crown has subjected him to.[9]

At this Election the Malice of the Enemies of the Lieut Governor was more apparent than usual. Otis the Father,[10] whose Enmity to the Lieut Governor is known to arise from personal Resentment, declared in publick, that he had rather be turned out of his Offices (which are the first in his County & given by me) & reduced to the lowest of the People, than that the Lieut Gov[r] should be elected into the Council: so much does private Malice prevail over public Considerations. This Declaration was made upon its being asserted that if the Lieut Governor was elected, the Governor would probably readmit M[r] Otis sen[r] into the Council to lay a Foundation for a general Reconciliation. As to the rest of the Election The Party turned out but 2 Councellors, the one a Friend of Government,[11] who will be as serviceable in the House; the other a Gentleman of no Consequence,[12] who happening to be Registrar of the Admiralty, was proscribed for holding an Office immediately from Great Britain. The other Councellors who were pushed at were saved only by 3 or 4 Votes;[13] the Opponent Party upon this Occasion appearing to have in other Cases 3 Majority of the whole Council & House; & in forming that Majority Six Councellors out of 22 joined.

As soon as the Election was over, some of the principal Members of the House waited on me to desire that I would continue to act as Governor; for it would not do to give up the Cause now. I readily assented to their Opinion and negatived 6 of the new List, 4 of which had been negatived before,[14] the other two new ones;[15] and I accepted one whom I had negatived before,[16] having Reason to think he was tired of his Party. I have thought proper to be particular in this narrative that your Lordship may see that I have no Choice in this Business. If I could be so indifferent to the Honour of the Crown as to admit into that Body called the Kings Council those Men who publickly profess an Intention of excluding all persons bearing the Kings Commission and would at present come in treading upon the Necks of the Kings Lieut Governor Secretary &c, yet the safety of the Kings Government would not suffer me to submit to a Compliance so dangerous & disgraceful. I have hitherto kept up the Authority of Government by supporting an Interest and maintaining a good Understanding with the Council. The Harmony which subsists between me and the Board has lately been evidenced by very full Testimonials, some of which have been unanimous, altho' I do not pretend to an equal Interest in every one of them. But if I had admitted all that have been elected to that Board, I should have had no Authority at it; and the Government would in Effect have been in the Hands of the Faction, who are now disputing the Authority of Parliament, & endeavouring to seperate themselves from great Britain in Regard to all real civil Power. I have therefore thought proper to keep still upon the defensive, untill the Effects of their late Remonstrances are known: I can at any Time make my own Terms by Concessions which I don't think myself at Liberty to submit to at present.

I hereby enclose my Speech at the opening of the Session. I have long ago left off making Speeches, unless upon some Occasion where an Expostulation is unavoidable, as at the End of last Session. As the Form of a Speech at the opening a Session must be kept up, I have some Time past, pitched upon some uncontroverted subject to turn 3 or 4 inoffensive Sentences upon.[17] By this Means I prevent their opening the Session with a Dispute, which they are fond of doing. In the present Instance Otis said it was the most exceptionable Speech I ever made; how so? why there is nothing in it to find fault with. I also enclose the Answer of the Council:[18] the House has as yet presented none;[19] as it is not determined what shall be done for their Defence in Regard to the Boundary Line with New York. I shall further inform your Lordship of what passes in the general Court as Occasion shall require.

I am with great Respect, My Lord your Lordships most obedient
and most humble Servant

Fra Bernard

The Right honble The Earl of Hillsborough

PS

To give your Lordship a Specimen of the unfair Means used to prejudice the Electors of the Council against the Lieut Governor & Secretary I send you a hand Bill circulated by the Faction about a fortnight before the Election and sent round the Country. It is printed with the same Letter with their newspaper[20] and appears to have been designed to be published in it; tho' afterwards a private Circulation might be thought better. The whole Artifice of it consists in setting the Lieut Governor the Secretary Mr Belcher Register of the Admiralty Court one of the Council for the last year, & Mr Auchmuty Judge of the same Court a fit Person for the Council and Mr Sewall Attorney general who ought allways to be of the Council, in the same List with the Commissioners of the Custom and the Officers of the Customs as low as Waiters; and by these Means to make the Crown Officers under the Charter as obnoxious to the People as the Custom House Officers sent from home. *This Paper was sent to Mr Belcher in a Cover and he has accordingly been left out of the Council.*[21]

The whole Purpose of these Proceedings is to divest the Crown of all its natural and constitutional Power in this government and fling all real Power into the Hands of the People. In some former Letters I gave my Opinion that the Lieut Governor and the Secretary were by Charter intitled to a Seat & Voice in the Council without being elected; and the obliging them to submit to an Election was an Usurpation.[22] I am now confirmed in that Opinion and shall be glad to give my Reasons for it when it shall be proper.

dupLS, RC   CO 5/757, ff 109-112.

In handwriting of Thomas Bernard. Endorsed: Boston May 30th: 1768. Governor Bernard (N[o]. 4 R 13. July. Dup[cle]. Original not reced) A.18. Enl[d].   Enclosed several newspaper extracts: a report on the election day procession and celebrations of 26 May 1768 and FB's speech to the Council and House of Representatives delivered the same day (taken from the *Massachusetts Gazette*, 26 May 1768); the address of the Council of 28 May and FB's reply of the same date (from the *Massachusetts Gazette*, 2 Jun. 1768); a letter "To The Public" concerning councilors proposed for election. CO 5/757, ff 113-114. Variants of letter: CO 5/766, ff 180-191 (L, RLbC); BP, 6: 304-311 (L, LbC).

FB opened the new assembly with a plea for brevity—"to avoid all Business that can well be postponed to the next Session."[23] Otis's ironic quip about FB's "exceptionable speech" was lost on FB, whose opening speech at the beginning of the previous legislative year had hectored representatives "to restore . . . mutual Confidence and Unanimity."[24] As it turned out, the first few days of the new session were FB's last days of peace in the province. For on 15 Jun., he received instructions from Hillsborough requiring the House to rescind the vote approving the Circular Letter on 11 Feb. At the same time, FB became embroiled in controversy occasioned by the seizure of John Hancock's *Liberty* on 10 Jun., and reconsidered the prospect of bringing British Regulars to Boston.

FB's influence in the Council declined rapidly following the election of 1768. His proposal to accept Col. Otis was not a serious overture, since FB knew from the 1767 contest that Otis would never accept TH's reelection. In the months ahead, Whigs James Bowdoin, James Pitts, and Royal Tyler emerged as leaders of the opposition in the Council, for the time being supported by moderates Samuel Danforth, John Erving Sr., and Harrison Gray. FB would have precipitated a major constitutional crisis had he refused to accept the election of all these men, for he would have been left with an inquorate rump of ten councilors.

---

1. James Otis Sr. and Nathaniel Sparhawk were elected to the Council in 1765 and negatived by FB the following year.

2. Jerathmeel Bowers (1717-99), who served Swansea from 1754 to 1774, and later; Samuel Dexter (1726-1810), Dedham's representative 1764-67, 1775, and later; Joseph Gerrish (1708-76), representative for Newbury, 1753-54 and 1766-74; Thomas Saunders or Sanders (1729-74), representative for Gloucester, 1761-69. See **No. 469**, *Bernard Papers*, 3: 151-154.

3. For FB's failed compromise with the Otises see **No. 549**, *Bernard Papers*, 3: 364-365.

4. These friends of government had probably undertaken to write to the secretary of state, for they were not in a position to persuade the House or assembly to petition the king.

5. Nathaniel Sparhawk (1715-76), who served in the Council until 1773.

6. See **No. 593**.

7. FB's explanation here clarifies that successful candidates required to win a majority of votes in either of the ballots: the first ballot for eighteen places and the second ballot for the remaining ten places. (See *Bernard Papers*, 3: 181n7.) A majority, as TH noted, was 71 votes, but he was three votes short, as FB here observes. Before the second ballot could take place, Otis and Adams intervened to accuse TH of being a "Pensioner." TH to Nathaniel Rogers, Milton, 31 May 1768, Mass. Archs., 25: 258-259, in Hutchinson Transcripts, 1: 256.

8. The Grafton administration had decided that TH was to receive his lieutenant governor's salary from the tea duty, with payment commencing in Jun. 1768. (It was probably an experiment intended to ascertain the colonial reaction.) The decision is not recorded in the Treasury's American papers (T 28/1). It was first reported in the Boston newspapers on 11 Apr., the news having been brought in

"private letters" from London carried by Capt. James Scott, master of John Hancock's brig *Lydia,* which docked on 8 Apr. Bernard Bailyn, *The Ordeal of Thomas Hutchinson* (Cambridge, Mass., 1974), 121n, 146-148; *Boston Gazette,* 11 Apr. 1768; *Boston Chronicle,* 4-11 Apr. 1768.

9. In in his brief account, TH notes that persons who had voted for him afterward gave their support to Artemas Ward (1727-1800), whose election FB vetoed. Thomas Hutchinson, *The History of the Colony of Massachusetts-Bay,* 3 vols., ed. Lawrence Shaw Mayo, (1764, 1767, 1828: Cambridge, Mass., 1936), 3: 141.

10. Col. James Otis Sr. FB's thesis of malice outweighing other motivation interestingly anticipates Bernard Bailyn on the primacy of ideology in the lead-up to the American Revolution. *The Ideological Origins of the American Revolution* (Cambridge, Mass., 1967).

11. John Chandler III (1721-1800) had been a councilor since 1765. He was a major landowner in Worcester County where he served as a probate judge, 1762-74; he occupied numerous local offices in Petersham, but was a single-term representative in the 1768-69 session.

12. Andrew Belcher (1706-71), a merchant by occupation, was first elected to the Council in 1764. Judging by FB's comment, it is unlikely Belcher was strongly partisan for either the Whigs or the friends of government.

13. This refers to the friends of government who were elected: Thomas Flucker, Thomas Hubbard, James Russell (who would soon side with the Whigs), Timothy Paine (d.1793) of Worcester, and John Worthington (1719-1800) of Springfield. Their attendance at Council meetings had been erratic on account of their residing out of Boston.

14. Bowers, Gerrish, Saunders, and Col. Otis.

15. John Hancock (1737-93) and Artemas Ward (1727-1800).

16. Sparhawk.

17. In his opening speech of 26 May, FB drew attention to Massachusetts's boundary dispute with New York, noting that he had sent to London the report of the joint boundary commission and (erroneously) expected it to be "confirmed." *JHRM,* 45: 9. See **No. 613**.

18. Address of the Council, 28 May 1768. CO 5/827, f 75.

19. The House did not directly answer FB's opening speech. Later responses to FB's messages were concerned with the rescinding controversy, starting with that of 30 Jun. *JHRM,* 45: 90-95.

20. Thus in manuscript.

21. Signed by "J. J." and addressed "To The Public," the list of councilors was ironically offered "to a manly and impartial Press; and which if adopted at the next general Election [*May 1768*] may take away all grounds of further complaint, and may possibly prove a healing and very salutary measure for the province." CO 5/757, f 114.

22. The House of Representatives had disputed FB's contention. See FB's letters to Shelburne, **Nos. 549** and **550**, *Bernard Papers,* 3: 364-369. After his defeat in the 1766 election, TH continued to attend Council meetings as lieutenant governor (though he was not an *ex officio* member) until growing criticism prompted him to desist. **No. 534**, ibid., 329-330.

23. *JHRM,* 45: 9.

24. Ibid., 8.

617 | To John Pownall

private

Boston. May 30. 1768

Dear S[r]

I herewith inclose to you my Speech at the opening of the Session; it is intended only to comply with form so as to afford no exception to ground a quarrel on; & in this Sense, it has been called by Otis a very exceptionable Speech, as it affords nothing to except to.[1] I was not able to bring them to a compromise in regard to the Election, tho' I went so far as to have it given out that if the Lieutenant Governor was chosen, The Governor would probably admit Otis Sen[r] into the Council, to lay a foundation for a reconciliation. The Old Man upon this occasion said that He would quit all his offices (which are the first in honor & profit in his County & of my gift)[2] & bring himself to the lowest of the People rather than the Lieut Governor should get into the Council.[3] However the Lieutenant Governor would have got in, if it had not been for the addition of ^to^ his salary of 200 £ lately order'd by the Treasury. This afforded Otis to say in the House that he was a Pensioner of Great Britain & was to recieve 200 £ per ann. out of the new Duties.[4] This was spoke in the house in the midst of the Election, when there was no time for confuting or explaining. I always thought it would be made use of for this purpose: between you & me this appointment is too small for a Salary or pension or compensation, & had better have been postponed, till it could have been done to more purpose. For I must question whether the Assembly here will admit of additions to their officers Salaries; what the Treasury gives they [then?][5] take away as far as they can, at least in their present humor. But It may be worth while to try the experiment.

In truth my good Freind, there seems to be wanting among your great people a right Idea of this Country, I mean, its present political State. If nothing but palliating measures are to be pursued, the present Idea, whatever it is, is as good as any. But If it should be thought high time, as it certainly is, to put a Stop to the political Enthusiasm which has been suffer'd to be blown up for above 2 Years past & is now running over the Country, the very best information of the State of this Country should be procured; & that can be had only from principal men free from the prejudices of the Country, & should be communicated, *vivâ-voce*,[6] as no Writing will be full enough or free enough for that purpose. I proposed myself for this Service above 2 years ago; but as Active Measures were then not thought proper, my offer was very rightly rejected. If active Measures shall still be thought unnecessary, I can be of no service, but if they are at length seen to be absolutely indispensable, I am sure I can be of more service as a Reporter at home than I can be as a Governor here. I have therefore wished that I had a discretionary leave (to be made use of accordingly as I should see it would be most for the Service) to come home before next Winter. I have signified this request to no one but my Lord Barrington, to whom I wrote upon the subject some time ago.[7] My Correspondence with my Lord Hillsborough has, by the delay of packets, been open'd so very lately, that I have had no time to write to him on this account, nor will it ^now^ be proper untill I see the Events of this Session: & by that time it will be too late to expect an answer time enough to embark before winter; & I hope I shall not be obliged by a positive order to take a Winter voyage. I have therefore no chance of going home this Year, unless what I have already wrote to Lord Barrington shall have procured an order before this arrives, or what I write now shall have effect immediately afterwards for if I do not recieve leave by the end of September or the beginning of October I must give it up for this Year.

The political Barometer stands here pretty much as it did, only there is less appearance of violence than there was some time ago. Otis said t'other day that there was no intention or desire to quarrel with the Governor. I have had some hints that I might make my own terms, if I would give up the Lieut. Governor & admitt their Councellors; that is, if I would put my self in their hands. But then I must sacrifice the Government & its freinds, myself & my honour. I choose rather to keep upon the Defensive till I can see what will be done at home: Vigorous measures there may give a great turn to the politicks of this place. The Faction keeps up its party now by assurances of success in their opposition to parliament; if they should recieve any great check, it might give a turn to the balance, which is now nearer an equilibrium than it has been.

I am &c

J Pownall Esq_{r.}

AL, LbC   BP, 6: 115-119.

Enclosed a copy of FB's speech to assembly of 26 May 1768 (not found), for which see *JHRM*, 45: 9.

This letter describes the last occasion when FB considered compromising with the Otises in order to bring TH back into the Council (see also **Nos. 617** and **619**). FB was outwardly disdainful of the Otises' political progress, but inwardly regretful of his own conceit in once supposing that James Otis Jr.'s mad "reign" was "quite over." (**No. 552**.)[8] The arrangement proposed depended upon Col. Otis accepting TH's restoration in return for his own reelection, but the elder Otis twice refused to accept that condition, in 1767 and 1768.

---

1. The only item of business raised by FB was to inform the assembly that he had transmitted to the Board of Trade copies of the printed report prepared by the commission on the province boundary with New York (**No. 613**).

2. James Otis Sr. (1702-78) was a former Speaker of the House, 1760-61, and had been a member of the Governor's Council from 1762 to 1766, when FB vetoed his election. In 1764, FB had appointed him chief justice of the court of Common Pleas in Barnstable County.

3. FB probably communicated the proposed compromise via "some principal Members of the House," as he had at the Council elections in 1767. **No. 549**, *Bernard Papers*, 3: 364.

4. See **No. 616**.

5. Obscured in the binding.

6. Meaning by word of mouth, person-to-person.

7. **No. 609**.

8. *Bernard Papers*, 3: 373.

618 | To John Corner

Province house June 6

S[r]

    I have received yours dated this Day, & am sorry for the Contents thereof. I can do nothing in a Business of this kind without the Advice & Assistance of the Council. I shall communicate your Letter to them on Wednesday next in the forenoon.[1] In the mean Time I shall be glad to have the most exact Account of this Riot that can be procured, and especially the Names of the Persons who flung Stones, if they can be obtained. If a Discovery of this kind can be made, the Offenders shall be brought to Justice.

I am &c.

Capt[n] Corner.[2]

L, LbC   BP, 5: 263-264.

In handwriting of Thomas Bernard.

    Capt. Corner's ship, HMS *Romney*, was a fifty-gun, fourth-rate ship constructed in 1762 for duty in North America, and was the largest and most powerful Royal Navy warship patrolling the continental waters. Leaving Halifax on 9 May, the *Romney* anchored in Boston harbor on 17 May, and participated in the 4 Jun. celebrations marking the king's birthday. At noon, after the guns on Castle William and at the town batteries were fired, the *Romney* issued a royal salute (which today can encompass sixty-two rounds). Meanwhile, the governor presided over a muster of his honorific bodyguard (the Company of Cadets) and the Boston militia in King Street, where the artillery discharged their "new field pieces" and the militia, under Col. Joseph Jackson's command, fired three volleys; afterward the artillery train, commanded by Capt. Adino Paddock, "performed the exercise of a mock fight, during which their soldier-like behavior . . . and the good order observed, gave general satisfaction to a numerous crowd of spectators." The governor, the Council, the House of Representatives, and the militia officers convened at the Council Chamber to toast the king and the royal family, while the militia captains hosted "genteel dinners" for their officers and the town gentry.[3]

The loyal sentiments may have been heartfelt, but for some Whigs the conviviality was a veneer. For Capt. Corner had already angered townsfolk by sending press gangs ashore. The incident alluded to in this letter occurred on the afternoon of Sunday, 5 Jun. when townspeople and local sailors "prevented" the press gang boats from landing at the waterfront by throwing stones and missiles. Three sailors were impressed in the coming days, one of whom was rescued by a crowd. While these incidents did not provoke a riot, they indubitably contributed to the ill-feeling toward Crown servants and naval officers that surfaced during the *Liberty* riot of 10 Jun.[4]

1. In the event, FB did not present the letter to the Council when it met on 8 Jun., probably because the Council had already, on 31 May, appointed a committee (comprising James Bowdoin, William Brattle, and Royal Tyler) to examine Corner's complaints. CO 5/827, f 46.

2. John Corner had taken command of HMS *Romney* in Mar. 1767, serving in the North Atlantic Station under Admiral Samuel Hood.

3. *Boston Chronicle*, 30 May-6 Jun. 1768.

4. Hoerder, *Crowd Action in Revolutionary Massachusetts*, 165-166. Popular concerns about impressment did not abate, however, when the Royal Navy warships gathered in Boston harbor in the autumn. FB had to intervene on at least one occasion to try to secure the release of sailors illegally taken from "Coasting Vessels." FB to Samuel Hood, Province House, 18 Nov. 1768, BP, 7: 215. Resistance to Royal Navy press gangs was manifest in Boston during the wars with France, notably in a riot of 1747 which undermined future "in-harbor" operations to fill British vessels with American sailors. Nicholas Rogers, *The Press Gang: Naval Impressment and its Opponents in Georgian Britain* (London, 2007), 86-90.

619 | To Richard Jackson

Boston June 6. 1768.

Dear S[r]

Since ^I wrote^ my last to you of Mar 14:[1] I have recieved yours of Mar. 11.[2] I was in hopes to have been able to have wrote fully to you by this packet: but my time will not permit it. However I must give you a short account of the opening of the new Assembly.[3]

It was in general apprehended that the Lieutenant Governor would be elected; but the Otises took infinite pains to prevent it, & the elder of them never showed a more unrelenting malice than he did upon this occasion. I had it given it out (not as directly from me) that if the Lieut Governor was elected the Governor would most probably consent to Mr Otis Senr. coming into Council. The Old Man upon that declared that he had rather be turned out of every place he had & be reduced to the very bottom of the people than that the Lieut Governor should get into Council. Nevertheless He was very near it, having at the first poll got to be within the 18; but wanting 3 of a Majority of the Electors as is required in elections here, He was obliged to Stand another poll.[4] Then Otis[5] sprung a Mine he had in reserve: he declared that the Lieut Governor had a pension from Great Britain charged upon the new duties, ~~have~~ upon which he had a warrant for 200 £ a Year. There was no denying the fact, but it might have been explained so as to exculpate the Lieut Governor, namely that it was an addition to his Salary as Cheif Justice which was before scandalously mean.[6] But the Hurry of the Business they were about left no time for any explanation: so upon the second poll many that had voted for him before fell off; & his friends were obliged to give him up.

When the first advice of this grant arrived here, it gave ^neither^ pleasure to the friends of the Lieut.-Governor, ^nor^ encouragement to the Officers of Government. It was so unequal to any purposes it could be intended for, that it could neither be deemed a Salary of the Officer nor a confiscation to the Man, whereas it was sure to be improved to make him obnoxious to the people. I immediately saw that it would be the Cause of his losing his Election, tho' I did not imagine he would come so near. But It was owing to me that he did make so good a figure; for I took uncommon pains to engage the friends of Government to exert themselves on this Occasion; & if there had not been an extraordinary non attendance of some of the Cheif of them, it would have been carried with ease. The Faction also attacked several other Councellors who were distinguished as supporters of Government; but they failed in the principal of them by a few votes & turned out only 2 one a Man of no Consequence,[7] the other one who will get into the House where he will be as serviceable as in the Council.[8] In short the Friends of Government are quite tired with waging so unequal a War, whilst the Enemy is permitted to raise continual ~~Commotions~~ disturbances in the Government by frequent insults of the Administration & parliament of Great Britain. They therefore say that they must lie by till the Faction receive a sufficient check from home. I send you my Speech & the Councils address thereupon. I have long ago left off making reel Speeches; such as[9] these are only calculated to keep up the form without giving any opportunity for a dispute.

I am D^r S^r

R Jackson Esq_r.

AL, LbC   BP, 6: 119-122.

⮞⮞⮞ 176 ⮜⮜⮜

THE PAPERS OF GOVERNOR FRANCIS BERNARD

Enclosures (not found): FB's speech to the Council and the House of Representatives, 26 May 1768 (for which see *JHRM*, 45: 9); the House's answer delivered on 31 May (ibid., 17); the Council's address to FB of 31 May (see CO 5/827, f 75).

This account of the proposed compromise with the Otises amplifies that given earlier to Hillsborough in **No. 616** and John Pownall in **No. 617**.

---

1. **No. 598**.

2. Not found.

3. The session ran from 25 May until 30 Jun. 1768.

4. For a brief summary of the procedure see **No. 616** and *Bernard Papers*, 3: 158n8, 181n7.

5. James Otis Jr.

6. The chief justice was granted £150 annually by the General Court.

7. Andrew Belcher.

8. John Chandler III (1721-1800).

9. First written as "are".

620 | *To William Dalrymple*

Boston June 10 1768

S^r:

When I had the Pleasure of seeing you at Boston I asked if Mr Palmer[1] the Chaplain of your Regiment might have Leave to come to Boston if I could procure for him a Church to serve: I understood there would be no Difficulty. Such an Opportunity offers now: Christ Church (one of the Churches of this Town)[2] will in a few Days will be destitute of a Minister. Their Rector is lately gone to England;[3] they are now served by Mr Kneeland Chaplain of the Garrison at Louisbourg; he is to depart in a few Days, and then they will be glad to have the same Assistance from your Regiment & will esteem the Favour. Churches in this Country subsist entirely by voluntary Association and Subscription; and if their is any long Interruption of the Ministry of the Church it endangers the being of the Society. You will therefore consider this request as well for a public Service as a private Favour.

I was to wait upon you at your Lodgings the noon of the Day you left Boston. It was to pay my Compl^{ts} to you, as to deliver you the Letter I bespoke your Care of & to speak to you on the forementioned Subject and on another Affair I cant write upon.[4] I should not have delayed it so long, if I had not observed the Wind all the while full against you, and thereby assured myself of seeing you. I suppose you yourself was hurried so as to have no Time to give me notice of your Departure.

I am &c.

Col Dalrymple[5]

L, LbC   BP, 5: 265-266.

In handwriting of Thomas Bernard.

---

1. The Rev. Hugh Palmer had been chaplain since 1756. FB also wrote Palmer on 10 Jun. suggesting he become the acting minister of Christ Church, which would provide him with one guinea "each Sunday for this occasional Service." BP, 5: 264-265.

2. Closing parenthesis supplied.

3. Thus in manuscript. At Easter 1768, Mather Byles Jr. (1735-1814) was invited to become minister of the Anglican Christ Church (more commonly known as Old North Church) in Boston's North End. In the absence of an American bishop, he was obliged to sail to England for ordination by the bishop of London, and returned to Boston on 28 Sept. to minister to around "one hundred families." Henry Burroughs, *A Historical Account of Christ Church, Boston, an address, delivered on the one hundred and fiftieth anniversary of the opening of the church, December 29th, 1873* (Boston, 1874), 23. Rev. Byles was a recent convert to Anglicanism. His father Rev. Dr. Mather Byles (1707-88) was the Congregational pastor of Hollis Street Church, Boston, a published poet, and one of the province's leading intellectuals. Father and son were both committed Loyalists. Arthur W. H. Eaton, *The Famous Mather Byles: the noted Boston Tory preacher, poet, and wit, 1707-1788* (Boston, 1914).

4. Col. Dalrymple left Boston for Halifax, N.S., on board the *Little Romney,* 27 May. *Boston Post-Boy and Advertiser,* 30 May 1768. Doubtless the Rev. Palmer's appointment was not uppermost in FB's mind: he probably wished to discuss with Dalrymple the prospect of obtaining Regulars or the logistics of transporting them from Halifax to Boston.

5. William Dalrymple (1736-1807) had been commissioned lieutenant colonel of the 14th Regiment of Foot (West Yorkshire Regiment) on 27 Mar. 1765 and commanded the regiment when it was located to Boston in Oct. 1768.

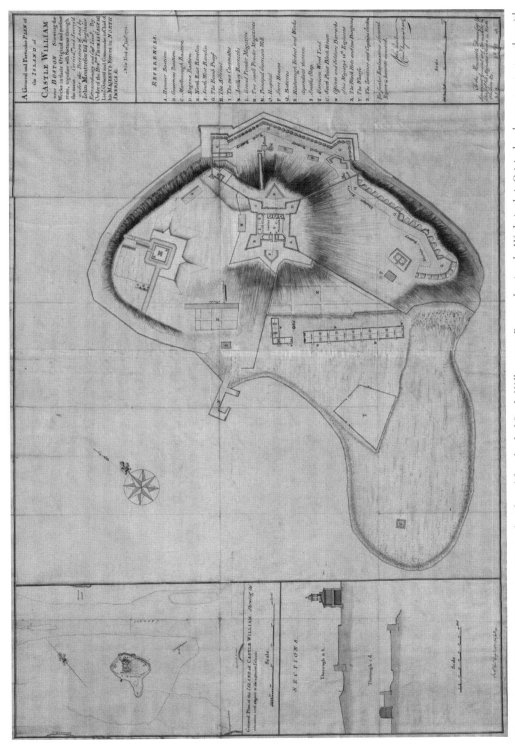

Map of Castle William. "A General and Particular Plan of the Island of Castle William near Boston, shewing the Works in their Original and present state, together with Sections through the same," 1771. By John Montresor. MR 1/19, TNA.

621 | From the American Board of Customs

Sir,

As soon as your Excellency signified to us by your Note to M[r]. Hulton, that you met this Morning in Council, our Officers, who were attacked last Night by the Mob, were directed to prepare an Account thereof.

We are now to acquaint your Excellency that M[r]. Harrison the Collector[1] & M[r]. Hallowell the Comptroller[2] have been so violently hurt, that the former is confined to his Bed, and the latter to his House; and on that Account your Excellency cannot be furnished with their Informations so soon as we could wish; but when they are prepared your Excellency shall receive the same by our Secretary.

We are &c.

Boston 11th. June 1768.

John Robinson[3]
Henry Hulton[4]
J. Temple[5]
W[m] Burch[6]
Chas. Paxton.[7]

L, Copy   CO 5/766, ff 203-204.

Entrybook title: N[o]. 1. To Gov[r]. Bernard. &c. &c.   A copy of this letter was enclosed with **No. 630**.[8]

This was the first letter FB received from the commissioners of Customs in the wake of the *Liberty* riot on 10 Jun. (which FB reported in **No. 623**).

---

1. Joseph Harrison, collector of Customs at Boston.

2. Benjamin Hallowell (1724-99), comptroller of Customs at Boston, 1764-70, and a commissioner of Customs from 1771.

3. John Robinson was an American-born former collector of Customs at Rhode Island, and had been in dispute with FB over the governor's response to a riot and rescue at Taunton, Bristol Co., in the spring of 1765. He chaired meetings of the American Board of Customs after the *Liberty* riot. See *Bernard Papers*, 2: 251-258.

4. Henry Hulton (1730-91), the senior commissioner, was the most experienced administrator on the Board, having been a clerk in the London Plantation Office and a customs officer in Antigua. Hulton came to see FB as politically naïve and ineffective, though he strove to work with him during the crisis. See Neil Longley York, *Henry Hulton and the American Revolution: An Outsider's Inside View* (Boston, 2010).

5. John Temple (1731-98). Temple's decision to remain in Boston while the other commissioners retreated to Castle William, jeopardized his relationship with his colleagues, who came to suspect him of colluding with the Whigs to embarrass both them and the governor.

6. William Burch (d.1794).

7. Charles Paxton (1704-88), surveyor and searcher of customs at Boston, 1760-67. Paxton was FB's only firm friend on the Customs Board.

8. According to CO 5/766 f 203.

622 | From the Earl of Hillsborough

(Nº 10.)

Secret.

Whitehall June 11th, 1768.

Sir,

Since my Letter to you Nº 7, I have received there from you addressed to the Earl of Shelburne Nº 7, 8, & 9,[1] and have laid them with the Inclosures, before the King.

It was evident, from what passed in the House of Representatives at the latter End of their last Session, that the Settled Purpose of those Men, by whose Influence the Proceedings of the Assembly seem to have been guided, was to inflame the Minds of the People and thereby to defeat every conciliating Measure; which the true Friends to the Constitution of this Kingdom and the Colonies were pursuing, in order to restore that Peace and Harmony, upon which the mutual Happiness of both so much depends.

What has happened since has shown too plainly the Success of their Endeavours, and the Negative which the Grand Jury of the superior Court of Boston put upon a Bill of Indictment against the Printers of the Boston Gazette in the Case you mention;[2] after themselves had directed the Attorney-General to prepare such a Bill, is but too striking an Evidence of the Influence of those, who seek to disturb the Public Peace and persist with so much Obstinacy and Malevolence in sowing the Seeds of Disorder and Discontent.

His Majesty trusts however that the Steadiness and Resolution, which have so eminently distinguished your own Conduct and that of the Chief Justice, will at length prevail over the Attempts of those, who endeavour to establish Credit to themselves by exciting popular Jealousy, and sacrifice even Justice itself and the due Course of Law to the Encouragement and Support of their seditious Purposes.

His Majesty observes with Pleasure what you say of the spirited and proper Conduct of the Council[3] in the last Session & of the Zeal they showed to promote His Majesty's Service; and although it should seem by your Letter N° 8,[4] that the Propositions made by you, on your Apprehensions of the Disorders and riotous Proceedings which were likely to happen in the Town of Boston on the Anniversary of the Repeal of the Stamp-Act, were, if not discountenanced, at least received with a Coldness inconsistent with a proper Regard to the Preservation of the public Peace; yet His Majesty observes with Satisfaction, that the Council was in some Degree justified in their Opinion by the Event, for though the Behaviour and tumultuous Rejoicings of the Populace, on that Day and Night, were marked with many indecent Circumstances of Insult and Disorder, they happily did not proceed to any Acts of Violence.

I hope you will not think from what I have said, respecting the Proceedings of Boston on the 18th of March, that I entertain an Opinion that the Vigilance and Attention shown by you on that Occasion, or the minute Detail you give of what passed on that Day, were unnecessary or improper. In Time of public Disorder a vigilant Attention to the Preservation of the public Peace is highly becoming in every Office and Magistrate, and the Duty of Persons in your high Station requires that they should communicate to the immediate Servants of the Crown every Information relative to the State of their Governments, in the most circumstantial and confidential Manner; and therefore I cannot but wish that in those Parts of your Letters, where you speak of what had passed at Town Meetings, and Meetings of the Merchants, (which appear to me to be of far greater Moment than the less deliberate Proceedings of a Mob) you had been more explicit as to the Objects of their Councils and Measures. If any Man or Set of Men, have been daring enough to declare openly, that they will not submit to the Authority of Parliament, it is of great Consequence that His Majesty's Servants should know who and what they are: And I trust, Sir, you will believe that I mean only the most friendly Admonition when I say, that a very full and confidential Communication of what you have heard, concerning the Designs and Intentions of those, whose Opposition to Measures of Conciliation render them justly suspected as Enemies to all Government, would have been more satisfactory than the alarming and dark hint you give, when you say, *that you dare not to repeat what you have heard, till their Purposes become more apparent.*

It is but too evident, not only from the Accounts contained in your last Letters, but also from a Revision of the State of your Government for some Time past, that the Authority of Civil Power is too weak to enforce Obedience to the Laws, and preserve that Peace and good Order, which is essential to the Happiness of every State; and His Majesty has thought fit, upon the most mature Consideration of what has been represented by yourself, and by the Comm^rs of the Customs established at Boston, to direct the Commander in Chief of His Majesty's Forces in America to station One Regiment at least in the Town of Boston, and to garrison, and if necessary to repair, the Fort or Castle of William and Mary, and he would probably have received some Directions, with regard to such other Forts and Fortifications, as have been usually kept up in the Province under your Government, if the Situation and Number of them had been known.[5]

His Majesty's Pleasure hath been also signified to the Lords Commissioners of the Admiralty,[6] that they do forthwith order one Frigate, two Sloops, and two Cutters to repair to and remain in the Harbour of Boston, for assisting and supporting the Officers of His Majesty's Customs in the Execution of their Duty; and I am to acquaint you, Sir, with His Majesty's Commands, that you do co-operate with the Commander in Chief, in taking all necessary Steps for the Reception and Accommodation of the Troops.

As I observe in many Parts of your Letter's Expressions of Doubt and Difficulty, whether you can or ought in any Case, to act without the Advice and Opinion of the Council, I think it necessary to take Notice, that I cannot find, upon the most careful Perusal of your Commision and Instructions, upon what Part of them this Opinion is founded; and it does seem to me, that the Admission of a Right in the Council to be consulted on all Occasions would be to establish in that Body a Power & Authority, inconsistent with the Spirit of the Constitution, as it is you, to whom the Crown has delegated its Authority, and you alone are responsible for the due Exercise of it.

As I understand you wish for a conditional Leave of Absence, I have laid your Desire before His Majesty, who is graciously pleased to gratify you in it, and I will take Care to have the necessary Instrument transmitted to you, which you may consider as in your Possession.[7]

You will see from the Nature of this Letter how necessary it is to keep the Contents entirely secret, till you hear from the Commander in Chief.

I am Sir your Most Humble & Obedient Servant

Hillsborough.

LS, RC   BP, 11: 187-196.

Endorsed: Nᵒ. 12 Earl of Hillsborough r Sep 14 1768 d June 11 Directions as to his Conduct of Correspondence.   The RC was carried by the June mail packet, which was six weeks overdue when it arrived at New York, on 7 Sept., having left Falmouth on 16 Jun.[8] FB received this letter seven days later, on 14 Sept. It is likely, but not certain, that the letter was carried to Boston by an express rider. However, FB had already received the duplicate on 3 Sept., (carried in the July mail) to which he replied with **No. 672** on 9 Sept. Variants: CO 5/757, ff 83-86 (LS, AC); CO 5/765, ff 9-14 (L, LbC). Extracts were laid before both houses of Parliament of Lords on 28 Nov. 1768. HLL: American Colonies Box 1.

Hillsborough's letter served notice that British policymakers were taking a firmer line toward Massachusetts. By the time Hillsborough wrote FB, orders had already been dispatched to Gen. Gage, on 8 Jun. (**Appendix 4**), to relocate two regiments to Boston. British historian Peter D. G. Thomas observed that "the ministry was not blindly risking confrontation."[9] This probably accounts for the contemplative nature of Hillsborough's letter to FB, and likely reflected the cabinet's discussions on the merits and possible repercussions of deploying soldiers to Boston. Hillsborough's ruminations in this letter did not challenge the probity of FB's accounts but nonetheless questioned their reliability; the request that, in future, FB tender substantive evidence concerning insurrection signaled that Hillsborough was attuned to the consequences of military intervention if not fully cognizant of the possible repercussions. Hillsborough's orders did not reach Gage until c.3 Sept., whereupon the general dispatched the 14th and 29th Regiments of Foot stationed at Halifax to Boston; one company of the 59th Regiment and one artillery company with five field pieces were also sent to Boston. On 30 Jul., Hillsborough ordered two other regiments to Boston, the 64th and 65th Regiments stationed Ireland and originally intended as relief for the Halifax garrison (for which see **No. 661**).[10]

---

1. **Nos. 596, 600,** and **601**.

2. In **No. 596**.

3. **No. 596**.

4. **No. 600**.

5. **Appendix 4**.

6. The earl of Hillsborough to the lords commissioners of the Admiralty, Whitehall, 11 Jun. 1768, CO 5/757, ff 81-82.

7. **No. 636**.

8. The *Lord Hyde* packet "had a long Passage occasioned by many head Winds, Calms, and Lee Currants." *New-York Gazette*, 12 Sept. 1768. The date of departure was noted in the *Boston News-Letter*, 18 Aug. 1768.

9. Thomas, *Townshend Duties Crisis*, 82.

10. The British military redeployment is best followed in Archer, *As If an Enemy's Country*, 104-106 and passim; Zobel, *Boston Massacre*, 93-107.

623 | *To the Earl of Hillsborough*

N° 5

Boston June 11th. 1768.

My Lord,

I am sorry to inform your Lordship that a great Riot happened in this Town last Evening which had very bad consequences, tho' happily there were no Lives lost.[1] The Collector & Comptroller of this Port seized a Sloop for openly & forcibly Landing a Cargo of Wines without paying Duty, and by means of assistance from the Romney Man of War secured her. Upon their return home they were attacked by a Mob; with Clubs, Stones and Brick-bats. Mr Harrison the Collector was much bruised particularly in the Breast, but kept his Legs so as to escape through an Alley. Mr Hallowell the Comptroller[2] was knocked down and left on the Ground covered with Blood: he has many Wounds & Bruses, but none dangerous to life. Mr Harrison's Son, a young Gentleman not in any Office,[3] who accompanied his Father, was knocked down and dragged by the hair of his head, and would have been killed if he had not been got into a House by some Standers by. In another part of the Town Mr Irwin[4] an Officer under the Board of Commissioners was attacked by another Mob, very much beat and abused, and would probably have been killed if he had not been rescued by two of the Mob, and enabled to escape through an House. This Gentleman was no ways concerned in the Seizure.

After this they went to M^r. Hallowell's House[5] and began to break the Windows and force an entry; but were diverted therefrom by assurances that Mr Hallowell was almost killed and was not at home. They then went to Mr Harrison's and broke his Windows: but he not being at home, and the owner of the House entreating them to depart, they left it. Then they went to Mr Williams House[6] (one of the Inspector Generals who was then at a distance from Boston) and broke near 100 panes and did other damage to the House; but on Mrs William's appearing and assuring them he was absent, and only she was at home, they departed. Happily they did not break into any House, for if they had got at a Cellar the Mischiefs would have been greater and more extensive.

After this they went to a Wharf where lay a pleasure Boat belonging to Mr Harrison, built by himself in a particular and elegant manner. This they took out of the water, and Carried it into the Common, & burnt it. By this time there were above 500 some say 1000 Men gathered together. Whilst the Boat was burning some Gentlemen who had an Influence over them, persuaded them to depart; this was debated and put to the Vote; Whereupon proclamation was made "each Man to his Tent:" Before this they were harangued by a Leader,[7] who among others used these words as they have been reported to me, "We will support our liberties depending upon the Strength of our ^own^ Arms and God."[8] Whilst they were upon the Common they got some Rum & attempted to get more; if they had procured it in Quantity, God knows where this Fury would have ended.[9] And now the Terror of this night is over it is said to be only a Prelude to greater Mischiefs the threats against the Commissioners & all the Officers of the Board being renewed with as great Malice as ever.

This Morning I got the Council together as soon as I could, and laid the affair before them. After a long altercation about what should be done, in which appeared a disposition to meddle with it as little as possible, it was advised & ordered that such of the Council as were Justices of the Peace should assist me in ascertaining the Facts by the Examination of Witnesses;[10] and Monday Morning at 9 oClock is appointed for proceeding upon this business.[11] When this is done I shall be able to give your Lordship a more full and particular account of this affair. At present what I send is only the Heads of it; which I dare say will ^not^ vary materially from the most authentic Narrative.[12] And I write this at present in Order to send it by the Post to New York to take the Chance of the Packet which it ^will^ probably just hit the time of.

I am My Lord Your Lordship's most obedient humble serv.ᵗ

(signd). Fra.ˢ Bernard

R.ᵗ Honble Earl of Hillsborough

P.S. 13.ᵗʰ June

This Morning early I received a Letter from the Commissioners[13] informing me of some particulars, from whence they concluded that they were immediately exposed to further Violences, and therefore they on Saturday evening took shelter onboard the Romney Man of War. That it being necessary to provide for their future security, they desire that they, their Families & Officers may be received accommodated and protected at the Castle. I immediately answer'd this by inclosing an Order to the Captain of the Castle to receive them accordingly.[14]

This Morning a Paper was found stuck up on Liberty Tree, inviting all sons of Liberty to meet at 6 o' clock to clear the Land of the Virmin which are come to devour them &c.ᵃ &c.ᵃ, I have been in Council all this Morning to consider of preventing an Insurrection tonight.[15] No Resolution has been or will be taken before I send away this. Perhaps the Commissioners retiring may assist our purpose.[16]

L, RC   CO 5/757, ff 115-117.

In handwriting of clerk no. 7. Variants: BP, 6: 311-315 (L, LbC); CO 5/766, (L, RLbC), ff 191-195; Coll. Mass. Papers, 1768 (L, Copy); *Letters to the Ministry* (1st ed.), 20-22; *Letters to the Ministry* (repr.), 26-29. The autograph original (which has not survived) and copies were carried to London by Benjamin Hallowell. Extracts were laid before both houses of Parliament on 28 Nov. 1768. HLL: American Colonies Box 1. Hillsborough replied with **No. 661**.

FB's reporting of the *Liberty* riot of Friday, 10 Jun., and its aftermath partially accounts for the British government's decision of 30 Jul. to send a further two regiments to Boston. The several reports of the American Board of Customs were also instrumental in persuading the Chatham administration to shore up the imperial establishment in Massachusetts.[17]

The rioters of 10 Jun. were ostensibly protesting the seizure of John Hancock's sloop *Liberty*. The seizure proceeded on the basis of information provided by tidesman Thomas Kirk, who claimed that on 9 May he had been detained and threatened to prevent him reporting that Hancock's crew were smuggling wine. Kirk only broke his silence following the death of his principal assailant. The accuracy of Kirk's account cannot be established, and the suspicion remains that the Customs commissioners were plotting to humble Hancock, whom they considered a serial and brazen smuggler. Be that as it may, Kirk provided the necessary evidence for customs officers Hallowell and Harrison to seize the *Liberty* at its berth on Hancock's Wharf. Expecting trouble, they requested assistance in advance from Capt. Corner of HMS *Romney* at anchor in the harbor. Sometime between 6 and 7 PM a crowd of traders and sailors on the waterfront observed boats from the HMS *Romney* tow the *Liberty* alongside the warship, and set out in small boats to disrupt the maneuver. The rescue failed. But when the customs officers returned ashore a crowd some three to four hundred strong, set upon them throwing missiles as well as insults.

The letter printed above (**No. 623**) documents FB's initial reactions to the riot, which he supplemented with a more a detailed account (**No. 630**). The narrative in **No. 623** correctly establishes the sequence of events, yet nevertheless fails to link them to Bostonians' underlying discontent arising from the impressment practiced by Capt. Corner (see **No. 618**). After leaving the waterfront, the customs officers passed through streets lined with near two thousand people, according to Hoerder. FB fails to mention (though he did not know all the relevant details at this point in time)[18] that another crowd of townsfolk intervened to guard the officials' houses (in addition to protecting young Harrison) and to prevent Benjamin Hallowell being subjected to a sustained assault (which Hallowell later claimed might have killed him). While FB captured for Hillsborough's benefit, the customs officers' manifest fears, the evening's proceedings hardly justified his depiction of them as a "great Riot" (in this letter) or "great disorders" (at the Council meeting the following Monday). Indeed, it was soon rumored that the governor, the Customs commissioners, and Capt. Corner had deliberately provoked a riot in order to besmirch Boston's reputation.

On Saturday 11 Jun., John Hancock initiated negotiations with the Customs Board for the return of the *Liberty*, to which the commissioners seemed amenable. The commissioners probably supposed that releasing the vessel would calm the local populace. Hancock might have been permitted to compound for the vessel's return, by which he would pay any duties owing on the cargo and agree to a fine, though he would remain liable for any other charges brought against him personally. Hancock, meanwhile, incurred the wrath of fellow Whigs James Otis Jr. and Samuel Adams for discussing such a compromise and abandoned the discussions on the Sunday evening. The Customs Board soon resolved to pursue Hancock in the courts, a decision that many historians have interpreted as a vendetta following the collapse of the action arising from the bungled inspection of the *Lydia* that April.[19]

On 22 Jun., the advocate general, Jonathan Sewall, commenced *in rem* proceedings to seize the *Liberty*'s cargo of oil tar. The actual charges are unknown but, as the editors of the *Legal Papers of John Adams* have demonstrated, would have encompassed one or more of three complaints: landing goods ashore before entering them at the Customhouse, failing to post a bond for the cargo, or unloading the cargo without permission. For the first offence the vessel alone was forfeit, for the second the vessel and cargo, and for the last the cargo alone would be confiscated. Hancock contested the libel, but Robert Auchmuty, the judge of the Vice Admiralty Court, on 17 Aug. decreed the *Liberty* forfeit on the basis of the first offence. The vessel was sold by order of the court and purchased by the American Board of Customs (ironically by Harrison, whose own boat had been destroyed by the rioters) for use as a cutter.[20] Meanwhile, sympathy for the *Liberty* rioters was such that an attempted prosecution by Sewall, in his capacity as attorney general, failed to proceed beyond an indictment (see **No. 672**).

However, William de Grey (1719-81), the English attorney general (whose opinion had been sought by the commissioners), advised the Customs Board that criminal proceedings could be instituted against Hancock. Consequently, on 29 Oct., Advocate General Sewall filed *in personam* libels against Hancock and five of his men (including Daniel Malcom) for smuggling wines, seeking a penalty of £9,000 (three times the value of the wines landed). Bail was set at £3,000. There is little doubt that the pursuit of Hancock was politically motivated, and driven by the Customs commissioners, yet it also became a test of imperial authority.[21] The trial, which commenced on 7 Nov., was sensationalized by the realization that Sewall (as prosecutor) and FB (as governor) stood to profit from one-third of the inordinately high penalties if Hancock and his men were convicted. John Adams defended Hancock, but while Hancock's "innocence is open to question," as Adams's editors noted, the prosecution failed to produce sufficient witnesses or evidence and Sewall withdrew the action on 25 Mar.[22]

---

1. Samuel Adams later accepted that "there was a riot on that evening, which is by no means to be justify'd," but proceeded to deliver a masterly critique of FB's overblown account of the disturbance in this letter. *Appeal to the World*, 9.

2. This was the second major incident of crowd action in which Benjamin Hallowell was targeted, his mansion house in Hanover Street having being looted during the Stamp Act riot of 26 Aug. 1765 (and he was also chased by a mob in 1774). *Bernard Papers*, 2: 319-325.

3. Richard A. Harrison (d.1813).

4. Thomas Irving (1738?-1800), inspector of imports and exports for the American Board of Customs. For his career and impact see John J. McCusker, "Colonial Civil Servant and Counter-revolutionary: Thomas Irving 1738?-1800 in Boston, Charleston, and London," *Perspectives in American History* 12 (1979): 315-350.

5. Probably Hallowell's house in Hanover Street, though FB appears to think that someone else was now the proprietor.

6. John Williams, inspector general of Customs.

7. The identity of this person is unknown, but there are two likely candidates. The first is Samuel Adams, who, about this moment in time, reputedly spoke to a group of seven people urging armed insurrection. **No. 732**, *Bernard Papers*, 5: 167-171. There is nothing to suggest that Adams went on to address the

large assembly mentioned by FB. The second candidate is William Molineux (c.1717-74). Of all the town's merchants, Molineux was the most closely involved with crowd action, directing mobs who visited importers and later participating in the Boston Tea Party. As an English-born Anglican he might have found it easier to establish normative relations with British customs officers, including Joseph Harrison, to whom he wrote on the morning of 15 Jun. Anticipating Harrison's surprize that a radical should contact him at this juncture, Molineux stressed that the communication came from "Gentlemen Worthy" of Harrison's notice; that the customs officer was in fact "Esteemd by the trade" and that the assault on his person and the burning of his boat he should attribute to the "frenzy of the Night . . . Such sort of People Inhabit every Great City Perhaps in the World." The actions of these criminally-minded denizens, he continued, ought not to be construed as a prelude to the "Greater Evils" Harrison's colleagues would surely imagine. William Molineux to Joseph Harrison, Boston, 15 Jun. 1768, NEP, 3: 1.

8. The leading historian of Massachusetts crowd action rendered the phrase as:

> We will defend our Liberties and property, by the Strength of our Arms and
> the help of our God; to your Tents O Israel.

Hoerder, *Crowd Action in Revolutionary Massachusetts*, 168.
   In fact, the speaker was citing a well-known passage of scripture: "to your Tents O Israel!" 1 Kings 12:16 or 2 Chronicles 10:16. The passage recounted the story of the divided kingdom, when ten of Israel's twelve tribes (all northern tribes) rebelled against the rule of King Rehoboam (a son of Solomon), dividing the kingdom between the northern tribes and the tribes of Judah and Benjamin, who remained loyal to the dynasty of David and Solomon. To FB, the citation was an indicator of Bostonians' rebellious instincts. Later generations of Americans would prefer the wisdom of the gospels that any house divided against itself cannot stand (Matthew 12:25 and Mark 3:23).

9. FB's suggestion that the mob resembled a lawless, drunken rabble was unfair, since, as Hoerder pointed out, there was nothing to have prevented the rioters looting the wine cellars of other officials, as they did to Hallowell's in 1765.

10. FB asked the Council to consider "as a matter of public notoriety, the great disorders" that occurred the previous day. The councilors forming the committee were William Brattle, Samuel Danforth, Samuel Dexter, Benjamin Lincoln, Jeremiah Powell, and Nathaniel Sparhawk, CO 5/827, f 48.

11. Ibid., ff 48-49.

12. He continued the account in **No. 630**.

13. Probably, **No. 624**, written the day before, which he received at 5 AM. FB would have received **No. 621** sometime after he commenced writing this letter. After reading the Customs commissioners' letter to FB (**No. 624**), Samuel Adams commented on FB's postscript:

> Here we see the Intelligence which the Governor represents to his Lordship as having been receiv'd by him from the Commissioners, he first communicated *to them*; and thereupon they grounded their pretended Fears in their letter *to him*, and Desire the Protection of the Government. This is all of a Piece, and may serve to explain the *frequent Rumours* of an insurrection mentioned in a former letter [**No. 600**], and from what quarter these frequent Rumours came.

Appeal to the World, 13.

14. FB to [John Phillips], Jamaica Plain, 13 Jun. 1768, CO 5/766, f 207.

15. Samuel Adams: "Could the Governor think, that but the Vermin that were come to Devour the Land, they meant his Excellency and the Commissioners?" *Appeal to the World*, 15.

16. That is to say, FB assumed that the retreat of the commissioners would remove the immediate threat of violence, and with it the imperative (as he saw it) of asking the Council to consider measures to prevent civil disorder.

17. Between 11 and 16 Jun, the American Board of Customs sent to the Treasury several detailed reports on the *Liberty* riot in which they enclosed copies of correspondence with FB, depositions (in order of dispatch) from Thomas Kirk, Joseph Harrison, Richard A. Harrison, and Benjamin Hallowell, together with a memorial of Thomas Irving, and correspondence between the Board and Capt. Corner. T 1/465, ff 129-186. The best account of the riot is Hoerder, *Crowd Action in Revolutionary Massachusetts*, 166-169.

18. **No. 621**. At sunset, FB left Boston for his country house at Jamaica Plain. **No. 630**.

19. For example, see Oliver M. Dickerson, "John Hancock: Notorious Smuggler or Near Victim of British Revenue Racketeers?" *Mississippi Valley Historical Review* 32 (1946): 517-540; Harlow G. Unger, *John Hancock: Merchant King and American Patriot* (New York, 2000), 122-123. On the *Lydia* incident see the source note to **No. 678**.

20. *Legal Papers of John Adams*, 2: 176-177.

21. Prosecutions *in rem* were brought under the Navigation Acts: 12 Car. 2, c. 18, (1660); 15 Car. 2, c. 7 (1663); 22 & 23 Car. 2, c. 26, (1670); 6 Geo. 3, c. 52, (1766); and 3 & 4 Anne, c. 10, (1704). The *in personam* charges were brought under the Sugar Act, 4 Geo. 3, c. 15, (1764). *Legal Papers of John Adams*, 2: 177, 181. In discussing the inordinately high penalties Hancock and his accomplices were facing, TH (drawing upon his knowledge of the tea trade) wrote that

> none of whom I dare say knew they were liable to this or any other consider-able penalty there never having been a prosecution upon this Act [*4 Geo. 3, c. 15*] except in one instance in my memory and that was against the Own-ers only. It is high time that it should be known and that the Acts of Trade should be more generally observed. The reduction of the Duty upon Tea has not had the proposed Effect. They who have been used to smuggling still continue it tho with less profit and large quantities of Tea are brought from St. Eustatia and other ports to which it is shipped from Holland.

TH to unknown, Boston, Nov. 1768, Mass. Archs., 26: 324-325, in Hutchinson Transcripts, 2: 673.

22. *Legal Papers of John Adams*, 2: 181-191, quotation at 185.

624 | From the American Board of Customs

Copy of a Letter from the Honble Commissioners of His Majesty's Customs to Govr. Bernard.

Sir,

As we found by Mr Secretary Oliver's Letter yesterday[1] that no immediate Measures were taken in Council for securing the peace of the Town, tho' there was the strongest Reason to expect further Violences, and your Excellency acquainting Us that you could give Us no Protection, and that Boston was no place of Safety for Us, and having received a verbal Message from the People by a Person of Character to this Effect "That if the Sloop that was seized was brought back to M^r.

Hancock's Wharf, upon his giving Security to answer the Prosecution, ^the Town^ might be kept quiet"; Which Message appearing to Us as a Menace, we applied to Capt. Corner to take Us on board His Majesty's Ship under his Command,[2] where we now are; and being this day further informed that some of the Leaders of the People had persuaded them in an Harangue to desist from further Outrages till Monday Evening, when the People are to be left to use their own Discretion, if their Requisitions are not complied with, We acquaint your Excellency, that we cannot consistent with the Honour of our Commission act in any Business of the Revenue whilst under such an Influence, and think it necessary to provide for our future Security, and therefore request your Excellency to give Directions, that the Commissioners may be received into the Castle, and that they may have Use of the Accommodations there for themselves, their Families and the Officers of the Board, and that your Excellency will please to give Orders for their Protection and Security whilst they may remain there.

On board His Majesty's Ship Romney 12 June 1768.

signed John Robinson.

H. Hulton.

W. Burch.

C. Paxton.

L, Copy   T 1/465, ff 143-144.

Docket: Copy. Boston 12th June 1768 Copy of a Letter from the Hon[ble]. Commiss[rs] of the Customs to Gov[r]. Bernard. The transcript is based on the commissioners' own copy of this letter because it was an enclosure to the Board's memorial to the Treasury of 16 Jun. **Appendix 6**. The other extant file copies were all made by third parties; the copy in CO 5/757 may have been prepared by a British government clerk rather than by FB. Variants: CO 5/757, ff 191-192 (L, Copy); CO 5/766, ff 204-26 (L, RLbC); Temple Papers, 1762-1768: JT Letterbook, 331-332 (L, RLbC); Coll. Mass. Papers, 1768 (L, Copy); BL: Add 38340, f 261 (L, Copy); *Letters to the Ministry* (1st ed.), 96; *Letters to the Ministry* (repr.), 128-129. FB received the commissioners' letter at 5 AM on the morning of 13 Jun. and replied with **No. 625**. A copy of **No. 624** was also enclosed with **No. 630** (according to CO 5/766 f 203).

As this letter indicates, the commissioners, their subordinates, and their families—some sixty-seven people—took refuge on HMS *Romney* fearing that they might become the target of popular violence. The exact time of their retreat is uncertain, but the "Major Part" of the Customs Board left town on Saturday afternoon, 11 Jun.; they would not have been able to keep the relocation secret, even if the commissioners were able to conceal their own movements.[3] FB may not have been aware of the commissioners' flight when, toward sunset, he left for his house at Jamaica Plain. (On the other hand, their movements could have been co-ordinated in advance, although there is no evidence for this.) FB received a personal visit from the Harrisons on Sunday afternoon, requesting refuge at Castle William; it is most unlikely that the Harrisons would have been unaware of the Board's retreat to the *Romney* or that they would have kept this from FB. (But if FB had hatched a plan with the commissioners he would have concealed this from the customs officers.) Whatever the case, FB received formal notification of the Board's relocation early in the morning of Monday 13 Jun. (**No. 626**). The commissioners and their families would have been received first, with the remainder of their staff and officers from the Customhouse following afterward. Boston customs officers Benjamin Hallowell and Joseph Harrison went also, but Commissioner John Temple remained, the clearest indicator to date that he supposed his colleagues exaggerated the threat to their persons posed by Boston's crowds.[4] On 20 Jun., the Board's entourage moved to the Castle, where they remained until mid-November.

1. Andrew Oliver to John Robinson, chairman of the Board, 11 Jun. 1768, T 1/465, ff 139-140.

2. American Board of Customs to John Corner, 11 Jun. 1768, T 1/465, ff 141-142.

3. "On Saturday Afternoon finding Ourselves utterly insecure in Town, the Major Part of Us were obliged to seek for an Asylum." **No. 626**. However, TH reported that "The Commissioners . . . remained pretty easy Saturday and Sunday but Monday morning early they sent a card to the Governor to let him know that were going aboard the Romney." TH would not have been immediately aware of the Board's movements, given that he was resident at his country house at Milton, and assumed that the Board's notification of their retreat (**No. 626**) was the first that FB knew of their relocation to the *Romney*. TH to Richard Jackson, 16 Jun. 1768, Mass. Archs., 26: 310-312.

4. Hoerder, *Crowd Action in Revolutionary Massachusetts*, 61.

625 | To the American Board of Customs

Copy of a Letter from Governor Bernard to the Commissioners of the Customs.

Council Chamber 13 June 1768.
forenoon.

Gentlemen,

Having communicated your Letter of the 12th Instant[1] to the Council, They observe with Concern, that you say, "That no immediate Measures were taken in Council for securing the Peace of the Town, Tho there was the strongest Reason to expect further Violences." They cannot but be apprehensive that this Sentence if it should pass unnoticed must tend to charge them with a Neglect of their Duty, in not advising me to take proper Measures for preserving the Peace of the Town. They therefore have desired me to acquaint you that during the Sitting of the Council on Saturday Morning so far from their having the strongest Reason to expect further Violences, there was no Reason at all given for such Expectation, and there was no Apprehension either in the Governor or Council of an immediate danger of further Violences. It was therefore the general opinion that they might take time to ascertain, the facts of the Riot on Friday Evening before they proceeded to order the bringing the offenders to Justice or to prevent the like offences for the future. I have this morning informed them of the present Apprehensions of further Violences & they are now taking the same into Consideration,

I am Gentlemen Your most obedient Humble Servant

Signed Francis Bernard.

To the Honble the Comm^{rs} of the Customs.

L, Copy   T 1/465, ff 153-154.

Docket: 14 Boston Council Chamber 13 June 1768 forenoon. Copy of a Letter from Governor Bernard to the Commissioners of the Customs. The RC is not extant, and this copy was enclosed in the memorial of the American Board of Customs, 16 Jun., (No. 14 on the list of enclosures to **Appendix 6**). Variants: CO 5/766, ff 207-209 (L, Copy); BL: Add 38340, f 279 (L, Copy); Coll. Mass. Papers, 1768 (L extract, Copy); *Letters to the Ministry* (1st ed.), 98-99; *Letters to the Ministry* (repr.), 132-133. Copies of the version enclosed with **Appendix 6** were laid before both houses of Parliament on 28 Nov. 1768. HLL: American Colonies Box 1.

The letter printed here is a formal reply by the Governor and Council to the Customs commissioners' letter of 12 Jun. FB presented the commissioners' letter to the Council on Monday morning, 13 Jun. (The commissioners of Customs responded with **No. 626**.) As FB reveals, the Council were irked by the imputation that they had been neglectful, advising FB to inform the commissioners that when they considered the commissioners' predicament (and appointed a committee of inquiry) they were "under no apprehensions of fresh disturbances." The commissioners' retreat to the *Romney*, however, manifestly demonstrated their lack of confidence in anything the Council might do to ensure their safety. Lest he too be accused of dereliction of duty, FB "acquainted the Board, that he was under apprehensions of fresh disturbances."[2] Nevertheless, despite these differences, FB and Council agreed to postpone an enquiry, and after the "matter being fully debated," the Council advised FB to refer any enquiry to a joint committee of the assembly (as the House requested). CO 5/827, f 48; *JHRM*, 45: 53. FB provided details of the afternoon's debates in the Council chamber in **No. 630**.

---

1. **No. 624**.

2. Samuel Adams interpreted the exchange as evidence of a settled plan "to perswade the Council if possible into a Belief . . . [*of an insurrection*], or if not, to form a Complaint to the Ministry, that they were negligent of their Duty in not advising to proper Measures for the Protection of the Commissioners; and from thence to enforce a Necessity of military Force to restore and support Government in Boston." *Appeal to the World*, 13.

626 | From the American Board of Customs

Copy of a Letter from the Commissioners of the Customs in Boston to Governor Bernard.

Sir

When your Excellency met in Council last Saturday[1] we were in hopes to have heard that effectual Measures would have been taken to aid and protect Us and our Officers in carrying on the Service of the Revenue, and for preserving the Peace of the Town, but we were much surprised to find that a Committee only was appointed to ascertain the facts attending the Tumult of the preceding Night and that your Council was not to sit again till this Day.

On Saturday Afternoon finding Ourselves utterly insecure in Town, the Major Part of Us were obliged to seek for an Asylum where we now sit as a Board, being persuaded of the Danger of attempting to proceed in our Duty in Town.

The Disorders of the Town we are sorry to observe are encreasing to such an enormous Pitch as to give it the Appearance more of an Insurrection than a Riot, and We find Ourselves obliged to apply to your Excellency to grant Us such Aid and Protection as may enable Us and our Officers to proceed in our Duty, and that we may be in some degree enabled to judge whether the Aid and Protection you'll think proper to grant, will be adequate to the distressed & embarassed State of the Service, We ^must^ request that You will let Us know what kind of Aid and Protection we may expect to receive.

(signed) Hen Hulton
J Temple[2]
W. Burch
C. Paxton
J. Robinson

On Board His Majestys Ship Romney 13th. June 1768

L, Copy   T 1/465, ff 157-158.

Docket: 13 June 1768 Copy of a Letter from the Commissioners to Gov.ʳ Bernard.__   The RC is not extant and this copy was enclosed in **Appendix 6**. Variants: CO 5/757, ff 205-206 (L, Copy); CO 5/766, ff 209-210 (L, Copy); BL: Add 38340, f 275 (L, Copy); *Letters to the Ministry* (1st ed.), 100; *Letters to the Ministry* (repr.), 133-134. This letter was a formal response to **No. 625**. FB's rejoinder is **No. 627**. Copies of the version enclosed with **Appendix 6** were laid before both houses of Parliament on 28 Nov. 1768. HLL: American Colonies Box 1.

The Customs commissioners' letter could be read as challenging FB to resolve their predicament. For it assumed that the harrasment and beatings administered to customs officers after the seizure of the *Liberty* warranted direct intervention to protect the commissioners from retribution. FB could have deployed the militia, but the Boston regiment had proven unreliable in facing Whig protestors during the Stamp Act riots; the only realistic, though provocative, military option was to bring British Regulars to Boston, as the commissioners and governor both knew. The letter should be read, therefore, as a tacit request that the governor should make such an approach to Gen. Thomas Gage at New York. In this respect, the operative phrase was the commissioners' assertion that they would "judge whether the Aid and Protection" FB could "grant, will be adequate to the distresses and embarrassed State of the Service." FB presented the commissioners' letter to the Council on the morning of 13 Jun. In the afternoon, he announced that he "was ready to do it,"— write to Gage for troops—but only with the agreement of the Council, he noted in **No. 630**. The commissioners may not have colluded with FB in collecting documentation to justify their flight from Boston, but they were were fully aware that FB agreed with their prognosis that Regulars were necessary for the Customs Board's future protection (see the source note to **No. 632**). The problem from FB's perspective was persuading the Council to co-operate; and so, while he endeavored to obtain the Council's agreement both he and the commissioners laid a paper trail that might also be used to persuade the British government to assume responsibility for sending in the troops.

---

1.   11 Jun.

2.   Temple did not sign the commissioners' letter to FB sent the previous day (**No. 624**). It is possible that the strident tone of this second letter (**No. 626**) conveyed the antipathy of FB's old enemy. Temple, however, did not accompany his colleagues to Castle William and resided in Boston for the duration of their retreat.

Thomas Gage. By John Singleton Copley, c.1768. Inscribed in yellow paint, lower right: "GENERAL THE HONB^{LE}. THO^S. GAGE/OB^T. 1788." (In fact, Gage died at home in London on 2 Apr. 1787). Yale Center for British Art, Paul Mellon Collection.

627 | To the American Board of Customs

Jamaica plain June 13. 1768

Gentlemen,

I am very sorry that you think yourselves so much in danger in Boston as to make it unsafe for you to reside there. As you judge it necessary to your Security to resort to the Castle, I hereby inclose orders to the Captain of the Castle[1] to receive you & your families and the Officers of your Board and to accommodate you there and to give you all the Protection and Security in his power.

I am, Gentlemen, your most obedient humble Servant

Fra Barnard.

To the honorable the Commissioners of his Majesty's Customs.

L, Copy   T 1/465, ff 159-161 (L, Copy).

Docket: Copy of Governor Bernards Letter of 13 June 1768 to the Comm[rs]: of his Majesty's Customs. N° 17.   Enclosed a copy of FB to the captain of Castle William [TH], Jamaica Plain, 13 Jun. 1768 (available at CO 5/766, f 207). The RC is not extant and this copy was the seventeenth in the list of items enclosed with **Appendix 6**. Variants: CO 5/757, ff 207-208 (L, Copy); CO 5/766, f 26 (L, Copy); BL: Add 38340, f 277 (L, Copy); Coll. Mass. Papers, 1768 (L, Copy); *Letters to the Ministry* (1st ed.), 100; *Letters to the Ministry* (repr.), 134. This letter is a reply to **No. 626**, the first of two sent that day.[2] Copies of the version enclosed with **Appendix 6** were laid before both houses of Parliament on 28 Nov. 1768. HLL: American Colonies Box 1.

---

1. Lt. John Phillip (1712-97) had been commander of the Castle William garrison since 1759, TH being the honorary captain. Phillip relinquished the position in 1770 when the fort was brought under the direct administration of the governor and garrisoned by British Regulars.

2. The second was **No. 628**.

628 | To the American Board of Customs

Boston 13th. June 1768.

Gentlemen

In answer to that part of your Letter of this day[1] wherein you desire me to grant you such aid and protection as may enable you and your Officers to proceed in your Duty. I can only inform you that after several hours deliberation of the necessity of taking some measures to preserve the peace of the Town & what those Measures should be, the Council have come to a resolution that as there appears to be no immediate danger of further Violence, they are of opinion that it would be best to refer this matter to the Consideration of a Committee of both Houses. I therefore cannot at present let you know what kind of aid & protection you may expect to receive.

I am Gentlemen your most obedient hum[ble]. Servant

(Signed) Fra. Bernard.

To the Hon[ble]. Commissioners of His Majestys Customs

L, Copy   T 1/465, ff 161-162.

Docket: Boston 13th. June 1768_____ Copy of Gov[r]. Bernards Letter to the Comm[rs]. The RC is not extant and this copy was the eighteenth item in the list of enclosures to **Appendix 6**. Variants: CO 5/757, ff 209-210 (L, Copy); CO 5/766, f 211 (L, LbC); BL: Add 38340, f 271 (L, Copy); extract in Coll. Mass. Papers, 1768; *Letters to the Ministry* (1st ed.), 100; *Letters to the Ministry* (repr.), 135. This is the second of two replies to **No. 626**, both dated 13 Jun.[2] Copies of the version enclosed with **Appendix 6** were laid before both houses of Parliament on 28 Nov. 1768. HLL: American Colonies Box 1.

---

1. **No. 626**.
2. The first was **No. 627**.

629 | *Petition of the Boston Town Meeting*

Province of the Massachusetts Bay — [*14 Jun. 1768*]

To His Excellency Francis Bernard the Esq. Governour and Commander in Chief, in and over said Province and Vice Admiral the same.[1]

The Inhabitants of the Town of Boston in Town Meeting legally Assembled —

Humbly Shew

That your Petitioners consider the British Constitution as the Basis of their safety and happiness; By that is established no Man shall be govern'd nor taxed but by himself or Representative legally and fairly chosen; and in which he does not give his own consent. In open violation of these fundamental Rights of Britons, Laws & Taxes are imposed on us to which we have not only not given our consent but against which we have most firmly Remonstrated — Dutiful Petitions have been preferred to our most gracious Sovereign, which (though to the great consternation of the People, we now learn, have been cruelly and insidiously prevented reaching the Royal Presence)[2] we have waited to receive a Gracious answer to, with the greatest attention to the publick peace, untill we find ourselves invaded with an armed force, Siezing, impressing the Persons of our fellow Subjects contrary to express Acts of Parliament.[3] Menaces have been thrown out, fit only for Barbarians which already effect us in the most sensible manner, and threaten us with Famine & Desolation, as all Navigation is obstructed, upon which alone our whole support depends, and the Town is at this Crisis in a Situation nearly such, as if War was formally declared against it. To contend with our Parent State is in our Idea the most shocking and dreadful Extremity; but tamely to relinquish the only security we and our Posterity retain of the enjoyment of our Lives & Properties, without one struggle is so humiliating and base, that we cannot support the Reflection; we apprehend Sir, That it is at your option, in your power, and we would hope in your inclination, to prevent this distressed and Justly incensed People, from effecting too much, and from the shame and reproach of attempting too little.

As the Board of Customs have thought fit, of their own motion to relinquish the exercise of their Commission here, and as we cannot but hope, that being convinced of the impropriety and injustice of the appointment of a Board, with such enormous power, and the inevitable distruction[4] which would ensue from the exercise of their office, will never reasume it. We flatter ourselves your Excellency will in tenderness to this People, use the best means in your power, to remove the other grieveance, we so Justly complain of, and issue your immediate Order to the

Commander of his Majestys Ship Romney, to remove from this Harbour, 'till we shall be ascertained of the Success of our Applications. —

transcript, PC   *Reports of the Record Commissioners of Boston,* 16: 254-255.

Variants: CO 5/757, ff 143-145 (Ms, Copy), which FB had sent under cover of **No. 632**; this was copied into CO 5/766, ff 223-227 (Ms, Copy); there is an extract in ADM 1/483, f 96. The town meeting published a copy in the *Boston Gazette*, 20 Jun. 1768 and other newspapers along with FB's reply of 15 Jun. It was also printed in the *Public Advertiser*, 29 Jul. 1768 (a British newspaper). FB replied with **No. 631**. The petition was laid before both houses of Parliament on 28 Nov. 1768.

Since the beginning of the year, FB had focused on holding in check, as far as he might, opposition in the House of Representatives. This petition signaled a re-emergence of opposition in the Boston town meeting, not that it had been silent; the anger of the townsfolk was palpable in the denunciation of illegal impressment by Capt. Corner. Exasperation that the assembly's petition to the king had been ignored doubtless encouraged the meeting to condemn unpopular imperial "Laws & Taxes" that together seemed to threaten their destruction; thus was the petition framed in the confrontational language of radical Whigs. The petition's antimilitaristic allusions, moreover, gave form to anxieties about the prospect of British Regulars being sent to Boston one day (the order, in fact, had already been given a week earlier), though some (such as the lawyer and future Loyalist Samuel Quincy, noted below) would have had deep misgivings about any mention of having to "contend with" the "Parent State" even if such were deemed "the most shocking and dreadful Extremity" imaginable.

> That it is at your option, in your power, and we would hope in your inclination, to prevent this distressed and Justly incensed People, from effecting too much, and from the shame and reproach of attempting too little.

The town had not sought FB's assistance since the Stamp Act Crisis, and rumors concerning the Regulars might account for the approach to the governor, as much as the impressment controversy and the flight of the Customs Board both explain the petition's timing. A twenty-one man committee, including leading radicals (James Otis Jr., Joseph Warren, and Samuel Adams) and two or three moderates (like Samuel Quincy) was instructed to carry the petition to FB, then residing at his estate at Jamaica Plan, and thereafter prepare a "true state" of recent events in the town for the edification of the House agent, Dennys DeBerdt. (See **No. 630**.) From a Whig perspective, these undertakings were partly conceived to mollify popular discontent and rumors of violence.[5] They complemented the investigations of the assembly's committee into popular "Apprehensions" without suggesting any rapprochement with the governor over and above the request to intercede with Capt. Corner. FB promised to do what he could to "regulate" impressment, iterating that he had no authority to issue orders to Corner to stop the practice (see **No. 630**). HMS *Romney* did not leave Boston harbor until 17 Oct.[6]

1. The title and place name have been relocated.

2. The House of Representatives, petition to the king, 20 Jan. 1768, *JHRM*, 44: 217-219. The petition was not transmitted by FB but submitted by the House agent DeBerdt, a breach of protocol that justified the British government's refusal to accept it. See **No. 712**, *Bernard Papers*, 5: 115-118.

3. Two acts of Parliament prohibited the impressment of sailors from vessels engaged in the American trade: the East India Goods Act, 6 Anne, c. 37, sect. 9 (1707) and the Sugar Trade Act, 19 Geo. 2, c. 30, sect. 1 (1746). Cited from Hoerder, *Crowd Action in Revolutionary Massachusetts*, 170; Boston town meeting, instructions to representatives, 17 Jun. 1768, *Reports of the Record Commissioners of Boston*, 16: 259. However, the king's attorney general in England subsequently advised that 6 Anne c. 37 was no longer in force. **No. 661**.

4. CO 5/757: "Destruction".

5. Hoerder, *Crowd Action in Revolutionary Massachusetts*, 170-171.

6. *Boston Chronicle*, 17-24 Oct. 1768.

630 | *To the Earl of Hillsborough*

(N°. 6.)

Roxbury near Boston, 14th June 1768

My Lord,

By my Letter N°. 5[1] I informed Your Lordship of a Riot which happened on the 10th. of June in the Evening & that upon my laying the matter before the Council, they had advised that such of the Board as were Justices of the Peace should assist me to ascertain the facts; afterwards the whole should be taken into consideration. I should have added that there was then no apprehension in the Council that there would be a repetition of these violences. Nor indeed did any such immediate danger appear to me whilst I staid in Boston, which was till Sun-set, when I went to my Country House about four Miles from Boston.

The next Day being Sunday, I heard some loose Reports that there was to be another rising. Early in the Afternoon the Son of Mr. Harrison the Collector came to me & said that His father apprehended that his Life would be in danger if he staid in Boston, & advised that I would give an order that he should be received at the Castle: I accordingly gave him such an order. The next morning, being Monday the 13th, a little after 5 O Clock, I received a Letter from the Commissioners which is mentioned in the P. S. of my last;[2] a Copy of which, together with my answer & my order to the Commander of the Castle, I herewith inclose. Immediately after I went to Town, & ordered the Council to be summoned to meet at 9 O' Clock. Before I went to Council, the Sheriff came to inform me that there was a most violent and virulent paper stuck up upon Liberty Tree, containing an Invitation to the Sons of Liberty to rise that Night to clear the Country of the Commissioners & their Officers, to avenge themselves of the Officers of the Custom-house, one of which was by name devoted to death:[3] There were also some indecent Threats against the Governor, if he did not procure the release of the Sloop which was seized. Afternoon as I came to the Town-house, where the Council Chamber is, I found several handbills, which have been circulated round the Town, stuck up there; an exact Copy of which follows.

Boston, June 13th, 1768.

"The Sons of Liberty.

"REQUEST all those, who in this time of oppression &
distraction, wish well to, & would promote the peace, good
order & security of the Town & Province, to assemble at
Liberty Hall, under Liberty Tree, on Tuesday the 14th. instant,
at Ten O'Clock forenoon precisely."

When I got into the Council Chamber in the Morning, after waiting for a full Board,[4] I told them that there was no time to enquire of the particulars of the former Riot which was accidental, when we were immediately threatned with new disturbances premeditated. I therefore laid before them the informations I had received,[5] & desired that they would take into consideration the necessity of providing for the peace of the Town, & the proper means of doing it. But notwithstanding all, I could not bring them to any conclusion or even to state a question. All that was done in the Morning was to conjure an expression in the Commissioners Letter ^which obliged me to write the Letter the 2ᵈ of that date.[6] About one O'Clock they desired me to adjourn the Council till 4 O'Clock in the Afternoon, that in the mean time they might inform themselves of the probability of new Disturbances arising.

In the Afternoon, the printed paper[7] was laid before the Council, but it was not considered as an implication of danger, neither was the impropriety of the Sons of Liberty appointing a meeting to secure the peace of the Town, when the Governor & Council were sitting upon that Business, & seemingly to little purpose taken much notice of.[8] I laid before them the Letter of the Commissioners of that day; but a disposition to censure it rather than answering it appearing, I postponed the consideration of that Letter 'till after the determination of the main question. Fresh attempts were made to get rid of the Business, & it was again proposed, as it had been in the Morning, that I should lay the Business before the General Court by a Message to both Houses.[9] I called for the Journal of the House and showed them that when I pursued this method, upon the Stampt-Act Riots, with the advice of the Council, I was told by the House that it was the Business of the Executive Government to quell Riots and the Legislature had no right to interpose, unless new laws were wanted.[10] That there was as much reason for them to give the same answer now; & I did not care to receive it twice. But the Bias still running this way, I was obliged to give it up, & leave it to the Council to raise a Committee of both Houses to consider of this Business; although I had many objections to this measure, but I could not help myself.[11]

In the course of these debates I told them that if this had been the first Business of the kind, I should have asked their advice whither I should not send to the General for Troops; but having tried it at a time when there was at least as much danger as now, & found them utterly averse to it, let the danger be ever so great & imminent, it would be in vain to repeat the question: however I was ready to do it, if any one Gentlemen would propose it. I was answered, that they did not desire to be knocked on the Head. I said that I did not desire that they or I should; but I was ready to take my share of the danger if they would join with me, tho' I could not act alone in so unpopular a measure, for if I did, I must quit the Government, at least for the present. I added, that tho' I was well-assured that if I put this question, every Gentleman would answer in the negative, yet I doubted not but every one would be glad to see the peace of the Town restored by this method, if it should appear to be the only one left. No answer was given.

By the removing this Business into the General Court, it is taken out of my hands any further than the final Consent or Dissent to what shall be sent up to me. It is not with my approbation, nor entirely to my dissatisfaction, for as I cannot conduct the Business as it ought to be, it may be best for me to have little hand in it. I am,

> My Lord, Your Lordship's most obedient humble servant

> (signed) Fra[s]. Bernard

Earl of Hillsborough.

P.S.

As I have not been able to proceed in the enquiry, I hereby inclose Depositions taken by the Commissioners.

The Meeting of the Sons of Liberty in my next.

ALS, RC   CO 5/757, ff 118-120.

Endorsed: Boston June 14. 1768. Gov[r] Bernard. (No. 6) R 19th July. A. 20.   Enclosed copies (not found) of **Nos. 624** and **625**; FB to captain of Castle William, Jamaica Plain, 13 Jun. 1768 (entered in CO 5/766, f 207);[12] copies of the depositions of Joseph Harrison,

Richard A. Harrison, and Benjamin Hallowell that were enclosed with **Appendix 6**. This letter, together with **Nos. 623**, **630**, and **633**, were carried to London by customs officer Benjamin Hallowell, who, on 19 Jul., personally delivered to the Treasury the memorial of the American Board of Customs also dated 16 Jun. (**Appendix 6**). Variants of the letter in: CO 5/766, ff 196-23 (L, RLbC); BP, 6: 315-319 (L, LbC); *Letters to the Ministry* (1st ed.), 22-24; *Letters to the Ministry* (repr.), 29-32. Extracts of the original autograph letter together with the enclosures were laid before both houses of Parliament on 28 Nov. 1768. HLL: American Colonies Box 2. Hillsborough replied with **No. 661**.

The *Liberty* riot had left FB fearful that the Sons of Liberty would attempt a more daring demonstration of popular opposition to the Townshend Acts. As this letter indicates, rumors of violent plots against the Customs commissioners and the governor circulated freely in the aftermath of the riot. This may account for FB's persistence in trying to persuade the Council that British Regulars were necessary for the support of government. He had no desire to invite popular retribution by requesting troops from Gen. Gage on his own authority, as he could, and wished always in this matter to act jointly with the Council; such would have clearly signaled the provincial government's unequivocal condemnation of popular opposition to imperial law. Popular concerns that the *Liberty* riot would provoke the British into dispatching Regulars to Boston were reflected in the deliberations of the House as well as the Council (which fears were not misplaced, as it turned out). While a joint committee of the House and Council (formed on 13 Jun.) deliberated the "State of the Province" (reporting on 30 Jun.) another joint committee (appointed on 18 Jun.) brought the prospect of military intervention to center stage (**No. 632**n27).

---

1. **No. 623.**

2. **No. 624** in **No. 623**.

3. FB also mentions the offensive paper in **No. 623**. The identity of the death-sentenced customs officer is unknown.

4. On Monday13 Jun.

5. Presumably FB is referring to the letter from the commissioners, **No. 624**.

6. **No. 625**.

7. The handbill quoted above.

8. Samuel Adams:

> But surely, if the Governor and Council could be supposed to be sitting *upon such Business*, at *such a time, and seemingly to little purpose*, there could be no great Impropriety in other Peoples undertaking it. But without adopting by any Means the Measure, Is not here a striking Instance of the Disposition of Governor Bernard, and some others, to receive with the greatest Avidity the most aggravated Accounts of every trifling Occurrence that has happened, and without any Enquiry, to paint them to the Ministry in the deepest colours!

Appeal to the World, 16.

9. For a brief discussion see the source note to **No. 625**.

10. The House had responded to FB's contention in a speech of 25 Sept. 1765 that resistance to the Stamp Act was threatening to undermine the power of government. In a long answer, dated 24 Oct., the

House refuted the imputation that the Stamp Act riots necessitated extraordinary measures (referring by implication, to the deployment of British Regulars) and professed that "laws are already in being for the support" of government.

> Surely you cannot mean, by calling the whole legislative in aid of the executive authority, that any new and extraordinary kind of power should by law be constituted, to oppose such acts of violence as you[r] Excellency may apprehend from a people ever remarkable for their loyalty and good order; tho' at present uneasy and discontented. If then the laws of the province for the preservation of his Majesty's peace are already sufficient, your Excellency we are very sure need not to be told, to whose department it solely belongs to appoint a suitable number of majestrates to put those laws in execution, or remove them in case of failure of their duty therein.

JHRM, 42: 130-138.

11. The joint committee was appointed to consider the "State of the Province" on 13 Jun., at the suggestion of the House. JHRM, 45: 53. Meanwhile, FB collected copies of depositions submitted by the customs officers caught up in the riot, and enclosed them with this letter. The Council later accused him of undermining the assembly's enquiry from the outset by assisting the Customs commissioners collect their own evidence for the British government. **Appendix 4**.

12. According to CO 5/766 f 203.

631 | *To the Boston Town Meeting*

[15 Jun. 1768]

Gentlemen

My Office and station make me a very incompetent Judge of the rights you claim against Acts of Parliament; and therefore it would be to no purpose for me to express my opinion thereupon. All I can say is, that I shall not knowingly infringe any of your Rights and Privileges, but shall religeously maintain all those which are committed to me as a servant of the King. —

In regard to the impressing men for the Service of the King in his Ships of war, it is practised in Great Britain, and all other his Majestys Dominions and therefore I cannot dispute it in this part of them. But I shall use my utmost endeavors to get it regulated so as to avoid all the inconveniences to this Town, which you are apprehensive of; and from the knowledge I have of Capt. Corner,[1] I have no doubt of my succeeding therein. —

I cannot pretend to enter into any dispute between you and your Parent State; I desire to be a faithful servant in regard to both; and I shall think myself most highly honoured, if I can be in the lowest degree an Instrument in preserving a perfect Conciliation between them, I can assure you that if it was as much in [my]^2 power as it is in my will it would always be preserved.

I am obliged by all kinds of duty, by my general Instructions; and by his Majestys special orders to protect aid and assist the Commissioners of the Customs (appointed under the Great Seal of Great Britain in pursuance of an act of parliament) and their Officers in their Persons and Offices.[3] And whether they shall or shall not relinquish the exercise of their commission, I must not fail to give them all the protection aid and assistance in my power If in so doing I shall give offence, I shall be sorry for it, but I shall never regret the doing my duty. —

I have no command over his Majestys Ships, and therefore cannot issue such orders as you desire nor indeed any order to the Commander of his Majestys Ship the Romney. And it would be highly improper for me to make a requisition to him to remove from this Harbour, when I know he is stationed here by a superior Officer, and cannot remove from hence but by his Orders —

Fra Bernard

transcript, PC   *Reports of the Record Commissioners of Boston*, 16: 256-257.

FB was replying to the town's petition of 14 Jun. (**No. 629**). A copy was enclosed in **No. 632** (according to CO 5/766, f 222) and copied into CO 5/766, ff 228-234. The town meeting published FB's reply in the province newspapers, including the *Boston Gazette*, 20 Jun. 1768.

FB met with Capt. Corner on 17 Jun. requesting that he and his officers cease impressment (see **No. 632**).

---

1.   Printing error corrected.

2.   Editorially supplied.

3.   Commissioners of Customs Act, 7 Geo. 3, c. 41 (1767).

632 | To the Earl of Hillsborough

(Nº 7)

Copy

Boston June 16ᵗʰ, 1768.

My Lord,

I come now to give your Lordship an Accoᵗ: of the meeting at Liberty Tree in pursuance of the printed notice, a Copy of which I inserted in my last.[1] Your Lordship must know that Liberty Tree is a large Old Elm in the high Street upon which the Effigies were hung in the time of the stamp Act, & from whence the Mobs at that time made their Parades. It has since been adorned with an Inscription and has obtained the Name of Liberty Tree, as the Ground under it has that of Liberty Hall.[2] In Augᵗ: last just before the Commencement of the present troubles they erected a Flag-Staff, which went thro' the Tree and a good deal above the top of the Tree. Upon this they hoist a Flag as a signal for the Sons of Liberty as they are called. I gave my Lord Shelburne an Accoᵗ: of this Erection at the time it was made.[3] This Tree has often put me in mind of Jack Cade's Oak of Reformation.[4]

Upon this Staff the Flag was flying early on the Morning of Tuesday:[5] at the time appointed there was assembled, they say at least 4,000 Men, many having come out of the Country for that purpose; some of the principal Gentlemen of the town attended, in order to engage the lower people to concur in Measures for peace and Quiet.[6] One of the select Men was chosen Moderator or Chairman: when it was found that they could not do business there they adjourned to the Town-Hall.[7] Here it was objected ^that^ they were not a legal Meeting; to obviate this they adjourned to the Afternoon, that in the mean time the Select Men might call a town Meeting to legalize[8] the Assembl[y.][9]

In the afternoon they met in a large Meeting House,[10] the Town Hall being not large enough for the Company; and Mr Otis was chosen Moderator. Many wild and Violent proposals were made, but were warded off.[11] Among these were that every Capt: of a Man of War that came into this Harbour should be under the Command of the Genˡ: Court? another was that if any person should promote or assist the bringing Troops here he should be deemed a disturber of the peace and a Traitor to his Country? but nothing was done finally but to pass a petition to the Govʳ:[12] and appoint a Committee of 21 Persons to resort to his Country House[13] (where I then was) and present it to him and to appoint a Committee to prepare Instructions for their Representatives, and a Letter to Mʳ. Deberdt as their Agent, after which they adjourned to the next Day.[14]

The same Evening the Committee which was in general very respectable attended me in a Train of 11 Chaises. I received them with all possible Civility, and having heard their Petition I talked very freely with them upon the Subject, but postponed giving a formal Answer till the next Day, as it should be in writing. I then had Wine handed round and they left me, highly pleased with their Reception, especially that part of them, which had not been used to an Interview with me.[15] The next Day M[r]. Otis having received my Answer in writing[16] reported the whole, took notice of the Polite Treatment they had received from me, & concluded that he really believed I was a well-wisher to the Province.[17] This from him was uncommon and extraordinary. The answer was universally approved so that just at this time I am popular: whenever my Duty obliges me to do any thing which they don't like, theres an End to my popularity, and therefore I don't expect to enjoy it a Week. I should here mention that I am not sure that the appointment of the Committee for preparing Instructions &c[a]: which I have mentioned to have been done on the first Day, was not on the Second[18] but it is not material, they then adjourned to Friday next in the Afternoon.[19]

There was but one thing mentioned in the Petition that I could do ^and that I had promised the Select Men, two days before, that I would do;^[20] this was to settle with Capt: Corner Commander of the Romney a Regulation for impressing Men, so that might not hurt the Town. And this I had settled long before, only there happened to be one single breach of it by an inferior Officer against his Orders. And indeed the Mob of the Town had lately used him and his Officers so very ill that he was disengaged from any promise he had made, if he had desired it. I accordingly went on board the Romney attended by 3 of the Council[21] and had a full conference with the Captain in which he acted with the utmost Candor and good Nature and after recapitulating the Injuries he and his Officers had received renewed the Engagement concerning pressing & professed a Desire of making that Service agreeable to the Town. In the Afternoon I went to the Council and having sent for the select Men I reported to them what had passed with the Captain, and after having shewn them how much it was the Interest of the Town to cultivate a good understanding with the Commanders of the King's Ships I exhorted them to use their Influence over the Common people so as to dispose them to treat the Captain his Officers and Men in such a Manner, as might procure his favour, at least avert his resentment: and one of the Gentlemen, who accompanied me engaged to attend the Town Meeting, and repeat what had passed at this Interview as of his own accord, it being not thought proper that the Gov[r]. and Council should appear to have any correspondence with a Meeting so originated & composed, as this was.

June the 18th. 1768.

I am now able to proceed in my Narrative of the Town Meeting. Yesterday in the Afternoon they met according to their adjournment. The Gentleman of the Council who had engaged to ^report^ Our Proceedings with Cap: Corner, did it in such a manner as gave great Satisfaction both in regard to me & the Captain.[22] But no Message was voted either to me or Cap: Corner: to me indeed it was useless; but to him requisite, as they have in a manner interdicted him and his Officers of the Town.[23] All they did was to instruct their Representatives; the only Instruction I hear of is to enquire if any Persons have been writing for the King's Ships or Troops to come here and who? that they might be distinguished as Enemies to the Country. They broke up quietly and there is an End of the Meeting.

The Comm[rs]: and their families and Officers are still on board the Romney, where they proceed in their Business. The Town won't hear of their return to Boston; and it is much better that they should not untill the Question is determined. I hear that they are to fix their Residence at the Castle next Monday.[24] The Romney is fell down and now lies off the Castle towards the Town; there is also a Sloop of War of 16 Guns just come in, which being stationed on the other side the Castle will complete the Command of all the approaches to the Castle; there are also other Ships of War expected in. So that the retreat of the Commissioners has been very timely and well circumstanced & their security is now effectually provided for. Your Lordship may wonder at my dwelling upon this; but if there is not a Revolt the Leaders of the Sons of Liberty must falsify their Words & change their purposes.[25] For my part when I consider the Defenceless State of this Town I cannot think they will be so mad as to attempt to defend it against the King's Forces: but the Lengths they have gone already are scarce short of Madness. I send you Copies of Papers stuck upon the Town House; they may be the Work of very few Individuals.[26]

I am &c[a].

Fra: Bernard.

P.S.

The Instructions of their Representatives which passed at the Town Meeting yesterday have this Morning produced a Vote in the House of Representatives to the purpose following.

> "Ordered that M[r]. Speaker M[r]. Otis &c[a]. with such as the honble Board shall join, be a Committee to enquire into the Grounds and Reasons of the present apprehension of the People that Measures have been

taken, or are now taking for the Execution of the late Revenue Acts of Parliament by a Naval or Military Force:" in which the Council have joined;

I will endeavour to get a Copy of the Instructions before I seal this.[27]

L, RC   CO 5/757, ff 138-141.

In handwriting of clerk no. 7. Endorsed: Copy of a Letter from Gov[r]: Bernard to the Earl of Hillsborough Dated Boston June 16th: 1768. (N[o]. 7) R 19th July. A.21.   Enclosures: copies of papers "stuck up" in Boston, Jun. 1768, CO 5/757, f 142;[28] petition of the Boston town meeting, 14 Jun. 1768, CO 5/757, ff 143-145 (MS, Copy), for which see **No. 629**; and a copy of **No. 631** (not found) Benjamin Hallowell carried the package to London. Variants of letter in: CO 5/766, ff 212-221 (L, RLbC) with enclosures at ff 221-227; BP, 6: 319-324 (L, LbC); *Letters to the Ministry* (1st ed.), 25-28; *Letters to the Ministry* (repr.), 33-37. Extracts of the original letter together with the enclosures were laid before both houses of Parliament on 28 Nov. 1768. HLL: American Colonies Box 2. Hillsborough replied with **No. 661**.

 FB's account of his intercession with Capt. Corner and his momentary popularity confirmed that the governor remained a vital instrument of royal authority, at least in negotiating the end of impressment by the Royal Navy. But from the people's perspective too there had also been a shift, FB reported, with attention focused on the question of who "might have been writing for the King's Troops and Ships." Despite this, FB expected that the province would still accept him as a "mediator" in the dispute over the circular letter issued by the House of Representatives in February (**No. 633**).

---

1. **No. 630**.

2. The tree was at the junction of Essex and Orange streets in the South End. For a description of the tree's adornments see *Bernard Papers*, 3: 387n10. This may record an early usage of the term "Liberty Hall," which was soon commonplace on both sides of the Atlantic; it was used in Oliver Goldsmith's play *She Stoops to Conquer* (1773) and gave an opera its name (1785), by Charles Dibdin.

3. **No. 557**, *Bernard Papers*, 3: 640-648.

4. Samuel Adams observed this was an "awkward and inconsistent Description of the Tree," probably in recognition of the symbolism that FB ascribed to it, than his description of it. *Appeal to the World*, 17. The history of English peasant rebellions resonated loudly in the phrase "Oak of Reformation," instantly locating the symbolism of Boston's Liberty Tree within a larger tradition. The phrase would have immediately alerted Hillsborough to FB's anxiety that the *Liberty* riot and the town's deliberations about impressment presaged a large-scale popular revolt (as his figures on crowd numbers, and the comments on rural activism were also designed to convey). The oak tree was the adopted symbol of the Kent rebellion of 1450 led by Jack Cade. But by the eighteenth century the "Oak of Reformation" was more commonly associated with the 1549 revolt against land enclosures in Norfolk led by yeoman farmer Robert Kett; an oak tree was the central meeting place of the rebel camp at Mousehold Heath before the rebel army of c.16,000 peasants invested Norwich, then one of England's largest cities. On the significance of trees as emblems of "ancient folk rights of freedom and liberty" see David Hackett Fischer, *Liberty and Freedom: A Visual History of America's Founding Ideas* (Oxford, 2005), 25; also Frederic William Russell, *Kett's Rebellion in Norfolk being a history of the great civil commotion that occurred at the time of the Reformation, in the reign of Edward VI* (London, 1859), 41, 52.

But mention of Cade also served to signal FB's alarm at the prospect of a violent insurrection during the early summer of 1768 (and which included Massachusetts's rural as well as urban populations). During the first days of Jul. 1450, Cade's supporters directly confronted royal authority forcing the king and his government to retreat from London. The rebel force, 20,000 strong and including port-town laborers and sailors as well as peasants, executed royal officials and looted the capital before they dispersed upon encountering protracted resistance by townsfolk and soldiers loyal to King Henry VI. Paul Murray Kendall, *The Yorkist Age: Daily Life During the Wars of the Roses* (New York, 1962), 468-472. FB was probably most familiar with Cade's bloody rebellion from Shakespeare's *Henry VI, Part 2*. Shakespeare's Cade is the obscure mercenary tool of the king's enemy, Richard Plantagenet, the duke of York (4:2). He also unleashed class conflict by marshaling

> a ragged multitude
> Of hinds and peasants, rude and merciless . . .
> All scholars, lawyers, courtiers, gentlemen,
> They call false caterpillars, and intend their death.

> (*Henry VI, Part 2*, 4:4. 33-34, 37-38).

5. 14 Jun.

6. It is noteworthy that FB should not comment on some of the wilder speechmaking purportedly made at the Liberty Tree on 14 Jun. Samuel Adams reputedly advocated insurrection: "If you are Men, behave like Men; let us take up arms immediately and be free and spend our last drop." The comments and quotations proffered by FB later in the letter indicate hostility to any such radical outbursts. Adams quoted in Harlow G. Unger, *John Hancock: Merchant king and American Patriot* (New York, 2000), 121, c.f. Miller, *Sam Adams*, 144-145.

7. Faneuil Hall.

8. Samuel Adams: "he should have said, broke up; and the selectmen . . . called a Town-meeting, agreeable to the Directions of the Law, to meet in the afternoon." *Appeal to the World*, 17.

9. Manuscript torn.

10. The Old South Meeting House.

11. Samuel Adams: "It ought here to be observed, that Governor Bernard constantly represents Bodies of Men, even the most respectable, by Proposals made by Individuals, which have been misrepresented by Pimps and Parasites, and perhaps aggravated by himself, instead of allowing them to stand or fall by their own Conclusions—Can any Thing be more base, more contrary to Equity than this?" *Appeal to the World*, 18.

12. **No. 629**.

13. At Jamaica Plain, four miles outside Boston.

14. The town meeting's proceedings of 14 and 17 Jun. were printed in the *Boston Gazette*, 20 Jun. 1768. See also, *Reports of the Record Commissioners of Boston*, 16: 257-259. The town's instructions to its representatives (Otis, Cushing, Adams, and Hancock), 17 Jun. 1768, are in ibid. 259; there is a copy of the town's letter to DeBerdt, approved on 15 Jun. in the Adams Family Papers, MHS (record number: 010495). .

15. The cavalcade set out from John Hancock's Beacon Hill mansion. Those members whom FB had met frequently in the course of public business were (in given order): James Otis Jr. (moderator), Joseph Jackson (militia officer), John Hancock, Thomas Cushing, and Samuel Adams (Boston representatives), Samuel Quincy (lawyer), and Royal Tyler (councilor). Of the others to whom this comment refers we might exclude the merchant John Rowe (whom he did meet socially) and include physicians Thomas Young, Joseph Warren, and Benjamin Church; justices of the peace Joshua Henshaw, John Ruddock, and Richard Dana, the lawyers Josiah Quincy Jr. and Benjamin Kent, and the merchants Samuel Pemberton, Henderson Inches, Edward Payne, Daniel Malcom, and Melatiah Bourn. From his own account, it may be deduced that FB controlled his anger towards Capt. Malcom for his past

obstructiveness and knew nothing of Joseph Warren's part in the writing the "True Patriot" letter he had found so offensive. FB's self-congratulatory account of the meeting was designed to remind Hillsborough of his value as a negotiator, in marked contrast to the grisly execution of the royal officials sent to parley with English rebels Jack Cade in 1450 or Robert Kett in 1549. *Reports of the Record Commissioners of Boston*, 16: 255; William M. Fowler, Jr., *The Baron of Beacon Hill: A Biography of John Hancock* (Boston, 1980), 88-89.

16. FB's letter (not found) was considered at the meeting held at 4 PM on Wed. 15 Jun. at the Old South Church.

17. Samuel Adams on moderator Otis's view of FB: "Thus saith Governor Bernard, but no one remembers or believes it." *Appeal to the World*, 19.

18. FB's correction is accurate, the instructions being approved on 17 Jun.

19. At 4 PM, Friday 17 Jun. at Faneuil Hall.

20. Insertion relocated from left margin.

21. The delegation likely included councilors James Bowdoin and Royal Tyler, both ardent Whigs.

22. The councilors wrote FB requesting that he intercede with Capt. Corner to release the man impressed (as FB reported) by Corner's "inferior Officer against his Orders". For "the peace of the Town seems in a great measure to depende upon it. If this application sh^d. Fail, it will be apprehended to be to no purpose to make a future one in any similar case." James Bowdoin and Royal Tyler to FB. 18 Jun. 1768, (ADft), Bowdoin and Temple Papers, Loose MSS.

23. The clause "as . . . Town" omitted from the LbC, probably in error.

24. 20 Jun.

25. Samuel Adams: "Perhaps he would have been more consistent if he had imagined these Letters would ever have seen the Light." *Appeal to the World*, 20.

26. Thus Samuel Adams concluded that having identified the potential for rebellion, FB was leading Hillsborough to only one possible conclusion: "the *favorite point* will not be carried, till the long-wished for troops arrive, to enforce his arbitrary Designs, and suppress the Spirit of Liberty. And now is the Time, if ever, to press the Matter: Every Hand therefore must be set to work; and nothing will serve the Cause like continually holding up the Idea of an *Insurrection*." *Appeal to the World*, 20.

27. The joint committee's remit went far beyond an investigation of the *Liberty* rioters, proposing "to enquire into the Grounds and Reasons of the present Apprehensions of the People" and fearing "that Measures have been and now are taking for the Execution of the late Revenue Acts of Parliament by a Naval and Military Force." FB's enemies in the House were to the fore: Samuel Adams, Joseph Hawley, James Otis Jr., and Jedidiah Preble; of the four councilors chosen James Pitts and John Bradbury were the governor's adversaries, while Jeremiah Powell and Gamaliel Bradford were at best his tacit critics. *JHRM*, 45: 63-64; CO 5/828, f 103.

28. One described as an "Incendiary Paper", *HCJ*, 32: 75.

633 | To the Earl of Hillsborough

Nº 8

Boston June 17 1768

My Lord

I have the honor to receive your Lordship's Letters Nº 6 & 7[1] together with the duplicates &c inclosed in the cover of the first. Upon the receipt of them I consulted the Lieut Governor & the Secretary about the best Manner of executing the orders contained in Nº 7; and We all agreed that it would be best to stay till the Town meetings continued by adjournments were over & the people a little composed. I therefore shall not be able to communicate to the House his Majesty's requisition untill Tuesday or Wednesday next, according as the House fills; there being always a thin ~~attend~~ House on Saturday & Monday.[2]

I cannot foresee what will be done upon the occasion; whether Prudence will get the better of Faction, or not. I know not how to hope that they will comply; if they do not, your Lordship may depend upon it I will obey my orders. It happens a little lucky that I am at present seen in a Very favorable light by the people; and that may prevent my being charged as the Author or advisor of this measure, as at other times I should certainly be. I have lately caused it to be hinted that the Faction is likely to have disputes enough upon their hands without quarrelling with me; and therefore they had best reserve me for a mediator as they will certainly want one: I beleive some of them have listened to this.

However I shan't put too great confidence in them: I shall act with all proper caution & if I find myself obliged to dissolve the Assembly, I shall end the Session by prorogation & dissolve them by proclamation.[3] By these means the Shock will become gradual; & I shall be able to step out of the Way till the Wonder is over. Indeed I intreated when this Session was over to take a little relaxation; as I find that the Multiplicity of business of late, & the Attention which the importance of it has obliged me to give to it has impaired my health.

I am with great respect, My Lord, your Lordships most obedient & most humble Servant

Fra Bernard

The right honorable The Earl of Hillsborough

P.S. June 18

The Commissioners of the Customs having appointed M[r]. Hallowell Comptroller of the port of Boston to go directly to London to represent the present state of the officers of the Revenue,[4] I shall give him the charge of my present dispatches. And I shall give him a separate Letter to introduce him to your Lordship. He will inform you of the particulars of the late disturbances, as he bore so considerable a part in them.

ALS, RC   CO 5/757, ff 146-147.

Endorsed: Boston June 17th: 1768. Governor Bernard. (N[o]. 8) R 19th. July. A.22.   Variants: CO 5/766, ff 230-233 (L, RLbC); BP, 6: 324-326 (L, LbC); *Letters to the Ministry* (1st ed.), 28-29; *Letters to the Ministry* (repr.), 37-39. The RC was carried to London by Benjamin Hallowell. Extracts were laid before both houses of Parliament on 28 Nov. 1768. HLL: American Colonies Box 2. Hillsborough replied with **No. 661**.

On 15 Jun., FB received his instructions from Hillsborough to have the House of Representatives rescind the vote approving the Circular Letter. While he knew that the the requisition would precipitate an argument he feared that hotheads might attempt a revolt (**No. 634**). FB nevertheless supposed that he was viewed "in a Very favorable light by the people" for supposedly ending impressment, and, with tensions running so high, fancied that the people would turn to the governor to mediate an end to the crisis. In fact, the rescinding dispute fatally undermined support for the governor in the House of Representatives.

---

1. **Nos. 603** and **608**.

2. FB presented Hillsborough's instructions (**No. 608**) on Tuesday, 21 Jun. *JHRM*, 45: 68-69.

3. When the House refused to rescind the February vote approving the Circular Letter, FB dissolved the assembly on 30 Jun. *JHRM*, 45: 98. The proclamation was published in the *Boston Post-Boy and Advertiser*, 4 Jul. 1768 and the *Massachusetts Gazette and Boston News-Letter*, 7 Jul. 1768.

4. Hallowell's testimony complemented the reports on the *Liberty* riot and town proceedings that FB and the American Board of Customs sent to the British government. His deposition of 11 Jun. (T 1/465, ff 133-134), was sent to the Treasury along with a host of other papers enclosed in the memorial of the Customs Board, **Appendix 6**. Hallowell left Boston on 20 Jun., on the Brig *Nancy*, Capt. Brett, and was examined by the Treasury on 21 Jul. The papers he brought were then read in the House of Lords on 2 Nov. and the House of Commons on 28 Nov. 1768, and considered by the Privy Council on 26 Jun. 1770. *Boston Weekly News-Letter*, 23 Jun.1768; *PDBP*, 3: 25; *APC*, 5: 249-250. The transcript of Hallowell's examination has not been found although his corrections to the paper are filed in CO 5/767, f 138.

634 | To Lord Barrington

Boston June 18 1768

My Lord

I have just received your Lordships Letter dated April 16th, as I did that of Mar 10 in due Time,[1] which I waited to acknowledge 'till this Mail come in.

Your Lordship observes that Things are coming apace to a Crisis: I am sure they are with us; and I fear the Bostonians will get the Start of you. The Commissioners of the Customs and their Officers & the Officers of the Custom House are driven out of[2] the Town allready, the latter not without wounds & bruises & a narrow escape with life. The Commissioners & their officers are on board the Romney man of war: they are going to the Castle to wait[3] the Event of this, as soon as it shall be made defensible by the station of men of war about it. There are allready the Romney of 50 guns & the Beaver of 16: others are expected.[4]

I am myself on better terms with the people, than usual. A Civil Treatment of a petition of the Town to me, a plain friendly answer thereto[5] & some real Service by interposing with the man of war, have given me a little popularity.[6] But it wont last a week: as soon as I have executed the orders I have just recieved from the Secretary of State,[7] in the general Assembly, there will be an end of my popularity. And I dont know whether I shant be obliged to act like the Capt of a fireship, provide for my retreat before I light the fusee.[8]

I shall send this by M[r] Hallowell Controller of the Customs of this Port, who is sent home by the Commissioners upon this occasion. He will inform Your Lordship of all the particulars of the present transactions, as he has bore a great part in them. There seems at present determination to resist Great Britain, & preparations, I am told are made for it. We must wait for the Event.

I am &c.

The Right Honble The Lord Viscount Barrington.

L, LbC   BP, 6: 123-124.

In handwriting of clerk no. 3 except where noted. Dittography has been silently corrected. The RC was carried by Benjamin Hallowell, who left Boston on 20 Jun. on the Brig *Nancy*, Captain Brett.[9]

The pessimism of this letter to Barrington contrasts with the optimism evident in FB's recent correspondence with Hillsborough, wherein he envisaged mediating in the colonists' disputes with Britain. His despondency arose from anticipation of confrontation over royal instructions requiring the House to rescind the vote for the Circular Letter.

1. **No. 605**. Letter of 10 Mar. 1768 not found.

2. From the dateline to "driven out of" the handwriting is probably that of Thomas Bernard.

3. First written form indecipherable.

4. HMS *Romney*, Capt. Corner, had been anchored in Boston harbor since 17 May. The HMS *Beaver*, a sloop, Capt. H. Bellew, probably came into Boston from Halifax in early June, left the port later that month, then returned on 4 Jul. *New-Hampshire Gazette,* 15 Jul. 1768. Of the twenty or so vessels in the North Atlantic Station under the command of Commodore Samuel Hood (1724-1816) between 1767 and 1770, the following were sent to Boston: *Garland*, a fifth rate ship, at Boston 13 Jun.-4 Jul. 1768; *Glasgow*, a sixth rate ship, 27 Jun.-4 Jul.; *Viper*, an armed schooner, arrived 3 Jul.; the sloop *Bonetta*, Capt. J. Wallace, arrived 4 Jul.; *Senegal*, a sloop, arrived 6 Jul.; *Hope*, a schooner, arrived 6 Jul.; the schooner *Gaspee*, Capt. Murray, departed Boston 6 Jul.; the schooner *Little Romney*, at Boston 18-23 May, returning on 6 Jul. *Boston Gazette*, 23 May, 1768; *New-Hampshire Gazette,* 15 Jul. 1768.

5. **No. 629** and FB's answer of 15 Jun. (not found).

6. See **Nos. 632** and **633**.

7. **No. 608**, received on 15 Jun.

8. A detonation device.

9. *Boston New-Letter*, 23 Jun. 1768.

635 | Circular From the Earl of Hillsborough

Circular

(N° 11.)

Duplicate

Whitehall 21st: June 1768

Sir,

It having been represented, that the General Instructions, given by His Majesty to the Governors of the American Colonies, have, from a Variation in the State and Circumstances of the said Colonies, become in many Parts improper and unnecessary, or inadequate to the Object of them; I have the King's Commands to desire you will, with the greatest Attention and with all convenient Dispatch, consider those given to you for your Guidance and Direction in the Administration of the Government entrusted to your Care, and transmit to me, for His Majesty's Information, such Observations as shall occur to you upon those Articles, which may in your Judgement require such Alteration or Addition as may have the Effect to improve His Majesty's Interests and Revenue, add Strength and Dignity to His

Majestys just Authority, promote the Welfare of the Colony, and give Facility to the Administration of Government, conformable to the Constitution, as it stands established by His Majesty's Commission under the great Seal, and by such Laws as have been ratified by the Consent of the Crown.

I am, with great Truth and Regard, Sir, Your most obedient humble Servant

Hillsborough

Governor of the Massachusets Bay.

dupLS, RC   BP 11: 201-204.

Endorsed: No. 11 Duplicate circ: Earl of Hillsborough d June 21 1768 r Sep 30. Direct[g] him to Send home Observ[s] on his Instructions.[1] The original RC has not been found. The duplicate may have been the letter that Gen. Thomas Gage mentions forwarding to FB under cover of his letter of 26 Sept. 1768, BP, 11: 311-314. FB received both the original principal and duplicate on 30 Sept.

Hillsborough's circular was an information-gathering exercise with a view to reforming the contents but not the form of the royal instructions issued governors. On assuming their commission, governors were issued a set of general instructions, covering their duties and responsibilities as royal representatives and chief executives, and a set of instructions covering the trade laws. FB was presently operating under the authority of instructions issued in 1761 after the accession of George III on 25 Oct. 1760 (see *Bernard Papers*, 1: 453-496). It was symbolic, however unintentional, that in Hillsborough's circular the king's interests were accorded priority over the colonists', whereas the colonists, though still loyal, by their recent actions reversed that sequence. FB acknowledged receipt of the circular with **Nos. 672** and **673**, but the pressure of public business occasioned by the imminent arrival of British Regulars became his priority. He never responded directly to this circular, but took the opportunity to address the wider issue of reforming colonial government in **No. 736**.[2]

---

1. This line in the hand of Thomas Bernard.

2. *Bernard Papers*, 5: 185-188.

636 | *Instruction Permitting Leave of Absence*

George R.

Whereas Our Trusty and Welbeloved Francis Bernard, Esquire, Our Captain General and Governor in Chief of Our Province of the Massachuset's Bay, in America, hath humbly represented unto us, that his private Affairs may require his Residence for some Time in this Our Kingdom, and therefore hath humbly requested the We would be pleased to grant him a discretionary Leave to be absent from his Government, and to permit him to return into this Our Kingdom of Great Britain; We are graciously pleased to condescend to his Request, and accordingly do, by these Presents; give and grant unto him the said Francis Bernard, Our full and free Leave, Licence and Permission, to come from his said Government of the Massachuset's Bay into this Our Kingdom and to remain here until Our further Pleasure shall be signified. Given at Our Court at S^t: James's the Twenty second Day of June 1768 in the Eighth Year of Our Reign.

By His Majesty's Command

Hillsborough

Govr: Bernard Leave of Absence

LS, RC   BP, 13: 243-246.

Sealed and addressed: To Our Trusty and Welbeloved Francis Bernard Esqr Our Captain General and Governor in Chief of Our Province of the Massachuset's Bay in America.   Docket: Leave of Absence.

FB had made several requests for leave of absence following the Stamp Act. In the first instance he had approached Secretary of State Conway directly,[1] but during Shelburne's period in charge at the Southern Department had communicated through intermediaries, John Pownall and Lord Barrington;[2] and it was Barrington whom FB had approached most recently to ask the Colonial Secretary Hillsborough for a discretionary leave of absence (**No. 609**). He acknowledged receipt this particular instruction mid-September, together with the offer of the lieutenant-governorship of Virginia.[3]

---

1. **No. 447,** *Bernard Papers*, 3: 98-102.

2. See ibid., 104, 106, 124-125, 128, 213.

3. **No. 682**.

637 | *From Thomas Gage*

New York June 24th: <u>1768.</u>

Sir,

Having some Dispatches of Consequence to transmit to Halifax, I take the Liberty to address them to your Care, and to request the Favor of you to get them forwarded from Boston by the first safe Conveyance for Halifax.

It gives me concern to hear, that there has been some fresh Commotions in Boston. I have received a Letter from the Commissioners of the Customs to acquaint me, that the Collector, Comptroller, and other officers had been beat and abused in the Execution of their Duty, that they themselves were obliged to take shelter on board His Majesty's Ship Romney,[1] Captain Corner Commander; who at their Request put them on shore at Castle William, and remained near the Castle for their Protection.

They inform me of Applications they had made, but had received no Assurances of Protection:[2] and write to acquaint me of the very alarming State of Things at Boston: and leave it to my Judgement to act as I think proper for the honor of the Crown, and the Protection of its Servants.

As I have received no Letter from you on this Subject or any Requisition made by you, for the Aid and Assistance of His Majesty's Forces on this Occasion; I have not ordered any ^Troops^ to move into your Province. Nor do I think it proper to order any of His Majesty's Forces to march for the sole purpose of quelling a Riot; unless required thereto, by the Civil Power. You must be the best Judge of the situation of Affairs in your Government, and whether the Aid of Troops is wanted to enforce the Laws, and ^to^ preserve Peace and Tranquility in the City. The moment you shall judge it convenient to apply to me for the Assistance of the King's forces, I shall order such a number to march as you shall have occasion for.

I have the honor to be with great Regard, Sir, your most obedient, humble Servant,

Tho[s]. Gage.

ALS, RC   BP, 11: 205-206.

Endorsed by FB: Gen[l] Gage d June 24 r July 2 1768. Relating to the Sending The Troops to Boston.   Variants: CO 5/757, ff 352-352 (L, Copy); Gage (L, AC); the second and third paragraphs are extracted in CO 5/86, ff 134-136 (L extract, Copy); the duplicate has not survived. FB replied to Gage with **No. 641**.

Gage was probably bemused by the fact that FB had not made a direct request for military assistance, given the strong terms in which the commissioners of Customs had represented their plight to him and the failure of the civil authority to provide for their protection (**Appendix 5**). It is possible that FB had counted on the commissioners being able to convince Gage of the need to intervene. While it is extraordinary to think that a colonial governor could have expected the general to order troops to Boston without first consulting him, that may have been what FB wanted, as his reply to Gage implies. "I was certain that troops would come here, not from any knowledge of applications or orders, but from the sure consequence of effects from Causes . . . [*and*] I need not expose myself by Applying for them." (**No. 641**.) Gage, however, would only have acted unilaterally in an emergency and it was just such a scenario the commissioners aimed to paint when, as Gage noted above, they "leave it to my Judgement to act."

Gage was sufficiently alarmed to give FB sealed orders directing Col. William Dalrymple at Halifax to provide FB with military assistance (**No. 639** enclosing **Appendix 8**.) Gage expected FB to transmit the orders to Dalrymple at his own discretion (which FB did under cover of **No. 642**). Gage also expected FB to make a formal request of Dalrymple; FB chose not to do this, initially presuming (wrongly) that Gage had actually ordered Dalrymple to dispatch the troops direct to Boston. Neither did Gage privately direct Dalrymple to place the regiments in a state of readiness, for that was the purpose of the orders he prepared for Dalrymple.[3] Gage and FB were as yet unaware that Hillsborough had already issued orders for Gage to send the regiments at Halifax direct to Boston. (**Appendix 4** and **No. 622**.)

---

1. **Appendix 5**. American Board of Customs to Thomas Gage 15 Jun. 1768, CO 5/757, ff 217-218.
2. See **Appendix 5**.
3. As FB put it: "I am informed that the Orders to him are only to collect the troops together, but not to embark them till they are required by me." **No. 660**.

638 | To the Earl of Hillsborough

Duplicate

Nº 9

Boston June 25 1768

My Lord

By my Letter Nº 8[1] I informed your Lordship of the Reasons why I deferrd communicating his Majesty's Requisition to the House unto Tuesday following being the 21[th2] inst[t]. On that Day in the forenoon I sent a Message to the House (a Copy of which I inclose)[3] together with a Copy of the 2nd 3[d] & 4th Paragraphs of your Lordships Letter. I did not send a Copy of the 5th & 6th Paragraphs;[4] because I knew that the Faction would make Use of them to insinuate that the House was treated with Threats in the first Instance, before their Minds were known, and were not allowed Freedom of Debate concerning what was required of them. If I had sent no Extracts at all but incorporated the Substance of your Lordships Letter into my Message, they then would have called for the Letter itself and not proceeded 'till I had given a Copy of it. As it was, I steered this Business in the right Way.

In the afternoon when this Message was read a second Time, Otis made a Speech near two hours long of the most violent & virulent Nature. He abused all Persons in Authority both here and at home. He indeed excepted the Kings Person, but traduced his Government with all the Bitterness of Words. He said "that the King appointed none but Boys for his Ministers; that they had no Education but travelling thro' France, from whence they returned full of the slavish Principles of that Country; that they knew Nothing of Business when they came into their Offices, and did not stay long enough to acquire that little Knowledge which is gained from Experience; that all Business was really done by the Clerks, & even they were too frequently changed to understand what they were about; that the People in England did not know what the Rights of Englishmen capable of composing so elegant so pure and so nervous a Writing as the Petition to the King which passed the last Session." &c.[5]

I give your Lordship a Specimen of this Rhapsody: and it was remarked that in this general Censure of the Kings Government No Exception was made of the Minister who favoured America by the Repeal of the Stamp-Act[6] & by other Indulgences; by the Abuse whereof this very Faction has rose to this Head: All were involved in one common Obloquy. I quote these Sayings from the Mouths of those who heard them delivered in the House which was laid quite open, both Doors and Gallery, upon this Occasion. But neither they nor I can pretend to Exactness of Words; but the Substance I dare say does not vary Materially.[7] In another Part of the Speech, he passed an Encomium upon Oliver Cromwell and extolled the Times preceeding his Advancement and particularily the Murther[8] of the King. The Result was the appointing a Committee to take the Message &c into Consideration, which Committee consisted entirely of the most violent of the Heads of the Faction viz the Representatives of the Town of Boston & 3 of those whom I had refused to admit into the Council upon Account of their having been distinguished by their fomenting the Troubles of Government, with two others.[9] Thus the House seemed to prejudge this Business in the Appointment of a Committee: and indeed the Appointment of a Committee at all shewed a Disposition to argue rather than submit.

On Thursday Morning upon Application from the Committee a Message[10] was sent to me desiring Copies of my Instructions upon this Occasion, of your Lordship's Letter (of which I have given an Extract) and of a Letter of your Lordships (N° 6) which I had communicated to the Council[11] & Copies of my Letters to your Lordship upon the Subject.[12] The next Morning (June 24) I returned an Answer with a Copy of the 5th and 6th Paragraphs of the Letters which concluded the whole.[13] In my Answer I caution them to provide for the Tax Bill:[14] I had a hint given me that they intended to omit that Business on Purpose to oblige me, in case I dissolved the Assembly, by popular Clamour and real Inconveniences to call another Assembly immediately after, which I by no Means think proper nor myself at Liberty so to do. I therefore thought proper to counter-work this Intention.

June 28

Since the former Date I have been obliged to keep Watch upon the Proceedings of the House, having been told that the very reverse of disavowing the Proceedings of the ^late^ House is preparing. They have been much elated within these 3 or 4 Days by some Letters they have received in Answer to the circular Letter. I shall enclose printed Copies of what have been published in the Papers here. I am told that there is also a circular Letter from the Assembly at Virginia arrived; I had it from a Gentleman who said he saw it at Rhode Island. If it is other than the Letter from Virginia now published they keep it a Secret here: but I shall soon have a Copy of it.[15] I keep a look out in the House, that if upon the Report of the Committee[16] they should move for another Congress (as Otis in his Speech said he hoped would soon take Place) or another circular Letter or any thing that contravenes his Majesty's Requisition, I shall immediately put a Stop to their Proceedings without waiting for an Answer in Form. For which Purpose to bring this Matter to a Crisis as soon as may be, after having waited their Motions all this Morning. I put a Message[17] in the Secretary's hands to be delivered to them this Afternoon as in the inclosed Copy.

July 1st:

On the next Day June 29, The House sent me a Message[18] desiring me to grant them a Recess that they might consult their Constituents respecting the Requisition. I knew that such an Indulgence would be liable to great Abuse; but if I had thought it could have produced any good Effect, which I had not any Reason to expect, I did not think myself at Liberty to postpone the Consideration of this important Question.[19] I therefore returned an immediate Answer[20] that I could not consistently with my Sense of my Duty prorogue or adjourn the Court untill I had received an Answer.

The next Morning I went early to the Council to watch the Proceedings of the House, having been informed that they intended to originate an Invitation for another Congress: In which Case the Moment I got Intelligence of it I intended to dissolve them. The House kept themselves locked up all the Morning; the best Part of which was spent in preparing a Letter to your Lordship which I am told is very lengthy: but as I have not seen it and probably shall not be allowed a Sight of it 'till it is printed in the Newspapers,[21] I will say no more of it than that I am told it is in the old Strain, complaining that they have been misrepresented; tho' the present Censure arises from an Act of theirs which they have had circulated throughout his Majesty's Dominions: They then put the Question "rescind or not rescind" which was determined in the Negative 91 to 17:[22] among the Majority were many Members who were scarce ever known upon any other Occasion to vote against the Government Side of a Question; so greatly has infatuation and intimidation gained Ground.[23] They then settled the Answer to be given to me and appointed a Committee to deliver it.[24] After this a Motion was made to appoint a Committee to prepare an Address to his Majesty to desire him to remove the Governor and appoint another more agreeable to the People: this was carried by a Majority of 5, & with this ended the Business of the Morning.[25]

I had some Doubts with myself whether I ought not to dismiss the Assembly immediately after I knew for certain that the House had passed a Vote against rescinding. But upon a little Recollection I thought it best to wait 'till I had received their Answer, as I was not obliged to take Notice of this Vote 'till it was notified to me in Form. In this I was influenced by a Consideration respecting myself: the House had appointed a Committee to prepare an Address to get me removed: if I had dismissed them in a hasty unformal Way, whilst this Business was on the Carpet; it would have been said that I was affraid of the Enquiry. Whereas this is the third Time the Faction has moved to impeach me; the two former Times they had been obliged to give it up for Want of Materials;[26] and I was sure that they had acquired none since the last Attempt of this Kind. And this Motion ended in the same Manner as the two former: after having endeavoured for 2 hours together in the afternoon to cook up something to found this Application on, and finding that I would not interrupt them in it; as I believe they expected & desired that I should, they were obliged to give it up themselves. Upon this the Answer[27] which had all the while been detained, was sent up to the Council Chamber where I received it. Immediately after which I sent up for the House and prorogued the general Court intending to dissolve it by proclamation.[28]

Upon this Occasion there happened a Fracas in the Council sudden and unforeseen, but what probably will be improved by the Faction for their own Purposes. It seems that the Evening before the Council had appointed a Committee to consider the State of the Province: which Committee had prepared an Address to his Majesty concerning the late Duties, to be reported to the Board.[29] I had all along declared that I should dismiss the General Court immediately upon receiving the Answer from the House; I knew nothing of any Business being undone, not being acquainted with this; I had ordered the Secretary to prepare for the Prorogation by laying the Acts which had passed that Session on the Table, their Titles being to be read in the Presence of the whole Court as has been my Usage; and the Acts were accordingly laid in Order.[30] Whilst I was waiting to receive the Answer of the House The Committee of the Board introduced this Address: I testified my Surprize upon the Occasion and observed that they could not expect to go thro' that Business at that Time. Presently after the Committee from the House attended; they were admitted and delivered their Answer. As soon as that was done, I ordered the Secretary to call up the House: As soon as the House entered one of the Committee of the Council expostulated with me upon my calling up the House while the Council was proceeding on the Address and was so indecent as to appeal to the House. I silenced him: another Gentleman interposed; I stopt him also, and proceeded to the Prorogation.

When the House was gone out of the Council Chamber, I expostulated with these Gentlemen upon the Interruption they had given me in the Presence of the House in executing his Majesty's positive Commands. I told them that I should have thought myself blameable, if I had suffered 5 Minutes to intervene between receiving the Answer and dismissing the House: for I should have made myself answerable for all they did in the Interval. This Proceeding could not be justified and was really condemned by some other of the Council and was in some Measure apologised for: but it will not be in the Power of the Apologisers to prevent an ill Use being made of it. I then informed the Council that I had no Desire to stop any Representation which they wanted to make to the King, if it was conceived in decent and respectful Terms, as it seemed to me from hearing it read this was; I therefore would let them introduce this into the privy Council; and if it appeared to be inoffensive, I would lay it before his Majesty, tho I should not agree with them in Opinion as to all their Assertions, as I pointed out some where I should not. But this was not enough: it seems that when the Address was past, there was a Petition to the House of Lords and another to the House of Commons to be brought in. I told them I could have nothing to do with them; I could not pretend to communicate with those great Bodies; my Correspondence went no higher than his Majesty's Ministers. After some Altercation they submitted and were Content with this Address being brought into the privy Council, after it had received my Approbation. This Compromise was very expedient to obviate the Misrepresentations which this Business would otherwise be subject to.[31]

Having carried my Narrative to this Length I must suspend my Reflexions upon these Events unto a further Opportunity. I will however here observe that it may be suggested that I have not conducted this Business with Spirit: but it must be observed to what a Weakness this Government is reduced which makes the most gentle Way of doing any Business most advisable. I never intended to depart from his Majesty's Orders in the least: but upon many Accounts I thought I best to dissolve them by Proclamation. It was said it was well I dismissed them by Prorogation and not by Dissolution; why, I dont know: but if any Triumph arises from it, it will be but short lived; for the Dissolution will be published in the Papers at the same Time with the Prorogation.

I am with great Respect, My Lord, your Lordships most obed[t]
and most humble Servant

Fra Bernard

The Right honble The Earl of Hillsborough

dupLS, RC   CO 5/757, ff 256-262.

Endorsed: Governor Bernard Boston June 25. 1768. (N[o]. 9.) R 19 August. A.28.   There
were several enclosures: copies of FB's messages to the House of 21, 23, 24, 28 and 29
Jun. 1768, CO 5/757, ff 263-264; the answers of the House, 30 Jun., ibid., ff 266-268; an
extract of Hillsborough's letter to FB of 22 Apr. 1768 (**No. 608**) at ibid., f 263; copies of
the *Massachusetts Gazette*, 7 Jul. 1766 and *Boston Chronicle*, 27 Jun.-4 Jul. 1768, ibid., ff
271-275. The original letter was sent by express to Gen. Thomas Gage, to be carried by the
New York packet boat. The duplicates were carried by "Capt. Smith" whom FB noted sailed
for Glasgow on 4 Jul.[32] Variants of the letter are in: CO 5/766, ff 250-262 (L, RLbC); BP, 6:
326-335 (L, LbC); *Letters to the Ministry* (1st ed.), 29-35; *Letters to the Ministry* (repr.), 39-
46. Extracts of the letter together with the enclosures were laid before both houses of Parliament on 28 Nov. 1768. HLL: American Colonies Box 2. Hillsborough replied with **No. 679**.

FB's account of the debate on the rescinding of the Circular Letter placed James Otis
Jr. in the van of the opposition. Otis's influence had fluctuated since the Stamp Act Crisis,
and he evidently seized the opportunity to reassert his leadership. The *Liberty* riot and
the rescinding controversy revealed clear divisions between Otis and Samuel Adams. Otis,
according to his family's biographer, was a "moderate" Whig on the spectrum of opinion
concerning American affairs, evincing a kind of constitutional "dualism"—in that he denied
both Parliament's authority to tax the colonists and colonial aspirations for legislative independence. The Circular Letter, as approved by the House, thus "epitomized" Otis's views
(see source note to **Appendix 1**). Otis, however, distrusted Adams's brand of confrontational radicalism lest it aggravate relations with Britain.[33] Yet, Otis's vitriolic attack on the
king's ministers, as reported by FB, was as antagonistic as anything that Adams wrote and
was symptomatic of the colonists' exasperation with the Chatham administration over the
Townshend Acts. Otis did not mention Chatham in his tirade (he was hardly a "Boy," a
denigration more appropriate for his much less experienced secretaries of state Shelburne
and Grafton born in the early 1730s), but neither did Otis explicitly exempt Chatham from
the accusation, perhaps leaving his audience to conclude that the man whom the House
had recently lionized as a defender of American rights[34] had now abandoned them. FB
underlined the point about Hillsborough's prime minister.

> No Exception was made of the Minister who favoured America by the
> Repeal of the Stamp-Act & by other Indulgences; by the Abuse where-
> of this very Faction has rose to this Head: All were involved in one
> common Obloquy.

All of this suggests Otis's speech reflected the defiant mood of the House whilst inciting
their opposition. Otis was firmly with Samuel Adams in defending the colonists' rights of
Englishmen, though he was not yet committed to unseating the king's governor.

FB's portrayal of Otis as a demagogue might have blinded him to the opportunity of exhibiting differences among the Whig leadership, as he had done previously.[35] However, Otis's reputed embrace of Oliver Cromwell was FB's way of characterizing Otis as a radical of Adams's stripe, irrespective whether or not Otis actually "extolled" the regicide. Otis was probably drawing a comparison between King Charles I's ill-fated attempts to tax his subjects and Britain's recent colonial policies, albeit the analogy required the audience to consider the 1760s Parliament as the oppressor rather than the leader of the opposition to the king. Any colonist familiar with the Rev. Jonathan Mayhew's *Discourse on Unlimited Submission*, first delivered in Boston on the centenary of Charles I's execution in 1649, would not have struggled to appreciate English Civil War analogies; neither would FB, who had once accused Mayhew of admiring Cromwell, having suffered the pastor's barbs after publicly defending the Anglican Church against the objections of Mayhew and his fellow Congregationalists to an American episcopate.[36] Cromwell's reputation, following the Stamp Act Crisis, underwent what one historian has called a "rehabilitation," with some Whigs appropriating the Protector as an icon of Liberty.[37] Otis may have been imitating Cromwell's famous speech dissolving the Rump Long Parliament on 20 Apr. 1653, wherein he lambasted the members as a "factious crew" and "sordid prostitutes" bereft of "the least care for the good of the Commonwealth" and accused them of six years of misgovernment. But FB might not have appreciated the significance of this particular allusion if his source had missed it (as FB's digest of his verbal report seems to indicate).[38] FB's source was probably not a paid informer but a friend of government, and may have reported simply that Otis had emulated Cromwell. Thus FB probably took the reference at face value without supposing that Otis was parodying FB's attempted dissolution of the Massachusetts legislature and British misrule.

By refusing to rescind the Circular Letter, the House demonstrated its defiance of British colonial policy. The formal answer to FB's request, prepared in committee by some of his principal enemies (including Otis and Adams),[39] appealed to a broad base (as did most of the public documents issued by the House at this time). The Circular Letter, the House maintained, originated in the just cause of seeking "Redress" against Parliamentary taxation, and was in its language and purpose "respectful" of parliamentary authority. Protesting that FB (and Hillsborough) had damned the Circular Letter as the work of "faction," the House iterated what FB had hitherto failed to acknowledge when he reported on the defeat of the first motion to issue a circular (**No. 589**)—that his opponents were an unassailable majority. The vote of reconsideration was taken in a full House of around eighty members (about 73 per cent) and the measures protesting the Townshend Acts (notably the petition to the king) were adopted by a *"three to one"* majority. The remainder of the paper protested the logic of rescinding a vote when the Circular Letter had already been distributed and defended the House's constitutional rights to communicate with other assemblies and petition the king. The House wondered if FB was the source of "Misinformation and Misrepresentation" that had prompted the king's minister to issue such an unfair directive and to dissolve the assembly in the event of noncompliance.

> . . . we are constrained to say, that we are disagreeably convinced, that your Excellency entertains not that Parental Regard for the Welfare of the good People of this Province, which you have some Times been pleased to profess, and which they had at all Times an irrefragible Right to expect from their Governor. . . . In all this we have been actu-

ated by a consciencious, and finally, a clear and determined Sense of Duty to God, to our King, our Country, and to our latest Posterity: And we most ardently wish, and humbly Pray that in your future Conduct, your Excellency may be influenced by the same Principles.[40]

As FB indicates, before the House presented the answer to him the members debated whether or not to request the king to remove him. FB likened this to an impeachment. The province legislature had no jurisdiction to impeach him. The House was grandstanding, the implication being that the petition might lead to FB's prosecution before what Sir William Blackstone termed "the high court of Parliament."[41] At the same time, the House's letter to Hillsborough accused FB of trying "to impress the Royal Mind with the Jealousy of his faithful Subjects," assuring the secretary of state that an inquiry would "find that such base and wicked attempts have been made." (**Appendix 9**.) A majority of the House probably agreed with the sentiments expressed in the answer to FB and the letter to Hillsborough, although, as FB indicates, the Whigs commanded a majority of just five on the question of whether or not to petition the king for his removal. It would be another year before they commanded the same level of support for removing FB as they did for refusing to rescind.

Indisputably, however, FB's opponents were now firmly in the majority. The seventeen members who had voted in favor of rescinding were ridiculed in patriotic iconography while the Glorious Ninety-Two were celebrated. The rescinders included six stalwart friends of government; for three others the vote was the first substantive demonstration of their loyalty to FB.[42] Doubtless they shared the Whigs' concern about unbridled parliamentary taxation, but worried, as Williams put it, that all the recent controversy would "prosecute the dispute with the Supream Authority of the Nation" and "procure harder measures" from Britain.[43] Jonathan Sayward tried to encapsulate his and others' motivations: "I acted uprightly and [*according to*] what I thought best as one of that assembly and I think I had not any sinister views on so doing." But henceforth he would be "with the Stream."[44] Twelve of the rescinders, including Sayward, were not returned by their towns at the 1769 elections, leaving the friends of government in the House "reduced to a rump status from which they never recovered."[45]

---

1. **No. 633**.

2. Thus in manuscript.

3. Annotation in left margin: "**I**", referring to his message of 21 Jun. *JHRM*, 45: 68-69.

4. **No. 608**. The version presented to the House of Representatives is in *JHRM*, 45: 68-69. The paragraphs omitted from the copy laid before the House were actually the sixth and seventh, for FB chose not to count the introductory sentence as a single paragraph. In these particular paragraphs, Hillsborough (a) instructed FB to dissolve the assembly if the House did not rescind the vote approving the Circular Letter, then (b) promised FB that if "a faithful Discharge" of his duty should disadvantage him "proper Care will be taken for the Support of the Dignity of Government." FB probably took this sentence to mean that Britain would pay his salary if the assembly refused the annual grant.

5. Starting quotation marks editorially supplied. End marks are in the manuscript. FB later acquired a fuller report of Otis's speech on 21 Jun., for which see the source note to **No. 680**.

6. Probably William Pitt (1708-78), the earl of Chatham, and the nominal leader of the administration until his resignation in Oct. 1768, although the Stamp Act was actually repealed by the marquess of Rockingham's administration.

7. FB's second hand account is the only source for this speech by James Otis Jr.

8. Thus in manuscript.

9. The committee appointed on 22 Jun. comprised Boston representatives Thomas Cushing (Speaker), Samuel Adams, John Hancock, and James Otis Jr.; those subjected to the governor's veto were Jerathmeel Bowers (1717-99) of Swansea, James Otis Sr. (1702-78) of Barnstable, and Thomas Saunders (1729-74) of Gloucester; plus Walter Spooner (1720-1803) of Dartmouth and James Warren (1726-1808) of Plymouth. *JHRM*, 45: 70-71. This committee would also prepare the House's letter to Hillsborough, 30 Jun. **Appendix 9**.

10. Annotation: "**II**", referring to the message from the House of Representatives, 23 Jun, CO 5/757, f 263. The message was issued after the committee tasked with preparing an answer to FB's message of 21 Jun. indicated that "it would be of great Use to them" if they could inspect an unedited "*whole*" copy of Hillsborough's letter of 22 Apr. (containing the instruction requiring FB to have the House rescind the vote for the Circular Letter), together with copies of FB's letters to Hillsborough and Hillsborough's to FB about the matter (and listed in note 12 below) *JHRM*, 45: 72-73.

11. **No. 603**.

12. The extract of Hillsborough's letter of 22 Apr. (**No. 608**) presented to the House omitted the first sentence wherein Hillsborough indicated receipt of FB's letters **Nos. 589, 591**, and **593**. This detail was unknown to the House committee members at this stage (and probably until publication of FB's official correspondence in 1769).

13. Annotation: "**III**", referring to FB's message to the House of Representatives, 24 Jun., CO 5/757, ff 263-264. However, FB still did not release the first sentence, thus preserving, for now, the material evidence directly linking him to Hillsborough's instruction (see note 12, above). *JHRM*, 45: 75.

14. The Annual Supply Act was passed on Thursday 30 Jun., see note 30, below.

15. Peyton Randolph, (Speaker of the Virginia House of Burgesses) to Thomas Cushing, 9 May 1768, *JHRM*, 45, 104-107. Replies were also received from the speakers of the following assemblies: New Hampshire (dated 25 Feb.), New Jersey (9 May), Connecticut (11 Jun.), Georgia (16 Jun.), South Carolina (10 Jul.), and Rhode Island (5 Aug.). Ibid., 108-112. While New Hampshire praised the "Measures" taken by the Massachusetts House (indirectly referring to the petition to the king and letter to the House agent), Virginia was the only colony to reply that offered an exhibition of colonial rights and liberties; it harmonized with the Massachusetts Whigs' position in rejecting the constitutionality of direct taxation by Parliament. Such sentiments were expressed, respectfully, in Virginia's own petition to the king drawn up in April. The letters from Virginia, New Jersey, Connecticut, Georgia, South Carolina, and Maryland (dated 24 Jun.) were printed in the Massachusetts newspapers. *Boston Evening-Post*, 27 Jun. and 11 Jul.; *Boston Chronicle*, 27 Jun.-4 Jul.; *Boston Weekly News-Letter*, 30 Jun.; *Essex Gazette*, 9-16 Jul. 1768. The replies printed in one of the enclosures to FB's letter were those from Connecticut, Georgia, New Jersey, and Virginia. *Boston Chronicle*, 27 Jun.-4 Jul. 1768, CO 5/757, f 273.

16. That is the committee appointed on 22 Jun. see note 9 above.

17. Annotation: "**IV**", referring to FB's message to the House of Representatives, 28 Jun., CO 5/757, f 264. Noted in *JHRM*, 45: 85.

18. Annotation: "**V**", referring to the House of Representatives' message to FB, 29 Jun., CO5/757, f 264. Noted in *JHRM*, 45: 86-87.

19. In the summer of 1766, the House postponed consideration of a requisition on compensating the victims of the Stamp Act riots, in order to ascertain the views of constituents. Not only did the House significantly delay the award but it also challenged the authority with which FB had made a "Requisition." *Bernard Papers*, 3: 242-245, 284, 431-439. At the time, FB was able to exploit divisions that emerged, but evidently supposed that he would have less opportunity to do so in the summer of 1768 should towns be able to instruct their representatives on the rescinding issue.

20. Annotation: "**VI**", referring to FB's message to the House of Representatives, 29 Jun., CO 5/757, f 264. Noted in *JHRM*, 45: 88.

21. **Appendix 9**. Signed by Speaker Thomas Cushing, the House's letter to Hillsborough was read and approved on 30 Jun.; it was printed in the newspapers a week afterward and later as an appendix to the House journals. *JHRM*, 45: 89, 99-104; *Boston Weekly News-Letter*, 7 Jul. 1768.

22. This is an error: ninety-two voted in the negative on 30 Jun. *JHRM*, 45: 89-90.

23. Friends of government who voted against rescinding included: Elisha Adams, (1719-81) representative for Medway; Jonathan Bagley (1717-80), Almsbury; Stephen Hall (1704-86), Medford; John Noyes (1715-85), Sudbury; Sampson Stoddard (1709-77), Chelmsford; Joseph Tisdale (1736-68), Taunton; and John Wadsworth (1709-99) of Duxbury. Colin Nicolson, "Governor Francis Bernard, the Massachusetts Friends of Government, and the Advent of the Revolution," *Procs. MHS* 103 (1991): 24-113, at 110-113.

24. The committee appointed to deliver the House's answer included Jedidiah Preble (1707-84), whose authority as an Indian agent FB had once undermined, and Jerathmeel Bowers (1717-99), whose election to the Council FB had vetoed. However, the inclusion of Col. Richard Saltonstall (1732-85), who had voted to rescind and had been a loyal ally to FB, probably came as a shock if, by accepting the appointment, Saltonstall was demonstrating regret. On FB's relations with these men see *Bernard Papers*, 1: 431-432; 2: 327-332, 352; 3: 154n11, 176. The House's answer, prepared by the committee appointed on 22 Jun., is in *JHRM*, 45: 91-94.

25. The committee formed on 30 Jun. to draft the petition to remove FB comprised FB's enemies Samuel Adams, Jerathmeel Bowers, John Hancock, James Otis Sr., and James Otis Jr. *JHRM*, 45: 94. According to historian John K. Alexander, the committee probably worked from a draft already prepared by Samuel Adams, since a fair copy was presented to the committee at its first meeting—the same day on which the committee had been appointed. FB's dissolution of the assembly prevented any consideration by the House. The matter was raised again the following year, when the same committee members (minus Bowers) were joined by five other representatives (including Thomas Cushing and Jedidiah Preble) in preparing a petition to the king for the governor's removal, which was adopted, printed, and dispatched. *JHRM*, 45: 136, 148, 197-199. Adams's biographer assumes that the petition adopted on 27 Jun. 1769 was the largely the same as that proposed in 1768: that may have been the case, but the 1768 draft has not been found to prove the point. Alexander, *Samuel Adams*, 71.

26. FB is not referring to any particular vote of the House but to proposals that were aired in the course of debates over FB's correspondence with the earl of Shelburne, in which the governor was alleged to have misrepresented the province to the secretary of state. The first occasion was on 13 Nov. 1767 when the House considered Shelburne's letter of 13 Sept. 1766 (**No. 501**). *Bernard Papers*, 3: 223-225, 253, 272n16. The second occasion was from 16 to 22 Feb. 1768, when the House requested a copy of Shelburne's letter of 17 Sept. 1767 (**No. 566**). *JHRM*, 44: 147, 239-240, 250-251; source note to **No. 591**.

27. Annotation: "**VII**", referring to the House of Representatives' answer to FB's messages of the 24 and 25, dated 30 Jun., CO 5/757, ff 266-268. Printed in *JHRM*, 45: 91-94.

28. On 30 Jun., FB prorogued the assembly until 3 Aug. and dissolved it by proclamation on 1 Jul. *Acts and Resolves*, 4: 1032.

29. The committee comprised James Bowdoin, William Brattle, Thomas Flucker, Royal Tyler, and James Russell. They requested approval to "prepare" an address to the king and to send after FB's "consideration." CO 5/827, f 52.

30. Eighteen acts were passed in the session that commenced on May 25 and was dissolved on 30 Jun. For a full list see *Acts and Resolves*, 4: 1114-1115. The first was a grant of £1,300 for the governor's salary. The supply act for appropriating £18,000 for the Treasury was passed on 23 Jun. (thus ensuring that the ordinary expenses of government would be met); a continuation act for the payment of fees to government officers was passed on 28 Jun.; and the supply act appropriating £100,000 from taxes for the redemption of government securities due in 1769 was passed on 30 Jun. Ibid., 1024-1025.

31. James Bowdoin drafted the Council's petition to the king, which he reported to the Governor and Council on 7 Jul. Bowdoin and Temple Papers, Loose MSS. The engrossed copy is **Appendix 11**.

32. **No. 646**. Probably Capt. John Smith, master of the brig *Betty*, which cleared the Customhouse on 4 Jul. bound for Greenock, near Glasgow. *Boston Chronicle*, 27 Jun.-4 Jul. 1768.

33. John J. Waters Jr., *The Otis Family in Provincial and Revolutionary Massachusetts* (Chapel Hill, N.C., 1968), 173-175.

34. See *Bernard Papers*, 3: 161.

35. See *Bernard Papers*, 2: 262-263; 3: 152, 280-281.

36. Jonathan Mayhew, *A Discourse, Concerning Unlimited Submission and Non-Resistance to the Higher Powers with Some Reflections on the Resistance made to King Charles I. and on the anniversary of his death: in which the mysterious doctrine of that Prince's saintship and martyrdom is unriddled: the substance of which was delivered in a sermon preached in the West meeting house, in Boston, on the Lord's day after the 30th of January, 1749-50* (Boston, 1750). On FB and Mayhew, see Nicolson, *The 'Infamas Govener'*, 77.

37. Brendan J. McConville, *The King's Three Faces: the Rise and Fall of Royal America, 1688-1776* (Chapel Hill, N.C., 2006), 268-273.

38. I am grateful to Prof. McConville for providing this lead, ibid.

39. See note 9 above.

40. Message of the House of Representatives, 30 Jun. 1768, *JHRM*, 45: 91-94.

41. Impeachment, as FB and the Whigs would have known, was "a presentment to the most high and supreme court of criminal jurisdiction by the most solemn grand inquest of the whole kingdom." Sir William Blackstone, *Commentaries on the Laws of England*, 4 vols. (Oxford, 1765), 4: 256. The penalties for maladministration and malfeasance by colonial governors were immediate dismissal, a *sine die* ban on holding Crown office, and a fine of £1,000. Governors were, of course, also subject to the full penalty of law for any criminal act. Governors of Plantations Act, 11 Will., c. 12 (1698).

42. The stalwarts were Jonathan Bliss (1742-1822), Springfield; William Browne (1737-1807), Salem; Jacob Fowle (1704-71), Marblehead; Timothy Ruggles, (1711-95), Hardwick; Richard Saltonstall (1732-85), Haverhill; Israel Williams (1709-88), Hatfield. They were joined by John Ashley (1709-1802), Sheffield; Jonathan Ashley (1739-87), Deerfield-Greenfield; Dr. John Calef (1726-1812), Ipswich; John Chadwick (1717-90), Tyringham; Josiah Edson (1709-81), Bridgewater; Chillingworth Foster (1707-79), Harwich; Matthew Mayhew (1721-1805), Chilmark; and Jonathan Sayward (1713-97), York. The three new government men were probably Peter Frye, (1723-1820), Salem; William Jernigan, (1728-1817), Edgartown; and Joseph Root (1713-86), Sunderland.

43. Israel Williams to Thomas Hutchinson, Hatfield, 28 December, 1767 [1768], Mass. Archs., 25: 234-235.

44. John H. Cary, "'The Juditious are intirely neglected': The Fate of a Tory," *New England Historical and Genealogical Register* 134 (1980): 99-114, quoted at 104.

45. Nicolson, *The 'Infamas Govener'*, 165; Nicolson, "Governor Francis Bernard, the Massachusetts Friends of Government, and the Advent of the Revolution," 110-113.

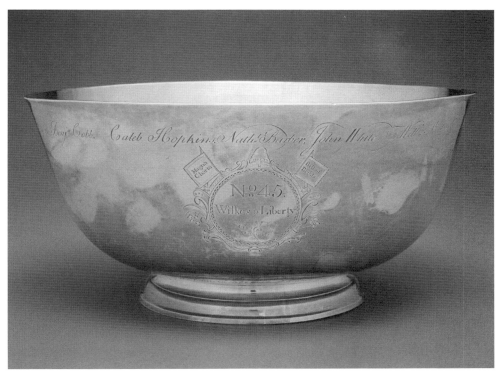

Engraved in script below the rim are the names of Sons of Liberty who commissioned silversmith Paul Revere to create this silver ornamental bowl commemorating the refusal of the House, on 30 Jun. 1768, to rescind the vote approving the Circular Letter. This side displays the Whig emblems of the Liberty Cap, Magna Carta, and the Bill of Rights. They adorn a badge labeled "No,, 45. Wilkes & Liberty," and sporting a torn copy of a general search warrant. The inscription on the opposite side included the dedication "To the Memory of the glorious NINETY-TWO" members of the House of Representatives who voted against rescinding. Photograph © 2015 Museum of Fine Arts, Boston.

639 | *From Thomas Gage*

Separate

New York June 25th 1768.

Sir,

As it is not possible from Reports to know the true situation of affairs at such a Distance as between this Place and Boston, I write you a separate Letter on the subject of the Tumults that have happened at Boston; and in Case the state of Affairs is such, as to require the aid and Assistance of His Majesty's Forces, in order to save time in your Application to me for them, I send you here with a Letter for the officer Commanding the King's Forces in Nova Scotia, which you will make use of, as you see occasion.

I have the honor to be with great Regard Sir, your most obedient, humble Servant

Thos. Gage

His Excellency Govr. Bernard Boston

ALS, RC   BP, 11: 209-210.

Endorsed by FB: Boston [Genl Gage] d June 25 1768 r July 2. Variants: CO 5/86, f 136 (L, Copy); Gage (L, AC). Enclosed orders to Col. William Dalrymple at Halifax placing him in a state of readiness to respond to any request from FB for military assistance (**Appendix 8**). FB replied with **No. 641**.

Gage appears not to have sent a copy of orders direct to Dalrymple. FB forwarded the orders to Dalrymple under cover of **No. 642**, assuming that they instructed the lieutenant colonel to send Regulars direct to Boston, without the Governor and Council having to make a formal request. As FB remarked to Hillsborough on 9 Jul., "I am mistaken, if there is not among them an order for at least one Regiment to come here." FB learned of his error on 16 Jul. (**No. 652**). Gage, meanwhile, reported to Hillsborough that

> Having afterwards Occasion to send some Dispatches to Boston to be forwarded to Halifax, I wrote two Letters by that Opportunity to Governor Bernard, on the Subject of these Commotions:[1] The last of which was a Separate Letter, in which I inclosed a Letter of Orders to the Officer Commanding His Majesty's Forces at Halifax, to embark with the whole, or such parts of the King's Forces under his Command as the Governor should require. By this means Time is saved, if Governor Bernard thinks it proper to demand the Aid and Assistance of His Majesty's Troops, and he may make use of the Orders as he sees Occasion.[2]

1. **Nos. 637** and **639**.

2. Gage to Hillsborough, New York, 28 Jun. 1768, CO 5/86, f 128.

640 | To Lord Barrington

Boston. June 29. 1768.

My Lord

I wrote to your Lordship a short Letter dated June 18, which went in the Care of Mr Hallowell.[1] Since that I have informed the Assembly of the orders I have received to require them to rescind & disapprove some resolutions of the late House in the ^last^ Session, & on their refusal to dissolve them. It is certain they wont comply; in the mean time they are putting off giving their answers, & perhaps meditating some other Act as bad as that which they are required to rescind. I am not at present an object of resentment, altho I have been abused in a speech of Otis's in common with the Government the Ministry, the parliament & the People of G Britain, & all persons in Authority on both sides the Water.[2] But I apprehend that I shall be drove to execute my orders in a manner that may make me personally offensive. Besides, one do^es^ not know what effects the Dissolution of the Assembly may have among the People, nor what turn it may take.

I therefore a good deal depend upon my obtaining leave of absence. I have not wrote to my Lord Hillsborough on this Subject: ever since my Correspondence has been opend with him I have had so many interesting Subjects to write upon, that I have not found room for myself. Besides, the Year has advanced so fast, that there is not Time left for me to recieve an Answer to a Letter wrote now, early enough to embark before the Winters sets in; tho I should venture much if I should meet with a good Ship, especially a Man of War. I must therefore rely upon what I have allready wrote & your Lordships kind offices therein.

It seems to me that my going to England is quite necessary for the improvement of the good disposition of the Minister towards me. Without an interview, there will be no End of doubts & difficulties, especially as my Ideas of an advantageous settlement lay a great stress upon health & the means to preserve it, a good Climate. I also want ease & rest, having been greatly too much overworked for 3 Years past, & I begin to feel it. I had therefore rather return to my old Government of New Jersey with a Salary of 1500 £: a Year (no more than is allowed to the Government of Nova Scotia) than go to a Southern or West indian Government (Barbadoes excepted) of twice or thrice the value. And I should think this might be effected by advancing Govr. Franklin & allowing an additional Salary to that Government.[3] As for my staying in this Government with an additional Salary, It would depend upon the treatment the People are to meet with here. If I was upon the spot where I could know what is to be done with this Goverment, I could quickly tell how advisable it would be for me to continue in it; & if I should be asked my opinion what should be done I might propose measures which would make my return to it by no means advisable. For tho' I conform to the Constitution of the Government, as it is at present my Duty, yet I cant be blind to its defects & the ill consequences which proceed from thence; & if I am called upon I must speak out. Upon the whole my having leave to go to England seems to be the first step to be taken.

June 30.

I have this day recieved the answer of the House, wherein they refuse to comply with the terms of the Kings requisition in a manner which will give great offence at home. I am also abused by them, altho' I have been meerly ministerial in this business.[4] I have therefore prorogued them to day & shall dissolve them to morrow by proclamation. I expect great resentment from England against this Town & province, & that much confusion will arise here & perhaps there may be an actual insurrection. Upon these accounts Leave for me to go to England becomes more & more desirable. I write fully to my Lord Hillsborough, & upon that Account must shorten this as I must make up my packet for a Ship which is to sail to morrow.[5]

I am with great &c

The Right Honble The Lord Viscount Barrington.

L, LbC   BP, 6 125-129.

In handwriting of clerk no. 3. Minor emendations not shown.

FB had solicited leave of absence during the Stamp Act Crisis, ostensibly to brief ministers on colonial opposition and the reform of colonial government, but also to obtain relocation to another post. Permission was refused, and in the late summer of 1767 FB concluded that "scarce one of the Reasons which induced me to sollicit it twenty Months ago are remaining now." (**No. 560**).[6] However, by the early summer of 1768, FB was convinced that his own well-being was now dependent upon getting out of Boston. FB did not make a direct request of Hillsborough, but relied on Barrington's intercession (**Nos. 587 and 609**). Hillsborough issued an instruction permitting FB leave of absence on 22 Jun. (**No. 636**). FB received that instruction in mid-September, together with the offer of the lieutenant-governorship of Virginia (which he acknowledged with **No. 682**).

---

1. **No. 634**.

2. See **No. 638**.

3. William Franklin (1730/31-1813) had been governor of New Jersey since 1762.

4.   That is to say, acting on the instructions of the secretary of state.

5.   FB was completing **No. 638**.

6.   *Bernard Papers*, 3: 394-395.

641 | To Thomas Gage

Roxbury July 2. 1768

S[r].

I received your letters together with the packets inclosed.[1] As I understood that there was no private ship ready to sail for Halifax I applied to Capt Corner commander of the Romney:[2] He has nothing under him but the Gaspee Cutter who cannot be spared from her station ^near the Castle^; but as soon as a Sloop which He expects shall come in, He will send the Gaspee with your dispatches, if I cannot find another Conveyance.

The State of Affairs in Boston is full as bad as the reports you have received can make it.[3] All real power is in the hands of the people of the lowest class; Civil Authority can do nothing but what they will allow. I have been obliged, after having in Vain applied to the Council for advice & assistance to tell the Commissioners of the Customs that I can give them no protection.[4] I have indeed ordered them to be received into the Castle: but that in its present state Cannot be called a place of Safety.

The Nature of this Government & the present State of the Town make it impracticable for me to apply for troops tho' the Occasion for them should be ever so urgent. For regularly I ought to have the advice of the Council for such a measure: but it will be impossible for me to obtain such advice tho' the Danger was ever so imminent & not to be avoided by any other means. For the nature of their Constitution & the intimidation they are under from the troops of the Sons of liberty make them incapable of pursuing effectual measures to restore the peace of the Town & the Authority of the Government.

I have heretofore in times of great Danger put the question to the Council whether I should apply to the General for troops, & have received such answers as have convinced me that it is in vain ever to put that question again.[5] And yet upon the late tumults I told the Council that I was ready to put the question for applying to the General for troops if Any two of them would propose it. I was answered that they did not desire to be knocked on the head. I told them that I did not desire it neither; but I was ready to take my share of the danger with them, and if they would advise this Measure I would carry it into Execution. But I would not act solely in this & take the whole resentment upon myself, attended with a charge of acting unconstitutionally in not taking the Advice of the Council.[6]

To show that the apprehensions of the Council are not groundless, I will mention a Fact. One of the chiefs of the Sons of Liberty (a Representative of the Town)[7] said in a mixed company about six weeks ago that if any person was known to apply for troops to come here, he would certainly be put to death.[8] A Gentleman in company expostulating with him, He repeated his words & said that he spoke this in publick that it might be known & people might take Warning.

Above a fortnight ago A Committee of both houses was appointed to enquire into the foundation of a report that troops were coming hither.[9] A Sub-committee was sent to me, who after Apologising for the question asked me if I had, or any one that I knew had applied for troops to come hither. I accepted the apology being desirous & prepared to answer the question. I told them that I neither had myself nor did I know that any one else had applied for troops; but that I was certain that troops would come here, not from any knowledge of applications or orders, but from the sure consequence of effects from Causes; and I beleived that when they did come, it would be Very satisfactory to most people of property in the Town, tho' perhaps, they won't own it. That for my own part I avoided as much as possible having Any hand in or knowledge of it: for if I wanted to have Troops here, I need not expose myself by Applying for them; the Sons of Liberty would save me that trouble.[10]

I have given this Capitulation that you see what it is that has prevented & still does prevent my applying for Troops from whence it will appear, that my not applying is no Argument that they are not wanted. It is above 3 months ago since I informed the Secretary of State of my Situation[11] & utter inability to preserve the peace of the Town or support the Authority of Government: but the Letter went too late for me to expect an Answer by this Mail.[12]

I must beg that you will keep this letter to yourself as much as you can, that is, wholly so on this side of the Water, for obvious reasons. I am, with great truth & regard

Sr Your most obedient & most humble Servant

Fra Bernard

His Excellency Genl. Gage.

ALS, RC   Gage, vol. 78.

Endorsed: Govr. Bernard Roxbury 2^d July 1768. Received July 9th. answered .   Variants: CO 5/757, ff 353-354 (AL, Copy) and BP, 5: 266-269 (L, LbC).

This was FB's first formal letter to General Gage following the *Liberty* riot. Gage had been alerted to the incident by the American Board of Customs in a letter of 15 Jun.[13] Gage wrote FB on 26 Jun. (**No. 637**); the letter printed here is one of two letters written in reply (the other being **No. 643**). These letters would have disabused Gage of any notion that the Customs commissioners were undermining FB's authority by asking for military protection on their own initiative. The letters also likely convinced Gage that the governor and the commissioners were generally of the same mind and, though acting independently, were actively cooperating (rather than tacitly colluding) to obtain military assistance for the support of civil government. FB now updated Gage on the situation in Boston, rendering politics in terms of class conflict: "All real power is in the hands of the people of the lowest class." Only British soldiers could redress the balance, he observed, stressing that "my not applying [*for troops*] is no Argument that they are not wanted." The penultimate paragraph of **No. 641** thus indicates that FB was hoping Gage would take charge of the situation and order a detachment of Regulars to Boston. That certainly was how Gage (in **No. 652**) interpreted FB's letter of 2 Jul. Gage's rejoinder (**No. 652**) reminded FB that the Governor and Council ought to make a formal request for military assistance. FB's reaction (in **No. 655**) to Gage's rejoinder expressed disappointment at the general not recognizing the "Necessity" of intervention.

---

1. **No. 639**.

2. **No. 644**. See also the source note to **No. 642**.

3. FB is referring not only to the newspaper reports but also to the Customs commissioners' letter to Gage, 15 Jun. **Appendix 5**.

4. **No. 628**.

5. FB had previously informed Gage of the Council's position on the matter, following the Stamp Act riots, in **No. 381**, *Bernard Papers*, 3: 332-333.

6. FB is referring to the Council meetings of 11 and 13 Jun. (described in **No. 630**), at which such matters were discussed but not recorded in the minutes. CO 5/827, f 48.

7. Most likely Samuel Adams, James Otis Jr., or John Hancock.

8. It is most unlikely that the allegation concerned Thomas Cushing, whose moderation had drawn praise from FB in the past. The other three Boston representatives (Adams, Hancock, and Otis) are likelier candidates. The comment when originally delivered (c.21 May by FB's reckoning) was probably not meant to be taken literally, as FB here implies. But the braggadocio was in keeping with the Boston Whigs' forceful rhetoric and domineering behavior, which FB had highlighted at the time. (**No. 614**). FB's careful dating of the alleged remark conveys some authenticity as to its impact upon him. It also demonstrated to Gen. Gage the depth of hostility FB faced. (This was more than a month before FB rendered himself a clear target for invective after proposing that the Council should join him in asking Gage for troops).

9. On 18 Jun., *JHRM*, 45: 63-64. The town's protests at Capt. John Corner's recent impressment of sailors probably heightened concern that FB would make such an application. *Boston Evening-Post*, 20 Jun.; *Boston Gazette*, 20 Jun. 1768.

10. See the account of these proceedings and exchanges in **No. 614**.

11. **No. 601**.

12. **No. 600**, to which Hillsborough replied with **No. 622**, received by FB on 14 Sept.

13. **Appendix 5**.

642 | To William Dalrymple

Roxbury July 3 1768

S[r]

I hereby send you some Dispatches which I received by Express from Gen[l] Gage on Fryday last.[1] I have reason to beleive that one of the Letters relates to Measures to be taken to restore Peace to the Town of Boston & Authority to the civil Power there; tho' by my receiving the Letter sealed I am happily not made acquainted with its Contents. You know that my Situation requires that I should appear to know as little of and act as little in the Proceedings of this Kind as can well be. I should therefore be obliged to you if in conducting a Business of this Kind you would let me appear a Stranger to it untill it becomes necessary to communicate it to me officially. In the mean Time any private hints conveyed to me by a safe hand will be acceptable. If I had seen you before you sailed this Letter would have been unnecessary.

I am &c.

Col Dalrymple

L, LbC   BP, 5: 272.

In handwriting of Thomas Bernard. Scribal emendations not shown. The RC[2] enclosed Gage's orders to Dalrymple, New York, 25 Jun. 1768 (**Appendix 8**). On 4 Jul., FB requested that Capt. Corner dispatch Dalrymple's orders promptly in a cutter (**No. 644**), and they may have been carried in the *Gaspee*, Capt. Murray, which departed Boston harbor on 6 Jul.[3]

As this letter indicates, FB likely assumed that Gage's sealed letter directed Dalrymple to provide military assistance to his government in Boston; that was not the case, as FB learned upon receiving another copy of Dalrymple's orders on 16 Jul., delivered under a flying seal, and enclosed in **No. 652**.

---

1. **No. 639** enclosing **Appendix 8**.

2. The copy of this letter that William Dalrymple made for Thomas Gage is probably in MiU-C: Gage, but has not been located.

3. *New-Hampshire Gazette*, 15 Jul. 1768.

643 | To Thomas Gage

Roxbury July 3. 1768

Separate

S[r].

I am obliged to you for your separate Letter, & am pleased that the Letter inclosed in it came sealed,[1] that I may be able to say, if there is occasion, that I know not the contents of any of the letters which I have forwarded: for I expect that these dispatches passing thro' my hands will occasion a good deal of talk. In my present situation I cant apply for troops nor can I prevent their coming.

I am, with great regard, S[r] Your most obedient & most humble Servant

Fra Bernard

His Excellency Gen[l] Gage.

You will learn from the papers that I have dissolved the Assembly by his Majesty's command: this may possibly create fresh disturbance.

ALS, RC   Gage, vol. 78.

Endorsed: Separate. Gov[r]. Bernard Roxbury July 3[d]. 1768. Received July 9th. Answered.   Variants: CO 5/757, f 354 (AL, Copy); BP, 5: 269 (L, LbC).

    This letter was a reply to **No. 641**. Gage's rejoinder is **No. 652**, in which he reminded FB that the proper civil authority (in this case the Governor and Council) was legally required to ask for military assistance if British Regulars were to be used "to quell Tumults and Riots"; in any such policing activity the army was subordinate to a civil command, in this case the governor.

---

1. The RC of **Appendix 8** enclosed in **No. 639**.

644 | *To John Corner*

Boston July 4 1768

S^r

Having by Reason of certain Rumours of their being an Intention in some desperate Men to attack or surprise his Majestys Castle William found it necessary to give Orders to the honble Thomas Hutchinson Esqr Captain of the said Castle to take proper Measures for defending & securing the said Castle; and having among other Things directed him to apply to you for your Aid and Assistance in such Case: I hereby transmit to you a Copy of the Order relating thereto and desire that if such Application should be made to you, you would comply with the Request and assist by all Means in your Power in the Defence and Protection of the Castle. And for that Purpose I desire that you would so station his Majesty's Ships under your Command which can be spared for this Service, as shall best serve for securing the Passages to the said Castle and repelling those who shall attempt to assail the same. And if such Attempt should be made in so sudden a Manner as not to Leave Time for the Commander of the Castle to apply to you, as aforesaid, I must desire that you would take the same Measures for the Defence of the Castle, as if such Application had been made to you.

I am S^r &c.

Captn Corner of the Romney

L, LbC BP, 5: 273.

In handwriting of Thomas Bernard. Enclosure not found. Variant: ADM 1/483, f 127 (L, Copy). Enclosed a copy of FB's orders to the captain of Castle William, Jamaica Plain, 13 Jun. 1768 (for which see CO 5/766, f 207).

FB did not expect Castle William to be invested but he treated the rumors seriously enough to warn Capt. Corner to protect Castle Island. At least four Royal Navy ships were anchored in the harbor on 3 Jul., with the *Romney* being closest to the Castle (probably in the shipping channel known as King's Road between Castle Island and Governor's Island). Several RN vessels left Boston harbor and others arrived, on or around 4 Jul. This was part of Commodore Hood's plan to provide protection to the American Board of Customs and provincial government.[1] There is no corroborating evidence to suggest that Corner wanted any of the ships out of harm's way, but the arrival of six navy ships probably precipitated further rumors about a conspiracy to "Storm" the Castle (described in **Appendix 10**).[2] FB continued his account in **No. 648**.

1. His Majesty's Ships *Romney*, *Garland* (departed 4 Jul.), *Glasgow* (dep. 4 Jul.), and *Gaspee* (dep. 6 Jul.). They were replaced by the vessels listed in note 2 below. The squadron's movements were reported in the *New-Hampshire Gazette*, 15 Jul. 1768. Commodore Samuel Hood, the commander of the North Atlantic Station, was responding to the entreaties of the American Board of Customs to keep a substantial Royal Navy presence anchored in Boston harbor. See source note to **Appendix 2**. Hood was not acting in direct response to Admiralty orders arising from Hillsborough's request that the Admiralty station a squadron in Boston harbor. The earl of Hillsborough to the lords commissioners of the Admiralty, Whitehall, 11 Jun. 1768, CO 5/757, ff 81-82.

2. His Majesty's Ships *Beaver*, *Bonetta*, *Little Romney*, and *Viper* arrived on 4 Jul., and *Hope* and *Senegal* on 6 Jul. The commissioners of Customs praised Commodore Hood for this "most seasonable" aid. American Board of Customs, memorial to the lords commissioners of the Treasury, Castle William, 11 Jul. 1768, T 1/465, ff 179-180.

645 | Circular From the Earl of Hillsborough

Circular. (N°. 12.)

Whitehall. July the 4th. 1768.

Sir,

As His Majesty has thought fit to direct that I should give constant Attendance in my Place at the Board of Trade, I shall not fail to lay before that Board such Matters, arising out of your Correspondence with me, as shall appear to be necessary for their Consideration; You need not therefore, for the future, be at the Trouble of transmitting their Lordships Duplicates of your Dispatches to my Office, but confine Yourself to One Channel of Correspondence, conformable to the Spirit & Intention of His Maty's Order in Council of the Eighth of August 1766.[1]

I am with great truth & Regard, Sir Your most obedient Humble Servant

Hillsborough

Governor of Massachuset's Bay.

LS, RC   BP, 11: 211-214.

Endorsed: Lord Hillsborough N° 2 circular d July 4 r Sep 3 1768. Docket by Thomas Bernard: Informing Gov[r] B& that Lord H sh[d] attend for the future the Board of Trade.

The Council of Trade and Plantations, commonly known as the Board of Trade, was an advisory body whose influence had declined in the past decade. Hitherto, the Board of seven or eight commissioners was presided over by the first lord commissioner. This office was discontinued by the Chatham administration, from 12 Jul. 1768, with the secretary of state for the Colonies becoming the Board's *ex officio* chairman.[2] Hillsborough had previously served as president of the Board, 1763-64 and 1766, before his appointment as colonial secretary. Initially, Hillsborough continued a practice established in 1766 whereby governors supplied the Board of Trade with copies of their correspondence with the secretary of state (**No. 582**); the letter printed here announced its discontinuation. Thereafter, the secretary of state's office, on Hillsborough's direction, presented selected items of governors' correspondence to the Board of Trade; in Massachusetts's case, presentation commenced on 1 Dec. 1769.[3]

Hillsborough thus exercised managerial control over the management and distribution of information on American affairs coming in from FB and other colonial governors. Of this he served notice to the governors with the circular **No. 651** and to FB with **No. 653**, wherein he reiterated his ministerial authority to lay in-letters before Parliament as and when he saw fit or when so requested by either house.

---

1. The order-in-council (and the subsequent instructions dispatched to colonial governors) required that colonial governors contact the secretary of state in the first instance and send "Duplicates" of their out-letters to the Board of Trade. BP, 11: 119-122.

2. J. C. Sainty, et al., *Officeholders in Modern Britain*, 3: 28-37.

3. *JBT*, 13: 125.

646 | To the Earl of Hillsborough

N° 10

Boston July 9 1768

My Lord

I gave your Lordship a full account of the issue of the proceedings upon his Majesty's requisition together with Copies of all papers relating thereto. I sent the original by a returned Express to Genl Gage to be forwarded by the packet. The duplicates I put into the hands of Captn Smith of the Brig [*blank*] which sailed last Monday for Glascow.[1] As there are other Ships now preparing to sail I shall inclose some printed copies of the papers from the Newspapers, some of which may come to your Lordships hands before either of my Letters. From these your Lordship will see that I dismissed the General Court by prorogation & dissolved them the next day by proclamation. This form of proceeding, tho' immaterial in the effect made this business pass more easily than I expected.[2]

The Sons of Liberty[3] keep up their Spirits still: on tuesday Evning last past,[4] a Number of them, between 50 & 60, went out of Boston at the close of day, & having divided themselves into two parties met on each side of an house in Roxbury about 3 miles from Boston which M[r] Robinson one of the Commissioners of the Customs has lately hired, with an intention, as is supposed from the manœuvre, they practiced, to surprise him there & prevent his escape. But he being at the Castle, where he has resided, since the Commissioners have been driven thither for safety, they did nothing but plunder his fruit trees & break off the branches thereof & break down some of the fences & trample down the garden; and did not, that I can learn, break into the House. After this, about Midnight they went back to Boston in a body huzzaing all the Way. This is called a Frolick of a few boys to eat some Cherries.

Last night about 30 Men came on board a Schooner lying at a Wharf which had been seized for having 30 hogsheads of uncustomed Molasses on board & was then in the custody of two customhouse officers, and having confined the two officers to the Cabbin carried off all the Molasses.[5] When the Sloop[6] was seized which occasioned the riot[7] in which the Custom house officers were ill treated & in consequence of which the Commissioners of the Customs were obliged to leave the Town, the Greatest part of the Resentment was expressed against carrying the Sloop from the Wharf & putting her under the Care of the Man of War. This, they said, was an Affront to the Town, as it contained an insinuation that the Sloop would not have been safe if it had been left at the Wharf in the Custody of a Customhouse Officer. Therefore When this Schooner was seized It was left at the Wharf under no other guard but 2 customhouse officers. It would have been Very easily secured by laying it in the stream & put^ting^ a guard on board either from the Romney or the Castle; but I suppose it was thought best to try the Experiment. As Evry seizure made or attempted to be made on land at Boston for 3 years past, before these two instances, has been Violently rescued ^or prevented^, it was easy to see what would be the Event of this & I foretold it as certain.[8] However the Experiment has been made.

I have not recieved any request from the Commissioners upon this occasion nor do I expect it: for they know I can do nothing. Your Lordship has observed in my letters N[o] 5 & 6[9] that I consulted the Council upon the great Riot on June 10, & after having, upon repeated adjournments, endeavoured to bring them to some resolution, the whole business was avoided by referring it to the general Court. After this a Committee of both Houses was appointed under the Specious title "to take the State of the province into consideration;" when after sevral meetings, as the two bodies had different purposes to serve, they could come to no conclusion.[10] And so this Matter rests: and I have no desire to revive it again; as, in the present state of things, the Advice of the Council will be timid & the Executive power of the Governor is perfectly impotent.

In regard to the Answer of the House[11] so far as it relates to me I will make but one observation upon it: It is *Felo de se* of it['s][12] own purport;[13] It pretends to be the Voice of the people & gives evidence itself that it is the Voice of a Faction. It charges the Governor with misrepresenting the generality of the people by asserting that the blameable Conduct of the House is to be imputed to a Faction prevailing there & not to the people in general. Now if this is not true All the injury the Governor has done the people is by setting them in a more favorable light than they deserve; and therefore if the people were to take notice of it there would be no occasion for passion or resentment. But it is otherwise with the Faction: If they are charged with more than belongs to them, it is natural that they should resent it: and therefore passion Malice and Abuse become them & are suitable to their Character & the Occasion. From this Criterion One may safely pronounce that this Answer is the Virulent Overflowing of a Faction & not the cool Voice of a people. And yet my Lord, I do not intend to give up my Opinion of the Faction or the People; not withstanding the high pitch to which the Wickedness of the former has raised the inflammation & infatuation of a great part of the latter.

I informed your Lordship that I had not seen nor probably should see, till it is printed, the Letter of the House to your Lordship, altho I am informed I am much intrested in the contents of it. But I shall soon have that satisfaction being informed that it is to be printed next Monday.[14] It seems that this Morning the two Consuls of the faction Otis & Adams had a dispute upon it in the representatives Room where the papers of the House are kept: which I shall write as a Dialogue to save paper. O. What are you going to do with the letter to Lord H? A. to give it to the printer to publish next Monday. O. Do you think it proper to publish it so soon that he may receive a printed copy, before the Original comes to his hands? A. What signifies that? you know it was designed for the people & not for the Minister. O. You are so fond of your own Draughts that you cant wait for the publication of them to a proper time. A. I am Clerk of the House & I will make that use of the papers which I please. __ I had this from a Gentleman of the first rank, who, I understood, was present.[15]

I have been under some concern for the safety of the Castle since the Commissioners retired thither, not upon[16] account of any intelligence I had of an intention to attack it (for that at most amounted but to idle rumours)[17] as from a consideration of the Weakness of the Garrison & the ease with which it might be surprised.[18] But I am relieved in this by the Care of Commodore Hood, who has so well supplied us with naval force, that there are now about the Castle one fifty gun ship[19] two sloops of 16 guns & two Cutters armed with swivell guns; so that I am under no concern for that place. Besides I have lately received by express from Gen¹ Gage some dispatches for Col Dalrymple at Halifax,[20] which I forwarded by one of the Kings Cutters: and I am mistaken, if there is not among them an order for at least one Regiment to come here; altho' Gen¹ Gage who knows my situation, where death is publickly denounced against those who are concerned in bringing troops here, is so kind as to conceal the contents of the dispatches from me. One Regiment will secure the Castle, but will not be sufficient to awe the Town. This Very morning the Select men of the Town ordered the Magazine of Arms belonging to the Town to be brought out to be cleaned, when they were exposed for some hours at the Town house. They were expostulated with for this impending Act; they excused themselves by saying, that those Arms were ordered to be cleaned *two* months ago. I have been much pressed to go to the Castle, when troops shall arrive here: I do not choose to show a want of resolution as I don't feel the firmness of my mind to fail; but I shall not ^unnecessarily^ expose myself to danger where I can foresee it. A short time will determine whether *Boston* is to be Subject to Great Britain or not; if the intention to dispute it is Any thing more than Talk.

I am with great respect My Lord, your Lordships most obedient & most humble Servant

Fra Bernard

The right honble The Earl of Hillsborough

ALS, RC   CO 5/757, ff 303-307.

Minor emendations not shown. Endorsed: ~~Copy of a~~ Letter from Governor Bernard to the Earl of Hillsborough dated Boston July 9th: 1768. R 24 August. (N°. 10). A.31.   Probably enclosed a copy of the *Boston Gazette*, 4 Jul. 1768. Variants of letter: CO 5/766, ff 264-267 (L, RLbC); BP, 6: 335-340 (L, LbC); T 1/465, f 190 (L extract, Copy); *Letters to the Ministry* (1st ed.), 38-41; *Letters to the Ministry* (repr.), 50-54. Extracts were laid before both houses of Parliament on 28 Nov. 1768. HLL: American Colonies Box 2. Hillsborough acknowledged receipt with **No. 679**.

No. 646 was crafted to elicit Hillsborough's sympathy and in the mistaken assumption that Gage had ordered troops to Boston (see source notes to **Nos. 642, 639**, and **Appendix 8**). By the time the secretary of state received this letter, he had already ordered a further two regiments of troops to Boston (**No. 661**).

While FB did not anticipate an attack on Castle William, the bravado display of muskets left him pondering the loyalty and resilience of the fifty officers and men who comprised the Castle garrison. However, there was a substantial Royal Navy presence in Boston in early July that would have intimidated all but the most reckless of would-be rebels (whose alleged conspiracy is described in **Appendix 10**). FB continued his account in **No. 648**.

1. **No. 638**.

2. The proceedings of the House of Representatives from 21 to 30 Jun. were printed in the *Boston Gazette*, 4 Jul. 1768. FB's proclamation for dissolving the General Court, "IN OBEDIENCE TO HIS MAJESTY'S COMMANDS," dated 1 Jul., was printed in the *Boston Weekly News-Letter*, 7 Jul. 1768.

3. L extract: from here to "they know I can do nothing."

4.   4 Jul.

5.   The cargo rescued on 8 Jul. was returned to the Customhouse, according to Samuel Adams, who claimed FB intentionally omitted that fact. *Appeal to the World*, 23.

6.   John Hancock's vessel the *Liberty*.

7.   On 10 Jun.

8.   Samuel Adams considered this "An Assertion so notoriously false, that few men could have made it without Blushing; and we may suppose even Governor Bernard himself would not have made it, had he apprehended it would have ever become Public." *Appeal to the World*, 22-23.

9.   **Nos. 623** and **630**.

10. The committee appointed on 13 Jun 1768 was reformed a year later, and proceeded to prepare a petition to the king calling for FB's removal. *JHRM*, 45: 53, 136.

11. Message of the House of Representatives, 30 Jun. 1768, *JHRM*, 45: 91-94. For a brief discussion see the source note to **No. 638**.

12. Editorially supplied.

13. *Felo de se* is a court verdict meaning suicide. FB suggested that the House had committed political suicide: by refusing to rescind the vote approving the Circular Letter, the House obliged him to dissolve the General Court as punishment.

14. Of 30 Jun., *JHRM*, 45: 89, 99-104. The letter to Hillsborough was printed in the *Boston Weekly News-Letter*, 7 Jul. 1768.

15. While FB probably exaggerated the differences between Otis and Adams, his claim of authenticity notwithstanding, there was distance between the Whig leaders. Otis was more conservative in demeanor, yet had taken the Whigs' constitutional arguments in radical directions. Adams was a radical activist, intuitively pragmatic in finding ways and means to advance the cause. For a recent discussion see Alexander, *Samuel Adams*, 28-30, 81.

16. LbC interlineation in FB's hand: "not so much upon".

17. For the rumors see **Appendix 10**.

18. The first sentence of this paragraph was later cited by TH in support of his suggestion that Boston radical William Molineux (c.1717-74) was the leader of a plot involving five hundred men to seize Castle William. TH noted "the governor mentioned [*the plot*] in one of his letters to the ministry,* but was not at liberty to make known the evidence of the fact. He believed it to be true." For this FB was later accused of misrepresenting the province. But, continued TH, "if it was true, the persons who brought the charge against him must have been privy to it." Hutchinson, *History of Massachusetts*, 3:121.
     * **No. 646** in *Letters to the Ministry* (1st ed.), 40.

19. HMS *Senegal*, which arrived on 6 Jul.

20. Thomas Gage to the Earl of Hillsborough, New York, 28 Jun. 1768, CO 5/86, ff 128-130.

647 | From John Pownall

Secry of States Office. Whitehall
July 9. 1768

Dear Sir,

As you will receive from me by this mail an official letter it would be unpardonable in me to suffer you to be informed of my publick situation without an assurance from me by private letter that no satisfaction that can attend it is greater than that which arises from a hope that it may afford me some opportunitys of testifying the zeal I have for your Interest and Service.

I have been long useless to myself & to my freinds but being now released from disagreeable restraint and acting in a respectable character under the protection of the best freind I ever had,[1] I cannot but cherish better hopes.

I understand that there is a Vessell for Boston next week if any thing occurrs that may be usefull to you, you will hear by her from

Your most faithfull & Obedt humble Servt

J Pownall

ALS, RC   BP, 11: 215-218.

Endorsed by FB. [_][2] Mr Pownall d July 9 1768 r Sep 3. His App^t as Under Secry. Variants: CO 5/757, ff 96-97 (L, AC); CO 5/765, f 16 (L, LbC). Enclosures: **No. 653** and **No. 651**; also enclosed an order-in-council of 29 Jun. and a letter from John Pownall, also dated 9 Jul., notifying FB of the disallowance of the provincial act to empower Abigail Conqueret of Lancaster, Worcester Co. (1767) (for which see CO 5/765, ff 16-18).

Pownall had earlier expressed anxieties about his career progression (**No. 577**) but the upbeat tone of this letter was the consequence of his appointment as under-secretary of state in the Colonial Department on c.24 Jun. 1768, which office he held until 5 Apr. 1776. FB warmly congratulated Pownall in **No. 684**.

---

1. That is, Hillsborough.

2. Obscured by tight binding.

648 | To the Earl of Hillsborough

N° 10. Supplement

Boston July 11 1768

My Lord

I find myself obliged to add a supplement to my Letter N° 10[1] which I sent away to day by a Brig to Liverpool, the duplicate whereof will be inclosed with this. I had there informed your Lordship that 30 hogsheads of Molasses which had been seized for illicit trade, together with the Schooner it was in had been taken from thence out of the Custody of the Custom house officers who had the care of it. This Very Molasses was on the next day returned & put on board the Schooner again. The Account I have of this affair is this: The people of the Town were dissatisfied that the assurances which they had made, that the Sloop, which had been seized before this & put in the Custody of the Man of War, would have been safe, if she had been left at the Wharf in the care of a single Officer, should be so ^soon^ falsified.[2] The select Men of the Town therefore sent for the Master of this schooner[3] & upon his denying that he knew any thing of the Molasses, told him that would not pass: for no body would take away his Molasses without his privity; they thereupon ordered him to return the Molasses directly under pain of displeasure of the Town: which was immediately done. I dare say, neither the Custom house officers nor the Judge of the Admiralty, nor the Chief Justice nor the Governor could have prevailed upon any one to run the risk of informing where this Molasses was consigned or to assist in recovering it, if it had been against the humour of the people. But to serve a purpose of the people The Selectmen in a Summary Way can do the business in a trice. So We are not without a Government: only it is in the hands of the people of the Town, & not of those deputed by the King or under his Authority

I am with great respect, My Lord, Your Lordships most obedient
& most humble Servant

Fra Bernard

The right honble The Earl of Hillsborough

The Letter to your Lordship is not printed in this days paper as was expected.[4] I inclose a Letter from Maryland which gives great pleasure to the faction.[5]

ALS, RC

CO 5/757, ff 307-308.

Minor emendations not shown. Endorsed: Boston July 11. 1768 Govr. Bernard. (N°. 10 Supplement.) R 24th August. A32.   Enclosures: duplicate of **No. 646**; a copy of the *Boston Evening-Post*, 11 Jul. 1768, CO 757, f 309. Variants: CO 5/766, f 268 (L, RLbC); BP, 7: 1-2 (L, LbC); T 1/465, ff 192-193 (L, Copy); *Letters to the Ministry* (1st ed.), 41-42; *Letters to the Ministry* (repr.), 55-56. Hillsborough replied with **No. 679**.

FB's account of the seizure made on 8 Jul. (also discussed in **No. 646**) stresses the resentment of the populace toward the Customhouse. This letter is notable for the intercession of the Boston selectmen in persuading the unknown smuggler to return to the custody of the Customhouse the cargo of molasses on which he had evaded paying duty.

1. **No. 646**.
2. Faint.
3. Not identified.
4. **Appendix 9**, printed in the *Boston Gazette*, 18 Jul. 1768.
5. Robert Lloyd, Speaker of the Maryland Assembly, to Thomas Cushing, 24 Jun. 1768, printed in the *Boston Evening-Post*, 11 Jul. 1768.

649 | To John Pownall

Boston July 11 1768

Dear S^r

I have had so much writing of late to the Secretary of State, that I have had no Time, amidst the Multiplicity of Business which the present dangerous State of the Province is continually creating, to write to my Friends.[1] The Information which I give you now must be by printed Papers with a little of handwriting.

We are now just entering into that critical Situation which I have long ago foreseen must come sooner or later; that is, the Time of Trial, whether this Town &c will or will not submit to Great Britain when She is in earnest in requiring Submission. Hitherto the Sons of Liberty have triumphed; the Commissioners of the Customs & their Officers are driven out of ^the^ Town; the Laws of Trade are executed no further than ~~the Sons of Liberty~~ as People are disposed to submit to them; and the civil Power is confined to such Business as does not interfere with the popular Pretensions.

The Sons of Liberty have publickly declared that whoever procures Troops to come here will be destroyed. That it should be left to any one ~~here~~ to ask for Troops to come here at this Time of Day, will be the Wonder of the future readers of the History of these Times. However it is now generally beleived that Troops are coming tho' from whence or when or in what Numbers is not known. And now the Question is whether they will be opposed, and in Consequence thereof a general Insurrection will happen or not? There is a great Division of Opinions upon this: but for my Part I don't beleive that there will be either an Opposition or Insurrection; tho I am well convinced that the Cheifs of the Faction are wicked enough and have really taken Measures to raise a Rebellion here; but I believe, when it comes to the Test their Hearts will fail them.[2]

For myself as I am obliged to continue in this disagreeable and dangerous Service without being allowed to retire but at my own Peril, I shall endeavour, as I don't find the Fortitude of my Mind fail me, to conduct myself so as to avoid Timidity on the one hand and rashness on the other. I have kept my Post hitherto and hope I shall still. I am much advised when it is certain that the Troops are coming, to retire to the Castle: I am unwilling to shew a Want of Resolution. Indeed it has not been a Place of Security 'till within these 2 Days; but it has now 5 Ships of the Kings, reckoning 2 Cutters, about it;[3] and I beleive may be now said to be out of Danger. What will be the Event of these Commotions I don't know; but a few ~~Days~~ ^Weeks^ will determine it.

I am &c

J Pownall Esq[r].

L, LbC   BP, 6: 130-131.

In handwriting of Thomas Bernard. May have enclosed a copy of the *Boston Evening-Post*, 11 Jul. 1768.

FB may not have believed rumors of a planned revolt, but now pondered the consequences of doing nothing to avert the possibility. The Council had hitherto protested that further disturbances were unlikely, but FB pressed upon them the fact that the Customs commissioners and their families had retreated to Castle William in fear. On 22 Jul., FB formally requested the Council's advice on the "unsettled State of Government." CO 5/827, ff 47-48, 52.

---

1. FB wrote several letters to Hillsborough in June and July reporting the *Liberty* riot of 10 Jun. and the House of Representatives' refusal to rescind the circular letter on 30 Jun.: **Nos. 623, 630, 632, 633, 638, 646,** and **648**.

2. FB was more explicit in a letter to Richard Jackson, written the same the day:

> The Faction has declared that the Kings Troops shall not come into this Town; and that the Country will rise to assist them in repelling them. They have also denounced Death against any one who shall be concerned in bringing them hither.

BP, 6: 133. He also mentioned the death threat in a letter to Barrington (ibid., 132). All three of his intimate correspondents could not have failed to appreciate that FB now believed himself to be danger.

3. See the source note to **No. 644**.

650 | *From the Earl of Hillsborough*

Duplicate (N° 14.)

Whitehall July 11th 1768.

Sir,

The Commissioners of His Majesty's Customs in North America residing at Boston having made further Complaint of Obstructions and Insults they and their Officers meet with in the Execution of their Duty, and having in a Memorial addressed to the Lords of the Treasury,[1] represented in particular that about 60 Pipes of Wine had been illegally unloaded from a Vessel in the Harbour of Boston owned by Mr Malcolm, and that the said Wine had been conducted into the Town at Night by a great Number of People, I am to signify to you His Majesty's Pleasure that you do give all the Assistance and Support in your Power to the Commissioners of the Customs and their Officers in the Discharge of their Duty, and especially in the discovering and bringing to Justice, all Persons who may have been guilty of any Breach of the Laws of this Kingdom either in the Case above referred to, or in any other whatever.

I am with great Truth and Regard, Sir, your most obedient, humble Servant,

Hillsborough

dupLS, RC   BP, 11: 223-226.

Endorsed: Duplicate N° 14 Earl of Hillsborough d July 11 1768 r Sep 30. Docket by Thomas Bernard: To assist the Commiss^{rs}.   An original was enclosed in **No. 647**. Variants: CO 5/757, f 100 (LS, AC); CO 5/765, f 23 (L, LbC). FB acknowledged receipt of Hillsborough's letter with **No. 672**. Daniel Malcom avoided prosecution and died the following year.

---

1. **Appendix 3**.

651 | Circular From the Earl of Hillsborough

(N°. 15.)

Circular

Whitehall July 11th 1768.

Sir,

As I observe that it frequently happens, that Intelligence of public Transactions in the Colonies is received by private Persons in this City, long before any official Communication of it comes to me for His Majesty's Information,[1] I conceive this Inconvenience must arise, in great Measure, from His Majesty's Governors not availing themselves of such casual Opportunities of writing by private Ships as frequently happen, but confining themselves to the Channel of the Packets only: For this Reason I desire that you will for the future send your Dispatches by the first Opportunity that offers, & Duplicates of them by the next Packet; or in Case the Packet shall be the first Opportunity that offers, then you will send your Duplicates by the next private Conveyance.

I am, with great Truth and Regard, Sir, your most obedient humble Servant

Hillsborough.

Governor of the Massachusets Bay.

LS, RC   BP 11, 227-230.

Endorsed: Lord Hillsborough N° 15 circ d July 11 1768 r Sep 3. Docket by Thomas Bernard: To send Letters by private Ships   Enclosed in **No. 647**. Copies were laid before both houses of Parliament on 28 Nov. 1768. HLL: American Colonies Box 2. FB replied with **No. 674**.

---

1. Hillsborough probably received his information at more or less the same time as private persons corresponding with the colonies (when he was not absent on his Ulster estates). For example, a letter from FB about the *Liberty* riot dated 14 Jun. was received on 10 Jul. (**No. 630**); others dated 19 and 30 May arrived on 13 Jul. (**Nos. 614** and **616**). But British newspapers could be up to three months behind in their detailed reporting of developments in the American Colonies. The *Public Advertiser* of 2 Jun. and the *Gazetteer and New Daily Advertiser* of 3 Jun. printed the proceedings of the Massachusetts House of Representatives of 22 Feb 1768, concerning FB's correspondence with Shelburne that FB had reported in letters which the secretary of state received on 15 Apr. (**No. 593**).

652 | From Thomas Gage

New York 11th. July 1768.

Sir,

Your Letters of the 2^d. & 3^d. Ins^t:[1] have been received, and I perceive that the Letter which I sent you directed for the Commander of His Majesty's Forces at Halifax was sealed up; instead of being sent you under a flying seals: I therefore inclose you a Copy of said Letter,[2] by which you will learn; that the order to the Officer Commanding at Halifax to embark Troops for Boston is Conditional in Case you should apply for the Assistance of the King's Troops.

It is needless for me to acquaint you, that it is contrary to the Laws and Constitution, for Troops to move to quell Tumults and Riots, unless Military Aid is required for those Purposes by the Civil Power; and that even then, the Troops cannot act by their own Authority, but are under the Command of the Civil Power, and must act solely in obedience thereto. My orders in these respects correspond with the Laws, and I could not give any other orders to the Officer Commanding at Halifax to embark Forces for Boston than those I suppose to have been forwarded to him, which empower him only to proceed in that Business, upon your Requisition to him for Military Aid.

I am much obliged to you for your Care to forward my Dispatches to Halifax, and hope to send the two Letters for England which you entrusted to my Care in a few Days, by the Opportunity of a London Ship commanded by Captain Borton.[3] And I shall take the same Care of any other Dispatches you shall commit to my Charge.

I have the honor to be with great truth and Regards, Sir Your most obedient,
& most humble Servant,

Thos. Gage

His Excellency Govr. Bernard

ALS, RC BP, 11: 107.

Endorsed: Genl Gage d July 11 1768 r July 16.   Enclosed a copy of **Appendix 8**, for FB's perusal. Gage was replying to **No. 641**. FB's rejoinder was **No. 655**.

Unaware that Hillsborough had already ordered British troops to Boston, FB had been trying to persuade Gen. Gage to send troops direct to the town. This letter disabused FB of the notion that Gage had ordered Dalrymple to provide military support from Halifax (see the source note to **No. 642**). Gage would not oblige unless he received a formal request from the Governor or the Governor and Council (**No. 655**). In fulfilment of that condition, Gage expected FB (a) to transmit the sealed orders to Dalrymple (**Appendix 8**)—which FB did in **No. 642**—and (b) specifically ask Dalrymple for the troops—which FB chose not to do without the Council's backing.

---

1. **Nos. 641** and **643**.

2. **Appendix 8**.

3. Possibly Benjamin Barton of St. Augustine, East Florida, a frequent visitor to New York.

653 | *From the Earl of Hillsborough*

N°. 13

Whitehall July 11ᵗʰ. 1768.

Sir,

I have received the Favour of your Letter N°. 1,[1] which contains Expressions of so much Partiality to me, that I felt distressed in the Performance of my Duty of laying it before the King. I take the first Opportunity to return you my Thanks for your obliging Congratulation upon the Honor His Majesty has done me, in entrusting to my Care a Department of so much Consequence to His Service, as that of His Colonies. His Majesty has been pleased also very lately to command me to preside at the Board of Trade, by which Arrangement, I trust, the Business of America will have quicker Dispatch than when the two Offices were in different Hands.[2] The reducing America into good Order as You justly observe, is a very arduous Task; I am not vain enough to think myself equal to it, but it is my Duty to exert my utmost Application to obey my Royal Master's Commands, and with His Gracious Support, and the active Assistance of His Majesty's other Servants, I trust His Business shall not be neglected; and give me Leave to say that so often as I shall have the Aid of Governors zealous able and active in promoting the just Purposes of Administration, as You have approved yourself to be, I shall find much greater Facility in the Discharge of my Duty.

Your Observation, with regard to the Impropriety of exposing the Letters of Government to Public View; which are in their Nature designed for the private Information of His Majesty's Ministers, is but too well founded. There are Times when Motions for laying such before Parliament cannot be resisted, but I will never give my Consent to any Thing of a Kind so unjust and unfair to the Writers, when I see any Probability of being able to resist; and with regard to Copies from my

Office, I will take especial Care that none shall be given: I hope therefore You will continue to write with the most entire Confidence. I am with true Esteem,

Sir, Your Most Obedient Humble Servant

Hillsborough

Governor Bernard

LS, RC   BP, 11: 219-222.

Endorsed by FB: Earl of Hillsborough N° 13 d July 11 1768 r Sep 3. Docket by Thomas Bernard: Approv[g] his Conduct Being in Ans[r] to N°. 1. Although annotated as "No. 13", this letter's summative content suggests that it may have been composed after the business-like letters of instruction (Nos. 14 and 15 in Hillsborough's series of out-letters) also enclosed with **No. 647**. Variants: CO 5/757, ff 98-99 (L, AC); CO 5/765, ff 21-22 (L, LbC). Copies were laid before both houses of Parliament on 28 Nov. 1768. HLL: American Colonies Box 2.

Hillsborough could not hope to keep FB's letters out of "Public View" when the government was obliged to defend its American policy to Parliament in Nov. 1768. Copies of FB's letters were then presented as evidence in justification of the administration's decision to send troops to Boston.

---

1. **No. 611**.
2. See source note to **No. 645**.

654 | To the Earl of Hillsborough

N° 11

Boston July 16 1768

My Lord

By my Letter N° 9[1] I informed your Lordship that at the time I dismissed the Assembly[2] The Council was beginning to proceed upon a petition to his Majesty, which Proceeding was interrupted by the prorogation of the general Court; and that, to takeaway all pretence to charge me with intending to stop any representation which they wanted to make to the King, I gave them leave to proceed in this business in the Privy Council;[3] and, if the petition was conceived in decent & respectful terms, I promised to submit the same to be laid before his Majesty, altho' I should not entirely agree with them upon the subject matter.

I have now the honor to transmit the petition enclosed to your Lordship & desire the favour that you would be pleased to lay the same before his Majesty for his most gracious consideration. I am not a party to it, nor could I think it proper that I should be: and therefore this Address is not quite regular in point of form.[4] But your Lordship will consider the circumstances before mentioned, that It originated in the legislative Council altho' it was not compleated there, and will receive it as an Act of that Body, to which the concurrence of the Governor is not necessary.

Your Lordship will observe that I am desired to recommend the prayer of the Petition. I have been allways tender in expressing my disapprobation of Acts of parliament, & was especially so in a Case where I thought the Act had better have been spared. But I can readily recommend that part of the petition which prays releif against such Acts as are made for the purpose of drawing a Revenue from the Colonies. For they are so little able to bear the drawing money from them, that they are unable at present to pay the whole charges of their own support & protection.

I am with great respect, My Lord, Your Lordships most obedient
& most humble Servant

Fra Bernard

The right honble The Earl of Hillsborough.

ALS, RC   CO 5/757, ff 316-317.

Endorsed: Boston July 16: 1768. Gov[r]. Bernard. (N[o]. 11) 1st. part.[5] R 26th August. A.34. Ent[d]:   Enclosed **Appendix 11**. Variants of letter: CO 5/767, ff 22-40 (L, RLbC); BP, 7: 2-7 (L, LbC); *Letters to the Ministry* (1st ed.), 42-43; *Letters to the Ministry* (repr.), 56-57. Copies of the letter together with the enclosures were laid before both houses of Parliament on 28 Nov. 1768. HLL: American Colonies Box 2. Hillsborough acknowledged receipt with No. 679.

FB's expression of support for the Council's petition (**Appendix 11**) was probably genuine. But he did not accept the Whigs' proposition that any parliamentary tax levied on the colonists for the "purpose of drawing a Revenue" was unfair or unconstitutional. By this phrase, as the last two sentences indicate, Bernard was referring to money being used to pay taxes, which, if paid in coinage would contribute to the American Colonies' chronic shortage of specie. The Council and James Bowdoin later accused FB of deliberately misrepresenting the Council's petition on this particular point. (See also **No. 717**.)[6]

---

1. **No. 638**.

2. On 30 Jun.

3. That is, to act as the Governor's Council, an executive body, as distinct from the Council acting without the governor as the upper legislative chamber.

4. In addition to the procedural issues mentioned in this letter and in **No. 638**, FB meant that the Council would not on its own normally petition the king; petitioning had hitherto been undertaken in conjunction with the House of Representatives; thus acting together, in a legislative capacity, as the province assembly.

5. Presumably the second part would be the petition enclosed.

6. **Appendices 3** and **4**, *Bernard Papers*, 5: 325-352.

655 | To Thomas Gage

Boston July 18th 1768

S[r].

I have received yours of the 11th inst[t] by which you inform me that the Troops at Halifax are not to move from thence untill I make a requisition of them.[1] They must then remain there: for upon a full consideration of my duty upon this difficult Occasion, I am convinced that It can not be expected of me, & that I ought not, to apply for Troops without the advice of, that is against the Opinion of, his Majesty's Council; and it is in Vain for me to apply to them for such advice. If I could make myself indifferent to the personal danger I should be exposed to by such a conduct, I cannot reconcile it to my Care of his Majesty's Government committed to me; which would be flung into the utmost confusion if the Governor was to be made an Object of popular fury by his introducing troops without the advice of the Council.

I quite agree with you that it is contrary to Law for troops to move to quell tumults & riots unless required by the civil power. And I should never think of applying to New York or Halifax for troops to quell a tumult or riot at Boston: the business would be done, & all would be over, long before the troops could arrive. It is to prevent tumults & riots & to enable the Civil power to punish those who create them, that Troops are Wanted here: and if the present state of this Town, wherein the Civil ^power^ is awed & controlled by a trained Mob, and Commissioners appointed under the great seal of Great Britain in pursuance of an Act of parliament are drove out of the Town, in which they were stationed by the King's Authority, & obliged to take refuge in the Castle, where they are defended by Ships of War for want of troops to garrison the place; if these Considerations do not show the expediency of stationing troops here; We must wait till it becomes more apparent.

I must add that it seems to me that the sending troops hither upon a requisition of the Governor & Council, if it could be obtained, is the Very Worst Way of introducing them. I cannot but think but that the better Way would be to station them here as in quarters, without assigning a requisition or any other reason for so doing except the disposition of a general Cantonment. And it should seem that the same power which enables the General to send a Regiment to Philadelphia or to New Jersey would authorise him to send one or more to Boston,[2] without being obliged to give any more reasons for the one than for the other. For my own part, I cant look back upon the 3 years last past, without wondering that there have not been Troops at Boston for the last 2 of them. I am sure they have taken pains enough ^at Boston^ to show the Necessity of such an Arrangement.

I shall communicate the subject of your Letter to the Council, without an expectation of any thing being done thereupon.[3] I will take care to forward the Letter to Col Dalrymple.[4]

I am, with great length & regard Your most obedient and most humble Servant

Fra Bernard

his Excellency Majr General Gage

P.S

There was a Riot last fryday which was quieted without any mischeif done: I am just told that there will be one tonight which will not be so easily quelled.

ALS, RC   Gage, vol. 78.

Endorsed by Thomas Gage: Governor Bernard. Boston 18th. July 1768. Received 26th. July.____ Variants: BP, 5: 274-276 (L, LbC); *Letters to the Ministry* (1st ed.), 43-44; *Letters to the Ministry* (repr.), 57-59. Gage replied with **No. 669**.

Having tried and failed to persuade Gage to send troops to Boston, FB now had options of (a) doing nothing, (b) persuading the Council to join him in asking Lt. Col. Dalrymple at Halifax for military assistance, or (c) writing Dalrymple on his own authority, knowing that the colonel was primed by **Appendix 8** to respond. FB's mention of instituting a "general Cantonment" of Boston indicates that he thought a garrison of troops would be beneficial primarily as a deterrent to law breakers. On this point he was more explicit in a letter to Barrington of 20 Jul., in which he also ruminated on his own discomfort and anxieties (**No. 658**).

---

1. **No. 652**.

2. British regiments were currently quartered in New Jersey and Philadelphia.

3. On 27 Jul. For a summary see **No. 660n9**.

4. FB is referring to the copy of **Appendix 8** that Gage had enclosed with **No. 652**.

656 | To the Earl of Hillsborough

Boston 18th. & 19th. July 1768.

N°. 12.

My Lord,

The dangerous State which this Government is in, makes it necessary for me to inform your Lordship of every little disturbance which happens here, as one cannot foresee the Tendency of any of the Movements of the Sons of Liberty & must expect the worst Consequences from each of them.

I sent your Lordship a Copy of a Paper stuck up on the Town House[1] inviting the Sons of Liberty upon Mr. Williams (one of the Inspectors of the Customs) [on] his Return to Town to make him resign his Office or quit the Town. Mr. Williams returned from his Circuit about the middle of last week. On friday last an Attack upon his House was planned; & to effect it, according to a preconcerted Signal, they rung the fire bells & cried out fire; & then directed the People to Mr. Williams's House. A Mob soon assembled there & began to break into the Courtyard there; Mr. Williams appeared at the House upon the Defensive with fire Arms, afterwards went into the Court & there parlyed with them. The Mob demanded that he should meet them at Liberty Tree the next day at Noon & there resign his Commission: He refused to do either, but said He would be upon the Change[2] the next day at Noon, & would there be ready to give an answer to any thing which should be objected to him. By this time some of the Magistrates & other Gentlemen of the Town had got to the place, & they persuaded the Mob to accept of this offer & disperse.

The next day Saturday[3] Mr. Williams attended by several Gentlemen, among whom were some of the Council, went about Noon into the Council Chamber. There were about 1500 People assembled about the Town House. Mr. Williams went into the Balcony of the Council Chamber & told that People that he was come according to his promise to answer them any objections which were urged against him. Nothing was offered after a Quarter of an Hour's Interval, He repeated his proposal; again nothing was said except by an ignorant fellow, whose Absurdity created Laughter. After a little stay they all departed in seeming good Humour; & Mr. Williams returned to his House accompanied by the Gentleman who had attended him, in Peace & Quiet.

This Transaction has flung great disgrace upon & given great Chagrin to the Faction; & I am told they are determined to retrieve it. The truth is, the Directors of the Mob durst not shew their faces at this Place & upon this Occasion, lest they should thereby acknowledge that they had spirited them up to the last Night's

Work. They now gloss it over, by giving it out that the Mob of that Night were not the true Sons of Liberty, & acted without Authority; & an Advertisement is published in the Boston Gazette signed by a pretended Secretary of the Sons of Liberty disclaiming the requiring M^r. Williams to appear upon Change, & threatning the Printer who shall make use of the Name of the Sons of Liberty *without an authentic order*. Something is to be done, & soon to recover the Spirit of the Sons of Liberty. I am told that some of the Chiefs of them are this day to go to M^r. Williams & advise him as a friend, if he will not resign his Commission to retire to the Castle; if he does not, his House will be destroyed & himself killed, what will be the end of this, We must wait to know.

July 19

Since I wrote the foregoing I have seen M^r. Williams; He confirms this Account & adds that the Mob expressed great satisfaction that those who set them on did not appear to talk for them. Several of the Mob & particularly the Captain a noted Mob Leader, have declared their Approbation of M^r. Williams's Conduct, & that they will defend him against any other Attack. On the other Hand great pains are taken to drive him out by Intimidation. Private Letters have been sent to him without a Name; & one of the Chiefs of the Faction declared publicly against his Fool-hardiness in staying in this Town. But M^r. Williams declares he will not go out of the Town unless he is drove out by Force. He tells me he fears no danger & I am inclined to think he will succeed in his defiance of the Faction & their Tools. If he does, he may do good Service in lessening the Terror which the Troops of the Faction have occasioned here.

I am, My Lord, Your Lordship's, most obedient humble Servant

signed Fra^s Bernard.

Earl of Hillsborough

P.S. Observing that there was no Account in any of the Newspapers of the Riot on Friday night, or the Meeting at the Town House on Saturday, I asked the Reason of it, & was told that the Sons of Liberty have forbid all the Printers publishing any thing of it. If the *King's* Government should assume such a Power, what would they say?

L, RC   CO 5/757, ff 326-327.

In handwriting of clerk no. 9. Endorsed: Boston 18th. & 19th July 1768.[4] Govr. Bernard (N°. 12) R 26. Aug: A. 36.   Enclosed a transcript of a handbill accusing John Williams of being "an Actor in the Conspiracy formed against his ^native^ Country" and announcing a meeting with the "Friends of Liberty"[5] at the Town House on 16 Jul. CO 5/757, f 328.

Variants of letter: CO 5/767, ff 40-45 (L, RLbC), with enclosure at f 45; BP, 7: 8-10 (L, LbC); *Letters to the Ministry* (1st ed.), 44-46; *Letters to the Ministry* (repr.), 59-62. Copies of the letter and enclosure were laid before both houses of Parliament on 28 Nov. 1768. HLL: American Colonies Box 2. Hillsborough replied with **No. 679**.

With this letter, FB reverted to a seemingly disjointed style of reporting that he had employed with Shelburne:[6] that of providing detailed accounts of particular events apparently of no immediate concern to the secretary of state or the business of his office. FB was not being devious and served notice of purpose in this letter: that he intended to link his meanderings to a political narrative about the Sons of Liberty and how the group was driving resistance to British colonial policy.

---

1. Enclosed in **No. 632**, but not found.

2. The Merchants' Exchange was on the first (or ground) floor of the Town House.

3. 16 Jul.

4. First written as "1769".

5. The nomenclature is consistent with the Sons of the Liberty's reputed desire to dissociate themselves from the meeting.

6. See *Bernard Papers*, 3: 21-22.

657 | *To the Earl of Hillsborough*

N⁰ 13

Boston July 18 1768

My Lord

I have now an opportunity of sending your Lordship a printed Copy of the Letter of the House to your Lordship;[1] the dispute concerning publishing it having only delayed it for a week. As It is professedly intended for the people more than for your Lordship, so it is accompanied with comments much more calculated to prepare the people to resent the disallowance of their pretensions than to induce your Lordship to endeavour to procure an allowance of them.

I never saw this Letter untill it was in print: I find nothing in it that requires my Answer. I am abused upon a supposition of my having misrepresented them in the business of the circular letter; I have looked over my letters upon this subject, & find nothing in them which is not admitted in the letter to your Lordship. I never said that there was a thinner house when the Circular Letter passed than when it was rejected. I said that the Way was proposed for this second vote by tampering with & influencing particulars:[2] this was as Notorious as that there was a house.

There was another reason for this contradictory Vote, which I did not assign, that altho the Number of the House was the same yet it consisted of ^many^ different persons; which as the Number was less than two thirds of the whole & there was a fourtnight intervening between the two Votes, may be easily conceived. The highest charge ag^st^ them, the eracing the Journals of the House to serve this purpose, they admit: this surely is a Very unjustifiable proceeding.

The general charge against me for misrepresenting them is false, & has not been supported by any one instance. It has been my misfortune to be Governor of this Province during a time when the most favorable representation of the proceedings of the Assemblies & the doings of the people must occasion his Majesty's displeasure. Before this time I scarce ever met the Assembly without receiving from them testimonials of their approbation of my Conduct. For these 3 years past It has been impossible to reconcile the Duty of the Governor with pleasing the people: and ^it^ would have been so, if a Man of greater ability, than I pretend to, had been in my place. Nothing less than a general Sacrifice of the rights of the Sovreign state can make a Governor popular in this Place at this Time.

I shall continue writing to your Lordship untill I have communicated all I think necessary for your Lordships information: When that will be, God knows. My Ideas are become too numerous & extensive for writing & are fitter for a conference than a Series of Letters. My Letter, as intended, upon the Subject of calling another Assembly will be lengthy Comprehensive & important; but it does not require haste as yet.[3] The Newspapers which I inclose contain a Variety of Sedition & Calumny, besides that which this Letter dispenses.

I am, with great respect, My Lord, Your Lordships most obedient
and most humble Servant

Fra Bernard

The right honble The Earl of Hillsborough.

ALS, RC   CO 5/757, ff 330-331.

Minor emendations not shown. Endorsed: Boston July 18th. 1768. Governor Bernard. (No. 13) R 26. August. A.37.   Enclosures: a copy of the *Boston Gazette*, 18 Jul. 1768, CO 5/757, ff 332-333, containing a copy of Thomas Cushing (for the House of Representatives) to the earl of Hillsborough, 30 Jun. 1768 (not found, but see **Appendix 9**); *Boston Evening-Post,* 18 Jul. 1768, CO 5/757, ff 334-325. Variants of letter in CO 5/767, ff 46-48 (L, RLbC) and BP, 7: 11-12 (L, LbC). Copies of the letter were laid before both houses of Parliament on 28 Nov. 1768. HLL: American Colonies Box 3. Hillsborough acknowledged receipt with **No. 679**.

1. **Appendix 9**.

2. FB in **No. 589**: "The Party therefore resolved to make another effort, & having prepared the way by privately tampering with, & influencing particulars, they moved that all the former proceedings upon this business should be obliterated out of the Journal."

3. **No. 663**, dated 6 Aug. 1768.

658 | To Lord Barrington

Boston, July 20, 1768__

My Lord_

We continue in the same uncertain Situation now as when I wrote last: the Crisis waits for the arrival of Troops; & I now learn that there are none coming. Genl Gage has now inaformed[1] me that his Orders to Halifax are that the Troops shall be collected & kept in readiness, but are not to move till I require them.[2] I answer that then they will never move: for I shall not make such a requisition without the Advice of Council; & I never expect to obtain that; neither their popular Constitution nor the present intimidation will permit it. He says that Troops never are sent to quell Riots & Tumults but at the desire of the Civil Power. I admit it; & say that I sh^d never think of sending to New York or Halifax for Troops to quell a Riot at Boston: the Business must be over before they can arrive; & no Troops can be of any Service in quelling a Riot or a Tumult, that are not previously quartered near the Place.

In Short, my Lord, Troops are not wanted here to quell a Riot or a Tumult, but to rescue the Government out of the hands of a trained mob, & to restore the Activity of the Civil Power, which is now entirely obstructed. And if an open Defiance of the Authority of Great Britain; a persecution of all those who are supposed to be maintainers of that Authority; The Expulsion of ^the^ King's Commissioners appointed under the great Seal in pursuance of an Act of Parliament out of the Town where they have been stationed by the King's Authority; & obliging them to take refuge in a Castle & there remain under the Protection of Men of War for want of better Security; If all these are not sufficient to show the Expediency of quartering Troops at Boston, we must wait till it becomes more apparent.

In truth, The sending Troops to Boston sh^d be a Business of quartering, of Cantonment: it is now no secret that this ought to have been done two years & a half ago. If it had, there would have been no Opposition to Parliament now, & above all no such Combinations as threatnens (but I hope vainly) the Overthrow of the British Empire. If Provision was to have been made against Faction & Sedition, the head quarters should have been secured. Instead of which Regiments have been sent into Quarters at Philadelphia & new Jer[sey][3] where the People are principled [in] peace & Submission to civil [O]rder; & Boston has been left under the uninterrupted Dominion of a Faction supported by a trained mob from Aug[st] 14, 1765 to this present July 23, 1768[4]

And now all the Burthen is to be laid upon me and, as if I was not at present sufficiently loaded with Dangers & Difficulties, I alone am to be made answerable to the Fury of the People for introducing Troops here illegally & unconstitutionally; for so they will call the requiring them without the Advice of Council. Otherwise I am to be made answerable to the King for all the ill Consequences which shall follow the Want of Troops here. I must say that this bringing me between two Fires is very hard; and I would add very cruel, if I was not convinced that it did not arise from any Intention to hurt me: for I am well assured that Gen[l] Gage has none but friendly Intentions towards me; tho' possibly he may act in this Business with t[oo] much Caution, or probably may be confined in his general Orders.

To discharge myself as well as I can of being answerable for Consequences I have ordered a general Council to meet on Wednesday next when I shall lay before them the Substance of Gen[l] Gages Letters, and require them to give me their Advice whether I shall or shall not send for the Troops which the Gen[l] has ordered to [be] ready at Halifax:[5] And according to their Advice I will act. I should not have chosen to have made this Communication: for I expect little Assistance from a Council popular & timid; and I have but lately tried them upon this very Question: for but I am drove into this Measure. As soon as the Determination is over, I shall acquaint Lord Hillsborough with it: In the mean Time I have thought it proper to state this Business to your Lordship, that if it should be brought upon the Carpet to my Disadvantage your Lordship may be informed of the true State of the Case.

I am &c

The Right honble The L[d] Visc[t] Barrington

AL, LbC   BP, 6: 136-139.

In handwriting of FB on pp. 136-137 and of clerk no. 3 on pp. 138-139.

This letter summarized FB's expectation that British Regulars could be used to deter rioters and expressed his frustration at being unable to acquire them. FB updated Barrington on the situation in a letter of 30 Jul. (for which see the source note to **No. 659**).

---

1. Thus in manuscript, meaning "informed." The letterbook entry appears to have been written in haste.
2. **No. 652** with FB's reply **No. 655**.
3. Obscured by an ink blot here and below.
4. Hereafter the letter is in a scribal hand.
5. 27 Jul. 1768. CO 5/827, ff 52-53.

659 | To Thomas Gage

Boston July 30 1768

S^r.

I have ^laid^ your letters offering me troops from Halifax before a Very full Council; and they have unanimously advised that I do not require troops.[1] And now the Question is answered in form, I shall think myself bound not to make such a requisition, whatever may be my Opinion of the expediency of it. For my own part, if no mischeif should happen in the Mean time, I can be well contented to wait till orders shall come from England; which will be more effectual & Authoritative than Any that can originate here.

I am, with great truth & regard, S^r your most obedient humble Servant

Fra Bernard

His Excellency Maj gen^l Gage.

ALS, RC   Gage, vol. 79.

Endorsed: Govr. Bernard. Boston 30th. July 1768 received 8th. August. __ Variant in BP, 5: 276-276 (AL, LbC). Gage replied with **No. 669**.

FB was more forthcoming in a letter to Barrington.

> But tho' I was prepared for this Answer, I was not for the high Strain of the present Popularity with which this Question was treated; from whence I am, convinced that I am no longer to depend upon the Council for the Support of the small Remains of royal & parliamentary Power now left . . . . But I desire by no Means to be understood to blame Genl Gage, whom I consider to be very friendly to me. I make no Doubt but he can as well vindicate himself for not sending Troops here without my Requisition as I can for not requiring them without the Advice of Council. All I desire is that we may both appear to have acted right.[2]

While FB's frustration was focused on the Council, criticism of Gage for placing him in that predicament was also implied, notwithstanding FB's profession of empathy.

---

1. 27 Jul. 1768. CO 5/827, ff 52-53.
2. FB to Barrington, Boston, 30 Jul. 1768, BP, 6: 139-141.

660 | To the Earl of Hillsborough

N° 14

Boston July 30 1768

My Lord

Since the first beginning of the troubles of this Town to the present time I have frequently represented to your Lordship's office the impracticability of my apply-ing for Troops either for the support of the Authority of the Government or the power of the Magistracy; both of which have been continually insulted and made contemptible for near 3 years past. The great Difficulty which has attended this Measure has been that I could by no means get the Council to advise or concur in it: and neither by the due consideration of my instructions & the rules of other Governments nor by the forms of this Government where the Governor is more connected with & restrained by the Council than in the Governments which are meerly royal, did I think my^self^ authorised to introduce troops into a Town not used to them upon my own opinion only & contrary to that of the Council, whom I am directed to consult & advise with in all matters of importance. And I have never imagined that It would be expected of me, that I should separate myself from the Council upon this occasion & make myself solely answerable for the consequences of the introducing troops here or the not introducing them: especially as I have allways understood that, since the repeal of the stamp act, the intention of the Administration was that all Appearance of forcible & compulsive Measures should be avoided. And as I have constantly sent home accounts of all occurrences which could influence this question I have concluded that a change of Measures must originate at Westminster & that the first orders for quartering troops in Boston would come from thence.

In my letter to the Earl of Shelburne, N° 8 of this year par 6, I treat this subject particularly, as it relates to the Commissioners of the Customs.[1] In my letter to your Lordship N° 6,[2] which gives an account of the riot on June 10 & the Com-missioners leaving the Town; I inform of what passed between me & the Council concerning sending for troops, from which it will appear to what little purpose it is to put a question upon that subject to the Council. However this Business is now brought to such a crisis, that I could no longer avoid putting such question in form: It has become necessary to my own justification & the acquitting me of the consequences, if any bad should arise, of this Town remaining destitute of troops: & to give an account of this transaction is the business of this letter.

On the 2[d] of July I received a letter from Gen[l] Gage, with two packets for Col Dalrymple at Halifax inclosed, informing me that He had received an Account of the tumults at Boston, & had sent an order to the commanding Officer at Halifax for Troops, if they were wanted at Boston.[3] I sent both Letters away, & wrote to the general[4] setting forth the reasons why I could not apply for troops: but that I had sent both the letters forward; for tho' I thought it improper for me to require troops, It was full as improper for me to prevent them coming if they were otherwise orderd. In answer to this the Gen[l] has sent me a Copy of the Letter to Col Dalrymple,[5] by which I am informed that the orders to him are only to collect the troops together, but not to embark them untill they are required by me. I have thereupon wrote to the General,[6] that if the troops are not to move from Halifax ^till I require them,^ they are like to continue there. For I cannot think it proper for me to make such a requisition without the advice of Council; & there was no probability of my Obtaining such advice: However I would lay it before the Council. I have been less explicit on these letters as I shall enclose Copies of them.

On Saturday July 23 I held a Council[7] when having in part opened the Matters I had for their consideration, they advised tha[t] in regard to the importance of the business I would order all of the Council who lived within a days journey of Boston to be summoned to meet on the Wednesday following & the Council to be adjourned till then. On Wednesday the 27th, there were 14 met;[8] & We proceeded to business that day & fryday following. As the Minutes of the Council are extended more than ordinarily, they will be sufficient to explain what was done.[9] There was some Altercation which is scarce worth remembring:[10] but I am obliged to take notice, that I observed with concern that the Popular Spirit upon this occasion showed itself higher in the Council, than I have known it heretofore; & my endeavouring to moderate it subjected me to treatment different from what I have been used of late to receive from that board. But these Considerations are more proper for another subject & place.

I shall inform Gen[l] Gage of the result of this Council,[11] by which all expectation of troops coming to Boston, untill orders arrive from England is over. Perhaps, if no great Mischeif is done in the mean time, it may be much better for them to be ordered from England than to be brought here by the order or requisition of any one in America; as they will be introduced in a manner Much more Authoritative. For my own part I have acted herein for the best, according to my judgement.

I could not require troops, against the Opinion of the Council, without making myself an object of popular resentment, which would probably, if it had produced no worse effects, have obliged me to quit the Government. Now, my Lord, as I have no leave of absence to justify my departure I must have staid till I was drove out by force or apparent danger. And if such an Event had happened, how could I have justified myself in doing an Act, with a doubt of the regularity of it, & a foresight of its ill consequences, which should produce such a convulsion in the state as obliging a Governor to quit his post?

I am with great respect, My Lord, Your Lordships most obedient
& most humble Servant

Fra. Bernard

The Right honble The Earl of Hillsborough.

P.S. Your Lordship will observe that in the Answer of the Council[12] there is nothing proposed or provided for the return of the Commissioners to Boston & their protection in the execution of their office there. It seemed to be the general Opinion, that it was quite impracticable for them to return & be protected in the execution of their Office. One Gentleman[13] said that He was convinced that they never would return to Boston & resume their functions; & gave for reason that Great Britain had too much employment at home in keeping her own unruly people ^in order^, & ballancing the parties which harasst the Government & weakened the Administration, to think of meddling with America or endeavouring to enforce the Execution of an Act of parliament which the Americans had declared against.

ALS, RC   CO 5/757, ff 349-351.

Endorsed: Boston July 30th. 1768. Governor Bernard. (No. 14.) R 19th: Septber A.39. Encld   Variants: CO 5/767, ff 56-61 (L, RLbC); BP, 7: 12-17 (L, LbC); *Letters to the Ministry* (1st ed.), 35-38; *Letters to the Ministry* (repr.), 46-50.[14] Enclosures to the RC: a copy of Gage to Hillsborough, 26 Jul. 1768 (not found, for which see the RC in CO 5/86, ff 128-130); copies of **Nos. 637, 641,** and **643** in CO 5/757, ff 352-354; [Observations of the Council on the *Liberty* riot, extracted from the Council minutes], 29 Jul. 1768, ibid., 358-362, and FB's commentary upon this document, "Observations upon the Answer of the Council," c.29 Jul. 1768, ibid., ff 366-367; minutes of the Massachusetts Council of 27 Jul. 1768, ibid., ff 363-365. Copies of the letter and the enclosures were laid before both houses of Parliament on 28 Nov. 1768. HLL: American Colonies Box 3.

Having failed to persuade Gen. Gage to send troops to Boston, FB now concentrated his efforts upon persuading Hillsborough to take the initiative. He changed tactics: where earlier letters had focused on the upsurge in colonial opposition and crowd action, FB now suggested that the conciliatory and lenient aspects of British policy, principally the repeal of the Stamp Act in 1766, had encouraged the opposition and undermined imperial authority despite his best efforts to preserve it. FB knew the politically experienced fifty-year-old Hillsborough, was perfectly capable of dissociating himself from the mistakes of his predecessors in the Rockingham and Chatham administrations; but FB probably supposed that he might be tempted to boost his reputation by taking a harder line against the Americans along lines suggested by FB. In this letter, FB's criticism of previous secretaries and administrations was implied rather than forthrightly expressed, as it was in a private letter (written afterwards) to Lord Barrington, Hillsborough's friend and ally.

> it is all over now: the indifference which has been shown in England to the checking the Demagogues of America for so long a Time has at length so effectually discouraged the Friends of Government, that they have been gradually falling off, 'till at length the Cause is become desperate.[15]

As **No. 661** revealed, however, Hillsborough had no intention of abandoning conciliatory measures that might elicit the support of colonial moderates and friends of government, and spurred FB to bring to justice the "wicked, designing, and . . . self-interested Men" behind the troubles. Thus, while FB hoped he might transfer onto Hillsborough the onus of resolving the Imperial Crisis by punitive measures, Hillsborough had already directed FB to find political and legal solutions.

---

1. "Since first these Tumults were apprehended, the Commissioners, with whom (I mean 4 of the 5) I am upon the most intimate Terms, have often asked me what Support to their Office or Protection for themselves I can afford: I answer none in the World." **No. 600**.

2. **No. 630**.

3. **No. 637**. FB fails to mention that he received a separate letter from Gage (**No. 639**), enclosing the orders for Dalrymple (**Appendix 8**) and that he had discretion to transmit them or not. This omission cannot have been accidental. The phrase "had sent an order" implies that Gage had sent the orders direct to Dalrymple (which he had not) and was probably intended to obscure the errors of fact and judgment in his letter to Hillsborough of 9 Jul., wherein FB stated that "at least one Regiment" had been ordered to Boston (para. 7 **No. 646**). Gage explained the procedure to Hillsborough in a letter of 28 Jun. CO 5/86, ff 128-130.

4. **No. 641**.

5. A copy of **Appendix 8** enclosed in **No. 652**.

6. **No. 655**.

7. In fact these proceedings took place on Friday 22 Jul. CO 5/827, f 52.

8. James Bowdoin, William Brattle, Samuel Danforth, John Erving, Thomas Flucker, Harrison Gray, Thomas Hubbard, Benjamin Lincoln, Timothy Paine, James Pitts, Nathaniel Ropes, Isaac Royall, James Russell, Nathaniel Sparhawk, and Royal Tyler. By delaying the meeting until the Wednesday, FB was thus able to ensure the attendance of friends of government who lived up to a day's journey from Boston (especially Paine and Ropes), yet the Whigs were in a firm majority with James Bowdoin having recently emerged as a group leader.

9. On 27 Jul., FB did not expressly request the advice of the Council on whether or not troops were necessary to preserve law and order. The minute indicates that he requested the Council's advice on what measures could be taken (a) "to protect" the commissioners of the Customs and their officers; (b) to ensure the Customs Board's safe return to Boston; (c) to "punish" the rioters of 10 and 13 Jun., and (d) to "preserve the peace of the Town & the Authority of the Civil Power." After debate, the Council advised that the matter should be laid before the General Court, whereupon FB postponed consideration. The remainder of the minute amounts to a list of position statements. The Council had previously supported the formation of a joint committee of the assembly to examine the state of the province, and likely supposed that this committee might be resurrected to consider FB's question. For his part, the minute recorded FB's concern that the Council's inertia "will certainly be taken notice of at home" by the Privy Council and "probably" by Parliament. FB put the question a second time, stressing that he had not written Gen. Gage about the "late troubles" though he had transmitted orders from Gage to the British commanding officer at Halifax, William Dalrymple. Whereupon, FB explained to the Council, he had promised Gage "that he would inform the Council of this order, and if they advised him to require these Troops, he should do so, and if they should not advise him to require them he should not." Only then did FB put the question about whether or not he should request troops, from Halifax. Then, at the request of the Council, the meeting was adjourned to Friday 29 Jul. CO 5/827, ff 52-53. The minute does not record that FB presented a "a Paper relative to riot" with the "injunction" that it remain secret, as the Council later claimed (in **Appendix 4,** *Bernard Papers,* 5: 329-352). This "Paper" doubtless concerned the *Liberty* riot and may have reprised his letter to Gage of 18 Jul. or included an extract from it (**No. 655**), in which he asserted he would never request military assistance without the advice of the Council. We must assume—if FB did show this particular letter—he would not have revealed its last sentence wherein he noted that he was "without an expectation of any thing being done thereupon" by the Council.

 Samuel Dexter was the only additional councilor who attended on 29 Jul. when the Council formally answered FB. After a preliminary declaration that the attorney general should prosecute rioters and the governor should issue a proclamation to encourage the apprehension of law breakers, the Council delivered a lengthy reply prepared in advance by James Bowdoin. The "popular spirit" that FB espied in the address was testament to Bowdoin's influence, for the document Bowdoin drafted reflected much of what Boston (in **No. 629**) had already stated with the regard to the *Liberty* riot being "magnified" by the governor and the Customs commissioners. The Council flatly rejected "any neglect" in responding to the commissioners' predicament, protesting that the commissioners retreat to the HMS *Romney* and the Castle were "voluntary" acts, not triggered by any specific violence. Moreover, the Council condemned the commissioners (but not FB, as the House did in **Appendix 9**) for misrepresenting the province, "especially if they have endeavoured to procure Troops to be sent hither." Lastly, the Council proffered their unanimous advice "That His Excellency do[es] not require any Troops." CO 5/827, ff 53-56.

10. LbC: "mentioning".

11. **No. 659**.

12. See the summary of the address of 29 Jul. in note 9 above.

13. Not identified.

14. Wrongly dated 30 Jun. in this edition.

15. FB to Barrington, Boston, 30 Jul. 1768, BP, 6: 139-141.

661 | From the Earl of Hillsborough

(N°. 16.)

Whitehall 30th July 1768.

Sir,

I am commanded by the King to acquaint you that, in consequence of the Advices contained in your Letters to me, of the 11th. 14th. 16th. 17th. and 18th. of June, numbered 5, 6, 7, 8,[1] His Maty has thought fit, after taking the Opinion and Advice of His Principal Servants thereupon, to signify His Pleasure, that the Troops intended for the Relief in North America in the next Spring, consisting of Two Regiments from Ireland,[2] should be immediately sent over to America and landed at Boston. Transport Vessels are preparing with all possible Dispatch, in order to proceed to Corke to take on board the said Regiments, which are to be augmented by Draughts to 500 Men each; and I am to signify to You His Majesty's Commands, that you do, in Concert with the Commander in Chief, take every necessary Step for the Reception and Accommodation of these Troops.

I am further commanded to acquaint you, that the Frigate[3] which will convoy the Transports from Ireland to Boston, together with a Ship of the Line now preparing for the Reception and Conveyance of Lord Botetourt, whom His Majesty has thought fit to appoint His Lieutenant and Governor General of Virginia, will have Orders to remain in those Seas, in Case the Commander in Chief of His Majesty's Forces shall be of Opinion that His Majesty's Service requires it.

The Disposition which has appeared in the Town of Boston for some Time past to resist the Laws and to deny the Authority of Parliament; and the illegal & unwarrantable Measures, which have been pursued for opposing the Officers of the Revenue in the Execution of their Duty and for intimidating the civil Magistrate, shew the Necessity of strengthening the Hands of Government; and his Majesty finds Himself called upon by every Consideration of Regard to the Safety of His People, and to the Preservation of the Constitution, to interpose His Authority and exert such Powers as that Constitution has placed in His Hands, for the Support of the civil Magistrate and for the Protection of His Officers of Revenue in the Discharge of their Duty; and I have His Majesty's Directions to acquaint You, that the Commanders of His Forces by Sea and Land in North America will be fully instructed that they do, when properly and legally called upon, give all necessary Aid and Assistance to the civil Magistrates of every Degree.[4]

After these Measures which the King has thought fit to pursue for inducing a due Obedience to the Law, it is the civil Magistrate alone who must stand responsible for the Peace of the Town of Boston, and for the Protection of the King's Subjects and Officers. — No Remissness of Duty will be excusable, upon Pretence of Terror and Danger in the Execution of Office and His Majesty relies upon your Firmness for the Punishment of it, particularly where it shall appear to proceed from Principles of Disaffection or Opposition.[5]

The total Want of Spirit, and ^the^ Neglect of Duty, which have appeared in the Magistracy of the Town of Boston, on occasion of the frequent Riots & Disturbances there (but more especially of that of the 10th of June last)[6] call for some Reform in the Commission of the Peace for that Town; it is therefore His Majesty's Pleasure that you should immediately make such Reform; in the doing of which you will consider whether it may not be advisable to remove all such Persons in the Commission as are known to be infected with Principles of Disaffection to the constitutional Authority of Parliament, and by what means others of different Sentiments and of the most considerable Weight and Influence may be induced to accept that Office, which will, under such Circumstances be supported with Dignity and executed with Effect; and if such of the Members of the Council as are Well-wishers to public Peace, and real Friends to the mutual Interests of Great Britain and her colonies, could be prevailed upon to act in this Capacity, it might possibly be a means of restoring the Commission to its proper Authority: But at all Events it will be a most advantageous Circumstance to the Public, and to you in the Execution of the important Commands I signify to you from His Majesty in this Dispatch, that you have the Assistance and Advice of the Lieutenant Governor, who in his Character of Chief Justice has shown so much Ability, Resolution and Integrity, and has already, and His Majesty makes no Doubt will continue to set an Example to every other Magistrate of that firm and dutyfull Regard to Law and the true Principles of our excellent Constitution, which best manifest a true Affection for and Attachment to the real and permanent Interests both of Great Britain and her Colonies.

The next Part of your Duty will be to set on foot a due Enquiry, both at the Council-Board and by the ordinary civil Magistrate, into the Causes of the Riots & other unlawfull and tumultuous Assemblings which have disturbed the Peace in the Town of Boston; that every legal Method may be taken for discovering and bringing to Justice those who shall appear to have been most active and forward in the Violences which were committed on the 10th. of June; and if in the Course of these Examinations it shall appear that there are any Persons, who shall, in the Prosecution of the unwarrantable Steps, which have been taken for encouraging a Resistance to the Laws, be found to have committed any overt Act that may justify their being brought to England to be tried here in the King's Bench, under the Authority of the Act of Parliament of the 35th. of Henry the 8th. cap. 2. you will in that Case make a full Report thereof, as well as of all your other Proceedings in the Execution of His Majesty's Commands, to the End that His Majesty may take such further Measures as shall appear to be requisite.[7]

It is evident from what has happened at Boston and from your Representation of the State of the Town, that while it continues in the Possession of a licentious & unrestrained Mob, it is impossible that either the Council or House of Representatives can proceed in their Deliberations with that Freedom which is incident to their Constitution. What has already passed shews plainly the Influence which they have been under, of Terror on the one hand, and Prejudice on the other, and therefore it is the King's Pleasure, that upon the first Occasion which shall occur of assembling the Council and House of Representatives, you do exert the constitutional Authority vested in you of summoning them to meet at Salem, Cambridge, or such other Place within the Province as you shall think most convenient and advisable, and where the Members of all the Branches of the Legislature may perform their respective Functions, and give their Advice in full Freedom and without Hazard of their Lives, which His Majesty observes is the Plea urged by the Council in particular for declining to apply for Assistance from the Commander in Chief.

These, Sir, are the Measures which I have in Command from His Majesty to recommend to your Attention, and His Majesty trusts, that in the Execution of them, and of every other Measure which your own Discretion may suggest to you as necessary for restoring Peace & supporting the Officers of the Revenue in the Discharge of their Duties, you will act with equal Temper and Firmness, not suffering any groundless Apprehensions of Want of Support in the Performance of your Duty to discourage you in the Pursuit of the great Object of inducing a due Obedience to the Laws, and Submission to the just and constitutional Authority of the Legislature.

I shall forbear on this Occasion entering into any Remarks on the unwarrantable Assertions and false Doctrine set up in the Petition of the Town of Boston to you, and in their Instructions to their Representatives,[8] or on what is set forth therein in respect to the impressing of Seamen by Captain Corner, the Circumstances of which are no where stated in your Letters.

How far impressing Men in America is or is not irregular, is a Consideration for other Departments, but it is my Duty to observe that the Plea set up that it is illegal because contrary to the 9th. Section of the Act of the 6th. of Queen Anne, cap. 37. is not to be maintained or admitted, it appearing from Opinions of Law of the greatest Authority, which I now inclose[9] and which were given upon similar Pretensions in the other Colonies, that the Act referred to is not in Force, having expired at the Conclusion of the War,[10] in which and for the Purpose of which it was enacted.

I have only to add that it is His Majesty's Commands, that you should communicate to the Commissioners of the Customs the Particulars of the Directions which have been given in Consequence of your and their Dispatches, relative to the Obstructions they have met with from Time to Time in the Execution of their Duty, & also such further Instructions as may hereafter be thought necessary to be sent to you on that Occasion.

But I ought not to conclude this Letter without expressing to you His Majesty's tender and benevolent Wishes, that His mis-led Subjects of the Massachusett's

Bay may be brought back to their Duty by lenient and persuasive Methods, by being made to understand that the erroneous Doctrines and dangerous Principles inculcated with so much Art and Diligence by wicked, designing, and probably self-interested Men, tend only to the Introduction of Anarchy and Confusion, to the Subversion of our Constitution, and to the Destruction of the British Empire; the Defence and Protection of whose Liberties can be no where so safely placed as where the Constitution has placed it, in the Hands of the supreme Legislature.

It will be most pleasing to His Majesty to hear that the People of Boston have been, by means such as these, led to a proper Sense of their Duty, & that the Commissioners of the Customs have been allowed to resume the Execution of their Office in the Town without Resistance; which at all Events however they must do, for the Crown will support the Laws, and the Subject must submit to them.

I am with great truth & esteem Sir Your Most Humble and Obedient Servant

Hillsborough

LS, RC   BP, 11: 235-248.

Endorsed by FB: Earl of Hillsborough d July 30 r Sep 18 1768. Docket by Thomas Bernard: Informing him of the Troops being ordered to Boston, & giving Direction for his Conduct— Parts of paragraphs 1, 4, 5, 6, 8, and 9 are marked by a line (possibly contemporaneous) in the left margin. Enclosed: a copy of the opinions of Sir Edward Northey (attorney general, 1710-18), Dudley Ryder (attorney general, 1737-54) and John Strange (solicitor general, 1737-42), CO 5/757, f 249. Variants of letter in: CO 5/757, ff 241-247 (LS, AC); CO 5/765, ff 24-33 (L, LbC); a triplicate (not found) was sent under cover of Hillsborough's letter of 13 Aug. 1768 (No. 17 in the secretary of state's series of out-letters).[11] Copies of the letter together with the enclosures were laid before both houses of Parliament on 28 Nov. 1768. HLL: American Colonies Box 3.

Hillsborough's letter was prompted by FB's several letters on the *Liberty* riot (for which see note 1) and a memorial of the commissioners of Customs (**Appendix 6**). These documents were delivered personally by Benjamin Hallowell on 19 Jul. and were reviewed by the Treasury on 21 Jul., then by the secretary of state for the Colonies on 23 Jul., and considered by the cabinet on 27 Jul.[12] The corresponding orders Hillsborough sent to Gen. Gage are in **Appendix 12**. Hillsborough assumed that FB would remain in post to oversee the settlement of the Regulars, reminding him that any "Remissness of Duty" would not be tolerated; however, he did not withdraw FB's leave of absence.

With regard to Hillsborough's instructions, FB addressed the reform of the provincial magistracy in **Nos. 711** and **724**.[13] The inquiry into the *Liberty* riot was undertaken by Attorney General Jonathan Sewall, but the rioters were not prosecuted ostensibly because of a lack of evidence (**No. 719**).[14] FB did not have an immediate opportunity to summon the assembly to meet outside of Boston, when, acting on other instructions from Hillsborough (**No. 608**), he dissolved the assembly after the House refused to rescind the vote approving the Circular Letter on 30 Jun.

On 19 Sept., one day after receiving Hillsborough's letter, FB "communicated" (i.e. read) an extract to the Council intimating the departure of the regiments from Ireland. At the same meeting he formally told them of Gen. Gage's letter (**No. 676**) indicating that two regiments were on their way from Halifax.[15] (New Englanders were already aware of this.) A reasonably accurate summary of Hillsborough's letter was published in the *Boston Weekly News-Letter* on 3 Nov.,[16] purportedly from a copy in the province secretary's files. No such copy has been found, though it is likely that FB permitted Andrew Oliver to make one after the Council meeting; either that or someone had access to FB's own files.

---

1. **Nos. 623**, **630**, **632**, and **633**.

2. The 64th and 65th Regiments of Foot arrived in Boston on 17 Nov.

3. HMS *Hussar*.

4. Hillsborough's orders to Gage are in **Appendix 12**.

5. While the phraseology of this warning was reminiscent of the stern language of royal instructions, it had specific meaning to FB's situation. Pownall would have briefed Hillsborough upon FB's past anxieties, probably revealing his fears of having to quit the province (for which see *Bernard Papers*, 2: 391; 3: 7); while Hillsborough himself would have read of FB's apprehensions of sedition in the letters listed in note 1 above.

6. The *Liberty* riot.

7. Recourse to the Treason Act of 1543 (35 Hen. 8 c. 2) was one means identified by the British government of overcoming the practical difficulties in the way of prosecuting leading Whigs in a colonial court. Colonial law officers and governors would never have been able to persuade a colonial grand jury to indict Whigs on criminal charges or high crimes and misdemeanors, yet any treason trial in Britain ran the risk of precipitating colonial resistance, as legal historian J. P. Reid noted.

    > Had British officials in prerevolutionary Massachusetts . . . one . . . means for bypassing the grand jury they might not have stemmed whig sedition, but they could have disrupted it. Surely several whig leaders would have seen the inside of a jail. Yet we may wonder if they would have remained there long.

    Reid, *In a Defiant Stance*, 50. Moreover, colonial Americans defined resistance to the Henrician statute in terms of their right to a fair trial (as might he expected from those Whigs anxious about being arraigned) and their right to be tried at the place of the alleged crime (as might also be expected from colonists schooled in English law). Thus later, in protesting King George III's endeavors to transport Americans "beyond seas" for trial, the American Declaration of Independence of 1776 gave form to concerns first raised in the mid-1760s, when trial at venue first became an issue of dispute in British-colonial relations, as J. P. Reid has also noted. Yet, while Hillsborough's instructions did not figure in the colonists' configurations at the time—because they were secret—it is possible that Americans obtained from England some idea of what Hillsborough's letter contained, though how and from whom is impossible to establish. (This may explain why Reid did not establish Hillsborough's letter to FB as a source of these worries). John Philip Reid, *Constitutional History of the American Revolution: the Authority of Rights* (Madison, Wis., 1986), 25, 54; idem, *Constitutional History of the American Revolution: the Authority to Legislate* (Madison, Wisc., 1991), 283-285.

8. **No. 629**.

9. This would have been abstracted by the current attorney general of England, William de Grey (1719-81), who held office from 1766 to 1771.

10. The War of Spanish Succession or Queen Anne's War as it was known in the American Colonies, 1702-13.

11. Receipt noted in BP, 11: 285.

12. Thomas, *Townshend Duties Crisis*, 85-86.

13. *Bernard Papers*, 5: 111-114, 145-146.

14. Ibid., 134-138.

15. CO 5/827, ff 59-60.

16. There was also a summary in the *Boston Evening-Post*, 8 Nov. 1768.

662 | *From John Pownall*

Secry States Office July. 30. 1768

Dear Sir,

The publick dispatch you will receive with this is so full in answer to your Letters by Hallowell[1] and so explicit as to the measures to be taken that I have scarce Subject for 2 sentences.

I dare say that former Letters from the Secry of State will have induced a beleif if what this will convince you, that what you and I have always thought serious is now considered so by Gov[t]., that the officers of the Crown will be no longer left a sacrifice, and that there was no necessity for that despondency of which there is a strong colour in your Letter nor for that doubt so strongly expressed of not committing yourself in measures of vigour without the advice of your Council.[2]

I who have long known your situation & can see your difficultys can make allowance for many things that to others might have the appearance of a want of Confidence in Govt, happily however such an impression is not general[.] Lord Hillsbro[h] enters fully into your embarressments, & has so explained your situation as to induce a reliance upon your firmness & resolution in the execution of whatever may be necessary to create entire Submission to the constitution——I need not say more to mark out to you the part which your own honour & my freinds Credit in the very full & entire confidence that is placed in you requires.

I wish I had time to prattle to you a little about old freinds & connections, but that is impossible. I should have as much pleasure in it as an old Pensioner of Chelsea has in fighting over his Battles,— for to say the truth I am grown an old man— I wish I was a wise one; but that I never shall be tho[t] I always shall be

Your most faithfull & Aff[t] humble Servant

J Pownall

ALS, RC   BP, 11: 249-252.

Minor emendation not shown. Endorsed: Mr Sec Pownall July 30 1768. Docket: doubts of Gov B's Spirit.[3]   Pownall enclosed a letter from Hillsborough (**No. 661**) intimating that an additional two regiments had been dispatched to Boston. FB replied to Pownall with **No. 684**.

---

1. **Nos. 623**, **630**, **632**, and **633**.

2. **No. 630**.

3. Docket probably in the hand of Thomas Bernard.

663 | To the Earl of Hillsborough

N.º 15

Boston Aug 6. 1768

My Lord

   Your Lordship will observe from my Letter N.º 9[1] & its inclosures that I signified to the House that if I should be obliged to dissolve the Assembly, I should not think myself at liberty to call another untill I received his Majesty's orders therefor. I was asked in Council whether I had received a special order for that purpose, or whether I drew it by implication from any part of your Lordships letter.[2] I answerd that I drew it from two passages in your Lordship's letter:[3] **1**. I am order'd, if I dissolve the Assembly, to send an Account of their proceedings that his Majesty may lay the same before his parliament to prevent such conduct for the future. Now if I was to call another Assembly without order, It might not be in the power of the King or the parliament to prevent such conduct for the future; for it would probably be repeated before any provision could be made against it. **2**. Your Lordship signifies to me that if the Dissolution should operate to the discontinuance of any necessary establishments, Care will be taken for the support of Government. By this It is plain that your Lordship does not expect that I should call a new Assembly: for in such Case your Lordship would have directed me to call upon the new Assembly to renew the discontinued establishments.

   But if your Lordship's intention had not appeared so plain, my own Discretion would have directed me not to have called another Assembly soon after the dissolution of the former. Such a proceeding has scarce ever failed to produce bad consequences: in the present case It would have the Worst; the cheif Alteration in the House would be in the exclusion of those few Members, or a great part of them, who in the late question dared to side with the King, & have since been held up in the public papers as objects of the resentment of the people.[4] It were to be wished that a New Assembly might not be called untill the people had got into a better temper & had gained truer Notions of their rights & intrest than they have at present. When that time will come God knows: it will depend more upon what is done at Westminster, than upon any measures that can be pursued here. I can therefore only state to your Lordship the inconveneinces[5] which will attend the not calling the Assembly untill the next general Election, & wait your Lordships orders.

The usual time for the Assembly's meeting for the Winter Session has of late been about the Middle of January. The Session has usually lasted above 2 months, great part of which has been lately spent in political squabbles rather than in real business. The ordinary business of this Session has been, to elect officers viz Treasurer, Commissary & impost officer & some lesser of no great significance; to grant Salaries to the Judges & other Officers & to the president & professors of the College &c; and to pass the Act of Tonnage & impost.[6] The Election of Officers may be postponed: for in such case they would continue in their Offices by their former Appointment; & by the Election is Nothing More but the Continuance of the same Officers. The grants of Salaries may be postponed without any other inconvenience than a delay of payment for about 3 months. The not renewing the impost bill would, I beleive, discontinue that revenue for about 2 months; but I cant be certain of it, as I have not the bill by me. These are the principal ordinary inconveniences which would arise from the not calling another Assembly before next May;[7] they must be ballanced by the Advantages proposed from the suspension; and the whole will be governed by the Measures which are to be taken for the restoration of the Government. And I must beg your Lordships favor that I may receive orders whether I am or am not to call the Assembly: for when the usual time shall come It will be quite necessary that the Governor should be able to Vouch positive orders for his not calling the Assembly, if he is not to do it. In regard to the calling the New Assembly in May, it will require much consideration: but there is time enough for that as yet.

There is another Matter for consideration in calling a new Assembly, which I cannot overlook because it is a common subject of reflexion; and yet I must own I dare not give my advice in it with that freedom, with which I could wish to act in all public business. It is, whether when a New Assembly is called it ought to meet at Boston or at some other Town.[8] People imagine that the principal part which Boston ^(distinguished from other Towns)^ has taken in raising & fomenting the present troubles of the province & the Continent will probably incur & deserve the Censure of having the Government removed from it. Others say that if Boston is subjected & brought into order the Inconveniences which the Government now feels by being seated there would be removed. For my own part, I could speak upon this subject, where I could explain myself occasionally; but I know not how to write upon it. All that I can ^now^ say is that if the prevailing Faction should be effectually checked, & the Terror of the mobs removed, It might be better to keep the Government here: but undoubtedly for these 3 years last Government has suffered Very much by it's being seated here. There are no ^two^ Towns on the Continent more contrasted in regard to respect & Duty to the Kings Government both at home & here, than Boston & (the second Town in the province) Salem. And yet I could not recommend the removing the Government to Salem otherwise than as a temporary Censure. But this is a subject too delicate for public letters.

   Having gone thus far I find a great deficiency from the Want of a proper representation of the present state of this Government, which is brought so low, that It can never recover itself by any internal means without a sacrifice of the rights of the imperial Power. This is a nice Task; & I wish I could do it in person: if I can not, I shall have much difficulty to represent it in writing & will overcome it as well as I can.

I am with great respect My Lord, Your Lordship's most obedient
& most humble Servant

Fra. Bernard

the right honble the Earl of Hillsborough

ALS, RC   CO 5/757, ff 368-370.

Minor emendations not shown. Endorsed: Boston Augst. 6th. 1768. Governor Bernard (N°. 15). R 27th. Sep^r: A40.   Variants: CO 5/767, ff 63-68 (L, RLbC); BP, 7: 19-23 (L, LbC); *Letters to the Ministry* (1st ed.), 46-49; *Letters to the Ministry* (repr.), 62-65. Copies of FB's letter were laid before both houses of Parliament on 28 Nov. 1768. HLL: American Colonies Box 3. Hillsborough replied with **No. 702**.[9]

---

1. **No. 638**.

2. **No. 608**.

3. These proceedings took place in Council on 29 Jul., CO 5/827, f 55.

4. The rescinding controversy generated considerable newsprint in the summer of 1768, much of it aiming to discredit both FB and Hillsborough. The first accounts were reprints of the official proceedings of the House between 21 and 30 Jun. These were compiled by the House clerk, Samuel Adams, and released to the *Boston Gazette* for publication on 3 Jul. and the *Boston Weekly News-Letter* on 7 Jul. Other newspapers provided factual digests or extracts, including the *Boston Evening-Post*, 27 Jun. and 3 Jul. The official roll giving the names of the seventeen representatives who voted to rescind the House's vote approving the Circular Letter, and the ninety-two who refused, was first printed in the *Boston Gazette* and the *Boston Post-Boy and Advertiser*, 11 Jul. Town resolutions expressing support for the patriotic and loyal "Ninety-Two" and disapprobation of the "rescinders" were published over the

summer, including Marblehead (*Boston Evening-Post*, 15 Jul.), Ipswich (ibid. 15 Aug.), Charleston, S.C. (*Boston Gazette*, 11 Jul.), and Philadelphia (ibid., 22 Aug.). Whig polemicists roundly denounced the rescinders for being tools of FB and willing to sacrifice colonial liberties at the behest of ministerial directives, while also criticizing Hillsborough for withholding the House's petition to the king. See for example, "Roger Martyn," *Boston Gazette*, 18 Jul.; "Anti-Rescinder," *Essex Gazette*, 16 Aug.; "Wyman," *Boston Gazette*, 6 Sept.

5. Thus in manuscript.

6. For a full list of legislation see *Acts and Resolves*, 4: 1114-1115.

7. The exigencies and circumstances discussed here indicate that FB anticipated further instructions from Hillsborough regarding the assembly. It was not until 4 Jan. that FB received clarification from Hillsborough until that the assembly should meet as planned on 31 May 1769. **No. 702**, *Bernard Papers*, 5: 85-86. FB's proclamation summoning the assembly was printed in the *Boston Weekly News-Letter*, 30 Mar. 1769.

8. **No. 661**, which FB received on 18 Sept., permitted FB to call the assembly to meet at Salem, Cambridge, or another place outside Boston.

9. *Bernard Papers*, 5: 85-86.

664 | To the Earl of Hillsborough

Nº 17.

Boston Aug. 9 1768

My Lord

I think it proper to inform your Lordship that for above a week past there has been agitated among the Merchants of this Town a Subscription against importing English Goods. It was begun by two principal Merchants[1] who have all along abetted the purposes of the faction: at first they met with Very little success but persevering ^in^ it & ways & means being used to push it on, It was last night reported ^at their third meeting^ that there was a sufficient Number ^of subscribers^ to carry the Matter into execution; that there were 40 who would not Subscribe but would observe the restriction; & 35 who would neither Subscribe nor observe. The latter I suppose are to be brought to reason by Mob Law; otherwise 35 importers only will defeat the Scheme.

There was the like Subscription set about at the beginning of March last, of which I gave an Account in my Letter to my Lord Shelburne Nº 9.[2] That was defeated by the Merchants of Philadelphia refusing to concur in the Measure, & the Merchants of New York thereupon declining it also: Upon which those of Boston were obliged to give it up. But now I suppose they assure themselves of better success at those places & expect to raise a combination formidable enough to alarm Great Britain at the meeting of the Parliament. But, My Lord, the Futility of this threat will be exposed by an Enquiry into the quantity of goods which have been lately ordered from Great Britain, which has exceeded & anticipated the usual quantities & times, in order to provide for an abstinence from importation for a year. This is professed by some & is undoubtedly true of others who are too attentive to their own interest to desist from importation without taking care not to have occasion for it. But the non subscribers, among which are Some of the principal importers of the Town,[3] will effectually defeat this Scheme, if they are Sufficiently secured from Mobs, which it is supposed they & all others will be before the first of Janry next.

> I am, with great respect, My Lord, Your Lordship's most obedient
> & most humble Servant

> Fra Bernard

the right honorable the Earl of Hillsborough

See my letter Nº 9 before mentioned par last but one

ALS, RC   CO 5/757, ff 375-236.

Endorsed: Boston August 9th. 1768. Governor Bernard (Nº. 17). R 27th. Septber. A.42   Enclosed a copy of the *Boston Gazette*, 15 Aug. 1768, CO 5/757, ff 377-378. Variants of letter in: CO 5/767, ff 69-71 (L, RLbC); BP, 7: 23-24 (L, LbC); *Letters to the Ministry* (1st ed.), 49-50; *Letters to the Ministry* (repr.), 66-67. Copies were laid before both houses of Parliament on 28 Nov. 1768. HLL: American Colonies Box 3. Hillsborough replied with **No. 702**.[4]

The Boston merchants had been at the forefront of colonial opposition to the Townshend Acts. They first proposed a nonimportation agreement on 1 Mar., subsequently placing an embargo upon the importation of enumerated goods from Great Britain beginning 1 Jun. and continuing for eighteen months or until the Townshend duties were repealed.[5] What complicated enforcement of the Boston agreement, however (as FB indicates), was that its continuation was explicitly dependent upon the compliance of Boston's commercial competitors at New York and Philadelphia. The New York merchants had agreed not to write for any goods after 14 Jun. or receive any sent from England after October, but did not approve nonimportation until 27 Aug., while the merchants of Philadelphia did not adopt nonimportation until the following February. Meanwhile, at a meeting on 8 Aug., the Boston merchants unanimously voted a series of amendments for instituting a unilateral boycott from 1 Jan. 1769 to 1 Jan. 1770, irrespective of what the New Yorkers would do. Traders were requested to forego placing orders for British "Goods or Merchandizes" in the five months before the new agreement took effect. Coal, salt, and "some Articles necessary to carry on the Fishery" were exempt, but the items taxed by the Townshend Revenue Act—tea, glass, paper, lead, and painter's colors were boycotted until the act was repealed. FB's comments in this letter indicate widespread discontent with the agreement's new provisions, though by 10 Aug. some town hundred and eleven merchants and shopkeepers had signed the subscription with only sixteen refusing.[6]

1. FB may be referring to John Hancock (1737-93) and William Phillips (1722-1804).

2. **No. 601**.

3. For example, Thomas Amory (b.1722) opposed nonimportation, although the firm of Thomas's brothers John (1728-1805) and Jonathan Amory (1726-97) supported it. The same was true of the Boylston brothers: Nicholas Boylston (1716–71) opposed the scheme, while Thomas Boylston (1721-98) approved it. While politics divided families it is possible that some calculated it was politic to be on both sides of this dispute.

4. *Bernard Papers*, 5: 85-86.

5. See **No. 601**. The best accounts of the Boston nonimportation movement are Tyler, *Smugglers & Patriots*, 109-170; Archer, *As If an Enemy's Country*), 144-163; Nicolson, "A Plan 'to banish all the Scotchmen'" 55-102.

6. According to the *Boston Evening-Post*, 8 May 1769, which reprinted a copy of the August agreement.

John Hancock. By John Singleton Copley, 1765. Photograph © 2015 Museum of Fine Arts, Boston.

665 | *From Lord Barrington*

Cavendish Square Augt. 11th. 1768.

Dear Sir,

In my last Letter to you[1] I made you an offer from Lord Hillsborough of the Lieu^t. Government of Virginia if it were agreable to you; but an Event has since happen'd which put an end to this Plan. The Representations of that Colony to the King and Parliament show such an alarming disposition there, that it was thought necessary a *Governor* and a man of great distinction should reside there. Sir Jeffery Amherst declining to go to America in that capacity, Lord Botetourt has been appointed in his room, a man every way fit for the business he has undertaken. I hope this will not prove a disappointment to you, and that some other advantagieous establishment will be found out for you in case Boston continues a disagreable Government, of which there is but too much appearance.[2]

It is now evident to all the world that the Civil Magistrate in the Massachusets should be assisted by troops, in maintaining Peace & supporting Law. The Regiments in North America being thro' a most fatal Policy dispersed so, as that no considerable number can be assembled, two Regiments are going from Ireland to that part of the world; but of this I need say no more, as your publick dispatches will fully apprize you of it.[3]

I understand from Lord Hillsborough that in your dispatches you mention leaving your Government on account of health or something of that sort, but in the present juncture I am perswaded you will not stir from thence on any Account tho' you have leave of absence. I know & lament the uneasyness of your situation and hope in God it will not long continue. I am with my best Comp^t to all my Cousins Dear Sir

Your Excellency's most faithful & obed^t. Servant

Barrington.

ALS, RC   BP, 11: 277-280.

Endorsed: Lord Barrington d. Aug 13 1768 r. Oct 23. Variant in BP, 11: 281-284 (dupALS, RC).

FB had responded positively in **No. 666** to Hillsborough's offer of the lieutenant-governorship of Virginia, unaware of the appointment of Lord Botetourt. He replied to Barrington with **No. 705**.[4]

1. **No. 610**.

2. News of Francis Fauquier's death on 3 Mar. may have sparked Hillsborough's interest in moving FB to Virginia (which Barrington communicated to FB in **No. 610**) but the ministry moved quickly to get a new governor in place without waiting for FB's views. Lord Botetourt was offered the full governorship on condition he reside in Virginia. Described by Barrington as a "man of great distinction," Botetourt was deemed by colonial newspapers to be the only peer of the realm to have been appointed a colonial governor. Botetourt received his royal governor's instructions on 12 Aug. 1768 and arrived in the colonies on 25 Oct. *Boston Evening-Post*, 17 Oct. 1768; *New-York Gazette, and Weekly Mercury*, 14 Nov. 1768. FB acknowledged his appointment in a letter of 23 Jan. 1769, BP, 7: 216.

3. In Hillsborough's letter of 30 Jul., **No. 661**, received by FB on 18 Sept. The regiments' departure from Ireland was noted in *Lloyd's Evening Post*, 24 Aug. 1768. The War Office had originally intended that the 64th and 65th Regiments of Foot would relieve the garrison at Nova Scotia, before orders were issued to send them to Boston instead.

4. *Bernard Papers*, 5: 92-95.

666 | *To Lord Barrington*

Boston Aug 27 1768

My Lord

I am honoured with your Lordship's Letter of May 9th which arrived at Boston the 20th of Aug. that is 14 Weeks after it left London.[1] I mention this that there may be no Imputation of Negligence in me in not acknowledging the Favour by the earliest Opportunity.

I am truly sensible of the high Honour I receive from my Lord Hillsboroughs Estimation of me and your Lordship's Attention to improve it in the best Manner for my Advantage. The unexpected Offer of a Title strikes me too forcibly not to occasion some Deliberation. If indeed it was to be determined by myself upon selfish Considerations, I should have no Doubt of declining it. But in a Business of so great Concern to my Family others are to be consulted besides myself. M[rs] Bernard is at present at a mineral Spring 90 Miles from hence to which she has been sent by her Physicians.[2] I have also an intimate Friend & Relation in England who has my Intrests so much at her Heart, that I can't excuse myself advising with her. So, my Lord, you must not be surprised, if by making Use of a female Council I should be led into an Act of Vanity. But at present I think the Objections I have to accepting the Honour are unsurmountable. If I consult my political Friends about accepting this Honour, I know they will labour for the affirmative with great Earnestness upon political Considerations. It will be urged that the conferring this Honor on me will afford a true and proper Triumph over those Enemies which my Adherence to the Rights of Great Britain has created; that it will hold out a Light to other Governors and Crown Officers and teach them that their true Intrest leads to adhering to their Duty and not temporising at the Expence of the Rights of the Crown; and that it will tend to cast a Disgrace upon the Faction which has of late prevailed here, and to lower its Estimate with the People of the Country. I own, my Lord, that these Arguments will have some Weight with me, who am used to consider every Event, with its Relation to the Service of the Crown. You see, my Lord that it is impossible for me to come to a Resolution at present, and therefore I can only desire your Lordship to present my most respectful and grateful Compl^ts to my Ld Hillsborough and to beg his Indulgence of further Time ^for^ to consider of the Propriety of my accepting the great Honour he intends for me.

In Regard to the Government of Virginia I have much less Difficulty or indeed none at all. It is certainly much more valuable than this, even tho' the contingent Profits, which this has been deprived of for 3 Years past & more, should be restored. I speak this upon a Presumption that the Lieutenancy will be held upon the same Terms with the principal as it was by Mr Fauquier; which I understand was by paying 1500 pounds sterl^g in England clear of all Charges. As for the Title of Lieut Govr it matters not whether the Governor is called his Honor or his Excell^cy.; tho if it signified any Thing the latter Title might be given to the Lieut Govr by a special Commission that should not be derogatory to the Commission in cheif: and I have often wondered it was not done; as this is in Effect a principal Government. The Govr of Maryland has long ago taken the Title of his Excell^cy, by what Authority I dont know, unless it is by a Commission from his Majesty: for surely a Proprietor can confer no such Title. As for the Climate which your Lordship knows is a principal Consideration with me, cheifly upon Account of Mrs Bernard, I have learned enough to satisfy me that tho it is too southerly, it is not unhealthy and will probably suit with her. I must therefore desire your Lordship to signify my most grateful Acceptance of this Offer for the present; by which I mean a Reserve of Liberty to apply for something else, if I should be disappointed in the Climate or Income of this Government. If I am not, I may probably set down with Pleasure for the rest of my Life: for it is high Time that my Peregrination should be determined.

It will be extremely agreeable to me to be succeeded here by the Lt Govr, as indeed it will upon many Accounts promote his Majesty's Service. Such an Appointment will effectually discourage the Faction, who are more inveterate against him than against me; and are most offended at me for taking his Part; And it will afford another great Instance of rewarding faithful Servants of the Crown. I shall treat this with all the Confidentiality your Lordship recommends, and shall not acquaint him with the Assurance I have of this Intention. But I must tell him that I hope and expect that he will succeed me; as it will be necessary to enter into Concert with him about many Matters previous to this Change, and to take his Opinion concerning several Regulations which I have had in my Thoughts to propose.

I shall avail myself of Leave to return with all due Expedition: Many Things both public & private concur in making it expedient. I have not yet received my Ld Hillsborough's Letter for that Purpose;[3] the June Packet is not come in, tho it is now 11 Weeks since it left London: It is become a most dilatory Conveyance. I now communicate to your Lordship my Sentiments as they arise: when I have the Honour to wait upon your Lordship I shall determine upon every Point. The Question of the Government may receive a considerable Alteration if Genl Amherst should require new Terms from the new Lieut^t:, which might impair the Beneficiality. But I dont expect it as it would probably open a Door for Disputes which had better be avoided.

I am &c

The Right honble The Lord Visc^t Barrington

L, LbC   BP, 6: 141-145.

In handwriting of Thomas Bernard.
    FB's hesitation about accepting a baronetcy was driven by the cost of purchasing the patent to the title. He might also have worried that the offer could be withdrawn if the ministry decided to recall him. FB's leave of absence was granted by **No. 622**, and while he did not secure the lieutenant-governorship of Virginia (**No. 665**), Barrington managed to persuade Hillsborough to pay for the patent (**No. 754**).[4]

---

1. **No. 610**.

2. Probably Stafford Springs, Conn., about 78 miles from Boston.

3. Hillsborough's letter of 4 Apr., which FB received on 20 Aug., did not address the issue of leave of absence. However, **No. 610** from Barrington, which also came in the April mail packet, intimated that FB would be appointed to a baronetcy and transferred to Virginia. From this, FB had deduced that leave of absence would be forthcoming.

4. *Bernard Papers*, 5: 229-231.

667 | To Samuel Hood

Boston Aug 27 1768

S^r:

I have received by the last mail[1] a Letter giving me Intimation that by the next Packet I may expect a discretionary Power to go to England if I shall think it proper.[2] In such Case I shall judge it most convenient for his Majesty's Service for me to embark as soon as possible. Upon this Occasion I beg Leave to ask the Favour of you, that if it shall be convenient for any of his Majesty's Ships or Sloops to return to England this Fall, you would be so good as to order me a Passage in her. I am under the greater Necessity to make this Request as I know of no Ship preparing to sail from hence but one, whose Cabbin is allready engaged. At present I make a Secret of this Purpose and shall keep it so as long as I can.

I am &c

Commodore Hood

L, LbC   BP, 7: 191.

In handwriting of Thomas Bernard.
1. **No. 610**.
2. Granted by **No. 622**.

668 | To the Earl of Hillsborough

N° 18

Boston Aug 29 1768

My Lord

I have received your Lordship's letters N° 8 & N° 9;[1] & think it proper to advise your Lordship by the first Ship which sails from hence that they did not arrive here till Aug 20 that is full 14 weeks from London. Also the June mail is not yet arrived being now in its 12th week from London. I mention these, that there may be no imputation of neglect in me, either as to acknowledging or executing your Lordship's orders.

I shall lay the letter N°8 with it's inclosures before the Council & consult with them of the best means to apprehend the Murtherer,[2] if He should come in to this Province. In regard to the Letter N° 9, I have allways given the Commissioners of the Customs & their Officers all the Assistance & support in my power. But that Power is now reduced so low, that I can be of very little Service in that respect.

I inclose the printed Account of the celebration of the 14th of Aug being the day of hanging the stamp officer in effigy & destroying his house in reality. This is the third Anniversary celebration of this day: At the head of the procession were 2 principal Merchants who have all along abetted the parades of the Sons of Liberty. In the procession, as I have been informed by sevral Persons, was one Moore, who was a principal hand in pulling down the Lieut Gov[rs] House, was committed to Goal for it, & rescued from thence by a Number of people in the night. This Man is now at liberty to celebrate those exploits, by which He legally incurred the penalty of Death.[3]

I am with great respect, My Lord, Your Lordship's most obedient
& most humble Servant

Fra Bernard

The right honble The Earl of Hillsborough

ALS, RC   CO 5/757, ff 379-380.

Endorsed: Boston August 29th: 1768. Governor Bernard (N°. 18) R 9th: October. A.43. Enc[d]. Enclosed a copy of the *Boston News-Letter, Postscript,* 25 Aug. 1768.[4] Variants: CO 5/767, ff 71-72 (L, RLbC); BP, 7: 25-26 (L, LbC); *Letters to the Ministry* (1st ed.), 50; *Letters to the Ministry* (repr.), 67. Copies of the letter together with the enclosures were laid before both houses of Parliament on 28 Nov. 1768. HLL: American Colonies Box 3.

---

1. From the earl of Hillsborough, Whitehall, 30 Apr. 1768, BP, 11: 175-176; **No. 612**.

2. Melchisedec Kinsman was being sought for the murder of William Odgers, a customs officer of Penzance, Cornwall. Hillsborough suspected Kinsman of having fled England for America. The Governor and Council agreed to offer a reward for Kinsman's arrest, if the British Treasury could promise reimbursement. Hillsborough to FB, 30 Apr. 1768, BP, 11: 175-176; CO 5/827, ff 57-58; FB to Thomas Bradshaw, Boston, 31 Aug. 1768, T 1/465, ff 199-200. Bradshaw's reply of 11 Nov. has not been found.

3. Will Moore had been arrested for participating in Boston's second Stamp Act riot, that of 26 Aug. 1765. Hoerder, *Crowd Action in Revolutionary Massachusetts,* 112n81. For FB, Moore's attendance at the open-air dinner held under Liberty Tree on 15 Aug. was the most newsworthy feature of that year's celebration of the first Stamp Act riot, especially since the dinner was attended by Moore's social superiors ("a very large Company of the principal Gentlemen and respectable Inhabitants of the Town"). (Moore's attendance was not recorded in the newspaper account that FB read, and there was no reason why it should have been.) The toasts numbered forty-five in total (in recognition of John Wilkes's controversial *North Briton,* No. 45): the first toasts were to the king and the royal family, then glasses were raised, *inter alia*, to the parliamentary friends of America (principally those Rockinghamites and

Pittites who had urged the repeal of the Stamp Act), the defeat of "sinister . . . Oppressors, both in Great Britain and America," Pascal Paoli the Corsican patriot, "The memorable 14ᵗʰ of August, 1765," the repeal of "unconstitutional" acts of Parliament, the "Pennsylvania Farmer", the "glorious NINETY-TWO" who had refused to rescind, Irish patriots, Dennys DeBerdt, the colonial assemblies, the king of Prussia, and so forth. A performance of John Dickinson's "Liberty Song" was a particular highlight for both dinner guests and the "Concourse of People of all Ranks" who swelled the nearby streets. In the late afternoon, the "whole Company" proceeded to Roxbury for an "agreeable Excursion round Jamaica Pond," visible from FB's farm, and were greeted by a "Discharge of Cannon" arranged by a "friend to the Cause" (perhaps one of FB's Whig neighbors), before returning to town at 6 PM.

There is no documentary record establishing that FB was in residence at Jamaica Farm to witness the procession. He had been at the farm during the first few days of August before returning to Boston by 6 Aug. The absence of any out-letters dated between 10 and 26 Aug. suggests FB had taken a break from official business following the Council meeting of 10 Aug. Jamaica Farm seems a more likely retreat than Castle William, where the family had spent previous summers, for the last of his letters to be inscribed Castle William is dated 28 Aug. 1767. On the other hand, if FB was in residence he might be expected to have commented on the procession and perhaps drawn a comparison with committee of twenty-one who presented him with Boston's petition on 14 Jun. or the (more threatening) crowd that visited the Province House on the night of 15 Aug. (when he was not in residence). *Boston News-Letter, Postscript*, 25 Aug. 1768; *Bernard Papers*, 2: 304.

4. Listed as "Extract from the *Boston Gazette*" in *HCJ*, 32: 76.

669 | *From Thomas Gage*

New York August 31ˢᵗ: 1768.

Sir,

It is not necessary to trouble you with any Answers to your Letters, and I only acknowledge the Receipt of them.[1] I am now to acquaint you, that I have received orders to send Forces to Boston,[2] and would regulate the number to be sent, agreeable to your opinion of the number that will be necessary. Captain Shirreff[3] my aid de camp goes to Boston under Pretence of private Business, and will deliver you this Letter. He is directed to settle this matter with you; and you may rely on his Discretion, Prudence and Secrecy. I have entrusted him with a Letter of orders, to the commander of His Majesty's Forces at Halifax to embark with the 14ᵗʰ. Regᵗ: and left a Blank in the Letter for Captain Shirreff to fill up with the like order for the 29ᵗʰ: Regᵗ:, in case you shall Judge it proper to have the whole, or any part of the 29ᵗʰ: Regᵗ:, as well as the 14ᵗʰ: and not think one Regiment as sufficient Force.[4] When you shall have fixed this matter with Captain Shirreff you will be so good to send me immediate Notice that I may without Delay write you a publick Letter to demand Quarters for the numbers that will be ordered into your Province. The Contents of this, as well as your answer and everything I now transact with you, will be kept a profound secret, at least on this side of the Atlantick.

It is submitted in my Letters, whether it would not be advisable, as Troops will probably continue at Boston, to take Possession of Castle William, which being a Place of some Strength, may in case of emergency be of great Service, and it is said to belong to the Crown.

You will be so good to fix with Captain Shirreff whether you would have the whole or any part of the Troops ordered to Boston, quartered in Castle William. As you should be of opinion that Troops stationed there will not answer the Intention of sending them to Boston, for the Purpose of enforcing a due Obedience to the Laws, and protecting and supporting the Civil Magistrates and the Officers of the Crown in the Execution of their Duty, part may be stationed there, and part in the Town. Should you require both the Regiments from Halifax; one of them, or three or four companys of one of them, might be quartered in the Castle, and you would then have an entire Regiment and five Company's & another in the City. I mention this, but leave it to your Determination and you will regulate this matter with Captain Shirreff, according to the number of Troops you think necessary to be sent to Boston. you will be pleased to give me notice of your Resolves on this head.

I don't know if you can supply Bedding for such of the troops as you would choose to be lodged in the Castle; if not Captain Shirreff will write to Lieut Col° Dalrymple, to bring Bedding with him from Halifax, sufficient for the number of men, you shall fix upon, for the garrison of Castle William.

I have the honor to be with great Regards, Sir, your most obedient, humble Servant,

Thos. Gage.

His Excellency Govr Bernard Boston

ALS, RC   BP, 11: 287-290.

Endorsed: Genl Gage d Aug 31 1768 r Sep 3.   FB replied with **No. 671**.

Capt. Sherriff arrived on 3 Sept., with Gage's letter,[5] bringing news FB had long been hoping for: that British Regulars were on their way to Boston from Halifax. In the mail packet from England was a duplicate of Hillsborough's letter of 11 Jun. (**No. 622**)[6] granting him a leave of absence, which he trusted would allow him to get out of Boston before the troops arrived. However, Hillsborough's letter of 30 Jul. (**No. 661**), announcing the departure of two further regiments from Ireland, which FB received on 18 Sept., also intimated that the ministry expected FB to remain in place. (Ostensibly to await the arrival of the British soldiers but also to reform the province magistracy and conduct investigations into treasonable activities.) FB was in full possession of the facts concerning the British orders respecting the Regulars when he announced to the Council, on 19 Sept., the imminent arrival of the two regiments from Halifax.

---

1. **Nos. 655** and **659**.

2. **Appendix 4**.

3. William Sherriff had been a captain-lieutenant in the 47th Regiment of Foot since 1761, and, on 25 Jul. 1768, was promoted to major and appointed deputy quartermaster general of British forces in North America. Gage occasionally rendered his surname as "Sheriffe" and "Sherreff." *Boston Post-Boy and Advertiser*, 19 Sept. 1768.

4. Thomas Gage to William Dalrymple, 31 Aug. 1768, MiU-C: Gage, vol. 80.

5. The newspapers suggested 4 Sept. *Boston Chronicle*, 29 Aug.-5 Sept. 1768.

6. According to **No. 671**.

670 | *Circular From the Earl of Hillsborough*

Circular

(N°. 18.)

Duplicate.

Whitehall 2ᵈ. September 1768.

Sir,

The King having observed that the Governors of His colonies have, upon several occasions, taken upon them to communicate to their Councils and Assemblies, either the whole or parts of letters which they have received from His Majesty's Principal Secretaries of State; I have it in command from His Majesty to signify to you that it is His Majesty's pleasure, that you do not, upon any pretence whatever, communicate either to the Council or Assembly any copies or extracts of such letters as you shall receive from His Majesty's Principal Secretaries of State; unless you have His Majesty's particular directions for so doing. I am, Sir,

your most Obedient Humble Servant

Hillsborough

dupLS, RC   BP, 11: 291-292.

Endorsed by FB: Earl of Hillsborough dated 2 Septʳ. 1768 reᵈ. Jan. 4. 1769. Docket by Thomas Bernard: Orderᵍ not to communicate ^to Council &c^ Extracts of Secʸ of States Letters .   The RC (not found) was enclosed in **No. 679**.

Previous contests between FB and the Massachusetts House of Representatives over the contents of FB's correspondence with Secretaries of State Shelburne and Hillsborough[1] was a principal reason why this directive was issued to colonial governors.

---

1. FB had presented Hillsborough's letters **Nos. 603** and **608** to the House of Representatives on 31 May and 22 Jun. respectively. In **No. 638**, he described to Hillsborough the accusation of misrepresentation the House had levied against him in their address of 30 Jun. and in their letter to the secretary of state of the same date (**Appendix 9**). *JHRM*, 45: 20, 72, 75-76, 86. On Shelburne see *Bernard Papers*, 3: 255n, 271n, 272n, 369.

671 | To Thomas Gage

Jamaica Farm near Boston Sep 5 1768

S[r]

I have received your Letter by Capt[n] Sherriff and have had some Talk with him upon the Subject thereoff.[1] I should be ~~much~~ embarrast with having the Number of Forces to be sent left to me, if I was not directed by the Secretary of States Letter to me, which says that the Commander in Cheif ~~has~~ ^is^ Ordered to station one Regiment *at least* in the Town of Boston, and to garrison the Castle.[2] Under these Directions and with Regard to the Uncertainty how these Troops will be received at Boston, I can by no Means take upon me to draw off any Men from the two Regiments which have been prepared for this Purpose. I have therefore[3] told Capt[n] Sherriff that less than two Regiments will not, as it seems to me, answer the Idea of the Secretary of State for this Service; especially as there have been other Disturbances of more Consequence ~~that~~ which he was not then acquainted with.

The distributing these Troops between the Town & the Castle will be another Question. At first it might be best to order one Regiment in the Town & the other into the Barracks at the Castle. If the first were received quietly & treated civilly they might continue in that Proportion. If they should be insulted & threatned, it might be proper to reinforce them with the greatest Part of the other Regiment leaving about two Companies at the Castle. At the Castle it would be best to put the Regiment or such Part of it as shall be stationed there into ^the^ Barracks which are roomy & Commodious.[4] The Fort there tho a regular Fortification, is of so small Dimensions, that it will but hold the present Garrison of 50 Men; & as the Officers & Men have not shown the least Disposition to favour the Sons of Liberty but have to all Appearance expressed a proper Sense of their duty, I would not have so great a Slight put upon them as to be dispossest of the Fort; as the Security of the whole will be as well ^perhaps no better^ provided for by stationing the Troops in the Barracks. Besides I would not at this time give ~~Cause~~ Umbrage or afford any Cause of Jealousy to the Province, which could be avoided, especially so alarming a one as removing the Provincial Garrison from the Fort.

I shall be glad to receive your public Letter[5] by Express rather than by the Post; as it will come to me 2 or 3 Days sooner, and I shall have Time to lay it before the Council before the Week is out.[6] I expect great Difficulty at that Board; and therefore I should be obliged to you if you would intimate in your Letter that this Movement is made by Order of his Majesty signified by his Secretary of State:[7] for I would have it bring as much Authority with it as possible: I yesterday communicated to Capt[n] Corner[8] the Purport of Capt[n] Sherriffs Dispatches. And he, as he had before declared his Intention, upon the Occasion resolved to carry them himself, both [to?][9] add his Ship to the Transports & encrease the Parade. But he has this Day informed me that there is a Difficulty raised by the Commissioners, who think they shall not be safe in [if] the Romney should be removed. But Capt[n] Corner intends to prevail with the Commissioners to let him go, if he can: if he cannot he will send away a Cutter early tomorrow morning. I should have mentioned before that it will be proper to intimate in your Letter that the Orders are to state one Regiment at least in the Town: otherwise the Council may Advise me to quarter them all at the Castle. I must add that I am more and more convinced that under the present Exigencies of the Times, it will be improper to put a regular Garrison in the Fort. What is done should be by Way of putting Troops into Barracks.

I am &c

His Excell[cy] Gen[l] Gage

L, LbC   BP, 7: 191-194.

In handwriting of Thomas Bernard. The RC was personally delivered to Gage by Capt. William Sherriff. Variants: BP, 7: 191-194 (L, LbC); CO 5/86, ff 178-179 (L extract, Copy).

---

1. **No. 669**.

2. FB is alluding to a duplicate of **No. 622**, received on 3 Sept.

3. CO 5/86: the extracted passage is "I have therefore . . . . Garrison from the Fort."

4. See the Map of Castle William, 179.

5. **No. 675**.

6. FB presented **No. 676** to the Council on Monday 19 Sept. CO 5/827, ff 59-60.

7. Gage omitted adding this phrase, or a variant thereof, to **No. 676**, mentioning only that the troops had been "ordered into your Government."

8. FB probably met Corner in Boston to discuss these matters.

9. Obscured by tight binding.

672 | To the Earl of Hillsborough

Nº 19.

Boston Sep 9 1768

My Lord

The July Mail arrived here last Saturday Sep. 3 which brought me the Duplicate of your Lordships Letter Nº 10[1] & the Originals of Nº 11, 12, 13, 14, & 15.[2] The June Mail which tomorrow will have left London 13 weeks[3] is not yet come here: by it I expect to receive the original of Nº 10.[4]

Your Lordship's observation of the intention of the Faction to defeat all conciliating measures will be fully confirmed, if it is not allready. Their Influence over the Courts of Justice especially at Boston is carried to an enormous length, of which there has been lately a most extraordinary instance. On Monday Aug 22 being the day before the sitting of the Superior Court there came out in the Boston Gazette a most Virulent Libell against the Cheif Justice,[5] in which He was threaten'd, that if he gave any more such charges as at the former Session, his private Life & Conversation should be exposed in that paper by which he is to be rendered odious to the people. The next day when the Court was opened the grand Jury was found to have among them sevral of the abettors of the Boston Mobs & particularly the famous Captain Malcolm, who having twice in a forcible manner set the Laws of trade at defiance with Success,[6] has thereby raised himself to be a Mob Captain; & was actually the raiser of the Mob which abused the Custom house Officers on the 10th of June last. This Man was thought a fit person to be upon a grand Jury before whom his own Riots were to be enquired into. To account for this your Lordship must know that in this Government Juries both grand & petty are not returned by & at the Election of the Sheriff, but by the appointment of the sevral Towns & returned by the Constables.

This being the Case, It was to no purpose for the cheif Justice to enter into particulars concerning the late riots: he therefore made his charge general, except only Vindicating himself from an infamous lie published in the Boston Gazette, asserting that he had received a Commission from England appointing him Cheif Justice. The Attorney general had been ordered by me with the advice of Council to prosecute the rioters on the 10th of June. But when He came to lay it before the grand Jury, no Evidence could be procured against any one man. There had been 2 or 300 people who paraded & did great part of the Mischeif in the public streets in the day time; and yet no Man ^could be found who^ dared to charge any of them. And it is no wonder, whilst the Head of the Mob sat upon the grand Jury ready to mark those who should testify against his Mob. And I suppose the Attorney-general was not Very earnest in endeavouring to procure Evidence; as he must see that before such a grand Jury there was no probability of getting a bill found.[7]

I am sorry, My Lord, that I cannot continue to give the Council that Credit, which I have done in former letters. Immediately after the Vote in the House for not rescinding &c, The Council suffered so great a change that they don't appear to be the same persons: and I can no longer depend upon them for that assistance, which I have been used to expect & often to receive from them in support of the rights of the Crown. They seem to have caught the general intimidation, to look upon the Cause of the present Government to be desperate, and to think that it is high time that they should take care of their intrests with the prevailing party of the people. And yet I am convinced that these Gentlemen or the greatest part of them are in their hearts friends to Government & would choose to be numbered among them, if they were independent of the people. But It is a melancholick Truth that this Government, after a three years War, is at length subdued, & in my Opinion, will never recover itself, untill some amendment is made in the constitution especially in the appointment & stability of the Council. I shall not produce instances in support of these assertions now: they will ^be^ fully explained hereafter.

I am far from thinking my conduct perfect; and therefore I shall allways be pleased with your Lordship's animadversions upon it. I have ever endeavoured to be as explicit as possible; but in some cases it is Very difficult to speak out: to explain this I will quote the Very instance which your Lordship refers to. I have kept up an acquaintance with some of the Sons of Liberty; by which means I sometimes get at useful intelligence: To procure this I am obliged to give the strongest assurances that their Names shall ^not^ be quoted nor any communication made of it which can make them Suspected. One of these persons informed me last Winter that his party had applied to the Sons of Liberty in other Colonies for support against Great Britain;[8] and If they had good Assurances of such support they would oppose the British ^troops^ entring this province. I learned from the same quarter that Emissaries were sent throughout the province to engage the People to rise and come to the assistance of Boston if Any of the Kings troops arrived there; and I was told that if any troops came to Boston, I should get out of the way as fast as I could; for if I staid, my Life would be in danger. Now, my Lord, If I had sent an Account of all this intelligence as it came to me, if My letter had been intercepted here (which is easily done by corrupting a Master of a Ship) or if It was made publick at home, and I was called upon to Verify my information, I could not do it: for I could not call upon my informer's without a breach of faith; & in such Case they would undoubtedly think themselves justified in denying that they ever told me so. The Case of using Names is attended with no less difficulty: where Names are used It is a kind of accusation which the Accuser is expected to support with proof. But in the present state of the Town Facts of the greatest Notoriety cannot be proved: One may have an exact account of Speeches & Declarations, in common conversation; but if it is offered to reduce it to evidence they immediately know nothing of the matter. Otis's Speech upon the Question of rescinding was the most Violent insolent abusive treasonable Declamation that perhaps was ever delivered; It was spoke in the presence of an 100 or 200 people besides the Members of the House. And yet I could not get one person out of a dozen, which I had application made to, to give any minutes of it: so fearful were they of their being made use of as Evidence: However I have procured some memoranda of this celebrated Oration, some part of which may possibly be Authenticated, if needful.[9] I could urge other things in justification of the deficiencies of my informations such as they are; but I hope they will all be supplied by my answers Upon a personal Enquiry.

It is certainly best that the Orders for sending troops to Boston should originate in England; especially as no great Mischeif has been done in the interval. The Generals Orders are gone to Halifax for two Regiments, and I expect a Letter from the General requiring quarters for them before the End of next week.[10] There will be a disturbance more or less upon this occasion: but upon a full Consideration I have thought that there was more danger from the troops coming suddenly than after expectation; and that an Opposition was more like to arise from inconsiderateness than deliberation. I have therefore purposely let it transpire that I expect to receive orders for providing quarters for 2 regiments. It has occasioned some alarm; and a Town Meeting is appointed for next Monday. I hope it will be for the best; but can't be answerable for Events in ~~the~~ so precarious a business as a popular assembly. I shall inform your Lordship of the result.

I have not considered my obligation to consult the Council upon intresting Matters so much upon the footing of my Commission & Instructions, as I have upon the traditional Notions of the Connection between the Governor & Council which have prevailed in this Government & are much warranted by Actual restraints laid upon the Governor by the Charter; upon the particular complexion ^of the time,^ which is favorable to all impeachments of the Conduct of the Governor & the rights of Government; & upon the danger of bad consequences following particular Measures, which it would be Very hard to lay upon the Governor's shoulders alone acting without, that is contrary, to the Advice of Council. This was the Case in my not sending for troops, tho' I was not blind to the Want of them: Of this I have allready explained the difficulties & Embarrasments it has occasioned. I admit that the Governor of Mass Bay is responsible for the due exercise of the royal Authority delegated to him, as much as the other royal Governors. But great Allowance must be made for the Constitutional Disability which he is put under; and to expect of him to support the royal Authority effectually with a Council who will not join with him & he cannot separate him^self^ from, would be to require him to make bricks without straw.

I am much obliged to your Lordship for procuring his Majesty's leave of absence for me. I shall avail myself of it immediately: for I am certain that in the present state of affairs, I can be of more service at Westminster than I can at Boston; especially as I shall leave the Government in the hands of a Gentleman who will not depart from my System, & will conduct himself with as much resolution as I have done & possibly with better Success. It has been unfortunate that the June Mail has been so delayed, as It has lost me 3 or 4 weeks & will fling my Voyage more into the Winter than I could have wished.

I am, with great respect, My Lord Your Lordships most obedient
& most humble Servant

Fra Bernard

The right honble The Earl of Hillsborough

ALS, RC   CO 5/757, ff 388-391.

Endorsed: Boston Sepr. 9th. 1768. Govr Bernard (N° 19) R 2^d Novr. A.45.   Enclosures: a copy of the *Boston Gazette*, 29 Aug. 1768, CO 5/757, ff 392-393; [an account of James Otis Jr.'s speech of 21 Jun. 1768] (not found, but see the transcript below). Variants of letter in: CO 5/767, ff 77-84 (L, RLbC); BP, 7: 26-33 (L, LbC); *Letters to the Ministry* (1st ed.), 50-52; *Letters to the Ministry* (repr.), 68-70. Hillsborough acknowledged receipt with **No. 712**.[11] Copies of the letter were laid before both houses of Parliament on 28 Nov. 1768. HLL: American Colonies Box 3.

FB was replying to Hillsborough's long-delayed letter of 11 Jun. (**No. 622**), the duplicate of which he received on 3 Sept. and the original on 14 Sept. While FB was pleased to learn that troops were on the way to Boston, and to receive a leave of absence, he was concerned by the prospect of having to delay his voyage home until after the Regiments were quartered. FB also labored to explain the difficulties in prosecuting the rioters during the *Liberty* riot and procuring evidence of sedition.

Hillsborough wished FB "had been more explicit" (**No. 622**) in describing what had been said by those radicals who "openly" defied parliamentary authority. In response, FB revealed that he was receiving key information from within the Whig camp. This came from two principal sources: the first was someone close to the Whig leadership, whom he described as a Son of Liberty; this person was not a spy, but a concerned citizen, fearful of mobbism and insurrectionism who (as he observed in this letter) "sometimes" provided "useful intelligence." FB knew the identity of his source and he was sufficiently valuable (and prominent) for the governor to pledge to keep his name out of all business. FB mentioned having "acquaintance" with other Sons of Liberty, but clearly valued this person more than the others. He likely received information through a third party, which raises the possibility that the third party was relaying information without the full knowledge of the source. Likely third parties were current and former senior government officers who maintained regular personal and professional contact with local Whigs, notably Jonathan Sewall, the present attorney general, and Edmund Trowbridge, attorney general until 1767, and for whom political allegiance was no barrier to wider social interaction.

The second source of information was friends of government who attended Boston town meetings and political gatherings. Two of these informants can be identified: Richard Silvester, an innkeeper, and Nathaniel Coffin, appointed deputy-cashier of Customs on 7 Nov. 1768. Both men had strong local ties. See **Nos. 732** and **733**.[12]

A shadowy third source was paid informers. While FB did not operate a spy ring, he had been using informers for some time, and their political activities probably grew out of their traditional role of helping to apprehend smugglers (many of whom were Whigs), for which they could be rewarded with a third share of profits from fines and the sale of forfeited property.[13] One of them may have supplied FB with "the memoranda" of James Otis Jr.'s "celebrated Oration" of 21 Jun. referred to in this letter. (The friends of government, FB intimated, were too timid to commit an account to paper.) A copy of indeterminate provenance exists.[14]

> Being in the Gallery a few days before the Assembly was dissolv'd, I heard Mr Otis make a long Speech, part of the substance of which was (as near as I can remember) couch'd in the following Terms. Respecting the Nobility of Great Britain he observ'd as follows.
>
> Pray what are those Men? — They have Titles' tis true, they are rais'd above those whom they are pleas'd to stile the vulgar — they have Badges to distinguish themselves — the unthinking Multitudes are taught to reverence them as little Deities — for what? — not their Virtues sure. — this cannot be the Case — 'tis notoriously known there are no set of People under the Canopy of Heaven more venal, more corrupt and debauch'd in their Principles — Is it then for their Superiour Learning? no, by no means — tis true they are sent to the Universities of Oxford and Cambridge — and pray what do they Learn there? — why — nothing at all but Whoring, Smoking and Drinking — a Pious setting out truly — Seven or Eight Years spent to a fine Purpose indeed — Let us attend them a little further — as a finishing stroke they are finally sent to France — what do they see there? — why —the outside of a Monkey— what are they when they return Home again? Compleat Monkeys themselves.
>
> Shall we now take a view of their House of Commons — what are those mighty Men that affect to give Laws to the Colonies? Surprizing! — a parcel of Button-makers, Pan-makers, House Jockeys, Gamesters, Pensioners, Pimps and Whore Masters.
>
> We have now before us a Letter from Lord Hillsborough — from the stile one would conclude it to be the performance of a School Boy — they are pleas'd in their Wonderful Sagacity to find fault with our Circular Letter I defy the whole Legislature of Great Britain to write one equally correct.

Otis caricatured the British aristocracy in self-consciously egalitarian terms, and, if the informer's account is accurate, is an excellent example of how the Whigs contrived to sustain their defiance of Hillsborough's instructions with socially-conscious satire.

1. **No. 622**.

2. State papers Nos. 11 to 13 and 15 are transcripts **Nos. 635, 645, 653,** and **651**. State paper No. 14 from Hillsborough is a sign manual for leave of absence dated the Court at St. James's, 23 Mar. 1768, BP, 12: 73-76; it was enclosed in **No. 757,** *Bernard Papers,* 5: 234-235.

3. That is, 10 Jun.

4. FB received the original on 14 Sep.

5. On 22 Aug. the *Boston Gazette* printed an article asserting that TH had received a royal commission as chief justice and annual salary of £200 for the office of lieutenant governor. In the following edition, published on 29 Aug., the printers admitted that the news of the royal commission was unfounded. In fact, the British government had proposed giving TH a salary as lieutenant governor, although this was never implemented. Bailyn, *Ordeal of Thomas Hutchinson,* 147.

6. See **No. 504,** *Bernard Papers,* 3: 232–235; **Appendix 3**.

7. This comment implies criticism of Attorney General Jonathan Sewall, suggesting he lacked enthusiasm for pursuing the rioters, even though FB appreciated the systemic problems that hindered Crown law officers in bringing rioters to justice. Sewall, who had been appointed attorney general in Nov. 1767, was further exasperated by Hillsborough's instructions in **No. 661** to undertake investigations of treasonable activities, for he was convinced of the impracticability of gathering sufficient evidence to secure prosecutions on the libels presented to the grand jury on 23 Aug.

8. See **No. 575,** *Bernard Papers,* 3: 424-425.

9. See **No. 638** for FB's own rendition of Otis's speech of 21 Jun.

10. **Nos. 675** and **676**.

11. *Bernard Papers,* 5: 115-118.

12. *Bernard Papers,* 5: 167-173.

13. *Bernard Papers,* 3: 94.

14. The account is appended to a report of the Boston town meeting of 12 Sept. 1768 (for which see **No. 680**). NEP, 3: 81.

673 | To the Earl of Hillsborough

N° 20

Boston Sep 10 1768

My Lord

I have received your Lordships letter N° 11,[1] by which I am ordered to consider his Majesty's instructions with attention & observe what Alterations & Additions may, in my opinion be effectual for his Majesty's intrests. This is a great task & to do it effectually will take up time. I will proceed upon it with the best dispatch: at present I have a good deal of public business upon my hands & more coming in; but I will get thro' it as fast as I can.

I have also received your Lordship's letter No 14,[2] by which I am ordered to assist & support the Commissioners of the Customs & their Officers, especially in discovering & bringing to justice all persons guilty of a breach of the Laws of Great Britain. My Power & that of the Civil Authority is at present reduced Very low: such as it is, it shall be exerted to the utmost for the said purposes.

I am, with great respect, My Lord, Your Lordships most obedient
& most humble Servant

Fra Bernard

The right honble the Earl of Hillsborough

ALS, RC CO 5/757, ff 394-395.

Endorsed: Boston Sept[r]. 10th. 1768 Gov[r]. Bernard (N°. 20) R 2[d]. Nov[r]. A.46.   Variants: CO 5/767, f 85 (L, RLbC) and BP, 7: 33-34 (L, LbC). Hillsborough acknowledged receipt of this letter with **No. 712**.[3]

---

1. **No. 635**.
2. **No. 650**.
3. *Bernard Papers*, 5: 115-118.

674 | To the Earl of Hillsborough

N° 21

Boston Sep 10 1768

My Lord

By your Lordship's Letter N° 15[1] I have directions concerning the dispatching my Letters to your Lordships Office. I have allready pursued the Method pre-scribed by your Lordship: I very seldom send any letters by the packet; for, as it is managed, it is a Very inconvenient carriage of letters from hence to your Lordship's office. It would be often be of great use in returning immediate Answers to letters arrived by the packet. But We are deprived of this benefit, by the returning packet being ordered away before Letters in answer to those received at Boston can reach New York: And this Hurry never gains more than a week, sometimes not more than 4 days time; but it wholly deprives Boston of the use of the returning packet.

But the Service suffers still more by the delay of the packets from England; of which We have now 2 extraordinary instances. The May packet did not arrive at Boston till at the end of 14 weeks from London; the June packet is not arrived yet & is now in its 14th Week.[2] This is indeed extraordinary: but the usual time of Letters passing by the packet from London to Boston is 10 weeks which allowing for the land carriage exceeds the usual time of the passage of Merchant ships; & in regard to Boston a Conveyance by a Merchant's Ship saves the land carriage.

I cannot therefore but think that as the Expedition of a Letter is often of great consequence to the use of it, It would be of great service to send duplicates of all such letters as require expedition by Merchant men ready to sail, inclosing the letters with a list of them to the post master of the intended port & taking a receipt of the Master of the Ship for the packet. I have a good deal conversed & thought of the inconveniences arising from the present Management of the packet ^boats^ & shall probably trouble your Lordship with my ^further^ thoughts upon it.

I am, with great respect, My Lord, Your Lordship's most obedient
& most humble Servant

Fra. Bernard

The right honorable the Earl of Hillsborough

ALS, RC

CO5/757, ff 396-397.

Endorsed: Boston Sept[r]. 10th. 1768. Gov[r] Bernard (N° 21) R 2 Nov[r]. A.47.   Variants: CO 5/767, ff 85-87 (L, RLbC) and BP, 7: 35-36 (AL, LbC). Hillsborough acknowledged receipt with **No. 712**.[3]

One frustrating aspect of transatlantic communications was that FB was unable to dash off a timely reply by the mail packet. He would have liked to have been able to provide London with more timely updates. The best he could do, as Hillsborough realized (**No. 651**), was reply by the first merchant ship leaving port, though FB doubted the security of such a conveyance. Otherwise he tended to wait for a trusted captain or write fuller dispatches by return of the next packet.

The American Board of Customs had raised similar complaints about the inadequacy of the mail packet, suggesting that merchantmen from London were usually twice as fast as the packet from Falmouth to New York. The Board proposed that Rhode Island would make a better terminus than New York, for ships could get there two days quicker. Also, the internal postal system was such that it took six days for the carriage of overland mail between Boston and New York. The typical post rider, the Board noted, covered about 160 miles in a single journey, only traveling in daylight "and frequently loiters to distribute Letters from his private bag, and to do other business upon the Board."[4]

---

1. **No. 651**.

2. While FB was writing this letter, Hillsborough's original letter notifying him that British troops were being sent to Boston (**No. 622**) was being carried overland from New York. That letter was probably among the June mail carried by the *Lord Hyde* packet, which after a long delay arrived at New York on 7 Sept. FB received it on 14 Sept. However, he received the duplicate of **No. 622** four days earlier than original, it having been brought in the July mail packet.

3. *Bernard Papers*, 5: 115-118.

4. American Board of Customs to the lords commissioners of the Treasury, Boston, 12 May 1768, T 1/465, f 60.

675 | From Thomas Gage

New York Septem[r]. 12. 1768.

Sir

Having received his Majestys Commands to order Troops forthwith to Boston, I am to acquaint you that in obedience thereto, I have directed his Majestys 14[t[h]].[1] & 29th. Regiments under the Command of Lieu[t]. Coll[o]. Dalrimple to embark at Halli-fax and proceed to Boston as soon as possible. One of the Regiments is ordered for the present to Castle William the other to the Town, and I am to beg the favor of you to see that the said Troops are provided with Quarters on their arrival in your Government as by Law directed —

I have the Honor to be with great Regard Sir Your most obed[t]. hum. Serv[t].

Thomas Gage

His Excellency Governor Bernard

transcript, PC

Reports of the Record Commissioners of Boston, 20: 309.

The original has not been found. There is an AC in MiU-C: Gage, vol. 80.[2]

In **No. 671**, FB had requested Gage to send him a "public letter" that could be shown to the Council and the Boston authorities to expedite the quartering of the soldiers. But that letter, printed above, did not specify, as FB had requested, that the orders for the troop movement originated with the secretary of state. Gage probably assumed that acting by "His Majesty's Command" would suffice.

---

1.   Editorially supplied.

2.   The AC was not available for inspection whilst this volume was in preparation.

676 | From Thomas Gage

New York Sep[t] 12th 1768

Sir,

I send you my publick letter[1] by Express as you desired in your's by Cap[t] Shireff,[2] who returned here with great Expedition. And doubt not that it will come to your Hands in due time. The officer Commanding the Troops, ordered into your Government, is informed that he is sent thither to strengthen the Hands of Government in the Province of Massachusett's Bay, enforce a due obedience to the Laws, and protect and support the Civil Magistrates and the officers of the Crown, in the Execution of their Duty. And is directed to give every legal assistance to the Civil Magistrate in the Reservation of the publick Peace, and to the Officers of the Revenue in the Execution of the Laws of Trade and Revenue.

The use that shall be made of the Troops to effect there Purpose I am to leave to the Direction and Management of the Civil Power and am with great Regard,

Sir, Your most obedient humble Servant

Tho[s] Gage

I send some Letters for L[t] Col[o] Dalrymple, which I beg the dower of you to deliver him on his arrival.

His Ex[cy] Gov[r] Bernard

ALS, RC   BP, 11: 297-300.

Endorsed: Gen[l] Gage. Sep 12 1768.   There is a variant in MiU-C: Gage, vol. 80. Enclosed **No. 675**, which FB had requested Gage send him in order to expedite preparations for the arrival of the British regiments. FB presented **No. 675** to the Council on 19 Sept. (CO 5/827, ff 59-60) and replied to Gage with **No. 680**.

---

1. The private letter was **No. 669**.
2. FB had requested the "public letter" in **No. 671**.

677 | To a Committee of the Boston Town Meeting

[12 or 13 Sept. 1768][1]

Gentlemen

My apprehensions that some of his Majestys Troops are to be expected in Boston, arise from information of a private nature; I have received no publick Letters notifying to me the coming of such Troops, and requiring Quarters for them; whenever I do I shall communicate them to his Majestys Council. The Business of calling another Assembly for this Year is now before the King; and I can do nothing in it, untill I receive his Majestys Commands.

Francis Bernard

transcript, PC
Reports of the Record Commissioners of Boston, 16: 261.

The distinction between "private" and "publick" letters was disingenuous. FB had received notification of the troop orders on 3 Sept., in a private letter from Gage dated 31 Aug. (**No. 669**). Gage dispatched the public letter from New York on 12 Sept., and FB presented it to the Council on 19 Sept. (**No. 676**).

---

1. The letter was reported to the town meeting at 10 AM Tuesday 13 Sept. *Reports of the Record Commissioners of Boston*, 16: 261.

678 | From the American Board of Customs

Sir

As Mr Sewall attorney General of this province had complained to Your Excellency and several other persons that we had made reports to Government at home greatly to his disadvantage, and in his letter to us[1] particularized several matters said to have been the subjects of our memorials against him, We were induced to desire Your Excellency to peruse the said letter, and every matter which had gone from this Board wherein he was mentioned, in expectation that he would be satisfied from your report, of the falsity of the representations that had been made to him, and of what he had thought proper to charge us with, as facts, and that from his regard to the service he would enable us to guard against any persons who had maliciously endeavoured to sow discord amongst the Servants of the Crown;[2] but as Mr Sewall has not thought proper to give us satisfaction in this matter,[3] We find o[urs]elves[4] obliged to request Your Excellency, that taking into consideration the reports you may have heard from Mr Sewall, what you have seen in his letter to us, and our correspondence respecting that Gentleman, you will do us the Justice you may think we deserve, as from a regard to our own Characters and the good of the service, we judge it necessary to lay the whole of this matter before Government for their information.

We are with great Regard Sir Your Excellency's most obedient humble Servants

Chas Paxton
Hen. Hulton
Wm Burch
John Robinson

Castle William Boston Harbour 13. Sept 1768

To His Excellency Governor Bernard &c^a &c^{a5}

LS, RC Mass. Archs., 56: 553-554.

There is a copy in T 1/471, f 35.

The Customs commissioners' letter alludes to their long-running dispute with Jonathan Sewall, simultaneously advocate general of the Vice Admiralty Court and attorney general of Massachusetts. While historians have paid little heed to this episode, it nonetheless illustrates the tensions within the imperial elite and the problems of enforcing unpopular laws.[6] Sewall's discontent probably undermined the legal pursuit of John Hancock, whose arraignment on charges of breaking the trade laws resulted in one of the most controversial trials during the Imperial Crisis. For the Customs Board, the case was probably the culmination of a scheme to disgrace a leading Whig merchant. Sewall did not object to prosecuting Hancock but he questioned the legal rationale and political imperatives behind it. The letters concerning the affair printed in this fourth volume of *Bernard Papers* (**No. 678**) and in the fifth (**Nos. 710** and **728**)[7] illustrate the complex and lengthy negotiations to resolve the dispute between Sewall and the Customs commissioners. The letter printed above (**No. 678**) was part of the commissioners' initiative to compromise with Sewall. For these reasons it is important to provide extended commentaries to this and some of the other relevant correspondence.

The commissioners' dissatisfaction with Sewall's performance (according to Sewall's biographer, Carol Berkin) arose from their insistence that he should be prepared to "compromise . . . the execution of professional responsibilities to satisfy political obligations."[8] FB and the British government expected Sewall to work closely with the American Board of Customs in the prosecution of smugglers, but the commissioners resented the fact they had no operational control over Sewall: as advocate general, Sewall's appointment rested with the Admiralty, and, as attorney general, with the province (whereas the Customs commissioners were Treasury appointees). Several of the Board members further objected to Sewall's close relationship with FB, Sewall's superior. Sewall (according to his biographer) "repeatedly disappointed" the Board with legal opinions that (in Sewall's words) objected to a "rigid adherence to the strict Letter" of parliamentary acts. The Board favored a "Liberal Construction" of technical and procedural matters governing enforcement and seizure of contraband.[9] But Sewall's legal opinions threatened to jeopardize the commissioners' efforts to enforce the trade laws rigorously and improve the collection of revenue.

The Customs commissioners reported their initial concerns to the Treasury in a memorial of 12 Feb. 1768 (**Appendix 2**). Just six seizures had been made since the Stamp Act Crisis, only one of which was successfully prosecuted; the rest never made it to court (when the vessels and cargo were rescued by mobs) or were acquitted. The people's licentiousness and the government's impotency, the commissioners continued, were epitomized by the defiant stance of Boston trader Daniel Malcom who, pistols in hand, had successfully prevented officers armed only with writs of assistance from searching his premises for contraband. "No measures have been taken to punish the Offenders or to strengthen the hands of Government" or to ensure the province magistracy protected customs officers. Sewall was not named in the memorial but when the commissioners' complained about the "want of support from Government" having "greatly discouraged" their officers, the imputation was that the province's chief law officer and governor were somehow responsible for the current situation.[10] A second memorial, of 28 Mar., highlighted the commissioners' apprehension that they might become the targets of community violence. The commissioners contended that opposition to parliamentary taxation was the root cause of popular discontent, manifest in rowdy celebrations of the Stamp Act's repeal on 18 Mar. While the Treasury agreed with this assessment, Sewall's subsequent concerns that he had been misrepresented stemmed from the apprehension that ministers and officials could have concluded from the commissioners' reports that the province's law officer was unwilling or unable to assist the American Board of Customs implement the Townshend Revenue Act.[11]

Matters came to a head when the Customs Board attempted to instruct Sewall in the prosecution of unnamed men who had obstructed customs officers searching for contraband aboard John Hancock's vessel the *Lydia* on 8 Apr. The commissioners proposed that the attorney general should file an "information" in the Superior Court detailing the "Certain Resistance" encountered by the officer, Owen Richards. (He had been physically ejected after searching the *Lydia* below deck for some three hours, but was unharmed and did not resist when he was carefully carried out of the hold by Hancock's men.) While it was perfectly reasonable for the Board to expect the attorney general to prosecute law breakers, the note from the Board's secretary made it clear that Sewall would be instructed by the Board's solicitor in assembling the "Evidences" of criminality. Moreover, Sewall was asked to initiate legal proceedings by filing an "Information" in the Superior Court "if" he considered there was "good Ground" to do so.[12] The problem was not the request as such, but the nature of the legal procedure that the attorney general was being asked to undertake on the Board's behalf. An "information" was a declaration made by an informer on behalf of the king and himself; it was commonly used by customs officers bringing smugglers to trial in the juryless Vice Admiralty Court and by the attorney general when pursuing known criminals. In this case, the commissioners' viewed the procedure as an alternative to bringing an indictment before a grand jury in the Superior Court. The job of the grand jury was to decide if the indictment offered sufficient *prima facia* evidence to warrant a prosecution, and in this case the Board assumed that the jurymen would be biased toward Hancock, given his high political profile. An information, on the other hand, assumed a person's criminality and could be presented to the court. While the Customs Board was concerned to overcome systemic failings in the pursuit of smugglers, they were also determined to make an example of Hancock. Sewall, moreover, was equally determined that the province's chief law officer should not be subordinated to the Customs Board's agenda.

The substantive points of law raised by Sewall in an opinion of 23 Apr. were that (a) the case did not warrant proceeding on the basis of an information, and (b) to do so would establish an unwelcome procedural precedent. According to O. M. Dickerson, Sewall's opinion may be the only surviving legal opinion by a colonial law officer, and reveals Sewall's firm understanding of what the Navigation Acts permitted customs officers to do when boarding and searching vessels. Sewall served notice of the "political independence of colonial law officers when it came to applying fundamental law," though in doing so risked damaging his chances of further advancement.[13] Sewall's opinion ended the proposed action against Hancock. Laymen like the commissioners (versed in the political furor surrounding John Wilkes's challenge to general search warrants in England but not in the finer points of admiralty law), privately might have thought Sewall's opinion a studied attempt to undermine imperial authority, and even indicative of Whig sympathies.

In their memorial to the Treasury of 12 May, reporting the *Lydia* affair, the commissioners appraised the likely consequences of Sewall's opinion: "that if Mr Sewall should be thought right in his opinion, there is a necessity that our Officers should have further powers, otherwise the service cannot . . . be carried into effect." While the commissioners did not recommend Sewall's dismissal (and had no authority to do so) they left the Treasury in no doubt that Sewall's opinion significantly complicated procedures for conducting searches. Without a salary to incentivize them, the commissioners continued, "Crown lawyers . . . dare not exert themselves in the service of the Revenue, as they look to the people for their support, and not to Government." The exercise of his duty was "certain" to render Sewall "obnoxious" to the people "and therefore it is not to be expected that an Attorney

General should be sollicitous for the interest of the Revenue." An unfavorable comparison with Judge Robert Auchmuty[14] ("who exerted himself in the worst of times") raised the criticism of Sewall to a personal level. At the same time the commissioners argued the necessity of somehow bringing down the "infatuated" John Hancock.[15]

Sewall was unaware of these memorials until July (see **No. 728**).[16] In the meantime, customs officers seized John Hancock's *Liberty* and the commissioners by-passed Sewall in seeking the opinion of the English attorney general, William de Grey, for a dual action against Hancock. The commissioners proposed and de Grey approved that the Massachusetts advocate general should initiate both an *in personam* prosecution of Hancock using informations (that is, against the person, over and above the property seized) and an *in rem* action against his vessel and cargo. Upon learning of this, Sewall submitted his resignation from both his offices,[17] for the proposed procedure contradicted the opinion he had given in the *Lydia* case. While FB dissuaded Sewall by pledging his support, Sewall tried to conduct his own investigation into the Board's allegations against him. That was not an easy undertaking: while the Customs Board was in retreat at Castle William,[18] Sewall had restricted access to the commissioners and no official access to the Board's papers, leaving him reliant upon what information he could wheedle from two senior Customs' officials: the Board's secretary (Samuel Venner) and its solicitor (David Lisle), with whom Sewall had established contact by 20 Jul. (**No. 728**).[19]

The dispute—which embarrassed the commissioners, undermined Sewall's morale, and led to the suspension of Venner and Lisle—can be followed in detail in the papers of the British Treasury. The Customs Board sent numerous papers and several memorials to the Treasury between Feb. 1768 and Jan. 1769 (T 1/471, ff 1-88, 435-436). The commissioners first learned of Sewall's grievances around 5 Aug. and considered the matter at a Board meeting on 8 Aug.; the minute of that meeting further reveals that the Board had engaged a senior lawyer, Samuel Fitch (1735-89), to assist Advocate General Sewall in preparing the case against Hancock. The Board immediately conducted an investigation, collecting a wealth of testimony from all parties, and engaged FB, TH, and Robert Auchmuty to intervene and allay Sewall's concerns; but the commissioners also demanded that Sewall reveal the source of his information. Sewall's reluctance to accept their assurances that he had not been maligned puzzled his biographer, Carol Berkin. She portrayed Sewall as a proud lawyer and principled government officer, unwilling to compromise until he had seen the evidence for himself among the commissioners' papers.[20] The Board's memorial of 12 May certainly questioned Sewall's competence (though Sewall probably never saw this document in full). Sewall was determined to prove his point and defend his own integrity. The Board came to blame Venner and Lisle for turning Sewall against the Board, but this, as Berkin has shown, amounted to a convenient face-saving solution. Indeed, it could be inferred that Sewall's explanation[21] and Venner's subsequent denial[22] indicated that Sewall was acting upon information received from parties unknown, from within and without the Customs Board. It is beyond the scope of this volume to speculate on who that might have been, and it would be erroneous to assume that John Temple was involved from the outset. Equally, it is also possible (if perhaps seemingly implausible) that there were no informers, and that Sewall had concocted the story about informers to justify his accusations.

From FB's perspective, the affair was a troublesome distraction from more serious matters of state. Nonetheless potentially it could have destabilized his administration further if it deprived him of his chief law officer and publicly exposed tensions manifest within the imperial elite. As the dispute dragged on into autumn, it was TH not FB who assumed the peacemaker's role. While it was in FB's interest to retain Sewall's services and aid his protégé, he was preoccupied with the imminent arrival of the British regiments from Halifax. But Sewall, as TH indicated, also had grounds for suspecting that the governor was not fully engaged. In a letter to the Customs commissioners dated 17 Sept. (the day before FB received news that two additional regiments were on their way from Ireland), TH reported that Sewall had approached him six to eight weeks previously complaining that the commissioners' memorials had misrepresented "him as a person very unfit for the place of Advocate [general] and praying that he might be removed." Sewall had spoken with FB, in July, on that occasion threatening to resign (**No. 678**). In seeking TH's intercession, Sewall was not undermining the governor but probably acting upon his suggestion to bring TH on side. TH privately approached "one or more" of the commissioners who willingly supplied FB with extracts of "all they had ever wrote relative to Mr. Sewall." But Sewall, acting on information that suggested the extracts "were very different" from the originals, demanded to see the official copies. Sewall did not doubt the veracity of his "Informers" reports, thinking his sources "actuated by meer friendship." The commissioners, however, allowed TH (along with FB and Auchmuty) to view the Board's records concerning Sewall, and he found "nothing" in them to "give the least grounds" for Sewall's claims about misrepresentation. While they did not permit Sewall to access the material, the commissioners nevertheless provided him with a signed letter declaring that they had not written anything about Sewall that TH did not see. In fact, the Board's minutes reveal that TH, Auchmuty, and FB were not shown the full evidence: they were permitted to view the Board's memorial of 12 May—the one document directly critical of Sewall—and their secretary's letters to the Treasury dated 12 May and 7 Jun.; they were not shown the memorials of 12 Feb. and 18 Mar. wherein the commissioners professed to lack confidence in the provincial government and its law officers.[23]

TH's letter of 17 Sept. was a watershed moment in the dispute. If the commissioners' declaration was correct, then TH did not regard the Board's substantive criticism of Sewall's opinion in the *Lydia* case as challenging Sewall's competency. Such an interpretation, however, missed the point, for Sewall believed his personal honor and professional integrity were now at stake in what he deemed a "most mysterious unaccountable Affair." Thus Sewall refused to give up his complaint until he was allowed to read the Board's papers, convinced that the Board had maligned him. While TH's delay in contacting the commissioners is unexplained, he nevertheless proffered a ringing endorsement of Sewall's capabilities and character, and reported his case to the commissioners:

> that he was not conscious of any unfaithfulness, he had acted in every affair according to his best judgment and he thought himself very unfortunate in having such representations made without his being heard or having any opportunity of exculpating himself.

TH's key comment was that public knowledge of the dispute would "increase the prejudice" prevailing against the Board. Thus, TH left it to the commissioners to satisfy Sewall's concerns, both he and the governor having tried and failed. He finished on an intriguing note.

> I said but little to Mr. Sewall concerning his discovering his Informers knowing the Governor had discoursed with him upon that Subject. In general I remember that he seemed to think he should violate the Laws of Friendship in making such a discovery until he was fully convinced that the persons informing had willfully misrepresented facts to him.[24]

1. Demanding to see the commissioners' memorials, Sewall had written:

> I am truly sorry to find myself under a necessity of assuring the honble Board, that without being guilty of a direct violation of the Rules of Honour & Friendship, as I now apprehend, I cannot comply with the Condition upon which they are pleased to offer me that Evidence, which alone can convince me that my information is false. I sincerely wish I were at Liberty to deal in all respects openly & ingenuously in this matter, & to mention names with the same Freedom that I can declare Facts, but to betray those who in confidence have appeared to be my Friends, before I have full evidence that they are Ennemies disguised, must, in the Judgment of the Comm^{rs}. be infamous & base. I therefore take this opportunity to declare my fixed resolution, be the consequence what it will, never to divulge their names to the Board, untill they themselves give me leave, or the Information they have given me be clearly proved to be false.

Jonathan Sewall to the American Board of Customs, Cambridge, 5 Aug. 1768, T 1/471, ff 21-22.

2. The Board directed their secretary Samuel Venner to write Sewall denying that the commissioners had ever misrepresented him in letters to the Treasury; they also promised to show "such parts" of their memorials and papers that "relate to him" not to Sewall but to FB, TH, and Robert Auchmuty, who might then reassure Sewall that he had not been disparaged. (At this stage, the commissioners had not accused Venner of being Sewall's informer.) Minute of the Customs Board of 8 Aug. 1768, T 1/471, f 8. There is a copy of Venner's letter to Sewall in T 1/471, ff 23-24.

3. Sewall replied to Venner's letter on 10 Aug. protesting that the commissioners "should insist as a preliminary, on betraying my author!" In defending his informers. Sewall wrote:

> If they have told me the Truth, I have too high a sense of the obligation I am under to them, ever to suffer their names to be tortured from me, by any power on Earth, until I can see the propriety of divulging them.

T 1/471, f 25.

4. Smudged.

5. The letter was also intended for TH and Robert Auchmuty, whose intercession the commissioners had hoped would satisfy Sewall.

6. The best account is Carol Berkin, *Jonathan Sewall: Odyssey of an American Loyalist* (New York, 1974), 45-67. But see also Zobel, *Boston Massacre*, 72, 83; Reid, *In a Defiant Stance*, 51-52.

7. *Bernard Papers*, 5: 109-111, 154-158.

8. Quoted in ibid., 46.

9. Berkin, *Jonathan Sewall*, 50.

10. American Board of Customs, memorial to the lords commissioners of the Treasury, Boston, 12 Feb. 1768, T 1/465, ff 21-24. **Appendix 2**.

11. American Board of Customs, memorial to the lords commissioners of the Treasury, 28 Mar. 1768, Boston, T 1/465, ff 25-27.

12. Samuel Venner to Jonathan Sewall, 15 Apr. 1768, National Archives of Canada: Sewall Papers, Correspondence, ff 225-226.

13. Opinion of Jonathan Sewall in the case of the *Lydia*, 23 Apr. 1768, T 1/465, ff 70-71. It is printed in full in Oliver M. Dickerson, "Opinion of Attorney General Jonathan Sewall of Massachusetts in the Case of the Lydia," *WMQ* 4 (1947): 499-504. For the technical aspects of the opinion and the legislation cited by Sewall see Dickerson op. cit.

14. Robert Auchmuty (1724-88), judge of the Vice Admiralty Court in Massachusetts.

15. American Board of Customs, memorial to the lords commissioners of the Treasury, Boston, 12 May 1768, T 1/465, ff 64-65.

16. *Bernard Papers*, 5: 154-158.

17. See **No. 728**, *Bernard Papers*, 5: 154-158. William De Grey, case and opinion of the attorney general of England, 29 Jul. 1768, T 1/463, ff 27-28.

18. After the *Liberty* riot of 10 Jun., the American Board of Customs sought refuge on board HMS *Romney* and shortly afterward moved operations from the Boston Customhouse to Castle William, taking with them their families and a retinue of officials. The Board did not return to town until c. 8 Nov.

19. *Bernard Papers*, 5: 154-158.

20. See Berkin, *Jonathan Sewall*, 45-67.

21. See note 1 above.

22. Memorial of Samuel Venner, 29 Apr. 1769, protesting his suspension as secretary to the Board. T 1/471, ff 491-502.

23. Samuel Venner, however, was instructed to procure any other material from the Board's papers pertaining to Sewall, and this would have included the papers not shown to FB, TH, and Auchmuty. Minute of the American Board of Customs of 22 Aug. 1768, T 1/471, f 9.

24. TH to the American Board of Customs, Milton, 17 Sept. 1768, Mass. Archs., 25: 272-273 (AL, LbC). There is a copy in T 1/471, ff 39-40.

679 | *From the Earl of Hillsborough*

(Nº: 19.)

Whitehall 14ᵗʰ: Septʳ: 1768

Sir,

As no Packet will sail for America 'till the 5ᵗʰ: of next Month, I avail myself of Mʳ: Rogers's return to Boston[1] to acquaint you that, since my dispatch of the 30ᵗʰ: of July, I have received your Letters numbered 9, 10, 11, 12, 13, & have laid them, with their Inclosures, before the King.[2]

His Majesty is concerned to find that the House of Representatives has not thought fit to comply with the Requisition you had in command from His Majesty to lay before that House.[3]

His Majesty trusted that the same regard for the Constitution, which had induced a negative to the first Proposition of writing to the other Colonies,[4] would have prevailed with the new Assembly to have restored the Resolution which had been entered upon the Journals on that occasion, and that the King would not have been disappointed in His Royal Wishes, of being enabled to lay before His Parliament, so becoming a testimony of reverence in the Colony of Massachuset's Bay, to the supreme legislative Authority.

The King has nothing more at Heart than that the Constitution should be preserved in it's utmost privity, and as it appeared to his Majesty that the Resolution
of the Assembly for erasing out of the Records a proceeding in the former part of
the Session, in which the House had shewn its respect for that Constitution; and
the substituting in the place of it a measure of a direct contrary tendency, might
not only have the effect to expose the Colony to the censure of Parliament, but was
in itself very irregular;[5] His Majesty therefore thought that he could not shew a
greater testimony of condescension as well as of paternal regard for His Colony of
Massachuset's Bay, than by giving the new Assembly a fair Opportunity of returning to a proper Sense of their Duty, and at the same time ^of^ doing credit to
themselves, by rescinding the Resolution of writing to the other Colonies in Terms
that not only questioned but openly denied the Authority of Parliament, so recently
declared by a solemn Statute, and by the provision of which Statute such resolution & proceeding upon it were null and void.

The King approves your conduct upon this occasion in every part of it, except
the communication of my Letters to the Assembly, which, tho' considered by His
Majesty with the most indulgent Allowances for the peculiar delicacy of your Situation, His Majesty does nevertheless apprehend to be an irregular proceeding,
& having observed that the same thing has been done in other Colonies, I have
signified His Majesty's Commands thereupon in circular Letters, one of which you
will receive herewith.[6]

Your Letters N°. 10, 12 and 13, do not appear to require any particular Answer,
& therefore I have only in command from His Majesty to repeat to you; the concern
He feels at the continuance of the seditious publications which have disgraced the
Government, & of the disorders which have so long disturbed the peace of the
Town of Boston; His Majesty trusts however, that the measures he has thought fit
to pursue[7] will encourage the Magistrates to do their Duty with becoming zeal and
spirit, which cannot fail of restoring publick peace and Tranquility, as is evident
from the consequences of M^r: Williams's spirited and proper conduct,[8] of which
His Majesty expresses great approbation.

The humble Petition of the Council transmitted with your Letter No 11,[9] has
been received by His Majesty in the most gracious manner; The King observes
with great satisfaction, the very decent and becoming manner in which they have
expressed their Sentiments in respect to the operation of the Law they complain
of, and I have it in command from His Majesty that you should acquaint the Council that this Petition, together with your reinforcing in support of it, will have full
consideration before the meeting of Parliament, which is appointed for the 8th: of
November.

I am Sir Your Most Obedient Humble Servant

Hillsborough

Governor Bernard.

LS, RC   BP, 11: 301-306.

Endorsed by FB: Earl of Hillsborough N° 19. 14 Sepr 1768. Docket by Thomas Bernard: Sundries. Enclosed the RC of **No. 670**. Variants of letter: CO 5/757, ff 346-348 (LS, AC); CO 5/765, ff 39-42 (L, LbC). Copies of the letter together with the enclosure were laid before both houses of Parliament on 28 Nov. 1768. HLL: American Colonies Box 3.

Hillsborough's letter underlined that FB had the full backing of the king and his ministers, despite the House of Representatives' efforts to undermine his reputation in London (see **Appendix 9**).

---

1. Nathaniel Rogers was a passenger on board the *Thames,* which arrived in Boston on 17 Nov. *Boston News-Letter*, 17 Nov. 1768.
2. **Nos. 638**, **646** and its supplement **648**, **654**, **656** and **657**.
3. Communicated to Hillsborough in **No. 638**.
4. The first motion for a circular letter to the colonial assemblies was defeated on 21 Jan. FB reported these proceedings in **Nos. 585** and **589**.
5. The vote of 21 Jan. was expunged from the House journals on 4 Feb. 1768. See **No. 585**n7.
6. **No. 670**.
7. In **No. 661**.
8. See **No. 656**.
9. **Appendix 11** enclosed in **No. 654**; both were presented to Parliament on 28 Nov.

680 | To Thomas Gage

Jamaica Farm near Boston
Sep 16 1768 2 o clock

S[r]

I have just received your Letters of Sep 12[1] with the inclosed for Col Dalrymple; and think it best to dismiss your Messenger without ~~suffering~~^letting^ him go into Boston. I shall go to Boston tomorrow & communicate your Letter to the Council & manage the Business in the best Manner I can;[2] for I expect to meet with much Difficulty. I must not however neglect cautioning you against the Probability (or, as I rather hope, the Possibility) of Events happening here which might require a Reinforcement.

As the Sons of Liberty kept continually declaring that no Kings Troops should enter Boston, I was apprehensive that the sudden Appearance of Troops would produce temporary Mischeifs Before the Troops could get ashore to prevent them. I therefore thought it best that the Expectation of them should gradually precede their Arrival; & therefore suffered a Report to be spread that I had said I had private Intelligence of Troops being ordered here tho I had received no public Orders for that Purpose. This gave a great Alarm to the Sons of Liberty who immediately procured a Town Meeting to be summond for Monday;[3] in the Mean Time, as I am informed at a general ^meeting^ it was agreed to rise in Opposition; & at a private Meeting it was agreed to attack and take the Castle. On Saturday Night a Barrel was put up upon the Beacon Pole, an empty one as it has proved. On Monday there was a Town Meeting consisting cheifly of Sons of Liberty, such other Gentlemen as came there being neutral. This it is said prevented the intended Attack of the Castle as well as the Insurrection. But as to the first I beleive the Station of the Romney Man of War was the principal Discouragement.[4] You will see an Account of the Proceedings of this Town Meeting, as published by themselves in the inclosed Paper. All I have to add is that the Tenor of the Speeches made upon this Occasion,[5] which seemed to be all precomposed & arranged, was that the King had no Right to station Troops in this Province; if he did they ought to & should be resisted: for which Purpose you will see a formal Argument in the Paper inclosed. In the middle of the Hall[6] where they met were many Chests of Arms, they say containing 400, belonging to the Town, which some Months ago were removed from the Lumber Rooms cleaned & put into the Floor of the Hall. It was moved that these should be delivered out to the People; but that being overruled, they were pointed to by M[r] O[7] & other Orators as explanatory of what was intended tho they did not speak out. Upon the whole it was understood that Resistance & the Confusion which must follow was to be expected; but on Wednesday Afternoon

Advices arrived by a Ship put in at Marblehead of Preparations made in England for bringing the Bostoners[8] to Reason; so that the Faction has been much cowed thereby & things at present seem to be quiet.

This is a true tho short State of these Proceedings thro which there have been so many public & private Declarations of their Intention to resist the Forces of Great Britain when they can do it ^to^ Advantage that I think no Time should be lost to provide against them. There have also been Riots at Salem and Newbury against the Custom House Officers of so violent a Nature that it will require a military Force to bring the Rioters to Reason.[9] And upon the whole I think it will be necessary for his Majesty's Service that you should order considerable Reinforcements to the Troops here; and that Col Dalrymple should have sufficient Power to strengthen himself from Halifax if any Resources remain there.

I have had for some Time a discretionary Leave to go to England, when I saw Occasion. If I had any Hopes that by staying here, I could be of service in composing the Troubles of this Province, I would stay. But as I now dispair of any Thing being done in a conciliatory Way, I intend to set out for England probably in 3 Weeks;[10] & shall be glad to be favoured with your Commands.

I am &c

Gen[l] Gage.

L, LbC   BP, 7: 196-198.

In handwriting of Thomas Bernard. Enclosures (not found): probably enclosed a copy of the *Boston News-Letter*, 15 Sept. or the *Boston Gazette*, 19 Sept. 1768, both of which printed the proceedings of the Boston town meeting of 12 Sept. Gen. Gage received the RC on the morning of Wednesday 21 Sept.[11]

FB had likely commenced writing to Hillsborough (**No. 682**) when he received the letter from Gage (**No. 676**) that prompted him to compose this reply, and in which he summarizes the contents of the letter to Hillsborough. Gage was doubtless irritated by FB's self-validating declaration that he hoped shortly to be returning to England, leaving Gage and Dalrymple to negotiate the landing and settlement of the Regulars coming from Halifax. FB was obliged to remain in post when, two days later, he received Hillsborough's most recent instructions (**No. 661**) concerning the departure of two additional regiments from Ireland. On 24 Sept., FB informed Gage that he would not be leaving (**No. 687**). Even so, his determination to leave Boston probably reinforced Gage's perception that Boston was on the verge of revolt (**No. 689**). While FB's actions suggested he feared an insurrection of some kind, TH labored to remain sanguine, declaring—though only after the troops had landed unopposed—that "I cannot think in any Colony . . . people . . . have ever been so mad as to think of a Revolt."[12]

---

1. **No. 676**; Gage's orders to Dalrymple of c.12 Sept. 1768 have not been found.

2. See **No. 686**. The next Council meeting was held on Monday 19 Sept. at the Province House. CO 5/827, ff. 59-60.

3. 12 Sept.

4. HMS *Romney* had been anchored in Boston harbor since 17 May.

5. See the account in **No. 732**, *Bernard Papers*, 5: 167-171.

6. Faneuil Hall.

7. James Otis Jr.

8. The ship probably brought news of the British government's decision to send over two regiments from Ireland (conveyed to FB in **No. 661** and received on 18 Sept.)

9. For a brief account see Hoerder, *Crowd Action in Revolutionary Massachusetts*, 189; *Boston Evening-Post*, 19 Sept. 1768; *Essex Gazette*, 20-27 Sept. 1768. FB's anxiety stemmed from the probability that this was the first time during the Imperial Crisis that protestors had tarred and feathered officers working for the Custom House: Robert Wood, a minor officer at Salem, and Joshua Vickery and Francis Mignot at Newburyport. Tarring and feathering was uncommon, with around ten or eleven incidents recorded in Massachusetts during the Imperial Crisis. For a short summary see Nicolson, "A Plan 'to banish all the Scotchmen,'" 98-99n.

10. FB received the duplicate of **No. 622**, granting him leave of absence, on c.3 Sept. and the RC on 14 Sept. Fresh instructions in **No. 661** obliged FB to remain in post.

11. According to **No. 689**.

12. TH to Thomas Whately, Boston, 5 Oct. 1768, Mass. Archs., 25: 281, in Hutchinson Transcripts, 1: 277.

681 | To the Earl of Hillsborough

N° 22

Boston Sep 16 1768

My Lord

In the Boston Gazette of the 5th inst appeared a paper containing a System of Politicks exceeding all former exceedings. Some took it for the casual ravings of an occasional enthusiast: but I persuaded myself that It came out of the Cabinet of the Faction and was preparatory to some actual operations against the Government.[1] In this persuasion I considered that if the Troops from Halifax were to come here of a sudden, there would be no avoiding an insurrection, which would at least fall upon the Crown officers, if it did not amount to an Opposition to the troops. I therefore thought it would be best that the Expectation of the troops should be gradually communicated, that the Heads of the Faction might have time to consider well what they were about, & prudent Men opportunity to interpose their advice. I therefore took an occasion to mention to one of the Council, in the Way of discourse, that I had private advice that troops were ordered hither, but I had no public orders about it myself. This was in the 8th inst: & before night it was throughly circulated all over the town.[2]

The Faction immediately took the alarm; & at first nothing was to be heard among them but declarations that the troops should not enter the Town.[3] But nothing was done in public, but appointing a Town Meeting on Monday following. In private there were, as I am told, two meetings, the one a large one on fryday Night (the 9th) where it was the general Opinion that they should raise the Country & oppose the troops[:][4] the other meeting, as I am informed, was very small & private on Saturday Night, at the House of one of the Cheifs;[5] and there it wa[s] resolved to surprise & take the Castle on the Monday night following. I dont relate these Accounts as certain facts but only as reported & beleived.[6] On Saturday night an ^empty^ turpentine Barrel was put up upon the pole of the beacon, (which had been lately erected anew in a great hurry by the Selectmen without consulting me).[7] This gave a great alarm, the next day, and the Council sent to me on Sunday afternoon to desire I would order a Council, which I held at a Gentleman's House[8] halfway between me and Boston. Here It was debated what Means should be used to take the barrel down; & it was resolved that the Select men should be desired to take it down: but they would not do it.

On the Monday at the Hall[9] the Faction appeared surrounded with all its forces: there were very few of the principal Gentlemen there; such as were, appeared only as curious & perhaps anxious spectators.[10] The Meeting was opened with speeches much to the same purpose as the paper enclosed and first mentioned.[11] Nothing was then resolved but to put 2 questions to me, which your Lordship will see in the printed Account;[12] and to appoint a general Commit[tee] to consider & report. The next day the Reports were made, upon which followed a Set of speeches by the cheifs of the faction & no one else; which followed one another in such order & method, that it appeared as if they were acting a play, evry thing, both as to matter & order, seeming to have been preconcerted before hand. As they have printed their own Account to circulate it round the province, I shall only add to it an Account of some of these Speeches, from the tenor of which the general intention of the whole transaction will be fully explained.

I should have mentioned before that in the middle of the Hall where they met, were deposited in chests, the Town Arms, amounting as it is said to ^about^ 400. These, as I have before informed your Lordship, about 4 or 5 months ago were taken out of the lumber rooms, where they had lain for some years past, to be cleaned; & have since been laid upon the floor of the Town hall to remind the people of the use of them.[13] These Arms were often the subject of discourse & were of singular use to the Orators in the way of Action. As the Subject of their debates turned upon arming the Town & Country against *their Enemies*, The probability of a French War was mentioned as a pretence for arming the Town & a Cover for the frequent use of the Word *Enemy*. It was said that the *Enemy* would probably be here before the Convention met, that is within 10 days; It was moved that the Arms should be now delivered out to oppose the *Enemy*; this was objected to for that ^they^ might fall into hands who would not use them. But this flimsy Veil was not allways kept on: it was often said that they had a right to oppose with arms a military force which was sent to oblige them to submit to unconstitutional Laws; and when it was required to be more explicit, the Chairman[14] said that they understood one another Very well, & pointing with his hand added "there are the Arms; when an attempt is made agst your liberties they will be delivered; our Declaration wants no explication:" and indeed it does not.

When first it was moved that the Governor be desired to call an Assembly, it was said to be to provide for the Safety of the province & put it in a posture of defence: it was thereupon observed that that would make troops necessary; & it was immediately struck out. One cried out that they wanted a Head; this was overruled: for indeed it was rather too premature. Another, an old Man, protested against evry thing but rising immediately & taking all power into their own hands. One Man, very profligate & abandoned, argued for massacring their Enemies: his argument was short. — Liberty is as pretious as Life; if a Man attempts to take my Life, I have a right to take his; ergo, if a Man attempts to take away my liberty, I have a right to take his Life. He also argued that when a Peoples Liberties were threatened, they were in a state of War & had a right to defend themselves. And He carried these Arguments so far that his own party were obliged to silence him.

I will now make one observation on one passage in the printed declaration,[15] to show to what length is capable of being carried a pretension to an exemption from the Authority of Great Britain. It has been heretofore argued that the parliament has no authority over the American Colonists, because they are not represented in the parliament of Great Britain; and in Consequence, that the provincial Assemblies are to all intents & purposes the parliament in regard to the subjects of the respective Colonies. This has been heretofore applied only to the raising & disposing of public Money: And now Observe a large stride to a Very different business. Because it is declared in an Act of the first of Willm & Mary[16] that no standing Army shall be kept up in the Kingdom in time of peace, but by consent of parliament, therefore the King shall not keep any part of the standing Army raised & supported by the parliament in any American province, without the Consent of the provincial Assembly. And this Exemption is pleaded in Virtue of a Charter granted by King William &c without the Authority of parliament,[17] & consequently according to true Revolutional principles not to be pleaded against the parliament; as according to such principles the King has no power, by his own Act only, to exempt Any Subjects of Great Britain from the Authority of parliament.

I herewith inclose a blank Copy of the precept which the Select men of Boston have used in calling together the Convention.[18] Surely so daring an Assumption of the royal Authority was never practised by Any City or Town in the British Dominions even in the times of greatest disorder; not even by the City of London when the Great Rebellion was at the highest, & the Confusion arising from thence most urgent for some extraordinary Measures.[19] How large this Meeting will be & what they will do at present can only be guest at. But as they have hitherto pursued the Dictates of the Paper in the Boston Gazette, It may be supposed that they will go thro' with them; & exclude the *Crown officers* & resume *the first original Charter* which has no ingredient of royalty in it.[20] It certainly will be so, if it is not prevented by power from without: and I much doubt whether the Force allready ordered ^by Genl Gage^ viz 2 regiments will be sufficient. For my own part, if I had any place of protection to resort to, I would publish a proclamation against the assembling Convention: but I dare not take so Spirited a step without first securing my retreat.

It is now a great question whether the Kings troops will be suffered to enter the Town or not: the general Opinion is in the affirmative. The Design against the Castle is now so well known that it is probable that the Very Names of the people who were enrolled for that Service to the Number of 500, or of the Chief of them, will be discovered. The Cheifs of the Party now own that it will be impossible for them to hold the Castle or the Town, tho' they should seize & Garrison them for the present. They therefore, at least some of them, seem content that the troops shall stay here, till the parliament has determined upon their remonstrances: as, they say, the troops cannot remain here for 2 years, if the parliament refuses to do them justice.

I am with great respect, My Lord, Your Lordships most obedient and most humble Servant

Fra Bernard

The right honorable The Earl of Hillsborough

ALS, RC   CO 5/757, ff 405-408.

Endorsed: Boston Septr. 16. 1768. Govr Bernard, (N°. 22). R 2 Novr. A.49.   While the letter is dated Boston 16 Sept., it is possible that FB commenced writing it at Jamaica Plain. It was there, at c.2 PM, he started writing **No. 680**, in which he summarized the contents of this letter to Hillsborough and stated his intention of returning to Boston the following day; postage of **No. 681** was delayed long enough for FB to include a newspaper dated 19 Sept. Enclosures: circular from the Boston Selectmen to the Massachusetts towns, CO 5/757, ff 408-409; copies of the *Boston Gazette*, 5 Sept. and the *Boston Post-Boy and Advertiser*, 19 Sept. 1768.[21] Probably also enclosed the minutes of the town meeting of Boston, 12 Sept. 1768, prepared by an informer (not found), of which there is a copy in NEP, f 81. Variants of letter in: CO 5/767, ff 87-96 (L, RLbC); BP, 7: 37-43 (L, LbC); Coll. Mass. Papers, 1768 (L, Copy); *Letters to the Ministry* (1st ed.), 52-56; *Letters to the Ministry* (repr.), 70-75. Hillsborough acknowledged receipt with **No. 712**.[22] Copies of the letter together with the enclosures were laid before both houses of Parliament on 28 Nov. 1768. HLL: American Colonies Box 3.

FB's report of the Boston town meeting of 12 Sept. relied on the eye-witness account of an informer, transcribed below in full, and which was probably enclosed with this letter.

> At the Town Meeting of ^Septemb[r] 12 1768^ at Faneul Hall before the arrival of the Troops, it was observ'd by M[r] Otis that the Times were then very alarming. That they had information of Troops being sent from Hallifax for this Town, tho' he beleived in his own Mind there was no such thing intended, as there was no manner of occasion for them. It was afterwards propos'd that the Inhabitants should Arm themselves, the reason assigne'd, was, that a French War would certainly commence soon, and probably this Town might be invaded by a Foreign Enemy; (on this being mention'd there was a general Smile) Those that had no Arms of their own were reminded, that there were then plenty in Faneul Hall belonging to the Province, which would on application, be deliver'd to those who had none of their own. on this being hinted, another Gentleman of the Town observe'd, that Arms in the hands of undisciplin'd Men were but of little use, and that it would be requisite to Train the Inhabitants at least once or twice a Week, and offere'd his own service for that Purpose; this Motion was unanimously approv'd of. Fanuel Hall being too small to contain the People it was propos'd to adjoin to Doct[r] Sewalls Meeting House,[23] which they did accordingly to the number of about three thousand as I then concluded; M[r] Otis was chosen Moderator, and at the request of the People, made his Harangue from the pulpit, The substance of what was then spoke tended to this purpose, That in case Great Britain was not dispos'd to redress their Grievances after proper applications, that the Inhabitants had then nothing more to do, but gird the Sword to the thigh[24] and shoulder the Musquet.[25]

---

1. This particular piece by "Clericus Americanus" comprised a series of nine queries, each expecting a positive response from the reader. The central thread of the argument was that the colonists rights and liberties were enshrined in the colonial charters, thus predating the doctrine of parliamentary supremacy and conferring on the colonies the right to "dissolve" the "political union" with Great Britain. The seventh query contained a provocative hypothesis:

   > Whether such men, (whether they are the King's ministers at home, or his Representatives in the Colonies), as are forming such plans and endeavouring to bring them into execution, which tend directly and immediately to dissolve the union of *Great-Britain* and the *Colonies*, and to bring the *Colonists* into a state of slavery, ought not to be considered and treated, both by *Great-Britain* and the Colonists, as avowed enemies to the *British Empire*?

Boston Gazette, 5 Sept. 1768. The author was the Rev. John Cleaveland of Ipswich, Essex Co., Mass, according to the Dorr Collection, 2: 227. Of the province's Congregational pastors, Cleaveland was one of most active on the side of the protest movement and Patriots during the Revolutionary War. See Christopher M. Jedrey, *The World of John Cleaveland: Family and Community in Eighteenth-Century New England* (New York, 1979).

2. Here FB unequivocally states that he relayed this information to a councilor (whose identity is not known). In addition, as Richard Archer noted, FB also informed merchant John Rowe. *As If in an Enemy's Country*, 99, 245n37; Anne R. Cunningham, ed., *Letters and Diary of John Rowe* (Boston, 1903), 174.

3. Samuel Adams: "By this he would insinuate that the better Sort of the People, and even the Generality of the Town, were well enough pleas'd with it. If the faction *only* took the Alarm, the Generality of the Town must have been included in the Faction . . . For in Truth, he had the Mortification of seeing the while Body of the People . . . thoro'ly awakened and alarmed at the sudden expectation of a military Force." *Appeal to the World*, 24.

4. Obscured in the fold of the binding, here and below.

5. The identity of this person is unknown.

6. Samuel Adams: "To what Purpose then did he relate them at all! It seems that he was full as *designing*, in communicating to Lord Hillsborough, as he was in communicating to the People, tho' his Designs were different: for the People were not to be told the *whole* that the Governor knew to be true; but his Lordship was to be induc'd to believe *more*:— In either case if the purpose could be served, Sincerity was out of the Question." *Appeal to the World*, 25.

7. The beacon was to warn the town and inland villages of invasion. A pole had first been erected on Beacon Hill in 1634.

8. The house of Captain George Erving (1738-1806), location unknown. Erving, a son of councilor John Erving, was a merchant and Whig who later broke with the protest movement to become a Loyalist.

9. Faneuil Hall.

10. Samuel Adams: "his own *few partizans*, who yet must be stiled '*the principal gentlemen*,' though expecting every Moment to be 'surrounded with all *their* Forces,' appeared inquisitive and *anxious* for the event!" *Appeal to the World*, 24.

11. This account partly follows the minute of the Boston town meeting of 12 Sept. reprinted in the *Boston Post-Boy and Advertiser*, 19 Sept. 1768.

12. Samuel Adams:

    > The main Question to the Governor was. Whether he had certain Expectation of the Troops? To which he answered with an artful Ambiguity, that he had private Advice, but no publick Orders about it. His private advice might have been *certain*; or he might have had *authentick* publick advice without public Orders about it . . . Being however somewhat press'd by the Committee who waited on him, he discovered a Duplicity for which he has a peculiar Talent, and said, that he would not have the Town *certainly* expect the troops; although he then expected them himself, and fully believed they were on their passage to from Halifax; and in this letter to Lord Hillsborough he tells him that it was at that very time his intention to communicate these Expectations of them *gradually*.

Appeal to the World, 26.

13. Samuel Adams:

> the simple truth of the Matter is, these Arms had for many Years been
> deposited in the Chests and laid on the Floor of the town hall; but the
> [*Faneuil*] Hall itself being burnt a few Years ago [*1761*], the arms were . . .
> carried to the Town House: after the Hall was Re-built [*1762*], the Town
> ordered their Removal there; and tho' it happened to be done at a Juncture
> when the Governor . . . talked much of the town's *revolting*, there was no
> other Thought in the minds of any.

Appeal to the World, 27. The order for returning the weapons to Faneuil Hall, to which Adams refers, is not recorded in the town minutes.

14. James Otis Jr.

15. *Reports of the Record Commissioners of Boston*, 16: 261-263.

16. An act declaring the rights and liberties of the subject, and settling the succession of the Crown, 1 Will. and Mary, c. 2 (1689), popularly known as the Bill of Rights. Samuel Adams: "The Governor indeed takes notice of our claim to a certain clause in the bill of rights . . . but as we are free British subjects, we claim all that security against arbitrary power, to which we are entitled by the law of God and nature, as well as the British constitution. And if a standing army may not be posted upon the subjects in one part of the empire, in a time of peace, without their consent, there can be no reason why it should in any other." *Appeal to the World*, 27.

17. Massachusetts's Province Charter (1691).

18. The selectmen's circular letter was one of the few documents obtained by the provincial government that was seditious, in as much as the selectmen exceeded their legal authority in summoning a convention of Massachusetts towns. FB contested that any such meeting was an illegal combination. See **No. 691**. TH agreed, observing that the circular was the product of several "weak but very criminal votes" taken in the town meeting. TH to Thomas Whately, Boston, 5 Oct. 1768, Mass. Archs., 25: 2 in Hutchinson Transcripts, 1: 281-282.

19. Samuel Adams: "Here then is the treason and misprision of treason, or a part of it least, about which there has been such an Eclat of late." But the selectmen's precept "was nothing more than a *friendly circular letter* . . . [*a*] very innocent measure. . . . Here is the burden of the song—*extraordinary measures!*" *Appeal to the World*, 28-29.

20. The Charter of Massachusetts Bay (1629).

21. The proceedings of the Boston town meeting of 12 Sept. printed in this newspaper probably alarmed British politicians when it was received in London on 27 Oct. The printers Edes and Gill later euphemistically reported that "the Expectation of People in general of the Consequence of those Proceedings was much raised." Such "Expectation" was "increased" by news of the Convention of Towns until apprehensions of disturbances in Boston were allayed by news brought in by Capt. James Scott on 5 Nov. that the British troops "were quietly landed" in Boston. *Boston Gazette*, 30 Jan. 1769.

22. *Bernard Papers*, 5: 115-118.

23. Joseph Sewall (1688–1769), minister of the Old South Meeting House, 1713–69.

24. "Gird thy sword upon *thy* thigh, O *most* mighty, with thy glory and thy majesty." Psalms. 45:3, KJV.

25. Minutes of the town meeting of Boston, 12 Sept. 1768, NEP, f 81. The first line of the document could imply that the original was written after the Regulars' arrival, which is unlikely given FB's reference to its contents in the letter printed above. Alternatively, the date might have been added for clarification by historian and Board of Trade clerk George Chalmers, whose late eighteenth-century transcription is the only surviving copy of the informer's report. Appended to this transcript was a report of a speech by James Otis Jr., reproduced in the source note to **No. 672**.

682 | To the Earl of Hillsborough

Private

Boston Sep 17 1768

My Lord

I beg your Lordships ^favor^ in accepting my most grateful Acknowledgements of my Sense of the Honor your Lordship has done me by the Intimation of your kind Intentions towards me by my Lord Barrington.[1] My whole Merit consists only in doing my Duty; if it is inhanced by the Difficulties which have attended it, I owe it in a great Measure to Accidents which have given me an Opportunity of showing those Principles, which ever have & I hope ever will form the Rule of my Conduct. It will be therefore with the greatest Humility that I shall receive the further Marks of His Majestys Favour by which he shall be pleased to distinguish me.

As to the Honor proposed for me, all private Considerations would induce me to decline it.[2] But there is a Consideration of a public Nature which has influenced me to examine how far the Difficulties which lie in the Way of my accepting this Honor are capable of being removed. This is a Reflexion on the Nature & Use of Honours accompanied with a little Self Flattery that even in my insignificant Person an Example might be held forth to encourage other Governors to adhere to their Duty, & discourage a ^the^ People from attempting to ru[in?] a Governor for his Fidelity to the King; in which within this Province they have more than once succeeded. Upon this Account I have desired some Time to consider of this Proposal.

The Offer of the Government of Virginia I most thankfully accept, supposing I shall hold it on the same Terms as the immediate Predecessor. I want Peace & Quiet; & it becomes Time that I should have them. For tho my Constitution is pretty good, & the firmness of my Mi[nd][3] has never failed me, so that I have borne the Insolence of the Faction, which has harrast this Government for above 3 Years, better than most Men would have done; yet I find that I am worn & want a little Rest; which it seems I may expect in Virginia. Besides it is high Time, wh[ile] I remain fit for Business, that I should make so[me] better Provision for my large Family than I have hitherto done; this Government being never much more than a Subsistence, & for these last 3 Years having fell short of that.

The Leave of Absence which your Lordship has been so good as to procure for me comes very Opportunely; when fresh Troubles are arising, which will make my Service here of very little Use to his Majesty: For in my Opinion all hopes of restoring Peace to this Government by conciliatory Measures are over. Nor is it less timely as to the Use I may be of at Westminster. For it seems to me that the true

State of this Country has never been well understood there[,] at least untill the Idea that your Lordship seems to have of it, took Place. I therefore shall embark by the first Opportunity, which I hope wont exceed a fortnight.

I am &c

The Earl of Hillsborough

L, LbC   BP, 7: 43-45.

In handwriting of Thomas Bernard. Minor emendations not shown. This letter was probably never sent, for reasons explained below, and FB substituted **No. 683** instead.

    With FB now making ready to leave Boston for England before the Regulars arrived from Halifax, he eyed the prospects of the baronetcy and the lieutenant-governorship of Virginia with some relish. But he was obliged to give up his plans upon receiving **No. 661** on 18 Sept. announcing the departure of two regiments from Ireland and Lord Botetourt's appointment as Virginia governor.

---

1. **No. 610**.

2. FB's principal concern was the cost of the commission, up to £400, as Barrington acknowledged in **No. 610**. He had asked Barrington for time to consider the offer (**No. 666**).

3. Obscured by tight binding here and below.

683 | *To the Earl of Hillsborough*

Private

Boston Sept 18 1768

My Lord

    I had just finished a Packet to your Lordship the last Letter of which I wrote Yesterday.[1] In this I took the Liberty to address your Lordship with my most grateful Acknowledgements of my Sense of your Lordship's kind Intentions towards me as signified by ~~your~~ ^my^ Lord~~ships Letter~~ Barrington.[2] This Afternoon I received your Lordship's Letter No 16,[3] which contains Orders of so important a Nature that I must consider my Leave of Absence which I had obtained thro' your Lordships Recommendation to be suspended until the Orders I have now received shall be so far executed as to restore Authority to this Government. This will probably prevent my returning before this Winter: for I shall fully consult the Exigencies of his Majesty's Service In the Use I make of that Indulgence.

I am also informed by your Lordship's Letter of the Appointment of Lord Botetourt to be his Majesty's Lieutenant & Governor General of Virginia.[4] This I understand defeated the Expectation which had flattered me upon the Receipt of my Lord Barrington's Letter of May 9, which I answered immediately after its Receipt. I must not conceal from your Lordship that this is a Disappointment to me; But I am so used to consider his Majesty's Service as the first Concern that I shall chearfully submit to this Intervention, especially as I am so well assured of your Lordships kind Intentions towards me. And indeed my Lord what I have said in the former Letter of Yesterday is too true; I am so worn by the severe Service which I have gone thro' for above 3 Years past; that I fear my Health & Spirits will not last thro much more of the like. And yet probably much more is to come before the Province is brought into Order. I will endeavour to execute his Majesty's Commands in such a Manner as shall preserve the Credit I have gained with your Lordship & will inform you of the Success from Time to Time.

I am &c

The Right honble The Earl of Hillsborough

L, LbC   BP, 7: 45-46.

In handwriting of Thomas Bernard. FB sent the RC of this letter in place of **No. 682**.
    FB did not surrender all hope of being moved to Virginia. TH noted that "the Governor I fancy will not determine whether to go home or not until Lord Botetourt arrives. I rather think he will go but it is far from certain."[5]

---

1. **No. 682**.

2. **No. 610**.

3. **No. 661**.

4. In fact Botetourt was appointed as a full governor, on the understanding that he remain in residence (whereas previous governors were absentees).

5. TH to Richard Jackson, 5 Oct. 1768, Mass. Archs., 25: 282, in Hutchinson Transcripts, 1: 281-282.

684 | To John Pownall

Boston Sep 20 1768

Dear S[r]

I have received both your kind Letters of July 9 & 30[1] and am much obliged to you for your friendly Professions of an Attention to my Intrests. I am sensible that you never have been without it; and must congratulate myself that you are placed in a Station which will afford you frequent Opportunity of exercising your Regard for me.

The Hint you have given me of my appearing to want Confidence in Government has been partly explained in some private Letter[s] which have ^been^ communicated to me. I learn that my Speech, my Answer to the Town, My giving Way to the Populace &c have done me much Injury, so that my Want of Spirit in conducting the new Measures is much suspected. As for my Speech (I know not which is meant) & my Answer to the Town,[2] I would ask what Concessions have I made that I ought not to have done; or what else is blameable in them except using civil Words; & of what Service at that Time would have been the Use of harsh Words? As for giving Way to the Populace (in whose Hands, be it observed, I have been left for above three Years) I would again ask what have I given up to them which I could maintain? And how would it have served his Majesty's Cause for me to have provoked the People, in whose Power I was, to have knocked me on the Head or drove me out of the Town.

They who suspect my Want of Spirit should go back to the latter End of the Year 1765 & the beginning & greater Part of 1766; when my Friends in Vain endeavoured to persuade me to consult my Safety at the Expence of my Duty; let them read my Speech on Oct 25 1765,[3] of which the L[t] Gov[r] said some time after, that he was surprised to see me in the Province so long after I had made that Speech. In this spirited Conduct I persisted till I found it did not agree with the System at Home, which required lenient Measures & soft Speeches to bring about Conciliation without Correction. I knew that this would not do with the People I had to deal with; but I could not dispute about it: And now the System is changed, & spirited Measures are found necessary, why should it be supposed that I cannot reassume such a Conduct under the Assurance of being supported, when I so readily assumed upon my own Judgement only, without knowing whether I should be supported or not? All the Reason that I see for such a Suspicion is, that I was not, at 3,000 miles distance, acquainted with the political Change at the Time it took Place at London; & continued to act upon the old System before I was well informed of the new one.[4]

I am indeed a good Deal worn with my former Service, which has been severe & dispiriting for 3 Years past; & I had Expectations that I was even now going to receive my Reward in being placed in a Station where I should have Health Peace & Competence. I carried my Expectations so far as to engage a Cabbin & fix upon a Day for embarking. But since the Kings Service requires that I should continue here in further station, I submit cheerfully to my Destination; & hope I have Strength enough to serve another Campaign. If the Dispute lasts much longer, it will be too much for me. I therefore hope that my Lord Hillsboroughs kind intentions towards me will be kept alive till they have their full Effects & that at no ^great^ Distance of Time.

I am &c

J Pownall Esq[r]

L, LbC   BP, 6: 146-148.

In handwriting of Thomas Bernard. Minor emendations not shown. A red line in the left margin marks the second paragraph to the closure. Variant in *Select Letters*, 61-63.

Disappointed at having to remain in Boston, FB vented his frustration at an unnamed British correspondent who had criticized his "Want of Spirit." In this letter he also alludes to the earl of Shelburne's policy of "lenient Measures & soft Speeches" that he believed were unsuited to the rigors of imperial administration.[5] He held Shelburne responsible for British failings to support his government properly in the aftermath of the Stamp Act Crisis. Shelburne resigned the secretaryship of the Southern Department on 21 Oct. 1768, leaving Grafton's cabinet. It is possible that this letter was read by Grafton's cabinet, whose favorable reaction was noted by John Pownall in **No. 714**.

1. **Nos. 647** and **662**.
2. **No. 677**.
3. This is an error. He meant 25 Sept. 1765. *JHRM*, 42: 118-123.
4. See Shelburne's letter approving FB's conduct as governor, **No. 566**, *Bernard Papers*, 3: 407-409.
5. See **No. 501**, *Bernard Papers*, 3: 224-225.

685 | To the Massachusetts Convention of Towns

By his Excellency FRANCIS BERNARD, Esq; Captain General and Governor in Chief of the Province of *Massachusetts-Bay*, and Vice-Admiral of the same.

To the Gentlemen assembled at *Faneuil* Hall under the
Name of a Committee of Convention.

As I have lately received from his Majesty strict Orders to support his constitutional Authority within this Government,[1] I cannot sit still and see so notorious a Violation of it, as the Calling an Assembly of the People by private Persons only. For a Meeting of the Deputies of the Towns is an Assembly of the Representatives of the People to all Intents and Purposes; and it is not the calling it a Committee of Convention that will alter the Nature of the Thing.

I am willing to believe that the Gentlemen who so hastily issued the Summons for this Meeting were not aware of the high Nature of the Offence they were committing; and they who have obeyed them have not well considered of the Penalties which they will incur if they should persist in continuing their Session and doing Business therein. At present Ignorance of Law may excuse what is past: A Step farther will take away that Plea.

It is therefore my Duty to interpose at this Instant, before it is too late. I do therefore earnestly admonish you that instantly and before you do any Business, you break up this Assembly and separate yourselves. I speak to you now as a Friend to the Province, and a Well-wisher to the Individuals of it.

But if you should pay no Regard to this Admonition, I must as Governor assert the Prerogative of the Crown in a more public Manner. For assure yourselves, (I speak from Instruction) the King is determined to ma[in]tain[2] his entire Sovreignty over this Province; and whoever shall persist in usurping any of the Rights of it, will repent of his Rashness.

FRA. BERNARD.

Province-House, Sept. 22d, 1768.

newspaper, PC   CO 5/757, f 433.

Transcribed from the copy printed in the *Boston Gazette*, 26 Sept. 1768 and enclosed in **No. 691**. The RC has not survived. Also printed in the *Boston News-Letter*, 29 Sept. 1768. Thomas Cushing, on behalf of the Convention, replied with **No. 688**.

With the province assembly having been dissolved, the Boston selectmen organized a congress of representatives from the Massachusetts towns, meeting at Faneuil Hall between 22 and 29 Sept. Attended by one hundred delegates (of whom fewer than half had been elected to the House of Representatives that year), the Convention did not pretend to function as an assembly, despite what FB alleged in in this letter. Behind FB's accusation was the imputation that in ignoring protocol, which demanded that the king's governor summon any assembly, the Convention was acting as if royal power was in abeyance. (FB might have drawn upon the historical analogies of the seventeenth-century English convention parliaments, see source note to **No. 691**). The Massachusetts Convention ignored FB's threats and proceeded to business. Shortly after receiving this letter the Convention petitioned FB protesting the imminent arrival of the British soldiers and warships and demanding that the General Court be summoned.[3]

---

1. **No. 661**.

2. Correction to a typographical error in the original.

3. The Convention's petition of 22 Sept. was printed in the *Boston Gazette*, 26 Sept. 1768.

686 | *To the Earl of Hillsborough*

N.º 23

Boston Sep 23 1768

My Lord

Upon the receipt of your Lordship letter N.º 16[1] I ordered a Council to be called on the morning of Monday last: at which time I communicated the two first paragraphs of your Lordship's letter, & also a Letter from Gen.l Gage to me wherein he writes that in obedience to his Majesty's commands He had ordered 2 regiments from Halifax to Boston, the one to be quartered at Boston, the other at Castle William; and desiring that quarters might be provided for them.[2] The Council instantly resorted to the Act of parliament[3] & there it was read that if there were no Barracks, The troops should be quartered in the public houses,[4] & if they were not sufficient, then the Governor and Council or in their default the Justices of peace should hire barnes outhouses &c for them. They therefore said that as there were no Barracks, they had nothing to do with it; for it was the Business of the Constables to billet them in the public houses, & the Council had nothing to do till the public houses were full. I answered, that they must be sensible that this Act of parliament (which seemed to be made only with a View to marching troops) could not be carried into execution in this Case. For if these troops were to be quartered in public houses

& thereby mixt with the people their intercourse would be a perpetual Source of affrays and bloodsheds; and I was sure that no Commanding officer would consent to having his troops separated into small parties in a town where there was so public & professed a disaffection to his Majesty's British Government. And as to hiring barnes outhouses &c it was mere trifling to apply that clause to Winter quarters in this Country; where the Men could not live but in buildings with tight walls & plenty of fireplaces. Therefore the only thing to be done was to provide barracks; and to say that there were none was only true, that there was no building built for that purpose; but there were many public buildings that might be fitted up for that purpose with no great inconvenience. At last what I said produced a Committee of Council to confer with the Selectmen about providing quarters for the troops: and the Council was adjourned.[5]

I had no Opinion of this refere[nce][6] but could not avoid consenting to it. I considered that the Selectmen were the tools of the Faction; & the Design of the latter was to embarras the business of providing quarters so as to oblige the Officers to make good their own quarters; & from thence to ground an insurrection of the people against the invaders of their property. I was told 2 or 3 days before this Council met, that Otis explained the Plan at the Town meeting (or at some other Meeting about the same time, I forget which) in the following manner. "There are no Barracks in the Town; and therefore by Act of parliament they must be quartered in the public houses. But no one will keep a public house upon such terms, & there will be no public houses. Then the Governor and Council must hire Barnes Outhouses &c for them; but no body is obliged to let them; no body will let them; no body will dare to let them. The Troops are forbid to quarter themselves in Any other manner than according to the Act of parliament, under severe penalties. But they can't quarter themselves according to the Act: and therefore they must leave the Town or seize on quarters contrary to the Act. When they do this, when they invade property contrary to an Act of parliament We may resist them with the Law on our side."[7] So here is a System to make an Act impracticable & then to oppose the Kings Troops for not observing it. Indeed the Act is impracticable enough without all this contrivance. But what is most surprising is that So many persons of consideration & property should join in supporting a Scheme, which if it is carried into it's full Execution, must involve this Town into universal Desolation & Ruin, in order to save a few desperate & wicked Men from being made answerable for their Crimes. And yet your Lordship will find the forementioned System of reasoning adopted by Men, from whom One could not expect to have heard it seriously mentioned.

At the next Council, which was yesterday,[8] the Committee reported that the Selectmen had given for Answer that there was an Act of parliament for the quartering troops & they had nothing to do with it; but gave it for their Opinion that it would be most for the peace of the Town that the two regiments expected from

Halifax should be quartered at the Castle. That in regard to the Troops expected from Ireland, It was time ^enough^ to think of them; as it would be a long time before they would arrive; & ^most^ probably they would not come here before Winter: for Mr Hancock one of the selectmen had told them, that he had advice from London, that the troops ordered from Ireland would not sail till after the parliament met. And the Gentleman who reported said that if they were to sail this fall it would be so late, that probably they would not get in [in] these Seas till Winter was set in & then they would be drove off the Coast. __ In this manner was your Lordship's positive Notice of the ordering these Troops to embark immediately & his Majestys orders thereupon treated.[9]

After the Report was made, followed sevral Speeches all tending to give reasons why they could not provide barracks for the reception of the Troops. It was strongly urged that the Act of parliament directed how to quarter the troops & they could not depart from it. I reminded them that at the last Council it was generally agreed that it would never do to quarter the Troops in public houses; for it would produce the utmost disorder throughout the Town; and they must be sensible that Troops could not live in the Winter of this Country in barnes outhouses &c. That I did not want them to act against the Act of parliament, but to carry into Execution the first part of it which recommended the troops being put into barracks as the most preferable disposition; & thereby avoid resorting to the latter parts of it which had been admitted by them to be impracticable. They Answered that if they were to follow the Act of parliament, the Barracks at the Castle ^which were in the Town of Boston^ must be filled before they could demand other quarters. That the barracks at the Castle would hold the whole of the 2 regiments from Halifax. I observed that they confounded the Words Town & Township; that the Castle was indeed in the Township of Boston but was so far from being in the Town that it was distant from it by water 3 miles & by land 7. Besides in the generals orders there was an express distinction between the Town & the Castle, one regiment being to be quartered in the Town & the other at the Castle; that it could not thereby be intended that both should be quartered at the Castle. And in your Lordships orders that the 2 regiments from Ireland should be landed at Boston It could not be conceived that your Lordship imagined that the Castle; which was known to stand upon an Island some miles distant from Boston was in Boston & that in executing those orders it would be sufficient to land those regiments at the Castle. But It was insisted that Town & Township was the same, and that the Castle was in the Town of Boston; and that as the Act had directed the Barracks to be first used, neither the General's ^nor your Lordships Letters^ could alter the Law: and one Gentleman added that If there had been other Barracks in the Province tho' at 50 miles distance, they must be filled, before any quarter could be demanded at Boston. I told them that this fallacious way of reasoning, however it might flatter them, would not pass elsewhere; and particularly they never would be able to persuade the Commanding Officers, who are ^ordered^ to land their troops at Boston, to land them at the Castle. And therefore as the Officer would certainly bring their troops into the Town, if no barracks were provided for them they would in their own defence be obliged to take possession of some of the public buildings & make barracks for themselves. I was then told by one Gentleman that ^as^ It was sup[osed] that the troops would be under my command, if they should come into the town & take quarters contrary to Law, I should be charged as the Author of it. I replied that whatever power I might have over the Troops, I certainly should not have that of requiring them to disobey their Orders. On the other hand I desired them to consider what they would have ^to^ answer for, if by refusing to concur with me in providing barracks for the troops, they should oblige them to provide their own quarters, & thereby afford a pretence for the Enemies of the public peace to draw the people into an opposition to the Kings troops, which they had in Vain attempted to bring about previous to this landing. I then gave them the Account of the declaration of Otis upon this subject as mentioned in pa 2 & 3 of this letter: and I might have added that it was long ago since I first heard that it was the intention of the Faction to embarras the business of quartering the troops & thereby set them and the people together by the Ears. In the Course of this dispute It was frequently urged on the side of the Council, that they had no power to draw money out of the Treasury for building or fitting up barracks. This Argument was allways ready at hand when any plan was proposed for the purpose. As I saw We were like ^to rise^ without doing any thing I was reduced to make a proposal as my ultimate effort. I observed that Col Dalrymple with the two regiments from Halifax were expected evry day; that the Barracks at the Castle, altho' they had held 1000 men for a short time in the Summer, yet they would not hold much more than a regiment ^with convenience^, & Col Dalrymple certainly would not consent to take less than a regiment to Boston. Therefore Accommodations for one regiment ought immediately to be provided. That there was the Manufactory house (a brick building belonging to the province) now wholly unappropriated, and inhabited only by self settlers who are ready to go out at a days Warning.[10] This building with a ^small^ addition to it for Officers, would hold a regiment. I therefore desired that they would authorise me to fit up this building with the addition; & I would assure them, that if the Assembly should refuse to allow this Expence I would engage to recommend it to the Kings Ministers, so that it should be paid by the Crown & they should be indemnified from it. When this was done we should have time to consider of providing for the two regiments from Ireland. If they refused this, I did not see how they could clear themselves from being charged with a design to embarras the quartering the Kings troops nor of the Consequences which might follow the obliging the troops to make good their own quarters. I spoke this so forcibly, that some of them were stagger'd, & desired further time to consider of it: I therefore adjourned the Council to this day, & since on account of the Weat[h]er to tomorrow. I have since spoke with sevral of them & they all tell me that I shall never get a Vote for providing barracks for the Troops at Boston. One of them pleasantly said, "what can you expect from a Council who are more affraid of the people than they are of the King?"[11]

Sep 24

The bad weather continuing, I am obliged to postpone the Council to another day as sevral of them come out of the Country & would not attend on this day. And as there are 2 ships ready to sail as soon as the storm is over,[12] I shall probably send away this letter and its duplicate before I can bring this business to a conclusion. I am sorry I am obliged to give your Lordship a detail so disgraceful to the body which is the Subject of it. But it is necessary as well to my Vindication, as to give your Lordship a true Idea of the present State of this Government. I shall pursue this Narrative till I have finished it. In what I shall have to write upon o[ther] parts of your Lordships letter I shall have frequent occasion to observe how impossible it will be for me to execute his Majesty's commands according to his expectation, untill I have a Council more dependent upon the King than the present is.

I am with great respect, My Lord, Your Lordships most obedient
and most humble Servant

Fra Bernard

The right honble The Earl of Hillsborough

P.S. Sept 24

After I had finished this letter, I received a Message from the Council to inform me they were ready to give an Answer to my proposal made at the last Council. I accordingly met them & received the Answer, in which they positively refuse to do any thing for providing for the troops expected from Halifax except fitting up the barracks at the Castle. And for the troops expected from Ireland they absolutely refuse to make any provision, but shall leave them to be billeted according to the Act of parliament; which they know to be impracticable under the present Circumstances of the Town.[13] I am sorry to see this Spirit got so high in the Government: It can end in nothing else but obliging the Troops to prov[ide][14] their own quarters. I cannot act in this myself: all that there is left for me to do is to give up the Manufactory house for the use of the Troops. This I will do without the Council, tho' I foresee it will create a clamour. They have taken back their Answer to correct some mistakes. I shall receive it tomorrow & will send your Lordship a Copy with my observations on it.

I am with great respect My Lord, Your Lordships most obedient
and most humble Servant

Fra Bernard

ALS, RC   CO 5/757, ff. 414-418.

Endorsed: Boston Sept[r] 23[d]: 176[8] Gov[r] Bernard (N[o] 23) R 3[d] Nov[r]: A.50. Variants: CO
5/767, ff 97-98 (L, RLbC); BP, 7: 47-56 (L, LbC); *Letters to the Ministry* (1st ed.), 56-62;
Letters to the Ministry (repr.), 75-83. Copies were laid before both houses of Parliament on
28 Nov. 1768. HLL: American Colonies Box 3.
    The Council delivered their objections to quartering the soldiers in a lengthy answer
to FB on 26 Sept., printed in the *Massachusetts Gazette* the same day.[15] FB discussed this
document in **Nos. 690** and **693**.

---

1. **No. 661**.

2. **No. 676**.

3. Parliament was obliged to renew the Mutiny Act of 1703 annually (as with 5 Geo. 3, c. 7, for example).
A Mutiny Act was also passed specifically for the American Colonies, 5 Geo. 3, c. 33 (1765); widely
known as the Quartering Act, it provoked sustained opposition from the New York Assembly during
1766. The discussion in this letter refers to the provisions of this particular act. During FB's governorship, the Quartering Act was continued by 6 Geo. 3, c. 18 (1766), 7 Geo. 3, c. 55 (1767), 8 Geo. 3, c.
19 (1768), and 9 Geo. 3, c. 18 (1769).

4. That is inns and taverns or "uninhabited" buildings owned by the province or local authority, but not
private dwelling houses. The first section of 5 Geo. 3, c. 33 stated:

> civil officers as aforesaid, are hereby required to billet and quarter the offi-
> cers and soldiers, in his Majesty's service, in the barracks provided by the
> colonies; and if there shall not be sufficient room in the said barracks for
> the officers and soldiers, then and in such case only, to quarter and billet
> the residue of such officers and soldiers for whom there shall not be room
> in such barracks, in inns, livery stables, ale houses, victualing houses, and
> the houses of sellers of wine by retail to be drank in their own houses or
> places thereunto belonging, and all houses of persons selling of rum, bran-
> dy, strong water, cyder or metheglin,* by retail, to be drank in houses; and in
> case there shall not be sufficient room for the officers and soldiers in such
> barracks, inns, victualling and other publick ale houses, that in such and no
> other case, and upon no other account, it shall and may be lawful for the
> governor and council of each respective province in his Majesty's domin-
> ions in *America*, to authorize and appoint, and they are hereby directed and
> impowered to authorize and appoint, such proper person or persons as they
> shall think fit, to take, hire and make fit, . . . for the reception of his Maj-
> esty's forces, such and so many uninhabited houses, outhouses, barns, or
> other buildings, as shall be necessary, to quarter therein the residue of such
> officers and soldiers for whom there should not be room in such barracks
> and publick houses as aforesaid.

The Council, therefore, in following the letter of the law had found one means of obstructing the relocation of soldiers to public buildings within Boston, and leverage to get them put into barracks on Castle Island.

* Spiced mead.

5. The Council proceedings of Monday 19 Sept. are in CO 5/827, ff 59-60. The committee comprised James Bowdoin, John Erving, Thomas Flucker, Harrison Gray, Thomas Hubbard, James Pitts, and Royal Tyler.

6. Obscured in the fold of the binding.

7. FB did not quote or cite James Otis Jr. at the Council meeting, whose proceedings he accurately summarized in this letter.

8. 22 Sept. 1768, in CO 5/827, f. 60.

9. The Boston selectmen reported to the Council committee on 21 Sept.

> The Selectmen having considered the Motion of a Committee of the Council of this Province respecting the Regular Troops soon expected from Hallifax, waited on said Committee this Day and acquainted them that it was their Opinion that the Act of Parliament relative to Billeting Troops, points out, that when any Barracks are provided by any of the Colonies where Troops shall be sent, that such Troops shall be quarter'd in those Barracks; and further that the Barracks Erected on Castle Island at the Province Charge for the purpose aforesaid are fully sufficient to receive the said Troops.

Reports of the Record Commissioners of Boston, 21: 308-310.

10. Earlier in the year, the town of Boston and local merchants had tried unsuccessfully to establish a linen manufactory using the workhouse poor, under the direction of John Brown and funded by public subscription. *Reports of the Record Commissioners of Boston*, 16: 249-250. Richard Archer notes that, at 140 foot in length and with two stories, the building was sufficiently spacious to accommodate an entire regiment. *As If an Enemy's Country*, 108.

11. Closing quotation marks supplied.

12. It was reported as "a smart N. E. storm with rain" which lasted from Thursday 22 Sept. until Sunday 25th. *Boston Chronicle*, 26 Sept. 1768.

13. CO 5/827 ff. 60-61.

14. Manuscript torn.

15. This was a special issue of the *Massachusetts Gazette* by Richard Draper (1726/7-74), proprietor of the *Boston Weekly News-Letter*. He altered his newspaper's title in recognition of a commission from the Governor and Council to print government documents: the *Massachusetts Gazette and Boston News-Letter* ran between 22 May 1766 and 19 May 1768, and the *Massachusetts Gazette and the Boston Weekly News-Letter* from 28 Sept. 1769 to 7 Sept. 1775. The record-book version of Council's address is in CO 5/827, ff 61-62.

687 | To Thomas Gage

Boston Sep 24 1768

S^r

Last Sunday I received a Letter from the Earl of Hillsborough[1] informing me that his Majesty had ordered two regiments from Ireland to be sent over immediately to America & landed at Boston & commanded that I do, in concert with you, take any necessary Measure for the reception & accommodation of these troops. Before I wrote to you I was desirous of learning what dependance I could have upon the Council to assist me in this business. I therefore on Monday[2] laid this letter & also your letter of Sep 12,[3] which I had deferred to that time, before the Council & enforced their providing for the Service in the best manner I could.

You must know that there are no Barracks at Boston, that is, no building appropriated as such. And you must observe that where there are no barracks the Act[4] directs that they shall be quartered in public houses; & where those fail the Governor & Council are to hire Barns, Outhouses &c for quartering the soldiers. Now It is obvious that neither of these methods will do at this time & in this place. For if the soldiers were quartered in public houses & thereby intermixed with the Towns people in the humour they are in at present, it would occasion perpetual feuds & affrays between the Soldiers & the People; it would occasion frequent desertion, for which no encouragement would be wanting, as has been declared to be intended. It has been also publickly declared that when the Soldiers came to be quarter'd in public houses, All persons keeping such houses would give up their Licenses & there would be no publick houses. And it has been also said that when the Governor & Council come to hire buildings, No one would, no One should let them any. And then It is concluded, Let the Soldiers come into private houses if they dare. This Plan has been laid some time ago & has been very lately explained in public.

At the meeting of the Council I urged these and other Reasons to show that there was nothing to be done upon this occasion but to fit up some of the public buildings for barracks & named some that might be evacuated without much inconvenience; or in part to run up slight barracks for the present: for that It would be very dangerous to quarter the Soldiers so as to intermix them with the people. This was generally agreed to; but how to fit up barracks was the question, as they had no command of the public money. At length it was agreed to confer with the Select men of the Town upon the Occasion.

On the Thursday after it was reported that the Selectmen would do nothing in the business but left it to the Act of parliament.[5] And the Council after declaring that the Barracks at the Castle were in the Town of Boston (as they are within the bounds of the Township) notwithstanding it entirely contradicted his Majesty's orders in both respects they refused to do any thing at present but fit up those barracks, alledging that they will hold the two regiments from Halifax. And as for the two regiments from Ireland, it would ^be^ time enough to provide for them when they came.

Being unwilling to let them part without doing something, I proposed to them that If they would authorise me to fit up the Manufactory House (a brick building belonging to the province & now unappropriated) to hold one of Col Dalrymple's Regiments; I would engage, that if the Assembly should refuse to pay the charge, I would recommend it to be paid by the Crown. They desired time to consider of it & have this day, in a writing condemning [6] the Ordering troops to Boston, refused to concur with me in fitting up that building or even consenting to the appropriating it to this Service; & adhere to doing nothing but fitting up the barracks at the Castle, which is 3 miles from Boston by Sea & 7 miles by land & therefore cant answer the purposes intended by sending troops to Boston.

I will however of my own Authority appropriate the Manufactory house, but have Nothing to fit it up with. And when I have done this, which will make a clamour, I have done all I can: for I know not of any other public building that I can pretend a command over. There will then remain difficulties on evry side: One cannot think of dispersing the Men about the Town, or quartering them otherwise than in a body; if they make good their own quarters, as might be done in the workhouse & the poorhouse it would be improved for the worst of purposes: and yet I dont see how the Kings Orders can be executed without it. There seems to be but one alternative, which is to run up hasty barracks at the Expence of the Crown. This would disappoint the whole combination: But this must be done by order of your Excellency: for I have neither money nor Authority for it. When Col Dalrymple comes I will introduce him to the Council: but I dont expect He will have more weight with them than I have; for I have left nothing unsaid. But they fear the People more than they do the King.

I am with great regard, S[r] your most obedient and most humble Servant

Fra Bernard

His Excellency Gen[l] Gage

ALS, RC   Gage, vol. 81.

Minor emendations not shown. Endorsed: Govr Bernard. Boston Sep[t]. 24th. Received Oct[r] 1st: answered ___   Variants: BP, 7: 199-22 (L, LbC) and CO 5/86, ff 209-212 (L extract, Copy). Gage replied with **No. 697**.[7]

The Council delivered their objections to FB on 26 Sept., here printed in full:[8]

The Board have taken into their further consideration General Gage's Letter and the Extract from Lord Hillsborough's Letter communicated by his Excellency on the 19th. instant relative to the reception and accommodation of the Troops in the said Letter and Extract mentioned, and have also considered his Excellency's proposal of the 22nd. instant relating to the Manufactory House in Boston that they would authorize him to take measures for fitting up the said Building for the reception of so many of the said Troops as it will conveniently accomodate. They have also attentively considered the act of Parliament providing among other things for the Quartering and Billetting the said Troops, and they find that the Civil officers in the said Act mentioned and no others are thereby impowered and "required to Quarter and Billet the Officers and Soldiers in his Majesty's Service in the Barracks provided in the Colonies; and if there shall not be sufficient Room in the said Barracks for the Officers and Soldiers then & in such case only to Quarter and Billet the residue" of them in such manner as in the said act is further and very particularly directed. Now it appears by this paragraph of the said act that in any Colony where there are Barracks the said Officers and Soldiers in his Majesty's Service shall be Quartered and Billetted in such Barracks and in no other place unless there shall not be sufficient room in the Barracks. With respect to this Colony the Government of it in the begining of the late War by their Order caused Barracks to be built at Castle William for the very purpose of accomodating his Majesty's Troops whenever it should be necessary for them to come hither; under which order the Governor and Council are authorized to provide Quarters in the said Barracks for such Troops; and those Barracks are sufficient to accomodate about one thousand Men, which number it is said the two Regiments ordered from Halifax will not exceed. Those Regiments therefore which are the first expected the said Act of Parliament requires to be quartered in the said Barracks.

General Gage however in his Letter aforesaid mentions that one of the said Regiments is ordered for the present to Castle William, the other to the Town of Boston: But it will be no disrespect to the General to say that no Order whatsoever coming from a less authority than his Majesty and Parliament can supersede an Act of Parliament. And it is plain the General had no intention that the said Order should, as he concludes his Letter by desiring the Governor to see that the said Troops are provided with Quarters on their arrival in this Government as by Law directed. The said Act also provides, "that if any Military Officer shall take upon himself to quarter Soldiers in any of his Majesty's Dominions in America otherwise than is limited and allowed by this act, or shall use or offer any menace or compulsion" & he shall be "*ipso facto* Cashiered and be utterly disabled to have or hold any military employment in his Majesty's Service." His Excellency therefore as the Board apprehend must clearly see by examining the said Act that it is not in the power of the Board to provide Quarters for the said Regiments destined 'till the Barracks at Castle William and the Inns Livery Stables and other Houses mentioned in the said Act shall be full; (in "which and no other case and upon no other account it shall and maybe lawful for the Governor and Council" to take the measures they are directed to by the said act for the reception of His Majesty's forces;) nor of consequence to authorize his Excellency to take measures for fitting up the Manufactory House agreable to his proposal.

The Quartering of Troops in the body of the Town before the Barracks are full is not only contrary to the Act of Parliament, but would be inconsistent with the peace of the Town whose peace and welfare, as also the peace and welfare of the Province in general, it is the duty, Interest and inclination of the Board to promote, and which in every way consistent with Law they will endeavour to promote to the utmost of their ability.

As the Board on the 19th instant when the Letters abovementioned were first communicated to them advised that his Excellency give proper Orders for the accomodation of one of the Halifax Regiments in the Barracks at Castle William, so they now further advise that his Excellency give like Orders for the accomodation of the other Halifax Regiments in the said Barracks.

With regard to the two Regiments ordered from Ireland to Boston, the Board doubt not that provision will be made for their accomodation agreable to the Act aforesaid.

That the Board might be better able to give their advice in regard to the Regiments ordered hither they thought it necessary that the whole of Lord Hillsborough's Letter so far as it related to the said Regiments and to the occasion and design of their coming should be communicated to them, and they accordingly desired his Excellency to communicate it. But though His Excellency was pleased to tell them he should very probably lay the whole of it before the Board in such parcels and at such times as he thought proper, yet as they apprehend the propriety their own conduct in a great measure depends on the communication of the whole of it together, they again request his Excellency to favour them with it.

With regard to the occasion of the said Regiments being ordered to Boston, his Excellency being asked informed the Board that he apprehended the Halifax Regiments were ordered hither in consequence of the Riots in March last, and the two Irish Regiments in consequence of that of 10th June last. On which the Board are obliged to observe that they are fully persuaded his Majesty's Ministers could never have judged it either necessary or expedient to go into such extraordinary measures as those of sending Troops hither unless ^in^ the Representations made from hence by some ill minded persons the said Riots had been greatly magnified and exaggerated.

With respect to what happened on the 18th March which was a day of Rejoicing and on such days disorders are not uncommon in populous places, it was too inconsiderable to make it a subject of Representation, and could not have been made the subject of so injurious an one but by persons disposed to bring misery and distress upon the Town and Province.

In regard to the Riot of the 10th. of June of which the Board have repeatedly expressed their abhorrence and have advised that the perpetrators of it should be prosecuted by the attorney General, the Board have in their answer to his Excellency's Representation laid before them the 27th. of July last given a just account of the last occasion of that Riot; and as they apprehend it necessary that the said account together with all the proceedings at that time should be made public, they again desire his Excellency will order the said Representation and Answer to be Printed as soon as may be in the public Newspapers.

---

1. **No. 661**, received on Sunday 18 Sept.

2. 19 Sept. 1768, in CO 5/827, ff 59-60.

3. **No. 676**.

4. The Quartering Act, 5 Geo. 3, c. 33 (1765).

5. *Reports of the Record Commissioners of Boston*, 20: 308.

6. FB objected to some of the passages in the first draft agreed on 24 Sept. But he gave permission for the Council to redraft the paper without requiring presentation at another meeting. However, the meeting to approve the new draft on 26 Sept. (from which FB was absent) was disputatious as FB's enemies tried to push through a draft highly critical of him. See **Nos. 686** and **689**.

7. *Bernard Papers*, 5: 71-73.

8. CO 5/827, ff 61-62.

688 | *From Thomas Cushing*

May it please your Excellency

The Committees from a Number of Towns in this Province, now conven'd at Faneuil-Hall, having received from your Excellency a Message[1] containing a Remonstrance against our thus Meeting, and an Admonition to break up and seperate ourselves instantly, and before we do any Business, have taken the same into our serious and attentive Consideration; and we assure your Excellency, that tho' according to the best of our Abilities, we have considered the Matters that are hinted by your Excellency as the Foundation of your Message yet we are not able to collect sufficient Information therefrom, to place our present Meeting and Proceedings in the same Light in which they seem to lie in your Excellency's Mind. We do assure your Excellency most fully, that neither the Views of our Constituents in sending us, nor the Design of any of Us in thus Meeting, was to do, propose or consent to any Thing oppugnant to, or inconsistent with, the regular Execution of Government in this his Majesty's Province; and that tho' the Letters from the Selectmen of the Town of Boston, to the respective Towns from which we come, might first give Rise to our being chosen and sent; yet that neither the said Letter from the Selectmen of the Town of Boston,[2] nor any Votes of the said Town accompanying the same, were considered by our respective Towns in the choosing, nor by us in our assembling, as the Foundation and Warrant of our convening.[3] But, may it please your Excellency, being assured, that our Constituents, as well as our selves, have the most loyal and affectionate Attachment to the Person and Government of our rightful Sovereign King GEORGE the Third, we beg Leave to explain to your Excellency the real Cause and Intention of our thus convening.

Your Excellency cannot be unacquainted with the many difficulties under which his Majesty's Subjects on the whole Continent of America, apprehend themselves to labour, and of the Uneasiness which his Subjects in this Province have repeatedly expressed on the same Account. The minds of the People who have sent us, are greatly disturbed that the humble and dutiful Petition of their Representatives[4] for the Removal of those Difficulties has not been permitted to reach the Royal Ear; and they are greatly agitated with the Expectation of a Standing Army being posted among us, and of the full Exertion of a Military Government; alarm'd with these Apprehensions and deprived of a House of Representatives, their Attention is too much taken off from their daily Occupations; their Morals and Industry are in Danger of being damaged, and their peaceable Behavior disturbed for want of such Persons as they can confide in, to advise them in these Matters, and to make Application for their Redress.

Your Excellency will further naturally conceive that those of his Majesty's Subjects who live remote from Boston, the Center of their Intelligence, and whose Occupations do not admit of much Knowledge of public Affairs, are subjected to many Misrepresentations of their public Concerns, and those generally of a most knowing Persons among us to wipe off the pernicious Effects of such Rumours, without the Appearance of a public Enquiry.

Induced by these Motives, and others of the same Kind, our Constituents thought it no Ways inconsistent with good Order and regular Government, to send Committee-Men to meet with such Committees as might be sent from the several Towns in the Province, to confer upon these Matters, and learn the Certainty of those Rumours prevailing among us, and to consult and advise as far as comes legally within their Power to such Measures as would have the greatest Tendency to preserve the Peace and good Order among his Majesty's Subjects, and promote their due submission; and at the same Time to consult the most regular and dutiful Manner of laying our Grievances before our most gracious Sovereign, and obtaining a Redress of the same. This we assure your Excellency is the only Cause and Intention of our thus convening; and we are exceeding sorry it should be view'd by your Excellency in an obnoxious Light.

Your Excellency may be assured, that had our Constituents conceived, or did their Committees thus conven'd, conceive this Proceeding to be illegal, they had never sent us, nor should we pretend to continue our Convention: But as your Excellency in the Message with which you have been pleased to favour us, has not been so explicit in pointing out the Criminality of our present Proceeding as we could have wished, but has left us to our own Judgment and Understanding, to search it out, we would with all Duty to your Excellency, as the Representative of our rightful Sovereign, request your Excellency to point out to us wherein the Criminality of our Proceedings consists, being assured we cautiously mean to avoid every Thing that has the least Appearance of Usurpation of Government, in any of its Branches, or any of the Rights of his Majesty's Sovereignty even a mental Disaffection to the Government by Law established and exercised.

Your Excellency will be pleased in your well known Knowledge of human Nature, and the Delicacy of British Privileges, to be sparing in your Frowns on our present Proceeding, we being at present inclined to think, 'till better inform'd that if Criminality be imputed to us, it will be applied only to our Doings, and not to be the professed manner and Design of our Meeting: But if your Excellency has a different Apprehension of the Matter, we intreat an Explanation of the same; and assure your Excellency we shall deliberately attend to it. Nothing could give us more Uneasiness than a Suggestion that our Proceedings are criminal; not so much from a Fear of personal Punishment, as from fix'd Aversion we have to any Thing inconsistent with the Dignity of our Sovereign, and the Happiness of his extended Dominion; and we flatter ourselves that when the real Designs of this Convention is understood, it will prove an argument to evince the intire Loyalty of his Majesty's Subjects in this Province, and their Disposition to Peace and good Order.

In the name and Behalf of the Committees of a number of Towns in this Province, and conven'd in *Boston*— *September* 24th, 1768.

Thomas Cushing, Chairman

newspaper extract, **PC**   CO 5/757, f 433.

Transcribed from the copy extracted from the *Boston Gazette*, 26 Sept. 1768 and enclosed in **No. 691**. The RC, which was a reply to **No. 685**, has not survived. Cushing's letter was also printed in the *Boston News-Letter* and the *Boston Evening-Post*, 29 Sept. 1768.

Thomas Cushing's letter was delivered to FB by a committee on Saturday 24 Sept. It was prepared in response to a message from FB instructing the Massachusetts Convention of Towns to disperse on the grounds that it was an illegal combination (**No. 685**).[5] The

Convention challenged the governor to prove the "Criminality" of their proceedings, since the assembled delegates did not purport to assume the authority of the dissolved House of Representatives, and knew that FB would struggle to acquire firm evidence of any treasonable action on their part. As the last paragraph shows, the Convention assumed that FB would examine the Convention's proceedings for evidence of treason, and probably did not expect that the governor would exhibit the selectmen's circular summoning the Convention (**Appendix 13**). The Convention dispersed when the British flotilla of transports started arriving in Boston harbor.[6]

1. **No. 685**.

2. **Appendix 13**.

3. Such an argument could have been used by defense counsel in the event of treason charges being brought against the Boston selectmen, which proceedings the Convention evidently feared.

4. The House of Representatives, petition to the king, 20 Jan. 1768, which Hillsborough had refused to present to the king. See **No. 712n6** and **No. 730n7**, *Bernard Papers*, 5: 117, 163. The petition is in *JHRM*, 44: 217-219.

5. See also FB's brief discussion in **No. 691**.

6. For the proceedings see the *Boston Gazette* on 26 Sept. 1768.

689 | *From Thomas Gage*

New York Sep.[t] 25th: 1768.

Sir

your Letter of the 16th Ins.[t][1] was delivered to me on the 21st in the morning: and on the Evening of the same Day a number of Letters from Boston were received by People in this Town,[2] to acquaint them of the noble Resolutions taken at the Town meeting held at Faneuil Hall.

Whatever may be my private Opinion, concerning the Firmness of your Sons of Liberty, when the Day of tryal comes, I shall prepare for the worst. And you may be assured that I shall exert all my Powers, as far as I can exert them with Propriety in support of the Rights of the King and Kingdom of Great Britain; and to defeat all Traiterous Designs against them.

Should any Body of Rebels have gained Possession of the Castle, thro' the Treachery of the Garrison before the Troops arrive, The ships of war, from the Reports made to me of the Situation of the Castle, will soon be able to drive them out of it. From what has happened, I can no longer be leader of putting the King's Troops in Garrison in the Castle,[3] and fortifying it as well as we can; for which Purpose I have sent an Engineer[4] to attend the Troops in that Business, and given

Powers to Lieu⋅. Col⁰. Dalrymple to order a Detachment of the Royal Regᵗ: of Artillery from Halifax, together with such military stores as he shall have occasion for, and Such further Reinforcements of Troops, as Nova Scotia can supply.

The Colonel will be always able whatever number of Rebels may rise or however great their Determination, to secure Castle William, till larger Reinforcements can be collected and I am taking every measure to collect them as speedily as possible, and to prepare them for service.

I am with great Regard Sir, your most obedient, humble servant

Thoˢ Gage

His Excellency Govʳ. Bernard

ALS, RC   BP, 11: 307-310.

Endorsed: General Gage Sepʳ 25ᵗʰ 1768. The letter was personally delivered by Capt. John Montresor on 30 Sept.[5]

FB's letter of 16 Sept. (**No. 680**), in which he announced his intention to leave Boston before the Regulars arrived, left Gen. Thomas Gage worried that Bostonians were planning to resist the landing of the troops. New York was also awash with rumors that the Bostonians "had revolted," as Capt. Montresor later explained to FB, and that the Sons of Liberty aimed to seize Castle William.[6] Gage's patronizing depiction of the Boston resolutions as "noble" imputed the tragedy of Bostonians being led into conflict by leaders whose own "Firmness" in standing up to British Regulars he very much doubted. He certainly had no doubts about Col. Dalrymple's willingness to use force against the inhabitants if necessary.

---

1. **No. 680**.

2. Also, the proceedings of the Boston town meeting of 12 Sept. were reported in the *New York Journal*, 24 Sept. 1768.

3. Presumably, Gage had thought seriously about coming to Boston shortly after Col. Dalrymple had landed the troops. He did not come to Boston until 15 Oct.

4. John Montresor (1736-99) was a captain in the 48th Regiment of Foot, and a British military engineer with considerable experience of designing North American fortifications.

5. According to **No. 695**, *Bernard Papers*, 5: 68-70.

6. See **No. 694**, *Bernard Papers*, 5: 63-68.

690 | To the Earl of Hillsborough

Nº 24

Boston Sep 26 1768

My Lord

I now send your Lordship a Copy of the Councils Answer to me concerning providing barracks for the troops, & what is extraordinary, in print; which shall be explained in order. In the ps of my last,[1] I informed your Lordship that the Council sent to me on Saturday[2] to desire that I would meet them to receive their Answer to my proposal of setting up the Manufactory House. At that time there was a Violent Storm of Wind & Rain & I was at my Country house at Roxbury 5 miles from Boston.[3] I thought by their being in such an hurry that they intended to do something; and as there was no time to be lost, I determined not to regard the Weather but set out immediately for Boston: and I therefore was surprised to find that I was sent for in such a storm meerly to receive a refusal. For I was not in the secret then, & did not know that all this hurry & drawing me thro' the worst Weather I allmost ever travelled in was to get their Writing thro' so that they might print it in the public papers on Monday.

I mentioned to your Lordship that they had taken back their Answer to correct some mistakes. These Mistakes were, mentioning sayings of mine which I never said & couching insinuations which I did not deserve. Upon my explaining these passages, it was said that nothing was intended against me, & that they would alter the passages to my satisfaction; and they offered to do it directly. I told them that I had rather that they should take it back & reconsider the whole: for it seem'd to me that it wanted alteration upon their Account as well as upon mine. It was objected that it would cause the unnecessary trouble of calling another Council: I answered that as there was nothing to be advised or ordered, I would consent that they should deliver the paper, when corrected, to the Secretary, without calling a council in form.[4]

They met early next Monday morning in the Council chamber, when they made some little alterations to remove what I had excepted to, which however was not done fully. After which It was moved (neither myself nor the Secretary being present) that this Answer should be printed in one of the papers of that day. This was opposed & occasioned some little debate, when the Question was put & determined in the affirmative 7 to 3: among the 7[5] was one Gentleman who rather acquiesced[6] than Approved; the other 6 being firm[7] in this System. In the course of this debate & also in the first bringing in this paper one Gentleman argued against it & protested[8] against some parts of it. Another took him[9] aside & said "you had better not distinguish yourself in this Opposition; the Council are determined not to alter a Word in this paper; they are resolved to adhere to the people." The same last mentioned Gentleman, in arguing for the printing, said, "I have no immediate communication with them (meaning the Sons of Liberty) but I know pretty well what is going on by my intimately conversing with many of the middling people. I say it again ^& again^ & would have it well understood, that if We dont print the Answer to the Governor this day, there will soon be no Government."

Accordingly they immediately sent for one of the printers of the Government Gazette & ordered him to stop his press, & gave the only Copy of the Answer to him, to set the press by, immediately after it was finished. I came into the Council chamber a little after 11 & there I found[10] one of the Council with the printer correcting the press: after which & not before, the paper was delivered to me.[11] I told the Gentleman that I would immediately represent this to his Majesty as the highest insult that ever was put upon a Kings Governor. He answered that there was no intention of affronting me. I replied that most probably there was not ^personally^; for I had never deserved to be ill used by them: but there was a great affront put upon the King in his representative; and it was my business to resent that.

To show the high Nature of this usurpation, I must observe that the Council (except in their legislative capacity) have no activity of their own without the Governor; they are by Charter appointed to advise & assist the Governor, & therefore they cannot meet without the Governor nor can act in Any business but what he proposes. Indeed it is has[12] been usual to appoint Committees to prepare papers for the Council; but then such papers are reported to the Governor in Council and have no Validity untill they are confirmed there. But for a Council to meet without the Governor, to appoint a Committee, to meet again & receive the report of the Committee, to admit a Motion for printing their proceedings & put the Question upon it, & to order the proceedings to be printed without the Governors consent or knowledge & even before it was reported to him, is alltogether a transaction never known or imagined before, & wholly illegal ^& unconstitutional^. There is but one way to make it regular, & that is to consider the Council as meeting in their legislative Capacity; this indeed will make all right; & they will form an upper house to the Assembly of Representatives now sitting in Convention;[13] and then there will be nothing wanting to render it a compleat general Court but the Authority ^and Representative of the King^. If All this coming together does not operate so as to produce an amendment (at least) of the Charter, Wise & Good Men who want to see the Authority of the Kings Government restored, or rather rebuilt upon a more ^firm^ foundation, will be disappointed. There is but one rational Way of accounting for these proceedings of the Council so contrary to their conduct about 7 months ago: and this is, that they are desirous to lend an hand to the Convention to bring about a forfeiture of the Charter; which, considering how they have heretofore been treated by their constituents, they may well be supposed to desire.

As to the Answer, I have little to say about it, having fully explained the System it is founded upon in my letter immediately preceeding. If it wants any thing more I will add a paragraph, which one of the Council proposed to be inserted in their answer to me, but it was rejected. This paper has by chance fell into my hands in the hand^writing^ of the proposer; and I will inclose a Copy of it.[14] It fully shows that there is an Intention of opposing the Troops by embarrassing their quarters & attacking them afterwards by means of such embarrassment; to justify which a formal System of Law is allready prepared. As to what the Council have desired for the printing a former Answer to me which I sent a Copy of to your Lordship with my Letter N⁰ [*blank*],[15] your Lordship must understand that since the Council (I mean the Majority of them in & about the Town of Boston) have gone over to the popular party, (the day of which revolt is precisely fixed) they have been Very fond in imitation of the Faction of the House, to do business by writings calculated for the press. The paper referred to[16] was plainly written for that purpose: but I prevented it's being published hitherto; & shall, notwithstanding this public ^call^ added to many private. In regard to the present publication, Upon the first opening this business I charged their proceedings with Secrecy; and the only pretence to Evade this charge is that I did not renew that charge at ev'ry adjournment, tho' the same business was continued.

And now, My Lord, I consider this Government as intirely subdued. The Outworks have been taken by degrees. The Citadell ^(the Council)^ however remained to the King untill within these 3 months. Now, that is surrendered; and the Garrison has joined the Enemy. To speak plain, Now the Council cooperate with the Opponents of Government, & they whose business it is to advise & assist me do all they can to embarrass me; they who ought to join with me in executing the Kings commands are at the head of those who oppose them. What can I do? Circumstanced as this Government at present is, *Ipsa Salus non potest servare hanc rem publicam.*[17] If the 3 Regiments ordered to Boston were now quietly in their quarters, (which I don't see how they are like to be by the means of the civil power only) It would not follow that the Civil Government could resume its functions: It will take sometime to recover that intimidation & *Lacheté*[18] which has pervaded all orders of Men. I shall write more particularly upon this subject when I write in an answer to the other parts of your Lordships letter, which the present emergencies prevent.

I am, with great respect, My Lord, your Lordships most obed^t
& most humble Servant

Fra Bernard

The right honble the Earl of Hillsborough.

ALS, RC   CO5/757, ff 419-422.

Endorsed: Boston Sept: 26. 1768. Gov[r] Bernard (N[o]. 24). R 3[d] Nov[ber]. A.51.   The annotations refer to the names provided in the enclosed "List of the Council who passed upon
the Answer [*of the Council of 26 Sept. 1768*]," CO 5/757, f 429. Enclosures: [*proposed
addition to the draft answer of the Massachusetts Council of 26 Sept.*], CO 5/757, ff 423-424;
copies of the minutes of the Massachusetts Council of 19 and 22 Sept. 1768, attested by
Andrew Oliver, ibid, ff 423-428; a copy of the Answer of the Massachusetts Council of 26
Sept., printed in the *Massachusetts Gazette*, 26 Sept. 1768, ibid., f 430; and a "List of the
Council who passed upon the Answer," ibid. f 429; a postscript dated 30 Sept. (**No. 693**).[19]
The packet carrying the RC sailed on 28 Sept.[20] Variants: CO 5/767, ff 108-114 (L, RLbC);
BP, 7: 56-62 (L, LbC); *Letters to the Ministry* (1st ed.), 62-65; *Letters to the Ministry* (repr.),
83-88. Hillsborough acknowledged receipt with **No. 712**.[21] Copies of the letter together
with the enclosures were laid before both houses of Parliament on 28 Nov. 1768. HLL:
American Colonies Box 3.

FB had lost influence with the Council following the nonelection of TH and Andrew
Oliver in 1766. This document further reveals that moderates like Thomas Flucker were
being courted by their more radical colleagues, preeminently James Bowdoin and Royal
Tyler, and joined them in drawing up the Answer of 26 Sept. rejecting FB's request to find
quarters for the British soldiers. FB refused to accept (as Tyler insisted to Flucker) that the
Council were driven by the imperative to placate a restless a public. What unsettled FB,
of course, was that in absolving themselves of any responsibility for bringing the troops to
Boston, the Council (like the House) necessarily blamed FB for precipitating the crisis.
Hereafter, a core group of ten or eleven councilors dominated proceedings, aiming to frus-
trate FB in virtually all matters pertaining to British colonial policy.

---

1. **No. 686**.

2. Saturday 24 Sept.

3. One newspaper reported that on Thursday 22 Sept. "came on here, a smart N. E. storm with rain"
    which continued until the Sunday. *Boston Chronicle*, 19-26 Sept. 1768.

4. The Council's draft was composed by Bowdoin, Gray, and Tyler and is filed with the minutes of the
    Massachusetts Council, 22 Sept.-5 Oct. 1768, Bowdoin and Temple Papers, Loose MSS. FB probably
    objected to a passage proposed and written by James Bowdoin and included in the final version:

    > his Majesty's Ministers would never have judged it either necessary or ex-
    > pedient to go into such extraordinary measures as those of sending Troops
    > hither unless in y[e] representations made from hence by some ill-minded
    > Persons the s[ai]d had been greatly magnified and exaggerated.

5. Authorial annotation in left margin: "1.7.8". These particular numbers indicate, respectively, that coun-
    cilors Samuel Danforth, Thomas Flucker, and James Russell voted in the negative.

6. Annotation: "5.": Thomas Hubbard.

7. Annotation: "3.4.6." and line below "[8.]10." The first set refers to William Brattle, James Bowdoin, and
    Harrison Gray; the second set to James Russell and James Pitts.

8. Annotation: "7": Thomas Flucker.

9. Annotation: "9": Royal Tyler.

10. Annotation: "4": James Bowdoin.

11. The address appeared in the *Massachusetts Gazette*, 26 Sept. 1769.

12. Thus in manuscript.

13. Summoned by the Boston selectmen, the Massachusetts Convention of Towns which gathered at Faneuil Hall between 22 and 29 Sept. was not a reconstituted House of Representatives, as FB suggests, for its membership was substantially different and the meeting did not purport to assume legislative powers. See Richard D. Brown, "The Massachusetts Convention of Towns, 1768," *WMQ* 26 (1969): 95-104.

14. Whigs Bowdoin, Pitts, and Tyler are the likely authors. While the proposed addition stated that any resistance to the Regulars as they came ashore was rebellion and high treason, it reasoned that

> yet if upon a sudden Quarrel, from some Affront given or taken, the Neighborhood should rise & drive the Forces out of their Quarters, that would be a great Misdemeanour, and if Death should ensue it may be Felony in the Assailants, but it will not be Treason, because there was no Intention against the Kings Person or Government.

CO 5/757, ff 423-424. In light of what happened in Boston eighteen months later and what modern scholars know about the risks of employing regular soldiers in a policing role, the councilors' advice seems sensible, though FB supposed it indicative of secret plans to assail the Regulars in their quarters.

15. After refusing quarters for the British soldiers, the Council's answer of 26 Sept. reviewed the disturbances in Boston of 18 Mar. and 10 Jun. which had prompted Secretary of State Hillsborough to dispatch the Regulars. At the meeting on 26 Sept., FB had refused to show the Council his correspondence with Hillsborough (**Nos. 622** and **660**)—though he declared his willingness to do so in the future. The Council then insisted that FB should order the printing of the Council proceedings of 27 Jul., the meeting at which he had first put the question to them whether or not the civil government should request military assistance; FB had sent a copy of these proceedings with **No. 660**.

16. The Council proceedings of 27 Jul.

17. Trans: "Even salvation herself cannot save the commonwealth." The quotation is probably an adaptation of T. Maccius Plautus, *Captivi* (*The Captives*), 3.3: "*ipsa si velit Salus, servare non potest,*" translated by Henry Thomas Riley, as "Salvation itself cannot save them." *The Comedies of Plautus* (London, 1912), accessible via the Perseus Digital Library (http://www.perseus.tufts.edu/hopper). I am grateful to my colleague John Taylor for his advice in this matter.

18. Italian for "the chat." Presumably "idle and irrelevant insolence" is meant.

19. According to CO 5/767, f 115.

20. According to **No. 694**, *Bernard Papers*, 5: 68-70.

21. *Bernard Papers*, 5: 115-118.

691 | To the Earl of Hillsborough

N.º 25

Boston Sept.ʳ 27. 1768

My Lord

In my letter N.º 22[1] I informed your Lordship of the Origination of calling an Assembly of Representatives under the Name of a *Committee of Convention*: notwithstanding that is the name of the body, the Members also all called Committees. So that for distinction sake We must call the body the Convention. This Convention is now sitting: they met on Thursday & did nothing that morning but choose a chairman & a Clerk, viz, the late Speaker & the Clerk of the House.[2] The same Morning I prepared a Message to this Convention & left it with Mr Oliver the Sec.ʳʸ to deliver in the afternoon. I wrote it wholly in my hand & my Name so written was in the title: but as it was not undersigned by me they refused to receive it.[3] This was only to gain time to send me a Message before they acknowledged the receipt of mine.[4] As they print what they do, your Lordship will have their own account of these proceedings. The 3 days last week they kept open doors; Otis was then absent. The two days this week they have kept the doors shut; Otis is with them. Whatever farther transpires I will inform your Lordship of it.[5]

It is now made a great Question in what manner Great Britain will resent this proceeding: for certainly, at the fountainhead it was ~~certainly~~ intended to provoke a resentment; the great principle of the faction being to raise & blow up fire. Some say, & especially in the Convention itself, that the persons assembling would be by Act of parliament ^render'd^ incapable of serving in any public office. But this seems to be at once too confined & too general a Censure. The Towns who chose these Deputies (next to that who issued the Summons) are answerable for this Convention; and, if they are a Majority of the Towns who send Members, as their own Accounts at the lowest assert, the Province is answerable. It is therefore concluded that the most probable Consequence will be the forfeiture of the Charter. If this is the worst, It is an Event most devoutly to be desired by evry well wisher to the province.

I am with great respect, My Lord, Your Lordships most obedient
and most humble Servant

Fra. Bernard

The right honble the Earl of Hillsborough.

ALS, RC

CO 5/757, ff 431-432.

Endorsed: Boston Septr. 27th. 1768 Govr Bernard (N° 25) R 3^d. Nov^ber A.52.　　Enclosed a copy of **No. 688**. Variants of letter in BP, 7: 62-64 (L, LbC); *Letters to the Ministry* (1st ed.), 65-66; *Letters to the Ministry* (repr.), 88-89. The packet carrying the RC sailed on 28 Sept.[6] Hillsborough acknowledged receipt with **No. 712**.[7] Copies of the letter together with the enclosure were laid before both houses of Parliament on 28 Nov. 1768. HLL: American Colonies Box 3.

　　The Massachusetts Convention of Towns was summoned by the Boston selectmen and met in lieu of the House of Representatives, but it was not its substitute, either in design or composition. Yet FB fully expected the British government to consider the Convention as meeting in defiance of royal authority to summon the province legislature. The assembling of delegates as a "convention" offered uncomfortable historical allusions to the English convention parliaments that had met without a royal summons in 1660 and 1689: the former had declared Charles II king while the latter proclaimed the abdication of King James II. The Glorious Revolution of 1688-89 offered another historical parallel: the Boston revolt that unseated King James's governor of New England, Sir Edmund Andros (1637-1742), in a bloodless coup. FB feared a demonstration and confrontation of some kind when the British soldiers arrived, and suspected the radicals of plotting to remove him from office.

---

1. **No. 681**.

2. Thomas Cushing and Samuel Adams.

3. **No. 685**. FB declared the Convention illegal and insisted that it disperse.

4. The Convention refused FB's demand with **No. 688**.

5. The Convention's proceedings were printed in the *Boston Gazette* on 26 Sept. and the *Boston News-Letter* on 29 Sept. 1768.

6. According to **No. 694**, *Bernard Papers*, 5: 63-68.

7. *Bernard Papers*, 5: 115-118.

692 | *To William Dalrymple*

Castle William Sep 30 1768

S^r

　　As you have informed me this Day that you have received orders from Genl Gage,[1] to land both the Regiments under your Command in the Town of Boston and that you intend to incamp some of the Regiments upon the Common and are desirous[2] to put the other into Barracks; for which purpose you have requested of me the Use of the building called the manufactory house which is a building belonging to the Province and at present not leased or appropriated to any Person or Purpose. I am sorry that I am obliged to observe to you that I have for 12 Days past earnestly desired the Council to assist me in fitting up Barracks for such Troops as are ordered to be quartered in the Town of Boston, in order to avoid the many inconveniences which must arise from the troops being put into quarters in publick Houses and thereby intermixed with the people of the Town; but have constantly met with a Refusal.

I am also obliged to observe, that at a Council held Yesterday in this Place, after you had informed me and the Council that you had orders to march one of the Regiments into the Town of Boston & that you should certainly obey such Orders; and you had added that if you had barracks assigned for their quarters, so that you could keep them in close quarters under the ~~Officers~~ Eye of their Officers, you would be answerable for the peace^a^ble and orderly Behaviour of the Men, but you could not answer for it if they were placed in open quarters soon to be intermixed with the people of the Town; I did thereupon move the Council to to[3] reconsider a proposal I had before made without Success, to fit up the Manufactory House for barracks for one Regiment which it was supposed it would hold.[4] And no material objection being made to fitting up that House as Barracks, except that the Council apprehended they had no Power to draw upon the Treasury for the Charge of fitting. I did propose to the Council that the Charge should be on the Credit of the King; nevertheless they did refuse to join with or assist me in fitting up such building for such Purpose.

I find it no Purpose to make any further Attempt to prevail upon the Council to assist me in providing barracks for the Troops. Nevertheless as it is my Duty to preserve the Peace of the Town by all means in my Power, for which it is necessary to prevent an intermixture of the Soldiers and the People, as it must certainly give frequent occasions for the ^breaking the^ Peace, I do hereby assign & appoint the Manufactory house being a building appropriated to no use, & belonging to the Province; & I do authorise you to take possession of the same as & for a Barrack for the quartering the King's Troops. In regard to the encamping the regiment I know of nothing wanting of me but to signify that I have no objection to it. As to the demand of Straw &c I shall lay it before the Council by the first Opportunity.

I am &c

Lt Col Dalrymple

L, LbC   BP, 7: 207-209.

In handwriting of clerk no. 9.

After the troops entered Boston on 1 Oct. without encountering resistance, Col. Dalrymple concentrated on finding appropriate and sufficient quarters for his soldiers. FB authorized use of the Manufactory House, but townspeople quickly frustrated the soldiers' occupation of the building.[5]

1. Dalrymple's letter not found. Gage to Dalrymple, New York, 25 Sept. 1768, MiU-C: Gage, vol. 81.

2. First written as "desired".

3. Thus in manuscript.

4. The Council proceedings of 29 Sept. are in CO 5/827, f 62.

5. See **No. 706**, *Bernard Papers*, 5: 96-101.

693 | *To the Earl of Hillsborough*

[Boston, 30 Sept. 1768]

Having since the finishing that Letter had an opportunity to meet the Council I enquired of themselves of the proceedings on Monday[1] for printing their answer to me; and finding it vary[2] from my narrative in some particulars, I am desirous that it should be corrected, being unwilling that there should be any misrepresentations even of Matters indifferent.

1. They say that a formal Vote was not taken; but admit that Care was had that the Opinion of every Gentleman should be known.[3]

2. They say that the division among them was not upon printing in general, but upon the time of printing, whether then or hereafter; which one Gentleman explained by saying that he was against the Printing it before it was presented to me; But another Gentleman declared he was against printing it at any time.

3. It seems that the copy which I saw the Gentleman[4] correcting, together with the Printer,[5] was not the Letter press of the Printer, but a Copy wrote for the Printer, which it is admitted was delivered to the Printer, before the Original was delivered into the Secry's Office for the Governor.

How far these Variations are material is left to your Lordship; but they make no difference in the Arrangement of the 10 Councillors employed in this business, who may be divided thus,

3. 4. 9. 10	Four principal Managers.[6]
2. 6	Two Aiders & Abettors.[7]
1. 5. 7	Three Acquiescers overawed.[8]
8.	One Opposer & protester thro' the whole.[9]

But however this is, it is agreed on all hands that it is the greatest blow that has been given to the King's Government here for this long while; And it is the heavier, as it comes from so respectable a body, as to be called tho' very improperly, His

Majesty's Council. It has had two evil Effects: The One to persuade the People that Troops would not have been sent here, if they had not been misrepresented; And all Charges of Misrepresentation are naturally applied to the Governor. Whereas they do not believe that a misrepresentation is the Cause of sending Troops hither; they must know that the plain facts were sufficient for such an effect; & that a Falsification of them was neither necessary nor practicable, as accounts are transmitted by so many hands that a false one must have been detected.

The other is that the People are told that the Execution of the King's Orders is contrary to Law; And the People are thereby encouraged to resist with a notion that they shall act with the Law on their side. In this Sense, considering all Circumstances, the Nature of the King's orders, the Ill-Temper of the People, & the Wickedness of those who have worked up that Ill-temper, & above all the Authority of the Writers & Publishers, it is the most inflammatory Paper that has been published. These are not my own Words, but taken from the Mouths of prudent & sensible Men; among whom this Proceeding is universally censured. And it is not doubted but it will receive a severe Censure at Westminster.

F.B.

L, RLbC   CO 5/767, ff 115-117.

Letterbook entry: Inclosure 6. Supplement to the above Letter N°. 24.[10] dated Sept[r]. 30. 1768. The RC was enclosed in **No. 690**. The numbers refer to the names provided in "List of the Council who passed upon the Answer [*of the Council of 26 Sept. 1768*]," CO 5/757, f 429, enclosed with **No. 690**. Variant in BP 7: 64-67 (L, LbC). Hillsborough acknowledged receipt with **No. 712**.[11]

---

1.   26 Sept.

2.   Thus in manuscript.

3.   From this point onwards, the handwriting is of a second scribe.

4.   James Bowdoin.

5.   Richard Draper.

6.   Respectively: William Brattle (1706-76), elected to the Council, 1755-68, 1770-73; James Bowdoin (1726-90), 1757-68, 1770-73; Royal Tyler (1724-71), 1764-70; James Pitts (1710-76), 1766-74.

7.   John Erving (1692-1786), elected 1754-74; Harrison Gray (1711-94), 1761-72.

8.   Samuel Danforth (1696-1777), elected 1739-74; Thomas Hubbard (1702-73), 1759-72; Thomas Flucker (1719-83), 1761-68.

9.   James Russell (1715-98), elected 1761-73.

10. **No. 690**.

11. *Bernard Papers*, 5: 115-118.

APPENDICES

Appendix 1

THE HOUSE OF REPRESENTATIVES' CIRCULAR LETTER TO THE SPEAKERS OF THE COLONIAL ASSEMBLIES

Province of the Massachusetts Bay.

February 11th. 1768__

Sir

The House of Representatives of this Province have taken into their serious consideration the great difficulties that must accrue to themselves and their Constituents, by the operation of the several Acts of Parliament imposing Duties and Taxes on y^e American colonies.

As it is ^a^ subject in which every Colony is deeply interested, they have no Reason to doubt but your Assembly is duly impressed with its Importance, and that such constitutional Measures will be taken by them as are proper. It seems to be necessary that all possible care should be taken that the Representations of the several Assemblies, upon so delicate a point, should harmonize with each other: The House, therefore, hope that this Letter will be candidly considered in no other Light than as expressing a disposition freely to communicate their mind to a Sister Colony, upon a *common Concern* in the same manner as they would be glad to receive the Sentiments of your or any other House of Assembly on the Continent.

This House have humbly represented to the Ministry their own Sentiments; That his Majesty's high Court of Parliament is the supreme Legislative power over the whole Empire: That in all free States the Constitution is fixed; and as the supreme legislative derives its power and authority from the Constitution, it cannot overleap the Bounds of it without destroying its own Foundation: that the Constitution ascertains and limits both Sovereignty & Allegiance[,][1] and therefore his Majesty's American Subjects who acknowledge themselves bound by the Ties of Allegiance, have an equitable Claim to the full enjoyment of the fundamental Rules of the British Constitution.

That it is an essential, unalterable Right in nature, ingrafted into the British Constitution, as a fundamental Law, and ever held sacred & irrevocable by the Subjects within the Realm, that what a Man has honestly acquired is absolutely his own, which he may freely give, but cannot be taken from him without his Consent; That the American Subjects may therefore, exclusive of any Consideration of Charter Rights, with a decent firmness adapted to the Character of Freemen & Subjects assert this natural Constitutional Right.[2] It is moreover their humble opinion, which they express with the greatest deference to the Wisdom of Parliament, that the Acts made there, imposing duties on the people of this Province with the sole and express purpose of raising a Revenue, are Infringements of their natural Constitutional Rights; because, as they are not represented in the British Parliament, his Majesty's Commons in Britain, by those Acts grant their property without their Consent.

This House further are of Opinion that their Constituents, considering their local Circumstances cannot by any Possibility be represented in the Parliament, and that it will forever be impracticable, that they should be equally represented there, and consequently not at all; being separated by an ocean of a Thousand Leagues, and that his Majesty's Royal Predecessors for this Reason, were graciously pleased to form a Subordinate Legislative here, that their Subjects might enjoy the unalienable Right of a Representation[;] and that considering the utter impracticability of their being fully & equally represented in Parliament, and the great Expence that must unavoidably attend even a partial Representation there; this House think that a Taxation of their Constituents even without their consent, grievous as it is would be preferable to any Representation that could be admitted for them there.

Upon these principles, & also considering that were the Right in the Parliament ever so clear, yet, for obvious Reasons it would be beyond the Rules of equity, that their Constituents should be taxed on the manufactures of Great Britain here, in addition to the Duties they pay for them in England, and other advantages arising to Great Britain, from the Acts of Trade; this House have preferred a humble dutiful and loyal Petition to our most gracious Sovereign, and made such Representations to his Majesty's Ministers as they apprehend would tend to obtain Redress.[3] They have also submitted to consideration, whether any people can be said to enjoy any degree of Freedom if the Crown in addition to its undoubted authority of constituting a Governor, should also appoint him such a stipend, as it may judge proper, without the Consent of the people, and at their expence; and whether while the Judges of the Land & other civil Officers in the Province hold not their Commissions during good behaviour their having Salaries appointed for them by the Crown independent of the people hath not a Tendency to subvert the principles of equity & endanger the happiness & security of ye Subject.

In addition to these Measures the House have wrote a Letter to their Agent M^r. Deberdt;[4] the Sentiments of which he is directed to lay before the Ministry, wherein they take notice of the hardships of the Act for preventing Mutiny & Desertion,[5] which requires the Governor & Council to provide enumerated articles for the king's Marching Troops, and the people to pay the expence, and also the Commission of the Gentlemen appointed Commissioners of the Customs to reside in America, which authorizes them to make as many appointments as they think fit, and to pay the appointees what Sums they please, for whose mal Conduct they are not accountable—from whence it may happen that Officers of the Crown may be multiplied to such a degree as to become dangerous to the Liberties of the people, by virtue of a Commission which doth not appear to this House to derive any such advantages to Trade as many have been led to expect.

These are the sentiments & proceedings of this House; and as they have too much Reason to believe that the Enemies of the Colonies have represented them to his Majesty's Ministers, and to the Parliament, as factious, disloyal, and having a disposition to make themselves independent of the Mother Country[,] they have taken Occasion in the most humble Terms to assure his Majesty & his ministers, that with regard to the people of this Province, and as they doubt not, of all the colonies, the Charge is unjust.

The House is fully satisfied that your Assembly is too generous and enlarged[6] in sentiment to believe that this Letter proceeds from an ambition of taking the Lead, or dictating to the other Assemblies: They freely submit their Opinion to the Judgment of others, and shall take it kind in your house to point out to them anything further which may be thought necessary.

This House cannot conclude without expressing their firm Confidence in the King, our common Head and Father, that the united & dutiful supplications of his distressed American Subjects will meet with his Royal and favorable acceptance.

Signed by the Speaker

A true Copy

Att[r]:[7] Sam[l]. Adams Clk

Ms, Copy CO 5/757, ff 30-33.

In handwriting of John Cotton, deputy to the province secretary. Endorsed: Circular Letter from the Assembly of the Massachusets Bay, to the Speakers of the several Assemblys on the Continent of America. In Gov[r]. Bernard's (N[o]. 4) of 18th: Febry 1768.

The House appointed a committee on 4 Feb. "to prepare a Letter to be transmitted to the several Houses of Representatives and Burgesses on this Continent." Known subsequently as the Massachusetts Circular Letter, the committee probably worked with a draft prepared by Samuel Adams before presenting an amended version to the House on 11 Feb.,[8] which was approved and entered into the House journals. *JHRM*, 44: 236-238. (The voting is reported in **Appendix 9**.) While Adams drafted numerous papers for the consideration of House committees, the final versions adopted should always be considered the work of committees (for historians have a tendency to ignore the contributions of his colleagues). James Otis Jr. subsequently claimed to have written the Circular Letter (and other documents since attributed to Adams) and suggested that Adams's principal contribution was as an editor refining Otis's prose. Otis's biographer concluded that this was a "boast that masked [*Otis's*] uncertainty" in his relationship with Adams. Nevertheless

Otis probably had a major part in revising Adams's original draft.[9] Adams's file copy of the final version is not substantively different from the version in the House journals. Harry Alonzo Cushing, ed., *The Writings of Samuel Adams*, 4 vols. (New York, 1904), 1: 184-188. The transcript printed above is based on a version that the deputy province secretary copied from the House journals and which FB transmitted to London enclosed in **No. 589**. This is the variant that British ministers would have read first. A summary of the transmitted copy was entered in CO 5/766, ff 109-115 (précis, RLbC). There are numerous printed versions of the Circular Letter, most based on the version in the House journals. The widely-used copy edited by Alden Bradford modernized spelling and grammar; some of its phraseology is different from FB's copy. *Speeches of the Governors of Massachusetts from 1765 to 1775: and the answers of the House of Representatives to the same; with their resolutions and addresses for that period and other public papers relating to the dispute between this country and Great Britain which led to the independence of the United States* (Boston, 1818), 134-136.

FB's stated objections to the Circular Letter were that it fostered intercolonial opposition to the Townshend Acts and reiterated the principle that any parliamentary tax was an infringement of colonial liberty. (**No. 589**.) He also would have disputed the contention that justification for the colonial position could be found in natural rights or that the "unalienable Right" of representation could only be realized in the colonial legislatures, as the letter maintained. And he would be have been angered by the letter's attack on Crown salaries for colonial governors. While the Circular Letter professedly acknowledged parliamentary supremacy and stressed loyalty to the Crown, the fact that the colonists were unrepresented in Parliament—and never could be practically—meant that they could not consent to taxation by that body. This construction by Samuel Adams was partly intended to avoid alienating moderates concerned about offending ministers.[10] FB's blunt assessment of the letter's intent reflected his wider anxieties that the early formulation constructed by the "Pennsylvania Farmer" to undermine the Townshend Acts had become Whig orthodoxy.

---

1. Obscured in the gutter of the binding, here and below.

2. *JHRM*: new paragraph.

3. *JHRM*: new paragraph.

4. House of Representatives to Dennys DeBerdt, 12 Jan., 1768, *JHRM*, 44: 241-250. DeBerdt's name was omitted from Bradford's transcript.

5. The Mutiny Act, 5 Geo. 3, c. 33 (1765).

6. Bradford: "liberal".

7. Abbreviation for "Attributed."

8. Speaker Thomas Cushing, Jerathmeel Bowers, Samuel Dexter, Joseph Hawley, James Otis Jr., and Ezra Richmond (c.1721-1800). *JHRM*, 44: 148, 157.

9. Waters Jr., *The Otis Family*, 173.

10. Alexander, *Samuel Adams*, 66-67.

Appendix 2

AMERICAN BOARD OF CUSTOMS TO
THE LORDS COMMISSIONERS OF THE TREASURY

May it please Your Lordships.

By our Secretarys letters of the 21st. of Nov[r]. to M[r]. Bradshaw,[1] we had the honor to inform your Lordships of the arrival of such of Us as came from England, and when we entered upon business, with some other occurences: and M[r]. Robinson having arrived on the 28th. we have ever since had a full Board.

After acquainting our Officers with our Commission, and giving them the necessary directions on the occasion, we ordered a state of the different Ports to be laid before Us; that we may be enabled to proceed to regulate such matters as we shall find necessary, as well as to give particular instructions to our Inspectors General, against they enter upon duty.[2]

It already appears to Us, that our Officers in these northern parts, and particularly in the Charter Colonies,[3] have been greatly discouraged for want of support from Government.

Tho' smugling has been carried to a very great height, yet six seizures only have been made in the New-England Provinces, within the course of two years and a half;[4] and only one prosecuted to effect.[5] a second was rescued out of the custody of our Officers at Falmouth, who were at the same time attacked by a mob.[6] A third was rescued at Newbury, and the Officers greatly abused.[7] A fourth was carried off clandestinely at New-London, while under prosecution;[8] the fifth and sixth were acquitted at Rhode Island, thro' the combination and influence of the people.[9] The Officers of this Port were resisted in the summer 1766, at noon-day, when endeavouring to enter the house of one Malcolm, and finding themselves unsupported against a numerous mob that was assembled, they were obliged to retire without making the seizure.[10]

These several matters were communicated to the Commissioners of Customs in London, but no measures have been taken to punish the Offenders or to strengthen the hands of Government. The Smugler[s][11] therefore with reason triumph in their success, and the Officers of the Revenue are deterred from exerting themselves with that vigour, & spirit, which the service requires.

The better to explain to your Lordships the difficulties which our Officers labour under, we beg leave to submit to your consideration the present state of Government in this country.

On the 14th Augst. the Sons of Liberty met, to commemorate that day of outrage in the year 1765, when the opposition to the Stamp Act begun; and intelligence being soon after received that the Acts of the last session of Parliament respecting America were passed, the news-papers in this town began to retail the most licentious publications, denying the right of Parliament to lay any taxes whatsoever on the Colonies: and some went so far as to assert the most unlimited independence.[12]

The minds of the people scarcely composed after the late tumults, were susceptible of every impression, and these doctrines agreeing with their democratic principles, were received with applause; and in a little time the frenzy of the people of this town was raised to such a height, that a forcible opposition to the execution of the new Laws was threatned; but thro' the interposition of the sensible and moderate part, it was considerably allayed by the beginning of November, when such of Us as came from England arrived and no act of violence was then commited, tho' every inflammatory art had been practised, to stimulate the people thereto, and we have ever since remained in safety, tho' not without some apprehentions, Mr. Paxton having undergone the indignity of suffering in Effigy.[13]

As every publication, be it ever so exceptionable, is sure to find access into most American newspapers, the principles therein broached are propagated with great success. Thus, the spirit which first shewed itself in this town, was diffused thro' the neighbouring Provinces, where the people seem to be as ripe for riot, and mischief, as they are here.

At Rhode Island it was proposed in an advertizement posted upon the townhouse, to stop the revenue money, which the Officers there were about shipping home.[14] At New-York sundry seditious papers have been dispersed, stirring up the people to a resistance. At Philadelphia, a series of letters are publishing in the Chronicle, under the name of the Farmers Letters, denying the right of Parliament to lay any tax whatsoever on the Colonies, and as the author affects moderation, and a parade of learning, we consider them of the most mischievous tendency.[15] Every thing that is said, or published in England, in favour of the Colonies, is peculiarly prejudicial, as the people in this country are led to believe, that their cause is powerfully espoused at home.

In these popular Governments there are frequent assemblies of the people at large, under the name of town meetings, which were originally instituted to regulate the prudential concerns of the towns, but now they are converted to answer political purposes.[16] At these meetings the lowest mechanics discuss upon the most important points of government with the utmost freedom; which, being guided by a few hot and designing men, become the constant source of sedition.

Men of character avoid these meetings, as the strongest lungs have generally the best of the argument, and they coud not oppose any popular measure, without being exposed to insult, and resentment.

Instead of opposing the execution of the new Laws by violence, as had been threatned, a plan of *œconomy & industry*, was set on foot, at one of these town meetings; the apparent design of which is to allarm the trading and manufacturing people of Great Britain, and to engage them in their interest, so as to obtain a repeal of the Laws, rather than to answer the ends and purposes pretended.[17]

An association was accordingly entered into in this town, whereby the articles now charged with duties, with many others, were to be entirely disused, and encouragement was given to manufacture the same among themselves; the consumption of British manufactures in general was to be discountenanced, and a preference given to those of America.[18] That this spirit might extensively prevail, the proceedings of the town meeting were transmitted to every town of note throughout the Continent, and we find the same measures adopted in the neighbouring Provinces,[19] and the news-papers of each, echo to the other, their great tho' but imaginary progress in manufactures. Few of the principal people of the town signed the association, and very few of the subscribers conform to the terms of it, which serves to shew Your Lordships that it is such a policy as we before suggested.

At a subsequent town meeting, instructions were given to the Representatives of Boston, to promote a remonstrance from the General Assembly, against the late Laws.[20]

The General Assembly is now siting, and the lower House has so far entered into their views, as to address His Majesty, and write to His Secretary of state on the subject, and to influence the other provinces to pursue similar measures, it was voted, a few days ago, that an account of their proceedings shou'd be transmit[ted] to the Speaker of every House of Representatives on the Continent.[21]

From this conduct of the lower House Your Lordships may form a judgment of the general sense and disposition of the people of this Province. We must nevertheless observe, that there are many people of property in this town, who might be induced to shew their countenance in support of Government, if the executive power had strength to protect them: property however has but little weight and influence in these popular Governments, places of trust and authority being acquired, and maintained, by trimming with, and courting the people.

While it is the general received opinion that the Acts imposing the late duties are unconstitutional the people will be easily persuaded not to pay any. And we do not know how soon that period may arrive, after they find themselves disapointed in their expectations of a repeal, in consequence of their remonstrances.

Our Officers were resisted and defeated, almost in every attempt to do their duty, when the right of Parliament to lay external duties was acknowledged; now, that the right of Parliament to lay any taxes whatever on the Colonies is denied, we have every reason to expect that we shall find it totally impracticable to inforce the execution of the Revenue Laws, untill the hand of Government is properly strengthned. At present, there is not a Ship of War in the province, nor a company of Soldiers nearer than New-York, which is two hundred and fifty miles distant from this place.

We herewith transmit to Your Lordships, a collection of News-papers, filled with publications derogatory to the honor and authority of Great Britain, and subversive of all order, and government, which have nevertheless been hitherto circulated thro' the different Colonies with impunity.[22]

We have not made any one privy to the contents of this memorial, as a Subject of this delicate nature, requires the utmost secrecy in the present feeble, and unhinged state of Government.

Which is humbly Submitted.

W^m. Burch[23]
Hen. Hulton.
J. Temple.
Chas Paxton
John Robinson.

Boston Feb^{ry} 12. <u>1768</u>.

The R^t. Honble. the Lords Commissioners of His Majestys Treasury

LS, RC   T 1/465, ff 21-24.

The enclosed file of newspapers has been not found, but some of the content is discussed in note 22 below. Variants of the letter in Temple Papers, 1762-1768: Bound MSS (L, Copy); CO 5/757, ff 60-63 (L, Copy); CO 5/226, ff 95-99 (L, Copy) a copy was enclosed in **Appendix 4**. John Temple's copy noted that the original was sent by the schooner *Lovely Betsey*, master W. Wilson, sailing on 24 Feb., and that the duplicate was dispatched to New York on 3 Mar. for transmission to London. Thomas Bradshaw, the Treasury secretary, sent a copy of the memorial to the earl of Hillsborough on 7 May (CO 5/226, f 95). The Treasury Board considered the memorial on 30 Jun. (T 28/1, f 332) and the Board secretary replied on 8 Jul. (CO 5/226, f 105). The secretary of state for the Colonies reiterated governors' responsibilities to assist the American Board of Customs (**No. 612**).

The assertion (in the final paragraph) that the memorial had not been shown to anyone outside the Board did not mean that FB was without influence in its composition. Many of the incidents referred to had been already reported in FB's correspondence (for which see the notes below), as FB would have told the commissioners. John Temple and John Robinson also would have been able to brief their colleagues about events in the province since the Stamp Act Crisis. There is no indication in this letter that Temple and Robinson disagreed with their colleagues' analysis of provincial affairs despite their previous disagreements with FB.

The Customs Board's memorial initiated the policymaking process that was to result in the Chatham administration sending troops and ships to Boston to support FB's government and the Customhouse in their daily duties (**Nos. 622** and **661**). Meanwhile, the Customs Board copied their memorial to Commodore Samuel Hood, commander of the North Atlantic Station, requesting "immediate" naval protection for their officers. The HMS *Romney* left Halifax on 9 May and arrived in Boston harbor on 17 May, and HMS *Magdalene* and HMS *Little Romney* on the following day; eight other Royal Navy ships came and went in early July.[24] On 14 May, the Secretary of State Hillsborough dispatched a circular to colonial governors reminding them of their responsibility to provide the commissioners with "all the Assistance and Support" in their "Power."[25]

---

1. T 1/461, ff 266-267.

2. Thus in manuscript.

3. Massachusetts, Connecticut, and Rhode Island.

4. That is, since the summer of 1766.

5. The *Polly*, a Rhode Island vessel, was seized in Apr. 1765, condemned in the Vice Admiralty Court at Halifax, and sold in Jun. 1766. See *Bernard Papers*, 2: 244. John Temple's account of the seizure and rescue of the *Polly* at Taunton in May 1765 is in **Appendices 3.3** and **3.4**, *Bernard Papers*, 2: 502-516.

6. **No. 493**, *Bernard Papers*, 3: 204-205.

7. **No. 454**, ibid., 120-121.

8. Collector Duncan Stewart had seized fourteen hogsheads of illegally imported rum on 20 May 1767 at East Haddam, whereupon they were rescued from the Customs House store on 8 Jun. *Connecticut Gazette*, 3 Jul. 1767.

9. The "fifth" seizure was by John Robinson, collector at Newport, R.I., in Mar. 1767; the "sixth" seizure was made by John Nichols, the comptroller at Newport, and "acquited" by the Vice Admiralty Court later in the year. John Temple to John Robinson, Boston, 2 Feb., 1767; Temple to John Nicoll [*Nichols*], Boston 14 Sept. 1767. Temple Papers, 1762-1768: Unbound MSS.

10. Daniel Malcom (1724-69), a Boston trader whose defiance of customs officers and magistrates was reported in **No. 504**, *Bernard Papers*, 3: 232-235. Depositions relating to the Malcom affair, dated Sept. and Oct. 1766, are in T 1/446, ff 103-133.

11. Manuscript torn.

12. Of the five commissioners only John Temple was likely to have been present during the 1767 commemoration of the Stamp Act riot. The account here reflects the substance of what FB had reported to Shelburne in **No. 557**, and while he did not expressly accuse the Whigs of aiming at independence nevertheless implied such by noting that a "Civil War between the two Countries (if it may be allowed that Name) must be the consequence" of colonial repudiation of Parliament's legislative supremacy. The phrase "the most unlimited independence" used here implied construction as subjects of George III. *Bernard Papers*, 3: 385.

13. Reported by FB in **No. 567**, *Bernard Papers*, 3: 410.

14. The Newport town meeting voted a reward of £50 for information leading to the conviction of the author of an advertisement "fixed upon" the door of the court house on the night of Friday, 27 Nov. 1767. The town clerk reported that the advertisement called on the inhabitants to assemble on the following day and "seize the Money in the Custom-House," recently deposited by a Royal Navy ship, "by way of Reprisal for the Money due to this Colony from the Crown, the Payment of which is stopped by the Lords of the Treasury." *Newport Mercury*, 7-14 Dec. 1767.

15. See note 22 below.

16. FB would have advised the Board about such proceedings in Connecticut. See *Bernard Papers*, 3: 55, 58, 69-70.

17. See **No. 592**.

18. On 28 Oct., the town had voted to encourage American manufactures and discourage the use of foreign imports. But the first nonimportation subscription was not adopted until the following March. See **No. 601**.

19. The New York merchants signed a nonimportation subscription on 27 Aug. 1768, which was to take effect on 1 Nov. 1768. The town's tradesmen followed suit on 15 Sept., The Philadelphia merchants, however, did not agree upon nonimportation until 6 Feb. 1769. I am grateful to Christopher Minty for his advice on New York merchants.

20. On 20 Nov. 1767, the Boston town meeting voted to give "proper Instructions" to its four representatives "at this very critical Conjuncture of our public affairs (having postponed consideration on 28 Oct.). The vote did not specifically instruct representatives to support a remonstrance, which conclusion the commissioners drew from the various papers issued by the House in January and February (for which see *JHRM*, 44: 219-250). *Reports of the Record Commissioners of Boston*, 16: 225.

21. See **No. 589**.

22. In a letter to the Treasury of 16 Feb., the commissioners reviewed the following items in the file of newspapers enclosed with the memorial of 12 Feb. (A) an extract of Dennys DeBerdt's letter to James Otis Jr., 10 Jan. 1767, printed in *Boston Gazette,* 13 Apr. 1767. The Board complained that in "repeating . . . the sentiments" of an English lord upon the Malcom affair he (inadvertently) "gave spirits to the Smuglers" and "discouraged" customs officers in the province. (B) The "Letters from a Farmer in Pennsylvania," No. 4 "wherein he absolutely denies the power of parliament to lay upon these Colonies any Tax whatever", *Boston Chronicle*, 28 Dec. 1767-4 Jan. 1768. (C) The Farmer, No. 9, "wherein he says the passing an Act for settling the extent of the English Laws seems absolutely necessary for the public Security." *Boston Chronicle*, 8-15 Feb. 1768. Temple Papers, 1762-1768: Unbound MSS. With regard to enclosure (A), FB had previously sent a copy of DeBerdt's letter to Shelburne with brief comments under cover of **No. 542**, *Bernard Papers*, 3: 350. Also, by the time the commissioners had written this memorial, FB had sent copies of the Farmer's letters to John Pownall, **No. 579**.

23. Burch autographed the letter first, probably because he was in the chair when the memorial was approved by the Board; though Hulton was the senior commissioner, the chair was rotated.

24. American Board of Customs to Samuel Hood, Customhouse, Boston, 4 Mar. 1768, ADM 1/483, f 102. The navy patrols and movements can be traced in *Boston Gazette*, 23 May and *New-Hampshire Gazette*, 15 Jul. 1768.

25. CO 5/241, f 31.

Appendix 3

AMERICAN BOARD OF CUSTOMS
TO THE LORDS COMMISSIONERS OF THE TREASURY

May it please Your Lordships.

In our Memorial of the 12th of February[1] we laid before Your Lordships our Sentiments upon the present State of Government in this Country, and we are very sorry to say that from the Experience we have since had, we are confirmed in the Opinions we had then formed.

Having had Reason to think that the Persons employed in the out-door Business had been guilty of collusive practices, we thought it necessary to employ some extra Tidesman on board of Vessels arriving in this Port from foreign parts; This Measure gave Umbrage to the Merchants, and produced great Clamours among[s]t them, and they have since endeavoured to distress and embarrass our Officers; and those who shew a Disposition to pay the Duties are threatned by them. Several persons have applied to M[r] Williams Inspector General for the usual Indulgences, and among the Rest the famous M[r] Malcolm, and being answered that the full Duties would be required, he went away, and said he should take his own Measures[.] On the next day his Vessel arrived near the Harbour, where she was unloaded of about Sixty pipes of Wine into Lighters, which were conducted into Town at Night by a great Number of people; the Master nevertheless, the next day, reported his Vessel in Ballast, and though the Affair is notoriously known and our Officers have endeavoured to procure an Informer, yet no one dares appear.[2]

To give your Lordships a fuller Idea of the general Temper and Disposition of the People in this Country, we beg leave to submit to your Consideration some other Proceedings in this place.

On the 26th. February the House of Representatives in this Province passed Resolves similar to those of the Town Meeting in October last, to discourage the use of *Foreign Superfluities* and to encourage the Manufactures of this Province, and out of eighty two Members, Brigadier Ruggles was the only one who answered in the Negative.[3]

The Merchants have held several Meetings (at one of which the said M[r]. Malcolm presided)[4] to concert Measures to obtain a Repeal of the Laws; accordingly they have entered into an Association not to import any Goods from Great Britain for a limited Time, and a Committee of seven persons hath been appointed to correspond with the Merchants in the other Provinces, to excite them to adopt similar Measures, and those persons who refuse to subscribe are to be discouraged in the most effectual manner; We are now to observe to Your Lordships, as we did before in our last Memorial,[5] in regard to the proceedings of the Town Meetings, that we consider those Measures as a Policy calculated to alarm the Trading and Manufacturing people of Great Britain, and to engage them in their Interest, so as to obtain a Repeal of the Laws, rather than to answer the Ends and purposes pretended.[6]

On the 29th of February a most audacious Libel on Governor Bernard was published in the News papers printed by Edes and Gill of this Town, His Excellency communicated the same to both Houses but the lower House payed no Regard to it.[7]

The Chief Justice opened the Superior Court on the 8.th Instant with a very strong and pointed Charge in respect to Libels, the grand Jury nevertheless did not present the Publishers of the Libel on the Governor.[8]

Though the most seditious and inflamatory publications have been circulated through all the provinces of America for many Months past, no one Governor, as we can learn, has hitherto attempted to prosecute the Authors or publishers of them, and the political Doctrines avowed in them are now become the Principles of the Generality of the People; on the 11th. instant at an annual meeting for the Choice of Town Officers, the Thanks of the Town were voted to the Author of the famous Letters published at Philadelphia, the Motion was made by the aforesaid Mr. Malcolm, and it passed unanimously.

For several Evenings in the beginning of March a number of people armed with Clubs assembled about the Houses of some of the members of the Board, blowing Horns, beating Drums, and making hideous Noises, so that the Familys quitted their Houses expecting they would proceed to Violence, on the 17th instant we had certain Information that, on the next day, being the Anniversary of the Repeal of the Stamp Act, which has been observed as a Day of Triumph over great Britain, certain Images would be affixed to a Tree, called the Tree of Liberty, that the mob would assemble and bring the Commissioners and the Officers of the Board to the Tree, to oblige them to renounce their Commissions, accordingly at day break on the 18th. the Effigies of Mr. Paxton and Mr Williams were exhibited on the Tree, and after hanging a few Hours were taken down, the morning was ushered in with Guns firing, Drums beating, and a Display of Colours in several parts of the Town; That morning as soon as the Board met, we wrote a Letter to the Governor, and before we broke up we received a Minute of the Council, Copies of which are sent herewith; The Council met again in the Afternoon, as resolved in the Minute of the Morning, and adjourned without taking any Measures to secure the Peace of the Town, and here we think necessary to observe to Your Lordships, that even in the heighth of the Outrages in the Year 1765[9] the Council of this Province, who are annually chosen by the Representatives of the people, would not advise the Governor to apply to the Commander of His Majestys Troops for any Military Aid; In the Evening the mob made a procession through the Town, with Drums beating, and Colours flying, which was closed with a Cart, in which were placed four swivel Guns,[10] they went to Liberty Tree and after discharging several Guns they paraded through the Streets making hideous Cries and Noises at the Houses of the Governor and some of the Commissioners, and about nine O'Clock they proceeded to the House of M[r]. Williams Inspector General, who is become particularly obnoxious by being our immediate Instrument in regulating this Post, and annexed is the Copy of M[r] Williams's Letter to the Board acquainting us of the Attack made upon him by the Mob of that Evening.[11]

It does not appear that it is their plan to molest us immediately, as the last Mob was prevailed upon to desist from proceeding to outrage until the answer of Government to the Remonstrance of their Assembly[12] could be received [*blank*]; But of this we are well convinced, that Governor and Magistracy have not the least authority or power in this Place that the Mob are ready to be assembled on any Occasion, and that every Officer who exerts himself in the Execution of his Duty will be exposed to the Resentment of the Populace, without the least probability of receiving any Protection.

Though no immediate Outrage should be committed on ourselves or Officers, yet if the answer from Government to the Remonstrances of the lower House of Assembly should not be agreable to the people, We are fully persuaded that they will proceed to violent Measures; In the mean Time we must depend on the favour of the Leaders of the Mob for our protection and in such Circumstances we cannot answer for our Security for a day, much less will it be in our power to carry the Revenue Laws into Effect

All which is humbly submitted.

John Robinson

Hen. Hulton.

J. Temple.

W[m]. Burch

Chas Paxton

Custom H[o] Boston 28th. March 1768

LS, RC   T 1/465, ff 25-27.

Endorsed: Memorial of the Commissioners of the Customs in America To the Right Honourable The Lords Commissioners of His Majesty's Treasury 28th. March 1768 Read 30 June 1768. Transmit Copy to M[r] Pownall v: min:[13] Thank you sent. American Cont[14] 16   Enclosed two copies of **No. 599**; minute and resolution of the Massachusetts Council of 18 Mar.; John Williams to the American Board of Customs, Boston, 21 Mar. 1768, T 1/465, ff 28-38. The Treasury considered the memorials of the American Board of Customs dated 12 Feb. and 28 Mar. 1768 (**Appendices 2** and **3**) on 30 Jun. Thomas

Bradshaw acknowledged receipt of **Appendix 3** on 8 Jul. (T 28/1, f 332) and forwarded a copy to John Pownall at the Board of Trade, for the consideration of the secretary of state, the earl of Hillsborough (CO 5/226, f 105).

The commissioners' reporting of events covered much of what FB had said in his letters to Shelburne, notably that of 19 Mar. (**No. 600**). That letter, and a comment made earlier to John Pownall about both he and the commissioners of Customs being in "the most precarious Situation" (**No. 595**), does not prove collusion in the composition of their respective reports but certainly suggests it.[15] The Treasury's reply to the American Board of Customs, however, presumed that the Board and governor were acting independently. Bradshaw informed the commissioners that Secretary of State Hillsborough "will send the most positive Instructions" to FB to "assist" them in "bringing to Justice all Persons concerned" in offences that they described in the memorial (T 28/1, f 332). Thus Hillsborough addressed the matter of Daniel Malcom's smuggling in **No. 650** (acknowledging the commissioners' memorial of 28 Mar.). The secretary of state also addressed the wider law and order issues raised by the commissioners, by announcing in **No. 661** that the Regulars were being sent to Boston (but without acknowledging the commissioners' memorial).

---

1. **Appendix 2**.

2. Discussed in **No. 601**.

3. Nonimportation was first proposed at a town meeting on 28 Oct. 1767 and agreed at a town meeting held on 1 Mar. 1768. On the House of Representatives and Timothy Ruggles (1711-95) see **No. 598**n5 and **No. 593**n7.

4. On 4 Mar. 1768.

5. **Appendix 2**.

6. See **No. 601**.

7. "A True Patriot" [Joseph Warren], *Boston Gazette, Supplement*, 29 Feb. 1768. The Council and the House of Representatives considered the alleged libel on 3 and 4 Mar. *JHRM*, 44: 213-215; CO 5, 757, ff 47-49.

8. For this issue see **Nos. 596** and **593**.

9. In **No. 600**, FB also drew comparison with the Stamp Act Crisis, when the two English commissioners, Hulton and Burch, were not in Boston. "I have not the Shadow of Authority or Power. I am just now in the Situation I was in above two years ago."

10. This is the first recorded instance of fire-arms being displayed during popular demonstrations, though the rioters who undertook the rescue of goods and ships seized by customs officers would have been armed (as was Daniel Malcom when he defended his house and store in the fall of 1766). The guns may have been taken from one of the town batteries or an armed merchant vessel.

11. These events are discussed in **No. 600**.

12. House of Representatives, petition to the king, 20 Jan. 1768, CO 5/757, ff 82-85 (MsS, RC).

13. Abbreviation for "vide minute."

14. Abbreviation for "Continent".

15. By contrast, TH was more skeptical in evaluating the commissioners' judgment. He observed that the commissioners "make great complaints of the insufficiency of the laws in being for preventing illicit trade," though people "very unwillingly submit"; the commissioners' attitudes, he supposed, contributed to his own unease at living "under constant apprehensions of danger." TH to Richard Jackson, Boston, 18 Apr. 1768, Mass. Archs. 26: 300.

Appendix 4

THE EARL OF HILLSBOROUGH TO THOMAS GAGE

(N°. 71)

Secret and Confidential

Whitehall 8th. June 1768

Sir,

I transmit to you, for your private Information, Copies of a Letter from His Majesty's Commissioners of the Revenue to the Lords of the Treasury;[1] of my Circular Letter to the several Governors upon the Continent in consequence of it,[2] and of governor Bernard's three last letters to my Office.[3]

The Contents of these Papers will evince to you how necessary it is become that such measures should be taken as will strengthen the Hands of Government in the Province of Massachusetts Bay; enforce a due Obedience to the Laws, and protect and support the Civil Magistrates, and the Officers of the Crown in the Execution of their Duty.

For these purposes, I am to signify to you His Majesty's Pleasure that you do forthwith order one Regiment, or such Force as you shall think necessary, to Boston, to be Quartered in that Town, and give every legal Assistance to the Civil Magistrate in the preservation of the Public Peace and to the Officers of the Revenue in the Execution of the Laws of Trade & Revenue — and, as this appears to be a Service of a delicate Nature and possibly leading to Consequences not easily foreseen, I am directed by the King[4] to recommend to you to make choice of an Officer for the Command of these Troops, upon whose Prudence & Resolution and Integrity you can entirely rely.

The necessary measures for Quartering and providing for these Troops, must be entirely left to your Direction but I would submit to you whether, as Troops will probably continue in that Town, and a Place of some Strength may in case of Emergency be of great Service, it would not be adviseable to take Possession of, and Repair, if repairs be wanting, the little Castle or Fort of William and Mary, which belongs to the Crown.

I am &c^a

Hillsborough

ADft, Copy

CO 5/86, ff 80-81.

Docket: Dra[t]. to Major Gen[l]. Gage 8th. June 1768 (N[o]. 7) (Secret & Confidential). The original RC in MiU-C: Gage, vol. 77, enclosed copies of **Appendix 1**, **Appendix 2**, and the earl of Hillsborough, circular to the colonial governors, Whitehall, 21 Apr. 1768, and copies of three of FB's letters to Shelburne (from **Nos. 589**, **591**, **596**, and **601**). FB learned of Hillsborough's orders to Gage on 3 Sept., when he received Gage's letter of 31 Aug. (**No. 669**). The RC was not available for checking *in situ* at MiU-C or in facsimile before this volume of the *Bernard Papers* went to press. The transcript printed here is based on the draft author's copy filed at TNA.

---

1. Probably **Appendix 2**.

2. The earl of Hillsborough, circular to the colonial governors, Whitehall, 21 Apr. 1768, CO 5/241, f 28.

3. Probably three of the following: **Nos. 589**, **591**, **596**, and **601**.

4. The use of the "King" rather than "His Gracious Majesty" presumably was military as opposed to administrative protocol.

Appendix 5

AMERICAN BOARD OF CUSTOMS TO
THOMAS GAGE AND WILLIAM DALRYMPLE

Copy of a Letter from the Commissioners of the Customs at Boston to His Excellency Gen[l]. Gage at New York, And to Col. Dalrymple at Halifax.

Sir,

Finding it utterly impossible to carry on the Business of the Revenue in the Town of Boston from the outragious behaviour of the People who grossly abused and wounded ^the Collector^ and Comptroller, and other Officers in the Execution of their Duty on the 10th. instant, and still continue to threaten their and our Lives; We took Shelter on Board His Majesty's Ship Romney, and desired Captain Corner to put Us on Shore at Castle William, where we now are, and at our request Captain Corner will continue near to the Castle for our Protection.

The ferment amongst the People has greatly encreased since the 10th. instant, and we are persuaded that their Leaders will urge them to the most violent Measures, even to an open Revolt, for one of their Demagogues in a Town Meeting yesterday, said, if they were called on to defend their Liberties and Privileges, he hoped and believed, they would one and all resist, even unto Blood.

What Steps the Governor and Council may take we cannot tell, but having applied to them, we have received no Assurances of Protection, and we are persuaded the Governor will not apply for Troops without the Advice of his Council, which Measure We do not imagine they will recommend, and we now write, Sir, to acquaint your Excellency ^of^ the very alarming State of things at Boston, and leave it to your Judgement to act as you shall think proper for the Honour of the Crown and protection of its Servants here in the present Exigency.

Castle William Boston Harbour 15 June 1768.

Sent To His Excellency General Gage New York & To Col. Dalrymple at Halifax.

L, Copy   T 1/465, ff 167-168.

Endorsed: N° 21. Copy. 15 June 1768. Copy of a Letter from the Commissioners of the Customs at Boston to General Gage at New York, and to Col. Dalrymple at Halifax.   The version printed here is the copy sent to the Treasury enclosed in **Appendix 6**. The original RC is in MiU-C: Gage, vol. 78; another copy sent by Thomas Bradshaw at the Treasury to the secretary of state, on 22 Jul. 1768 is filed at CO 5/757, ff 217-218.

Gage replied on 21 Jun. reminding the commissioners that he could not send troops into Boston without the express permission of the civil government. Dalrymple replied two days later, stating his readiness to move troops upon receipt of orders.[1]

---

1. Copies of both replies were enclosed with the memorial of the American Board of Customs to the Treasury dated 11 Jul. Commodore Hood also responded to the commissioners, informing that he had ordered two schooners to Boston harbor: HMS *Beaver* and HMS *St. Lawrence*. T 1/465, ff 179-186.

Appendix 6

MEMORIAL OF THE AMERICAN BOARD OF CUSTOMS TO THE LORDS COMMISSIONERS OF THE TREASURY

Duplicate.

May it please your Lordships,

In our former Memorials to Your Lordship we represented the Disaffection of the People here to the Revenue Laws,[1] & from the many treasonable Publications that had been spread thro' all the Provinces, & the Correspondence carried on by the several Assemblies we were persuaded there had been a long concerted extensive Plan of Resistance to the Authority of Great Britain and we believe that the Seizure referred to in the incl^d. Papers has hastened the People of Boston to the Commission of Actual Violence, some that was attended.

From their outrageous Behaviour towards our Officers, & their repeated threats of immediate violence to our own Persons, we found it absolutely necessary in order to save His Majesty's Commission from further Insult, & to preserve our Lives, to take Shelter on board His Majesty's Ship the Romney in Boston Harbour, from whence we are removed into Castle William to carry on the Business of the Revenue till we can receive such Protection as will enable us to act in safety at Boston.

We herewith lay before Your Lordships Copies of our Minutes of the 13.th & 14.th instant, together with Copies of sev^l. Affidavits and Letters relative to our present Situation, agreeable to the Schedule inclosed, and we beg leave to submit our Opinion, that nothing but the immediate Exertion of military Power will prevent an open Revolt of the Town, which may probably spread throughout the Provinces.

Which is humbly submitted.

Hen. Hulton
J Temple.
Wm Burch
Chas. Paxton
John Robinson

Castle William, Boston Harbour, June 16th 1768.

LS, RC   T 1/465, ff 120-122.

Endorsed: Letter from the Comm.^{rs} of Customs in America to the Lords of The Treasury, dated Castle William, Boston Harbour June 16.th 1768. In Mr Bradshaws of 22^d July 1768.   A full list of enclosures to this letter is provided in **Appendix 7**. Thomas Bradshaw, secretary to the Treasury, forwarded a copy of the memorial to the secretary of state on 22 Jul., CO 5/757, ff 163-164; with the memorial at ff 225-226. There is another copy in Coll. Mass Papers, 1768. Bradshaw replied to the American Board of Customs on 28 Jul., T 28/1, f 332. Copies of the letter and enclosures were laid before both houses of Parliament on 28 Nov. 1768. HLL: American Colonies Box 1.

While the commissioners did not send FB a copy of their memorial, he would have been aware of its contents and the views of the commissioners regarding their preference for having British troops and ships stationed in Boston for the near future. He would have been annoyed by the manner in which the commissioners reported his handling of the situation to the Treasury and also (in the same terms) to Commodore Samuel Hood. Criticism was implied rather than overtly stated by the commissioners' perplexity as to "What steps" might ever be taken to ensure their safety.[2]

Acknowledging receipt of the commissioners' memorial, Thomas Bradshaw explained how it was personally delivered by Benjamin Hallowell on 19 Jul. and how the Treasury "immediately" transmitted an "exact Account" of the *Liberty* riot to Hillsborough, desiring the king's "Protection & Support" for the Customs Board and customs officers. Hillsborough, meanwhile, received other reports of disturbances in Virginia. Both matters were addressed at a cabinet meeting on 27 Jul., at which the British government authorized sending two further regiments to Boston (**No. 661**) and appointing Lord Botetourt as the resident governor of Virginia (replacing the absentee governor Sir Jeffrey Amherst). Hillsborough was the architect of both policy decisions, although, as Peter D. G. Thomas advised, "it is impossible to reconstruct the ministerial consultations before the policy decisions taken" by the cabinet.[3]

---

1. **Appendices 2** and **3**.

2. American Board of Customs to Samuel Hood, Castle William, 15 Jun. 1768, CO 5/757, f 286.

3. Bradshaw to the American Board of Customs, [London], 28 Jul. 1768, T 28/1, f 332; Thomas, *The Townshend Duties Crisis*, 91.

Appendix 7

SCHEDULE OF SUNDRY PAPERS ENCLOSED IN THE MEMORIAL OF THE AMERICAN BOARD OF CUSTOMS

Castle William Boston Harbour

June 15th. 1768.

Schedule of sundry papers inclosed in the memorial from the Commissioners of the Customs in America to the Right Honble the Lords Commissioners of His Majesty's Treasury.

N[o]. 1 Copy of the minutes of the Board 13 & 14th June[1]

2. . . . . of the Information of Tho[s]. Kirk Tidesman[2]

3. . . . . of the Deposition of Jos[h]: Harrison Esq[r] Collector of Boston[3]

4. . . . . D[o] . . . . of Benj[n]. Hallowell Jun[r]. Comptroller[4]

5. . . . . D[o] . . . . of R. A: Harrison Son of the Collr[5]

6. . . . . Memorial of Tho[s]. Irving Inspector of Imports & Exports.[6]

7. . . . . M[r]. Secretary Oliver's Letter to the Chairman 11th June[7]

8. . . . . The Comm[rs] Letter to Capt Corner 11th June[8]

9. . . . . D[o] . . . . to Gov[r] Bernard ——— 12th June[9]

10 . . . . Letter from the Coll[r] & Comp[r]. Boston 11th June[10]

11. . . . Letter to the Coll[r] & Comp[r]. of Boston 12th June from the Chairman[11]

12. . . . Letter from D[o].   in Answer 12th June.[12]

13. . . . Letter to D[o].   13th June 1768.[13]

14. . . . from Gov[r] Bernard 13 June 1768[14]

15. . . . to Capt Corner 13 June[15]

16. . . . to Gov[r] Bernard 13th June[16]

17. . . . from D[o]   13th June[17]

No 18   Copy of a Letter from Gov[r]. Bernard 13th June[18]

19. . . . from the Coll[r] & Compt[r]. 14 June[19]

20. . . . to Commodore Hood at Halifax 15 June[20]

21. . . . to Gen[l] Gage at New York & Colonel Dalrymple at Halifax.[21]

1. 2. 3 Extracts from three anonymous Letters[22]

Mem[l]: of Comm[rs]: Customs at Boston to the Lords of the Treasury transmitting the above

MS, RC   T 1/465, ff 122-123.

An enclosure to **Appendix 6**, this document lists all the other papers enclosed with the memorial of the American Board of Customs. The spacing of text has been editorially altered, including the number of suspension dots, in order to represent the layout of the manuscript.

---

1. T 1/465, ff 124-128.
2. Ibid., ff 129-130.
3. Ibid., ff 131-132.
4. Ibid., ff 133-134.
5. Ibid., ff 135-136.
6. Ibid., ff 137-138.
7. Ibid., ff 139-140.
8. Ibid., ff 141-142.
9. Copy of **No. 624** at ibid., ff 143-144.
10. Ibid., ff 145-146.
11. Ibid., ff 147-148.
12. Ibid., ff 149-150.
13. Ibid., ff 151-152.
14. Copy of **No. 625** at T1/465, ff 153-154.
15. Ibid., ff 155-156.
16. Copy of **No. 626** at ibid., ff 157-158.
17. Copy of **No. 627** at ibid., ff 159-161.
18. Copy of **No. 628** at ibid., ff 161-162.
19. Ibid., ff 163-164.
20. Ibid., ff 165-166.
21. Ibid., ff 167-168.
22. T 1/465, ff 169-176.

Appendix 8

THOMAS GAGE TO WILLIAM DALRYMPLE

New York June <u>25</u>[th] 1768

Copy

Sir,

Should Governor Bernard find Occasion to make Application to you, for the Assistance of his Majesty's Forces, you will immediately move with the Troops under your Command at Halifax, and proceed to Boston, or such other Place, as shall be pointed out to you by the Governor.—

There is now at Halifax, one entire Regiment, and five Companies of another, and if you have Time to put the Orders in execution, which are transmitted to you, concerning the withdrawing the Troops from Louisbourg, S[t]: Johns Island, and Fort Frederick,[1] before any Requisition is made for the Aid of the King's Forces; you will then have under your Command, and ready for immediate Service, a number of Troops equal to two Regiments, and three Companys. You will embark therefore, if your Assistance is required, with the Whole, or any Part of those Troops, as Governor Bernard shall demand, and if the Governor should be of Opinion, that it wou'd be requisite you should bring Artillery with you, the Detachment of the Royal Regiment of Artillery at Halifax, will be embarked at the same time, with such a Number of Pieces of Artillery, as they shall be Able to manage. You will pay no Regard, in effecting this Service, to the leaving Halifax without Troops: it will be sufficient, that you leave there one Company, or a Detachment equal to a Company.

As it is probable, the Assistance of the Commodore, would at the same Time be required, he will facilitate the Embarkation of the Troops, by taking them on board the King's Ships: But in every Case, you may depend upon the Aid in his Power to give you.

I am with great Regard, Sir, Your most obedient Humble Servant

(Signed) Tho[s]: Gage

Lieu[t]. Col[o]: Dalrymple 14th: Reg[t]: Officer Comm[g]: his Maj[s]: Forces. Nova Scotia at Halifax.

L, Copy   CO 5/86, f 138.

Endorsed: [_ _ _]² Gage to Lieuᵗ: Colᵒ: Dalrymple 14ᵗʰ: Regᵗ: or Officer Commandᵍ: his Majˢ: Forces in Nova Scotia at Halifax. Date New York June 25ᵗʰ 1768. Inclosed in a Letter directed to His Excellency Govʳ: Bernard at Boston. In Genˡ: Gage's (Nᵒ 6) of 28ᵗʰ June 1768. (5). The original set of orders that Gage prepared for Dalrymple was sealed and enclosed in **No. 639**, for transmission to Dalrymple as and when FB chose. Gage apparently did not communicate the orders separately to Dalrymple, leaving that decision to FB. FB thought he knew what these orders amounted to, though he would never have broken the seal to read them. He forwarded them to Dalrymple on 3 Jul., under cover of **No. 642**, wrongly assuming that Gage was ordering Dalrymple to send troops to Boston. The version printed here was a copy that Gage sent to the secretary of state. There is also an AC in MiU-C: Gage, vol. 78.

FB did not make any requisition of Dalrymple for military assistance which, as Gage's letter of 25 Jun. (**No. 639**) and Gage's orders to Dalrymple (**Appendix 8**) clearly state, was an express condition of troops being sent Boston. FB wrongly assumed that Gage had directed Dalrymple to send the troops (**No. 642**), which had it been true, would have removed the requirement of a civil requisition. FB did not learn of Gage's condition until 16 Jul., upon receiving a letter from Gage (**No. 652**) enclosing a copy of the orders under a flying seal. FB copied this set to Hillsborough (in **No. 660**).

---

1. Louisbourg on Cape Breton Island, N.S.; St. John's Island, renamed Prince Edward Island in 1798; Fort Frederick on the banks of the St. John's River, N.S.

2. Obscured by tight binding.

Appendix 9

THOMAS CUSHING TO THE EARL OF HILLSBOROUGH

Province of the Massachusetts Bay June 30th. 1768.

My Lord,

His Excellency the Governor of this Province, has been pleased to communicate to the House of Representatives, Extracts of a Letter he had received from your Lordship, dated Whitehall the 22nd: of April 1768;[1] wherein it is declared to be the Royal Pleasure, that he should require of them, in his Majesty's Name, to rescind the Resolution which gave Birth, to a circular Letter from the Speaker of the last House,[2] and to declare their Disapprobation of and Dissent to that rash and hasty Proceeding.

The House are humbly of Opinion, that a Requisition from the Throne of this nature to a British House of Commons has been very unusual: Perhaps there has been no such Precedent since the Revolution:[3] If this be the Case, some very aggravated Representations of this Measure must have been made to his Majesty, to induce him to require of *this* House to rescind a Resolution of a former House, upon Pain of forfeiting their Existence: For, my Lord, the House of Representatives, duly elected, are constituted by the royal Charter the representative Body of his Majesty's faithful Commons of this Province in the General Assembly.

Your Lordship is pleased to say, that his Majesty considers this Step "has evidently tending to create unwarrantable Combinations, and to excite an unjustifiable Opposition to the constitutional Authority of Parliament."[4] The House therefore thought it their indispensable Duty immediately to revise the Letter referred to; and carefully to recollect as far as they were able, the Sentiments which prevailed in that House, to induce them to revert to, and resolve on the Measure.

It may be necessary to observe, that the People in this Province have attended with a deep Concern, to the several Acts of the British Parliament, which impose Duties and Taxes on the Colonies, not for the Purpose of regulating the Trade, but as the sole Intention of raising a Revenue. This Concern, my Lord, so far from being limited within the Circle of a few inconsiderate Persons, is become universal: The most respectable for Fortune, Rank and Station, as well as Probity and Understanding in the Province, with very few Exceptions, are alarmed with Apprehensions of the fatal Consequences, of a Power, exercised in any one Part of the British Empire, to commend and apply the Property of their Fellow Subjects at Discretion! This Consideration prevailed on the last House of Representatives, to resolve on an humble, dutiful and loyal Petition to the King,[5] the common Head and Father of *all* his People, for his gracious Interposition, in Favor of his Subjects of *this* Province.— If your Lordship, whom his Majesty has honored with the American Department, has been instrumental in presenting a Petition, so interesting to the well being of his loyal Subjects here, this House beg Leave to make their most grateful Acknowledgements, and to implore your continued Aid and Patronage.

As all his Majesty's North American Subjects, are alike affected by these Parliamentary Revenue Acts, the former House very justly supposed, that each of the Assemblies on the Continent would take such Methods of obtaining Redress, as should be thought by them respectively to be regular and proper: and being desirous that the several Applications should harmonize with each other, they resolved on their circular Letter; wherein their only View seems to be, to advertise their Sister Colonies of the Measures *they* had taken, upon a *common* and important Concern, without once calling upon them, to adopt those Measures or any other.

Your Lordship surely will not think it a Crime in that House, to have taken a Step, which was perfectly consistent with the Constitution, and had a natural Tendency to compose the minds of his Majesty's Subjects of this and his other Colonies, until in his royal Clemency He should afford them Relief; after a Time when it seemed to be the evident Design of the Party to prevent calm, deliberate, rational and constitutional measures from being pursued, or to stop the Distresses of the People from reaching his Majesty's Ear; and consequently to precipitate them into a State of Desperation and melancholy Extremity! Thus my Lord, it appears to this House: and your Lordship will impartially judge, whether a Representation of it to his Majesty, as a Measure "of an inflammatory Nature" — as a Step evidently tending "to create unwarrantable Combinations", and to excite an unjustifiable Opposition to the constitutional Authority of the Parliament", be not injurious to the Representatives of this People, and an Affront to his Majesty himself.

An Attempt, my Lord, to impress the Royal Mind with a Jealousy of his faithful Subjects, for which there is no just Grounds, is a Crime of the most malignant nature; as it tends to disturb and destroy that mutual Confidence between the Prince and the Subjects, which is the only true Basis of publick Happiness and Security: Your Lordship, upon Inquiry may find that such base and wicked Attempts have been made.

It is an inexpressible Grief to the People of this Province, to find repeated Censures falling upon them, not from Ministers of State alone, but from Majesty itself! Grounded on Letters and Accusations from the Governor,[6] a Sight of which, though repeatedly requested of his Excellency, is refused. There is no Evil of this Life which they so sensibly feel, as the Displeasure of their Sovereign: It is a Punishment which they are assured his Majesty would never inflict, but upon a Representation of the Justice of it from his Servants whom he confides in. Your Lordship will allow the House to appeal to your own Candor, upon the grievous

Hardship of their being made to suffer so severe a Misfortune, without ever being called to answer for themselves, or even made acquainted with the matters of Charge alledged against them: A Right, which by the common Rules of Society, founded in the eternal Laws of Reason and Equity they are justly intitled to. The House is not willing to trespass upon your Patience: They *could* recite numbers of Instances, since Governor Bernard has been honored by his Majesty to preside over this Province, of their suffering the King's Displeasure, through the Instrumentality of the Governor, intimated by the Secretary of State, without the least previous notice, that they had ever deviated from the Path of their Duty. This they humbly conceive is just Matter of Complaint: and it may serve to convince your Lordship, that his Excellency has not that tender Feeling for his Majesty's Subjects, which is characteristick of a good Governor, and of which the Sovereign affords an illustrious Example.

It is the good fortune of the House to be able to shew that, the Measure of the last House referred to in your Lordship's Letter to the Governor has been grossly misrepresented, in all its Circumstances: and it is [a] Matter of Astonishment, that the Transaction of the House, the Business of which is constantly done in the open View of the World, could be then coloured; a Transaction, which by special Order of the House was laid before his Excellency, whose Duty to his Majesty, is, at least, not to misinform him.

His Excellency could not but acknowledge in Justice to that House, that Moderation took Place in the Begining of the Session: This is a Truth, my Lord; It was a Principle with the House to conduct the Affairs of Government in their Department, so as to avoid the least Occasion of Offence: As an Instance of their pacifick Disposition, they granted a further Establishment for one of his Majesty's Garrisons in the Province, rather to gratify his Excellency who had requested it, than from a full Conviction of its Necessity.[7] But your Lordship is informed, but this Moderation "did not continue"; and that "instead of a Spirit of Prudence and Respect to the Constitution, which seemed at that Time to influence the Conduct of a large Majority of the Members, a thin House at the End of the Session presumed to revert to, and resolve on a Measure of an inflammatory nature" — that it was an "unfair Proceeding", — "contrary to the real Sense of the House", — and — procured by Surprize. — My Lord, The Journal and Minutes of the House will prove the contrary of all this: and to convince your Lordship, the House beg Leave to lay before you, the several Resolutions, relating to these Matters as they stand recorded.

The House having their Petition to the King, and their Letters to divers of his Majesty's Ministers, a Motion was regularly made on 21st January, *which was the Middle of the Session*, and a Resolution was then taken to appoint a Time to consider the Expediency of writing to the Assemblies of the other Colonies on this

Continent, with Respect to the Importance of their joining with them in petitioning his Majesty at this Time. Accordingly on the Day assigned, there being eighty
^two^ members present, a number always allowed to be sufficient to make a full
House, the Question was debated; in Consequence of which a Motion took Place,
That Letters be wrote to the several Assemblies of the Provinces and Colonies on
the Continent, acquainting them that the House had taken into Consideration,
the Difficulties to which they are and must be reduced, by the Operation of the
late Acts of Parliament, for levying Duties and Taxes on the Colonies; and have
resolved on a humble, dutiful and loyal Petition to his Majesty for Redress; and
also upon proper Representations to his Majesty's Ministers on the Subject: and
to desire that they would severally take such constitutional Measures thereupon
as they should judge most proper. And the Question upon the Motion passed in
the negative. On Thursday the 4th. of February, it was moved in the House that the
foregoing Question be recommitted so far as to leave it at-large and conformable
to a standing Rule of the House, that no Vote or Order shall be reconsidered at
any Time, unless the House be as full as when such Vote or Order was passed;
the number in the House was called for, and it appearing about eighty two members were present,[8] the Question was put, and passed in the Affirmative by a large
Majority. And by an immediately subsequent Resolve the first Vote was ordered to
be erased. — The same Day the Resolution which gave Birth to the circular Letter
took Place; a Question being regularly moved and fairly debated, Whether the
House would appoint a Committee to prepare a Letter to be sent to each of the
Houses of Representatives and Burgesses on the Continent, to inform them of the
Measures which this House has taken with Regard to the Difficulties arising from
the Acts of Parliament for levying Duties and Taxes on the American Colonies,
and report to the House, which passed in the Affirmative; and a Committee was
appointed accordingly. This Committee after Deliberation a Week, reported the
Letter, which was read in the House, and accepted almost unanimously;[9] and fair
Copies of the same were ordered to be taken for the Speaker to sign and forward
as soon as might be: and this Day there were eighty three members in the House.

The Day following an Order passed that a fair Copy of the Letter be transmitted to Dennys Deberdt Esqr. in London;[10] The Design of which was, that he might
be able to produce it as necessity might require, to prevent any Misrepresentation
of its true Spirit and Design.

On Saturday, 13th. of February,[11] in Order that no possible Occasion might be
taken by the Governor to think that the Debates and Resolutions were designed
to be kept a Secret from his Excellency, the House came into the following Resolution, Vizt: Whereas this House hath directed, that a Letter be sent to the several
Houses of Representatives and Burgesses of the British Colonies on the Continent, setting forth the Sentiments of the House, with Regard to the great Diffi-

culties that must accrue, by the Operation of divers Acts of Parliament, for levying Duties and Taxes on the Colonies, with the sole and express Purpose of raising a Revenue; and there Proceedings thereon, in a humble, dutiful and loyal Petition to the King, and such Representations to his Majesty's Ministers, as they apprehend may have a Tendency to obtain Redress: And whereas it is the Opinion of this House, at all effectual Methods should be taken to cultivate an Harmony between the several Branches of this Government, as being necessary to promote the Prosperity of his Majesty's Government in the Province. Resolved, That a Committee wait on his Excellency the Governor, and acquaint him that a Copy of the Letter aforesaid, will be laid before him, as soon as it can be drafted; as well as of all the Proceedings of this House relative to said Affair, if he shall desire it. And a Committee was appointed, who waited on his Excellency accordingly. — On Monday following, the House resolved on the Establishment already mentioned; which is observed only to shew your Lordship, that there was at this Time no Disposition in the House "to revive unhappy Divisions and Distractions so prejudicial to the true Interest of Great Britain and the Colonies". —

The House beg Leave to apologize to your Lordship, for the Trouble given you in so particular a Narration of Facts, which they thought necessary to satisfy your Lordship, that the Resolutions of the last House, referred to by your Lordship, was not an unfair Proceeding, procured by Surprize in a thin House, as his Majesty has been informed, but the declared Sense of a large Majority when the House was full; That the Governor of the Province was made fully acquainted with the Measure, and never signified his Disapprobation of it to the House; which it is presumed he would have done, in Duty to his Majesty, if he had thought it was of evil Tendency: and that therefore that House had abundant Reason to be confirmed in their own Opinion of the Measure, as being the Production of Moderation and Prudence. And the House humbly rely on the ^royal^ Clemency; That to petition his Majesty will not be deemed by him to be inconsistent with a Respect to the British Constitution as settled at the Revolution by William the Third: That to acquaint their Fellow Subjects, involved in the same Distress, of their having so done, in full Hopes of Success, even if they had invited the Union of all America in one joint Supplication, would not be discountenanced by our gracious Sovereign, as a Measure of an inflammatory Nature: That when your Lordship shall in Justice lay a true State of these Matters before his Majesty, he will no longer consider them as tending to create unwarrantable Combinations, or excite an unjustifiable Opposition to the constitutional Authority of the Parliament: That he will then clearly discern, who, are of that desperate Faction, which is continually disturbing the publick Tranquility; and that while his arm is extended for the Protection of his distressed and injured Subjects, he will frown upon all those, who to gratify their own Passions, have dared even to attempt to deceive him.

The House of Representatives of this Province, have more than once, during the administration of Governor Bernard been under a Necessity of intreating his Majesty's ministers to suspend their further Judgment, upon such Representations of the Temper of the People, and the Conduct of the assembly, as they were able to make appear to be injurious. The same Indulgence this House now beg of your Lordship: and they beseech your ^Lordship^ to patronize them so far as to make a favorable Representation of their Conduct to the King our Sovereign. It being the highest ambition of this House, and the People whom they represent, to stand before his Majesty in their just Character of affectionate and loyal Subjects. In the Name and Behalf of the House of Representatives;

I am, My Lord, Your Lordship's devoted, and most humble Servant,

Thomas Cushing Spk[r].

The Right Hon[ble]: Wills Earl of Hillsborough.

ALS, RC   CO 5/757, ff 310-315.

Minor emendations not shown. Endorsed: Province of the Massachusets Bay. June 30th. 1768. Speaker of the House of Assembly. R. 25th: August. A.33. Encl[d].   In handwriting of Thomas Cushing, Speaker of the House of Representatives. No enclosures have been found. The letter was drafted by a House committee;[12] it was read and approved on 30 Jun. and printed in the newspapers a week afterward and later as an appendix to the House journals. *JHRM*, 45: 89, 99-104; *Boston Weekly News-Letter*, 7 Jul. 1768; *Boston Gazette*, 18 Jul. 1768. Hillsborough did not reply.[13]

In **No. 657**, FB defended himself against the accusation of misrepresentation made by the House. Hillsborough reported that the king approved FB's conduct during the controversy and condemned the House for refusing to rescind the circular letter and for expunging the record of the defeated motion of 21 Jan. **No. 679**.

---

1. **No. 608**.

2. **Appendix 1**.

3. That is, the Glorious Revolution of 1688-89.

4. The quotations here and below are from **No. 608**.

5. House of Representatives, petition to the king, 20 Jan. 1768. *JHRM*, 44: 217-219. The petition was sent to the House agent, Dennys DeBerdt, who passed it to Stephen Sayre to transmit to the secretary of state. **No. 712**n2, *Bernard Papers*, 5: 117. Hillsborough, DeBerdt reported to Cushing on 22 Jun., "by no means thinks proper to deliver to his Majesty at present . . . . He thinks the only thing that can be done to serve you at present, is to keep the matter of Right out of Sight, & only consider the good or bad effects the present Acts will have on the Interest of G. B. & her Colonies." The petition was never considered by the Privy Council or Parliament. Albert Matthews, "Letters of Dennys DeBerdt, 1757-1770," *Publications of the Colonial Society of Massachusetts* 13 (1911): 290-461, at 332.

6. **Nos. 589, 591**, and **593**.

7. Cushing is likely referring to the establishment for Castle William, of fifty officers and men totaling c. £1,051 30s for 1768-69. Provision was also made for Fort Pownall at £459. On 28 Jun. *JHRM*, 45, 80-82; *Acts and Resolves*, 18: 363.

8. Annotation. An asterix refers to a footnote: "The same Number as mentioned before."

9. **Appendix 1**.

10. Not found. But DeBerdt acknowledged receipt of the assembly's petition to the king and letters from Cushing's dated 11 Feb., 18 and 19 Apr. 1768. Matthews, "Letters of Dennys DeBerdt, 1757-1770," 332-333. Cushing's letter of 18 Apr. is printed in "Letters of Thomas Cushing from 1767 to 1775," *Collections of the Massachusetts Historical Society,* 4th ser., 4 (1858): 347-366, at 350-351.

11. *JHRM*, 44: 164.

12. The committee appointed on 22 Jun. were Thomas Cushing (Speaker), Samuel Adams, Jerathmeel Bowers, John Hancock, James Otis Jr., James Otis Sr., Thomas Saunders; Walter Spooner, and James Warren, *JHRM*, 45: 70-71.

13. A reply has not been found in Cushing's published correspondence, the *JHRM*, or the Mass. Archs.

Appendix 10

UNKNOWN TO [*JOHN ROBINSON*]

Boston July 7th. 1768

Sir

I make bold to trouble you with some of the particular proceeding last night & I have it from good authority I beg it may be some caution both to the Castle and his Majesty's ships in case of a Surprise which undoubtedly is their intention. There was a letter sent from Otis or Hanncok or both, to Esq[r]. Dexter of Dedham[1] and he convey'd it to Major Pond of Roxborough[2] with instructions to provide a Number of Men, to join the same in Boston and the Dorchester Company belonging to the Castle with their Arms, to Assist them to Storm both the Castle and His Majesty's Ships or take them by Surprise, in order for this adventure a number assembled in Town was join'd by men, so made up the usual armado of a Mob who was to be furnished with Vessels Convey them down; but some prudent Gent[n]. reason'd on the daring attempt they thought proper to refer it only destroying an innocent House with it's Garden.

Sir as it is in my power (though one affects to be of their party) to find the whole [*of?*] [*the*][3] Affair if it may be any advantage, but [_] you will take all possible care as I believe [*there?*] is something more intended. I am &[c].

The above was sent to one of the Commissioners [a]nd is said to Come from a trusty hand

J: C:

(a Copy)

L, Copy   ADM 1/483, f 128.

Enclosed in Samuel Hood to Phillip Stephens,[4] HMS *Launceston*, Halifax, 5 Aug. 1768.
Capt. Corner was transmitting a message given to one of the commissioners of Customs, most likely John Robinson, the present chairman of the Board, whose house at Roxbury had been damaged by rioters on the evening of 4 Jul. (for which see **No. 646**). FB did not take this particular intelligence seriously, and was more concerned by the "Weakness of the Garrison" (**No. 646**), which amounted to fifty officers and men, rather than their loyalty (despite the allegation concerning the Dorchester company of the Suffolk regiment).

1. Samuel Dexter (1726-1810), who had represented Dedham, 1764-67.

2. Eliphalet Pond (1704-95) a shopkeeper and justice of the peace of Dedham; he had been a selectman and town clerk and represented his home town in the province legislature in 1761 and 1763. Pond was colonel of the second regiment of Suffolk County militia, but would have relinquished authority over the Dorchester company when it was posted to Castle William, whose garrison was commanded by Lt. John Phillips (subordinate to the captain of the castle, Thomas Hutchinson). Judging by this report Pond was a radical, but in 1774 his Patriot neighbors obliged him to recant of his Loyalism.

3. Manuscript torn here and below.

4. Philip Stephens (1723–1809), first secretary of the Admiralty 1763-95.

Appendix 11

MASSACHUSETTS COUNCIL'S PETITION TO THE KING

[*7 Jul. 1768*]

To the **KING'S** most Excellent Majesty, The humble Petition of the Council of the Province of **MASSACHUSETTS BAY**.

We your Majesty's most dutiful and loyal Subjects the Council of the Province of Massachusetts Bay, deeply impressed with a sense of your paternal affection for all your Subjects, even the most remote of them, & your disposition to hearken to their Addresses with an attention Suited to the nature of them, humbly beg leave in behalf of your faithful Subjects of said Province to represent to your Majesty

That the first Settlers of New-England, more attentive to religion than worldly emolument, planted themselves in this Country with a view of being Secure from religious imposition, and not with any expectations of advancing their temporal Interests, which the nature of the Soil forbad them to indulge.

That they obtained a Patent of this Country from King Charles the first, which, though vacated in the unhappy times of James the Second, revived in the present Charter of the Province, which was granted in the succeeding glorious reign of King William & Queen Mary, who by said Charter confirmed to their Subjects in this Province divers important rights & privileges, which have been enjoyed to the present time.[1]

That from length and Severity of the winters; the inferiority of the Soil, and the great labour necessary to Subdue it, they underwent incredible hardships.

That beside the climate and Soil, they had to contend with a numerous and barbarous Enemy, which made frequent inroads upon them, broke up their exterior Settlements, and several times had nearly accomplished their utter destruction by which means they were kept in perpetual alarms, & their Country made the Scene of rapine and Slaughter.

That nothing but the most invincible fortitude, animated by the principles of religion, could have enabled them to sustain the hardships and distresses, that came upon them by these Causes_____ Nothing less could have induced them to persevere in the Settlement of a Country, from w^{ch}: in it's best estate they had only to expect a comfortable Subsistence; and that in consequence of their unremmited labour.

That by this labour, these hardships and distresses they dearly purchased the Rights and Privileges and the Country granted to them by Charter and which they have transmitted to their Children & Successors, the present Inhabitants Your Majesty's faithful Subjects, of this Province.

That the present Inhabitants, though more happily circumstanced than their Ancestors & tho' some among them especially in the trading towns, live in affluence, yet from the operation of the same causes, (the length & severity of the winters & the Stubborness and infertility of the Soil) are now able with all their labour to obtain but a comfortable Support for themselves and families, and many of them a very slender one: their Cloathing of which in this cold climate a great deal is necessary, and which except some small part of it, which they make themselves is wholly made of the woolens & other Manufactures of Great-Britain; the other necessary articles of Subsistence, and the yearly taxes upon their poles and on their real and personal estates, taking up the whole or nearly the whole produce of their Lands.

That by their means your Majesty's dominions have been enlarged; your Subjects increased; & the Trade of Great-Britain extended: all in degree envied by her Enemies, and unexpected by her warmest Friends; and all without any expence to her till the late War.

That in the late War, without recurring to the former Expeditions against Canada, to the Reduction of Nova-Scotia in 17 [*blank*][2] to the preservation of it several times since, to the Conquest of Louisbourg with it's dependent teritories in 1745, the reddition[3] of which was esteemed by France an ample Equivalent for all her Conquests during on her part a Successful War and gave peace to Europe, _____ upon your Majesty's requisition, and the requisitions of your Royal Grandfather[4] this Province in the last War yearly raised a large body of Troops in Conjunction with other Colony Troops to assist in reducing the French Power in America: the expence of w^ch^: was very great, & would have been insupportable, if part of it had not been refunded by Parliament from a conviction of our inability to bear the whole.

That the loss of Men in the several Campains of that War was great, & which to a young Country must be very detrimental, and could not be retaliated by Grants of Parliament, and to which those Grants had no respect.

That the acquisition of so large a part of America by your Majesty's Arms tho' a great national Good, & greatly benfic^i^al to the Colonies by freeing them from the hostilities of the French, and the Indians that were under their influence, has in several respects operated to the detriment of the Colonies: particularly in diminishing the value of real Estates, and drawing our People from us to Settle the new-acquired territory.

That the said Acquisitions have occasioned new and increasing demands for the Manufactures of Great Britain, & have opened to her Sources of Trade greatly beneficial: and continually enlarging the benefits of which center in herself, & which with the extensive territories acquired are apprehended to be an ample equivalent for all the Charges of the War in America; and for the expences of defending protecting and Securing said Territories.

That this Province in particular is still in debt on account of the charge incurred by the late War.

That the yearly taxes — excepting the present Year, on which no public tax has been laid by reason of a General Valuation of Estates through the Province which could not be compleated before the dissolution of the late General Assembly, but which will probably be resumed when a new Assembly shall be called__ That the yearly taxes upon the People for lessening said debt, tho' not so great as during the War, are nevertheless with more difficulty paid, by reason of the greater Scarcity of money.

That the scarcity of Money in the Colonies is owing to the balance of their Trade with Great Britain being against them: which balance without the operation of the several Acts of Parliament taxing the Colonies by laying certain Duties for the purpose of drawing a Revenue from them drains them of their money so as that their trade, which is the only source of their money, is greatly embarrassed.

That this embarrassment is much increased by the Late Regulations of Trade; and by the Tax Acts aforesaid, which draw imediately from Trade the money necessary to Support it: on the Support of which the payment of the balance aforesaid depends.

That the said Tax Acts operating to the detriment of the Trade of the Colonies must operate to the detriment of Great Britain by disabling them from paying the Debt due to her, & by laying them under a necessity of using less of her Manufactures.

That by using the Manufactures of Great Britain, which are virtually charged with most of the Taxes that take place there, the Colonies pay a considerable part of those Taxes.

That by several Acts of Parliament the Colonies are restrained from importing most of the Commodities of Europe except from Great Britain: which occasions her Manufactures and all Commodities coming from her to be dearer charged and is therefore equivalent to a Tax upon them. That the Colonies are prohibited from sending to foreign markets many valuable articles of their produce: which giving to Great Britian[5] an advantage in the price of them, is a proportionable & further Tax upon the Colonies.

That the exports of the Colonies, all their Gold & Silver & their whole powers of Remittance, fall short of the charged value of what they import from Great Britain.

That in evidence of this we humbly apprehend the Merchants of Great Britian Trading to the Colonies but especially such as send Goods to them on factorage, can declare their judgment: who from the difficulty of obtaining remittances, from the bad debts made, and from the rate of Exchange; which is generally above par, can form a very good One._____ That if it be considered what difficulties the Colonies encountered on their first Settlement; their having defended themselves (a few of them excepted) without any expence to Great Britain: the assistances given by them in the late War,[6] whereby the Empire of Britain is so greatly extended, and its Trade proportionally increased; the diminution of the Value of their Estates, and the Emigration of their Inhabitants occasioned by that extention; the loss of Men in said War, peculiarly detrimental to young Countries; the Taxes on them to support their own internal Government; the share they pay of the Duties & Taxes in Britain by the Consumption of British Manufactures, for which such valuable returns are made; the Restraints upon their Trade equivalent to a Tax; the balance of Trade continually against them and their consequent inability to pay the duties laid by the Acts aforesaid____ if these facts be considered, we humbly conceive it must appear that your Majesty's Subjects in the Colonies have been, and are as much burthened as those in Great Britain; and that they are whilst in America, more advantagious to Britain; than if they were transplanted thither and Subjected to all the duties and taxes paid there.

With great humility we beg leave to lay this Representation at your Majesty's feet, humbly praying your Majesty's favourable Consideration of it & that the Charter Rights, & Privileges of the People of this Province may be secured to them.

And if it should appear to your Majesty, that it is not for the benefit of Great Britain & her Colonies (over the whole of which your Paternal Care is conspicuous) that any Revenue should be drawn from the Colonies, we humbly implore your Majesty's gracious Recommendation to Parliament, that your American Subjects may be relieved from the operation of the Several Acts made for that Purpose, in such manner as to the Wisdom of your Majesty and Parliament may seem proper.

At a Council held at the Council Chamber in Boston, on Thursday July 7th 1768

Present in Council

His Excellency Fra: Bernard Esq. Governor.

Isaac Royall[7]	James Russell
John Erving	Thomas Flucker
James Bowdoin Esq[rs].	Royall Tyler
Thomas Hubbard	James Pitts.
Harrison Gray	

M[r] Bowdoin from the Committe appointed to prepare a humble Address to his Majesty having reported the foregoing Draft the same was accepted. And His Excellency was thereupon unanimously desired to transmit a fair Copy of the same to his Majesty's Sec[y]: of State with a Request that he would be pleased to lay it before his Majesty for his most gracious consideration, that his Excellency be Desired at the same time to recommend the Prayer of the said Petition.—[8]

Andrew Oliver, Secretary[9]

Ms, RC   CO 5/757, ff 318-323.

This engrossed copy of the petition was not signed but its authenticity was attested by the copy of the Council minute appended to it by Province Secretary Andrew Oliver. It was transmitted by FB under cover of **No. 654**. Variants: James Bowdoin's autograph draft is in Bowdoin and Temple Papers, Loose MSS; extracts of the engrossed copy were printed in *Letters to Hillsborough* (1st ed.), 54; *Letters to Hillsborough* (repr.), 106-107. Hillsborough received the petition on behalf of the king and in **No. 679** notified FB that he would present it to Parliament, which he did on 28 Nov. But by doing this Hillsborough denied the Massachusetts Council the opportunity of first communicating directly with His Majesty in Council. *HCJ*, 32: 75.

---

1. The first charter of Massachusetts Bay was issued by King Charles I on 4 Mar. 1629. It was revoked in 1684 by the future James II (as duke of York ruling the New England and New York colonies now incorporated in the Dominion of New England). Following the collapse of the Dominion of New England, the new Charter of the Province of the Massachusetts Bay in New England was issued on 7 Oct. 1691 and took effect on 14 May 1692.

2. The British conquest of Acadia in 1710, during Queen Anne's War (1702-13), and undertaken by an expedition commanded by Francis Nicholson.

3. Restoration and/or surrender. *OED*.

4. King George II.

5. Thus in manuscript, here and below.

6. The French and Indian War in North America, 1754-63, was part of global struggle for imperial supremacy between Britain and France known as the Seven Years' War, 1756-63.

7. Signatories (in alphabetical order) with dates of election to Council:* James Bowdoin (1726-90), 1757-68, 1770-73; John Erving (c.1692-1786), 1754-74; Thomas Flucker (1719-83), 1761-68; Harrison Gray (1711-94), 1761-72; Thomas Hubbard (1702-73), 1759-72; James Pitts (1710-76), 1766-74; Isaac Royall (c.1719-81), 1752-73; James Russell (1715-98), 1761-73; Royal Tyler (1724-71), 1764-70.
    *Elections were conducted at the beginning of the assembly's legislative year, which was in the last week of May. Votes were cast by the new House of Representatives and the outgoing Council. Appointments to the mandamus Council in Aug. 1774 have been excluded.

8. This paragraph is a copy of the Council minute of 7 Jul. 1768. CO 5/827, f 52.

9. Autograph signature.

Appendix 12

THE EARL OF HILLSBOROUGH TO THOMAS GAGE

(N⁰: 11)

Whitehall July 30th. 1768.

Sir,

In my Letter of the 8th of June last,[1] I communicated to you the Advices which had been received of the Disposition that appeared in the Town of Boston to deny the Authority & resist the Execution of Acts of Parliament; & His Maty has the fullest Confidence, that every prudent and proper Step will have been taken for carrying into due Execution the Orders contained in that Letter.

Since that Time further Advices have been received from Boston of great Riots & Disturbances in that Town, and that the Comm^rs. of the Customs have been obliged, from Hazard of their Lives, to seek Protection on board the Romney Man of War, & afterwards in Castle William.[2]

Upon these Advices; upon what has appeared in other Colonies of a like dangerous Spirit of Opposition to the Authority of the Laws of this Kingdom, and upon a full Consideration of the State & Distribution of the Troops under your Command, His Majesty has thought fit that the Hands of Government in His Colonies should be further strengthened by the Addition of Two Regiments from Ireland, and His Majesty's Commands are signified, that the 64th. and 65th. Regiments of Foot, which were intended for the usual Relief in N⁰. America next Spring, should be augmented ^by Draughts,^ to 500 each and sent immediately to Boston, [there][3] to be disposed of in such Manner as you shall think most advise[able] for the Purposes of supporting and protecting, when properly and legally called upon, the civil Magistrates & Officers in the Discharge of their Duty, and for inducing a due Obedience to the Laws of this Kingdom.

Transport Vessels are preparing with all possible Dispatch in order to take on board these Troops at Corke and to proceed with them to Boston, and I am to acquaint you that it is His Majesty's Intention, that when these Regiments are landed at Boston, such a Number of the Transports as shall be sufficient for the Reception of the 62d. Regiment, which is to be brought from the ceded Islands[4] to Ireland, should proceed to those Islands for that Purpose, and that the Remainder should follow such Orders as you may think proper to give them, either for their Return to England or otherwise.

I am further to signify to you, that it is not His Maty's Intention, that either one or both of the Regiments in N⁰. America, which would have been sent Home next Spring in the ordinary Course of Relief, should be immediately exchanged for the two Regiments now sent out, unless you think that His Majesty's Service in the present Situation of Affairs may safely admit of it,[5] in which Case you will avail yourself of the Transports that will remain after the Service in the West Indies has been provided for and make the usual and necessary Provision for their Passage Home on board such Transports.

At the same Time the King has thought fit, upon a Consideration of the present State of Affairs in Nº. America to augment His Troops by Land, His Majesty has also had a proper Attention to the State of the naval Force there; and I have signified His Majesty's Commands to the Lords of the Admiralty,[6] that the Frigate that convoys the Transports from Ireland to Boston, and also a Ship of the Line which is preparing for the Reception of Lord Botetourt, whom His Majesty has appointed to be His Lieutenant & Governor General of Virginia, should be ordered to remain in those Seas, if you shall judge it to be necessary.

As it may be of Use to you to be informed of the Instructions given to Governor Bernard, in relation to the present State of Affairs in his Gover^n^ment, I herewith inclose to you, for your private Satisfaction, a Copy of my Dispatch to him of this Day's Date, and am to acquaint you that your Letters to me, Nos. 3, 4, & 5,[7] have been duly receivd and laid before the King, and that I shall hope to be able to transmit to you His Majesty's Orders thereupon by the Pacquet of Saturday se'nnight.

Just as I had finished this Dispatch I received your Letter Nº. 6,[8] which was immediately communicated to His Majesty with the Papers inclosed, and [I][9] have it in Command to acquaint you that His Majesty entirely approves the Steps you have taken in consequence of the Application made to you by [the][10] Commissioners of the Customs.

I am &cª.

Hillsborough

Major Genˡ. Gage.[11]

L, Copy   CO 5/86, ff 124-127.

Enclosed a copy of **No. 661** (not found). Variants: CO 5/241, ff 48-50 (L, LbC); Gage, vol. 79 (LS, RC). Gage would have received the RC c.3 Sept.[12] Not printed in *Correspondence of Gage.*

1. **Appendix 4**.

2. **Nos. 623**, **630**, **632**, **633**, and **Appendix 6**. See source note to **No. 661**.

3. Manuscript torn here and below. Supplied from CO 5/241.

4. Islands in the Caribbean ceded to Great Britain by France under the Treaty of Paris, 1763, including Grenada and the Grenadines.

5. Annotation. Asterisk referring to left marginalia: "viz. the 9th. & 34th."

6. Hillsborough to the lords commissioners of Admiralty. Whitehall, 21 Jun. 1766, CO 5/86, f 92.

7. Gage to Hillsborough, New York, 16, 17, and 18 Jun. 1768, CO 5/86, ff 104-115.

8. Of 28 Jun. 1768, CO 5/86, ff 128-130.

9. Obscured in the fold.

10. Obscured in the fold.

11. Relocated from the first page.

12. **No. 669**. The RC was not available for transcription when this present volume was being prepared.

Appendix 13

CIRCULAR OF THE BOSTON SELECTMEN
TO THE MASSACHUSETTS TOWNS

BOSTON, September 14, 1768

GENTLEMEN,

You are already too well acquainted with the melancholy and very alarming Circumstances to which this Province, as well as *America* in general, is now reduced. Taxes equally detrimental to the Commercial Interests of the Parent Country and her Colonies, are imposed upon the People, without their Consent;— Taxes designed for the Support of the Civil Government in the Colonies, in a Manner clearly unconstitutional, and contrary to that, in which 'till of late, Government has been supported, by the free Gift of the People in the *American* Assemblies or Parliaments;[1] as also for the Maintenance of a large Standing Army; not for the Defence of the newly acquired Territories, but for the old Colonies, and in a Time of Peace. The decent, humble and truly loyal Applications and Petitions from the Representatives of this Province for the Redress of these heavy and very threatning Grievances, have hitherto been ineffectual, being assured from authentick Intelligence that they have not yet reach'd the Royal Ear: The only Effect of transmitting these Applications hitherto percievable, has been a Mandate from one of his Majesty's Secretaries of State to the Governor of this Province, to Dissolve the General Assembly, merely because the late House of Representatives refused to Rescind a Resolution of a former House, which imply'd nothing more than a Right in the American Subjects to unite in humble and dutiful Petitions to their gracious Sovereign, when they found themselves aggrieved: This is a Right naturally inherent in every Man, and expressly recognized at the glorious Revolution as the Birthright of an Englishman.

This Dissolution you are sensible has taken Place; the Governor has publicly and repeatedly declared that he cannot call another Assembly; and the Secretary of State for the American Department in one of his Letters communicated to the late House, has been pleased to say, that "proper Care will be taken for the Support of the Dignity of Government"; the Meaning of which is too plain to be misunderstood.

The Concern and Perplexity into which these Things have thrown the People, have been greatly aggravated, by a late Declaration of his Excellency Governor BERNARD, that one or more Regiments may soon be expected in the Province.

The Design of these Troops is in every one's Apprehension nothing short of Enforcing by military Power the Execution of Acts of Parliament, in the forming of which the Colonies have not, and cannot have any constitutional Influence. This is one of the greatest Distresses to which a free People can be reduced.

The Town which we have the Honor to serve, have taken these Things at their late Meeting into their most serious Consideration: And as there is in the Minds of many a prevailing Apprehension of an approaching War with *France*, they have passed the several Votes, which we transmit to you; desiring that they may be immediately laid before the Town, whose Prudentials are in your Care, at a legal Meeting, for their candid and particular Attention.

Deprived of the Councils of a General Assembly in this dark and difficult Season, the loyal People of this Province, will, we are persuaded, immediately perceive the Propriety and Utility of the proposed Committee of Convention: And the sound and wholesome Advice that may be expected from a Number of Gentlemen chosen by themselves, and in whom they may Repose the greatest Confidence, must tend to the real Service of our Gracious Sovereign, and the Welfare of his Subjects in this Province; and may happily prevent any sudden and unconnected Measures, which in their present Anxiety, and even Agony of Mind, they may be in Danger of falling into.

As it is of Importance that the Convention should meet as soon as may be, so early a Day as the 22d of this Instant *September* has been propos'd for that Purpose —and it is hoped the remotest Towns will by that Time, or as soon after as conveniently may be, return their respective Committees.

Not doubting but that you are equally concerned with us and our Fellow Citizens for the Preservation of our invaluable Rights, and for the general Happiness of our Country, and that you are disposed with equal Ardor to exert yourselves in every constitutional Way for so glorious a Purpose,

We are, GENTLEMAN, With the greatest Esteem, Your obedient humble Servants,

N.B. *The other two Selectmen are out of the Province.* }

To the Gentlemen Select-Men of

Prt, PC   CO 5/757, f 408.

Unsigned broadside. Listed in *Early American Imprints, Series 1,* no. 41799. This copy was enclosed in **No. 681**. Copies "*Signed by the Select-Men*" (minus the names) also appeared in the *Boston Evening-Post* and the *Boston Post-Boy and Advertiser* on 19 Sept. and the *Essex Gazette,* 12-19 Sept. 1768. The selectmen present at the meeting which approved the circular would probably have signed the copies distributed to the towns: Joseph Jackson, John Ruddock, John Hancock, and Samuel Pemberton. *Reports of the Record Commissioners of Boston,* 20: 308. The selectmen's circular was the only documentary evidence FB could produce that might warrant investigation, by virtue of the Boston selectmen having usurped royal authority in summoning an assembly of town representatives.

---

1. This word underlined, probably by FB or the recipient.

Appendix 14

LIST OF CORRESPONDENCE

The following list itemizes in chronological order Francis Bernard's extant in-letters and out-letters for the period covered by this volume. It excludes non-epistolary enclosures. The first item in each entry is the authoritative version; sub-entries show variant copies retained or made by the receiver, the author, or a third party (and which are also sorted by date of composition, if known).

To John Pownall, Boston, 8 Jan. 1768. BP, 6: 55-56 (L, LbC). **No. 577**.

To Richard Jackson, Boston, 8 Jan. 1768. BP, 6: 57-59 (L, LbC).

From Lord Barrington, Cavendish Square [*London*], 8 Jan. 1768. BP, 11: 111-114 (ALS, RC).

To Messrs. Etty, Offley and Co.,[1] Boston, N.E., 9 Jan. 1768. BP, 6: 60-62 (L, LbC).

To John Pownall, Boston, 9 Jan. 1768. BP, 6: 59-60 (L, LbC). **No. 578**.

To John Pownall, Boston, 16 Jan. 1768. BP, 6: 62-65 (L, LbC). **No. 579**.

To Richard Jackson, Boston, 16 Jan. 1768. BP, 6: 65-67 (L, LbC). **No. 580**.

To the Earl of Shelburne, Boston, 21 Jan. 1768. CO 5/757, ff 18-21 (ALS, RC). **No. 581**.

——CO 5/893, ff 33-36 (dupLS, RC).

——CO 5/766, ff 98-104 (L, RLbC).

——BP, 6: 256-262 (L, LbC).

——Coll. Mass. Papers, 1768 (L extract, three copies).

——HLL: American Colonies Box 1 (L extract, Copy).

——*Letters to the Ministry* (1st ed.), 3-5.

——*Letters to the Ministry* (repr.), 2-6.

Circular from the Earl of Hillsborough, Whitehall, 23 Jan. 1768. BP, 11: 123-126 (dupLS, RC).

——CO 5/241, f 2 (L, LbC).

To Lord Barrington, Boston, 26 Jan. 1768. BP, 6: 67-70 (L, LbC). **No. 583**.

To Peter Clausen,[2] Boston, 28 Jan. 1768. BP, 5: 256 (AL, LbC).

To Lord Barrington, Boston, 28 Jan. 1768. BP, 11: 127-136 (AL, AC). **No. 584**.

——BP, 6: 70-77 (Dft, LbC).

——*Select Letters*, 53-60.

To the Earl of Shelburne, Boston, 30 Jan. 1768. CO 5/757, ff 22-23 (ALS, RC). **No. 585**.

——CO 5/893, ff 37-38 (LS, RC).

——CO 5/766, ff 104-106 (L, RLbC).

——BP, 6: 263-264 (L, LbC).

——Coll. Mass. Papers, 1768 (L extract, Copy).

——*Letters to the Ministry* (1st ed.), 5-6.

——*Letters to the Ministry* (repr.), 6-7.

To Richard Jackson, Boston, 1 Feb. 1768. BP, 6: 77-81 (L, LbC). **No. 586**.

To the Earl of Shelburne, Boston, 2 Feb. 1768. CO 5/757, f 24 (ALS, RC).

——CO 5/766, f 106 (précis, RLbC).

——BP, 6: 264-265 (L, LbC).

——Coll. Mass. Papers, 1768 (L, Copy).

——HLL: American Colonies Box 1 (L, Copy).

——*Letters to the Ministry* (1st ed.), 6.

——*Letters to the Ministry* (repr.), 7-8.

To John Pownall, Boston, 2 Feb. 1768. BP, 6: 82 (AL, LbC).

From Sir Henry Moore, New York, 6 Feb. 1768. Mass. Archs., 4: 286 (ALS, RC).

To Lord Barrington, Boston, 7 Feb. 1768. BP, 6: 82-87 (L, LbC). **No. 587**.

To Richard Jackson, Boston, 8 Feb. 1768. BP, 6: 88-89 (L, LbC).

From John Osborne,[3] [Boston?], 13 Feb. 1768. Mass. Archs., 56: 536-538 (LS, RC).

From the Earl of Hillsborough, Whitehall, 16 Feb. 1768. BP, 11: 137-140 (LS, RC). **No. 588**.

——CO 5/757, ff 15-17 (LS, AC).

To the Earl of Shelburne, Boston, 18 Feb. 1768. CO 5/757, ff 28-29 (dupALS, RC). **No. 589**.

——CO 5/766, ff 107-109 (précis, RLbC).

——BP, 6: 265-268 (L, LbC).

——Coll. Mass. Papers, 1768 (L extract, Copy)

——HLL: American Colonies Box 1 (L extract, Copy).

——*Letters to the Ministry* (1st ed.), 7-8.

——*Letters to the Ministry* (repr.), 8-9.

To Lord Barrington, Boston, 20 Feb. 1768. BP, 6: 94-95 (L, LbC).

From the Earl of Hillsborough, Whitehall, 20 Feb. 1768. BP, 11: 141-144 (LS, RC).

To Richard Jackson, Boston, 20 and 22 Feb. 1768. 1768. BP, 6: 90-96 (L, LbC). **No. 590**.

To the Earl of Shelburne, Boston, 20 and 22 Feb. 1768. 1768. CO 5/757, ff 34-35 (dupLS, RC). **No. 591**.

——CO 5/766, ff 115-121 (L, RLbC).

——BP, 6: 269-273 (L, LbC).

To Benning Wentworth,[4] Boston, 27 Feb. 1768. BP, 5: 251 (L, LbC).

To Benning Wentworth, Boston, 29 Feb. 1768. BP, 5: 253 (AL, LbC).

To Sir Henry Moore[5], Boston, 29 Feb. 1768. BP, 5: 253-255 (L, LbC).

To Lord Barrington, Boston, 4 Mar. 1768. BP, 6: 96-99 (L, LbC). **No. 592**.

To the Earl of Shelburne, Boston, 5 Mar. 1768. CO 5/757, ff 38-41 (ALS, RC).
   No. 593.

——CO 5/766, ff 121-127 (L, RLbC).

——BP, 6: 272-277 (L, LbC).

——HLL: American Colonies Box 1 (L extract, Copy).

——*Letters to the Ministry* (1st ed.), 8-10.

——*Letters to the Ministry* (repr.), 10-13 (L extract, PC).

From the Earl of Hillsborough, Whitehall, 5 Mar. 1768. BP, 11: 149-152
   (dupLS, RC).

To Richard Jackson, Boston, 6 Mar. 1768. BP, 6: 11 (L, LbC). **No. 594**.

To John Pownall, Boston, 7 Mar. 1768. BP, 6: 99-100 (L, LbC). **No. 595**.

To the Earl of Shelburne, Boston, 12 Mar. 1768. CO 5/757, ff 64-65 (ALS, RC).
   No. 596.

——CO 5/893, ff 39-41 (dupLS, RC).

——CO 5/766, ff 146-150 (L, RLbC).

——BP, 6: 278-280 (L, LbC).

——HLL: American Colonies Box 1 (L extract, Copy).

——*Letters to the Ministry* (1st ed.), 10-12.

——*Letters to the Ministry* (repr.), 13-16.

From Lord Barrington, Cavendish Square, 12 Mar. 1768. BP, 11: 157-160
   (ALS, RC). **No. 597**.

To Richard Jackson, Boston, 14 Mar. 1768. BP, 6: 103-104 (L, LbC). **No. 598**.

To John Pownall, Boston, 14 Mar. 1768. BP, 6: 101-102 (AL, LbC).

From the American Board of Customs, 18 Mar. 1768. T 1/465, f 34 (L, Copy).
   No. 599.

——T 1/465, f 28 (L Copy).

To the Earl of Shelburne, Boston, 19 Mar. 1768. CO 5/893, ff 41-45
   (dupLS, RC). **No. 600**.

——CO 5/766, ff 150-160 (L, RLbC)

——BP, 6: 280-288 (L, LbC).

——HLL: American Colonies Box 1 (L extract, Copy).

——*Letters to the Ministry* (1st ed.), 12-17.

——*Letters to the Ministry* (repr.), 16-22.

To the Earl of Hillsborough, Boston, 19 Mar. 1768. CO 5/757, ff 66-71
   (L, Copy).

To the Earl of Shelburne, Boston, 21 Mar. 1768. CO 5/757, ff 74-77 (ALS, RC).
  No. 601.
——CO 5/893, ff 50-53 (dupALS, RC).
——CO 5/766, ff 160-168 (L, RLbC).
——BP, 6: 288-295 (L, LbC).
——HLL: American Colonies Box 1 (L extract, Copy).
——*Letters to the Ministry* (1st ed.), 17-19.
——*Letters to the Ministry* (repr.), 22-25.
——*Boston Evening-Post*, 21 Aug. 1768 (L extract).
——*Essex Gazette*, 15-20 Aug. 1769 (L extract).
——*Pennsylvania Gazette*, 31 Aug. 1769 (L extract).
——*Providence Gazette*, 19-26 Aug. 1769 (L extract).
To Michael Francklin, Boston, 24 Mar. 1768. BP, 5: 260-261 (L, LbC). **No. 602**.
From Sir Henry Moore, Fort George, New York, 25 Mar. 1768. Mass. Archs.,
  4: 300-302 (LS, RC).
——Mass. Archs., 56: 543-544 (LS, Copy).
——Prov. Sec. Letterbooks, 2A:172-173 (L, Copy).
To Lord Barrington, Boston, 28 Mar. 1768. BP, 6: 105-106 (L, LbC).
To John Pownall, Boston, 28 Mar. 1768. BP, 6: 104-105 (L, LbC).
From the Earl of Hillsborough, Whitehall, 4 Apr. 1768. BP, 11: 163-166
  (dupLS, RC). **No. 603**.
——CO 5/757, ff 26-27 (L, Copy).
——CO 5/765, ff 4-5 (L, LbC).
——HLL: American Colonies Box 1 (L extract, Copy).
To Nathaniel Ropes, Boston, 9 Apr. 1768. BP, 5: 258 (L, LbC). **No. 604**.
To Stephen Hopkins, Boston, 16 Apr. 1768. BP, 5: 260 (L, LbC).
From Lord Barrington, Cavendish Square, 16 Apr. 1768. BP, 11: 167-170
  (ALS, RC). **No. 605**.
From Benjamin Price, Montréal, 16 Apr. 1768. Mass. Archs., 56: 549-550
  (ALS, RC).
To Lord Barrington, Boston, 20 Apr. 1768. BP, 6: 106-107 (L, LbC). **No. 606**.
To Thomas Pownall, Boston, 20 Apr. 1768. BP, 6: 107-110 (L, LbC). **No. 607**.
From the Earl of Hillsborough, Whitehall, 22 Apr. 1768. BP, 11: 171-174
  (LS, RC). **No. 608**.
——CO 5/757, ff 55-57 (LS, AC).
——CO 5/765, ff 6-8 (L, LbC).
——HLL: American Colonies Box 1 (L extract, Copy).
——*JHRM*, 45: 68-69 (L extract, PC).
To Sir Henry Moore, Boston, 27 Apr. 1768. Mass. Archs., 56: 547 (LS, AC).
From the Earl of Hillsborough, Whitehall, 30 Apr. 1768. BP, 11: 175-176
  (dupLS, RC).

To Sir Henry Moore, Boston, 4 May 1768. BP, 5: 255 (AL, LbC).

From Lord Barrington, Cavendish Square, 9 May 1768. BP, 11: 183-186 (ALS, RC). **No. 610**.

——BP, 11: 177-180 (dupALS, RC).

To Lord Barrington, Boston, 9 and 12 May 1768. BP, 6: 110-115 (L, LbC). **No. 609**.

To the Earl of Hillsborough, Boston, 12 May 1768. CO 5/757, ff 88-89 (ALS, RC). **No. 611**.

——CO 5/766, ff 170-171 (L, RLbC).

——BP, 6: 295-297 (L, LbC).

Circular from the Earl of Hillsborough, Whitehall, 14 May 1768. BP, 11: 181-182 (dupLS, RC). **No. 612**.

——CO 5/241, f 31 (L, LbC).

To John Pownall, Boston, 17 May 1768. CO 5/893, ff 54-55 (ALS, RC). **No. 613**.

——BP, 6: 297-298 (L, LbC).

To the Earl of Hillsborough, Boston, 19 May 1768. CO 5/757, ff 104-106 (dupLS, RC). **No. 614**.

——CO 5/766, ff 172-177 (L, RLbC).

——BP, 6: 300-304 (L, LbC).

To the Earl of Hillsborough, Boston, 21 May 1768. CO 5/757, ff 107-108 (dupLS, RC). **No. 615**.

——CO 5/766, ff 177-180 (L, RLbC).

——BP, 6: 298-300 (L, LbC).

To Michael Francklin, Boston, 23 May 1768. BP, 5: 261-263 (L, LbC).

To the Earl of Hillsborough, Boston, 30 May 1768. CO 5/757, ff 109-112 (dupLS, RC). **No. 616**.

——CO 5/766, ff 180-191 (L, RLbC).

——BP, 6: 304-311 (L, LbC).

To John Pownall, Boston, 30 May 1768. BP, 6: 115-119 (AL, LbC). **No. 617**.

To John Corner, Province House, 6 Jun. 1768. BP, 5: 263-264 (L, LbC). **No. 618**.

To Richard Jackson, Boston, 6 Jun. 1768. BP, 6: 119-122 (AL, LbC). **No. 619**.

To William Offley, Boston, 8 Jun. 1768. BP, 6: 123 (AL, LbC).

To William Dalrymple, Boston, 10 Jun. 1768. BP, 5: 265-266 (L, LbC). **No. 620**.

To the Rev. Hugh Palmer, Boston, 10 Jun. 1768. BP, 5: 264-265 (L, LbC).

From the American Board of Customs, Boston, 11 Jun. 1768. CO 5/766, ff 203-204 (L, Copy). **No. 621**.

From the Earl of Hillsborough, Whitehall, 11 Jun. 1768. BP, 11: 187-196 (LS, RC). **No. 622**.

——CO 5/765, ff 9-14 (L, LbC).

——CO 5/757, ff 83-86 (LS, AC).

——HLL: American Colonies Box 1 (L extract, Copy).

From Lord Barrington, Cavendish Square, 11 Jun. 1768. BP, 11: 197-200
(ALS, RC).

To the Earl of Hillsborough, Boston, 11 and 13 Jun. 1768. CO 5/766, ff 191-195
(L, RLbC). **No. 623**.

——CO 5/757, ff 115-117 (L, Copy).

——BP, 6: 311-315 (L, LbC).

——Coll. Mass. Papers, 1768 (L, Copy).

——HLL: American Colonies Box 1 (L extract, Copy).

——*Letters to the Ministry* (1st ed.), 20-22.

—— *Letters to the Ministry* (repr.), 26-29.

From the American Board of Customs, HMS Romney, 12 Jun. 1768. T 1/465,
ff 143-144 (L, Copy). **No. 624**.

——CO 5/757, ff 191-192 (L, Copy).

——CO 5/766, ff 204-206 (L, RLbC).

——Temple Papers, 1762-1768: JT Letterbook, 331-332 (L, Copy).

——BL: Add 38340, f 261 (L, Copy).

——Coll. Mass. Papers, 1768 (L, Copy).

——*Letters to the Ministry* (1st ed.), 96.

——*Letters to the Ministry* (repr.), 128-129.

To the Captain of Castle William [Thomas Hutchinson], Jamaica Plain, 13 Jun.
1768. CO 5/766, f 27 (L, LbC).

To the American Board of Customs, Boston, 13 Jun. 1768. T 1/465, ff 153-154
(L, Copy). **No. 625**.

——CO 5/766, ff 207-209 (L, LbC).

——BL: Add 38340, f 279 (L, Copy).

——HLL: American Colonies Box 1 (L, Copy).

——Coll. Mass. Papers, 1768 (L extract, Copy).

——*Letters to the Ministry* (1st ed.), 98-99.

——*Letters to the Ministry* (repr.), 132-133.

From the American Board of Customs, HMS Romney, 13 Jun. 1768. T 1/465,
ff 157-158 (L, Copy). **No. 626**.

——CO 5/757, ff 205-206 (L, Copy).

——CO 5/766, ff 209-210 (L, Copy).

——BL: Add 38340, f 275 (L, Copy).

——*Letters to the Ministry* (1st ed.), 100.

——*Letters to the Ministry* (repr.), 133.

To the American Board of Customs, Jamaica Plain, 13 Jun. 1768. T 1/465,
ff 159-161 (L, Copy). **No. 627**.

——CO 5/757, ff 207-208 (L, Copy).

——CO 5/766, ff 206-206 (L, Copy).

——BL: Add 38340, f 277 (L, Copy).

——Coll. Mass. Papers, 1768 (L, Copy).

—— HLL: American Colonies Box 1 (L, Copy).

——*Letters to the Ministry* (1st ed.), 100.

——*Letters to the Ministry* (repr.), 134.

To the American Board of Customs, Council Chamber, Boston, 13 Jun. 1768. T 1/465, ff 161-162 (L, Copy). **No. 628**.

——CO 5/757, ff 209-210 (L, Copy).

——CO 5/766, f 211 (L, Copy).

——BL: Add 38340, f 271 (L, Copy).

——HLL: American Colonies Box 1 (L, Copy).

——Coll. Mass. Papers, 1768 (L extract, Copy).

——*Letters to the Ministry* (repr.), 135.

——*Letters to the Ministry* (1st ed.), 100.

To the Earl of Hillsborough, Roxbury, 14 Jun. 1768. CO 5/757, ff 118-120 (L, Copy). **No. 630**.

——CO 5/766, ff 196-203 (L, RLbC).

——BP, 6: 315-319 (L, LbC).

——HLL: American Colonies Box 2 (L extract, Copy).

——*Letters to the Ministry* (1st ed.), 22-24.

——*Letters to the Ministry* (repr.), 29-32.

To the Boston Town Meeting, 15 Jun. 1768. CO 5/766, ff 228-230 (Ms, LbC). **No. 631**.

To the Earl of Hillsborough, Boston, 16 and 18 Jun. 1768. CO 5/757, ff 138-141 (L, RC). **No. 632**.

——CO 5/766, ff 212-221 (L, RLbC).

——BP, 6: 319-324 (L, LbC).

——HLL: American Colonies Box 2 (L extract, Copy).

——*Letters to the Ministry* (repr.), 33-37.

——*Letters to the Ministry* (1st ed.), 25-28.

To the Earl of Hillsborough, Boston, 17 and 18 Jun. 1768. CO 5/757, ff 146-147 (ALS, RC). **No. 633**.

——CO 5/766, ff 230-233 (L, RLbC).

——BP, 6: 324-326 (L, LbC).

——HLL: American Colonies Box 2 (L extract, Copy).

——*Letters to the Ministry* (1st ed.), 28-29.

——*Letters to the Ministry* (repr.), 37-39.

To Lord Barrington, Boston, 18 Jun. 1768. BP, 6: 123-125 (L, LbC). **No. 634**.

From the Earl of Hillsborough, Whitehall, 21 Jun. 1768. BP, 11: 201-204
(dupLS, RC). **No. 635**.
From Thomas Gage, New York, 24 Jun. 1768. BP, 11: 205-208 (ALS, RC).
No. 637.
——MiU-C: Gage, vol. 78 (L, AC).
——CO 5/757, f 352 (L, Copy).
——CO 5/86, ff 134-136 (L extract, Copy).
To the Earl of Hillsborough, Boston, 25 and 28 Jun. and 1 Jul. 1768. CO 5/757,
ff 256-262 (dupLS, RC). **No. 638**.
——CO 5/766, ff 250-262 (L, RLbC).
——BP, 6: 326-335 (L, LbC).
——HLL: American Colonies Box 2 (L extract, Copy).
——*Letters to the Ministry* (1st ed.), 29-35.
——*Letters to the Ministry* (repr.), 39-46.
From Thomas Gage, New York, 25 Jun. 1768. BP, 11: 209-210 (ALS, RC).
No. 639.
——MiU-C: Gage, vol. 78 (L, AC).
——CO 5/86, f 136 (L, Copy).
To Lord Barrington, Boston, 29 and 30 Jun. 1768. BP, 6: 125-129 (L, LbC).
No. 640.
To Thomas Gage, Roxbury, 2 Jul. 1768. MiU-C: Gage, vol. 78 (ALS, RC).
No. 641.
——BP, 5: 266-269 (L, LbC).
——CO 5/757, ff 353-354 (AL, Copy).
To William Dalrymple, Roxbury, 3 Jul. 1768. BP, 5: 272 (L, LbC). **No. 642**.
——MiU-C: Gage, vol. 78 (L, Copy).
To Thomas Gage, Roxbury, 3 Jul. 1768. MiU-C: Gage, vol. 78 (ALS, RC).
No. 643.
——BP, 5: 269 (L, LbC).
——CO 5/757, f 354 (AL, Copy).
To John Corner, Boston, 4 Jul. 1768. BP, 5: 270 (AL, LbC).
——ADM 1/483, f 127 (L, Copy).
To John Corner, Boston, 4 Jul. 1768. BP, 5: 272-273 (L, LbC). **No. 644**.
——ADM 1/483, f 127 (L, Copy).
From the Earl of Hillsborough, Whitehall, 4 Jul. 1768. BP, 11: 211-214 (LS, RC).
No. 645.
To the Earl of Hillsborough, Boston, 9 Jul. 1768. CO 5/757, ff 303-306
(ALS, RC). **No. 646**.
——CO 5/766, ff 264-267 (L, RLbC).

——BP, 6: 335-340 (L, LbC).

——HLL: American Colonies Box 2 (L extract, Copy).

——T 1/465, f 190 (L extract, Copy).

——*Letters to the Ministry* (1st ed.), 38-41.

——*Letters to the Ministry* (repr.), 50-54.

From John Pownall, Secretary of State's Office, Whitehall, 9 Jul. 1768. BP, 11: 215-218 (ALS, RC). **No. 647**.

——CO 5/757, ff 96-97 (L, AC).

——CO 5/765, f 16 (L, LbC).

To the Earl of Hillsborough, Boston, 11 Jul. 1768. CO 5/757, ff 307-308 (ALS, RC). **No. 648**.

——CO 5/766, f 268 (L, RLbC).

——BP, 7: 1-2 (L, LbC).

——T 1/465, ff 192-193 (L, Copy).

——*Letters to the Ministry* (1st ed.), 41-42.

——*Letters to the Ministry* (repr.), 55-56.

To Richard Jackson, Boston, 11 Jul. 1768. BP, 6: 133-134 (L, LbC).

To Lord Barrington, Boston, 11 Jul. 1768. BP, 6: 132 (L, LbC).

To John Pownall, Boston, 11 Jul. 1768. BP, 6: 130-131 (L, LbC). **No. 649**.

From the Earl of Hillsborough, Whitehall, 11 Jul. 1768. BP, 11: 223-226 (dupLS, RC). **No. 650**.

——CO 5/757, f 100 (LS, AC).

——CO 5/765, f 23 (L, LbC).

Circular from the Earl of Hillsborough, Whitehall, 11 Jul. 1768. BP, 11: 227-230 (LS, RC). **No. 651**.

——HLL: American Colonies Box 2 (L, Copy).

From Thomas Gage, New York, 11 Jul. 1768. BP, 11: 231-234 (ALS, RC). **No. 652**.

From the Earl of Hillsborough, Whitehall, 11 Jul. 1768. BP, 11: 219-222 (LS, RC). **No. 653**.

——CO 5/757, ff 98-99 (L, AC).

——CO 5/765, ff 21-22 (L, LbC).

——HLL: American Colonies Box 2 (L, Copy).

From William Tyng,[6] Falmouth, 12 Jul. 1768. Mass. Archs., 56: 552 (ALS, RC).

To the Earl of Hillsborough, Boston, 16 Jul. 1768. CO 5/757, ff 316-317 (ALS, RC). **No. 654**.

——CO 5/767, ff 22-40 (L, RLbC).

——BP, 7: 2-7 (L, LbC).

——HLL: American Colonies Box 2 (L extract, Copy).

——*Letters to the Ministry* (1st ed.), 42-43.

——*Letters to the Ministry* (repr.), 56-57.

——*Boston Gazette*, 23 Oct. 1769 (newspaper extract, PC).

——*Newport Mercury*, 30 Oct. 1769 (newspaper extract, PC).

To Thomas Gage, Boston, 18 Jul. 1768. MiU-C: Gage, vol. 79 (ALS, RC). **No. 655**.

——BP, 5: 274-276 (L, LbC).

——*Letters to the Ministry* (1st ed.), 43-44.

——*Letters to the Ministry* (repr.), 57-59.

To the Earl of Hillsborough, Boston, 18 and 19 Jul. 1768. CO 5/757, ff 326-327 (L, RC). **No. 656**.

——CO 5/767, ff 40-45 (L, RLbC).

——BP, 7: 8-10 (L, LbC).

——HLL: American Colonies Box 2 (L, Copy).

——*Letters to the Ministry* (1st ed.), 44-46.

——*Letters to the Ministry* (repr.), 59-62.

To the Earl of Hillsborough, Boston, 18 Jul. 1768. CO 5/757, ff 330-331 (ALS, RC). **No. 657**.

——CO 5/767, ff 46-48 (L, RLbC).

——BP, 7: 11-12 (L, LbC).

——HLL: American Colonies Box 3 (L, Copy).

To Lord Barrington, Boston, 20 Jul. 1768. BP, 6: 136-139 (AL, LbC). **No. 658**.

To the Earl of Hillsborough, Boston, 21 Jul. 1768. BP, 7: 12 (L, LbC).

To Richard Jackson, Boston, 21 Jul. 1768. BP, 6: 135 (L, LbC).

To Thomas Gage, Boston, 30 Jul. 1768. MiU-C: Gage, vol. 79 (ALS, RC). **No. 659**.

——BP, 5: 276 (AL, LbC).

To the Earl of Hillsborough, Boston, 30 Jul. 1768. CO 5/757, ff 349-351 (ALS, RC). **No. 660**.

——CO 5/767, ff 56-61 (L, RLbC).

——BP, 7: 12-17 (L, LbC).

——HLL: American Colonies Box 3, HL/PO/JO/10/7/288 (L, Copy).

——Coll. Mass. Papers, 1768 (L, Copy).

——*Letters to the Ministry* (1st ed.), 35-38.

——*Letters to the Ministry* (repr.), 46-50 (Prt, PC).

To Lord Barrington, Boston, 30 Jul. 1768. BP, 6: 139-141 (L, LbC).

From the Earl of Hillsborough, Whitehall, 30 Jul. 1768. BP, 11: 235-248 (LS, RC). **No. 661**.

——CO 5/765, ff 24-33 (L, LbC).

——CO 5/757, ff 241-247 (LS, AC).

——HLL: American Colonies Box 3 (L, Copy).

From John Pownall, Secretary of State's Office, Whitehall, 30 Jul. 1768. BP, 11: 249-252 (ALS, RC). **No. 662**.

To Oliver Partridge,[7] Jamaica Farm, 3 Aug. 1768. BP, 5: 276-278 (L, LbC).

To the Earl of Hillsborough, Boston, 6 Aug. 1768. CO 5/757, ff 368-370 (ALS, RC). **No. 663**.

——CO 5/767, ff 63-68 (L, RLbC).

——BP, 7: 19-23 (L, LbC).

——HLL: American Colonies Box 3 (L, Copy).

——*Letters to the Ministry* (1st ed.), 46-49.

——*Letters to the Ministry* (repr.), 62-65.

To the Earl of Hillsborough, Boston, 8 Aug. 1768. CO 5/757, ff 371-372 (ALS, RC).

——CO 5/767, f 69 (L, RLbC).

——BP, 7: 17-18 (L, LbC).

To the Earl of Hillsborough, Boston, 9 Aug. 1768. CO 5/757, ff 375-376 (ALS, RC). **No. 664**.

——CO 5/767, ff 69-71 (L, RLbC).

——BP, 7: 23-24 (L, LbC).

——HLL: American Colonies Box 3 (L, Copy).

——*Letters to the Ministry* (1st ed.), 49-50.

——*Letters to the Ministry* (repr.), 66-67.

From William Alexander,[8] Baskenbridge, 10 Aug. 1768. CO 5/757, f 42 (L, Copy).

——CO 5/893, f 81 (L, Copy).

From Nathan Jones, Frenchman's Bay [*Mount Desert Island*], 10 Aug. 1768. BP, 11: 275-276 (ALS, RC).

To Edmund Quincy Jr.,[9] Jamaica Farm, 11 Aug. 1768. BP, 5: 278 (AL, LbC).

From Lord Barrington, Cavendish Square, 11 Aug. 1768. BP, 11: 277-280 (ALS, RC). **No. 665**.

——BP, 11: 281-284 (dupALS, RC).

From the Earl of Hillsborough, Whitehall, 13 Aug. 1768. BP, 11: 285-286 (dupLS, RC).

——CO 5/757, ff 254-255 (L, AC).

——CO 5/765, f 34 (L, LbC).

To Lord Barrington, Boston, 27 Aug. 1768. BP, 6: 141-145 (L, LbC). **No. 666**.

To Samuel Hood,[10] Boston, 27 Aug. 1768. BP, 7: 191 (L, LbC). **No. 667**.

To the Earl of Hillsborough, Boston, 29 Aug. 1768. CO 5/757, ff 379-380 (ALS, RC). **No. 668**.

——CO 5/767, ff 71-72 (L, RLbC).

——BP, 7: 25-26 (L, LbC).

——HLL: American Colonies Box 3 (L, Copy).

——*Letters to the Ministry* (1st ed.), 50.

——*Letters to the Ministry* (repr.), 67 (L extract).

To Thomas Bradshaw,[11] Boston, 31 Aug. 1768. T 1/465, ff 199-200 (ALS, RC).

——BP, 7: 34-35 (L, LbC).

From Thomas Gage, New York, 31 Aug. 1768. BP, 11: 287-290 (ALS, RC).
  No. 669.

Circular from the Earl of Hillsborough, Whitehall, 2 Sept. 1768. BP, 11:
  291-292 (dupLS, RC). **No. 670.**

To Thomas Gage, Jamaica Farm, 5 Sept. 1768. BP, 7: 191-194 (L, LbC).
  No. 671.

——CO 5/86, ff 178-179 (L extract, Copy).

——BP, 11: 293-296 (ALS, RC).

To William Alexander, Boston, 7 Sept. 1768. BP, 7: 194-195 (L, LbC).

——CO 5/757, ff 400-401 (L, Copy).

——CO 5/893, ff 84-85 (L, Copy).

To John Pownall, Boston, 8 Sept. 1768. CO 5/757, ff 398-399 (ALS, RC).

——CO 5/893, f 78 (dupLS, RC).

——BP, 7: 47 (L, LbC).

To the Earl of Hillsborough, Boston, 9 Sept. 1768. CO 5/757, ff 388-391
  (ALS, RC). **No. 672**.

——CO 5/767, ff 77-84 (L, RLbC).

——BP, 7: 26-33 (L, LbC).

——HLL: American Colonies Box 3 (L, Copy).

——*Letters to the Ministry* (1st ed.), 50-52.

——*Letters to the Ministry* (repr.), 68-70 (L extract).

From Lord Barrington, Cavendish Square, 6 Sept. 1768. BP, 11: 293-294
  (ALS, RC).

To William Alexander, Boston, 7 Sept. 1768. CO 5/757, ff 400-401 (L, Copy).

To John Pownall, 8 Sept. 1768. CO 5/757, ff 389-399 (ALS, RC).

To the Earl of Hillsborough, Boston, 10 Sept. 1768. CO 5/757, ff 394-395
  (ALS, RC). **No. 673**.

——CO 5/767, f 85 (L, RLbC).

——BP, 7: 33-34 (L, LbC).

To the Earl of Hillsborough, Boston, 10 Sept. 1768. CO 5/757, ff 396-397 (ALS,
  RC). **No. 674**.

——CO 5/767, ff 85-87 (L, RLbC).

——BP, 7: 35-36 (AL, LbC).

From Thomas Gage, 12 Sept. 1768. *Reports of the Record Commissioners of
  Boston*, 20: 309-309 (transcript, PC). **No. 675**.

——MiU-C: Gage, vol. 80 (L, AC).

From Thomas Gage, New York, 12 Sept. 1768. BP, 11: 297-300 (ALS, RC).
   No. 676.
——MiU-C: Gage, vol. 80 (L, AC).
From the Boston Town Meeting, Boston, 12 Sept. 1768. *Reports of the Record Commissioners of Boston*, 16: 260-261 (transcript, PC).
To the Boston Town Meeting, 13 Sept. 1768. *Reports of the Record Commissioners of Boston*, 16: 261 (transcript, PC). **No. 677**.
From the American Board of Customs, Castle William, 13 Sept. 1768. Mass. Archs., 56: 553-554 (LS, RC). **No. 678**.
——T 1/471, ff 35-36 (L, Copy).
From the Earl of Hillsborough, Whitehall, 14 Sept. 1768. BP, 11: 301-306 (LS, RC). **No. 679**.
——CO 5/757, ff 346-348 (LS, AC).
——CO 5/765, ff 39-42 (L, LbC).
——HLL: American Colonies Box 3 (L, Copy).
To Thomas Gage, Jamaica Farm, 16 Sept. 1768. BP, 7: 196-198 (L, LbC).
   No. 680.
To the Earl of Hillsborough, Boston, 16 Sept. 1768. CO 5/757, ff 405-408 (ALS, RC). **No. 681**.
——CO 5/767, ff 87-96 (L, RLbC).
——BP, 7: 37-43 (L, LbC).
——Coll. Mass. Papers, 1768 (L, Copy).
——HLL: American Colonies Box 3 (L, Copy).
——*Letters to the Ministry* (1st ed.), 52-56.
——*Letters to the Ministry* (repr.), 70-75.
To the Earl of Hillsborough, Boston, 17 Sept. 1768. BP, 7: 43-45 (L, LbC).
   No. 682.
To the Earl of Hillsborough, Boston, 18 Sept. 1768. BP, 7: 45-46 (L, LbC).
   No. 683.
To Thomas Gage, Boston, 19 Sept. 1768. BP, 7: 198-199 (L, LbC).
To John Pownall, Boston, 20 Sept. 1768. BP, 6: 146-148 (L, LbC). **No. 684**.
——*Select Letters*, 61-63 (Prt, PC).
To the Massachusetts Convention of Towns, 22 Sept. 1768. CO 5/757, f 433.
   No. 685.
To the Earl of Hillsborough, Boston, 23 and 24 Sept. 1768. CO 5/757, ff 414-418 (ALS, RC). **No. 686**.
——CO 5/767, ff 97-18 (L, RLbC).
——BP, 7: 47-56 (L, LbC).
——HLL: American Colonies Box 3 (L, Copy).
——*Letters to the Ministry* (1st ed.), 56-62.

——*Letters to the Ministry* (repr.), 75-83.

To Thomas Gage, Jamaica Farm, 24 Sept. 1768. MiU-C: Gage, vol. 81
 (ALS, RC). **No. 687**.

——BP, 7: 199-202 (L, LbC).

——CO 5/86, ff 209-212 (L extract, Copy).

From Thomas Cushing, 24 Sept. 1768. CO 5/757, f 433. **No. 688**.

——*Boston Evening-Post*, 26 Sept. 1768.

From Thomas Gage, New York, 25 Sept. 1768. BP, 11: 307-310 (ALS, RC).
 No. 689.

To the Earl of Hillsborough, Boston, 26 Sept. 1768. CO 5/757, ff 419-422
 (ALS, RC). **No. 690**.

——CO 5/767, ff 108-114 (L, RLbC).

——BP, 7: 56-62 (L, LbC).

——HLL: American Colonies Box 3 (L, Copy).

——*Letters to the Ministry* (1st ed.), 62-65.

——*Letters to the Ministry* (repr.), 83-88.

From Thomas Gage, New York, 26 Sept. 1768. BP, 11: 311-314 (LS, RC).

——MiU-C: Gage, vol. 81 (L, AC).

To the Earl of Hillsborough, Boston, 27 Sept. 1768. CO 5/757, ff 431-432
 (ALS, RC). **No. 691**.

——CO 5/767, ff 117-119 (L, RLbC).

——BP, 7: 62-64 (L, LbC).

——HLL: American Colonies Box 3 (L, Copy).

——*Letters to the Ministry* (1st ed.), 65-66.

——*Letters to the Ministry* (repr.), 88-89.

——*Boston Evening-Post*, 11 Sept. 1769.

To William Dalrymple, Boston, 30 Sept. 1768. BP, 7: 207-209 (L, LbC).
 No. 692.

To the Earl of Hillsborough, Boston, 30 Sept. 1768. CO 5/767, ff 115-117
 (L, RLbC). **No. 693**.

——BP, 7: 64-66 (L, LbC).

1. This company was probably a firm of wine merchants headed by London merchant William Offley (d.1789), a leading trader in Portuguese and Madeira wines, and possibly a relative of Amelia Bernard (née Offley). The Offley family had long been active in the Merchant Taylors Company. Norman R. Bennett, "The Golden Age of the Port Wine System, 1781-1807," *International History Review* 12 (1990): 221-224.

2. Peter Clausen, governor of the Virgin Islands, a Danish Crown colony (1766-71 and 1773-84). Clausen's out-going correspondence, 1774-84, is in the US National Archives, 55.2 Records of the Government of the Danish West Indies, 1672-1917.

3. John Osborne (1688-1768) a former councilor and merchant, and father-in-law to TH.

4. Benning Wentworth (1696-1770), governor of New Hampshire, 1741-66.

5. Sir Henry Moore (1713-69), governor of New York since 1765.

6. William Tyng (1737-1807), a merchant in Falmouth, Maine, and future Loyalist.

7. Oliver Partridge (1712-93), a wealthy farmer and former representative for Hatfield, and FB's business partner in several New Hampshire land grants.

8. William Alexander (1726-83) of New Jersey, a future American general. He claimed to be the sixth earl of Stirling of the Scottish nobility. He used the unconfirmed title to claim land between the St. Croix and Kennebec Rivers, for which see William O. Sawtelle, "Sir Francis Bernard and His Grant of Mount Desert," *Publications of the Colonial Society of Massachusetts* 24 (1920): 197-254, at 206-209.

9. Edmund Quincy and his partner John Staley operated a gold and silver mine at Mendon, Worcester Co., Mass.

10. Samuel Hood (1724-1816), a British naval officer and commander of the North Atlantic Station from Jul. 1767 to Oct. 1770. He did not see active service in the American War of Independence until his promotion to rear admiral and deployment to the West Indies in 1780.

11. Thomas Bradshaw (1733-74) was chief clerk to the Treasury between 1761 and 1767 and thereafter secretary to the Treasury until 1770. He was made a lord commissioner of the Treasury in 1772 and sat as an MP for Harwich (1767-68) and Saltash (1768-74).

INDEX

"A True Patriot" (anti-government writer), 117–19n, 372n
    assembly, considered by, 113
    cited, 123n
    Council, considered by, 113
    on FB, misrepresentations by, 112, 117n
    "flagitiousness" of, 112
    as libel, 115
    quoted, 118n
Acadia, 396n
Achilles, 86n
Adams, John
    on Adams, S., 75n
    on House of Representatives, papers of, authorship of, 75n
    Hutchinson, criticizes, 170n
    on Otis Jr., 75n–76n
    Tudor, letter to, quoted, 75n
Adams, Samuel
    Appeal to the World
        FB, comments concerning, 133n, 134n, 188n, 189n, 193n, 204n, 210–12n, 246n, 323–24n
        writes, 22
    biographers of, 163
    and *Boston Gazette*, 112, 115, 117n
    as Boston representative, 50n, 211n, 228n, 237n
    Boston town meeting, as committee member, 211n
    on Bostonians,
        alarm at arrival of troops, 323n
        arming of, 324n
    on British women, 133n
    and Council, 193n, 204n
    FB
        and, 2, 40
        character attacked by, 24, 163
        on conspiracy of, 22, 25, 133n, 323n
        on Customs commissioners and, 133n
        editorial comments concerning, 39
        as enemy of, 212n, 226, 229n, 237n
        investigated by, 88n
        on misrepresentations of, 134n, 188n, 189n, 211–12n, 246n, 323n
    on FB's correspondence with Hillsborough, 323n
    FB's views on, 164
    and Hancock, 187–188
    House of Representatives
        authors papers of, 12, 75n, 229n, 279n, 361, 362

    as clerk of, 2, 75n, 352, 353n, 361
    as committee member, 75n, 228n, 229n, 389n
    criticizes Hutchinson, 167, 170n
    identified, 75n
    as insurrectionist, 188–89n, 211n
    on Liberty Tree, 210n
    and Otis Jr.,
        differences, 25, 225, 246n
        disagreements, 244, 361
        similarities, 225–26
    Otis, quotes, 212n
    as political writer, 362
    portrait of, 111
    radicalism of, 12, 200, 225, 246n
    on rights and liberties, 324n
    as tax-collector, 2, 164n
    on treason, evidence of, 324n
    on violence, 134n
    Whig party, as leader of, 6, 12, 20, 163, 167
Administration of the Colonies (Thomas Pownall), 51n, 145n
    FB reads, 148–149
Admiralty Board
    and advocate general of Vice Admiralty, appointment of, 308
    clerks of, 43
    Hillsborough, letters from, cited, 184n, 241n, 399n
    Hood, orders to, 241n
    lords commissioners of, mentioned, 183
    orders Royal Navy to Boston, 183
    secretary of, xxvi, 390–91n
    secretary of state, letters from, 44
Admiralty Law, 18, 309
Advocate General of Vice Admiralty (Massachusetts), 17–18, 34, 52n, 154, 188, 307–08, 310
Alexander, Wiiliam
    identified, 416n
    letters to, listed, 413
Almon, John
    Collection of Interesting, Authentic Papers, relative to the Dispute between Great Britain and America (1777), 55n
Almsbury, Mass., 229n
American Board of Customs
    attorney general of England and Wales, seeks opinion of, 188, 310
    authority of, defiance to, 129
    Boston
        on civil order in, 127

CROWD ACTION

troops, as rationale for, 109–10, 154,
268–69
General Court, acts and resolves received,
158n
hostility toward, 99
House of Representatives, reponses to,
126n, 201n
lieutenant governor's salary, proposes, 300n
mentioned, 7, 147n, 205n
ministerial changes, 6, 8, 51n, 60, 76n, 78
ministers
FB, influenced by, 8, 11, 97, 106, 110,
151, 224, 234
FB, misled by, 24, 99
mentioned, xxv, 1–12, 16, 24– 29, 33,
51n, 59–60, 66, 72, 76n, 106, 131,
142, 145, 151, 225, 334, 361–62,
384–87
optimism of, 125n
Otis, Jr., disparaged by, 221
perceptions of, 5, 11, 24, 29, 85, 97, 151,
254, 308, 322n, 341, 350n, 360–61,
388
Northern Department. *See under* Secretary
of State (Northern Department)
officeholders, appointment of, dates, 55n
opposition to, 8, 85, 268
and Parliament, 41
and American representation in, 65
supporters in, 84, *See also* Barrington,
Lord
prime minister, 8, 27n, 50n, 61n–62n, 66n,
68n, 225
Southern Department. *See under* Secretary
of State (Southern Department)
and Townshend Acts, repeal of, 2, 7, 132
and Townshend Revenue Act, enforcement
of, 268
and treason, prosecution of, 275n
British Politics
and American affairs, 6– 11, 26–27, 51, 124,
133, 148
and factions, 268
Boston town meeting (12 Sept.), reactions
to, 324n
and colonial government, reform of, 124
developments in, 6
and FB, 6–9
FB's friends in, 7–8, *See also* Barrington,
Lord
general election (1768), 124–25n, 171n
and Hillsborough, 28

honors in, 156
and House of Representatives, 75n
satirized, 299
and Stamp Act, repeal of, 66n, 68n
and Townshend Acts, repeal of, 6
Whig dominance in, era of, 6
Bromfield (gentleman), 100
Bromfield, Henry, 103n
Bromfield, Thomas, 103n
Brompton, Richard, 62
Brooke, John, 27
Brown, John, 337n
Browne, William, 230n
Buildings, 2, 35, 38, 116n, 136, 139n, 207,
209, 211–12n, 245, 259, 260–61n, 318n,
322–24n, 330, 331, 334–35, 339–41, 345,
347, 351n, 353–54, *See also* Castle William
Bunch of Grapes Tavern, Boston, 134n
Burch, Ann
identified, 133n
mentioned, 108, 129–130
Burch, William
American Board of Customs, letters of, as
co-signatory to, 127, 180, 191, 194, 307,
366, 371, 377
as commissioner of Customs, 368n, 372n
crowd action, subjected to, 108, 129
family of, 108, 129
Province House, take refuge in, 130
identified, 110n, 128n, 181n
Buttons, 139
Byles, Mather, Jr.
England, travels to, 177
identified, 178n
Byles, Mather, Sr.
mentioned, 178n

Cade, Jack, 207, 210–12n
Cade's Rebellion (1450), 210–11n
Calef, John, 230n
Cambric, 139
Cambridge University, 299
Cambridge, Mass., 144n, 146–47, 273, 280n
Old Burying Ground, 146
Camden, Lord
American Colonies, taxation of, views on, 66
Chatham, confusion with, 67n
FB's reports of Stamp Act riots, praises,
66–67
House of Representatives, letter from
about, 67, 76
quoted, 67

royal colonies, appointments to, 92
royal commands, 77, 112, 150, 159, 182–83,
  206, 216, 224, 251, 254, 271, 272–73,
  277, 292, 298, 304, 306, 313–14, 327,
  330–31, 333, 335, 338, 339, 373, 378,
  383, 397–98, 400, *See also under* King,
  The: royal commands
royal commissions, 4, 71, 127, 140, 153,
  156, 168, 191, 199, 206, 217, 259, 260,
  286, 295, 297, 300n, 360–61, 363, 377
royal salute, 174
weakness of, 20, 265, 305, 335, 363
Governor and Council
  American Board of Customs requests pro-
    tection from, 127, 130, 375
  considered, 127–28, 130, 193, 198, 202,
    250
  authority of, 266, 297, 348–49
  and British troops, authority to request, 29,
    54n, 131, 232, 237, 239, 254, 257, 264,
    266–67, 276, 297–98
    Hillsborough advises on, 183
    instructions respecting, 54n
  House of Representatives, relationship with,
    72–73, 96
  Kinsman, arrest of, offer reward for, 289n
  meetings of, 38, 129, 180, 186–87, 192,
    195, 201–02, 208, 222–24, 264–65, 267,
    319, 331, 335, 338, *See also* Council:
    proceedings of (with given date)
    sequence of, 290n, 318n, 337n
  minutes of. *See under* Council:minutes
  printers to, 337n
  province agent, appointment of, excluded
    from, 50n
  Quartering Act, responsibilities under, 331,
    336–41, 360
  Stamp Act, repeal of, considers celebrations
    of, 127
Governor's Island, Boston Harbor, 240, 337n
  barracks at, 337n
Governor's Council. *See under* Council
Governors, Colonial
  and assemblies, relationships with, 9, 80,
    142, 348
  authority of, in decline, 10
  Barbados, of, 95n
  and Board of Trade, correspondence with,
    60, 72, 78, 242
  British government, communications with,
    protocol concerning, 72–73
  and British troops, authority to request, 54n

correspondence of, 4
Parliament, considered by, 157
as source of information, 9–10, 60, 73, 158
Hillsborough
  and, 28
  circulars from. *See under* Governors,
    Colonial: instructions to
    about, 367
    cited, 52n, 152n, 158n
    as enclosures. *See also* Hillsborough,
      Earl of: circulars from
    Massachusetts Circular Letter, con-
      cerning, 151
  communications with, about, 26, 44, 60,
    78, 242, 252
instructions to, 4, 76–80, 95n, 215–17,
  251–52, 275n, 285n, 292–93, *See also*
  Hillsborough, Earl of: FB as governor:
  instructions to
  American Board of Customs, on provid-
    ing assistance to, 26, 159, 366, 367
  assemblies, communication of official
    correspondence to, respecting, 292,
    293, 292–93, 314
  Board of Trade, communication with,
    respecting, 242n
  cited, 374n
  Hillsborough, on appointment of, 52n
  Kinsman, apprehension of, respecting,
    289
  manufactures, accounts of, respecting,
    166n
  Massachusetts Circular Letter, concern-
    ing, 12
  royal instructions, review of, respecting,
    216–17, 301
  secretary of state, communication with,
    respecting, 76–80, 242, 251–52
  cited, 26, 302
and juries, 275n
as king's representatives, 9, 71, 73, 254, 286,
  297, 325
legal penalties respecting, 230n
Massachusetts, of, 7, 51–52n, 148
mentioned, 80, 284
New England, of, 353
New Hampshire, of, 60n, 416n
New Jersey, of, 234n
New York, of, 60n, 92, 95n, 416n
North Carolina, of, 95n
Nova Scotia, of, 141n, 148
as politicians, 4

quoted by, 337
freedom of press, defends, 123n
and Hancock, 187
Hawley, disagreement with, 12, 89, 91n
House of Representatives
    authors papers of, 10, 12, 75n, 76n
    influence in, 12, 20, 75n, 101, 209,
        228–29n, 362n, 389n
        on Jackson's salary, 89
        newspaper libels, discusses, 119–20
        speeches
            on Camden, 68n– 69
            Conway, letters to FB from, de-
                mands, 104
            Council, attacks, 113
            FB, criticizes, 169–70, 172, 221,
                233
            FB's reports of, 221, 222, 225,
                228, 299, 300
            Hutchinson, criticizes, 172
            king, attacks, 225
            king's ministers, disparages, 221,
                225
            on rescinding, 227n, 297–300n
            Shelburne, letters to FB from,
                demands, 104
        on writs of assistance, 140
Hutchinson
    criticizes, 170n, 172
    opposition to, 175
Hutchinson's views on, 123n
identified, 177n
and insurrection, 390
intellectualism of, 2
jury, influence on, 121, 123n
"madman," behaves like, 113, 173
mental illness of, 91n
moderation of, 225
oratory of, 25, 35, 113, 117n, 221, 297
radicalism of, 12, 35, 102, 200, 225–26,
    246n, 297
as recreant, 12, 91n
and rescinding controversy, 225, 297
sedition of, 35
speeches
    about, 25, 35
    as enclosures, 298
Whig party, as leader of, 2, 6, 12, 25, 100,
    163, 167, 225
writings of, 90
and writs of assistance, 2, 140–41n

Otis, James, Sr.
    compromise with fails, 168
    Council, election to, vetoed, 167–68, 170n,
        174n, 228n
    Council, readmission to, 168, 170, 172–73,
        176
    in House of Representatives, 89
    as committee member, 229n, 389n
    Hutchinson
        enmity towards, 168, 172, 175–76
        opposition to, 170
    identified, 171n, 174n
    offices of, 171n, 174n
Oxford University, 299

Paddock, Adino, 174
Paine, Thomas
    Common Sense (1776), 64
Paine, Timothy
    as councilor, 117n, 269n
    as friend of government, 171n
Paint
    duties on, 281
Painters and Engravers, 62, 79, 111, 196, 231,
    283
Palmer, Hugh
    Christ Church (Boston), invited to, 177–78n
    letter to, listed, 406
    mentioned, 178n
Paper
    duties on, 281
Paper Mills, 136
Parliament
    America, friends of, 66, 289
    American affairs
    debates, 32, 41, 150
    dissention over, 83
    inquiry into, 25
    knowledge of, 116
    American Board of Customs, memorials and
        papers of, presented, 380
    American Colonies
        authority over, asserted, 7
            authority over, challenged, 63–64
        concessions to, 7
        hostility toward, 99
        impatient with, 65, 69, 71
        "Indulgence" of, 93
        intervention in, proposed, 11, 109, 266,
            278
        members' attitudes to, 20